THE
COMPLETE
REAL ESTATE
ENCYCLOPEDIA

THE
COMPLETE
REAL ESTATE
ENCYCLOPEDIA

THE COMPLETE REAL ESTATE ENCYCLOPEDIA

From AAA Tenant to Zoning Variance
and
EVERYTHING In Between

Denise L. Evans, JD
O. William Evans, JD

McGraw-Hill

New York Chicago San Francisco Lisbon
London Madrid Mexico City Milan New Delhi
San Juan Seoul Singapore Sydney Toronto

ISBN–13: 978-0-07-147638-6
ISBN–10:   0-07-147638-5

Product or brand names used in this book may be trade names or trademarks. Where we believe that there may be proprietary claims to such trade names or trademarks, the name has been used with an initial capital or it has been capitalized in the style used by the name claimant. Regardless of the capitalization used, all such names have been used in an editorial manner without any intent to convey endorsement of or other affiliation with the name claimant. Neither the author nor the publisher intends to express any judgment as to the validity or legal status of any such proprietary claims.

This publication is designed to provide accurate and authoritative information in regard to the subject matter covered. It is sold with the understanding that neither the author nor the publisher is engaged in rendering legal, accounting, futures/securities trading, or other professional service. If legal advice or other expert assistance is required, the services of a competent professional person should be sought.

—From a Declaration of Principles jointly adopted by a
Committee of the American Bar Association
and a Committee of Publishers

McGraw-Hill books are available at special quantity discounts to use as premiums and sales promotions, or for use in corporate training programs. For more information, please write to the Director of Special Sales, Professional Publishing, McGraw-Hill, Two Penn Plaza, New York, NY 10121–2298. Or contact your local bookstore.

Dedication

This book is dedicated to my parents, Norm and Pat Lier, who bought a set of encyclopedias for me when I was still a baby. Not that I was a prodigy—they just liked to plan ahead. Over the years, they bought more reference materials and dictionaries, and always told me to "look it up" when I had a question. They encouraged me to read anything, to learn everything, and to have fun with both. Then they threatened to punish me if I continued reading to my younger brothers, who were in danger of never learning the skill at all if I always insisted on doing it for them!

Thank you, Mom and Dad, for everything. You've been wonderful role models, tireless cheerleaders, and the finest parents imaginable. I'm sure you still have the receipt for that original set of encyclopedias. Maybe we can find the salesman, and sell him one of mine!

Contents

Foreword

Real Estate is a fascinating subject. It is absolutely captivating when you begin to understand it. With this book, Denise and Bill Evans have given the reader the primary tools of a great education in real estate, and an opportunity to share in our wonderful and exciting industry. Their encyclopedia includes not just definitions of the lingo of the real estate community, but also examples to put the language into understandable context. Many of the entries include practical advice about opportunities, pitfalls, and related concepts. This book is a terrific educational achievement that provides immense value for the real estate novice and the seasoned professional alike.

What gives me the right to say all this? I've been active in real estate for over 50 years, including work in construction, government, corporate America, and private legal practice.

As a young man, I needed to work during the "down times," finishing up undergraduate school at UCLA in June 1955 and waiting to go into the service in 1956. I found employment in the heavy earth-moving construction business in the fast-paced housing construction and office-industrial developments of southern California. I saw first hand the real world application of important real estate principles. In February 1959, I returned from active duty as an Air Force pilot to Orange County, California and started UCLA Law School the following September. Still intrigued with the real estate industry, I returned to the construction business part-time during the first year of law school. After completing law school and passing the bar exam in 1962, I joined an Orange County law firm that had a significant portion of its work in the real estate field.

In June of 1969 I was appointed Chief Deputy Commissioner of Corporations by Ronald Reagan, who was governor of California at the time. Because of my extensive real estate experience, I was, along with the Commissioner, responsible for drafting rules for real estate syndications in California. These rules were substantially adopted by the SEC and NASD.

In 1972, at the end of my term, I returned to private practice in Orange County, again concentrating on real estate–related matters. In 1982 I was contacted by the Century 21 real estate brokerage franchise to prepare a business plan for Century 21 to sell real estate syndication interests through the Century 21 brokerage offices nationwide, in each of the nine Century 21 regions.

Bill Evans was recommended to me as someone who could prepare, plan, and manage the training for the real estate syndications licensing program. Previously, Bill had been responsible for other real estate training programs throughout the southeastern United States, but this was his first national platform. He rose to the occasion, writing the textbooks and traveling the United States to conduct week-long courses, primarily to residential agents with no prior commercial real estate or securities experience. Over the course of 18 months, he took the program from absolutely nothing to successful real estate syndication licensing of over 700 candidates, which included their completion of a national securities exam. Miraculously, he found time to get married to Denise, and she eventually forgave me for keeping Bill on the road so much.

Since that time, we've each gone on to other endeavors outside Century 21, but we've all stayed active in real estate. Denise and Bill Evans are a great team in all their real estate related endeavors. I am confident that this book will herald another team victory.

James L. Kelly

Former President of Century 21
Real Estate Securities Corporation

Preface

This work started out as a simple dictionary, an attempt to explain complicated real estate and finance concepts in everyday language. Somewhere along the way we discovered that definitions were often not enough. People needed to know about related issues, sometimes a little practical advice, and places to look on the Internet for more in-depth treatment.

And so, the little dictionary grew to this encyclopedia. We hope you find it useful in your everyday life, and a much-used resource for refining your understanding of real estate in the United States.

Up until the final day allowed by the publisher, we were adding new words. There will always be new words, new ways to use old words, and fresh perspectives on tried-and-true concepts. On the other hand, we can't print new versions of the encyclopedia every week. That's why we're really excited about the commitment McGraw-Hill has made to this project, and to the maintenance of a Web site dedicated to the encyclopedia.

The Web site will contain real estate–related tools such as forms, formulas, and links to valuable Web sites. It will also provide new words and expanded definitions as those become available.* This book will grow as we grow. Please feel free to share your comments with us by sending an e-mail to dle@deniselevans.com.

---

*Take advantage of this additional information by going to mhprofessional.com/reencyclopedia.

Acknowledgments

We would like to thank Dianne Wheeler and McGraw-Hill for making this exciting new project possible. There is a tremendous risk in publishing a work of this stature, in a fresh new format not yet tried by any other company. They believed in us, made available their top people to provide editorial and production assistance, and committed to a Web site for this book before they had seen the first draft. Thank you for the vote of confidence. We look forward to seeing you gratified to learn it was well-placed.

Thank you, also, to J. Barry Mason, Dean of the Culverhouse College of Commerce and Business Administration at the University of Alabama, for making the resources available to us so we could research this encyclopedia. We appreciate all of his confidence and support, and the nurturing and supportive environment he has encouraged in the entire College among students, faculty, and staff.

THE
COMPLETE
REAL ESTATE
ENCYCLOPEDIA

Numbers

80–10–10 mortgage   A type of mortgage arrangement with 80 percent of the purchase price paid by a first mortgage, 10 percent paid by a second mortgage, and the final 10 percent in down payment; sometimes used in order to avoid having a 90 percent first mortgage and the required private mortgage insurance premiums.

203(b) loan   Standard FHA-insured fixed-interest rate mortgage loans for one- to four-family residential properties. The loan program features the ability to have down payments as low as 3 percent and to finance closing costs as part of the loan. There are limitations on the maximum size loan that can qualify. The limitations change over time and by geographic area. The comparable adjustable-rate program is called a 251 loan.

203(k) loan   Also called a HUD rehabilitation and repair loan, it is an FHA-insured loan obtained through independent lenders. Single-family to four-unit residential properties are eligible, as well as mixed-use properties with certain ratios of residential to commercial uses. Rehab money can be used for normal repairs or improvements, or to convert a single-family home to a multifamily dwelling (up to four units) or the reverse. Homes that have been demolished, or will be razed as part of the rehab, are eligible as long as some of the foundation structure remains. The maximum loan amount is 110 percent of the value of the property after rehab. (Do not confuse this type of loan with HUD's property improvement loan, also called a Title I loan.)

203(n) loan   FHA-insured loan for the purchase of a unit in a cooperative apartment building. [Program details are similar to that of a 203(b) loan.]

234(c) loan   FHA-insured loan for the purchase of a condominium unit. If the unit is in a building converted from apartments to condos, no insurance will be provided unless (1) the conversion was more than one year earlier, (2) the potential buyer was a tenant before conversion, or (3) the conversion is supported by a tenant's organization that represents a majority of the households in the project. Eighty percent of FHA-insured mortgages in the project must be to owner-occupants. [Otherwise, it is similar to the 203(b) program.]

234(d) loan   An FHA-insured loan for the construction or rehabilitation of housing projects intended to be sold as condominium units.

245 loan   An FHA-insured loan program also called the graduated payment mortgage. It allows home purchasers to begin with low monthly mortgage payments and then steadily increase them over the next 5 to 10 years, when they will remain constant.

245(a) loan   FHA-insured loan program also called Growing Equity Mortgage (GEM) Insurance.

251 loan   A standard FHA-insured mortgage loan for one- to four-family residential properties at adjustable interest rates. The comparable fixed-rate program is called a 203(b) loan.

501(c)(3)   A charitable organization, named after Internal Revenue Code, Section 501(c)(3), which gives such organizations tax-exempt status.

1031 exchange   (pronounced "ten thirty-one exchange") From Section 1031 of the Internal Revenue Code, the ability to exchange like-kind property and defer paying taxes on the gain realized. Under normal circumstances, if a party purchases Blackacre for $10,000 and then exchanges it for $100,000 in cash, there is a gain of $90,000 on which income taxes must be paid. But, because of §1031, if Blackacre is exchanged for like-kind property, then the gain is realized (meaning it occurs) but is not recognized (meaning no tax is due at that time).

The property given up is called the relinquished property, and the property received is called the replacement property. After the exchange, the basis in the relinquished property becomes the basis in the replacement party. In other words, the $10,000 purchase price for Blackacre, called the basis, becomes the basis of the replacement property. When the replacement property is sold later for $150,000, the gain would be $150,000 less $10,000, not $150,000 less $100,000. That is true unless you do another 1031 exchange at that time. There is currently no limit on the number of exchanges you can do in a lifetime.

The properties must be qualifying use properties, meaning that they have or will be held for income production (rental) or investment, or used in a trade or business. Personal residences and vacation homes are not qualifying properties.

Swapping properties is a very handy tax tool, but it is relatively rare to find property owners who want to exchange properties at a simultaneous closing. As a result, the IRS allows the use of a fiction, a type of like-kind property proxy. In the fiction, the owner of Blackacre may sell it for cash, but the money must be placed in the hands of a qualified intermediary to hold. It is said the taxpayer can never have his or her fingerprints on the cash—not to spend, not to borrow against, nothing. The taxpayer then has 45 days to identify a replacement property and complete a form with the identification information. After that, the taxpayer has a short time to close on the replacement property, for which the funds in the hands of the qualified intermediary may be used. If all this is done exactly right, the taxes will be deferred.

[This entry does not allow enough space for all the technicalities of a 1031 exchange. Specific details of a 1031 exchange can be found at the IRS Web site (www.irs.gov), "Publication 544, Sales and Other Dispositions of Assets" and "Form 8824, Like-Kind Exchanges" (PDF).]

1099   The IRS form for reporting payments made to independent contractors or interest earned on investments or bank accounts. The person completing the form supplies copies to the party receiving the payments and to the IRS and state and local taxing authorities. If one's tax return does not disclose income reported on a 1099, there is a high likelihood of an audit. Real estate agents typically receive 1099s from their brokers for commissions earned during the prior year.

A

AAA tenant   (pronounced "triple-A tenant" but written as AAA tenant) Commercial tenant with the best possible credit rating and the least likely possibility of default. Owners can secure better selling prices or better financing terms if they have such tenants in their property.

abandonment   An intentional surrender, disclaimer, or termination of ownership with no stated intention regarding who the next owner should be. Legally requires some external evidence of an intention to abandon; simply neglecting property will not suffice. Differs from surrender, which requires that someone accept the property, and from forfeiture, which is unintentional loss of property. Abandoned property will generally revert to someone with a prior claim, such as an abandoned leasehold reverting to the landlord or an abandoned easement reverting to the landowner. Sometimes abandoned property will escheat to the state.

abatement   A reduction or decrease. Local governments sometimes offer tax abatements to new businesses in order to attract them to the area. Commercial leases usually have clauses denying rent abatement if the leased property is partially destroyed and then rebuilt and made usable again.

able to purchase   Financially capable of gaining access to the necessary funds to complete a purchase. Real estate brokers with a written listing agreement are usually entitled to a commission if they produce a buyer who is "ready, willing, and able" to acquire the subject property at the asking price, even if the seller then refuses to go through with the sale.

abnormal sale   In appraisals, a sale that is not typical of the market at that place and time. Such a sale may be the result of family transactions, ignorance of true values, threat of foreclosure, or other unusual events and will not be used to determine the value of the property being appraised.

abode   Residence, home, domicile.

above building standard   Typically refers to items not included in a landlord's construction work letter. A new tenant can usually negotiate the landlord's agreement to pay for all construction expenses necessary to customize space to building standard, which might be hollow doors, inexpensive carpet, 2 ft × 4 ft ceiling tiles, and fluorescent light fixtures, depending on the building. Anything above building standard must generally be paid by the tenant.

abrogate   Withdraw, rescind, revoke, or cancel. Common usage implies an act done in a one-sided or high-handed manner, but this is not necessary to the definition.

absentee owner   One who does not personally occupy or manage their property.

absolute auction   A sale will be to the highest bidder, regardless of the amount bid. Common wisdom among auctioneers is that a property advertised as being sold at absolute auction will attract more bidders and higher bidding prices than one advertised with even a low minimum acceptable bid, or reserve price.

absolute net lease   Also called a triple net lease, in which the tenant pays rent plus all costs of ownership, such as insurance, real estate taxes, repairs, cleaning, and utilities.

absolute net rent   Rent payments that are pure income to the landlord, because they are not reduced by any operating expenses. When an owner quotes a figure as absolute net rent, it is a clue that the tenant will also have to pay all insurance, real estate taxes, repairs, cleaning, and utilities in addition to the monthly rent.

absolute title   A title to real estate without any competing claims such as IRS liens, prior mortgages, leases, easements, or spousal claims. A lender will usually require either clear title in the borrower, or waivers by other parties, so the lender will have absolute title if it has to foreclose. Also called clear title.

absorption rate   The rate at which vacant space is leased or purchased over a specified period of time. The absorption rate for commercial property is usually expressed in square feet per year; residential property is quoted in units (homes) per year.

abstract deed   Colloquial expression used to refer to the original deed from the government to the first private owner of a parcel of land. Other times, it is meant to describe a deed that recites all former owners and their dates of acquisition. Sometimes purchasers who request an abstract deed mean to communicate that they want title insurance or a title opinion in addition to the deed. Technically, there is no legal instrument called an abstract deed. (When you encounter this expression, ask questions in order to determine what is meant.)

abstract of title   Synopsis of all prior owners and important claimants to property, with the date and origin of their rights and date and manner of termination, together with all current owners, lienholders, easements, or other such claims against the property.

Sidewalk abuts the house

abut   Next to, touching, contiguous. Typically arises in the context of whether property owners have a duty to clean snow, ice, and debris from the sidewalks abutting their property.

A/C   Shorthand for air conditioning.

accelerate   To demand the full amount due under a contract even though the original agreement allowed payments over time. Almost all promissory notes and leases have acceleration clauses in the event of default. If it were not for such clauses, the lender or landowner could be required to file separate lawsuits when each payment was missed, or wait until the end of the term and sue for all at once.

accelerated amortization   Making additional mortgage payments so as to reduce the principal amount of the debt more quickly than originally contemplated in the parties' agreement.

accelerated cost recovery system (ACRS)   A method of tax accounting in which the IRS simplified the rules for depreciation of property. It has been replaced by the modified accelerated cost recovery system (MACRS), but you will still encounter references to ACRS.

accelerated depreciation   Depreciation methods that allow larger deductions in early years, trailing off to smaller deductions in later years. It is the opposite of straight-line depreciation, in which equal amounts are depreciated every year. Accelerated depreciation is not allowed for real property, but may be employed for certain components, such as fencing, security systems, carpet, or windows. The most common types of accelerated depreciation encountered in real estate are double declining balance, also called 200 percent declining balance, and the alternative 150 percent declining balance method.

Example: *Carpeting in residential rental properties may be depreciated over 5 years. Assuming $10,000 worth of carpeting is installed in an apartment building, this is each year's depreciation using the different methods:*

	Straight Line	150% Declining	200% Declining
Year 1	$2,000	$3,000	$4,000
Year 2	2,000	2,100	2,400
Year 3	2,000	2,000	2,000
Year 4	2,000	2,000	1,600
Year 5	2,000	900	0

acceleration clause   The clause in a promissory note or lease that allows immediate demand, upon default, for all sums due over the entire term.

acceptance   (1) The act of receiving something with the intention of retaining it. Transfer of title to real estate requires acceptance of the title. (One cannot secretly deed a toxic waste site to an enemy in hopes that the Environmental Protection Agency will make that person handle the cleanup.) (2) The act of agreeing to the terms and conditions of an offer, creating a contract by virtue of the acceptance.

Access Board   An independent federal agency that develops and maintains design criteria for buildings and other improvements, transit vehicles, telecommunications equipment, and electronic and information technology. It also enforces accessibility standards that cover federally funded facilities. The Access Board's Web site is www.access-board.gov.

accessibility (1) Evaluation of the convenience of a property relative to the people who will be using it. May refer to ingress and egress for customers or lack of obstructions for persons with disabilities. (2) Important component in pricing surveying services. The more difficult the terrain and the less accessible the site; the more expensive the fee.

accession The right to own things that become a part of something you already own. When a tenant adds built-in cabinetry or other fixtures to a building, they become the property of the landlord by virtue of accession. Also frequently encountered in the realm of riparian (water) rights, such as new land created by dry river beds or retreating tidal lands.

accessory building A secondary structure that exists for the benefit of the main building, such as a tool shed or a detached garage. When drafting an offer to purchase real estate, you should be sure to include accessory buildings in your description. Otherwise, easily movable sheds and other structures not permanently affixed to the soil might be removed before closing.

A greenhouse is an accessory building.

access right The right of owners to get to or from their property. Legally, no land may be landlocked. Therefore, if a parcel is cut off from all public roads and there are no easements for ingress and egress, then the owner may bring suit and have a court declare an easement of necessity over the land of another. (This is one of the rare times when private individuals are able to bring condemnation actions and force another to give them property rights.)

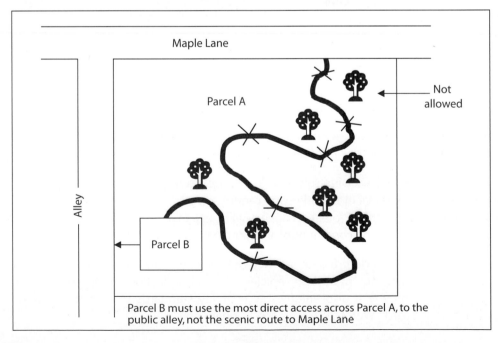

Parcel B must use the most direct access across Parcel A, to the public alley, not the scenic route to Maple Lane

> **Example:** *Parcel B is landlocked, but the owner is entitled to access rights to public roads and may force the owner of parcel A to provide an ingress and egress easement. The easement must be via the most direct route to the nearest public road, without being unduly burdensome on parcel A. The owner of parcel B may not force the owner of parcel A to provide a scenic route.*

accommodating party   A third party who holds money or other property for a short period of time in order to facilitate a tax-free exchange under Section 1031 of the IRS Code. The third party is called a qualified intermediary in the tax regulations.

> **Example:** *Jack sells his office building to Jill for $400,000. Jill pays the money to Larry Lawyer, who keeps it in his escrow account. Larry is the accommodating party. When Jack meets the timing requirements of Section 1031 and wants to buy an apartment building for $1,000,000, Larry will write a check to the seller for $400,000 and Jack will pay the remaining $600,000. In common language, Jack can't have his fingerprints on the money, so an accommodating party is necessary.*

accommodation party   One who signs a promissory note even though he or she receives no direct economic benefit from it. Typically, a financially strong party who must add his or her name to the transaction or the true borrower would not qualify for the loan. There is a widespread and mistaken belief among accommodation parties that they simply signed their name but will not be held responsible if the loan goes into default. This is incorrect; they will be held liable for the full amount of the loan if there is a default. (*Do not confuse with accommodating party.*)

Accredited Rural Appraiser (ACR)   A designation granted by the American Society of Farm Managers and Rural Appraisers (www.asfmra.org).

accretion   The addition of land through natural causes, such as gradual silting. You will often see accretion used to also describe the addition of land because of receding waters, but this is more properly called dereliction.

accrual method   An accounting method in which income is counted when it is earned (whether you receive the money at that time or not) and expenses are counted when incurred (whether you pay the bill at that time or not). It is the opposite of the cash method, in which income is counted when money is received and expenses are counted when the bills are paid. Most businesses use the accrual method because it allows income, and the expenses associated with generating that income, to be accounted for in the same period. (Many small businesses use the cash method because it's easier.)

accrue   To accumulate; grow. A $100,000 loan at 7 percent interest accrues interest at the rate of $7,000 per year, or $19.18 per day. The mortgage holder on a property being sold will typically tell the closing company a payoff amount accurate as of the anticipated closing date, with a daily accrual for each day closing is delayed.

accrued but unpaid   Money that has been earned, such as interest on a mortgage loan, but not yet collected.

accrued depreciation   The total depreciation claimed, to date, on a property. It is an entry on the balance sheet and is supposed to properly reflect that the property is becoming less valuable with the passage of time. Realistically, in the case of real estate, the property is usually becoming more valuable each year. As a result, you may have a book value of $200,000 but a fair market value of $2,000,000.

accrued interest   For every day that a loan remains unpaid by the borrower, it earns interest that must be paid to the lender. This process of earning interest with each passing day is called accrual, and the money earned is called accrued interest. It may not be payable until the first day of the next month, but it has already been fully earned by the lender. See also *nonaccrual*.

accumulated depreciation   Also called *accrued depreciation*.

acknowledge   To accept responsibility for something. In real estate, it means to sign an instrument in front of a notary public, who will certify that the signer stated the signature was an act of free will.

acknowledgment   A declaration by one signing an instrument, usually a deed, mortgage, or will, that their signature was free and voluntary. The declaration must be made before an authorized person, usually a notary public, but may also be designated court officials or others named by statute.

ACM   See *asbestos containing material*.

acquisition   The act of obtaining ownership of something. It may occur through derivative acquisition—procured from another who previously owned the thing—or though original acquisition, which is new creation such as land made when the ocean recedes.

acquisition cost   The price and all related expenses of obtaining property; may include closing expenses, survey, inspections, and paying off adverse claimants.

acquisition, development, and construction (ADC) loan   A loan made to allow a developer to buy land, install infrastructure such as streets and sewers, and build improvements. Because the value of the collateral depends on the development process adding significant value, these are considered somewhat risky loans. As a result, lenders limit the number of ADC loans they extend. A loan turndown from one lender may not be a stamp of disapproval for the project, but simply that lender's inability to extend any more ADC loans until others are paid off or converted to permanent financing.

acquisition loan   A loan made to acquire a property, also called a purchase money loan. In bankruptcy law, acquisition lenders receive some special priorities and benefits not granted to other creditors.

acre   Historically, the amount of land a yoke of oxen could plow in one day; today, a quantity of land containing 43,560 square feet. An acre can be any shape. Especially in the case of commercial properties, land values are usually expressed in terms of price per square foot rather then price per acre.

Example: *If you know that a 16-acre parcel recently sold for $10,000,000, you calculate the price per foot as follows:*

16 acres × 43,560 square feet per acre = 696,960 square feet
$10,000,000 ÷ 696,960 feet = $14.35 per square foot

acreage zoning   Zoning intended to reduce residential density by requiring large building lots.

acre-foot   A quantity of water, sand, or minerals equal to a volume 1 foot high over one hypothetical acre of land. It arises in the context of pricing water for irrigation purposes, estimating the value of minerals in place under the soil, and estimating numbers of fish per acre-foot of water.

ACRS   See *accelerated cost recovery system.*

action to quiet title   See *quiet title action.*

active participation   An IRS term relating to passive activity losses that can be deducted only against passive activity income, not against ordinary income. Rental activities are always passive, unless you are a real estate professional. There is a small loophole—if you or your spouse actively participated in a passive rental real estate activity, you can still deduct up to $25,000 in rental activity losses from ordinary income. As a result, taxpayers are eager to prove they have active participation in their real estate investments so that large depreciation expenses, for example, can shelter income from other sources. Active participation can be shown if you make bona fide management decisions such as approving new tenants, deciding rental terms, approving expenditures, and similar activities. (See IRS Publication 925, "Passive Activity and At-Risk Rules" at the IRS Web site www.irs.gov.)

active remediation   Engaging in some affirmative action to remove contaminants from soil or water. The alternative is passive remediation, which is usually accomplished by normal flushing processes occurring over time.

active solar heating   Method of heat that relies upon the sun to heat either air or liquids in a solar collector, and then distribute that heat throughout the structure. Contrast with passive solar heat.

Act of God   An act caused exclusively by the violence of Nature, without any intervention from humans. Many contracts contain clauses relieving the parties of responsibility if an Act of God delays or makes impossible the performance of the contract. Examples include earthquakes, floods, hurricanes, lightning, tidal waves, tornadoes. (With current controversy over the effects of global warming, and with allegations that deficiencies in the New Orleans levee system caused the massive flooding in 2005, we can expect renewed litigation concerning flooding as an Act of God or of humans.)

actual age   In appraisal, the true age of a property, as opposed to its effective age. A building might have an actual age of 25 years but an effective age of 3 years because of massive renovations made 3 years earlier. A house with six small children in the family might have an actual age of 2 years and an effective age of 18 years.

actual damages   Losses or injuries for which the law allows compensation as a means of reimbursement; used also to refer to the money awarded by a court as that compensation. Contrast with nominal damages, which would award $1, but recognize that the plaintiff's rights have been violated even though no economic, physical, or emotional harm occurred. Contrast also with punitive damages, which are not intended to compensate the victim but to punish the aggressor.

Actual damages may be

- Direct damages—those that flow directly and naturally from the wrong
- Consequential damages—those that flow from some consequence of the wrong

> **Example:** *Able agrees to purchase Baker's house. As a result of that contract, Baker agrees to buy a new condo under construction and pays a nonrefundable $5,000 reservation fee. Able then defaults and refuses to purchase Baker's house, even though Able has no justifiable reason for doing so. Two weeks later the stock market crashes, and Baker counts himself lucky when he is able to sell his house for $40,000 less than the original contract price. But, Baker is now unable to purchase the condo and loses his $5,000. Under the right circumstances, Able could be liable to Baker for actual damages consisting of the $40,000 difference in the two sale prices (direct damages) and for the loss of the $5,000 earnest money (consequential damages—more indirect and less predictable) and for punitive damages.*

actual eviction   Removing someone from property either by force or by legal process. Contrast with constructive eviction, in which property is rendered unusable because of some action or inaction of the landlord.

actual notice   Commonly means notice expressly and directly given to a person and received by that person. In legal documents, however, a requirement for actual notice may be satisfied through express notice or implied notice, but not by constructive notice. Express notice is given by actual delivery of the information to the person charged. Implied notice is satisfied if the person has sufficient facts available to cause him or her to ask further questions and thereby receive express notice. Constructive notice occurs when someone is charged by law with making inquiries such as would cause him or her to learn of facts giving rise to implied notice.

actual possession   The physical occupancy or control of property by someone. Contrast with constructive possession in which the law assumes possession because of legal rights to the property.

> **Example:** *One who has a deed to 40 acres of land, but uses only 1 acre for a house and yard, is said to have actual possession of 1 acre and constructive possession of the other 39 acres.*

actual value   The true market value of a property if it were offered for sale at a particular time to a buyer with sufficient information about the property to make an informed decision. Contrast with book value, which is the original purchase price, plus capital expenditures, minus depreciation. Contrast also with perceived value based on fraud.

ADA   See *Americans with Disabilities Act*.

ADC loan   See *acquisition, development, and construction loan*.

add-back   The amount added to the principal balance of a loan because the monthly payments are insufficient to pay all currently accrued interest; may be encountered with variable-rate, fixed-payment loans.

addendum   Something added as an attachment to a form contract, before contract execution; generally used to cover the particular circumstances of that transaction. Real estate contracts may have addenda (plural of addendum) to cover requirements relative to financing contingencies, property inspections, disclosure of the possible presence of lead-based paint in structures built before 1978, and other variables. Especially for properties with lengthy legal descriptions, an addendum will generally be used for the legal description of the property, rather than squeezing it into the small space available on the form. Contrast with amendment, which is an attachment added after contract execution in order to modify or expand upon the original contract.

additional charge mortgage   A mortgage instrument that recites on its face that it is used to secure present and future debts by the borrower to the lender. It serves to put new lenders on notice that the equity in the property may decrease in the future, as a result of additional money being advanced by the first lender. See *future advances mortgage* and *anaconda mortgage*.

additional rent   Amounts due under a lease in addition to the originally agreed upon base rent. Leases usually characterize all sums due to a landlord, including late fees, collection costs, and property damage, as additional rent. This gives the landlord some legal advantages as far as declaring a default, obtaining an eviction, and collecting sums due. Examples could include the tenant's share of property maintenance and insurance expenses and a retail tenant's obligation to pay a percentage of gross income in addition to base rent.

additional first-year depreciation   Also called bonus depreciation. An IRS provision that allows taxpayers to take more than the ordinary depreciation in the first year a property is placed in use. (After the 9/11 attacks, taxpayers could deduct up to one-half of the basis of their property in the first year. Ordinarily, only $1/39$ or $1/28$ of the basis could be deducted in the first year. Similarly, in the wake of the devastating 2005 hurricane year, some taxpayers could take additional first-year depreciation equal to one-half of the basis.) In addition, taxpayers may take larger than normal depreciation for some property, called Section 179 property, even it if results in effectively expensing the entire purchase price in the current year.(For more information, visit the IRS Web site www.irs.gov.)

add-on interest   An interest calculation sometimes used to avoid state usury laws (prohibitions against excessive interest) or to gain the equivalent of a prepayment penalty not otherwise allowed by law. The interest for the entire term of the loan is calculated as if no payments will be made until the loan matures. The total interest is added to the principal, and the borrower then makes equal monthly payments over the term of the loan. Even though the borrower reduces the outstanding principal balance with each payment, he or she is still paying interest on the whole amount borrowed. If the borrower prepays the loan, a calculation called the rule of 78s results in a disguised prepayment penalty.

Example: *The difference between 8 percent simple interest and 8 percent add-on interest for a $25,000 loan paid monthly for 4 years is*

Simple interest monthly payments	=	*$610.32*
Simple interest total interest paid	=	*$3,586.62*
Add-on interest monthly payments	=	*$687.50*
Total add-on interest paid	=	*$8,000.00*

adequate consideration   See *consideration*.

adequate public facilities ordinances (APFO)   A local law controlling growth by requiring completion of infrastructure—roads, sanitary and storm sewers, waterlines, and schools—prior to, or at the same time as, new private development that will need those services. Approvals for new subdivisions or commercial properties may be withheld until regulatory authorities deem there are adequate public facilities.

adhesion contract   A contract that is so grossly one-sided that courts will not enforce it, or will not enforce specific terms deemed to be unconscionable or oppressively unfair, especially if the consumer has no other choices in the marketplace.

adjacent   Nearby, but not necessarily touching; implies properties separated by a natural barrier such as a river, or by a street, but not separated by another property. Properties that touch each other are legally said to be adjoining rather than adjacent, but common usage includes such properties as within the definition of adjacent.

Adjacent to my property	
Maple Street	
My property	Adjoins my property

adjoining   Touching, as in properties that are not separated by any natural or human-made barrier nor by any other property. Contrast with adjacent, which means nearby, but not necessarily touching.

adjudication   A formal declaration by a court, addressing all issues raised by the parties.

Example: *The court's adjudication declared the seller in default, ordered the seller to execute a deed to the buyer, and further assessed attorney's fees and costs against the seller.*

adjunction   Adding something to property in such a manner that it loses its independent identity.

Example: *Personal property consisting of boards and nails will become part of the real estate by adjunction when they are used to build an addition to a house.*

adjustable mortgage loan   See *adjustable-rate mortgage*.

adjustable-rate mortgage (ARM)   An instrument granting a security interest in real property as collateral for a promissory note with interest rates that change from time to time, as specified in the note. The note should contain

- An initial rate, or the first interest rate to be charged.
- A reference number, called the index, to be used in calculating future interest rates. As the index increases or decreases, the loan interest rate will increase or decrease by the same amount.
- The index could be the Federal Reserve overnight funds rate plus a certain percentage, it could be the prime rate charged by CitiBank to its most credit-worthy customers (CitiBank Prime), or any number of other indices. You want to avoid any adjustable-rate note with references to vague generalities such as "market rate" or rates charged by small unknown lenders.
- A statement regarding the frequency at which the rate may change. Commercial loans typically change every time the index changes. Consumer loans usually change only once or twice a year.
- A statement regarding the maximum amount the interest may increase each time, called a periodic cap. (Consumer loans usually have periodic caps, but not commercial loans.)
- A statement regarding the maximum amount the interest may increase over the lifetime of the loan, called a lifetime cap. (Consumer loans usually have a lifetime cap around 5 percent; commercial loans usually do not have any lifetime caps.)

Many adjustable-rate mortgages for home loans have a conversion clause allowing (or even requiring) change to a fixed rate of interest after a specified period of time, usually 5 or 7 years. This gives the homeowner the ability to lock in a fixed rate without having to go through the trouble and expense of a refinance.

One type of adjustable-rate mortgage is the fixed-payment, adjustable-rate loan. With it, the consumer pays the same amount each month, even if interest rates rise to the point that the payment does not pay the currently accruing interest. The unpaid interest is added to the principal of the loan. In such a situation, the loan is said to be negatively amortizing, meaning the principal balance grows larger each month rather than smaller.

adjusted basis   A tax and accounting term referring to the original acquisition cost of a property, with the following adjustments:

- Depreciation, which reduces the basis
- Capitalized closing costs, which increase the basis
- Capital improvements, such as a new roof, which increase the basis

The difference between the adjusted basis and the ultimate sale price of a property will be the taxable profit on the sale. The adjusted basis is an extremely important tax concept, and one which it is important to master in order to comfortably evaluate properties.

adjusted sales price   In an appraisal, the answer obtained when the sales price of a comparable property is adjusted for factors that make it different from the property being appraised.

> **Example:**   *Property A is being appraised, and property B is a similar property that sold recently. Property B has some features that property A does not. The sale price of property B would probably be lower if it, too, lacked that feature, so a downward adjustment is made. Likewise, property B lacks some features present in property A. If property B had those features, it would have sold for a higher price, so an upward adjustment is made in property B's sale price.*

Example: Adjusted Sales Price Calculations			
	A	**B**	**Adjustments**
Sale price	—	$175,000	
Garage	Yes	No	+$40,000
Pool	No	Yes	−$25,000
Brick	Yes	No	+$8,000
Adjusted sale price of B			$198,000

adjusted tax basis   See *adjusted basis*.

adjustments   Closing: Debits and credits to the purchase price of a property because of items to be paid by the seller or the buyer. All adjustments should be reflected on a settlement statement. (The settlement statement used in home sales is a form, called a HUD–1, created by the Department of Housing and Urban Development.). In appraisal: See *adjusted sales price*.

administrative expenses   Compensation to management for operating or building a property; may include salaries and professional fees. Contrast with operating expenses, reserves for losses, and reserves for repairs.

administrator   A person appointed by a court to manage and distribute the estate of someone who has died without a will. Sometimes, the term refers to a male occupying that position, with a female being called an administratrix. Contrast with executor (male or gender-neutral) and executrix (female), who are persons named by a will to manage and distribute one's estate.

administrator's deed   A deed executed by one appointed by a court to administer another's estate; usually for someone who died without a will.

administratrix   Older term meaning a female appointed by a court to administer the estate of another, usually someone who died without a will. The male position was called an administrator. (Today, the term administrator is considered gender-neutral.)

administrivia   Slang term meaning the nondeal points contained in small print in documents written by lawyers, especially seemingly nonsensical items such as "The masculine shall include the feminine and the singular shall include the plural."

ADR   See *asset depreciation range.*

adult   One who has gained the age of majority, usually 18 or 21 depending on the state. Sometimes, younger people can take legal steps to remove the "disabilities of nonage," after which they will be treated as legal adults even though under the requisite age. Only adults have the legal capacity to enter into contracts or sell property. Minors may own real estate, but, because of the inability to enter contracts, they cannot effectively manage it, obtain a mortgage, or sell the property. If such actions should prove necessary, the child's legal guardian will usually have to ask a court for permission for the proposed action. The court will then appoint a guardian ad litem to represent the child's interests, in case the guardian has a conflict of interest or clouded judgment.

ad valorem tax   Literally means "according to the value." A tax placed upon property and calculated with reference to the value of the property. Ad valorem taxes usually have a super-priority, so that a sale for unpaid taxes will transfer title into the buyer, free and clear of any mortgages or other liens. On the other hand, lienholders are generally given the right to redeem property from tax sales, and regain all rights simply by reimbursing the purchaser for the sale price plus accrued interest.

advance   In construction financing, to disburse money from the allowable total amount of a loan in order to pay bills currently due, or to pay the builder or developer according to a previously agreed upon schedule of payments. Typically, a certain percentage will be advanced upon approval of plans and drawings, another amount at completion of all clearing and grubbing, at the end of final grading, when the structure is in the black (the roof decking has been completed), and then again at completion and final inspection.

advance payment annuity   A regular payment made at the beginning of each month, year, or other period. It is relevant to real estate because many financial calculations, such as those possible in Microsoft Excel or on a financial calculator, require entry of different formulas depending on whether you are solving for an advance payment annuity (also called an annuity due) or an ordinary annuity. Any time you want to solve an equation that involves a payment received at the beginning of a period, such as rent, you use the format for advance payment annuity. Any time you want to solve an equation that involves a payment received at the end of a period, such as mortgage payments, you use the format for ordinary annuity.

adverse claim   A claim against real property that is inconsistent with the purported owner's full ownership rights.

adverse financial change condition   In a loan commitment, a clause that allows the lender to cancel the commitment without penalty if the borrower's financial condition changes for the worse before loan funding.

adverse possession   Sometimes called squatter's rights; method of acquiring title to real estate when the true owner has neglected to assert his or her own rights for a specified period of time.

Commonly arises in the context of boundary line disputes. The next most common occurrence is when there is some technical defect in the title which can't be cured with a corrective deed because the person who must sign has disappeared, is dead, or refuses to sign. If one actually occupies property without permission, in an open and notorious manner, that is exclusive and hostile, and the true owner takes no action to dispossess the claimant, then the actual owner will be forever barred from asserting any rights to the property. The requirement of hostility does not mean there must be animosity between the parties, but simply that the adverse possessor claims ownership of the property, and therefore is legally hostile to any other claimants. The lack of permission refers to the absence of a lease or other such agreement granting possession but not necessarily title. The required time period, called the holding period, may vary from 10 to 20 years.

By law, one cannot adversely possess against the government.

> **Example:** *Seth and Rose are next-door neighbors and the best of friends. Seth erects a fence on what he believes to be their boundary line. For the next 10 years (or 20, depending on the jurisdiction) he mows the lawn up to the fence. Rose believes the fence marks the boundary between their two properties, but she is mistaken. Rose then sells her property to Greg, who orders a survey. The survey reveals that 20 feet of Emma's land is on Seth's side of the fence. In a lawsuit over the property line, Seth will usually claim that Greg's surveyor is mistaken and will also claim that even if the survey is correct, Seth has gained title to the 20 feet by virtue of adverse possession. It was Emma's responsibility to know the true location of her property lines. If she did not assert her rights during the 10- or 20-year time period, she, and all others coming after her, lose those rights.*

aesthetic value   A premium attached to the value of property because of its physical appearance or the scenic views that may be enjoyed from the property; the artistic worth of something, rather than its practical value.

aesthetic zoning   Zoning regulations that require new construction to conform to certain architectural and landscaping requirements. Examples include prohibitions against metal buildings, requirements that retaining walls be hidden behind shrubberies or trees, and restrictions on the location of off-street parking. Failure to investigate aesthetic zoning requirements can result in a project going substantially over-budget and possibly becoming economically disastrous.

affiant   A person who makes a written statement under oath by way of an affidavit.

affidavit   A written statement signed by the person making the statement—the affiant—and sworn to as true and accurate.

affirm   Confirm, ratify, positively acknowledge as correct. One may affirm a statement in an affidavit. Witnesses may affirm that all testimony to be given will be true and accurate.

affirmative lending   Obligation placed upon federally chartered lenders by virtue of the Community Reinvestment Act, and upon state-chartered lenders by similar state legislation. Requires lenders to exert efforts to match the demographic character of their loan portfolios to the demographic character of the community in which they operate.

affirmative marketing program   A voluntary program designed by the U.S. Department of Housing and Urban Development in order to further its fair housing goals. This program seeks to involve builders, developers, lenders, and the real estate industry in a wide variety of cooperative enterprises to improve communication, focus, and sensitivity. Signatories are contractually bound to abide by the requirements of the plan. Many local governments have their own versions of an affirmative marketing program. Developers may agree to be bound by the master plan, or they must present and obtain approval of their own plan before construction permits will be granted.

affordability index   See *housing affordability index*.

affordable housing   Housing for people whose income is a certain percentage below the median income for an area, as determined by the U.S. Department of Housing and Urban Development (HUD). National and local governments provide incentives and cash assistance to developers to build new affordable housing or rehabilitate older apartment buildings or other projects and offer housing at rates deemed affordable for the area.

Currently, HUD has three affordable housing programs. They are

1. HOME. Provides grants to state and local governments to fund their programs to meet the housing needs of low-income and very low income families.
2. SHOP. Provides funds to nonprofit organizations to acquire home sites and develop or improve the systems for delivery of sweat equity and volunteer-based homeownership programs for low-income families.
3. HOZ. Provides funds for communities to reclaim vacant and blighted areas and create home ownership zones of mixed income, pedestrian friendly neighborhoods.

after acquired property clause   A clause in a mortgage that "scoops up," as additional collateral, property acquired after the original loan. The intent is to protect the lender in case the borrower has a defective title to the property at the time of the loan, but later cures those defects and gains full legal title. It is also intended to gain a security interest in contiguous land purchased later, and having some practical relationship to the mortgaged land. (In practice, the clause is usually buried in the fine print and allows lenders to increase the value of their collateral when that was never the original intent of the parties.)

after-tax cash flow   A financial analysis of an income-producing property to determine cash benefits to the owner after paying all expenses, mortgage payments, and taxes, and after deducting amounts that must be taken into income for tax purposes, but which have not yet been collected. If the tax savings from depreciation or other tax shelters will result in tax losses, thus reducing taxes that must be paid on other income, then those savings are added back in, just as if they were additional income. The intent is to discover the amount of money that can be deposited in the bank at the end of each year.

Analysis of a Property Management Company for One Year

Financial Items	Profit	Cash Flow	After-Tax Cash Flow
Total billings	$80,000	$80,000	$80,000
Outstanding receivables as yet unpaid	N/A	(22,000)	(22,000)
Labor expenses	(35,000)	(35,000)	(35,000)
Office equipment depreciation	(4,000)	N/A	N/A
Loan principal payments	N/A	(6,000)	(6,000)
Loan interest payments	(1,200)	(1,200)	(1,200)
Net taxable income	39,800	N/A	N/A
Taxes on income	(9,154)	N/A	(9,154)
Net cash flow	N/A	15,800	N/A
Net cash flow after taxes	N/A	N/A	6,646
After-tax income	$30,646	N/A	N/A

N/A = not applicable.

after-tax equity yield Methods of financial analysis for an equity position in real estate, being the net return rate on an investment after deducting expenses, interest, and taxes.

> **Example:** *An investor buys a property with $100,000 down (equity) and $400,000 in financing. The investor receives $7,000 in cash flow each year, after paying income taxes on money earned from the investment. After 5 years, the investor sells the property and receives $150,000 after deducting mortgage balance, taxes, and sale costs. The investor received a return of the original $100,000 and a sale profit of $50,000 upon sale, plus the $35,000 received over the course of 5 years, for a total of $85,000.*

After quantifying the various components, one then calculates yield by using any of several formulas, such as cash-on-cash and internal rate of return.

after-tax income Income after deducting taxes. After-tax income is not the same thing as after-tax cash flow. The major difference between the two will usually occur because depreciation is a deduction from income but not cash flow. You don't write a check for depreciation. The other major difference arises because you write a check for mortgage principal payments, which reduces cash flow, but you can't deduct it, so it does not reduce taxable income.

Difference between After-Tax Income and After-Tax Cash Flow		
	After-Tax Income	**After-Tax Cash Flow**
Total rents	$10,000	$10,000
Operating expenses	(1,000)	(1,000)
Depreciation	(1,500)	N/A (not a cash item)
Mortgage interest	(1,000)	(1,000)
Mortgage principal	N/A (not deductible)	(500)
Subtotals	6,500	7,500
Taxes	(1,820)	(1,820)
Final number	$4,680	$5,680

N/A = not applicable.

after-tax proceeds from resale   The amount of money left for the investor upon a sale after deducting all sale costs and taxes. This is the money available for reinvestment in another property.

agency   A relationship in which the principal gives an agent the right to act on the principal's behalf and to exercise some business judgment and discretion. Agents owe very high degrees of loyalty, good faith, and confidentiality to their principals, often expressed as fiduciary obligations. Except for the agency coupled with an interest, agency relationships automatically terminate when the principal dies or becomes incapacitated. Agents do not have to receive payment for their services, and the agency agreement does not have to be in writing unless It relates to transferring an interest in real estate. The consequence is that many people enter into principal-agent relationships almost accidentally, being unaware of the responsibilities and obligations each has to the other.

- There is a great variety of agency relationships that arise in a number of ways. All states have statutes regulating real estate agents and defining their duties and responsibilities, but this is by no means the exclusive method of defining the relationship or its obligations.
- Agency by estoppel arises when a principal allows someone to engage in such activities that the public is justified in believing the person is acting as an agent, even if the person had no such authority. This becomes important when someone makes commitments he or she had no authority to make, and an innocent third party, relying on those commitments, suffers an injury. The principal will not be allowed to avoid the commitment by claiming the supposed agent had no authority, because the law will impose an agency by estoppel.
- Exclusive agency is a real estate sales relationship in which the owner of property grants a particular agent the exclusive right to market the property and secure buyers, but the owner retains the right to sell the property himself or herself and pay no commission at all. Contrast with an open listing, in which the owner agrees to pay a commission to any real

estate professional who brings a buyer to the closing table. Contrast also with an exclusive right to sell agreement, in which not only does the agent have an exclusive agency, but even if the owner sells the property, the agent receives a commission.

- General agency occurs when the agent is empowered to do all acts in connection with a particular trade, business, or employment. Contrast with special agency, in which the agent is authorized to conduct a single transaction or series of transactions not involving a continuing relationship. Real estate agents are special agents.
- Agency by ratification arises when one purports to act on behalf of a principal, without true authority, but the principal later learns of the act, ratifies it, and agrees to be bound. Requires some proof that the principal made a conscious decision to ratify the act. Contrast with agency by estoppel, in which the principal becomes bound because of his or her negligence, not because of any conscious decision.
- Agency coupled with an interest is a special relationship that arises when the agent also has an interest in the property with which he or she is dealing. This agency will not automatically terminate upon the death of the principal.
- Types of real estate agency:
  - A listing agent represents the seller of a property.
  - A selling agent works with the buyer, but may be a subagent of the seller or an agent of the buyer. Real estate agents must disclose which party they are representing, before someone accidentally reveals any confidential information.
  - A dual agent is supposed to represent both the buyer and seller, but this is virtually impossible for one person to do. The status arises most often when one real estate agent in an office represents the seller and another real estate agent in the same office represents the buyer; then the broker is technically considered a dual agent. In such situations the broker must take care that each agent not reveal confidential information to the other.
  - A transaction agent is technically no agent at all, but is simply a facilitator who uses superior knowledge of real estate customs and practices to assist buyers and sellers.

agency disclosure   State laws that require agents to disclose which party to a transaction they are representing. Some states also require agents to disclose all agency relationships offered by their firm.

agent   One who acts on behalf of a principal in an agency relationship. See *agency* for an extended discussion.

aggrieved party   A party who has suffered a wrong or an injury; one who has a grievance or a complaint against another.

agreed boundary   A doctrine that allows adjoining landowners to agree regarding the location of the true boundary line between themselves, if the line is in doubt. An oral agreement as to the location of the true boundary line is usually enforceable, despite statute of frauds laws that require all contracts relative to real estate to be in writing. In contrast, an oral agreement to compromise a boundary line, perhaps to "split the difference" and establish it someplace in the middle between two conflicting opinions, must be in writing to be enforceable.

agreement of sale   Typically refers to any real estate sales contract. In a few states, however, the term refers specifically to a type of seller financing also called a bond for title, land sale contract, or contract for deed. In that instance, the seller retains legal title to the property until the purchaser has made all payments over the term of the financing period. At the end, if there has been no default, the seller executes a deed to the buyer. This device is often used in high-risk financing situations because it can often avoid legal protections given to the buyer in the event of foreclosure or bankruptcy.

Agricultural Foreign Investment Disclosure Act   A law requiring foreign persons with an interest in more than one acre of agricultural land to report their ownership to the U.S. Secretary of Agriculture, using form FSA 153. The law is only one of a number of mechanisms for monitoring foreign investment in the United States, its effect on pricing Americans out of the market, and its concentration of critical resources into foreign hands. (For more information, go to the U.S. Department of Agriculture Web site www.usda.gov and search for "FSA 153.")

agricultural use exemption   In ad valorem taxes, an exemption that allows agricultural land to be valued at its current usage, rather than the possibly much more expensive highest and best use valuation. Oftentimes, the appraised value is then further reduced by a certain percentage to reach an assessed value, upon which the taxes are based. (Many say this is done as an incentive to maintain green spaces and agricultural land rather than developing it in order to generate money to pay extremely high real estate taxes. Others say the exemption is a result of powerful agricultural and timber lobbies.)

AIDS   Acquired immunodeficiency syndrome. Persons who are HIV-positive, or who have AIDS, are protected from discrimination by the Americans with Disabilities Act (ADA) and other federal and state legislation. This extends to decisions to buy, rent, or sell. Further, in many states it is considered a violation of privacy to reveal that a former tenant or owner was HIV-positive or suffered from AIDS.

AIDS Housing Opportunity Act   Legislation passed in 1990 to provide state and local governments with the resources and incentives to devise long-term comprehensive strategies for meeting the housing needs of persons with AIDS and the families of such persons.

air rights   Historically, property owners owned to the center of the earth and to the top of the heavens, which included the right to all the air above the property and the right to exclude trespassers from that air. Until the invention of aircraft, the matter typically arose only in disputes over the right to remove tree limbs extending over one's property. Today, aircraft constantly trespass into property owner's air space and violate their air rights. As an accommodation to modern technology, courts allow reasonable trespasses to air rights. Airports and governments frequently purchase air rights adjacent to an airport, called avigation easements, to provide glide paths for aircraft. (Because of the scarcity of prime real estate near city centers, many local governments are investigating and implementing plans to lease air rights above transit hubs to developers, for building hotels and other such projects.)

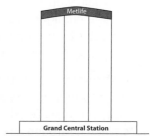

The 58-story MetLife building in New York City is built in air rights above Grand Central Station

air space   A three-dimensional slice of property above ground level. People who own condominiums own the rights to a specific air space.

ALDA   See *Asset Conservation, Lender Liability and Deposit Insurance Act of 1996*.

alienation   The act of transferring ownership or some partial interest in real property from one person to another. Voluntary alienation occurs when one executes a deed or a lease. Involuntary alienation occurs when there is a foreclosure, tax sale, or condemnation.

alienation by devise   Occurs when property passes by virtue of a will, and alienation by descent occurs when it passes by intestate succession in the absence of a will.

aliquot parts subdivision   Method of describing large parcels of lands as being entire sections, or regular percentages of sections. Under the public land survey system employed in most southern and western states, the states were divided into townships containing 6 square miles each. Townships were subdivided into 36 sections, and each section had 640 acres. Smaller parcels are described in terms such as quarters or halves of sections. All townships and sections are numbered, so it is fairly easy to identify a particular parcel of land by reference to its section township number, section number, and then its quadrant within the section.

W 1/2 320 acres	NE 1/4 160 acres
	N 1/2 of SE 1/4 80 acres
	N 1/2 of SW 1/4 of SE 1/4 20 a. / SE 1/4 of SE 1/4 40 acres
	S 1/2 of SW 1/4 of SE 1/4 20 a.

Subdividing a Section

alley   A path between buildings or behind buildings, usually with walls on both sides.

alligator property   Derogatory slang term referring to a property with negative cash flows that eat up large amounts of investor cash.

all-inclusive deed of trust   A purchase money deed of trust which is secondary to the seller's deed of trust to its own lender, which remains in place rather than being paid off at the time of sale. Now largely extinct because almost all commercial lenders have loan clauses allowing them to accelerate the note and demand all sums due immediately when a sale occurs. As a result, it is now virtually impossible to sell property without paying off the first mortgage or deed of trust, unless one engages in some type of fraud in order to prevent the lender from discovering the property has been sold. (Similar to a wraparound mortgage, but used in states that employ deeds of trust rather than mortgages.)

allodial system   A system of real property law in which individuals may fully own all the rights associated with property and dispose of that property as they wish. The system had been evolving for many centuries, but the theory and the term were first clearly articulated by Thomas Jefferson in 1774, when he argued against an attempted land grab by King George III and used the theory to provide one of the supports for the American Revolutionary War. Contrast the allodial system with the feudal system, in which the sovereign owned all land and could grant usage rights to others, but those rights were revocable at will.

allowance   An accounting term used to describe entries on a profit and loss statement for expenses that might become necessary in the future. Examples include an allowance for bad debt, in which a certain percentage of income is deducted because of the likelihood it will be uncollectible.

Alpha Sigma Gamma   A national real estate honorary for college students participating in real estate education programs. It is sponsored by the American Real Estate Society (www.aresnet.org/ASG/index.htm).

all-risks policy   An insurance policy that covers all perils except those specifically excluded in writing. Mortgage lenders typically require an all-risks policy on their collateral.

alluvium   The material deposited on land by virtue of the process of accretion. The accretion process occurs when rivers or other waters deposit silt and mud on land, and thus create more land; the silt and mud making up the new land is called alluvium.

ALTA   See *American Land Title Association*. The acronym is usually pronounced as a word—"all tuh"—and used to describe a particular type of survey or other requirements imposed by the lender at a real estate closing, for example, "The mortgage lender will require an ALTA survey." Although this expression is common, there is no such thing as "an" ALTA survey. There are various ALTA requirements for a survey, some or all of which might be demanded by a lender.

alterations   Physical changes to a property. Tenants are usually prohibited from making any alterations to the leased property. Disputes arise over whether something constitutes an alteration, or mere decoration or even repair.

alternative investments   See *specialty investments*.

alternative minimum tax   Tax reform enacted in 1969 as a result of the increasing financial burden of the Vietnam War. It was designed to impose a flat tax upon wealthy individuals who used all available tax shelters and loopholes in order to avoid paying any taxes at all. The treasury secretary at the time, Joseph Barr, warned against a taxpayer revolt once it became widely known that the country had 155 citizens who made over $200,000 per year but paid no income taxes at all, and 20 of them were actually millionaires! His predictions were accurate; more people wrote their congresspersons to complain about the 155 "tax cheats" than wrote to complain about the Vietnam War.

To remedy the situation, Congress revised the Internal Revenue Code so that complex calculations must be performed as if certain tax preference items were not deductible and then a minimum tax imposed on that figure so that "wealthy" individuals would pay their fair share of the tax burden. The problem with the system is that it is not indexed for inflation, so a 1969's wealthy individual is today's typical two-income middle-class family. The New York Times predicts that, by the year 2010, nearly 30 million taxpayers will have to pay the alternative minimum tax. There is increasing pressure to abolish the tax entirely, or to revise it to provide relief for middle-class Americans.

alternative mortgage instrument   Any mortgage other than a fixed-rate, fixed-term, fully amortizing mortgage.

alternative workspace   Various concepts relating to novel uses of space, including:

- Telecommuting. Working at home or on the road, with a computer network and possibly video links to a central office.
- Hoteling. Using office space on an as-needed basis via reservations, like a hotel room.
- Hot desking. In which telecommuters come into the office and use any available office or cubicle, without the need for reservations.
- Office sharing.
- Open office plans.

amendment   A change to an agreement; an attachment added after contract execution in order to modify or expand upon the original contract.

amenities   Particular features that add to the value of a property, such as a whirlpool tub and steam shower in a house, or swimming pool and tennis courts in a condominium project.

American Bankers Association   A trade organization for officers of commercial banks (www.aba.com).

American Institute of Architects   A professional association for architects, designers, and developers (www.aia.org).

American Institute of Real Estate Appraisers   A professional organization formerly associated with the National Association of REALTORS®. It merged with the Society of Real Estate Appraisers in 1991 to form the Appraisal Institute (www.appraisalinstitute.org). It awards two designations, the MAI (Member, Appraisal Institute) and SRA (Senior Residential Appraisal) to members who have completed rigorous experience and testing requirements. In common parlance, an MAI appraisal, being one performed by someone with the MAI designation, is supposed to be more accurate and more reliable than one prepared by a licensed appraiser without the MAI designation.

American Land Title Association   An association founded in 1907 as the trade association for the abstract and title insurance industry (www.alta.org).

American Motel Hotel Brokers Network   An association for real estate brokers who specialize in hotels, motels, resorts, casinos, bed and breakfasts, and assisted living facilities (www.amhbnetwork.com).

American National Standards Institute, Inc.   Founded in 1918, the organization (www.ansi.org) promulgates and oversees the implementation of a wide variety of standards, from acoustical devices to building measurements to livestock production. It also accredits programs that assess conformance to the ISO 9000 (quality) and ISO 1400 (environmental) management systems.

American Planning Association   A professional organization of regional and urban planners (www.planning.org).

American Real Estate and Urban Economics Association   An organization of scholars and practitioners concerned with the economic analysis of real estate activities. The association publishes Real Estate Economics, the oldest academic journal concentrating on the real estate industry. The organization's Web site, www.areuea.org, includes a searchable database of article abstracts.

American Real Estate Society   Describes itself as an "association of real estate thought leaders... dedicated to producing and disseminating knowledge related to real estate decision making and the functioning of real estate markets." Membership is open to anyone with an interest in real estate research. The society's Web site is www.aresnet.org.

American Society of Appraisers   A professional organization of appraisers (www.appraisers.org). It offers testing and accreditation in all appraisal disciplines, including

- Appraisal review and management
- Business valuation
- Gems and jewelry
- Machinery and technical specialties
- Real property
- Personal property

American Society of Farm Managers and Rural Appraisers   Founded in 1929 as an association of farm managers; it added rural appraisers in 1936. It confers the designation ARA (Accredited Rural Appraiser). The organization's Web site is www.asfmra.org.

American Society of Home Inspectors (ASHI)   A professional organization for home inspectors, founded in 1976. It is North America's oldest and largest professional society of home inspectors. The organization's Web site is www.ashi.com.

American standard   Shorthand for measurement methods used by the Building Owners and Managers Association and adopted by the American National Standards Institute Inc. (ANSI) so that there is uniformity in measuring and calculating office space.

Americans with Disabilities Act (ADA)   A federal law that grants civil rights protections to individuals with disabilities. It guarantees equal opportunity for individuals with disabilities in public accommodations, employment, transportation, state and local government services, and telecommunications.

- Real estate: The Act is most relevant in its provisions regarding public accommodation. Responsibility for compliance is placed on both landlords and tenants, as well as other property owners. Many commercial leases allocate the burden of ADA compliance so that the tenant must pay for any alterations or improvements necessary to bring a property into compliance.
- Places of public accommodation: These include a wide range of entities, such as restaurants, hotels, theaters, doctors' offices, pharmacies, retail stores, museums, libraries, parks, private schools, and day care centers. Private clubs and religious organizations are exempt.

- Accessibility for existing properties: Steps must be taken to remove barriers, if it can be done easily and without much expense. The evaluation of the expense depends on the size and financial strength of the entity.

- Accessibility requirements when a property undergoes alteration or renovation: For example, if during renovations a doorway is being relocated, the new doorway must be wide enough to meet the new construction standard for accessibility. When alterations are made to a primary function area, such as the lobby of a bank or the dining area of a cafeteria, an accessible path of travel to the altered area must also be provided. The bathrooms, telephones, and drinking fountains serving that area must also be made accessible. These additional accessibility alterations are only required to the extent that the added accessibility costs do not exceed 20 percent of the cost of the original alteration.

- Accessibility in new construction: The ADA requires that all new construction of places of public accommodation, as well as of "commercial facilities" such as office buildings, be accessible. Elevators are generally not required in facilities under three stories or with fewer than 3,000 square feet per floor, unless the building is a shopping center or mall; the professional office of a health care provider; a terminal, depot, or other public transit station; or an airport passenger terminal.

- Litigation: Private individuals may bring lawsuits to obtain injunctive relief to force compliance with the ADA and recover their attorneys' fees for the litigation, but may not obtain money damages. Citizens may also file complaints with the United States attorney general, who is authorized to bring lawsuits in cases of general public importance or where a pattern of discrimination is alleged. The suit can ask for money damages and civil penalties.

- The official ADA Web site is www.usdoj.gov/crt/ada/.

AMI   See *alternative mortgage instrument.*

AML   See *adjustable mortgage loan.*

amortization   (1) In mortgages, the gradual payment of a loan, in full, by making regular payments over time of principal and interest so there is a $0 balance at the end of the term. (2) In accounting, refers to the process of spreading expenses out over a period of time rather than taking the entire amount in the period the expense occurred. For example, some real estate closing expenses may be deducted on one's taxes in the current year, but others must be amortized over the life of the mortgage loan and only a small percentage deducted each year.

amortization schedule   A report that usually shows the principal and interest allocation of each monthly payment during the first year, the total principal and interest paid in each subsequent year, and the total interest that will be paid over the life of a loan. Download a template for creating loan amortization reports by going to the Microsoft Excel Web site at http://office.microsoft.com/en-us/templates.

Loan principal amount	$175,000.00	Annual loan payments	$13,971.36
Annual interest rate	7.000%	Monthly payments	$1,164.28
Loan period in years	30	Interest in first calendar year	$12,193.68
First year of loan	2007	Interest over term of loan	$244,140.80
First month of loan	January	Sum of all payments	$419,140.80

Year	Month	Beginning Balance	Payment	Interest	Cumulative Principal	Cumulative Interest	Ending Balance
2007	Jan	$175,000.00	$1,164.28	$1,020.83	$143.45	$1,020.83	$174,856.55
	Feb	$174,856.55	$1,164.28	$1,020.00	$287.73	$2,040.83	$174,712.27
	Mar	$174,712.27	$1,164.28	$1,019.15	$432.86	$3,059.98	$174,567.14
	Apr	$174,567.14	$1,164.28	$1,018.31	$578.83	$4,078.29	$174,421.17
	May	$174,421.17	$1,164.28	$1,017.46	$725.65	$5,095.75	$174,274.35
	June	$174,274.35	$1,164.28	$1,016.60	$873.33	$6,112.35	$174,126.67
	Jul	$174,126.67	$1,164.28	$1,015.74	$1,021.87	$7,128.09	$173,978.13
	Aug	$173,978.13	$1,164.28	$1,014.87	$1,171.28	$8,142.96	$173,828.72
	Sep	$173,828.72	$1,164.28	$1,014.00	$1,321.56	$9,156.96	$173,678.44
	Oct	$173,678.44	$1,164.28	$1,013.12	$1,472.72	$10,170.08	$173,527.28
	Nov	$173,527.28	$1,164.28	$1,012.24	$1,624.76	$11,182.32	$173,375.24
	Dec	$173,375.24	$1,164.28	$1,011.36	$1,777.68	$12,193.68	$173,222.32

Year	Beginning Balance	Payment	Principal	Cumulative Principal	Cumulative Interest	Ending Balance
2008	$173,222.32	$13,971.36	$1,906.07	$3,683.75	$24,258.97	$171,316.25
2009	$171,316.25	$13,971.36	$2,043.97	$5,727.72	$36,186.36	$169,272.28
2010	$169,272.28	$13,971.36	$2,191.73	$7,919.46	$47,965.98	$167,080.54

anaconda mortgage   A mortgage containing a clause saying it secures the debt originally intend-ed by the parties, and all future debts that may become due and owing in the future. Such clauses are sometimes called dragnet clauses or Mother Hubbard clauses. The effect is that a borrower with multiple loans—real estate, automobile, line of credit, checking account overdraft protection, busi-ness—may find that the lender will require all sale proceeds when the property is sold, even though the borrower might have substantial equity under the terms of the specific note originally secured by the mortgage. Debtors find themselves squeezed to death, like being encircled by an anaconda snake. The courts disfavor such clauses and usually refuse to enforce them unless there is some rela-tionship among the debts and some specific reference in later loan documents to the earlier anacon-da clause. Despite that, it is recommended that you ask mortgage lenders to delete the clause from their instrument before you sign.

anchor tenant   A major department store or chain store located in a shopping center so as to attract customers who will then shop at the smaller, satellite stores; sometimes referred to as a traffic generator or magnet store.

- Because of the critical importance of that traffic to the smaller tenants, wise shopping center owners in a position to negotiate terms will prohibit the anchor from going dark, meaning vacating its space. Otherwise, the anchor could move to a more desirable location, continue paying the rent for the old property, but effectively cause most of the other tenants to go out of business and default on their leases because of the lack of traffic. Unfortunately, important anchor tenants usually have the clout to refuse to sign a lease with such terms.

- Anchor tenants often reserve the right to dictate the selection of the satellite tenants and to prohibit ones which might be incompatible with their core philosophies (such as liquor stores) or who might compete with their merchandise sales.

- A related term is shadow anchor, used when a small shopping center wants to communicate that an important traffic generator is next door or directly across the street. An ad might read, "Subject property shadow anchored by Wal-Mart to the east and Target to the west."

ancient lights doctrine   Early English doctrine holding that one could not build a structure so as to block the sunlight from a neighbor's window. Despite the abundance of available land in this country, Americans love of high-rise architecture, coupled with a general unwillingness to expand private property rights to contiguous spaces, means that the concept never really caught on here. One exception occurs when a neighbor builds a spite fence for a malicious purpose to obstruct light; the courts will order removal of the fence. Recently, some courts are revisiting the doctrine and allowing application, especially as it relates to the use of solar-powered equipment. Such courts reason that public policy now disfavors unbridled development and favors use of alternative energy sources.

ancillary tenant   A shopping center tenant that occupies smaller space and is less important than an anchor tenant. See *satellite tenant*.

angel investors   See *venture capital*.

animal unit   A unit of measurement indicating the ability of land to support range animals. Generally, a 1,000-pound animal grazing 26 pounds of dry forage per day (a mature cow or equivalent) is equal to one animal unit. Livestock grazing permits are usually expressed in terms of animal units per area or total animal unit months.

annexation   The process of joining property to another. Arises in two contexts: (1) Personal property is annexed to real property, becoming a part of it, and must remain if the property is sold or if a leasehold interest comes to an end. (2) Local governments expand their jurisdictional limits and tax bases by annexing property. The process is usually accomplished through local ballot and is generally hotly contested by groups of property owners who do not want to lose their independence or see an increase in property taxes.

annual bumps   Slang for annual increases in such items as rent or operating expenses.

annual cap   An agreed-upon limit on the amount an adjustable-rate mortgage may increase the interest rate each year. Consumer mortgages usually have annual caps; commercial mortgages usually do not.

annual debt service   The total of all principal and interest payments made over the course of a year. This figure provides one of the analytical tools for mortgage lenders of income-producing properties, who compare net annual income of the property to annual debt service on the proposed mortgage to arrive at a debt service coverage ratio. Acceptable ratios depend on the particular industry and on lending market conditions at the time.

annual mortgage constant   The amount of annual debt service compared to the principal amount of a loan and then expressed as a dollar amount.

Annual debt service ÷ Mortgage principal = Annual mortgage constant

The constant tells you the total principal and interest payments per year per $100 of debt. (Before the widespread availability of simple financial calculators and computer spreadsheet templates, figures obtained from annual mortgage constant tables were the only quick and reliable way to calculate mortgage payments.)

annual percentage rate (APR)   Usually different from the quoted interest rate or face rate on a promissory note, the annual percentage rate is a creation of the federal Truth in Lending Act, which requires that certain loan expenses be treated as if they were additional interest paid over the life of the loan, and then a new interest rate calculated based on that assumption. The intent was to force standardization in calculating the cost of obtaining credit, so that consumers could shop wisely and make informed decisions without fear of hidden charges making credit more expensive than anticipated. In reality, there is no real consensus or practical guidance about the necessity to include or ability to exclude many loan charges from the APR calculations, resulting in continued widespread confusion about the cost of credit.

Annual Percentage Rate	Finance Charge	Amount Financed	Total of Payments
The cost of your credit as a yearly rate.	The dollar amount the credit will cost you.	The amount of credit provided to you on your behalf.	The amount you will have paid after you have made all payments as scheduled.
8.69%	$227,087	$125,000	$352,087

Sample disclosures required by the Truth in Lending Act for a $125,000 loan for 30 years at a quoted interest rate of 7.25% but a higher APR because of prepaid interest points and other charges

annuity   A sum of money received on a regular basis as one of a series of fixed payments. Real property is sometimes sold in exchange for a private annuity. The buyer guarantees a fixed monthly income to the seller for the seller's lifetime. The seller, of course, is gambling he or she will live much longer than anyone could expect, and thus ultimately receive far more than the property was worth.

The buyer is gambling that the seller will die sooner as opposed to later, and the buyer will have a windfall. Wise sellers will include a clause guaranteeing a minimum term for payments, even if they must be made to their estate or heirs. See *advance payment annuity* and *ordinary annuity*.

annuity due   See *advance payment annuity*.

anticipation, principle of   In appraisal, the concept that the value of property today is equal to the value of future income, discounted to present value. Discounting rests on the assumption that the right to receive $1 in the future is not worth $1 today, but something less than $1.

anticipatory breach   An affirmative statement or action indicating that a party has no intention of honoring his or her contractual commitments. This is important because one cannot ordinarily bring a lawsuit until there has been an actual breach of a contract. For tactical or other reasons, it may be important to avoid delays. If there has been an anticipatory breach, the aggrieved party may bring suit immediately.

antideficiency legislation   Laws in some states that protect consumers from deficiency judgments after foreclosure of a purchase-money mortgage on residential real estate. The lender may take the real property in satisfaction of the debt. If the property is worth less than the debt at that time, the lender suffers the loss and may not sue the borrower for the difference.

antitrust laws   State and federal laws designed to encourage competition and discourage or prohibit monopolies. Relevant in the real estate context because of the somewhat monopolistic power of local real estate boards, their ability to admit or exclude members, the possibility of de facto (informal) price fixing relative to real estate commissions, and their control of the Multiple Listing Service® database of properties offered for sale. This is an exceptionally complex area of law. (For more information, visit the Department of Justice Web site at www.usdoj.gov/atr/overview.html and the National Association of REALTORS® antitrust pages at www.realtor.org/libweb.nsf/pages/fg704.)

APA   See *American Planning Association*.

apartment (building)   A building with multiple residential tenants.

APFO   See *adequate public facilities ordinances*.

APN   See *assessor parcel number*.

APP   Shorthand for appreciation.

appeals board   A local board empowered to overturn decisions of a permitting, zoning, taxing, or other regulatory authority. Before embarking on any possibly contested activity in these areas, such as a zoning change request, it is extremely important to determine the name and requirements of the correct appeals board, should it become necessary to ask for reversal of a decision. Many boards have very limited and technical grounds for appeal that, if known in advance, can be factored into tactical decisions at the level below. In addition, the time limits for filing appeals are generally extremely short.

application fee   A fee charged by a lender, ostensibly for the time and trouble involved in processing a loan request, analyzing available data, and calculating what terms and conditions to offer. In reality, this view is a holdover from the days when consumers went to lenders, hat in hand, to plead for money. In today's very competitive lending market, where virtually every television show includes at least one mortgage lender as an advertiser, it is ludicrous to think that a consumer would pay someone for the opportunity to review a loan request. This fee will usually be waived upon request; it is simply another source of profit for the lender.

apportion   To divide into parts. Co-owners of property may decide to apportion maintenance costs among themselves, according to the percentage of ownership enjoyed by each. Buyers and sellers usually apportion real estate taxes so that the portion earned by local government before closing, but not yet paid because not yet due, will be paid by the seller in the form of a credit against the purchase price. When the property tax bill is later received by the buyer, he or she will pay the entire bill in full, but will have already received the equivalent of reimbursement through the credit at closing.

apportionment   Division into parts. Typically used when deciding how to allocate expenses relative to oil and gas leases, and when deciding that portion of the income of a company or utility that was earned in a particular state and thus subject to state income taxes. See *apportion*.

appraisal   The process of developing an opinion about a property's value. That opinion is supposed to reflect what a willing buyer would pay a willing seller after reasonable exposure to the marketplace, with neither buyer nor seller operating under any sort of duress or pressure. An appraisal is generally required when property is financed, and should be required before a real estate agent attempts to market anything significantly different from properties commonly and frequently sold in the marketplace. It may not be necessary to obtain an appraisal of a four-bedroom ranch house in a good school zone, but some assistance may be needed in arriving at a price to market an 11,000 square foot ski-lodge-type home in a small town.

- There are three common approaches to estimating the fair market value of a property. They are comparison, cost, and income.
- The comparison approach to appraisal seeks to obtain information about recent sales of comparable properties. It would be highly unlikely for the properties to be identical, so the appraiser will make adjustments in the sale price of the other comparable properties— called comps for short—in order to calculate what the sale price might have been if it were identical to the subject property. For example, if the subject property had no garage, but the comp had a two-car garage, the appraiser might subtract $50,000 from the sale price of the comp. The appraiser might then add $30,000 because the subject property has a finished attic providing more livable square footage, and another $15,000 because the subject property is brick while the comp is wood frame needing new paint. A residential appraiser will typically use three comps, commercial appraisers will employ more because it's generally difficult to find truly comparable properties, resulting in a large number of adjustments. The more adjustments, the more likely error will creep into the calculations. At the end of the process, the appraiser will have a value based on the comparison approach.

- Cost approach. This approach uses an estimate of the reproduction or replacement cost of the improvements, less depreciation, plus land value. The reproduction cost is the amount necessary to build exactly the same building. Replacement costs are those necessary to build an improvement with substantially the same usefulness using today's materials and techniques, but not necessarily the same exact characteristics.

- Income approach. This approach assumes that the value of the real estate is directly related to the value of the income generated by that real estate, such as shopping centers, apartments, and office buildings. The appraiser will calculate a net operating income (NOI) for the property by taking all possible income over the course of a year, and then subtracting operating expenses, insurance, real estate taxes, reserves for bad debts, a certain percentage for anticipated vacancies, and sometimes a certain dollar amount for the value of the owner's management and supervision. The bottom line number, the NOI, is then capitalized by dividing it by a certain percentage. That percentage rate is supposed to reflect the return an investor would expect on his or her money taking into consideration all the variables associated with the property. Variables could include the strength of the tenants, the likelihood of default, the remaining term on the leases, the prospect of future rent increases built into the leases, the likelihood of lease renewals at the expiration of current terms, the cost of financing to purchase the property, the availability of other investment sources and their rates of return, and other such factors. If a property had an NOI of $100,000 and a capitalization rate (cap rate for short) of 10 percent, then you divide $100,000 by 0.1 and arrive at a value of $1,000,000. Increasing the cap rate to 11 percent decreases the value to $909,090. Decreasing the cap rate to 9 percent increases the value to $1,111,111.

- Integration. Sometimes the appraiser will have to employ several methods in order to account for different aspects of the property. An income-producing property might include additional acreage for future development. The appraiser would value the current improvements using the income approach, and the surplus or excess land using the comparable approach.

- Reconciliation. At the end of the analysis, the appraiser will take all methods employed, as appropriate to the property, and reconcile the differing values into one value. This will then be the appraised value of the property.

appraisal review   A report that comments on the completeness and accuracy of an appraisal report. Lenders frequently employ in-house review appraisers as a check on the accuracy and honesty of third-party appraisals.

appraiser   One who performs appraisals of real or personal property. The various associations and organizations for real estate appraisers include:

- Appraisal Institute (www.appraisalinstitute.org). Offers the designation MAI, among others.
- National Association of Independent Fee Appraisers (NAIFA) (www.naifa.com). Founded in 1961.

- National Association of Master Appraisers (NAMA) (www.masterappraisers.org). Founded in 1982. It offers three designations: Master Residential Appraiser; Master Farm and Land Appraiser, and Master Senior Appraiser.
- National Association of Real Estate Appraisers (NAREA) (www.iami.org/NAREA/home.cfm). Founded in 1966.
- National Association of Review Appraisers and Mortgage Underwriters (NARA/MU) (www.iami.org/NARA/home.cfm). Founded in 1975.
- National Society of Real Estate Appraisers (www.nareb.com/affiliates/society_appraisers.shtml).
- American Society of Farm Managers and Rural Appraisers (www.asfmra.org).

appreciation   The process of increasing in value. As a practical matter, although the IRS allows taxpayers to depreciate real property improvements as if they were becoming less valuable over time and will eventually be worthless, real property generally appreciates over time with proper maintenance and repair.

appreciation return   Expressed as a percentage, the return generated by the appreciation of a property or portfolio over the period of analysis.

appropriation   (1) Taking private land for public use, as by condemnation. (2) Taking public property for private use, such as using water from a navigable river for irrigation purposes. (3) Legislatively designating government funds for a project.

appurtenance   That belonging to something of greater importance. Contracts usually describe a main structure and add a catchall for all appurtenances. (See figure on page 34.)

- In real estate law, easements, or the right to use another's property, may be appurtenant or in gross.
- If appurtenant, then the easement belongs to what is called the dominant estate (property) and passes to new owners for all time until the easement is abandoned. For example, an easement for ingress and egress over another's property is an easement appurtenant. The property that enjoys the easement is the dominant estate, and the property over which one may travel is called the servient estate. A sale of the dominant estate automatically includes a transfer of the easement, because it is appurtenant.
- Contrast with an easement in gross, which might be a right to park one's antique car at a friend's house and gain ingress and egress for purposes of using the car. This easement is personal and not tied to any particular real estate.
- This is a tricky area of the law that generally requires the assistance of a lawyer specializing in complex real estate issues. The seminal case on the subject is the 1850 English case of Ackroyd v. Smith.

APR   See *annual percentage rate.*

ARA   See *Accredited Rural Appraiser.*

arable   Able to be cultivated.

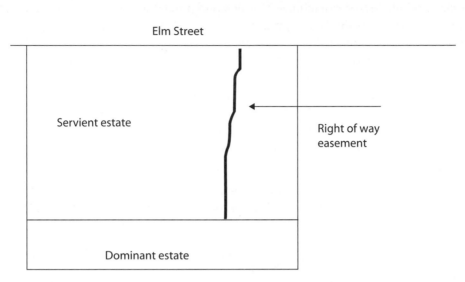

arbitrage   The simultaneous purchase in one market and sale in another market of a commodity, security, or monies, in the expectation of making a profit on price differences in the differing markets. Generally thought of as involving foreign currency exchanges, in which one enters contracts to buy euros and sell yen and hopefully make money in a moment in time when the exchange rates work out in one's favor (this is highly risky).

arbitraries   Shortened property descriptions used in title plants for indexing real properties, rather than the sometimes lengthy, technically accurate, surveyor's descriptions. Also called arbs.

arbitration   A method of nonjudicial or alternative dispute resolution (ADR) which long existed at common law but has recently gained renewed vigor because of the Federal Arbitration Act and the U.S. Supreme Court's pronouncements that the Act applies to all disputes involving matters in interstate commerce. Virtually every construction contract, architectural agreement, and mortgage loan document today contains an arbitration clause and is deemed to involve interstate commerce because of the nationwide impact of those industries. The American Arbitration Association maintains a Web site at www.adr.org.

The process relies upon aggrieved parties agreeing to one or more disinterested persons hearing their complaints and defenses and then coming to a conclusion establishing the rights and responsibilities of the parties and their damages, if any. In theory, at least, the arbitrators are skilled and knowledgeable in the particular field of the dispute and allowed to factor into their decisions their own knowledge and experiences. This is in contrast to the modern jury system, in which the law seeks to obtain a jury absolutely ignorant of any details of the industry or dispute, and willing to come to a conclusion based solely on the evidence presented by the lawyers.

- Pros. The process is usually much more informal than a traditional trial, allowing a leveling of the playing field when consumers attempt to represent themselves against lawyers representing the other side. In some markets, for some types of disputes, you can reach a hearing and resolution faster and more cheaply than in the court system. For others, a shortage of trained arbitrators for complex cases means the dispute might actually take longer. There are no formal rules of evidence, and the arbitrator simply factors in issues such as hearsay when deciding how much weight to give evidence, rather than excluding it entirely. Discovery is usually very limited in consumer cases so that extensive time and money is not spent searching for documents to produce, attending depositions, and other such matters. The final judgment is confidential and not publicly reported anywhere unless it is a money judgment not paid within the required time period, in which case the winner may record his or her arbitration award in the public records and attempt to enforce it.

- Cons. As a practical matter the arbitration award cannot be appealed or overturned, even if the arbitrator made obvious mistakes of law that directly resulted in a wrong decision. There are exceptions, but they are exceedingly technical, generally disfavored by appellate courts, and usually require a level of sophistication at the hearing level not enjoyed by most consumers. That is because, for most of the few allowable grounds of appeal, you must know those grounds and all their technicalities in advance and make tactical decisions at the hearing level that will preserve your rights to appeal. This lack of appellate rights was considered a trade-off for the ability to have an arbitrator knowledgeable about your field and supposedly able to reach a more fair decision than a jury. In reality, this rarely works out.

architecture   The science and art of structural design and construction supervision.

Architectural and Transportation Barriers Compliance Board   The former name of the Access Board.

architectural drawings   Project drawings provided by the architect, typically showing the floor plan; elevations (views of the various sides of the structure); finish schedules; and details of moldings, cabinetry, doors, and other such matters necessary for the builder to order the proper materials for construction. It typically does not include engineering drawings for heating and air conditioning, electrical, audiovisual, telecommunications, security, waste management or plumbing systems, or landscaping plans and topographical details. All such plans, obtained from other professionals, are typically combined with the architectural drawings into a set of working drawings.

area   A measurement of the square footage contained within certain boundaries.

ARELLO   See *Association of Real Estate License Law Officials.*

ARES   See *American Real Estate Society*.

AREUEA   See *American Real Estate and Urban Economics Association.*

Argus   A computer program widely used among real estate investors to analyze portfolio performance and purchase opportunities. It is becoming increasingly important for graduates of business schools to have working knowledge of the Argus software if they want to secure employment with large institutional owners and managers of real estate. (For more information go to Realm Web site at www.realm.com.)

ARM   See *adjustable-rate mortgage.*

arm's-length transaction   A transaction in which the parties have equal bargaining strength in order to protect their individual interests and are not related or involved in some other type of relationship that would tend to call into question the fervor with which they attempt to protect their interests. If the IRS determines that a sale of real estate was not an arm's-length transaction for fair market value, it may deem part of the value of the property as a gift, which could result in gift taxes.

arrears   (1) Being past due on a debt. (2) Paid at the end of the period rather than the beginning. Rent is usually paid in advance, at the beginning of the month for the coming month. Interest is usually paid in arrears, at the beginning of the month for interest accrued during the prior month. Real estate taxes are usually paid in arrears.

arterial street   Designed to carry traffic through an area as quickly and efficiently as possible in order to reach another destination. One might not want to locate a retail business on an important arterial street, because there would be limited ability for commuters to exit the artery and shop at the retail establishment. Arterial streets are designed for the benefit of the city as a whole, rather than the communities through which they pass. See *feeder road.*

artificial intelligence   The ability of a computer program to evaluate data and make decisions according to parameters set out in the software. Automated underwriting software is a type of artificial intelligence. The increasingly popular AVM—automated valuation model—uses artificial intelligence and related property data to create appraisals for lenders and for the IRS.

artificial person   A legal entity that is granted some of the rights and responsibilities of a natural person, such as corporations that may enter into contracts, partnerships that may sue and be sued, and church associations that may hold title to real estate. Almost all artificial persons enjoy the same rights and responsibilities as each other.

ASA   See *American Society of Appraisers.*

asbestos   A mineral fiber once commonly used for its fire-retarding and insulation properties. It was widely employed in insulation, roofing, floor tiles, household products, and appliances. After extensive studies, the Environmental Protection Agency determined that asbestos caused lung and stomach cancer in people exposed to it over long periods of time. If real property contains asbestos in it, most lenders will require removal, or a firm commitment for removal, before they will fund any loans to buy or renovate the property. Real estate agents are required to disclose the presence of asbestos on property, if known. Asbestos removal is generally accomplished by specially trained and licensed asbestos abatement contractors.

asbestos containing material (ACM)   Under Environmental Protection Agency regulations, any material containing more than 1 percent asbestos. There are different regulatory requirements depending on whether the ACM is friable or nonfriable.

as-built drawing   Not infrequently, the owner or contractor of a building under construction will make field modifications to the original architectural or engineering drawings. Ideally, all such modifications should be noted on one set of plans set aside for that purpose. At the completion of the project, the respective professionals will be asked to generate a new set of drawings showing the actual construction details, rather than original designs, so that future work can be planned and executed in a knowledgeable manner with reference to what already exists in the property. In the alternative, long after a building has been constructed, the owner may employ professionals to prepare plans showing all details of the building and its various systems. Both of these result in as-built drawings.

as is   In its current condition without any guarantees by the seller.

as-is value   An estimate of the value of real property in its current condition, which may be depressed because of necessary repairs and maintenance.

ASHI   See *American Society of Home Inspectors*.

assemblage   The process of putting together the purchase, or options for the purchase, of several small parcels from multiple owners in order to create a larger parcel of land. The goal is to obtain enough land for a particular development in mind, or to conduct the assemblage as a speculative venture, in order to sell the larger parcel for more money than it cost to purchase the smaller parcels. This increase in value due to the assemblage is called plottage value.

assessed value   The value of real property for the purposes of calculating property taxes and other similar charges such as school taxes and fire district dues; the tax appraiser will establish a fair market value for the property. The assessed value is then frequently calculated as a specific percentage of the appraised value. Oftentimes the percentage will vary depending on the use of the property and any applicable exemptions. In some states, for example, property is assessed at 20 percent of its fair market value. Persons residing on their property, and claiming a homestead exemption, may be entitled to an assessment of 10 percent of fair market value.

Example: Assessed Value of Real Property at 310 Main Street		
Appraised value	$370,000	
Assessment ratio of 10% for owner-occupied residential properties, results in assessed value	$37,000	
Tax rate of 2% of assessed value	$7,400	
Taxes due		$7,400

assessment   (1) The official valuation of property for tax purposes. (2) A one-time charge made against property owners for each one's pro rata share of the expense of repairs or improvements to be enjoyed by all of them in common, such as a condo association assessment to replace a roof, or a local government assessment to pave a dirt road. (3) Determination of the value of property in a condemnation case.

assessor   A public official charged with maintaining the property tax rolls and the accuracy of the appraised and assessed value of properties.

assessor parcel number (APN)   A number assigned by the local assessor in order to identify a particular property. Often used in real estate contracts until a more detailed legal description can be obtained, because each parcel has its own unique APN; deemed to be more reliable than a street address.

asset   Something of value. On a balance sheet or personal financial statement, assets will include the following items, typically arranged in order according to the ease with which they can be converted into cash:

    Cash and equivalents
        Cash on hand
        Cash in banks
        Marketable securities
    Receivables
        Accounts receivable
        Less reserves for bad debts
    Furniture, fixtures, and equipment
    Fine art
    Real property
    General intangibles
        Stock in closely held corporations
        Intellectual property rights
        Goodwill

When lenders examine balance sheets, they generally assume that individuals and small businesses overvalue the furniture, fixtures, and equipment and the general intangibles. Large entries for cash and equivalent assets will overcome a poor credit rating 9 times out of 10.

Asset Conservation, Lender Liability and Deposit Insurance Act of 1996   An amendment to the Comprehensive Environmental Response, Compensation and Liability Act (CERCLA) made in response to mortgage lender anxiety regarding statutory language that might make lenders liable for cleanup of contaminated sites, simply by virtue of their mortgage interest or as the result of a foreclosure. The amendments protect lenders from liability, preforeclosure, unless they participated in the contamination. It also shields them after a foreclosure, but only if they sell the property at the earliest practicable, commercially reasonable, time.

asset cost recovery system (ACRS)   See *accelerated cost recovery system*, which is the correct name for an outdated tax accounting methodology abbreviated as ACRS. Unfortunately, one often encounters this method erroneously described as "asset cost recovery system."

asset depreciation range (ADR)   An elective depreciation method allowed by the IRS after 1970 and before 1981. It had over 100 classes of property from which to choose appropriate depreciation periods. The entire system was a hotbed of taxpayer versus IRS controversy, so it was replaced by the

ACRS system in 1981, and then by the MACRS in 1987. One still encounters the ADR in literature, but it no longer exists.

asset management   The umbrella name for all phases and areas of expertise in the acquisition, management, leasing, operation, and eventual sale of real property assets.

assign   To transfer one's property rights or contract rights to another. In the context of real property, an assignment is commonly used in three circumstances: (1) An investor signs a contract to purchase real property and reserves the right to assign that contract to some business entity to be created in the future, but still owned or controlled by the same investor. (2) An investor wishes to purchase property anonymously because of fears the owner will increase the asking price if he or she knew the identity of the true purchaser. As a result, the investor employs a straw man to sign the purchase contract, and the contract is then assigned to the ultimate purchaser. (3) A speculative purchaser of condominium units or other property to be built in the future will sign a purchase contract for a fixed price, in the expectation that prices will increase dramatically by the time construction is completed. At that time the speculator may then assign their (below-market price) contract to another for a substantial profit.

assignee   One to whom a contract or lease has been assigned. See *assign*.

assignment of lease   Transferring all rights in a lease to real property to another. Leases typically contain prohibitions against assignment without landlord approval, but the approval may not be unreasonably withheld. Reasonable grounds may include a change in the creditworthiness of the tenant, an increase in the burden placed upon the property by the new tenant because of additional parking demands, or incompatibility with other tenants such as a liquor store coming into a small shopping center of family-oriented businesses. When a tenant assigns its lease, it remains liable for the entire lease term unless the landlord agrees to a novation, which is a declaration that the old lease is void and the landlord has entered into a direct relationship with the assignee.

assignment of rents   Additional collateral usually required by lenders for commercial properties. The lender may wish to take some step short of foreclosure if there is a default. By virtue of the assignment of rents, the lender may exercise its rights to contact all tenants and advise them to pay their rent directly to the lender rather than to the landlord borrower.

assignor   A person making an assignment.

associate broker   A real estate classification used in some states to describe someone who has obtained his or her broker's license and is thereby legally capable of heading a real estate office, but who works as a salesperson under the supervision and control of the lead broker, usually called the qualifying broker or a managing broker.

Associated Builders and Contractors (ABC)   A national trade association representing contractors, subcontractors, materials suppliers, and related firms. The organization's Web site is www.abc.org.

Associated General Contractors of America (AGCA)   A trade association for general contractors; established in 1918 after Woodrow Wilson expressed a need for such an organization. The organization's Web site is www.agc.org.

Association of Real Estate License Law Officials (ARELLO)   This association was organized in 1929 to facilitate the exchange of information and cooperation among regulators and policy makers in the area of real property. Today, the ARELLO mission statement is to "Support jurisdictions in the administration and enforcement of real estate license laws to promote and protect the public interest." Their Web site, www.arello.org, includes a consumer section with links to consumer protection agencies and to a database for checking whether persons selected by you have current real estate licenses in their jurisdiction.

assumable loan   A loan that can be taken over by a purchaser, who may then continue making payments in the same amount, at the same interest rate, for the remaining term of the loan.

History and background: Before the high interest rates and banking crises of the 1980s, most mortgage loans were freely assumable if the purchaser paid a small assumption fee. Problems arose when interest rates skyrocketed to nearly 20 percent, creating a lively market in people wishing to assume old 6 and 7 percent loans rather than obtain new purchase money loans at 20 percent. The lending industry also began to see a high percentage of non-credit-worthy purchasers, unable to obtain financing on their own, assuming loans. This all seemed good for consumers, but it was bad for lenders. Caught in the squeeze, many went under in the giant banking and savings and loan debacles of the era. To prevent future interest rate squeezes, and future underwriting disasters, lenders introduced a new loan clause called the due on sale clause. It stated that if the underlying property were sold or otherwise conveyed, the entire note would be due and payable immediately, even if it had not matured and there had never been a single default or late payment. California led the way of states antagonistic to this attempted infringement on consumer rights and outlawed the enforceability of due on sale clauses. The federal government, facing gigantic cash losses as a result of its lending industry bailouts, was strongly in favor of due on sale clauses so the current crisis would not repeat itself in the future. It passed legislation preempting states laws in the case of all federally chartered or federally insured (FDIC) financial institutions. The new law stated that due on sale clauses were enforceable and state laws to the contrary did not apply. The ability to assume mortgage loans is now effectively dead.

Today, some loans are still characterized as assumable, but the purchaser must meet all underwriting requirements necessary for an original loan, and the interest rate can usually be increased to market rates. In a true loan assumption, the original borrower remains liable on the promissory note, in addition to the purchaser of the property.

assumptions and limiting conditions   A recital of the assumptions on which an appraisal is based. These typically include matters such as: the appraisal is an accurate reflection of the value of the property, but only if there are no hidden defects, there are no boundary line problems, factual information obtained from others is correct, zoning allows the current or anticipated future use, and other such matters.

at-risk rules   IRS rules limiting the deductibility of some losses, which are not allowed to exceed the amount the taxpayer has at risk, meaning the total of cash contributions and liability on promissory notes. Under certain circumstances, nonrecourse loans secured by real property but not by the individual's guarantee or endorsement may still satisfy the at-risk rules. (For more guidance, go to IRS Web site www.irs.gov and download IRS Publication 925, "Passive Activity and At Risk Rules.")

attached housing   Housing that is attached to each other on at least one side. Contrast with detached housing, which is best exemplified by the traditional suburban home.

attachment   The legal process of seizing real or personal property for the payment of nonmortgage debts such as tax liens or judgments.

attest   To witness by observation and signature, as one who attests that another has signed a real estate contract. Contrast with acknowledgment, in which the signer states he or she signed the document voluntarily, and then a notary public or other such individual affixes his or her signature and seal as evidence of hearing the acknowledgment and witnessing the signing.

attorn   The act of a tenant formally agreeing to become the tenant of a new landlord, but for the same property. Usually occurs when there has been a sale or foreclosure of the leased property. The new owner will want to obtain an attornment in order to cut off defenses and claims the tenant might have against the old landlord, and to prevent the old landlord from muddying the waters by making claims for rent, even though no longer owning the real estate.

attorney-in-fact   A person authorized to act for another under a properly executed power of attorney.

attorney's opinion of title   The written opinion of an attorney regarding the identity of all current title owners, lienholders, and possible claimants to a particular parcel of land. Although lenders always require title insurance, which will pay off claims if the title opinion turns out to be inaccurate, many cash purchasers are content with simply the attorney's opinion of title. If other persons then assert claims in the future, the purchaser may suffer loss of the property, with the only recourse being to sue the attorney for malpractice, a difficult and expensive process and one further complicated by the general inability to find lawyers willing to sue other lawyers.

attornment   See *attorn*.

attractive nuisance   A concept in tort law holding that if a person creates or allows a condition to exist on his or her property that a reasonably prudent person would know presents a danger to children, then that person must take steps to protect children of tender years from the condition, especially if it is something known to be attractive to small children. Liability can also be imposed if someone creates such a condition on someone else's property or even in a public place. Examples would be a swimming pool on one's own property, a rope swing installed by a private individual over a pond in a public park, or even an old refrigerator dumped by the side of the road in a rural area, but which could trap and suffocate children inside. Many courts hold that an artificial body of water, such as a pool, is an attractive nuisance but a natural one, such as a pond, is not.

auction   A sales technique in which real or personal property is offered for sale and bidders make oral offers in varying amounts until one is accepted. Frequently used for involuntary transfers of real estate, such as foreclosures and tax sales. In some states, foreclosure auctioneers must be licensed. Where property is offered by the owner voluntarily for auction sale, the fine print in the auction terms usually contains a provision for a buyer's premium. The amount of the winning bid is automatically increased by the stated amount, and that percentage is used to pay the auctioneer's fees.

automated mortgage underwriting   Loan processing that is entirely or predominantly performed by computers using artificial intelligence, without human assistance or intervention. The computer has a complex set of instructions to follow depending on the data input by the consumer or by a data entry clerk, including ordering credit reports and other financial data and evaluating all borrower information against predetermined profiles for acceptable lending requirements.

automated valuation model (AVM)   Originally a computerized method of estimating large numbers of property values in an efficient, if not entirely accurate, manner; frequently used by tax appraisers to periodically reappraise properties for purposes of real estate taxes. A disgruntled property owner may appeal the valuation and present evidence the computer made a mistake in that particular instance. Today, AVM artificial intelligence has progressed to the level of respectability that lenders use it to appraise property for mortgage loan purposes and the IRS uses it to evaluate a taxpayer's assets.

automatic stay   A bankruptcy provision that stops all creditor actions, including foreclosures, immediately upon a debtor's filing for bankruptcy protection. There is then a breathing period during which no creditor action may take place. Afterward, a creditor may ask the court for permission to proceed, called a request to lift the automatic stay. To be successful, it must prove that neither the debtor, nor any other creditors, will be prejudiced if foreclosure or repossession is allowed to continue.

average downtime   An estimate of the length of time a leasehold property will remain on the market after the expiration of one lease term and before the commencement of a new tenant's lease.

average free rent   The number of months typically given as free rent in order to provide incentives for a tenant to vacate their old premises and move to new ones without being liable for double rent during the overlapping terms, or to provide competitive incentives for new tenants to rent in one building rather than another.

average rate of return   One way of measuring an investment's profitability. To calculate, one takes the total net earnings, divides by the total number of years the investment was held, and then divides that answer by the investment's initial acquisition cost.

> **Example:** *Rainer spent $800,000 to buy an apartment building. After deducting all operating expenses, real estate taxes, and insurance, she receives $65,000 in the first year, $71,000 in the second year, $69,000 in the third year, and $70,000 in the fourth year. The total net earnings are $275,000. Divide that number by the 4 years being analyzed, to reach $68,750 as an average*

annual return. Divide $68,750 by the initial $800,000 investment to calculate the average rate of return of 8.59 percent.

Drawback: The procedure does not take into account the time value of money. The $65,000 received in the first year was more valuable than the $70,000 received in the fourth year, because the $65,000 could have been invested to earn still more money.

avigation easement   An easement obtained by airport authorities, through purchase or condemnation, and used to provide clear access for low-flying aircraft on the glide path.

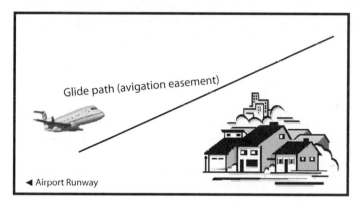

Avigation easement for a glide path for departing aircraft.

avulsion   A sudden and perceptible loss or addition to property as a result of the action of water either taking soil from one property and leaving it on another, or by virtue of a river or other running water changing the course of its bed. The rule is that boundary lines described with reference to the midpoint of the stream will remain at the midpoint of the old stream, and not the midpoint of the new stream. This is because of the sudden nature of the change, so that people may reasonably notice and mark the location of the old stream bed as a matter of reference.

axial growth   A growth pattern for cities, which typically expand outward along major arteries such as interstate highways or other controlled access roads. The population centers will appear star shaped, or like spokes in a wheel, when viewed from above.

B

bachelor apartment   A small rental dwelling unit that combines living and bedroom spaces into one room (and, sometimes, kitchen space as well). (Do not confuse with single-room occupancy, which generally has shared cooking or bathroom facilities.)

back-end ratio   One method of analyzing a borrower's ability to meet underwriting requirements for a home loan. This method takes into account existing long-term debt of the applicant, plus the payments on the requested loan, in order to arrive at a percentage of income that will be devoted to debt service. Lenders typically like to see ratios below 36 percent of take-home pay. Contrast with front-end ratio, which compares only the requested loan against take-home pay.

Example: Back-End Ratio	
Monthly take-home pay	$3,600
Auto loan payments	$480
Mortgage loan payments	$790
Total long-term debt	$1,270
Ratio of debt to take-home pay	35.28%
Back-end ratio	35.28%

backfill   In construction and excavation work, to fill something with additional dirt. When building foundation walls or retaining walls, one excavates a space large enough to build the walls and provide a comfortable work space, and then backfills with additional rock and dirt afterward.

back taxes   Unpaid property taxes, which remain a lien on property even after it is sold to another; could result in a forced sale.

back-to-back lease   One type of rental concession in commercial leases; encountered in markets with large amounts of vacant space on the market and no real prospect of filling the space with new entrants. As a result, landlords must resort to "stealing" tenants from each other. They will offer a back-to-back lease, agreeing to pay the tenant's rent at their old space until the expiration of the term, if the tenant will immediately vacate and move to the new space. In a strong rental market, a landlord may wish to attract a particularly desirable tenant from another building even though the landlord's vacant space could easily be filled from current market demand. In such a situation, the landlord will offer to buy out the entire current lease, paying a lump sum to the owner of the other building. The other building owner is generally motivated to accept the lump-sum payment, because he or she anticipates renting the vacant space to a new tenant fairly quickly and thereby gaining a cash windfall in the form of the buyout price.

backup contract   An offer to purchase that is accepted by the seller but is contingent on a prior contract failing to proceed to closing.

bad title   Title to real estate that has some defects or problems that prevent the owner from conveying the property free and clear of any liens or adverse claims.

bailment   A legal relationship is which a person (bailor) surrenders control of personal property to another (bailee), but with the agreement that the goods will be returned or accounted for upon request. Bailees are not insurers of goods and are responsible only for their own negligence in carrying out the terms of the bailment agreement, not for any third-party theft or vandalism, unless the bailees specifically represented they would protect the goods against third parties. Warehouse operations are typically bailments, as are records storage businesses. Most self-storage facilities, in which consumers retain their own lock, are not bailments.

balance, principle of   In appraisal, the concept that there is an ideal balance of factors for the development of real estate, such as will produce the greatest value.

> **Example:**   *A 10-acre parcel may be capable of being divided into a community of small garden homes with a profit margin of $10,000 each, but the legal fees and time spent for zoning changes and the costs of street and other infrastructure improvements may decrease the total project profitability to $250,000, thus affecting the value of the land. The developer may be able to build three luxury homes, instead, for a total profit of $500,000.*

balance sheet   A semi-itemized listing of all assets and liabilities of a person or a company in order to arrive at a net worth, which is the difference between the assets and the liabilities. Most lenders require a balance sheet as part of the loan application process. Short-term debt, which will be paid off in one year or less, is treated by lenders in a different manner than long-term debt when calculating their various ratios to determine loan eligibility. As a result, consumers would be well advised to separate the two types of debt when completing a balance sheet form provided by the lender.

> **Example:**
>
> *Assets:*
>
> | | |
> |---|---:|
> | Cash and equivalents | $23,400 |
> | Marketable securities | 87,300 |
> | Real property, nonhomestead | 312,000 |
> | Primary residence | 209,000 |
> | Art and collections | 19,000 |
> | Vehicles | 42,000 |
> | Furniture and accessories | 48,000 |
> | Total assets | $740,700 |

Liabilities:

Line of credit balance	$11,000
Credit cards	2,500
Mortgages, nonhomestead	118,000
Mortgage, primary residence	92,000
Accrued and unpaid taxes	13,000
Total liabilities	$236,500
Net worth	$504,200
Liabilities and net worth	$740,700

One of the primary weaknesses of a standard balance sheet is that it does not reflect any contingent liabilities—matters which may become liabilities in the future, but then again, may simply disappear. These are things like loans guaranteed for children, the results of pending litigation, and penalties and interest that may be imposed at the end of a current tax audit. In accounting, such matters are noted in footnotes. Some mortgage application forms specifically ask about contingent liabilities, and others do not. Obviously, the rosy picture presented in the preceding example balance sheet would change markedly if the owner disclosed involvement in a multimillion dollar lawsuit for which there was no insurance coverage, and which might result in a judgment in the future.

balcony   A platform that projects from a wall, usually surrounded by some sort of guard structure to prevent falls.

balloon mortgage   A real estate loan with monthly payments as if the loan would be paid in full over a period of time, usually 30 years, but the entire principal balance is due in a much shorter time, usually 5 or 7 years. This is a method for lenders to offer fixed-rate mortgages at rates very competitive with adjustable-rate mortgages, but without the risk that interest rates will rise dramatically in 6 to 10 years or longer, leaving the lender with a low-interest-rate investment in a high-return world. Balloon mortgages are usually quoted as something similar to "6.5 percent interest on a 30-year am [short for amortization] with 5-year balloon." Also called partially amortized loan.

balloon payment   The full principal amount due at the end of a balloon mortgage.

BANANA   A derogatory term; acronym for Build Absolutely Nothing Anywhere Near Anybody. Much stronger than NIMBY—Not In My Back Yard.

band of investment   An appraisal method used to arrive at a capitalization rate for the valuation of income-producing property. Appraisers determine the net operating income from a property, and then divide that figure by a number, called the cap rate or capitalization rate, in order to arrive at a property value. Conceptually, that value represents what an investor would pay to receive an income equal to that of the property. (The net operating income is fairly easy to calculate, but what cap rate do you use? There are no tables or standards. The appraiser must choose a figure that is justifiable.)

The band of investment method considers the interest rates currently available in the marketplace to finance the particular property. In commercial markets, interest rates may vary significantly depending on which lenders are trying to add what particular property types to their loan portfolios in order to achieve an optimum mix. After deciding on the property loan interest rate, the appraiser then calculates the amount of equity the purchaser would have to pay at closing, and what reasonable investors would expect for a percentage return on their equity each year. These two percentages are then blended according to the percentage of debt and percentage of equity typically seen when financing such properties. The blended number is the cap rate the appraiser will use to help determine value.

bank   An institution empowered by law to receive deposits, cash checks or drafts, discount commercial paper, make loans, and issue promissory notes payable to the bearer, known as bank notes. American commercial banks fall into two categories: (1) federally chartered and (2) state chartered. Federally chartered banks come under the regulatory and auditing supervision of the United States Comptroller of the Currency. State-chartered banks come under the control of the appropriate state banking authority. Typically the FDIC will audit state-chartered banks and the comptroller's office will audit federally chartered banks.

Bank Insurance Fund   The new name of the former fund of the Federal Deposit Insurance Corporation (FDIC). The FDIC is still alive and kicking, only the fund has changed names.

bank partitions   Cubicles; floor-fastened room partitions approximately 5 feet high, so named because they are common in banks.

bank rate   See discount rate.

bankruptcy   A common expression used to mean insolvency, being a condition in which one's liabilities exceed one's assets, or in which current cash flow is not sufficient to meet current debts. As a result of the condition, the debtor may take advantage of protections afforded by the Bankruptcy Code. Immediately upon filing, the law imposes an automatic stay which prohibits all collection activities. Over time, the stay may be lifted so that collection may resume, but the law does allow a breathing spell to allow the debtor and attorney to analyze their options. The Code underwent dramatic changes in November of 2005, with the Bankruptcy Abuse Prevention and Consumer Protection Act of 2005 (BAPCPA). Bankruptcy is now a much less consumer-friendly place than it used to be, and it places greater demands on bankruptcy lawyers. Some pertinent aspects of bankruptcy law are noted here.

- Chapter 7 bankruptcy. A case brought under Chapter 7 of the Code, with a goal of liquidating all assets, paying all liabilities as far as the money will go, and then obtaining a discharge and a fresh start. Some debts cannot be discharged at all, such as judgments for money damages for fraud, payroll withholding taxes, intentional damage, domestic obligations, and other items. In addition, because of past credit card abuses with debtors maxing out their credit cards and then filing for bankruptcy, there is now increased scrutiny of purchases prior to bankruptcy. Suspect purchases will be denied discharge. Debtors requesting Chapter 7 relief must complete government-approved credit counseling before filing, and may be forced to enter Chapter 13, rather than Chapter 7, if a "means test" determines they have the ability to repay some debts over time.

- Chapter 11. Commonly called reorganization, this is designed for businesses or for individuals who exceed the financial limitations for Chapter 13 eligibility. Businesses will continue operations and propose a plan to meet their obligations, or a plan to sell the business as a going concern rather than liquidate assets. The plans usually contemplate the sale of some assets, forgiveness of some debt, and a generous repayment schedule over time. Things rarely work out well for the debtor, and the vast majority of Chapter 11 cases either result in the largest lender owning the company at the end, or the company changing its plan to one of liquidation. Just because the goal is liquidation does not mean the debtor must convert to Chapter 7; they are said to be in a "liquidating 11."
- Chapter 13. Commonly called wage earners bankruptcy, but this is misleading, because anyone with regular income from some source may take advantage of the chapter. There are financial limitations for eligibility that, if exceeded, will result in the debtor taking advantage of Chapter 11 instead of Chapter 13. The debtor must complete government-approved credit counseling before being allowed to file. Once in Chapter 13, the debtor proposes a plan for repayment of debts, with payments stretching over 3 to 5 years. At the end of the time, if all agreements under the plan have been met, and if the person completes all required financial education, the debtor receives a discharge.
- Bankruptcy and real estate:
  1. Filing stops all foreclosure activities until and unless the lender is able to lift the automatic stay and obtain court approval to proceed. In some states where a debtor may redeem property after a foreclosure sale, the bankruptcy will enable the debtor to do so by making payments, rather than by paying the full cash price ordinarily required for a redemption.
  2. Transfers of real estate within the recent past may be reversed if they are for less than full value and deemed to be a fraud against creditors, even if there was no fraudulent intent.
  3. Listing agreements to sell property may be terminated, or cancelable, depending on the chapter.
  4. Tenants may reject burdensome lease obligations and secure early termination of their leases.
  5. Commercial lenders, who typically require that collateral be held in a single-asset entity, may be able to successfully argue against a plan of reorganization and force a foreclosure.
  6. Other lenders opposed to a Chapter 11 plan of reorganization may be forced to accept it in a procedure called the cram-down.

bargain and sale deed   A deed that contains only the name of the seller, the name of the buyer, a recital of consideration, a description of the property, and words of conveyance is a bargain and sale deed. In it, the seller makes no warranties regarding good title or any other matters, but simply sells to the purchaser whatever interest the seller might have had. Typically used in two situations: (1) When the seller obtained the property by law and is not in a position to make warranties because of lack of knowledge and lack of prior control. This would include deeds by administrators of estates, deeds from the IRS after a tax sale, or deeds from a lender after a foreclosure. (2) The second frequent instance is when someone is asked to sign a deed in order to clear up title defects that might or might not have given the seller some rights in the property. The seller is willing to give up any rights he or she might have but is not willing to issue any warranties that he or she owned anything at all. See *quitclaim deed*.

bargain purchase option   A right granted to a lessee, typically under a personal property lease such as for office equipment, but it could be a real property lease. The right, called the option, gives the lessee the ability to buy the property, at the end of the lease term, for a price substantially less than fair market value. The inclusion of a bargain purchase option in a lease contract is an indication that the contract is really a disguised seller-financing arrangement. As a result, "rent" payments previously written off in their entirety may be disallowed by the IRS because some portion of the rent was really payment of principal on a loan. In addition, under Sarbanes-Oxley, public companies may have to post such arrangements as liabilities on the company's balance sheets, contrary to prior custom and practices.

base and meridian   On May 7, 1785, Congress adopted the rectangular system of surveying properties, now called the public land survey system. It is based on a rectangular system of imaginary lines running across the country. The baselines run east and west, and the meridian lines run north and south. Properties are described by reference to the principal meridian and the baseline that controls that area.

base (expense) year   In commercial leases, the year used as a measure of a tenant's obligation to pay the pro rata share of ever-increasing building expenses over time. The rent for the first year is usually calculated by the landlord so as to pay currently known building expenses and provide a profit. This is usually the base year. As expenses increase over time, the amount they exceed the expenses of the base year is the figure the landlord uses to calculate the tenant's pro rata share of the expenses.

baseline   East-west lines in the public land survey system, part of the baseline and meridian line components. Each principal meridian has a baseline. Properties in the principal meridian's area are described by their bearing east or west of the meridian and north or south of the baseline.

base period   The point in time that serves as a reference for calculating financial and economic data. The base period value is usually set at 1.0 or 100, called the benchmark, for purposes of comparison, and then all other periods are either greater or less than the benchmark.

base rent   The minimum periodic rent specified in a lease. Additions could include the tenant's share of common area maintenance (CAM—pronounced as a word), share of building operating expenses, and percentage rent based on gross retail or food sales.

basis   A tax and accounting term referring to the original acquisition cost of a property; used to determine annual depreciation deductions and eventual gain or loss upon the disposition of the property. This concept is fundamental to almost all real estate analysis and real property tax planning, and an important one to master. Some of the key concepts are

- The basis may be increased by adding some acquisition and closing costs. Many taxpayers would prefer to write off those costs as deductible expenses, but that is not allowed.
- The basis may be increased as you make capital expenditures for the benefit of the property. Usually a capital expenditure is something that adds value above and beyond the slight increase experienced when things are repaired.
- The basis is decreased each year as you deduct depreciation expenses on your taxes.
- Property acquired by gift will have the same basis the donor had, plus any capital improvements made by the donee, plus any gift taxes paid by the donor.
- Property acquired by inheritance will receive a stepped-up basis valued as of the date of death or a date 6 months afterward, depending on which election is selected. While this may be good for the heir, it might be bad for the estate to value property at a high value and be required to pay estate taxes.
- Property acquired by virtue of a 1031 exchange will have the same basis as the property sold. If this doesn't make sense, refer to definition for 1031 exchange, which is too long to include here.
- The basis must be allocated between land and improvements. Land cannot be depreciated for tax purposes, but improvements can. There is no precise formula, and taxpayers are expected to use good faith in their allocation rather than setting artificially high improvement values in order to maximize depreciation deductions.
- Most consumers do not currently track the basis in their homes, nor the capital improvements such as a new roof, swimming pool, or new garage. This is because current tax code provisions allow individuals up to $250,000 in gain ($500,000 for married persons) on the sale of their personal residence without incurring any tax liability. However, the apparent large size of this number could easily be eroded by inflation, and Congress could easily change the tax laws.

basis point   A unit of measure used in finance, it is $^1/_{100}$ of 1 percent. Commercial lenders will typically quote rates as a certain number of basis points above an index, such as LIBOR (London InterBank Overnight Rate) or 10-year Treasury bonds. A fee of 50 basis points for a $3,000,000 loan is a fee of $^{50}/_{100}$ of 1 percent, or $^1/_2$ of 1 percent on $3,000,000, being $15,000.

basket loan   Financial institutions are heavily regulated regarding the types of loans they can make and the mixture of the types of allowable loans in the total portfolio. They are allowed to make a very small percentage of loans that would otherwise be prohibited for one reason or another. Such loans are scooped into the miscellaneous basket. The term "basket" is used in a wide variety of circumstances in law, finance, and general business dealings, and always refers to some sort of conceptual container filled with small items.

bay   (1) The smallest rentable tenant space in a strip center, usually defined by the front and rear exterior walls and fire walls at either side. (2) An unfinished area between rows of columns or load-bearing walls. (3) Loading areas in warehouse or industrial space. Ascertaining the number of bays necessary and available is usually critically important when working with buyers or potential tenants of such space.

bay depth   Represents the distance from the building's corridor wall to the outside window of the building. The bay depth will be a critical limitation when configuring space for the most efficient use. Because of the waste factor when bay depths result in larger than necessary offices, for example, a building with cheap per-square-foot rental rates but inefficient bay depths may be more expensive than one with higher rental rates but a more compatible design. In the diagram, the bay depth is 15 feet.

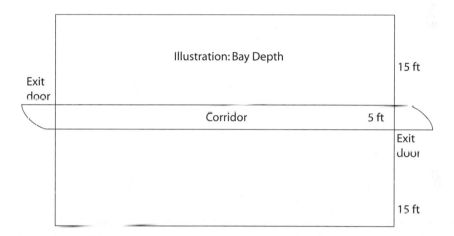

bay window   An arrangement of three or more windows that project outward from the exterior wall.

bearer instrument   A security that does not include the name of the owner or payee. Anyone in possession of the instrument may present it and receive payment.

bearing wall   A wall that helps support the weight of the upper floors and roof. See *load-bearing wall*.

bedrock   The solid rock under soil.

bedroom community   An area consisting primarily of commuter residences and small local establishments—grocery, laundry, limited dining, and other similar businesses catering to residents—but no large employers. Also called a dormitory town.

before-and-after rule   A rule of damages holding that the measure of damage to a thing is the difference between the value before the injury and the value after the injury. In a real estate context, this often arises in a condemnation case for eminent domain purposes. The government must compensate a property owner for the value of the property taken, but must also pay damages if the remaining property has been injured because of the loss of the other piece.

before-tax cash flow   The amount of money generated by an investment after collection of all revenues and payment of all bills, but without any deductions for depreciation or other noncash items, and before calculation of income tax consequences. An important figure in analyzing any investment, because properties with high depreciation expenses may show tax losses but positive cash flows. In the alternative, a property that requires expensive financing for acquisition or operation may show good net income figures for accounting and tax purposes, but have a negative cash flow requiring the owner to supplement the property with money from other sources.

below-market interest rate (BMIR)   Government-subsidized interest rate concessions offered to spur development, usually in a particular market segment, such as low-income housing, or in particular market areas, such as parts of the country heavily damaged by natural disasters. In the housing industry, the borrower is generally required to pass along the savings to consumers in the form of lower rents.

benchmark   A permanent reference mark, usually set in concrete or iron and used to establish the elevation above sea level or certain corners in a surveying system. All other measurements in the area should be checked for accuracy relative to the nearest benchmark, preferably against several nearby benchmarks to establish redundancy.

beneficiary   A person who receives the benefits from something although perhaps not the legal owner of the thing. In real estate, the term is usually encountered in the context of a trust, in which a trustee holds what is called bare legal title to the property, but the property itself and all sums gained from the property are held for the beneficiary. Care should be taken when buying, selling, or leasing property that involves a beneficiary, and, if at all possible, one should gain the beneficiary's signature even though it is not technically required. Otherwise, you could find yourself in the middle of litigation between the trustee and the beneficiary if the beneficiary claims the actions taken were illegal and not authorized.

benefit-of-the-bargain rule   A rule of damages that says if a person has been defrauded, that person may recover the difference between the actual value of the property and the value the property would have if it had been as represented.

benefits   In eminent domain cases, the concept of "benefit" comes into play because property owners may receive an enhancement in the value of their remaining property after the condemnation. If the enhancement is special to them, or only a very few owners, rather than the general betterment enjoyed by the public at large by the anticipated improvements, then any condemnation award to them may be reduced by the amount of the benefits.

> **Example:**   *Ken owns 5 acres of land near an eight-lane city thoroughfare. The only thing preventing him from having valuable road frontage is a 2-foot-deep strip of land still owned by Elsie. This is the only land remaining to Elsie after successive road widenings over the years. The city*

decides to widen the road again and takes all the rest of Elsie's land and a 15-foot-deep strip of Ken's land. The city is liable to Ken for the 15-foot sliver, but Ken suddenly has 5 acres of extremely valuable road frontage property. Ken probably won't receive a check from the city because of the special benefits he received from the condemnation.

bequeath   To leave personal property to another in a will. The word devise is used when referring to real property left by will.

bequest   A gift of personal property made by will.

berm   A small ledge or shoulder of dirt with some type of vegetation, designed to control water runoff, hide something unsightly such as a power substation, or provide a noise-control buffer between busy streets and residential areas.

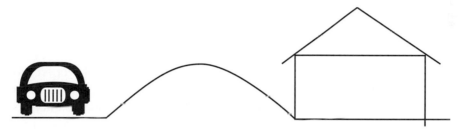

betterment   An improvement to real estate.

BFP   See *bona fide purchaser*.

biannual   Occurring twice a year. Contrast with biennial, which means occurring every 2 years. If an adjustable-rate mortgage provides for rate changes biannually or biennially, it's important to know the difference.

bid   (1) An offer to purchase at a specific price, usually at an auction or foreclosure. (2) An offer to complete specified work for a certain price, usually presented in the context of a request for sealed bids to complete government work.

bid bond   A type of bond required in some government construction projects. If required, it must be filed at the same time as the bid. This protects the agency in the event the bidder fails or refuses to enter into a contract after being offered it or withdraws the bid before the award. The bonding company will then pay the agency the difference between the defaulting low bid and the next highest bid, whose bidder will be given the contract.

bid shopping   The practice of a general contractor estimating the cost for subcontractors in order to prepare a bid for construction work, and then attempting to induce those same subcontractors to lower their price below the estimate.

biennial   Occurring every 2 years. Contrast with biannual, which means occurring twice a year. (It's important to know the difference if an adjustable-rate mortgage provides for rate changes biannually or biennially.)

big box   (1) Large square or rectangular building with ample parking, suitable for a wide variety of retail tenants. (2) Regular users of such space, such as Wal-Mart, Target, or Home Depot. An example of usage is, "I'm working with a big box and need to find 12 to 16 acres to buy. Do you have anything?"

bilateral contract   A contract in which each party promises to do something in return for the other's promise. If either party breaks its promise, the other may sue. This is the most common type of contract. A real estate purchase contract is a bilateral contract—the seller promises to sell, and the buyer promises to buy. Contrast with a unilateral contract, in which one party has an obligation but the other does not. Option contracts are unilateral contracts—the seller is obligated to sell if the buyer decides to buy, but the buyer is not obligated to buy at all.

bill of assurance   A name used in some states to describe the total collection of restrictive covenants that apply to a neighborhood.

bill of sale   A written instrument used to transfer ownership of personal property. Many buyers insist on a general bill of sale, in addition to a deed, to ensure that all property intended to pass in the sale actually does so. Some states have held that certain real estate–related interests are actually personal property, and attempted sales via deed were void.

binder   (1) Money given as earnest money for an oral contract to purchase real estate, to bind the parties until such time as they can complete the necessary written contract. (2) A written instrument giving immediate casualty coverage for property, even though the insured may not have paid a premium or received a policy. (3) A temporary contract of title insurance in which the insurer agrees to issue a final policy if certain exceptions, such as prior mortgage liens, are removed at or before closing.

biometrics   Increasingly popular building security system technology that relies on automated identification of physical characteristics such as fingerprints or retinal scans in order to determine access rights. The technology and the cost have both reached the point that consumer-level biometric security devices are available, such as for use in self-storage facilities and residences. Access codes, keys, and electronic cards are becoming outdated. Developers should bear this in mind when designing new construction and spend a minor amount of extra money necessary for wiring to accommodate biometric systems.

bird dog   Someone who regularly furnishes sales leads to another, but does not actually handle any of the selling. Successful real estate agents usually have many bird dogs.

biweekly loan   A loan that calls for payments every 2 weeks, rather than once a month.

Blackacre   Mythical property used as an example in nearly all explanations of legal concepts relating to real estate, such as, "If A owns an undivided $1/2$ interest in Blackacre… ." If more properties are needed, use Greenacre, and then Whiteacre.

black mold   Refers to Stachybotrys chartarum, called stachy for short, a greenish black mold that can grow in parts of a structure exposed to constant moisture. The fungus can produce toxins harmful or even fatal to humans and has been identified in the sick building syndrome. There are some very dark dematiaceous hyphomycetes that look very similar; confirmation of stachy must be made after miscroscope examination. This is an area of widespread litigation and should be a cause of concern to both buyers and sellers of real estate. (For more information, visit the Web site of the Centers for Disease Control and Prevention at www.cdc.gov/mold/stachy.htm.)

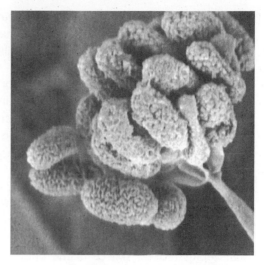

Black's Guide   A data source for office buildings in certain major markets, providing tenant and other information. Its primary competitor is CoStar. (For more information visit the Black's Guide Web site at www.blacksguide.com.)

blacktop   The asphalt paving used on many roads, and also the process of paving the road.

blanket   A single mortgage instrument covering two or more properties. It is most often encountered in property intended for development, with partial lien releases given as lots are sold and part of the sale proceeds used to pay down the loan. Contrast with cross-collateralization, in which two or more properties, each with their own mortgages, include the other properties as additional collateral.

bleeding a project   (1) In construction, charging excessive development and construction oversight fees, renting one's own equipment to the project at inflated prices, and perhaps putting family members on the payroll in order to bleed off as much money as possible. (2) In rental property management, refusing to make ordinary repairs and replacements in order to take as much cash flow as possible from the project, but with a resulting rapid deterioration of the property. In an area of limited consumer choices, such as communities with high concentrations of low-income housing, the landlord almost never suffers the consequences of this type of decision.

blighted area   A declining area suffering from seriously decreasing property values and not likely to recover without some outside intervention. More than simply a market slip, a blighted area can be identified by deteriorating buildings, increased crime rates, and decreased occupancies.

blind ad   An advertisement that does not include the identity of the person placing the ad, only a phone number or a post office box number. They are popular with employers placing help wanted ads in order to identify someone to replace a soon-to-be-fired employee. Blind ads are illegal in most states for real estate brokers or agents, who must not only identify themselves in all ads, but include enough information to alert the public of their status as a real estate professional.

block   An area bounded by perimeter streets. Many subdivision descriptions employ a subdivision name, and then a block number and a lot number to identify particular properties. The numbers are assigned when the subdivision developer files its plat plan with local authorities.

blockbusting   An illegal and discriminatory practice in which someone stampedes another into selling or granting a listing contract by trading on fears the neighborhood is changing with respect to race, sex, religion, color, disability, family status, or ancestry of the inhabitants. (For more detailed information, visit the U.S. Housing and Urban Development Web site at www.hud.gov and search on the term "blockbusting.") See panic peddling.

block numbering area (BNA)   A small, relatively perma-nent statistical subdivision within a county, generally con-taining 2,500 to 8,000 people and having readily identifiable borders. Similar to census tracts, but differing only in the local versus federal source of the data used to create the maps. Mapped and numbered by the U.S. government, which provides demographic information at www.census.gov. Third-party resellers of demographic information extrapo-late from the census tract data into more personalized demographic areas.

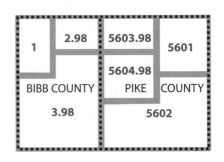

Blue book: Any number of pocket-sized reference books on a wide variety of topics. The ones most relevant to real estate are The Blue Book of Building and Construction (www.thebluebook.com), The Apartment Blue Book (www.apartmentbluebook.com), and The Realty Blue Book.

blue laws   Laws that prevent the transaction of certain business on Sundays, prohibit the sale of alcoholic beverages any day of the week; and/or place severe limitations on the manner and hours of sale of alcoholic beverages. These laws originated in colonial New England and were printed on blue paper. It is important to know and understand all local blue laws in a market area because, for example, many national restaurant chains will not open locations where Sunday liquor sales are pro-hibited.

blueprint   A detailed set of plans used as a guide for construction. Because of the economies of a very inexpensive method of creating and copying such plans, they were formerly characterized by white lines on blue paper.

blue-sky laws   A popular name for state securities laws intended to protect investors and aid them in making informed buying decisions rather than taking the word of a smooth-talking salesperson who "promises the sky."

blue stake   When a utility company (telephone, gas, electric, cable TV, sewer, or water, etc.) comes to the job site and locates and spray paints the ground and/or installs little flags or blue stakes to show where their service is located underground. See *utility notification*.

blue top   In excavating and in road construction, the practice of marking the desired final grade with a stake topped by blue fibers. The heavy equipment operator continues to move dirt until only the blue tops show above the ground.

B-note investors   In commercial real estate financing, purchasers of the subordinate tranches, or second and third mortgages. If a borrower defaults, the B-note investors will suffer losses before the investment-grade tranches. As a result, such investors scrutinize deals more thoroughly, charge higher interest rates commensurate with their increased risk, and typically retain powers to protect themselves somewhat in the event of default. These rights include

- The right to approve modifications to the agreement
- The right to insist on foreclosure in the event of default
- Certain limited cure rights to keep a loan current and avoid foreclosure

board-foot   A measure of lumber 1 foot square by 1 inch thick, being 144 cubic inches. In valuing timber land, it is usually important to calculate the number of board-feet that can be harvested from the standing timber. Often, however, timber is now sold by the pound rather than the board-foot.

board of directors   The governing body of an organization, charged with establishing policy and with taking steps to see that the policies are implemented. Except in small corporations or associations, the board typically does not involve itself in day-to-day business activities, those being more properly the role of the president. Many corporations have executive boards with true legal responsibilities, and advisory boards of largely ceremonial function designed to reward contributors, create strategic alliances, or gain expert insights into limited areas on an as-needed basis.

- In the real estate context, a director who acts as a broker in real estate transactions involving corporate property cannot accept a commission unless the board specifically authorizes it, even if the president previously granted the approval and would otherwise have had such authority to hire a third party.
- Lenders have legal limitations on the sizes of loans they can extend to their own directors. Large developers should consider this before accepting board positions.
- The board of directors in a cooperative apartment enjoys tremendous power in the approval of new members and in decisions to evict current members.
- The board of directors of a condominium association is charged with making sure the community always has adequate insurance. Because of the shared nature of ownership in the common areas, inadequate insurance could result in the imposition of liability on individual unit owners for an accident in a common area. Failure to maintain the proper level of insurance could subject board members to liability.

board of equalization   A local government board charged with the responsibility of ensuring equal property tax assessments. Normally, a property owner appeals to the board of equalization if dissatisfied with the tax assessment notice received for the year.

board of REALTORS®   A local association comprised of real estate professionals who are members of the National Association of REALTORS® (www.realtor.org and www.realtor.com) and the local or state board of REALTORS®.

board of zoning appeals   A local board empowered to overturn decisions of a zoning authority. Before embarking on any possibly contested activity in these areas, such as a zoning change request, it is extremely important to find out the name and requirements of the correct appeals board, should it become necessary to ask for reversal of a decision. Many boards have very limited and technical grounds for appeal that, if known in advance, could have been factored into tactical decisions at the level below. In addition, the time limits for filing appeals are generally short. See *appeals board*.

Boeckh Building Valuation Manual   A reference book that provides guidance for the replacement costs (substantially similar utility, but not identical methods of construction) or reproduction costs (identical) for various types of buildings. (For more information go to the Marshall & Swift/Boeckh Web site at www.msbinfo.com.)

boilerplate   A term used to refer to standard language appearing in almost all mortgages, leases, sale agreements, and other contracts. Important rights can be signed away by language lurking in the boilerplate; it is important to read all contracts thoroughly and not to skip anything.

boiler room   A lead-generating system usually characterized by large groups of people working in cubicles making cold calls to consumers in order to gauge interest in real estate investments, insurance products, refinance offers, or any number of other products. The leads are then sold to professionals for follow-up. Sometimes, the boiler room operation also engages in high-pressure sales techniques, which has lead many states to pass legislation allowing a cooling off period within which to reject and void any contracts entered into as a result of such tactics.

bollard   A pillar or post, usually consisting of a metal pipe anchored in concrete and then filled with concrete, placed near building corners, loading docks, entrance doors, and gas pumps in order to protect them from automobiles; may be left natural, painted, or covered with plastic bollard covers.

BOMA   See *Building Owners and Managers Association*.

BOMA measurements   Standards offered by the Building Owners and Managers Association for determining leaseable square footage and other such measurements. Many have been adopted by the American National Standards Institute, Inc. (ANSI).

bona fide purchaser (BFP)   One who purchases property in good faith and for a valuable consideration without knowledge, actual or constructive, of the seller's title defects. Under certain circumstances, BFPs may retain the property free and clear of the claims of others. (As a practical matter, it is difficult to be a BFP of real property because of the constructive notice provided by public filings of almost all real estate–related claims.)

bond   A certificate that provides evidence of a debt or obligation.

bond for title   A method of selling and financing real estate; also called a land sale contract or a contract for sale. The owner signs a contract agreeing to transfer the property to the buyer after the buyer makes all required regular payments over a certain period of time. Unlike a mortgage, the seller avoids many problems associated with foreclosure and possibly bankruptcy if there is a default. The practice is looked upon with disfavor by courts, which typically try to find ways to convert the relationship in some sort of equitable mortgage, and thus grant the consumer protections afforded by the law.

bonus depreciation   Additional depreciation deductions allowed by the IRS under certain circumstances and possibly in certain areas. After the devastating effect of the 9/11 attacks, business owners were allowed to take a first-year depreciation deduction of up to 50 percent of the basis of property placed in service between specified dates. This was in contrast to the normal deduction of 3.63 or 2.56 percent for real property, depending on whether it was commercial or residential rental. Again, after the 2005 hurricane season, the IRS allowed the same bonus depreciation for property placed in service in specifically named Gulf Opportunity Zone counties in the affected states.

book cost   The acquisition cost of a property as reflected on the books and records of a company.

book depreciation   The amount of depreciation expenses deducted for a property on the books and records of a company. Book depreciation may be charged at a faster or slower rate than allowed by the IRS, in order to provide management with a realistic view of the gradually diminishing value of the company's assets.

book value   The value of an asset as reflected on the books and records of a company, taking into account the original book cost of acquisition and then deducting depreciation expenses charged over the years and adding capital expenditures. Book value rarely bears any relationship to the true value of assets.

boomerangers   Generation-X aged persons who return home to live with their parents after being unable to find jobs that will provide adequate compensation to support them as well as their parents did.

boot   (1) Money or other property that is not like-kind and is given to make up the difference in value between two properties exchanged in a like-kind exchange under Section 1031 of the Internal Revenue Code. If a gain would otherwise be recognized on the transaction, except for the intervention of the 1031 vehicle, then gain must be recognized and taxes paid to the extent of the value of the boot. (2) Especially in Texas, it is common among property developers to require some type of boot to show that more than money is involved in their business transactions.

> **Example:**   *A seller might agree to sell prime property for $12,000,000, but only if the buyer throws in a particularly handsome bronze statue sitting on his desk.*

bootstrap financing   A funding expansion from internal sources, such as reducing expenses in the budget, collecting rents or other receivables more aggressively, delaying payments to vendors, or preselling units.

boring tests   Tests conducted to determine the soil's load-bearing ability to support a building or other improvement, and the size of the footings necessary. Also called compaction tests.

bottom feeder   A derogatory term for someone who buys distressed properties; one who profits from the misfortunes or poor management of others.

bottom-fishing   The strategy of offering ridiculously low prices for large numbers of properties because of the expectation that, statistically, someone is bound to "bite" and accept an offer.

bottomland   Lowlands located in a valley or other low area near rivers, streams, or bodies of water prone to flooding. Bottomland was especially prized by farmers at one time because of the constant deposit of nutrient-rich soils.

boundary   The perimeter of a property as fixed in the legal property description. Boundary line disputes are common, emotional, and often end up in years of litigation and sometimes mayhem. If one is buying property in a subdivision, it is advisable to have the seller locate and point out the markers at the corners of the property. These may or may not be consistent with fence lines, shrub-beries, driveways, or even structures built on the wrong side of the boundary. If buying nonsubdivi-sion property, employ the services of a licensed professional surveyor to determine the proper boundary.

boundary line disputes   Probably the most common type of lawsuit involving real estate, because it is the type least likely to result in settlement before trial. Problems generally arise as a result of some or all of the following four factors:

1. Formerly unsurveyed property owned by amicable neighbors passes into the hands of an outsider who orders a survey and discovers the boundary lines are in different places than previously thought.
2. Formerly amicable neighbors who did not care about a 10- or 20-foot discrepancy in boundary lines suddenly care when oil or gas is discovered under the land, or the property becomes so valuable that it is being sold by the square foot rather than by the acre.
3. Advances in surveying technology would have placed a property corner in a different loca-tion than the original surveyor placed it, and when this is discovered, the neighbors go to court.
4. Someone mistakenly builds a house or other improvement with a portion located on a neighbor's land. Words are exchanged regarding tearing down the trespassing improve-ment, and the parties resort to the court system to solve their differences.

There are very specific rules for resolving boundary line disputes:

1. Advances in technology make no difference because the property corners are where the original surveyor placed them according to his or her own state-of-the-art technology for the time, not at the absolutely accurate location according to today's technology.

2. If there are mistakes in the description, courts follow a hierarchy of things to consider and things to ignore if there is a conflict among descriptions within a deed.
3. If someone innocently builds an improvement that encroaches on another's land, most courts will figure out a way to either give the property to the encroacher or will order the other person to sell a minimal amount of land to the encroacher.

B-paper   Home mortgages for consumers with poor credit or other disabilities that prevent them from obtaining the best possible interest rates, percentage of financing, or other terms. The promissory notes are generally at high rates of interest commensurate with the higher risk of default assumed by the lender. The B-paper industry was largely unregulated for many years, but has now come under increasing scrutiny and even class action litigation because of widespread predatory abuses. On the other hand, the industry is predominantly honest and does fill a void in the home mortgage market, enabling millions of responsible persons to enjoy the benefits of homeownership.

branch office   Any secondary or ancillary place of business. Most states require branch offices of real estate companies to have their own broker-in-charge or qualifying broker, legally responsible for activities at that branch.

breach of contract   A violation of some or all of the terms of a contract. Most contracts spell out specific remedies in the event of breach, but include a basket granting any and all other remedies allowed at law or equity. Some states have statutes making defaulting parties liable for the attorneys' fees of the other side; other states do not have such laws and attorneys' fees are recoverable only if that right is granted in the contract.

- In a real estate context, some purchase contracts provide that a breaching buyer will lose his or her earnest money but not be responsible for any other damages. If not so specified as a limitation on damages, then a breaching buyer is fully responsible for all the seller's damages, which could include losses when the property is sold for a lesser amount, costs of remarketing the property, attorneys' fees, and possibly even consequential damages such as the seller's loss of opportunity to purchase something else. In extremely rare circumstances, the seller can obtain an injunction forcing the defaulting buyer to proceed with the purchase.
- If the seller defaults, the buyer may apply for an injunction to order the seller to proceed with the sale. This unusual remedy is because the law says that real property is so unique that money damages can never compensate one for its loss—only the property itself will suffice. Despite that, buyers may waive this remedy of specific performance and seek damages instead. Under some circumstances they may receive both.

breakdown method   In appraisal, the process of dividing depreciation into separate components, assigning a weight to each one, and then arriving at a depreciated value of the property. This has nothing to do with book depreciation or tax depreciation, but is instead intended to calculate the true current value of the improvements. The three types of property depreciation are:

1. Physical depreciation. What is the condition of the improvement?

2. Functional obsolescence. Loss of value because of physical factors other than deterioration, such as a poor floor plan, a one-car garage instead of a two-car garage, or high ceilings and multiple windows creating heating and cooling problems.
3. Economic obsolescence. Loss of value because of factors outside the property, such as noise pollution from nearby highways or an airport.

break-even point   In any project, the point at which revenue will be sufficient to pay all required expenses and debt service. Most industries have generally recognized rules of thumb for the appropriate break-even point. For apartments, it might be 80 percent occupancy, for self-storage it might be 55 percent occupancy, and for business center space it might be 75 percent occupancy. Most construction lenders require that a project at least reach the break-even point before construction lending can be converted to fixed-rate and lower-rate permanent financing. If preparing a pro forma for a project and your break-even point is dramatically different from the rule of thumb for your industry, it may be time to check your assumptions or your math.

bricks and mortar   A popular expression for a physical location, as opposed to intangible assets or even cyberspace.

bricks, clicks, and flips   Retail stores that have physical locations, Internet sale sites, and strong catalog sales. (A variant of "bricks and clicks" and "clicks and mortar.")

bridge loan   A short-term loan intended to bridge the gap between other transactions. (1) Temporary financing obtained at the end of a construction loan period but before permanent financing can be arranged. (2) A loan obtained by a home buyer when the equity from an existing home is necessary to provide the down payment for a new home, but the buyer has been unable to sell his or her old home as of that time (frequently offered by employers who transfer employees to new cities).

bring-down search   An additional title search to make sure nothing adverse has been recorded in the real estate records since the time of the original search and the recording of the deed or mortgage. This time period is known as the gap.

British thermal unit (BTU)   A unit of measure of heat, used in rating the capacity of air conditioning and heating equipment. One BTU is the amount of energy necessary to raise the temperature of 1 pound of water by 1 degree Fahrenheit.

broker   An agent employed to make bargains and contracts for compensation. In the real estate industry, a broker does not make contracts and bind his or her principal but, instead, acts as an intermediary between buyers and sellers.

- The broker-in-charge or qualifying broker in an office is responsible for setting office policies, supervising agents in the execution of their legal responsibilities, and complying with all regulatory requirements. All contracts with consumers are with the broker, who is the only one legally permitted to enter into such relationships. The broker may then delegate some responsibilities to agents or other licensed salespersons, but does not thereby relieve himself or herself of liability.

- Brokers have fiduciary responsibilities to their principals, called clients. They must exercise honesty, integrity, care, and skill in carrying out their duties. All other persons, called customers, are owed the duty of honesty.
- The broker must submit all written offers to the principal as soon as received and may not hold any offer while waiting for a more attractive one.
- All earnest monies coming into the possession of the broker must be deposited into an escrow account as soon as possible according to the instructions of the offer, but it may hold a check, undeposited, in a file if the offer states the check may not be deposited until the offer is accepted.
- All client monies, such as from property management activities, must be maintained in an escrow account and cannot be comingled with the broker's other funds.

brokerage   A real estate activity devoted to assisting buyers and/or sellers in the purchase of real property. In smaller communities, brokerage activities are conducted on a type of general practitioner basis. In larger communities, brokers generally specialize in certain price ranges or types of residential properties; or some combination of office buildings, retail space, food service, industrial, warehouse, farms and lands, or development land.

broker-in-charge   See *broker*.

broker price opinion (BPO)   In most states, only a licensed appraiser is authorized to offer a professional opinion as to the value of a property. Often, though, a real estate broker will be asked to offer an opinion regarding the price to ask when marketing a property. This is a fine distinction, but perfectly legal, as long as labeled as such. BPOs are frequently obtained by out-of-state lenders seeking to work out a sale of a distressed property.

broom clean   Containing no debris. Most apartment leases require that the premises be left broom clean.

brownfields   According to the Environmental Protection Agency, "a brownfield is a property, the expansion, redevelopment, or reuse of which may be complicated by the presence or potential presence of a hazardous substance, pollutant, or contaminant." The EPA's Brownfields program (initiated in 1995) supplies local grants to support revitalization efforts by funding environmental assessment, cleanup, and job-training activities.

brownstone   A row house built of reddish-brown sandstone; usually refers to one built in the nineteenth century, in a large city, with a narrow profile facing the street.

BTU   See *British thermal unit*.

BTXE   Toxic chemicals typically found as soil contaminants at former gas station or other petroleum-handling sites. Short for benzene, toluene, xylene, and ethylbenzene.

bubble   A period of rapid expansion and price increases, followed by a market slowdown and contraction. Many analysts claim a real estate bubble exists in some cities characterized by a price growth of more than 30 percent per year. Other analysts disagree. (For housing cost information in various states and cities, see the Office of Federal Housing Oversight Web site at www.ofheo.gov, and click on House Price Index.)

budget   (1) An itemized list of expected income and expenses over a period of time. (2) An estimate of particular monetary needs, such as a capital budget for construction or a development budget for construction and business ramp up to break even.

budget mortgage   Typically a residential mortgage, one that requires monthly payments for real estate taxes and insurance in addition to principal and interest payments.

buffer zone   (1) A transitional area between two areas of different zoning or characteristic land use. (2) Green space or other open or natural areas providing privacy and noise pollution control for a subdivision.

builders and sponsors profit and risk allowance (BSPRA)   An amount above the cost of constructing apartments that is allowed to be included in the project costs for purposes of determining the maximum loan amount in certain government-sponsored programs; generally calculated as 10 percent of the project development cost, less the cost of the land.

builders risk insurance   Fire, liability, and extended coverage protection to cover the risks encountered when a building is under construction.

builder warranty   A guarantee offered by the builder on the quality of construction.

building codes   Regulations established by local governments to specify minimum building standards for foundations, structural support, electrical and plumbing systems, fire retardation, accessibility, safety for small children and others, fire escapes, numbers of exits, numbers of parking places, and many other areas concerned with the health and safety of the population. The most widely employed building code is the standard known as the International Building Code. Some local governments still employ the Southern Building Code. (For more information go to the International Code Council Web site at www.iccsafe.org.)

building efficiency ratio   The proportion of leasable space in a building to the total space.

Building Energy Conservation Code   As a part of the National Energy Policy Act of 1992, Congress required that states incorporate energy-efficient requirements into their building codes for commercial buildings. Details regarding model codes may be obtained from United States Department of Energy Web site at www.energycodes.gov or a local building inspection office.

building height   The total height from the bottom of the ground floor to the highest structure or decoration on the roof. Local building codes or airport avigation easements may place restrictions on building height.

Example: *The Washington, D.C., building height restriction states that no building may be more than 20 feet taller than the width of the street in front of it, but exceptions may be granted for spires, towers, domes, minarets, pinnacles, and engineering structures such as ventilation shafts.*

building inspection   A physical review of a property in the various stages of construction, to ensure the builder has complied with all requirements of the local building codes. Failure to pass a particular inspection may halt progress until the condition has been corrected. For example, no construction may proceed on a building until it has passed its foundation inspection. The local inspections department will not issue a certificate of occupancy (C/O) until the property has passed fire marshall review and any other inspections that may be required in the locale. In order to provide de facto enforcement of the rule prohibiting occupancy without a C/O, many utility companies will not provide permanent service without proof that one has been issued and will disconnect temporary service at the end of the originally anticipated completion date.

building line   A setback line; the closest a building may be allowed to come to the property boundary line. Building lines may be set by local government or by subdivision building restrictions.

building loan agreement   A loan to finance construction. Funding is made either at preestablished stages or at completion, or upon submission and approval of invoices evidencing construction bills.

Building Owners and Managers Association (BOMA)   This professional organization (www.boma.org) is made up of persons who own or manage buildings, primarily office buildings.

building permit   Written permission from local government to proceed with construction, substantial repair, demolition, or sign erection on real property. The permit process serves several purposes:

- Revenue generation through permitting fees
- Early identification of potential problems, such as the need for historical district approvals
- Entry of the project into a tracking system to ensure code compliance through periodic inspections
- Estimation of the anticipated cost of the project, in order to assist local government with analysis of building and development trends
- Initiation of steps that will ultimately ensure all subcontractors have business licenses and correctly report their income for the year

(Developers typically include contingencies in their purchase contracts to allow for difficulties in obtaining building permits. Especially with large projects, which require extensive plan review before issuance of a permit, the permitting process can take many months.)

building restrictions   Zoning or subdivision restrictions on the size or type of building that can be erected.

building standard   A particular style and quality of building materials, finishes, and accessories used in a specific commercial building. Office leases will generally include a construction allowance or build-out allowance to complete space according to a tenant's space design and using building standard materials. If the tenant desires a better quality, the tenant may usually pay for the difference in cost and obtain it. The phrase also comes into play in circumstances when the landlord has agreed to be responsible for replacing all building standard lightbulbs in the leased space. If building standard is fluorescent, and the tenant has incandescent bulbs in spaces such as conference rooms, then the tenant will have to pay for replacement of those bulbs. This can be a significant expense.

build-out   Improvements to leased space to make it usable for a particular tenant's needs.

built-ins   Appliances, machinery, and other equipment installed as part of a building rather than left freestanding. Built-ins are considered fixtures, and fixtures are considered real estate. A contract to sell real estate automatically carries with it an obligation to leave all fixtures in place and included in the sale. There is usually a great deal of controversy over the exact nature of something as a built-in or not, such as a high-end refrigerator surrounded by custom cabinetry and with matching door insert panels. If in doubt, specifically list all appliances, machinery, and other such questionable items in the purchase contract.

built to suit   An arrangement in which a property owner agrees to construct a building according to a tenant's exact specifications, and then to lease the property to the tenant, preferably on a long-term basis.

bulk sale   Transfer of all or substantially all the assets of a business. Some states have bulk sales laws requiring notice to creditors before any such sales, so that a debtor may not liquidate all assets, pocket the money, and leave creditors holding the bag.

bulk zoning   Zoning designed to control density and overcrowding.

bullet loan   A loan with a 5- to 10-year term, no amortization, and the entire principal balance due at the end.

bundle   A package of shingles. Normally, there are three bundles per square and 27 shingles per bundle. Most roofing contractors charge by the square or by the bundle.

bundle of rights theory   A concept describing all the rights capable of ownership in real property. The bundle may be broken, and only some of the rights transferred and others retained, or they may be transferred to different people.

burden of proof   In court, the responsibility to come forward with credible evidence that a thing happened or did not happen. Normally, the party who complains about a wrongdoing has the burden of proof. In some circumstances, primarily under federal laws related to discrimination, the aggrieved party need only make an allegation of wrongful behavior and the defendant has the burden of proof that his or her behavior was reasonable under the circumstances. The burden of proof may be set at different levels for various types of litigation. For example:

- When contesting a property tax valuation, the owner must generally prove that the assessment was manifestly excessive, clearly erroneous, or confiscatory. This burden of proof is very high, much more than required to show the assessment was simply inaccurate.
- Housing discrimination cases involve a three-step process that moves the burden of proof back and forth. Under what is called the McDonnell Douglas test, plaintiffs have the burden of showing they are a member of a protected minority; they applied for and were qualified to rent or purchase property; and they were rejected and the housing or rental opportunity remained available afterward. That creates a presumption of discrimination, which shifts the burden to the defendants to prove they had legitimate, nondiscriminatory reasons for their actions. If successful, the burden shifts back to the plaintiffs to prove by a preponderance of the evidence (meaning, "more likely than not") that the offered reason was a pretext and there really was a discriminatory purpose.

Bureau of Land Management   An agency of the U.S. Department of the Interior, charged with the care, custody, and management of all land owned by the U.S. government, comprising approximately 261 million acres. It also maintains current and historical information regarding land ownership and use, maintains a geospatial (GIS) data clearinghouse, and manages and provides access to the public land survey system, also called the rectangular survey system employed in surveying real property. (The Bureau of Land Management Web site is at www.blm.gov.)

burned-out tax shelter   An investment that has exhausted most of its tax-sheltering benefits. For properties taking advantage of bonus depreciation of up to 50 percent for the first year placed in use, the shelter can be burned out by year 2.

business center   An office arrangement providing individual offices for local representatives of large companies, professionals, and small-business persons, with sharing of lobby space, conference rooms, support staff, telecommunications services, office equipment, and other amenities. Formerly called executive suites and shared offices. The industry trade organization is the Office Business Center Association International (www.obcai.org).

business day   A standard day for conducting business, excluding government holidays and weekends. Various notices required in real estate contracts, leases, or other agreements may have deadlines based on the passage of a certain number of days, or of business days. To count days, you start with the day after the triggering event, and count that as day 1.

business interruption insurance   Insurance that provides benefits if business is interrupted while repairs are conducted after an insurable loss.

business park   A development designed for warehouse, office or light-industrial use, with generous landscaping and open spaces.

business value   The intangible value of a business, over and above the value of the land, improvements, fixtures, receivables, and cash. Intangibles may consist of goodwill, franchise value, and proprietary systems and procedures.

buyback agreement   A provision in a contract requiring the seller to buy the property back for a stated price if certain conditions are met within a specified period of time. One wishing to purchase an existing automobile dealership may purchase the land first, with a buyback agreement requiring seller repurchase if the purchaser is unable to obtain manufacturer approval for transfer of the dealership itself.

buy down   To reduce the interest on a mortgage loan by paying discount points in order to buy down the rate. For residential loans, it rarely makes sense for borrowers to buy down their rate. In order to evaluate, ask for the amount of the monthly principal and interest payments with and without the reduced rate. Subtract the lower number from the larger number. This is the amount of your monthly savings. Divide your monthly savings into the price for the buy down. This provides the number of months you must pay on the mortgage before you will have saved enough money to pay for the discount points. Finally, ask yourself, "Do I realistically think I will own this property for that length of time?" If not, then do not pay the points.

buyer's broker   An agency relationship in which the broker represents the buyer rather than the seller. This is typical in commercial real estate transactions, but relatively rare in residential real estate brokerage. For residential brokerage, most agents "working with" buyers are actually subagents of the seller.

buyer's market   A market with more properties for sale than can reasonably be expected to be purchased by the available demand. As a result, sellers will have to compete against each other to attract buyers and will usually do so by lowering prices.

buyout   (1) Securing the removal of tenants from a building by paying cash incentives for the early termination of their leases. Owners may desire to buy out tenants in order to rehab the property to attract a better quality of tenant at higher rates; in order to sell the property to an owner-occupier; or to remove an objectionable tenant causing problems but not technically in default. (2) Securing the release of a tenant from lease obligations in another building so the tenant can rent in the owner's building. The other building's owner may permit the buyout if he or she believes the departing tenant can be replaced fairly quickly, thereby gaining a large windfall profit from the buyout payment.

buy-sell agreement   An agreement among partners or shareholders describing the circumstances and terms of sale if one or more wish to exit the arrangement or wish to sell their shares to an outsider.

bylaws   Regulations by which an organization conducts its governance activities. They typically provide for the timing and method of elections and regular meetings, number of directors and other officers, methods and notice necessary for special elections or meetings, number of votes required for different types of actions, establishment of standing committees, and a grant of authority to organize other committees, powers of the board, officers, and various committees. The developer of a subdivision or condominium project typically creates the first set of bylaws and appoints the initial board of directors.

by operation of law   A method of acquiring rights in real estate without any specific intention or even knowledge on the part of the owner. Spouses may gain rights through homestead, dower (widow's rights), curtesy (widower's rights), or community property statutes.

C

CAD   (1) See *cash available for distribution*. (2) See *central appraisal district*. (3) See *computer-aided design*.

cadastral   (1) A legal map for recording ownership of the various parcels of land within a jurisdiction. (2) The United States Cadastral System program within the U.S. Department of the Interior Bureau of Land Management, responsible for surveying and related activities. (For more information go to the Bureau's Web site at www.blm.gov.)

CAI   See *Community Association Institute*.

caisson   A casing or cylinder used to sink shafts into wet or unstable ground, or a watertight structure within which construction is conducted under water. Often used in bridge building; sometimes used in commercial construction.

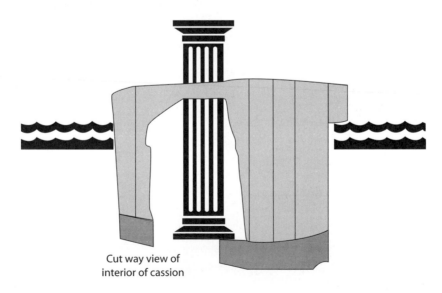

Cut way view of
interior of cassion

call option   See *call provision*.

call provision   A clause in a loan instrument that gives the lender the right to accelerate the debt upon the occurrence of certain conditions. These might include filing for bankruptcy (illegal, but it's in all the promissory notes anyway), reduction in value of the collateral, occupancy levels dropping below certain minimum levels in income-producing properties, or the catchall clause "whenever the lender deems itself insecure." As a practical matter, it would be an unwise lender who relies solely on the "deeming itself insecure" clause, because such action almost always results in litigation in which a jury, usually of the borrower's peers, gets to decide if it was reasonable under the circumstances for the lender to panic.

CAM   See *common area maintenance.*

cancellation clause   A clause in a contract or lease that allows one or either party to cancel it upon the happening of certain named events other than a default. It is most often encountered: (1) in the lease for a single-tenant commercial building or house, allowing the landlord to cancel the lease upon sale to another owner who wishes to occupy the property rather than use it as an investment, and (2) in a commercial lease for a small-space user who might stand in the way of expansion by a larger tenant. Well-negotiated leases include a provision for some sort of compensation to the tenant if this happens.

cantilever   A beam or overhanging architectural element that is supported at only one end. The most common examples are bay windows and swimming pool diving boards. The most famous example is a balcony that seems to be suspended in the air above a waterfall at Frank Lloyd Wright's architectural masterpiece, Fallingwater, in Pennsylvania (www.paconserve.org/fallingwaterhome.htm).

cap   A ceiling on the adjustments that can be made in the payments or interest rate of an adjustable-rate loan.

capacity   The legal ability of parties to enter into contracts.

- Full capacity. Having unlimited ability to enter into binding contracts of all types.
- Limited capacity. Having the ability to enter into binding contracts for certain things, such as a minor's contracts for necessities, but also having the ability to disaffirm other contracts upon reaching legal age, for example.
- No capacity. Having no ability to enter into contracts, such as one who has been adjudicated as mentally incompetent.

capital   (1) In architecture, the top part of a column. (2) In finance: (a) All the accumulated goods, possessions, and assets used for the production of income and wealth. (b) The amount invested in business.

capital asset   (1) All property held by a taxpayer except inventory or goods in process. (2) All property except that held for resale to others in the ordinary course of business.

capital calls   A call for additional equity investment by shareholders or partners in order to fund cash shortfalls in development or operations, or to compensate for the falling value of noncash assets and the need to increase cash so that liabilities do not exceed assets.

Corinthian capital.

capital expenditure   Money spent on capital improvements, being those that change the nature of property, extend its useful life, or otherwise improve it beyond the natural improvement to be expected with routine repairs and maintenance. This is an important concept because capital expenditures must be added to the basis and depreciated slowly over time, while noncapital expenditures for repairs may be deducted entirely in the current year on one's taxes.

capital gain   The taxable gain recognized from the sale of a capital asset. It is the difference between the sale price of the property and the adjusted basis. Tax laws routinely offer preferential treatment for long-term capital gains on property held for a certain period of time before sale. Capital gains may be offset by capital losses.

capital improvement   See *capital expenditure*.

capitalization rate   Usually called a cap rate, it is a number used in order to estimate the value of an income-producing property. There are no cap rate tables, no firm standards, and no universal formulas for arriving at one. Cap rates change frequently, depending on market demand for particular types of properties, lender appetite for particular types of loans, and prevailing interest rates. Most commercial real estate brokers, appraisers, and lenders know a range of cap rates for different types of properties. One divides the annual net operating income by the cap rate to arrive at a value. High-quality multi-tenant medical offices might sell for cap rates of 7 percent, and rundown apartment buildings with high turnover might sell for a cap rate of 13 percent. If both of them had gross rents of $300,000 per year with operating expenses of $60,000, then each would have a net operating income (NOI) of $240,000. By dividing the cap rate into the NOI, the medical offices would have a value of $240,000 ÷ 0.07, or $3,428,571. Using the same formula for the apartments, but the higher cap rate, $240,000 ÷ 0.13 gives a value of $1,846,153. It seems counterintuitive at first, but the higher the cap rate, the lower the value.

capitalize   (1) In finance: (a) To add an expenditure to the basis of property. (b) To provide funding to an enterprise. (c) To book something as an asset and depreciate it rather than writing off the money spent as an expense. (When one "cooks the books" for a business, extensive repairs might be capitalized as improvements in order to make the enterprise appear more valuable than it is in reality. This approach runs counter to the normal taxpayer desire to treat all repairs as expenses in order to gain maximum tax deductions in the current year.) (2) In appraisal, to estimate the present value of an income stream from a business or property.

capitalized closing costs   A taxpayer may write off as deductible expenses some of the closing costs associated with the purchase of property or the acquisition of a loan. Others must be deducted proportionately over the term of the loan, so that if the loan is for 30 years, $1/_{30}$ may be deducted each year. Still others must be capitalized, meaning treated as additional money spent on the purchase price when it comes time to calculate the gain on a later sale of the same property.

Tax Deductions for Home Purchase Expenses

	Deduct in Current Year	Amortize over Loan Term	Capitalize
Loan origination fee for primary home purchase	✓		
Buyer-paid loan discount points for primary home purchase	✓		
Seller-paid loan discount points for primary home (but only if the seller doesn't deduct them also)	✓		
Any of the above three, but for secondary home		✓	
Prepaid interest	✓		
Property tax prorates	✓		
Title insurance for owner			✓
Survey			✓
Legal fees for closing			✓
Recordation fees and transfer taxes			✓
Normal seller expenses you agree to pay, like real estate commission, back taxes, and unpaid assessments or dues			✓

For more information, consult IRS Publications 530 (Tax Information for First Time Homeowners), 523 (Selling Your Home), 587 (Business Use of Your Home), and 936 (Home Mortgage Interest Deduction) available at www.irs.gov or by calling 800-829-3676.

capitalized value of future income   The value today of the right to receive income in the future. The concept rests on the principle that no one would pay $120 today for the right to receive $120 one year from today. Neither would anyone pay $120 today for the right to receive $10 per month over the next 12 months. Add to that the idea that relative risk affects a person's decision making. You might place $120 in an FDIC-insured savings account today, in order to receive $140 in one year. But, would you pay $120 to an out-of-work student, in exchange for her promise to pay you $140 in one year? Probably not. These two concepts—the time value of money and the evaluation of risk— are at the heart of discounting. Discounting is the basic tool for reaching a capitalized value of future income. See *present value* or *discounted cash value*.

capitalized value of property   The acquisition cost of the property, plus expenses of acquisition and improvement. The choice between adding an item to the capitalized value or writing it off as an expense in the current year is one of the critically important decisions of any business or invest-ment property. It is important to have a grasp of the hard-and-fast rules and an understanding of the gray areas.

capital loss   A loss recognized upon the sale of a capital asset. It is the difference between the sale price of the property and the adjusted basis. Just like capital gains, capital losses can be either short term or long term. Long-term capital losses may be set off against long-term capital gains. Short-term capital losses may be set off against short-term capital gains; one may not recognize a capital loss on the sale of a personal residence.

capital markets   The markets in which equity is raised and long-term loans (over one year) are originated and traded. These include the stock market, the bond market, and the primary market. The primary market is any market in which the original issuer receives money, such as an investment house that purchases all securities for an original issue and then resells them on the stock market. Short-term debt instruments, for one year or less, are sold in the money markets, not the capital markets.

capital recapture   Return of the principal invested in a property, normally expressed as a dollar amount over a period of time.

capital recovery   See *recapture rate*.

capital stack   A description of the totality of capital invested in a project, including pure debt, hybrid debt, and equity. The stack is described as containing the most risk at the top, traveling down the stack to the position with the least risk. Higher positions in the stack expect higher returns for their capital because of the higher risk. Lenders and equity stakeholders are highly sensitive to their position in the stack. Typically, the stack is arranged as follows.

1. Sponsor equity
2. Preferred equity
3. Mezzanine investors (hybrid debt and equity)
4. Second and other junior mortgages
5. Investment-grade first mortgages

Capital stack.

capital structure   See *capital stack*.

cap rate   See *capitalization rate*.

capture rate   The sales or leasing rate of a project, which is usually compared to similar projects in the marketplace. There are various measurements, depending on the size of the units being sold or leased. When referring to commercial real estate space for lease, the capture rate might be expressed as an average number of square feet leased per month, quarter, or year. When referring to small space with short rental terms, such as self-storage or business center space, the expression is also used to communicate the number of units rented versus the number of inquiries per month, or sometimes the number of units rented versus the number of physical visits to the property per month. All these measurements allow management to compare its success to others in the marketplace and to make adjustments in pricing, advertising, or possibly even sales personnel as a result. They also allow management to make decisions about future development, in order to accurately anticipate the length of time it will take a project to reach stabilized occupancy or, the alternative, to break even.

Example: *The following table shows capture rates of square feet of space rented in each of the quarters of the past year, for three different buildings.*

Square Feet of Space Leased, per Quarter, in Three Different Buildings

Quarter	Building A	Building B	Building C
1st	5,000	0	500
2nd	10,000	0	10,000
3rd	18,000	42,000	12,500
4th	2,000	0	500

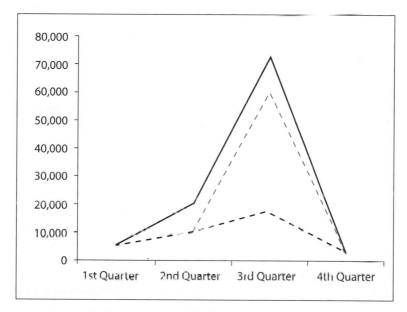

A quick glance at the chart shows that tenants seem to sign the most leases in the third quarter, although the negotiating process probably starts much earlier.

caravan   A group inspection tour of newly listed properties by local real estate agents; a field trip to view the competition's listings.

carport/car porch   An open-air roofed structure used to house vehicles at a residence. Contrast with a garage, which must be completely enclosed.

carry-back financing   Seller financing through the vehicles of a second mortgage, a wraparound mortgage, or a bond for title.

carrying charges   Costs incurred in owning property up until completion of a development, as opposed to the actual development expenses themselves. Carrying charges must be capitalized and then amortized, or expensed, over the next 10 years as tax deductions. Examples include interest accrued on development loans, and property taxes.

carryover basis   In tax accounting, the retention of an earlier basis (adjusted acquisition cost) in property even though the property has changed hands. This happens most often in two instances: (1) Someone acquires property by gift. The basis is the same as it was in the hands of the donor, adjusted upward for any gift taxes paid by the donor. (2) In a 1031 exchange, in which like-kind property is exchanged for other like-kind property in a sort of perfectly legal accounting sleight of hand, the basis in property acquired is the same as the basis in the property given up, even though both might currently have substantially different fair market values.

carve-out   An area of personal liability in an otherwise nonrecourse loan. A lender may be willing to accept property as sufficient collateral for a loan, without requiring personal liability on the part of the corporate or individual borrower in case there is a default and the collateral is insufficient to pay the debt. The exceptions, or carve-outs, are for things outside the ability of the lender to analyze during underwriting, such as borrower fraud or environmental claims.

cash available for distribution (CAD)   Encountered in REIT (real estate investment trust) and large corporation accounting, it is cash from operations after payment of all expenses and a reserve for taxes, repairs, and reasonably anticipated capital expenditures.

cash equivalent   (1) In finance, assets easily converted to cash. Lenders like to see large percentages of assets held in cash and cash equivalents rather than tied up in real estate or stock in small corporations. (2) In appraisal, the conversion of a sales price with favorable or unfavorable financing terms into the equivalent price if the consideration had been all cash. A seller might demand an above-market price for a property but be willing to hold the financing at below-market rates, for example. Such a transaction would require analysis for the cash equivalent sales price.

cash flow   (1) Noun: The cash available from an investment after receipt of all revenues and after payment of all bills. (2) Verb: The process of creating cash flow, as in "I think that property will start to cash flow in about a year." A property can have positive cash flow (good) or negative cash flow (usually bad). Cash flow is not the same thing as profitability. A property can be profitable, meaning gross income less expenses, depreciation, and interest on debts results in a positive number. That same property can have a negative cash flow because of the need to pay principal payments on loans or expend money for something that represents a capital expenditure, like a new roof.

cash flow mortgage   A loan workout tool in which all, or nearly all, of the cash flow from a property is used to service the debt for some period of time, even though this amount may be less than the amount originally expected by the lender.

cashier's check   An official check issued by a bank with itself as the drawer. Contrast with a certified check, which is one drawn on the bank customer's account, with the customer as drawer, but certified as good by the bank. Closing companies usually require a cashier's check for the purchaser's portion of all closing costs and purchase money. A cashier's check can be the subject of a stop-payment order. Because of widespread forgery of cashier's checks, many closing companies will not complete closing until funds are actually collected and in the closing company's escrow account.

cash method   An accounting method employed by individuals for preparation of their taxes, and often used by small businesses. Income is counted when the money is actually received by the taxpayer, and expenses are counted during the period in which they are actually paid. Contrast with the accrual method, in which income is counted when it is earned, whether or not it results in money during that period, and expenses are counted when they are incurred, regardless of when they are actually paid. Cash method accounting can dramatically skew financial statements, making properties appear profitable solely as a result of holding bills and not paying them until another period.

cash-on-cash   A tool for investment analysis, being a comparison of the cash flows taken from a property over some period, usually a year, as compared to the original cash investment.

cash-on-cash return   See *cash-on-cash*.

cash out   To liquidate an asset.

cash-out refinance   To refinance a property in an amount sufficient to pay off existing debt and provide cash to the owner. Because this is not a taxable event, it is a widespread way for investors to realize benefits from the growth in their assets without having to sell them.

cash purchase   A property acquisition with no financing. Even without a financing contingency, it is important for real estate contracts to specify if there will be a cash purchase or a financed purchase, because the two represent vastly different responsibilities on the part of the closing company.

cash throw-off   Same as the noun version of cash flow, but rarely used. It is common, however, to say that a property Is "throwing off cash."

castle, man's home as   A concept rooted in English common law, from the case of *Anonymous*, King's Bench, 1506, reported at Year Book, 21, H.VII 39, pl. 50, holding that a person was entitled to defend his premises against intruders because "a man's house is his castle and his defense, and where he has a peculiar right to stay."

categorical taking   A government regulation that deprives a property owner of all economically beneficial use of his or her property, and, as a result, constitutes a regulatory taking such as would justify requiring the government to pay the property owner for the loss.

caveat emptor   Means "buyer beware." The legal doctrine followed in some states that sellers of real property are not required to disclose any defects except those inherently dangerous and not easily discoverable by the purchaser. Contrast with seller disclosure states that affirmatively mandate written disclosure of a wide variety of named deficiencies, plus anything else that might be deemed a property defect.

caveats   Warnings. Frequently encountered in real estate disclosures or contracts with the words "to the best of the Seller's knowledge" or "but without aid of a structural engineer."

CBD   See *central business district*.

CCA   chromated copper arsenate; a pesticide that is forced into wood under high pressure to protect it from termites, other wood-boring insects, and decay caused by fungus.

CCIM   See *Certified Commercial Investment Member*.

C-corporation   A typical corporation that pays taxes on its income at the corporate level and then the shareholders are taxed on dividends distributed to them. Contrast with S-corporation, which has no taxes at the corporate level.

CCR   See *conditions, covenants, and restrictions*.

CD   See *certificate of deposit*.

cease and desist   An order from a government authority requiring one to stop engaging in some activity, such as construction without a proper permit. If issued from a court, it would be called an injunction.

ceiling   (1) The uppermost surface of a room or space. When a lease makes all improvements "below ceiling" the responsibility of the tenant, one must ask if "ceiling" means the concrete bottom of the floor above, or if it means the suspended grid system with ceiling tiles. The space in between the two is called the plenum. All the wiring, plumbing, and ductwork go through the plenum, so the choice of which surface is the "ceiling" could mean a substantial difference in tenant responsibilities. (2) An upper limit on something, such as the IRS ceiling of $1,000,000 worth of home mortgage debt for which one can deduct mortgage interest.

cemetery lots   A special land use designation authorized by statute. In many states, cemetery lots are exempt from real property taxes.

census tract   A small, relatively permanent statistical subdivision within a county, generally containing 2,500 to 8,000 people and readily identifiable borders. Similar to block numbering areas (BNAs), but differing only in the local versus federal source of the data used to create the maps. Mapped and numbered by the U.S. government, which provides demographic information at www.census.gov. Third-party resellers of demographic information extrapolate from the census tract data into more personalized demographic areas.

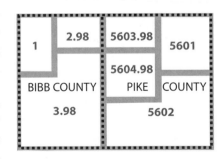

central appraisal district (CAD)   Employed when multiple entities are entitled to assess taxes based on the value of real property located within their shared borders. In order to avoid inconsistencies in appraisals and duplication of expenses, the multiple entities will organize and share the expenses of a central appraisal district.

central business district (CBD)   Typically the downtown section of a city, generally containing the finance, real estate, insurance, and legal headquarters for the city.

Century 21 page   A slang expression derived from the real estate franchise firm Century 21; describes a Web site that exists for no other purpose than to redirect you to another site. Web sites are often referred to as "real estate."

CERCLA   See *Comprehensive Environmental Response Compensation and Liability Act.*

certificate of completion   A document issued by an architect, engineer, or other qualified inspector attesting that the project has been completed in conformity with all plans and specifications; usually required before the construction lender will fund the final payment due under a construction loan.

certificate of deposit (CD)   A receipt for money deposited in a financial institution.

certificate of discharge   Also called a waiver of tax lien. An IRS release of tax lien so that property can be sold or foreclosed. (For more information go to the IRS Web site www.irs.gov and see Form 4422, "Application for Certificate Discharging Property Subject to Estate Tax Lien"; Form 783, "Instructions on How to Apply for a Certificate of Discharge of Property from Federal Tax Lien" (non-estate tax); and Form 786, "Instructions for Preparing Notice of Non-judicial Sale of Property & Application for Consent to Sale.")

certificate of eligibility   A certificate issued by the regional Department of Veterans Affairs in order to indicate a person's eligibility for a VA loan.

certificate of estoppel   See *estoppel.*

certificate of insurance   A document issued by an insurance company to certify the extent and limits of coverage. Usually required by landlords as evidence a tenant is in compliance with lease requirements to maintain certain minimum levels of property and liability insurance. Also required by general contractors as proof the subcontractors have adequate insurance.

certificate of no defense   Same as estoppel certificate. See *estoppel.*

certificate of occupancy (C/O)   Almost always referred to simply as a "C.O." A document issued by a local government certifying that a structure has passed all required inspections and is ready for occupancy. It is always required at the completion of any construction when repairs require a construction permit. It is also often required when a property changes character from residential to commercial, even if no construction takes place, and is sometimes required before issuance of a new business license when a property changes hands. As a de facto method of enforcement, many utility companies will not permit service until receipt of a valid certificate of occupancy.

certificate of reasonable value (CRV)   A document issued by the Department of Veterans Affairs as a prerequisite for a VA loan; it is based on an approved appraisal. It establishes the maximum value of the property for VA purposes and, as a result, the maximum size of the VA loan.

certificate of satisfaction   A document filed in the public records certifying that a recorded lien on real property has been paid in full.

certificate of title   A document issued by an attorney or title company certifying the status of title to real property and the absence or presence of title defects, liens, and adverse claimants. This is not the same as title insurance, because the preparer is liable only for negligence in the event of mistakes.

certified check   A check drawn on the bank customer's account, with the customer as the drawer and the check certified by the bank as payable.

Certified Commercial Investment Member (CCIM)   A designation awarded by the Commercial Investment Real Estate Institute after a member completes education, experience, and testing requirements. (For more information go to the Web site of the CCIM Institute at www.ccim.com.)

Certified General Appraiser   An appraiser qualified to appraise any type of property, under rules adopted by the Appraisal Foundation (www.appraisalfoundation.org).

certified historic structure   As defined by the IRS for purposes of the rehabilitation tax credit (popularly known as the historic preservation tax credit), any building, portion of a building, bridge, ship, railroad car, dam, or any other structure that is either listed in the National Register of Historic Places or located in a registered historic district and certified by the U.S. Department of the Interior as being historically significant to the district.

certified home inspector   A home inspector certified under state licensing or certification programs.

Certified Property Manager (CPM)   A professional designation awarded by the Institute of Real Estate Management (IREM) (www.irem.org), which is affiliated with the National Association of REALTORS®.

Certified Residential Appraiser   A state certification for residential appraisers.

Certified Residential Broker (CRB)   A designation awarded by the Council of Real Estate Brokerage Managers (www.crb.com), which is affiliated with the National Association of REALTORS®.

Certified Residential Specialist (CRS)   A designation awarded by the Council of Residential Specialists (www.crs.com), which is affiliated with the National Association of REALTORS®.

cestui que trust   (pronounced "seh tee kuh trust") The beneficiary of a trust.

chain   A unit of measurement formerly used in surveying and still seen in deeds with old property descriptions. One chain equals 66 feet.

chain of title   The history of all owners and lien holders of real property, together with the dates of their acquisition and the nature of their title, going all the way back to the first deed out of the government.

change order   A written order from the owner, architect, engineer, or other authorized person to depart from previously agreed upon plans and specifications for construction. Change order management is a critical aspect of any construction job, as change orders frequently change the cost of the job, usually in an amount in excess of what might otherwise be expected. Many sub-contractors bid jobs at break-even prices in order to secure the work, confident that numerous change orders will provide the profit necessary.

> **Example:** *An electrician might contract to perform all wiring and electrical work for a home for $2,000. Additional outlets added by change order might be billed at $65 each, even though the additional labor and materials might amount to only $5 each.*

charge off   To discontinue accounting for some or all of a promissory note and its accrued interest as an asset of the lender. If a loan is partially or totally uncollectible, then it is partially or totally worthless and cannot constitute an asset. This is an accounting function only; the lender may still pursue collection activities and then rebook the money as a cash asset when and if there is a recovery.

chattel   Tangible personal property.

chattel mortgage   A security interest in tangible personal property.

Check 21   Shorthand for the Check Clearing for the 21st Century Act; legislation that allows faster processing of checks by financial institutions by allowing them to process images rather than physical pieces of paper. The law also allows the creation of substitute checks that are processed immediately.

checkerboard development   A traditional subdivision design with straight streets at right angles to each other and houses on evenly sized square or rectangular lots. Contrast with *cluster development*.

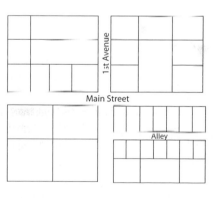

choice of law clause   Frequently employed by a national company with real estate relationships in many states, the clause will state that the law of the company's headquarters will control any disputes between the parties. This is because the lawyers back at headquarters know their own law and know how to write contracts to protect themselves. If all their nationwide contracts were interpreted under the laws of the different states, it could be chaotic. Choice of law clauses are usually accompanied by forum shopping clauses, which specify which state's courts will hear disputes between the parties.

chronologic age   The actual age of a thing, rather than its effective age.

circulation   Areas in an office space that are used to travel between offices, cubicles and the like; hallways and corridors.

cistern   A container for the collection of rainwater. Many historic homes had gutters and downspouts that routed all water into a cistern beneath the house to be used as a water source for cooking, cleaning, and in the event of fire.

civil law   A system of laws with its origins in Roman and French statutes rather than the judicial decisions of English common law. See *common law*.

Civil Rights Act of 1866   Passed after the Civil War, this Act declared that all persons born in the United States were citizens of the United States without regard to race, color, or previous condition of servitude. All citizens were entitled to enter into and enforce contracts, and to buy, sell, lease, inherit, and pass by inheritance real and personal property. It prohibited discrimination in housing, but provided no enforcement mechanism other than private lawsuits. It was not until 102 years later, with the passage of the Civil Rights Act of 1968, that antidiscrimination laws could be truly enforced through federal actions.

Civil Rights Act of 1964   On November 27, 1963, newly sworn-in President Lyndon Johnson called for the passage of a new civil rights bill, as a tribute to the late President John F. Kennedy, who had been assassinated only weeks earlier. The resulting bill was signed into law on July 7, 1964, with a stated purpose: "To enforce the constitutional right to vote, to confer jurisdiction upon the district courts of the United States to provide injunctive relief against discrimination in public accommodations, to authorize the Attorney General to institute suits to protect constitutional rights in public facilities and public education, to extend the Commission on Civil Rights, to prevent discrimination in federally assisted programs, to establish a Commission on Equal Employment Opportunity, and for other purposes." It has come to be identified with halting discrimination in public accommodations—restaurants, hotels, and other public facilities.

Civil Rights Act of 1968   Expanded upon prior civil rights acts, especially the Civil Rights Act of 1866 and the Civil Rights Act of 1964. The Act was passed one week after the assassination of Dr. Martin Luther King. One improvement was the provision of federal solutions to aid in stopping discrimination. Title VIII of the Civil Rights Act of 1968 is also known as the Fair Housing Act. Additional information is available at the Web site of the U.S. Department of Justice, Civil Rights Division, www.usdoj.gov/crt/crt-home.html.

claim   A demand, as of right.

Claritas   A commercial provider of market research and demographic data (www.claritas.com). When marketing commercial real estate, it is common for the agent to obtain 1-, 3-, and 5-mile-radius demographic information regarding population density, median household income, and median home price for the most recent census survey with estimates of current data and projections of future data.

class (building)   Subjective evaluation of the desirability of an office building based on its age, amenities, maintenance, and design. There are no hard-and-fast rules, and evaluations may change for a virtually identical building in two different markets. The classification is independent of the location; one commonly encounters comments such as "It's a class B property in a class A location," meaning a less desirable building happily situated at a great location and thus able to command higher rents than might otherwise be expected.

class A building   A building of high-quality and well-designed with above-average finishes and features and the ability to attract first-class investors and tenants. New tenants typically offered a build-out allowance to customize their space.

class B building   A building of good quality but without any extras; may have been designed as a no-frills building or may be a former class A building that has become dated in its design and finishes but is still well maintained. New tenants may be offered a build-out allowance, but it is typically sufficient only to repaint walls and replace floor coverings.

class C building   An affordable office space with average to below-average maintenance. New tenants typically take space "as is," although carpets might be shampooed before occupancy.

Clean Water Act   Legislation originally enacted in 1972, and amended several times since then, that establishes comprehensive national policies for water quality management. The laws are enforced by the Environmental Protection Agency (www.epa.gov).

clearance letter   Also called a wood infestation report, provided by a licensed termite inspection company and attesting the absence of any evidence of active termite infestation. (This letter is a requirement of most lenders before closing may take place.)

clear-cutting   The process of removing all vegetation from a site when harvesting timber, rather than cutting only the marketable trees. Some states require immediate reforestation of clear-cut timber lands. Purchasers of timbered land should be careful to word contracts so as to include the timber. In many states, once an owner signs a contract to sell timber, it ceases to become part of the real estate, is converted to personal property, and is not automatically covered under a sale contract for real property.

clearing and grubbing   The stage of development in which vegetation is cleared from land (clearing) and a root rake or similar device employed to remove roots remaining in the soil (grubbing). The next stage is cutting and filling.

clear span   The horizontal distance between supporting pillars, columns, or walls, being the maximum possible distance clear of obstacles. Especially when working with industrial properties, it is important to know the existing or required clear spans for clients.

clear-span facility   A building, most often a warehouse or airplane hanger, with vertical columns on the outside edges of the structure and a clear span for the entire interior area.

clear title   Good title; marketable title; title to real property without any defects, liens, mortgages or adverse claimants.

client   The person to whom an agent owes duties of integrity, confidentiality, loyalty, and hard work. Contrast with customer, who is owed the duty of honesty.

close corporation   A corporation comprised of a small number of individuals who contribute to the success of the business operations. Also called closely held corporation. Stock in close corporations is typically sale-restricted, so that shares must be first offered to the corporation or to the other shareholders before they can be sold to outsiders. Sale restrictions must be noted on the face of stock certificates, putting buyers on notice that an attempted sale may be void if all requirements have not been met.

closed-end mortgage   A mortgage loan in which all sums have been funded at closing. Contrast with open-end mortgage, in which the principal balance may increase over time. A home loan is typically a closed-end mortgage; a construction loan is typically an open-end mortgage.

closely held corporation   See *close corporation*.

closing   The process of obtaining all necessary signatures, making all required disclosures, and collecting and disbursing all monies in order to transfer title to real estate, execute a mortgage, or both. Closings are regulated by the Real Estate Settlement and Procedures Act.

closing agent   The person who performs a closing. The closing agent is typically not an agent of either party or of the lender, but simply the person entrusted to carry out all nonconflicting instructions from all parties.

closing company   A company or firm that conducts real estate closings, also called settlements. The closing company does not represent any party to the transaction, but merely ensures that all documents are properly signed and all monies collected and disbursed according to the parties' contract.

closing costs   Technically, only those fees and expenses necessary to close a sale or a mortgage, such as document preparation, the fee for the actual closing itself, and perhaps overnight delivery charges. In common language, though, the phrase has come to mean all expenses associated with a closing with the exception of the actual purchase price of the property and any lender fees. Rather than specifying that a buyer and seller will share closing costs equally, the better practice would be to spell out all anticipated expenses and the allocation for payment.

Examples of potential expenses include

- Preparation of closing documents
- Deed preparation
- Expenses associated with clearing title defects, such as preparation of affidavits or quit-claim deeds
- Title inspection
- Owners' title insurance
- Lender's title insurance
- Lender-required policy endorsements
- Deed recordation fees
- Mortgage recordation fees
- Transfer taxes (which can be sizable in the case of the New York mansion tax, for example)
- Closing agent fees
- Transfer fees imposed by condos, homeowners associations, or co-op boards

- Listing agent's commission
- Selling agent's commission
- Cost of wood infestation report and clearance letter
- Cost of survey
- Cost of appraisal
- Cost of required inspections
- Escrow fees
- Prepayment penalties
- Prorated real estate taxes, insurance, and/or dues

closing date   The date on which the seller delivers the deed to the buyer and the buyer pays the agreed-upon consideration. Purchase contracts typically specify a closing date no later than a certain number of days or no later than a certain date. If closing does not take place on or before the designated date, then the party causing the delay is in default. As a practical matter, unless the contract recites specifically that "time is of the essence," then closing may usually be delayed several days without penalty or loss. In a seller's market, however, the better practice is to ensure that closing takes place by the agreed-upon date, or the buyer will risk loss of the property and sale to someone else.

closing protection letter   Additional title insurance coverage insuring the lender against losses caused by errors or infidelity of the closing attorney or the closing agents in the handling of the transaction.

closing statement   Written itemization accounting for all funds changing hands at a real estate or mortgage loan closing.

closure   In a metes-and-bounds legal description of land, the necessity that the various calls and distances culminate at the point of beginning, so the shape described is "closed." If the shape is not closed and the property description is inaccurate in some regard, then the transaction violates the statute of frauds and the transfer is void. The drawing to the right is of a property description without closure.

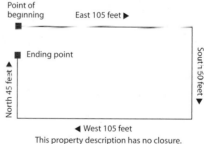

This property description has no closure.

closure document   A document written by a state environmental protection agency certifying that a previous environmental hazard no longer bears further scrutiny because it has been remediated.

cloud on title   Something that appears on its face to constitute a defect in title or a claim against property, but which may be cleared through the execution of affidavits, quitclaim deeds, or corrective deeds, or by means of a lawsuit called an action (or bill) to quiet title.

cluster development   A subdivision planning design in which housing is clustered together on relatively small lots with a larger amount of common area shared by all; also called open space development and conservation subdivision. Requires some sort of homeowners association with the ability to assess dues in order to maintain the common area. Contrast with *checkerboard development*.

cluster zoning   Zoning that specifies housing density for an entire area overall, leaving a developer free to use some space for high-density housing such as apartments or garden homes, and other space for low-density estate-sized lots. Contrast with traditional zoning ordinances that specify the same density for each and every lot within an area.

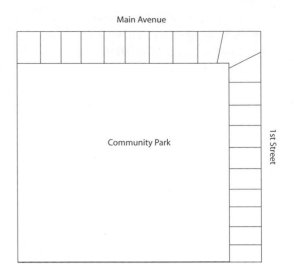

CMA   See *comparative market analysis.*

CMBS   See *collateralized mortgage backed securities.*

CMO   See *collateralized mortgage obligation.*

CMO REIT   A real estate investment trust that specializes in collateralized mortgage obligations.

C/O   See *certificate of occupancy.*

cobroker   See *cooperating broker.*

code   (1) Any systematic collection of laws, regulations, or rules. (2) Shorthand for any of the various building codes, such as, for example, "This historic property has been updated and meets all current code requirements."

code of ethics   Any written system of standards and ethical considerations for the persons bound. All state real estate licensing organizations have their own codes of ethics; most are based on that of the National Association of REALTORS®, which is available at www.realtor.org/mempolweb.nsf /pages/code?opendocument.

COFI   See *cost of funds index.*

coinsurance   A method of dividing financial responsibility for a loss between the owner and the insurance company. Coinsurance clauses exist within insurance contracts as a type of penalty for an owner who decides to gamble about the size of any potential loss and insure property for less than the full value in order to keep premiums low. They usually provide that an owner may not collect full policy limits for a loss unless the property has been insured to at least 80 percent of its value.

COLA   (pronounced like the beverage) See *cost-of-living adjustment.*

cold call   To make unsolicited contact with persons for the purpose of making a sale. In real estate, new agents will often cold call entire neighborhoods in an attempt to obtain listings.

cold canvass   See *cold call.*

collapsible corporation   A former tax-planning tool allowing conversion of ordinary income to capital gains through the vehicle of a corporation set up and then quickly "collapsed" by a sale or exchange of the stock or a liquidation. Today, the vehicle has been largely penalized out of existence by the IRS. If the corporation is collapsed and the stock sold within 3 years of formation, sale proceeds will be treated as ordinary income although such a holding period would otherwise qualify for capital gains treatment. See also *thin corporation*.

collateral   Security for a debt.

collateral heir   An heir who is not in a direct line from a decedent, but born from a collateral line, such as brothers and sisters, aunts and uncles, or cousins. Relevant in the context of intestate succession, being the order of distribution of property when one dies without a will. Contrast to lineal heirs.

collateralized mortgage obligation (CMO)   A security or bond backed (collateralized) by a pool of mortgages. The issuer of the security segmented the cash flow in such a manner that it could create bonds with maturities at differing dates and appeal to a broad spectrum of investors. Today, the CMO has largely been replaced by the REMIC—real estate mortgage investment conduit—although the terms are often used interchangeably.

collateralized mortgage backed securities (CMBS)   Derivative investments created by aggregating mortgage loans into pools and then selling interests, much like bonds, which entitle owners to payments over time until the debt is finally retired. (Note: Commercial mortgage backed securities, a specialized type of collateralized mortgage backed securities, are also known as CMBSs.) The concept is best understood by reference to the various parties involved:

- A loan originator, such as a commercial bank, mortgage banker, or insurance company originates mortgage loans.
- An investment bank acts as an intermediary and sponsors the conduit by purchasing the commercial mortgage loans and warehousing them until they are ready to be converted to securities.
- A rating agency rates the underlying mortgages as AAA, AA, A, BBB, and so on down to CCC, with AAA to BBB being classified as investment-grade and BB downward classified as below investment grade.
- The same investment bank previously mentioned now separates the mortgages into tranches, or classes, of bonds depending on their ratings. The tranches are then offered for sale as securities backed by the entire mortgage pool. One might buy investment-grade tranches, but they are backed by all the loans, not just the investment-grade loans.
- Investors purchase the securities. Investment-grade tranches are usually purchased by insurance companies, pension funds, mutual funds, money managers, and commercial banks. Below-investment-grade tranches are sold to real estate investment funds or CMBS servicing entities.
- A servicer collects mortgage payments, monitors delinquencies and defaults, engages in workout procedures or initiates foreclosure, and handles all accounting and reporting, paying over monies periodically to the trustee for distribution to the investors.

- The trustee, who represents the trust that holds legal title to the mortgages for the benefit of the certificate holders, pays out money to investors according to the terms of their securities. The most common arrangement is the "waterfall" payment, in which class A bond holders receive principal and interest payments in the early years, while class B and class C holders will receive only interest. After a fairly short predetermined period of time, the class A bond holders will have been paid in full, and their bonds will be retired. At that point, the class B holders will begin to receive principal in addition to interest, but the class C holders will still receive only interest. When class B holders have been paid in full, class C holders will begin receiving principal payments. As a result, the class C holders will suffer if there are significant defaults and not enough money to pay everyone in full. For that reason, class C holders generally receive a higher return on their investment.

colonia   Residential areas along the United States side of the border with Mexico and that may lack some of the most basic living necessities, such as potable water and sewer systems, electricity, paved roads, and safe and sanitary housing. The Environmental Protection Agency estimates there are more than 1,300 colonia in Texas and New Mexico alone.

color of title   The appearance of title to real property, such as a deed that turns out to be defective. Important because those with color of title are given more rights than those who have no color of title, but a mere possessory or other such claim.

Color of Title Act   This act, 43 U.S.C. §1068, authorizes the secretary of the interior to issue a patent—original deed from the government—to a person who has occupied a certain area of land for at least 20 years with color of title, under circumstances that would otherwise constitute adverse possession if it were not for the rule prohibiting adverse possession against the government. The occupier is able to tack his or her possession on to that of his or her ancestor or grantor, in order to arrive at a cumulative time of 20 years or more.

commencement of work   The readily observable date on which work commences on a construction project. This date is important in the context of mechanics' and materialmen's liens for unpaid construction bills, because the date of the lien is effectively backdated to the date of commencement of work, even though there may not have been a failure to pay bills until many months later. In many states, if there is a lien filed, and the commencement of work occurred before the construction mortgage was recorded, then the lienholder is in a first lien position and the construction lender is in second place, comparable to having a second mortgage rather than a first mortgage.

commerce clause of the constitution   Article I, Section 8, Clause 3 of the United States Constitution. This clause empowers Congress "to regulate Commerce with foreign Nations, and among the several States, and with the Indian Tribes." The commerce clause has provided the most powerful tool available to the federal government for spreading its legislative and regulatory reach into the lives of everyday Americans.

commercial bank   A financial institution authorized to receive both time (savings accounts, CDs) and demand (checking accounts) deposits, to make loans of various types, to engage in trust services, to issue letters of credit, to accept and pay drafts, to rent safety deposit boxes, and to engage in similar activities and ventures.

commercial creep   The gradual encroachment of commercial real estate into residential areas.

Commercial Investment Real Estate Institute   A professional organization, which is an affiliate of the National Association of REALTORS®; specializing in commercial real estate and offering the designation CCIM—Certified Commercial Investment Member. The name of the institute has now been changed to the CCIM Institute (www.ccim.org), but the old name is still frequently encountered.

commercial lease   A lease of space for nonresidential purposes.

commercial leasehold insurance   Insurance to cover the payment of rent in the event a tenant defaults.

commercial lender   An entity that routinely loans money as part of its core business. Contrast with a seller who loans money as part of a real estate transaction, or private investors who loan money sporadically as a good opportunity presents itself.

commercial mortgage backed securities (CMBS)   Collateralized mortgage backed securities with an underlying pool of commercial (non-residential) loans. See also *collateralized mortgage backed securities*.

commercial mortgage banker   A banker who specializes in originating commercial mortgage loans.

commercial mortgage loan   A loan secured by a mortgage on real estate that has a business or investment purpose.

commercial property   Property designed for use as offices, retail space, or wholesale, hospitality, or similar uses. Contrast with multifamily residential (apartments), residential development, or industrial property.

commercial real estate   Typically refers to office or retail space, or multifamily residential properties such as apartments. May include industrial real estate, but sometimes the phrase is meant to exclude industrial properties and must be read in context.

Commercial Real Estate Women (CREW)   A national organization (www.crewnetwork.org) founded in 1989 with the goals of "advancing the success of women in commercial real estate" and "achieving parity in opportunity, influence and power in the industry."

commingle   (also spelled co-mingle) It is illegal for real estate brokers to combine (or commingle) clients' funds with the broker's business funds in one account, even if all monies are accurately accounted for and there have been no other improprieties. Client funds do not have to be separated from each other, but can all be commingled in one escrow account.

commission   The compensation paid to a real estate broker for services rendered in connection with a sale, exchange, or lease of property. In order to be entitled to a commission, the broker must have a written contract for the services and must be licensed in the state. Generally the commission is fully earned if the broker produces a buyer who is ready, willing, and able to close at the terms specified in the listing agreement. This is true even if the seller elects not to accept the offer and withdraws the property from the market or increases the price.

Commission rates. Commissions are negotiated independently between the parties. Setting commission rates in advance by local real estate boards or other organizations is a violation of federal law. Most listing agreements now contain a disclaimer advising that commissions are separately negotiated on a case-by-case basis.

Sales commission amounts. Typically expressed as a percentage of the gross sales price of the property, usually ranging from 6 to 10 percent, although higher and lower percentages may be negotiated.

Leasing commissions. Compensation paid to an agent upon lease execution. It is usually calculated as a certain percentage of the total anticipated rent payments, up to a 5-year term.

> **Example:** *If the leasing commission is 4 percent on a 5-year lease at $12,000 per month, then multiply $12,000 by 60 months to arrive at $720,000 and the broker is paid 4 percent, or $28,800. The parties may negotiate a lesser percentage for a term longer than 5 years, to be paid at the 5-year anniversary date.*

Leasing commissions—lump sum. Sometimes negotiated to be equal to one or two month's rent, or even a certain amount per square foot. The drawback to this method is that the broker is compensated the same for a 3-year lease as for a 10-year lease.

Leasing commissions—payment over time. Occasionally, leasing agents prefer to receive their commissions as each payment of rent is made, rather than in a lump sum at lease signing. The effect is to provide a guaranteed income for many years.

commissioner   An officer charged with the administration of laws or regulations pertaining to a particular subject matter, such as a real estate commissioner. A directory may be found at the Web site of the Association of Real Estate License Law Officials (ARELLO) at www.arello.com.

commission rates   See *commission*.

commission splits   Listing brokers will typically split their commission with the selling broker— the person who provides the buyer for the property. One should always inquire, however, because some brokers refuse to split commissions, preferring to find their own buyers and keep 100 percent of the commission rather than work with other brokers in the area.

commitment (loan)   An agreement by a lender to extend a loan on certain terms and conditions and by a certain date. Language making the "commitment" subject to credit approval or underwriting are not true commitments at all, but merely quotes.

common area maintenance (CAM)   ("CAM" is pronounced as a word) Costs required for a tenant's pro rata share of the upkeep of common areas and amenities such as the parking lot, external lighting, trash removal, and street cleaning. When obtaining quotes for retail space or office space, one should always ask about tenant CAM expenses, because a lower per-square-foot rental rate at one location may be offset by high CAM expenses.

common areas   (1) In leaseholds, the area over which the landlord retains exclusive control and liability, such as stairwells and hallways. (2) In condominiums, all property except for the specific condominium units themselves. Common areas are owned by all condo owners in common with each other, except that access may be restricted for plumbing, electrical, and other such areas, or it may be semirestricted so that all condo owners own a portion of your balcony, but you are the only one entitled to use it.

common enemy rule   A rule of water management and rights followed in some states. It holds that excessive rainwater is a common enemy that damages property at random. Uphill property owners can take any steps to protect their land from the water, even if it causes damage to the property of others further down the hill. The downhill property owners are supposed to protect their own land, because water is the common enemy and everyone has to provide their own protection. Today, most states have modified rules that require everyone to act reasonably under the circumstances in order to protect their own property and avoid damaging the property of others.

common law   A law derived from common usage, ancient customs, or the pronouncements and interpretations of courts. Contrast with code law, or civil law, which relies on statutory enactments for the articulation of rights and responsibilities, and then judicial interpretation of those statutes. English law, and almost all American law, is based on common law. The law in France is based on the Napoleonic code, and the law in Louisiana is based on that code also. (Because of the completely different underpinnings of Louisiana law, it is rare to find a lawyer or real estate agent outside the state who will offer an opinion regarding real estate law within the state.) When reading definitions of words, one should pay attention to whether the definition recites "at common law" or "at civil law."

Community Association Institute   An umbrella association for condo associations, homeowners associations, and other community groups, providing information on management, governance, and legal issues. It estimates that 57 million Americans lived in association-governed communities in 2006. The Web site of the Community Association Institutes is at www.caionline.org.

community property   Property owned by a husband and wife, each owning an undivided one-half interest by virtue of the marital relationship and not by virtue of any deed or other document of specific intent. There are exceptions for family property inherited from one side or the other. The community property states are Arizona, California, Idaho, Louisiana, Nevada, New Mexico, Texas, and Washington.

Community Reinvestment Act (CRA)   An act passed by Congress in 1977 to encourage financial institutions to meet the credit needs of the communities in which they operate, including low- and moderate-income neighborhoods. Compliance is monitored via regular audits, and a poor record of CRA compliance is taken into consideration when the financial institution applies for deposit facilities, including mergers and acquisitions.

One may find a financial institution's rating for CRA compliance by visiting the Web sites of the various regulatory agencies that track compliance. A financial institution may appear on one list but not others, depending on which agency has responsibility for that bank and its CRA compliance. The possibilities are

Federal Reserve Board (www.federalreserve.gov)
FDIC (www.fdic.gov)
Office of Comptroller of the Currency (www.occ.treas.gov)
Office of Thrift Supervision (www.ots.treas.gov)

community shopping center   A shopping center of approximately 100,000 to 300,000 square feet and 20 to 70 retail spaces, designed for a mixture of retailers and food service establishments with a high convenience factor for a market area radius of 3 to 6 miles. Usually situated on 10 to 40 acres, with at least one anchor tenant; anchor(s) typically comprise 40 to 60 percent of the gross leasable space.

compaction   The process of compressing soil used to fill the low areas in a parcel of land. Developers typically obtain soil compaction reports before beginning development, but care must be taken to test more than the typical 6-foot depth. It is a common practice for excavating companies and unscrupulous landowners to use substandard fill material, such as tree trunks and other vegetation that will eventually decompose and reduce volume, and then properly compact only the top 6 feet of fill. Over time, the property will settle, possibly resulting in severe structural problems.

compaction tests   See *boring tests*.

comortgagor   An additional borrower with some interest in the real property that is the subject of the mortgage.

comparables   In an appraisal, recently sold or leased properties similar to the property under analysis, such that a review of the sales prices of the comps will assist in determining a value of the subject property. The properties need not be identical, as long as they are reasonably similar and the appraiser can make adjustments for features that differ. These may include property amenities, age of the improvements, traffic counts and market area, time and conditions of the sale, and anything else recognized by the market as having value.

comparative market analysis (CMA)   An analysis of the value of property by taking only a very few market indicators, such as price per square foot for land or price per unit for apartments, and then extrapolating to the property under analysis. This does not constitute an appraisal, but may give prospective sellers a basis for setting a sales price for listing purposes.

comparative negligence   A legal theory in some states that evaluates the negligence of a wrongdoer against any negligence of the injured party that contributed to its injuries, and then assigns a pro rata responsibility for the harm suffered.

> **Example:** *If a property owner allows a loose step to remain unrepaired, and a guest loses his or her balance and falls, the property owner has been negligent. If, however, the guest was*

intoxicated, a jury might decide the guest was 25 percent responsible for the injuries. In such a case, the jury will calculate a dollar value for the injury and associated expenses and will then reduce it by 25 percent in order to arrive at an award.

Contrast with contributory negligence, which denies any award at all if the injured party was at all negligent under the circumstances.

comparative unit method   An appraisal technique in which direct and indirect costs are totaled and then divided by an appropriate unit to obtain a cost per unit.

Examples include

- Land compared on a value per square foot
- Land compared on a value per front-foot
- Self-storage facilities compared on a value per unit
- Hotels compared on a value per room

comparison method   See *market comparison approach*.

compensation   (1) Payment for goods or services. (2) Damages necessary to restore an injured party to his or her position before the wrongdoing. (3) In eminent domain, payment to property owners for the value of the property taken and any damage caused to the value of the remaining property.

compensatory damages   Damages intended to compensate the injured party for the harm suffered. Contrast with punitive damages to punish the wrongdoer, and nominal damages awarded to recognize that a right was violated or a duty breached, but no harm done.

competent   (1) Duly qualified; having sufficient ability or authority. (2) Having the legal ability to testify about a particular subject. In real estate, the concept is important because property owners are usually competent to testify about the value of their property before a loss and the value of their property after a loss. In other words, it is not legally necessary to hire an appraiser to testify, although it is prudent as a practical matter.

competitive market analysis   See *comparative market analysis*.

complete appraisal   An older term rendered obsolete by the July 1, 2006, changes to the Uniform Standards of Professional Appraisal Practice, but still frequently encountered. The term used to mean an appraisal that did not resort to using any of the departure provisions of the old rules. Previously, all clients had to be provided with a complete appraisal unless the client signed off and approved a limited appraisal noting specific appraisal methods not employed because they were perhaps not relevant to the specific property. Today, the new scope of work rule allows the appraiser to choose the analytical methods necessary to meet the client's objectives and the scope of work, but the client does not have to approve the methodology.

completion bond   A fidelity bond posted by a contractor or developer to guarantee that a particular project will be completed according to plans and specifications, on time, and without any liens incurred as a result of unpaid bills to subcontractors and suppliers; usually required as a condition of performing government work. It provides more coverage than a simple performance bond, which ensures that one party will perform if the other will perform, usually by payment. The completion bond is independent of any underlying contracts and any defenses to those contracts.

compliance inspection   (1) An inspection by a government official to ensure that a building or project complies with all relevant building codes and zoning regulations. (2) An inspection by the representative of a lender to ensure that all lending institution requirements have been met as a prerequisite to a loan or as a condition of funding advances on a construction or development loan.

component building   A building made of prefabricated components that are then delivered to the construction site and assembled. In housing, the modular home is an example, although a man-ufactured home that is assembled elsewhere and delivered to the site would not be a component building. Components could include tilt-up concrete walls popular with commercial construction, and structural insulated wall and roof panels (providing rigidity, sheathing, insulation, wire chases, and sometimes even outside and inside finishes all in one product) for residential construction. The ultimate component building is an apartment building of self-contained apartment rectangles built elsewhere and then stacked together like children's building blocks.

component depreciation   A former practice of separating a building into its various compo-nents—walls, roof, etc.—and then depreciating each component separately, some more rapidly than others, in order to generate large tax deductions. (This is no longer allowed by the IRS, except in a modified form called cost allocation.)

compound interest   The process of charging, or earning, interest on interest. Interest accrued in prior periods is added to the principal, and then interest in the current period is calculated on the total.

> **Example:** *If you saved $100 per month, starting at age 25, at an earnings rate of 5 percent per annum, you would have $144,959 by age 65, only $48,000 of which would be money you contributed. To perform your own calculations, use the following formula to create a Microsoft Excel spreadsheet:*
>
> *=FV(Interest Rate, Number of Years, Savings per Year)*–1*

For Interest Rate enter the cell address where you will note the interest rate you expect to earn; for Number of Years enter the cell address where you enter the number of years you expect to save the same amount each year; and for Savings per Year enter the cell address where you will enter the amount you expect to save each year.

	A						
1	0.05						
2	40						
3	1,200						
4	=FV(A1,A2,A3)*–1						

Comprehensive Environmental Response Compensation and Liability Act (CERCLA)   Federal laws passed in 1980 and known commonly as the Superfund. The law imposes strict liability for cleaning up environmentally contaminated land—one's liability does not depend on any fault or responsibility, but simply on one's status as any of the following:

- A past or current owner of a facility
- A past or current operator of a facility (such as a tenant or property manager)
- A generator of hazardous substances
- A transporter of hazardous substances

Because of potential cleanup liability for the actions of previous owners, it is essential that any purchaser of commercial property investigate a property history for evidence of manufacturing processes, petroleum-related businesses such as gas stations, dry-cleaning plants, transmission repair shops, and any number of other activities. In the alternative, one may order a Phase I Environmental Report from a licensed engineer. As a practical matter, most lenders will require the report as a condition of providing funds for purchase.

At one time, there was some confusion over a mortgage lender's potential exposure to liability by virtue of possibly being considered an "operator" when involved in management decisions during a loan workout. There was also great fear about lender liability after foreclosure, when the financial institution became an "owner." This has largely been cleared up through CERCLA amendments providing limited lender immunity provided there is appropriate due diligence before credit extension. Due diligence is usually resolved through requiring a Phase I Environmental Report from a licensed engineer, and then a Phase II report if the Phase I report indicates any suspicious evidence. After foreclosure, the lender can avoid liability if it takes steps to sell the property as soon as possible.

When selling or buying property, it is important for the sales documents to include a provision allocating financial responsibility in the case cleanup is necessary in the future. Parties may not disclaim responsibility under CERCLA, but they may contractually agree regarding who will bear the ultimate cost of a cleanup.

For more information regarding this complex subject, visit the Superfund pages of the Environmental Protection Agency Web site at www.epa.gov/ebtpages/cleasuperfund.html.

comps   Shorthand for comparable properties, used in appraisal.

computer-aided design (CAD)   The use of computer software to assist in performing standard architectural and engineering design services. Products range from the most basic shareware home design and landscaping software to sophisticated systems with three-dimensional flyover and walk-through capabilities, project budgeting, and timeline creation.

computerized loan origination (CLO)   A computerized network of major lenders that uses artificial intelligence to evaluate loan application data entered online by agents and determine loan eligibility and terms. HUD has approved the procedure as long as there is full disclosure of the fee, multiple lenders are displayed on the screen to give borrowers freedom of choice, and the fee charged is a dollar amount rather than a percentage of the loan.

concession   (1) A discount, rebate, or abatement. Lease concessions may consist of free rent, below-market rent, a larger than normal build-out allowance, reserved parking, 5-year anniversary renovation allowance, or any number of other economic incentives to induce one to lease in a particular building. When investigating the purchase of an income-producing property, one should examine each and every lease in its entirety to determine the existence of any lease concessions that would adversely affect an economic analysis of the property, and one should also obtain estoppel certificates from tenants so that there are no agreements outside the terms of the written leases. (2) A business that operates within the confines of another business or on another property, but usually without a lease. Examples include a shoe-shine concession at the airport, the hot-dog concession at the ball park, or the designer fragrance concession in a department store.

concession burnoff   The process of rent concessions becoming less frequent, smaller, or both, so that the market sees growth in overall rental rates because of the discontinuance of temporary concessions, not because of a true increase in market rates.

conciliation agreement   A settlement or compromise agreement between a regulatory agency and an individual or entity charged with violating rules, regulations, or laws. The agreement evidences an acknowledgment of past wrongdoing and an intention to correct the consequences of the past actions and to desist from future violations.

concurrent ownership   Ownership by two or more parties at the same time. The most common examples of concurrent ownership are

- Tenants in common
- Joint tenants with right of survivorship
- Tenants by the entireties
- Community property interests
- Tenants in common with cross-contingent remainders

condemnation   (1) A proceeding to obtain private property for public use through the exercise of the government's rights of eminent domain. Historically considered possible only for public improvement projects such as roads, schools, and courthouses, the landmark U.S. Supreme Court case of *Kelo v. City of New London*, 125 S.Ct. 2655 (June 23, 2005) held that local government could condemn land belonging to one private party in order to convey it to another private party as part of an economic development plan to increase government revenues, add jobs, and improve the quality of life in a depressed area.

In a condemnation case, the government will order an appraisal of the property and then offer the owner the appraised price, or perhaps a negotiated amount in excess of the appraisal but taking into account the savings realized by not having to litigate the issue. If the property owner does not accept, the government must escrow the amount of money determined by its appraisal and may then proceed with condemnation of the property. The parties may then go to court to contest the amount of the required award, but the contest will not prevent or delay condemnation of the property.

Specialized tax rules apply whether property is condemned, sold to the government under threat of condemnation, or sold to a third party under reasonable fear of impending condemnation (see IRS Publication 544 at www.irs.gov). Taxpayers may defer income realized in a condemnation award by purchasing replacement property within 2, 3, or 5 years, depending on the particular circumstances.

Payments to cover the costs of relocating are not part of the condemnation award and are not taxable income. Severance damages awarded because of damage caused to the remaining property are not part of the condemnation award. The amount of damages will reduce the basis in the remaining property. If it reduces the basis to $0, then any excess must be reported as gain, but taxation can be deferred.

(2) A decision by local government that property owned by another is no longer safe and must be repaired or demolished. It is not a defense that the owner is making no use of the property and is not exposed to any danger, so long as the public at large may be exposed to danger. If the owner fails to make the necessary repairs or take any other action, the government authority may conduct the demolition itself and place a lien upon the property for the costs of demolition.

condemnee   One whose property is condemned.

condemnor   One who condemns property.

condition   A future and uncertain event that determines whether or not there will be a contractual obligation or liability. Conditions may be express or implied, possible or impossible, lawful or unlawful, affirmative or negative, precedent or subsequent, positive or negative, and, finally, single, copulative, or disjunctive. Each type of condition has different legal consequences.

Examples of the most common types encountered in real estate are

- Express. If the purchaser cannot obtain financing, the purchaser may cancel the contract.
- Implied. If the seller burns down the house the day before closing, the purchaser may cancel the contract.
- Lawful. If the broker produces a buyer willing and able to pay the asking price, the seller will pay a commission of 6 percent of that price.
- Unlawful. If the broker produces a buyer willing and able to pay at least $125,000, the broker will be paid all the purchase price in excess of $125,000.

conditional commitment   An agreement by a lender to extend a loan with specified terms, but only if certain conditions are met, such as retention of occupancy rates at a certain level until the time of closing, securing of key man insurance for an important manager-owner, release from a contingent liability that might impair the borrower's financial condition, or any number of other conditions.

conditional offer   An offer to buy real estate conditioned on the occurrence of one or more things before the purchaser is obligated to buy. Examples include zoning changes or the ability to secure a contiguous property.

conditional sales contract   (1) A sales contract in which the buyer is given possession and use of the item sold, but the seller retains legal title until all payments have been made in full. Equipment leases for a term of years, at the end of which the buyer pays $1 to buy the property, have been characterized by the IRS as conditional sales contracts rather than true leases. As a result, the taxpayer is not allowed to deduct the full lease payments each year, but only an amount equal to the depreciation available if the property had been purchased for cash, plus an allocation for interest. This amount is usually less than the annual lease payment. (2) If pertaining to real estate, commonly called a bond for title, land sale contract, or contract for deed.

conditional use permit (CUP)   (pronounced "cup") A permit granted to a property owner to make use of real property in a manner allowed under current zoning regulations, but only in accordance with conditions to be applied by the zoning authority. Houses of worship may be allowed in areas zoned for residential use, but the applicant may be required to obtain a conditional use permit that can be predicated on size, off-street parking availability, indirect nighttime lighting, and other such factors determined on a case-by-case basis. Contrast with variance, in which the property owner is given permission to use the property in a manner inconsistent with current zoning regulations.

conditions, covenants, and restrictions (CC&Rs)   Rules incorporated by reference into the deeds of condominiums and individual lots in subdivisions with homeowners associations and/or restrictive covenants. The CC&Rs set out restrictions on the use of property, and even on the behavior of residents.

condo cowboys   A derogatory term among condominium developers used to refer to inexperienced persons with little training, experience, or capital, but who decide to engage in condo construction or conversion. Such people often ignore established methods and principles of development and marketing, frequently encounter financial difficulties requiring additional financing at high interest rates, and then dump units on the marketplace with little or no profit margin but with the net effect of forcing down prices in the entire market.

condominium   A system of ownership in a multiunit development allowing individual ownership of some areas and common ownership of all other areas. The identifying feature is the legality that common areas (entrance, hallways, elevators, swimming pool, parking, etc.) are owned by all members of the community in common with each other, rather than being owned by a separate corporation or association. Residential condominium projects may be multistory apartment-style residences or may resemble traditional detached housing or garden home communities.

condominium conversion   The process of converting a building with tenants, or a cooperative building with tenant-shareholders, into a community of individual owners of specified units and common owners of all common areas. Many states have laws protecting tenants in a building scheduled for conversion. Protections may include lengthy notice periods regarding the plans to convert, prohibitions against drastic rent increases designed to force tenant flight from the building, an exclusive period during which only the tenant may purchase the unit before exposure to the general market, and special protections for the elderly and disabled.

condominium declaration   The document that establishes the legal existence of the condominium project and the ability to divide airspace into horizontal layers of ownership. The condominium declaration must be filed with the designated public official for the state or county where the land is located.

condominium owners association   An association that automatically includes as members all persons who own condominium units in a defined project. Unlike subdivisions, in which the home-owners association often owns the common lands, the condominium owners association does not own the common areas—the unit owners own them in common with each other. The association does enforce the provisions of the covenants, conditions, and restrictions and manages the financial, legal, and maintenance business of the community.

condotel   A relatively recent concept involving a melding of a resort hotel with condominium ownership. Initially became popular after September 11, 2001, when it became difficult to obtain financing of more than 50 percent of the cost of acquisition or development of a hotel property. To raise the additional necessary capital, developers sold individual units to investors and users, with the promise to rent the units to hotel guests and pay over profits to the individual owners. In recent years the practice has become less common with regular hotels, but remains strong with resort developments. The Securities and Exchange Commission, and several plaintiffs' law firms, have recently taken the position that such relationships involve the sale of securities, thereby requiring registration, disclosure, adherence to strict accounting standards, and many other requirements.

conduit   A metal pipe through which electric wiring is run. Building codes often require that all electric wiring for commercial buildings must be in conduit and securely attached to the ceiling, not suspended from dropped-ceiling supports or other building components.

conduit financing   A method of providing loan money through a debt instrument that blends fea-tures of a traditional pass-through mortgage security and a bond. Traded on Wall Street as securities known as REMICs—real estate mortgage investment conduits. For real estate borrowers, the single most important feature of conduit financing is the very large prepayment penalty imposed on all such transactions. The success of the entire securitization process depends upon trustee receipt of regular monthly income for distribution to bondholders according to a prearranged schedule. If a borrower pays off the loan early, that loan will no longer earn any interest, which affects the money available for payment to investors. In order to compensate, the trustee will have to go out into the marketplace and purchase an investment to replace the mortgage paid off. That investment may cost a premium price, so the prepayment penalty is used to offset the premium.

conduit tax treatment   Income passing through an entity without taxation at that level, but only at the recipient's level. A subchapter S-corporation, a partnership, and a limited liability company are all examples. Contrast with a C-corporation, which pays income taxes on profits and then uses after-tax dollars to pay dividends to shareholders, who pay taxes on the dividends.

confirmation of sale   A court approval of a sale by a trustee, executor, administrator, guardian, or bankruptcy trustee. Sales contracts by such persons are always specified as contingent on court approval.

confiscation   Seizure of private property by the government without compensation to the owner, usually as a consequence of the owner being convicted of a crime.

conflict of interest   A situation that presents the possibility of having to choose which side in a transaction will receive the better service, deal, terms, or representation. The conflict may be choosing between two other parties, such as an agent attempting to represent both buyer and seller in a particular transaction, or it may be between the party and another, such as a real estate broker wishing to purchase property listed with that same broker. Rules regarding handling conflicts of interest generally provide a solution through full disclosure to all parties involved or withdrawal from the situation entirely.

conforming loan   A loan that meets the underwriting requirements necessary for sale to Fannie Mae (FNMA—Federal National Mortgage Association) or Freddie Mac (FHLMC—Federal Home Loan Mortgage Corporation). There is nothing derogatory about a nonconforming loan; it may be too large, it may be for a property flipped within the prior 90 days, or any number of other disqualifying reasons besides creditworthiness or value of collateral.

conformity principle   An appraisal principle holding that the more a property's components are in harmony with the surrounding properties or components, the more they contribute to value.

> **Example:** *A 5,000-square-foot home with a three-car garage and an inground pool is more valuable in a neighborhood filled with similar properties than it would be in a neighborhood of 2,500-square-foot homes with two-car garages and no pools.*

congregate housing   Also called supported housing, with private living quarters and shared dining and social areas. Housing for the elderly and disabled is generally congregate housing, as are dorm rooms for students.

consent decree   A judgment in which the defendant agrees to take some action, or to cease doing something the plaintiff deemed objectionable, but without admitting any wrongdoing.

consequential damages   (1) Damages that do not flow directly from some wrong, injury, or taking. A buyer who refuses to proceed to closing for no legal reason may be liable for the seller's *direct* damages of the difference between the agreed-upon purchase price and the price ultimately obtained for the property, or the interest on the money if the sums are identical, plus any additional costs of marketing. The buyer might also be liable for the seller's *consequential* damages consisting of its loss of earnest money on another property, but only if the buyer knew the seller was depending on the closing to fund money for the seller's new home. (2) In a condemnation award, consequential damages are those suffered when the remaining property is injured because of the loss of the condemned property. A farmer's fields may be too small for efficient cultivation by large machinery after the county condemns enough land for roads to cross through the fields. A storekeeper's business may suffer as a consequence of its parking lot being taken for construction of a fire station.

conservation easement   A voluntary restriction on land preventing development on the property in order to retain its natural condition. The restriction will remain on the property for all subsequent property owners unless it can be successfully removed by court order or by agreement of all affected parties. See *easement*.

conservation subdivision   A housing development where homes are clustered together on smaller lots to preserve the surrounding natural area or farmland, which is often then owned and managed by the community.

conservator   A guardian, receiver, or other protector appointed by a court to manage the assets of someone suffering from a permanent or temporary disability that prevents the person from managing his or her own affairs. A person need not be adjudged mentally incompetent to have a conservator appointed, and the appointment does not disqualify the person from entering into contracts, making or changing wills, or any other such legal rights.

consideration   An act or a promise given by one person in exchange for an act or a promise from the other. The values do not have to be equal, and it has been said that one may promise to give a barleycorn in exchange for the promise to deed a castle, and it will be sufficient. It is a common misperception that earnest money is the component that makes a real estate contract enforceable. In reality, the promise to buy, and the promise to sell, is sufficient consideration. Consideration is an essential element for contract enforcement.

Consideration substitutes. Sometimes the law will permit enforcement of a contract even though one side or the other did not give consideration, if there was an allowed consideration substitute. The most common one is detrimental reliance, in which one person promises to do a thing gratuitously and another worsens his or her position in reliance on that promise. Under ordinary circumstances this would be a mere promise to make a gift, and unenforceable. Because of the detrimental reliance, however, it may become an enforceable contract.

Adequate consideration. If this is required by law, the consideration must be reasonably close to the value of the thing promised or exchanged.

Good consideration. The consideration is based on natural duty and affection or a moral obligation, such as property sold for "love and affection."

Consideration of support. It is not uncommon for elderly parents to transfer property to their children "in consideration of care and support." In most states, such transfers are voidable if the care and support are not forthcoming.

consideration of support   See *consideration*.

consignment   The practice of accepting possession of goods for another with the intention of selling the goods and remitting payment to the owner, less any agreed-upon fees. Ownership of the goods remains at all times in the consignor, not in the shopkeeper (consignee). Landlords may not obtain liens in the goods, and lenders may not gain security interests under blanket liens, if they have been put on notice that the party engages in the sale of consigned goods.

consolidated metropolitan statistical area (CMSA)   See *metropolitan area*.

consolidation loan   A new loan that pays off two or more existing loans or indebtednesses, usually resulting in lower payments. Home equity lines of credit are often marketed as consolidation loans, urging consumers to pay off high-interest-rate credit cards and automotive debt for lower-interest-rate, tax-deductible, mortgage debt. While the practice does reduce monthly payments significantly, it replaces relatively short term debt with long-term debt and results in higher total interest payments over time.

constant   The annual payment required to pay the principal and interest due on a $1 loan for a specified repayment term at a specified interest rate. Before the widespread availability of computers and extremely affordable financial calculators, it was common to use mortgage constant tables to calculate monthly payments. One would refer to the table for the proper loan term, such as 30 years, and then within that table find the loan constant for the anticipated interest rate. See the following example. The constant is the monthly payment on $1. To find out your own monthly payment, you multiply the constant by the number of dollars in your loan, and the answer is what your monthly payments would be.

Example:

Monthly Loan Constants for a 30-Year Mortgage Loan

Interest Rate (%)	Constant
5.00	0.00537
5.25	0.00552
5.50	0.00568
5.75	0.00584
6.00	0.00600
6.25	0.00616
6.50	0.00632
6.75	0.00649
7.00	0.00665
7.25	0.00682
7.50	0.00699
7.75	0.00716
8.00	0.00734
8.25	0.00751
8.50	0.00769
8.75	0.00787
9.00	0.00805
9.25%	0.00823
9.50	0.00841
9.75	0.0085

If the loan is $145,000 for 30 years at 6.75 percent interest, then

$$0.00649 \times 145,000 = \$941.05$$

constructed wetlands   A system of artificially created marshy-type areas of vegetation with frequent flooding, designed to treat wastewater through natural biological processes. The Environmental Protection Agency is a strong proponent of this method of cleaning water and has many additional resources on its Web site at www.epa.gov; search on "constructed wetlands."

construction allowance   As a leasing incentive, an amount budgeted for a tenant to spend on improvements to the space leased. When one is engaged in negotiations, care should be taken to define the tenant's obligations and the landlord's obligations with reference to the construction allowance. Also called tenant improvements allowance or TI for short.

> **Example:**   *If the lease gives the tenant responsibility for all improvements "below ceiling," then the considerable cost of adding or replacing ceiling tiles and light fixtures must be borne by the landlord and will not be deducted from the construction allowance. One should also negotiate the disposition of any unused construction allowance dollars and provide for their use as a credit against future rent or for them to be retained by the landlord in the account of the tenant and used at some point in the future for rehab expenses such as replacing worn carpet or repainting internal corridors.*

construction contract   A contract for construction services. A good one should contain the following information:

- The names of the parties
- The contractor's registration number
- A general description of the work to be performed
- A statement of the quality, such as "standard practices of the trades"
- A set of blueprints and engineering plans
- A set of specifications
- A description of responsibilities for oversight and management
- A timetable
- A fixed price for the work or a formula such as time and materials
- Definitions of terms, such as "time to exclude/include commuting time"
- The process for pricing and approving change orders
- Payment schedules
- The process to be used for dispute resolution
- Remedies in the event of default
- The terms of any warranties

construction loan   A loan originated for the purposes of providing payment for construction work or subdivision development. See also *building loan agreement*.

construction to permanent loan   A construction loan with provision for automatic conversion to a fully amortizing permanent loan upon completion of construction.

constructive eviction   The circumstance arising when, through no fault of the tenant, the premises are rendered unusable for the purposes for which they were leased, resulting in the de facto equivalent of an eviction. The concept is available as a defense for consumer tenants breaking their leases and vacating the premises as a result of claimed constructive eviction. It is not generally available to commercial tenants.

constructive fraud   A breach of some duty that results in a tendency to deceive others, with no requirement of a showing of intention to deceive or moral wrongdoing. A broker may be charged with constructive fraud if that person had a duty to disclose a known dangerous defect and failed to do so.

constructive notice   Notice that is deemed to have been received by a person, whether or not the person actually received it.

- All citizens are presumed to have constructive notice of the law.
- All persons have constructive notice of the contents of documents recorded in the public real estate records.
- The owner of property has constructive notice of any persons in actual possession of the property and claiming adversely to the owner.

constructive possession   Legally considered to be in possession of property even though not physically occupying it or using it in any manner. If one has a house on 40 acres of land, but rarely ventures outside the house and yard, one is in actual possession of the house and yard and in constructive possession of the remainder of the 40 acres.

constructive receipt   An IRS concept that the unrestricted right to receive money is the same as actually receiving it for purposes of calculating income. This has nothing to do with accrual methods of accounting versus cash methods of accounting, but, rather, with timing of depositing checks and similar concepts.

Consumer Credit Protection Act   See *Truth-in-Lending Act*.

consumer mortgage   Usually a home mortgage loan, but sometimes also refers to mortgages on rental houses.

consumer price index (CPI)   A Bureau of Labor Statistics' (www.bls.gov/cpi/) inflation calculator; it is the most widely known index for measuring economic performance and inflation in the United States. The CPI measures and compares the total cost of a statistically determined "typical market basket" of goods and services consumed by U.S. households against the cost for the same goods and services consumed in the base period 1982–1984. The contents of the "market basket" are determined by the Consumer Expenditure Survey of about 10,000 families and their spending habits over a period of time.

contamination   A condition of impurity resulting from mixture with a foreign substance.

contiguous   Next to, actually touching, at something greater than a point. The identification of contiguous parcels is important in the following circumstances:

- In adverse possession, a party in actual possession of property that has a defective deed is considered in constructive possession of the remainder of the parcel, but not of contiguous parcels, even if described in the same deed.
- Bankrupt debtors may claim homestead rights in contiguous parcels of land and are not limited to the single parcel on which their home sits, assuming other legal requirements are met.
- Under the Uniform Land Security Interest Act (model legislation not necessarily passed by all states) a mortgage lender's after acquired property clause is unenforceable except as to contiguous property.

A	B
C	D

Elm Street

E

Parcel C is contiguous to parcels A and D, but only adjacent to parcels B and E. But, in some jurisdictions, if the corners of the properties touch, this is sufficient to make the properties "contiguous."

contingency clause   A clause that allows cancellation of a contract without penalty if a certain described thing happens (e.g., an inspection report reveals necessary repairs estimated to cost in excess of $1,000) or fails to happen (e.g., failure to obtain satisfactory financing). A contingency clause contains a condition for contract performance.

contingent liability   A liability that is not currently a liability but may become one upon the happening of some future event. If a father guarantees the student housing lease of his son, then the son is liable for the rent but the father may become liable if the son defaults. Other common contingent liabilities are guarantees of the debts of others, potential adverse judgments in litigation, and currently contested tax liabilities or audits. Lenders sometimes request a list of all contingent liabilities when evaluating a borrower's financial strength.

contingent offer   See *conditional offer.*

continuing care retirement community   See *life-care facility.*

continuous occupancy clause   A clause frequently contained in the lease of a shopping center anchor tenant requiring it to remain open and in business for the entire term of its lease. The anchor is important not just because of its own rent payments, but also because it attracts customers who will shop at the other retail establishments in the center. If the anchor goes dark by moving out, all the remaining tenants will suffer, causing a possible domino effect of defaults.

continuous operations clause   Similar to a continuous occupancy clause, but with better drafting. The continuous operations clause in the lease of a shopping center anchor tenant requires the tenant to remain open at a contractually defined level of operations sufficient to generate the traffic flow necessary to attract ample customers for the other shopping center tenants.

contour map   A map that displays the hills and dales of a site as determined by a topographical survey. The contours of the land are represented by curved lines along which the height above sea level is relatively constant. The map will contain a linear scale indicating the dimensions of the site, and a contour scale indicating the elevation difference between contour lines, such as 5 feet. Lines that are widely spaced indicate a slow change in elevation; lines that are closely spaced indicate a rapid change in elevation.

contract   A legally enforceable agreement. Its requirements are

- Competent parties
- Subject matter
- Legal consideration
- Mutuality of agreement (also called "meeting of the minds")
- Mutuality of obligation

As a general rule, oral contracts are enforceable unless they relate to real estate or are incapable of performance within one year, guarantee the debts of another, or are evidenced by some writing signed by the person sought to be charged ("This is to confirm our agreement…") There are other exceptions, but they are not relevant here. It is often difficult to enforce oral contracts because the parties usually have differing recollections of the exact terms of the agreement.

contract for deed   See *bond for title.*

contract for purchase or sale   A contract for the sale of real property. There is no one form for this purpose, although local boards of REALTORS® typically draft model contracts for customization and use by their members.

contractor   One who supplies labor and materials to provide services in connection with the construction of an improvement on real estate. General contractors must typically be licensed by the state. An exception is made for property owners who act as their own general contractors or for general contractors of projects below a certain dollar limit.

contractor grade   Usually an inexpensive quality of building materials; it is generally equated with the cheapest components possible.

contract price   A tax term used in the calculation of gain realized on an installment sale. It is the selling price, minus any mortgage debt assumed by the buyer, plus the excess of any such liens collected in addition to the seller's equity in the property.

contract rate   The face rate of the interest on a promissory note; typically the interest rate quoted, as opposed to the federally mandated calculation of annual percentage rate (APR) which treats certain prepaid loan costs as additional interest.

contract rent   The rent stipulated in a lease. Contrast with *economic rent*.

contribution   (1) An appraisal principle that says the value of an improvement is the amount it adds to the value of the property as a whole, not the value of the improvement standing alone in a void. A backyard workshop in a prestigious neighborhood might not add any value at all and could be considered an eyesore detracting from value, but might be worth $10,000 in a different neighborhood. (2) A legal principle holding that if a judgment is collected against one who was held guilty of negligence, assault, defamation, fraud, or some other tort, then that person may obtain a contribution from others against whom the same judgment was rendered, for their proportionate share of the judgment. Likewise, persons jointly liable for a debt, such as partners or cotenants, are responsible to pay their share to the other if one pays the entire amount.

contributory negligence   A legal theory of negligence followed in some states (often called "contrib." for short). Under this theory, if someone was guilty of negligence that caused injury to another person, but the injured person was also negligent in any manner at all that contributed to his or her injuries, then there will be no recovery.

> **Example:**   *If a contractor built a deck with supports in the soil instead of in concrete, the contractor would be guilty of negligence. If the homeowner routinely left a hose dripping at the base of one of the supports, leaching out the soil and rotting the wood, the homeowner would also be guilty of negligence. If the deck collapsed, then in a contributory negligence state the home owner would not be allowed to recover any damages at all from the contractor. In a comparative negligence state, the homeowner's recovery would be reduced, but not eliminated.*

controllable expenses   Real estate expenses one may manage and keep as low as practical under the circumstances. For an office building, controllable expenses would be things like janitorial services, office personnel, and, to a limited extent, electricity. The most common noncontrollable expense is real estate taxes. Most contracts or leases will define what they mean by controllable expenses, without regard to what the common understanding of the phrase might be. The phrase is important because many commercial leases require tenants to pay their pro-rata share of increases in building expenses each year. Wise tenants will negotiate an upper limit on the contributions; wise landlords will insist that the "cap" apply only to controllable expenses.

controlled business arrangement (CBA)   A business arrangement recognized under the Real Estate Settlement and Procedures Act (RESPA) allowing a real estate brokerage office to provide financing, title insurance, and hazard insurance through the vehicle of subsidiary companies that operate within the brokerage office. Restrictions include the requirement that written disclosure of the affiliation be made to consumers, an estimated charge for the services is provided, consumers are free to obtain the services elsewhere, and referral fees are not charged among the various subsidiary companies.

control premium　　An amount paid to gain enough ownership interest to control a corporation or other entity. This would typically be an amount in excess of the simple fair market value of the shares sought to be purchased; used in business valuation calculations.

convenience center　　An open shopping center with fewer than half a dozen stores offering day-to-day necessities, such as basic groceries, dry cleaners, liquor stores, and video rental stores.

convenience store (C-store)　　A retail store that sells daily purchase items such as milk and beverages and impulse purchase items such as snacks and small gifts, usually in conjunction with gasoline sales. Convenience stores are attractive investments because the IRS allows rapid depreciation over a 15-year time period rather than the normal 39-year period required of typical commercial real estate.

conventional home　　Also called a stick-built home; a home built on-site, as opposed to a manufactured home (built elsewhere) or a modular home (components built elsewhere and assembled on-site).

conventional loans　　A mortgage loan without government participation in the form of insurance (such as the FHA) or guarantee (such as the VA).

conversion　　(1) The process of changing a property into condominium ownership. (2) Wrongfully taking property of another, or denying that person access to his or her property. If a self-storage facility overlocks a tenant unit in the mistaken belief the rent is past due, when in reality the rent was credited to the wrong person's account, then the facility is guilty of conversion.

conversion clause　　(1) A clause in a mortgage loan that allows the borrower to convert from an adjustable-rate mortgage to a fixed-rate mortgage, or that allows the borrower to convert from interest-only construction financing to a lower interest rate and usually fully amortizing permanent financing. (2) A clause sometimes seen in leases and real estate sales contracts providing that any personal property left on the premises after lease expiration or after real estate closing may be discarded or retained, as the real estate owner desires, and will not constitute a conversion. (In other words, the owner has no responsibility to keep the property in a safe place and/or attempt to return it to the former occupant.)

convertible ARM　　An adjustable-rate mortgage loan that the borrower may convert to a fixed-interest rate during a predetermined time period, at an interest rate calculated according to a formula set out in the note.

convey　　To transfer title to real estate to another.

cooling off period　　A time period within which a person may change his or her mind about a contractual agreement and cancel it without penalty. The right must be granted within the contract itself or by virtue of consumer protection statutes because it does not exist at common law.

co-op　　(1) Short for cooperative apartment, being a method of owning real estate in which a corporation owns a building and related facilities and persons who buy stock in the building are entitled to rent a particular unit, called a proprietary lease, at rates significantly below market rents. (2) An arrangement between two real estate agents for the sale of a property and splitting of the commission, usually as a result of one agent having the listing with the owner and another agent bringing the buyer to the closing table.

cooperating broker   A broker who agrees to split a real estate commission with another broker in return for services rendered in connection with a particular piece of real property.

cooperative apartment   See *co-op.*

core-based statistical area (CBSA)   A concept developed by the federal Office of Management and Budget in order to standardize geographic and population descriptions so that data from one federal agency may be reliably related to data from another federal agency without having to recheck definitions used by each agency. In the Year 2000 census definitions by the United States Census Bureau, a core-based statistical area is a functional region based around an urban center of at least 10,000 persons. These definitions replace the Year 1990 census definitions of metropolitan area, metropolitan statistical area, and consolidated metropolitan statistical area, although the older terms are still used in common parlance. CBSAs are further grouped as follows:

- Metropolitan statistical area. Contains at least one urbanized area of 50,000 people or more.
- Micropolitan statistical area. Contains at least one urbanized area and a population of 10,000 to 50,000 people.
- Metropolitan divisions. Divisions in metropolitan statistical areas with a single core of 2.5 million people or more.
- New England city and town areas (NECTAs). Geographic areas defined by cities and towns in New England, but still segregated according to the 50,000 people per size cutoff.

core factor   In an office building, the percentage of common area space such as lobbies, restrooms, and corridors as compared to the total net rentable square footage in the building. See *loss factor.*

CORENET Global   An association of corporate real estate executives and related professionals, organized in 2002 by the merger of the International Development Research Council (IDRC) and the National Association of Corporate Real Estate Executives (NACORE). The Web site for CORENET Global is at www.corenetglobal.org.

core space   In an office building, the common area space such as lobbies, restrooms, and corridors.

corner influence   The effect on the value of real estate by its proximity to the intersection of two streets.

corner of Main and Main   The most important intersection in a community or in a downtown office area. Some drug store chains have a simple site-selection preference for the "corner of Main and Main," no matter what the cost.

corporation   A legal entity created by filing documents with the local secretary of state, commissioner of corporations, or similar official. It may have as few as one shareholder, must begin life with some minimal amount of assets gained as a result of the shareholder(s) paying for shares of stock, may be stipulated as having a limited life span or perpetual existence until formally dissolved, and may be designated as having the powers to do only limited types of things or anything allowed by law. The entity thus created will enjoy all the rights and responsibilities of natural persons, including owning and renting real estate, and suing or being sued in the courts. The IRS allows corporations to be segregated into three main types for tax accounting purposes:

1. **S-corporation.** A small corporation that is allowed to file information returns only. It pays no taxes on its income but, instead, sees all income taxed to the shareholders according to their pro rata share of the corporation.
2. **C-corporation.** Any corporation that does not meet the limitations for an S-corporation, or one that otherwise qualifies for S-corporation status but elects to be treated as a C-corporation. The corporation files its own tax returns, pays taxes on income, and then distributes dividends to shareholders who pay taxes on the dividends.
3. **501(c)(3) corporation.** A not-for-profit corporation authorized by Section 501(c)(3) of the Internal Revenue Code, which files an information tax return but pays no taxes.

corporeal   Tangible real or personal property; things you can touch. Contrast with incorporeal property such as easements (a right to use, but not a right to, property) and goodwill.

correction deed   A deed executed to correct some defect in the original, such as the misspelling of a name or a mistake in a property description. Correction deeds are usually exempt from transfer taxes imposed by the recording authority.

correction lines   Provisions in the public land survey system made to correct for the curvature of the earth; one cannot have perfect rectangles over a curved surface. Every fourth township line (24 miles apart) is used as a correction line on which the spaces between the east and west range lines are corrected to a full and proper 6 miles. The effect is that the grid lines do not match up until they meet at the principal meridian.

23	24	19	20	21	22	23	24	19	20	21	22	23	24	19
31N01E				31N02E						31N03E				
26	25	30	29	28	27	26	25	30	29	28	27	26	25	30
35	36	31	32	33	34	35	36	31	32	33	34	35	36	31
1	6	5	4	3	2	1	6	5	4	3	2	1	6	5	4
12	7	8	9	10 30N02E	11	12	7	8	9	10 30N03E	11	12	7	8	9 30N04E
13	18	17	16	15	14	13	18	17	16	15	14	13	18	17	16
14	19	20	21	22	23	24	19	20	21	22	23	24	19	20	21

correlation   A former appraisal term, replaced by reconciliation.

correlative water right   A theory of riparian rights—water rights—that holds an owner who has rights in a common source of water is entitled to take only a reasonable amount of water for the beneficial use of the land. Contrast with appropriative rights, in which the owner has the exclusive right to take all the water for the beneficial use of the land.

cosigner   A person who signs a promissory note in such a capacity that he or she has equal and primary liability with another. Contrast with a guarantor, who is liable only if the original obligor defaults. A cosigner must list the promissory note as a liability on financial statements; a guarantor has only contingent liability which may never ripen into full liability.

cost allocation depreciation   A tax method of depreciating property by separating a functional unit—such as an office complex—into allowable components that may be depreciated over a shorter time period than otherwise permitted for the whole. For example, nonresidential real property improvements must be depreciated over 39 years. One may allocate the cost of some components, such as fencing, lighting, security systems, and carpet into categories that can be depreciated over 5 or 7 years, providing larger tax deductions.

cost approach   An appraisal method that estimates the cost to reproduce or replace an improvement and then subtracts an amount for depreciation to reach the current condition of the property. Of the three approaches—comparison to comparable properties, capitalization of income, and cost—cost is the one deemed least reliable overall, but most necessary in the case of unusual properties with no realistic probability of a tenant.

CoStar   A commercial provider of information about commercial real estate in most major markets across the United States and the United Kingdom. The information provided includes the ability to take a virtual drive down a designated street; to see street-level views of all the properties; and to click through to obtain information regarding ownership, management, vacancy rates, tenant information, lease expirations, and asking rents. Other information includes a property listing service, data regarding sales prices of properties, and advertising services for real estate firms. The CoStar Web site is at www.costar.com.

cost basis   The original cost of a property. After increases for capital improvements made over the years, and decreases for depreciation deductions or involuntary conversions such as condemnation, the number becomes one's adjusted basis.

cost-benefit analysis   A decision-making tool that evaluates all the hard-dollar and economic consequence costs associated with pursuing a course of conduct against all the hard-dollar and economic consequence benefits reasonably to be expected from that decision, and comparing the two to see if they make economic sense.

> **Example:** *Riverdale Apartments is experiencing increased competition because of the abundance of new apartment projects being built nearby. In order to compete more effectively, it is considering adding a sophisticated security system with Web cameras allowing residents to monitor gate access; areas around the buildings; and common areas such as the laundry room, swimming pool, and playground. The hard costs of $270,000 can be partially defrayed by*

charging rental rates $15 per month higher than other properties. Spread across 200 apartments, this results in an additional income of $36,000 per year. In addition, the system is anticipated to result in the ability to retain occupancies at 95 percent rather than an expected short-term drop to 75 percent until the new apartment buildings fill up and begin charging market rents in about 2 years. Calculations may attach a value of $36,000 per year to this consideration. Finally, the security system will result in significant insurance premium reductions amounting to $20,000 per year. The total short-term economic benefit is $92,000 per year for 2 years and $56,000 per year each year afterward (without adjusting for inflation or the cost of money). As a result, the initial $270,000 investment can be recouped in about 3¹/₂ years and will show a profit afterward. After completing this cost-benefit approach, management will probably decide to spend the money for the improvements.

cost of funds index (COFI)   A yield index based on the cost of funds to savings & loan institutions in the San Francisco Federal Home Loan Bank district. It is one of the indexes commonly used to set the rate of adjustable-rate mortgages.

cost-of-living adjustment (COLA)   A change in payments, such as rent in subsidized housing, based on a change in the index that measures inflation.

cost-of-living index   An indicator of the current price level for goods and services as compared to a base year. The base year is always set at a value of 1.0 or 100. As the cost of living increases (inflation), the number will increase, so that a cost of living index of 150 means things cost 50 percent more than they did in the base year. As the cost of living decreases (recession or depression) the number will decrease, so that a cost of living index of 93 means things cost only 93 percent of what they cost in the base year. The consumer price index is one such cost of living index.

cost-plus-percentage contract   A compensation method for a construction project, in which the contractor is paid a specified percentage over and above construction costs. This percentage may be pure profit to the contractor, or it may be the contractor's gross compensation from which must be paid general overhead expenses such as clerical help, phone lines, and general business insurance. It is important to determine the difference, because if the contractor expects the percentage to be pure profit, then normal business operating expenses will have to be accounted for somewhere in the construction contract as expenses.

cost recovery   A tax concept commonly called depreciation, but technically different in ways that don't matter to most taxpayers. The explanation is that depreciation is a calculation determined by starting with the acquisition cost of a property and then subtracting the anticipated salvage value when the property's useful life is over. That number is then divided by the number of years one can reasonably assume the property will have a useful life. The resulting figure is the annual depreciation for the property. Because of constant arguments, audits, and litigation over the correct salvage value and the correct useful life for various properties, the IRS replaced the whole depreciation system with the cost recovery system that assigns a useful life to various classes of property, assumes the property will be worthless at the end, and then allows deductions over the course of the useful life.

cost to cure   The amount of money necessary to remedy something that is depressing the value of real property. If the cost to cure a parking lot filled with potholes is $12,000, but the current parking lot condition depresses the value of the property by $20,000, then the defect is said to be curable.

cotenancy   A form of property ownership in which two or more persons or entities own undivided interests. The interests do not always have to be in equal shares.

Council of Real Estate Brokerage Managers   An affiliate of the National Association of REAL-TORS®; it confers the Certified Real Estate Brokerage Manager (CRB) designation. The Web site of the Council is www.crb.com.

Council of Residential Specialists   An affiliate of the National Association of REALTORS®; it confers the designation Certified Residential Specialist (CRS). The Web site of the Council is www.crs.com.

counseling   A relatively new career within the real estate industry that involves providing independent and unbiased advice on a variety of real estate–related issues. Membership in the Counselors of Real Estate (www.cre.org) is by invitation only. Another trade organization is the National Association of Counselors (http://nac.lincoln-grad.org/).

counselor   One who provides counseling services.

Counselors of Real Estate (CRE)   See *counseling.*

counteroffer   An offer that differs from the previous offer in some significant detail. A counteroffer rejects the prior offer by operation of law, and instead makes a new offer that must either be accepted or rejected by the other party.

> **Example:**   *A seller offers to sell her home "as is" for $250,000.*

- A buyer offers to buy the home for $240,000, but the seller must replace the roof and recarpet the house (counteroffer)
- The seller replies that she will sell for $235,000 "as is" (another counteroffer).
- The buyer replies that he will pay $210,000 "as is" (another counteroffer).
- The seller sees things going downhill and says, "Wait, wait, I accept your first counteroffer of $240,000 and I will repair the roof and carpet." However, the seller cannot do this, because that offer no longer exists and cannot be accepted.

county   A political subdivision within a state. It is usually the largest government body within the state. In Louisiana, the equivalent is called a parish.

coupon book   Formerly, a booklet given to investors with coupons that were clipped out and mailed in to receive that period's income. This was the source of the expression "coupon clipper," meaning a person of leisure with investment income. Today, a coupon book is the booklet given to mortgage borrowers, containing coupons with account and payment information, to be mailed in with monthly mortgage payments.

court   An organ of government belonging to the judicial department and charged with resolving disputes among parties. Courts generally have jurisdictional requirements providing that only certain disputes among described parties for certain amounts of money may be heard. If you file your grievance in the wrong court, you may be prejudiced when the case is dismissed for lack of jurisdiction and the time period during which to file in the proper court has expired.

covenant   An agreement. For example, one can make a "covenant not to compete" a provision of a business sale, or one can write a restrictive covenant regarding the use of real property into the real estate records, which binds all owners whether it is contained in their specific deed or not.

covenants, the usual   The use of this expression in a real estate contract refers to the seller's obligation regarding the type of deed the seller will execute. The three usual choices are a general warranty deed, a special warranty deed, or a quitclaim deed. The general warranty deed gives assurances and promises regarding the quality of the title being transferred; a special warranty deed merely promises that the seller has not done anything to injure the title, but makes no promises about other parties and their possible claims; while a quitclaim deed merely transfers any interest the seller might have, not that the seller is saying he or she owned anything at all. As a general rule, courts have construed contract language requiring execution of a deed "with the usual covenants" to mean a general warranty deed with the covenants of seisin, right to convey, against encumbrances, quiet enjoyment, warranty, and further assurances.

CPI   See *consumer price index.*

CPM   See *Certified Property Manager.*

CRA   See *credit reporting agency* and *Community Reinvestment Act.*

cradle-to-the-grave management   A phrase used to describe the Resource Conservation and Recovery Act, which is a federal law establishing a system for managing hazardous wastes in an environmentally sound manner from the point of origin to the point of final disposal.

cram down   A bankruptcy tool used by debtors to force creditors to agree to a plan of reorganization in Chapter 11. If the requisite minimum number of votes have been obtained to approve a plan of reorganization, and if the plan provides better protections or payments to the nonconsenting creditors than they would receive in a liquidation, then the court may "cram down" the plan and all will be bound by its terms.

CRE   See *Counselor of Real Estate.*

creative financing   Any financing arrangement other than the traditional one of obtaining a loan from a commercial lending institution.

credit   (1) In finance, the availability of money. (2) In accounting, a liability or equity entered on the right side of the page in double-entry accounting. The concept is confusing to most consumers because an accounting "credit" does not mean more "stuff" such as property or money; it merely indicates the side of the page on which the entry is posted. The other entry is called a debit.

credit bid   The amount a lender can bid at a foreclosure sale under one of its mortgages, representing the total of all amounts due under the promissory note.

credit bureau   See *credit reporting agency*.

credit enhancement   A method of reducing the risk of extending credit to a borrower. It can include requiring collateral, a stand-by letter of credit, a comaker, a guarantor, or any other means.

credit history   An individual's history and experience regarding repayment of loans and use of revolving credit such as credit cards.

credit life insurance   Insurance that pays to a lender the full principal balance of a loan in the event of the death of the borrower. It is illegal for a lender to require credit life insurance (or credit disability insurance) as a condition of making a loan.

credit limit   The maximum loan amount a person may receive on a particular instrument or from a particular lender. A revolving line of credit might have a credit limit of $50,000. Banks have limits on the amount of credit they can extend to single borrowers, based on the size of the bank, and limits on the credit they can extend to officers and directors.

creditor   One who is owed a debt.

credit rating service   See *credit reporting agency*.

credit report   A history of all information on file at a credit reporting agency about a particular individual or business. By law, consumers are entitled to receive one free credit report per year from each of the three major credit reporting agencies—Experian, Equifax, and TransUnion, but may request and pay for as many as they choose. Requesting one's own credit report does not decrease the score. You may obtain a copy of your report by going to the official Web site at www.annualcreditreport.com or calling 1–877–322–8228. (Beware: The Web site www.freecreditreport.com is not the official, federally mandated Web site.)

credit reporting agency (CRA)   An organization that maintains credit history information and sells reports and scores to authorized credit grantors. Regulated by the Federal Trade Commission under the requirements of the Fair Credit Reporting Act.

credit scoring   The process of rating potential borrowers based on their overall credit history, current debts, and frequency of application for credit. The most commonly used score, by far, is the FICO score.

credit tenant   A national or large regional tenant with excellent credit. Although local tenants may also have excellent credit, oftentimes better than their national counterparts, only the larger companies are called credit tenants. A lender will offer more attractive financing terms for a development with a certain amount of space preleased or currently leased to credit tenants.

credit union   A nonprofit organization in which qualified persons may make deposits and obtain loans. Formerly, membership was strictly defined so as to limit it to persons in a particular industry or trade organization, but those rules are now largely obsolete. Bankers believe that credit unions enjoy an unfair advantage in the marketplace by virtue of paying no income taxes as a result of their nonprofit status. The lack of any income tax expenses allows the credit unions to offer somewhat higher rates on deposits and somewhat lower rates on loans.

CREW network   See *Commercial Real Estate Women.*

crib   Slang for one's dwelling place.

cross-collateralization   The process of tying two or more mortgages together so that the security of one note stands as security for the other notes. A step often taken in a debt workout after default so that the creditor may enhance the amount of collateral available for a debt and also increase the hostage value of property, thereby discouraging any plans the debtor might have to simply turn in the keys and abandon mortgaged property to the creditor.

cross-defaulting clause   A provision in many mortgages that a default in any mortgage on the property, or any loan by the same lender to the same borrower, will constitute a default in the one containing the clause, even if all note payments are current on that particular mortgage. Used as a method for early triggering of remedies before things are allowed to deteriorate to a point that could seriously impair the value of the collateral.

> **Example:** *A borrower may default on a second mortgage but not suffer foreclosure because the second mortgage holder believes the property has insufficient equity to make it worthwhile. Technically, this does not affect the first mortgage lender, but is a good indication of worsening financial conditions and possible cessation of routine property maintenance by the borrower, possible insurance cancellations, potential lawsuits from other creditors which might force a bankruptcy, and other matters generally unpleasant to contemplate by the first mortgage holder. It may be preferable to declare a default immediately and proceed to foreclosure rather than wait until the borrower misses payments on the first mortgage.*

CRS   See *Certified Residential Specialist.*

CRV   See *certificate of reasonable value.*

C2P   See *construction to permanent loan.*

CTL   Shorthand for credit tenant lease. See *credit tenant.*

cubic yard   A measurement used to measure concrete, gravel, or earth. It measures 3 ft × 3 ft × 3 ft, which is equivalent to 27 cubic feet. Usually shortened to simply "yard," as in "It will take 12 yards of dirt to fill that hole."

culvert   A waterway for rainwater or other runoff; may be a ditch or a pipe. If ditches along the side of a road channel runoff, then property owners must install culverts under driveways in order to prevent the formation of dams. One must usually obtain highway or road department permission to install a culvert because the location will generally be in a road right-of-way.

curable depreciation   Depreciation that can be cured at a cost less than the value that will be added.

curb appeal   The subjective evaluation of the aesthetic appeal of a house or other building, as viewed from the street.

cure rights   In bankruptcy, the right to fix a default so that a creditor cannot pursue its remedies. For example, a debtor may file for bankruptcy moments before foreclosure, stop the foreclosure, and then propose a plan to cure the default and past due sums. Usually the plan involves small monthly payments over the course of several years. Of course, it is not enough to cure the default, the debtor must also stay current on future obligations, but bankruptcy will sometimes allow for a renegotiation of those obligations.

current use   See *highest and best use*.

curtail schedule   See *amortization schedule*.

curtesy   The right of a husband to some interest in his deceased wife's real estate, even if the wife died without a will or left all property to another in her will. The same rights granted to a widow in her deceased husband's property are called dower. As a result of these rights, mortgage lenders may require a spouse to sign a mortgage instrument giving security in the real estate, even though the spouse has not signed the promissory note and so has no personal liability to repay the debt. Many states have abolished the ancient rights of dower and curtesy.

curtilage   The enclosed space of ground and buildings immediately surrounding a dwelling, or a conceptual amount of space reasonably attached to the use of a dwelling. This is an important concept in law enforcement in determining whether (a) an area is within the curtilage and thus searchable under a search warrant for the dwelling, (b) an officer's presence in an area for surveillance purposes is within the curtilage and thus an unlawful entry, and (c) despite the determination of (a) and (b), there is no expectation of privacy in garbage left within the curtilage for pickup, so it may be searched without a warrant.

cut and fill   The process of contouring land to more easily develop it, accomplished after clearing and grubbing.

cyberpark   A large area of land where computer and technology companies are concentrated, or that has been constructed with a high-tech communications infrastructure such as loop redundancy, fiber optics, and perhaps even belowground network bunkers of reinforced concrete.

D

damages   Compensation for an injury for which the law provides a remedy. Following are highlights of some of the law of damages as it relates to real property:

- The measure of damages to property is the difference in the value of the thing before the injury and after the injury. The cost to make repairs is usually not a valid measure of damages.
- Parties may not contractually agree to a penalty for default, such as late completion of a construction project. Penalties are illegal. Parties may, however, agree that the damages for default will be difficult to measure exactly, so they will agree to liquidated damages in a certain agreed-upon amount. This is the reasoning behind contracts that allow retention of the earnest money if the buyer defaults.
- In breach of contract cases, injured parties are required to take such actions as are reasonable to minimize their damages and will be denied any damages at all if they do not take such mitigation steps. If a tenant breaches a lease, the landlord must try to release the premises to another, and the value of any damages will be diminished by the value of the new lease.
- Consequential damages, which are damages not as a direct result of the wrong, but flowing from some of the consequences of the wrong, are recoverable only if the wrongdoer had some reason to know of the consequences. A person who allows something unsafe to remain on the premises (such as a wet floor) may be responsible for the injury to a guest who slips and falls. However, the person may not be liable for the consequential damages when the guest becomes addicted to pain medication.
- Punitive damages are intended to punish the wrongdoer and deter future similar conduct. Because of the preponderance of multimillion-dollar punitive damage jury verdicts in recent years, the United States Supreme Court has recently held that excessive punitive damages are a violation of the "cruel and unusual punishment" clause of the Constitution, and so may be reviewed in the federal court system and set aside even though the original lawsuit was brought in a state court system.
- Treble damages are allowed under many federal statutes rather than allowing the jury to calculate punitive damages.
- Damages received for personal bodily injury are not income and not taxable; other types of damages may be taxable depending on what they represent.
- Damages are recoverable for emotional distress. The addition of a claim for emotional distress is often enough to trigger an insurance company defense of a lawsuit. Although there may not be insurance coverage for an award, it will pay for the lawyers.

Davis-Bacon Act   A federal law requiring certain minimum levels of wages for all workers involved in construction on federal projects or federally funded projects. The purpose was to give local contractors an opportunity to participate in government contracts, even though out-of-town contractors might have access to cheaper labor and would therefore enjoy a competitive advantage in bidding. The other purpose was to prevent contractors from paying lower wages than currently prevailing in the local marketplace, thereby reducing wages for the entire area. The Act is looked upon as one favoring unions, although that was not the intent. In fact, the Act had an unsavory beginning, introduced by Representative Bacon in 1927 as a reaction to a contractor who hired poor black laborers from Alabama to build a veterans hospital in Bacon's district of Long Island. The Act does not require payment of union wages, merely payment of wages consistent with those prevailing in the community. Today, the Act is still alive and well, and garnered tremendous public support when President Bush attempted to temporarily suspend it for contractors working in hurricane-damaged parts of the country.

d/b/a   (Also written as "dba.") Means "doing business as." Some states require dba registration with a central office, and others do not.

DBH   Means "diameter breast-high"; the diameter of a tree at a point $4^1/_2$ feet above the ground.

Many homeowners associations prohibit cutting trees of a certain DBH on one's own land, unless the property owner receives prior approval.

When selling timber, purchasers generally need to know the average DBH for the trees. The information is also necessary to calculate tonnage of timber, which is the more modern way of pricing, rather than calculating board-feet.

DCR   See *debt coverage ratio.*

DDA   See *demand deposit account.*

dead load   The weight of a building, not counting the occupants and furnishings.

dead man's statute   A law of evidence employed in many states. One version says that a witness may not testify about oral statements made by a decedent (someone who has died) if the effect of the testimony would be to make the decedent's estate larger or smaller, even if the witness would not benefit one way or the other. Another version says witnesses cannot testify about statements made by a decedent if the witness would benefit from those alleged statements. (Be sure to clearly understand which is being used in a specific case.)

dealer   In tax law, persons who buy and sell property for their own account, whether that property consists of silver spoons, trading cards, or real estate. Investors want to avoid dealer status because:

- Gains on sales are treated as ordinary income rather than the more favorably treated capital gains, no matter how long you hold a particular piece of property.
- Dealers have to pay self-employment taxes on their income.

- Dealers cannot take advantage of installment sales provisions that allow others to pay taxes over time, as they receive installment payments from the purchaser. Dealers must pay income taxes on the entire profit, even if they receive payments over many years.

dealer status   See also *dealer*. Determined by the intent of the party. The courts have arrived at several areas they will examine in order to determine intent. The most significant are

1. Taxpayer's purpose for the acquisition and sale
2. Number and frequency of real estate sales
3. Duration of ownership
4. Time spent by taxpayer in promoting the sale
5. Use of outside brokers in making the sale
6. Extent of taxpayer improvements to the property

debenture   An unsecured note or bond.

debit   (1) On a closing statement for a real estate sale, an item that is charged to a party. (2) In accounting, an entry that appears on the left side of the page. It is the opposite of a credit. In accounting, a credit does not necessarily indicate more money and a debit does not necessarily indicate less money or an expense.

debt   An obligation to pay another.

debt capital   Money borrowed on a long-term basis and used to purchase an investment such as real property.

debt coverage ratio (DCR)   The ratio of net operating income compared to annual debt service, which includes principal and interest payments. The ratio is used by lenders to evaluate loans on income-producing property. A ratio of 1.2 or better will usually support the extension of credit.

Example:

Annual revenues	=	*$100,000*
– Annual operating expenses	=	*50,000*

= Net operating income	=	*50,000*

Annual debt service on proposed loan = 11,000

$$\$50,000 \div \$11,000 = DCR \text{ of } 4.54$$

debt/equity ratio   The ratio of mortgage debt to the owner's equity in the property. Typical home mortgage lenders require a debt/equity ratio of 80 percent—meaning they will loan up to 80 percent of the value of the home. Higher ratios can be obtained by purchasing private mortgage insurance. Commercial lenders have varying requirements depending on particular market circumstances at the time.

debtor   (1) One who owes a debt. (2) In bankruptcy, the person who requests protection under the bankruptcy laws.

debtor in possession (DIP)   (To pronounce the abbreviation always say each letter; it is not pronounced as a word.) In bankruptcy, a Chapter 11 debtor who remains in possession of his or her property and continues to operate a business or sell the property. The DIP must still obtain court approval for nonroutine transactions but is able to conduct business, receive monies, and pay bills, including a reasonable salary for the debtor. Contrast with the situation in which a bankruptcy trustee is appointed; in this case the trustee is then in control of all assets of the debtor.

debt relief   The forgiveness of a legal obligation, in whole or in part. In real estate, it occurs most frequently when a mortgage lender agrees to accept a deed to the property rather than go through a foreclosure, and further agrees to accept the property as full payment for the loan, even though it is not worth the full amount of the loan. In such a situation the borrower has received debt relief and must report that as income for tax purposes. There is a loophole: if the debtor was insolvent immediately before the debt relief, and insolvent immediately after the debt relief, then he or she need not declare income to the extent of the insolvency.

> **Example:**
>
> *The debtor owes $125,000 on his home and 20,000 on credit cards. The debtor's only asset is his home, which is worth $110,000.*
>
> *Netting assets and liabilities before the debt relief results in the debtor being insolvent by $35,000.*
>
> *After giving the home to the bank and receiving forgiveness of the balance of the mortgage loan, the debtor now still has credit card debt of $20,000 and no assets at all. The debtor is insolvent by $20,000.*
>
> *Because the debtor is still insolvent, and the debt relief did not cure his condition of insolvency, there is no taxable income.*

See also Publication 17, "Your Federal Income Tax," Chapter 12, "Other Income," available at the IRS Web site, www.irs.gov.

debt service   The amount necessary to make principal and interest payments on a loan. It does not include amounts collected each month as a reserve for insurance or real estate taxes and does not include payments for private mortgage insurance.

debt service constant   See *mortgage constant*.

debt service ratio   The ratio of debt payments to disposable income; used in evaluating one's eligibility for a mortgage loan. National averages, calculated quarterly for every year since 1980, are provided at the Web site of the Federal Reserve Board, www.federalreserve.gov/releases/housedebt/default.htm.

debt to equity ratio   See *debt/equity ratio*.

decedent   One who has died. The legal subject "decedent's estates" deals with all the law related to the collection, preservation, and disposition of property formerly belonging to a decedent.

declaration   The legal document a condominium developer must file in order to create the vehicle for condominium ownership. All states have fairly similar laws setting out the requirements for what must be in the declaration. They are sometimes called uniform condominium acts or horizontal property acts.

declaration of condominium ownership   See *declaration*.

declaration of homestead   A document signed by a homeowner and filed with the tax assessor's office in order to take advantage of homestead exemptions reducing real estate taxes.

declaration of restrictions   A document filed in the real estate records of the county where property is located, and incorporated by reference into the deeds of every property located within the described area, setting out the rules and regulations pertaining to those properties. It is commonly used to spell out restrictive covenants in neighborhoods, such as minimum building size, setback lines, prohibitions against home-based businesses, and restrictions against boats or motor homes parked in view of the street.

declaration of trust   A written statement that one who holds the legal title to property does so in trust for another, being the beneficiary.

decree   Technically, the judgment of a court of equity. Today, states have abolished the distinctions between courts of law, which followed fairly strict rules of law and awarded damages to injured parties, and courts of equity, which generally tried to do what was fair and just (equitable) and issued decrees to people ordering them to do something, or to stop doing something. Causes of action are grounded in law or equity, but the same court and same judge now hear everything.

decree of foreclosure and sale   An announcement by a court establishing the amount of a mortgage debt and ordering the foreclosure of the property to pay the debt; employed in states that must follow judicial foreclosure in order for a lender to sell mortgaged property.

dedicated circuit   An electric circuit that serves only one appliance (e.g., a dishwasher) or a series of electric heaters or smoke detectors. It is an important point of lease negotiations to agree upon the number and size, in amps, of dedicated circuits to be provided to a tenant. Most leases of large and modern office buildings contain restrictions on the electrical load a tenant can place upon the building.

dedication   An owner's gift of land, or an interest in land such as a right-of-way, for the public's use, coupled with the public's acceptance of the gift by making use of it. A dedication may be express, as when the owner specifically states an intention of dedicating land for a park. Alternatively, a dedication may be implied because of the owner's conduct and the reasonable conclusions to be drawn from that conduct. When one sees news stories about protestors attempting to block development of a valuable vacant lot previously kept clean and mowed by neighbors and used by children as a park, one is seeing an attempt to have a court declare that the owner made an implied dedication for the public use.

deed   A written document properly signed, acknowledged, and delivered, and bearing a description of specific property and words of conveyance for that property.

deed books   Records containing copies of recorded deeds and other instruments affecting title to land located within the jurisdiction.

deed indented   See *indenture deed*.

deed in lieu of foreclosure   An instrument transferring title to real property to a mortgage lender without the necessity of going through the foreclosure process. Called the deed in lieu (pronounced "loo") for short, the procedure is attractive to lenders because of the speed, lack of any defenses, and removal of anxiety about last-minute borrower bankruptcy. It is attractive to borrowers because there is no foreclosure to appear on the credit records. There is some risk to the lender if there are intervening liens, because a deed in lieu transfers title to property subject to the effect of any junior liens. Usually a foreclosure destroys other liens, if they were recorded after the mortgage or deed of trust.

deed of reconveyance   A method of extinguishing lender's rights in real property in a state that uses the deed of trust procedure rather than the mortgage procedure.

deed of trust   A security instrument used to grant rights in real property to a lender. It is used in some states; other states use mortgages to accomplish the same goal. With a deed of trust, title to the property is transferred to a trustee, who holds it in trust for the borrower's benefit until such time as the loan has been paid in full. At that time, the trustee will transfer legal title back to the borrower by way of a deed of reconveyance. If there is a default and foreclosure, it is the trustee who conveys the property to another.

deed poll   A deed signed only by the grantor. This is the typical type of deed, but one rarely hears it called a poll deed or deed poll. Contrast with a deed indented, also called an indenture deed, which contained promises, representations, or warranties by both the seller and purchaser and so required both signatures. The documents were distinguished because the deed poll had a "polled" or clean-cut edge, while the deed indented had an indented or jagged edge.

deed restriction   A provision placed in a deed restricting or limiting the use of the property In some manner. It may include subdivision or similar restrictions common to many properties in the neighborhood, or it may be something personal to the grantor such as a requirement that the purchaser resell to the seller before offering to anyone else.

deed to secure debt   A type of mortgage used in a few states; the title to the property is transferred to the lender until the debt is paid in full. Contrast with deed of trust which is employed in states called title theory states, and with true mortgages which are employed in states called lien theory states. The deed to secure debt is a hybrid of the two theories.

de facto   In fact, in actuality, as things are really done. The phrase is used to express a state of affairs or condition that might not be technically legal, but which has the same effect as the legal condition. Here are two examples:

- When an apartment complex allowed the power to be disconnected for nonpayment and failed to secure a reconnection, it amounted to a de facto eviction of all the tenants (also called a constructive eviction).

- The IRS has ruled that a long-term lease of property with the right to purchase for $1 at the end of the term is not a true lease, but a de facto installment sale.

defamation of title   Wrongfully causing some cloud—problem—to be placed on the title of another, such as a lender failing to satisfy a mortgage that has been paid in full.

default   The failure to meet one's obligations in a timely manner. There are several important concepts relating to defaults in the real estate field:

- Leases and mortgages often differentiate between monetary defaults, such as failure to pay money when due, and nonmonetary defaults such as a failure to provide proof of insurance or copies of monthly financial statements. If so, there will be different notice provisions and grace periods for each.
- Unless a sale contract contains language that "time is of the essence," or one party has made the other aware that time is critical, then a court will ordinarily award a purchaser a reasonable amount of time to complete closing, even if it is past the contract date.
- Some states have statutes allowing collection of attorneys' fees when there has been a default in the contract. Other states require specific language in the contract allowing for collection of attorneys' fees.

default point   The total revenues necessary from a project to pay all the bills with nothing left over—the point at which $1 more in revenues creates a profit and $1 less forces one to default on paying creditors unless additional capital is injected into the project. See *break-even point*.

defeasance   The process of legal title being transferred back to a borrower once all payments and other requirements in a mortgage loan have been completed.

defeasance fee   A prepayment penalty; in a commercial loan, money that must be paid to the lender when a mortgage is paid off earlier than the specified maturity date.

defeasible fee   A real property title that can be revoked or undone upon the happening of a named event. (The whole area of real estate law, regarding things that might happen in the future to grant or take away title to property, is called future interests. The rules are exceptionally complex and not often encountered in the real world.)

defect in title   A recorded instrument that would prevent a grantor from giving good or clear title to property.

defendant   The party sued in an action at law. Contrast actions in equity, in which the party sued is called a respondent. Today, these distinctions are largely irrelevant, but they may be encountered when reading old legal decisions.

deferred charges   An accounting and tax concept in which nontangible costs that are expected to provide value over a number of years are booked as assets and then reduced each year by a pro rata amount as they are charged to expenses.

Example:

Acme Inc. pays a broker $75,000 to negotiate a 10-year lease on very favorable terms.

Year 1, day 1: Acme writes a check for $75,000 and books an asset for $75,000.

Year 1, day 2: Acme enters an expense for $7,500 (one-tenth of the total amount) and reduces the asset by $7,500. The net result is that, at the end of year 1, Acme has $75,000 missing from its bank account, but this is balanced by an asset of $67,500 and an expense of $7,500.

Years 2 through 10: Continue the same process as year 1, day 2 until the deferred charge is finally $0 and the last $7,500 is expensed.

If you do not properly account for such deferred charges on your taxes, you risk an audit, disallowance of expenses, penalties, and interest.

deferred commission   A real estate commission paid at a later date or over time. See *residual*.

deferred exchange   The correct name for a real estate transaction which is often erroneously called a tax-free exchange. See *1031 exchange*.

deferred gain   In a tax-deferred exchange, the amount of gain that escapes current taxation and is deferred until a later date, when the replacement property Is sold. See *1031 exchange*.

deferred maintenance   A physical deterioration of a property due to lack of periodic repairs, routine maintenance, and necessary replacements. Commenting that a property has deferred maintenance issues is a polite way of saying it appears shabby and needs work.

deferred payments   Payments to be made at some point in the future. Some leases have deferred payment provisions rather than free rent concessions. With deferred rent payments, the tenant pays no rent for the first 3 to 12 months, but then will pay higher-than-market rent for the balance of the lease term as the tenant makes payments on the rent that accrued in the early months.

deficiency   The amount due on a mortgage loan after adding all expenses of foreclosure and accrued interest to the principal balance of the loan and then deducting the sale price or lender-bid price for the property. The balance remaining, if any, may be collected by the lender by means of taking a deficiency judgment, unless prohibited by law or contract. Deficiency judgments may be collected just like any other judgment, through seizure of other assets or garnishment. There are two circumstances when a lender may not collect any deficiency:

1. In states with consumer protection statutes that outlaw deficiencies on first mortgages on a borrower's principal residence.
2. With mortgage loans designated as nonrecourse, meaning the lender and borrower agreed in advance that the property would stand for the debt and there would be no deficiency allowed in the event of foreclosure.

deficiency judgment   A lawsuit and judgment against a debtor for the remaining balance due on a promissory note after giving credit for any repossessed or foreclosed collateral.

Example: *Sarah has a mortgage for $200,000 on her home. She defaults on her loan, and the bank forecloses. The bank sells the home at a foreclosure auction to a third party who bids only $160,000 because the home has been allowed to deteriorate and needs many repairs. Sarah still owes the bank $40,000 unless she lives in a state that does not allow deficiencies on home loans. The bank may sue Sarah and obtain a judgment for $40,000, called a deficiency judgment.*

definition of value   In a formal appraisal, the bottom line—the statement with the appraiser's estimate of value, after all calculations, comparisons, and reconciliations.

delayed (tax-free) exchange   See *1031 exchange.*

delinquency rate   The number of loans with delinquencies divided by the total number of loans; also calculated alternatively as the total principal balances of loans with delinquencies divided by the total principal balances of all loans. Commercial lenders look at historical and current delinquency rates for differing types of properties—apartments, office buildings, warehouses, and others—as part of the analysis for the interest rates and terms they will offer on a particular loan.

delinquent   Past due.

delivery   The transfer of possession from one person to another. Deeds and leases require delivery before they are effective. Delivery does not depend on manual transfer, but does depend on the intent of the parties. Deeds are delivered when placed within the possession or control of the grantee in such a manner that the grantor cannot regain possession or control.

demand deposit account   A checking account. One may demand payment of the money on deposit without penalty. Contrast with a certificate of deposit, in which one must pay a penalty if the money is withdrawn early.

demand loan   A loan that states it is due upon demand, rather than on any certain date or upon the happening of a certain event. For purposes of calculating the statute of limitations within which to sue on a demand loan, it is treated as if demand were made and default occurred on the very first day the loan was made, even if that did not truly happen in fact.

de minimis PUD   A planned unit development (PUD) in which the common areas have minimal value; a no-frills project.

de minimis settlement   A settlement agreement between the Environmental Protection Agency (EPA) and a property owner who may be technically liable for cleanup under the strict liability provisions of the Superfund, but who did not create nor contribute to the contamination and who acquired the property without knowing or having reason to know of the earlier contamination. Although a de minimis settlement is always a possibility, the EPA is by no means required to offer such a deal, so it is truly "buyer beware." See *CERCLA.*

demise   A transfer of an interest in real property for a certain number of years, for life, or at will. This is why leases often refer to "the demised premises." The use of the word demise in an instrument automatically triggers the grantor's liability for the warranty of quiet enjoyment.

demised premises   The property leased. See *demise*.

demising partition or wall   A wall separating two tenants or separating a tenant's space from a corridor or other common area space.

demographic   Pertaining to characteristics of the population, such as race, age, household income, median home price, and number of inhabitants per household. The U.S. Census Bureau (www.census.gov) collects a wealth of demographic data.

Example: *Families without insurance, 2003 and 2004:*

	2003			2004		
Family Income	Total (in millions)	Number Uninsured (in millions)	Percent Uninsured	Total (in millions)	Number Uninsured (in millions)	Percent Uninsured
All	288,280	44,961	15.6%	291,155	45,820	15.7%
Less than $250,000	73,881	19,603	26.5	73,012	19,437	26.6
$25,000 to $49,999	74,278	13,221	17.8	73,791	13,565	18.4
$50,000 to $74,999	53,672	6,018	11.2	54,982	6,373	11.6
$75,000 or more	86,449	6,119	7.1	89,371	6,445	7.2

demography   A study of the characteristics of people living in an area.

demolition   A destruction and removal of some or all of an existing structure. The process of demolishing something is usually shortened to the verb *demo*, as in, "We're going to demo that space next week to prepare it for the next tenant." A demolition usually requires a permit from the same local government agency that issues construction permits.

demolition clause   A clause that allows landlords to cancel a lease in the event they decide to demolish the building.

density   In zoning, the number of things allowed per unit of land, such as number of houses, occupants, or families per acre.

Department of Housing and Urban Development (HUD)   Created as a cabinet-level agency in 1965, the stated mission of HUD (www.hud.gov) is "to increase homeownership, support community development and increase access to affordable housing free from discrimination. To fulfill this mission, HUD will embrace high standards of ethics, management and accountability and forge new partnerships—particularly with faith-based and community organizations—that leverage resources and improve HUD's ability to be effective on the community level."

The most common HUD-related activities are

- Acquisition and sale of all FHA-insured homes that are foreclosed on
- Involvement in moderate-income and low-income housing
- Removing barriers to minority ownership of homes
- Community planning and development
- Native American housing

Department of the Interior (DOI)   A department of the federal government, established in 1849 to take charge of the country's internal affairs. Lightheartedly referred to as the "department of everything else" at one time, it was originally responsible for all affairs not handled by the Department of Foreign Affairs (now the State Department), Treasury Department, and War (now Defense) Department. Today, it is responsible for Indian affairs, national parks, wildlife management, and surface mining, to name a few areas. More information is available at its Web site, www.doi.gov, which includes Webcams for several national parks and the city of Washington, D.C.

Department of Veterans Affairs (VA)   Established on March 15, 1989, to replace the former Veterans Administration, it is currently the second largest of the 15 Cabinet departments and is headed by the secretary of veterans affairs. It provides a wide variety of programs, including guarantees of mortgage loans received by eligible veterans.

departure provision   An older term rendered obsolete by the July 1, 2006, changes to the Uniform Standards of Professional Appraisal Practice (USPAP), but it is still frequently encountered. It refers to the ability of an appraiser to render less than a complete appraisal in certain limited situations and only if the person reading the appraisal would not be misled or confused. Omissions might include particular appraisal methods deemed unreliable or impractical under the circumstances.

depletion   An accounting and tax term referring to deductions made to account for land becoming less valuable because of the removal of natural resources, including timber and geothermal deposits of hot water or hot rocks.

Examples of items eligible for the IRS depletion allowance under 26 U.S.C. §613(b) are

Borax	Marble	Carbon dioxide
Mollusk shells	Clay	Oil and gas
Coal	Potash	Copper
Sand	Gold	Silver
Granite	Shale	Gravel
Slate	Iron	Stone
Iron ore	Sulfur	Limestone
Timber		

For more information, see Publication 535, "Business Expenses," Chapter 10, "Depletion," available at the IRS Web site, www.irs.gov.

deposit   Money paid to ensure performance under a written or oral contract. Many states require that lease and other such deposits be maintained in escrow accounts and earn interest which must be paid to the party when the deposit is refunded. All real estate brokers must place earnest money deposits in escrow accounts. One must carefully examine the particular contract language relative to deposits in order to determine the circumstances under which they may be withheld from the depositor.

Deposit Insurance Fund   An entity under the control of the Federal Deposit Insurance Corporation, with two subfunds called the Bank Insurance Fund and the Savings Association Insurance Fund. Depositors are insured to the extent of $100,000 of deposits per depositor per insured institution. Bank customers who buy securities offered by the financial institution do not receive insurance for those securities. By law, one should see prominently displayed on all such literature: "Not Insured by FDIC."

deposition   Out-of-court testimony under oath by a witness or other party either during the pendency of a lawsuit or in order to preserve evidence in the event of a lawsuit. The testimony is recorded and transcribed by a court reporter, and the deponent (the person giving the deposition testimony) then signs the transcript to confirm that it is a true and accurate record of the questions asked and the answers given. Deposition testimony is admissible in court under some circumstances if the deponent is unavailable to testify. Especially when dealing with elderly persons, if there is some dispute over title to real property or the effects of adverse possession, it is good practice to obtain deposition testimony.

Depository Institutions Deregulation and Monetary Control Act of 1980   Federal legislation that accomplished phenomenal deregulation of federally chartered financial institutions, leading to state deregulation so that state-chartered financial institutions could compete with their federal cousins. Regulation Q phased out the former limits on interest that could be paid on deposits. Many analysts say that the resulting unbridled competition for depositors' money, leading to a bidding war to gain depositors, drove financial institutions to make ever riskier loans in order to obtain the high interest rates necessary to service the deposits. According to such analysts, this legislation was one of the primary factors in the savings and loan crash, the banking crisis, and the FDIC bailout of the mid to late 1980s.

depreciable basis   See *basis*.

depreciable life   See *accelerated cost recovery system*.

depreciable real estate   Property capable of supporting depreciation deductions. As a general rule of thumb, improvements may be depreciated but land may not. Land may be depleted, however, if minerals are extracted.

depreciated cost   See *book value*.

depreciation   (1) In accounting, the process of deducting some portion of the acquisition cost of property over time, as an expense against income, to reflect the fact that the property is becoming less valuable and will eventually require replacement. One cannot allow a $3,000,000 building to remain on the books for 35 years as an asset at the same value and then, suddenly one year, demolish the building, write off $3,000,000 against income for that particular year, and then construct another building or move. (2) In appraisal, a reduction in the calculations for the reproduction cost of an improvement, in order to arrive at a value of the improvement in its current state, not as it would be if it were reproduced and brand new.

depreciation methods   Various accounting tools for calculating depreciation. The most common is the straight-line method, in which equal pro rata shares are deducted each year until one reaches $0 or a salvage value, as the circumstances may warrant. The second most common is the double-declining balance method. Some accountants still use the sum-of-the-years-digits method, although this is no longer allowed for tax purposes.

> **Example:** *Following are three graphs representing the depreciating value of a $10,000 asset with a useful life of 5 years and a salvage value of $0, using the three different methods.*

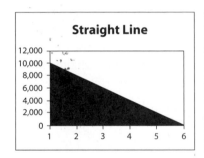 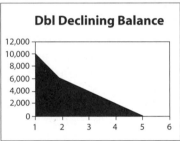 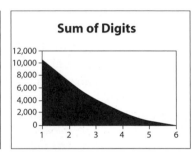

depreciation recapture   A tax law provision that some depreciation expenses taken on real property must be "recaptured" upon a sale of the asset and taxes paid at ordinary income rates rather than capital gains rates. Ordinarily, property held for more than one year and then sold will qualify for capital gains tax rates, which are lower than ordinary income tax rates.

There are two exceptions in which some or all of the gain must be taxed at ordinary income rates:

1. If depreciation was taken on personal property, that portion of the gain that is equal to total depreciation taken over the years will be taxed at ordinary income rates.
2. If accelerated depreciation was taken on real property (see *depreciation methods* for an explanation), then that portion of the gain represented by the difference between straight-line depreciation and the accelerated depreciation will be taxed at ordinary income rates.

depth   The distance between the front and the rear property line of a lot. Because local government rights-of-way for streets and sidewalks may exceed the actual width of the pavement, the lot depth may be less than the visible yard.

depth tables   In a tax assessment appraisal, a set of tables that evaluate the relative value of artificially defined slices of property as one proceeds at greater depths from the street frontage. The first, and most simple, table is the 4–3–2–1 table. It describes the front quarter of a parcel as representing 40 percent of the total value, the next quarter as representing 30 percent of the value, the next quarter as representing 20 percent of the value, and the rearmost quarter as representing 10 percent of the value. Commercial appraisers consider the use of depth tables unreliable.

Example: *Here is an example of a depth table.*

$10,000	
$20,000	Total value of parcel: $100,000
$30,000	
$40,000	

Skyland Blvd

deraign   To prove ownership of land; to trace the chain of title.

dereliction   The gradual receding of water to leave dry land.

derivative acquisition   See *acquisition*.

derivative investments   Investments that rely on the performance of underlying assets in order to establish value and return profits.

descent   A method of acquiring real property, when the prior owner dies without a will and the laws of intestate succession determine the person or persons who will acquire title by descent.

description   The information in a deed that will precisely identify the land being conveyed, in such a manner that it cannot be confused with any other land. It is not appropriate to use a street address or a tax parcel identification number in a deed, except as additional information to aid in the description. There are three predominant types of description:

- Metes and bounds. Includes an independently verifiable starting point, distances of lines and directions, and angles between lines.
- Aliquot parts. Uses portions of one or more sections (640 acres), half sections (320 acres), quarter sections (160 acres), or quarter-quarter sections (40 acres).
- Subdivision plat. Makes reference to subdivision plats, such as "Lot 9, Block 3 according to the plat or map of Sunny Acres as recorded in the County records at Plat Book 182, Page 79."

designated broker   See *principal broker*.

detached housing   Homes with freestanding walls not shared with any other house. Contrast with row house, duplex, or townhome.

determinable fee   See *future interest* and *fee simple determinable*.

detrimental reliance   Taking an action or failing to take an action because of a representation made by another person that turned out to be untrue.

> **Example:** *Jake called his mortgage company to find out the remaining balance due on his home loan. The lender sent Jake a letter advising him the payoff was $28,312. The sum was small enough that Jake decided to sell his car to pay off the home loan, quit his job, and take a year off to write a novel. After he sent the money in, the mortgage company advised him that it had made a mistake and the payoff was really $48,312, so he needed to pay an additional $20,000 to satisfy the mortgage. A court may apply the theory of estoppel against the mortgage company and force it to satisfy the loan without any additional money, because Jake had detrimental reliance on the mortgage company's representations.*

developer   One who transforms raw land into improved real estate.

developer profit   The increase in value caused by the efforts of a developer.

development   The process of improving raw land.

development impact fee   See *impact fees*.

development loan   A loan used to develop real property, which includes not just construction of the improvements, but also excavation work, infrastructure such as storm sewers and roads, and the holding costs of the property until such time as it can be sold or can support fully amortizing permanent financing. Contrast with a construction loan, for building improvements only.

devise   A transfer of real property by virtue of the provisions in a will. Contrast with descent, which is a transfer by virtue of statutory provisions controlling ownership of real estate when one dies without a will.

devisee   A person who inherits real property by virtue of provisions in a will.

diffused surface waters   Water that comes from rain, melting snow, or underground springs and that spreads over the surface of the land. The concept is important because

1. Applicable local environmental laws may require developers to provide siltation and erosion control for diffused surface waters traveling over disturbed land.
2. In some states, called common enemy states, property owners may do what they want with diffused surface waters—impound them and deny water to lower landowners, or dam one's own land to prevent a watershed and cause flooding to the upper landowners.

3. In other states, using the civil law rule, property owners may not dam diffused surface waters to the damage of upper owners, nor may they impound diffused surface waters and deny water to lower property owners.

4. Still other states use the common enemy rule for urban land and the civil law rule for rural land.

diluvion   The gradual washing away of soil along a watercourse. Contrast with accretion, the gradual adding of soil to land along a watercourse.

DINK   An abbreviation for "dual income, no kids." A slang expression for a particular income market.

dinosaur pen   A traditional mainframe computer room complete with raised floor, special power, and its own ultraheavy air conditioning.

DIP   See *debtor in possession*.

direct capitalization   Dividing the net operating income of a property by a selected capitalization rate to arrive at a value. Contrast with *yield capitalization*.

direct costs   Construction costs that are readily identifiable, such as labor, materials, and construction management fees. Contrast with indirect or soft costs which cover an allocation for overhead plus all expenses spent away from the construction site, such as legal, accounting, permitting, and construction period interest. Sometimes called hard costs.

direct endorsement   A mechanism that allows HUD-approved lending institutions to approve FHA mortgage insurance themselves, without having to submit paperwork to HUD and wait for approvals.

directional growth   The direction in which a city or town seems to be growing. This is important in appraisal and in making decisions to purchase speculative real estate to hold for later sale or development.

direct participation program (DPP)   An investment vehicle that allows parties to directly participate in the cash flows and tax benefits of the underlying property, without requiring any active management by the investor. The investment will be shares of a partnership, a subchapter S-corporation, a limited liability company, or some other entity that files an informational return with the IRS but does not itself have any taxable income or deductible losses.

direct reduction mortgage   A mortgage loan in which at least a portion of each month's payment is used to reduce the principal balance of the loan—there is a direct reduction of the principal balance, resulting in next month's interest being smaller. When a borrower makes a fixed payment each month according to a fully amortizing loan schedule, the entire loan balance will eventually be paid by the anticipated maturity date. That is the most common type of direct reduction mortgage, but a wide variety of other options is possible.

direct sales comparison approach   Formerly known as the market data approach, this is an appraisal method in which the property being appraised is compared to sales of similar properties in order to arrive at a value. The appraiser identifies the comparable properties as being similar in time and somewhat similar in size, quality, use, and amenities, among other considerations. The appraiser then makes adjustments to the sales price of the comps, based on how they differ from the specific property.

> **Example:** *A home with a three-car garage might be reduced by $25,000 in order to make it comparable to the subject home with a two-car garage. After making the adjustments, the appraiser then reconciles all the comparables to arrive at an opinion of value for the subject property.*

disbursement   Payment of money.

discharge in bankruptcy   The release of a debtor from the payment of any and all debts except those specifically approved by a bankruptcy court.

disclaimer   (1) The refusal or rejection of a right, as a disclaimer of an inheritance of environmentally contaminated property. (2) The limitation of a warranty or responsibility.

disclosure statement   (1) Also called the Reg-Z box, information required by Regulation Z of the federal Truth in Lending Act. (2) Any other federally required or state-required document designed to inform consumers of rights, responsibilities, or property defects.

Annual Percentage Rate	Finance Charge	Amount Financed	Total of Payments
The cost of your credit at a yearly rate	The dollar amount the credit will cost you	The amount of credit provided to you or on your behalf	The amount you will have paid after you have made all payments as scheduled
A%	$**B**	$**C**	$**D**

A: The annual cost of the loan, as a percentage. Usually higher than the quoted interest rate because of the additional cost of prepaid interest and other finance charges.
B: If all payments are made on time, and the loan is paid in full over its expected term, "B" is the total of all interest, prepaid interest, and mortgage insurance payments over the life of the loan.
C: The loan you applied for, less prepaid interest and other up-front finance charges such as commitment fees, origination fees, or mortgage insurance premiums paid up front.
D: The total of all payments (principal, interest, and mortgage insurance) if the loan is paid in full over the entire term.

Disclosure is required by the Truth in Lending Act.

discount   To sell at a reduced value, such as selling a $100,000, 30-year, 8 percent mortgage for $90,000 in order to raise immediate cash.

discount broker   A real estate broker who offers limited services in return for a commission rate lower than what is generally available in the marketplace. The most common service offered is listing a property on a multiple listing service, but all prospective buyers are then referred directly to the owner.

discounted cash flow   Also known as a present value analysis; an approach to analysis of an income-producing property by calculating the present value of a future income stream with the use of a discount rate. The two most common methods are the internal rate of return method and the present value method.

discounting   The appraisal method of computing the value of an income-producing property by calculating the present value of anticipated cash flows.

discount points   Mortgage fees charged by the lender and treated as additional interest above the face rate in the promissory note in order to obtain an effective rate higher than the stated rate. One point is equal to 1 percent of the loan.

discount rate   The rate at which the Federal Reserve loans money to lenders to cover short-term cash needs, usually for overnight loans. Increases or decreases in the discount rate almost always signal similar increases or decreases in bank loan rates to customers, even though the two are not directly tied to each other.

discrimination   (1) The act of making generalized distinctions among groups of people or things without inquiry into the specific characteristics of individuals within the group. This includes illegal discrimination such as that based on race, color, sex, age, disability, religion, or family status (protected classifications) and legal discrimination such as a builder's bias for or against local subcontractors. Federal and state laws prohibit denying or discouraging housing or credit choices for persons in protected classifications. (2) The unintentional but still illegal effect of barring certain groups of people from access to housing, credit, goods, or services because of their race, color, sex, age, disability, religion, or family status. This is called disparate impact. An example would be a prohibition against tenants having animals in their units, which would work a hardship to the sight-impaired who rely on guide dogs. (3) Specific federal laws addressing discrimination include the

- Americans with Disabilities Act
- Fair Housing Act provisions of the Civil Rights Act of 1964
- Equal Credit Opportunity Act

disintermediation   The situation that exists when depositors withdraw their savings from financial institutions and invest the money directly in the marketplace, usually because they can obtain a higher yield even though also running a higher risk of losing their money.

disparate impact   A legal doctrine in discrimination cases whereby the plaintiff demonstrates a type of discrimination that is perhaps not intentional, but which has the effect of barring certain citizens from full access to rights, property, or experiences. The courts may examine a policy that appears neutral on its face but which has a different (disparate) impact on a protected class than others. Once a plaintiff in a lawsuit proves that a disparate impact exists, the defendant must then prove there is a valid and nondiscriminatory reason for the statistical imbalance.

disposal field   The area where wastewater from a septic tank drains into specially prepared ground for further purification.

disposition costs   The seller's expenses of sale.

dispossess proceeding   One name for the legal proceeding commonly known as an eviction.

disseisin   The wrongful deprivation of possession of real property; a wrongful eviction.

dissolution   A termination, as of an agreement, contract, corporation, or partnership.

Distinguished Real Estate Instructor (DREI)   A designation granted by the Real Estate Educators Association (www.reea.org).

distraint   The legal right of a landlord to obtain a court order and seize tenants' possessions to pay for back rent.

distressed property   Real property that suffers a reduction in its market price because of pressures operating on the owner, such as threatened foreclosure, divorce, settlement of an estate, or fear of economic changes that might decrease the value.

distressed sale   The sale of real property under circumstances creating great urgency on the part of the seller, such as impending foreclosure, divorce, relocation to another city, or any other such pressure.

distribution real estate   The modern term for industrial real estate, because most industrial operations today involve assembling components and/or distributing goods rather than the old smokestack manufacturing uses.

divided interest   An interest in some portion of the bundle of rights in real estate, such as a leasehold interest or a remainder interest. (This does not mean a particular percentage of interest or a cotenancy.)

doc-in-a-box   A popular term for a neighborhood or other retail-type medical office specializing in walk-in patients.

dock-high building   An industrial building with loading docks at the height of a delivery truck, opening to a floor at the same height.

dockominium   Condominium ownership of a boat slip or dock. The owner sometimes obtains a deed to the small parcel of land under the water and has the right to use the common elements consisting of the docks and perhaps some storage space, bathroom facilities, parking, and other such things. The concept is still relatively new and is meeting legal challenges from people claiming that it is inconsistent with doctrines of public trust and riparian rights. According to opponents, navigable waters are not subject to private ownership and, as a result, no one can sell condo-type rights in a boat slip upon the waters. (Before investing in a dockominium, it might be wise to check out the status of this emerging area of the law.)

documentary evidence   Traditionally, evidence in the form of written papers or documents. Today, many government agencies, such as the IRS, accept printed versions of electronic documents when regulations require documentary evidence. See also *Uniform Electronic Transactions Act.*

documentary letter of credit   Used somewhat like cashier's checks, but with more safeguards. The typical documentary letter of credit will allow payment to a vendor upon the vendor's presentation of the letter and certain documents, such as proof the goods were placed on board a vessel for shipment to the United States.

Dodge, F.W.   A company that provides a wide variety of reports and services relevant to the construction industry. Its Web site is at www.fwdodge.construction.com.

dog   Slang for an undesirable property.

domicile   The place of one's principal residence.

dominant tenement (or estate)   Land that benefits from an easement that burdens another property, called the servient tenement.

donee   One who receives a gift.

donor   One who gives a gift.

dormitory town   See *bedroom community.*

dotal property   An archaic term meaning the property the wife brings into a marriage in order to assist her husband in setting up the household.

double declining balance   An accounting method employed to approximate the situation of an asset losing value (depreciating) more rapidly in the early years after acquisition and then more slowly in later years.

double escrow   A process of flipping a property in a simultaneous closing. If anybody defaults, then everybody defaults.

double-load corridor   A building design in which there are apartments or other individual units on both sides of a passage corridor. Contrast with single-load corridor.

double taxation   A situation said to exist when a corporation must pay taxes on income, make dividend payments to shareholders on after-tax dollars, and then the shareholders must again pay taxes on the dividends. This is the situation with normal corporations, called C-corporations, that do not qualify for S-corporation (small corporation) status. S-corporations file reports allocating pro rata shares of all income to the individual shareholders, who then pay taxes on that number. The corporation itself does not pay any taxes.

dower   A widow's rights in the real property of her deceased husband. The similar right of a widower in his deceased wife's property is called curtesy. Many states have abolished these rights and replaced them with a more generic homestead right or surviving spouse's share.

down payment   The balance of the purchase price for property after credits for money contributed by lenders. See *equity*.

downzoning   The process of changing the zoning on a parcel to a use that is less intensive than formerly allowed. Property once zoned for multifamily residential use might be downzoned to single-family residential use.

dragnet clause   A clause in a mortgage loan that spreads a dragnet, which, in fishing, is a large net dragged across an area in order to capture everything it encounters. Similarly, a mortgage dragnet clause attempts to capture as much as possible for the lender. There are three types; some or all may appear in a mortgage loan. One seeks to make all debts of the borrower includable in the mortgage so that even a checking account overdraft may be deducted from sale proceeds when the property is sold. Another type attempts to extend the mortgage to other properties acquired by the borrower at a later date. In addition, a dragnet clause can provide that default in any other loans will constitute a default in the mortgage loan, even if the mortgage payments are current. Courts disfavor dragnet clauses and tend to scrutinize them very carefully in order to limit their reach, or sometimes they even find them unenforceable. If opposed to a dragnet clause in a promissory note or mortgage, one should request its deletion.

drainage rights   Legal principles regarding the ability of a property owner to divert the natural flow of water onto another property. Whether it is allowed or not depends on the state, sometimes on whether the land is urban or rural, or on what's reasonable under the circumstances.

draw   (1) A request that a lender advance funds under a construction or other future-advances loan. (2) A periodic request by a contractor or subcontractor for a portion of the contract price for a job, usually according to the percentage of completion of the work and the cost of materials and labor.

DREI   See *distinguished real estate instructor*.

dresser drawer title   See *trunk title*.

drill track   A segment of rail track that connects various individual industrial spurs to the main railway. When negotiating for the purchase or lease of industrial property, one should make sure there are provisions for a drill track, which usually requires easements over the properties of other owners.

drive-by appraisal   A value estimate made without examining the interior of a property. There is nothing inherently wrong with such an appraisal, as long as it is disclosed.

Drug Enforcement Act   Relevant to real estate as it allows seizure of real property if illegal drug activities take place on it. Innocent owners may successfully contest the seizure after expending large sums of money to lawyers to prove that the owner had no involvement and no knowledge of the drug activity or took steps to stop the illegal activity but was unsuccessful. (The lesson for property owners is that if you are suspicious about drug-related activity in your apartments or other properties, you cannot take a "live and let live" approach to the problem.)

dry closing   A closing that is completed except for the disbursement of money and delivery of documents. Often used when a buyer delivers a personal check at the closing and the closing company must wait until the funds are collected in order to complete closing.

dry hole clause   A provision in an oil and gas lease that specifies rent payments in the event of a dry well.

dry in   To install black roofing felt (tar paper) on a roof. When completed, one says the building is "in the dry" or "in the black."

dry mortgage   A nonrecourse mortgage, in which the lender looks solely to the property for recovery in the event of default and has no rights to sue the borrower for a deficiency judgment if the property is worth less than the loan balance at the time of foreclosure.

Dryvit   A brand name for a particular exterior insulation and finish system (EIFS) that resembles stucco. There has been extensive class-action litigation as a result of claimed deficiencies in the system as a whole, not just the Dryvit brand. Unfortunately, Dryvit has come to be synonymous with the entire industry, much the same as Xerox for copiers and Kleenex for facial tissues.

drywall   Also called wallboard or gypsum board, it is a panel of gypsum covered on both sides with paper and used as the primary wall material in home construction. Commonly also called by a particular brand name, Sheetrock.

dual agency   A relationship in which an agent represents two principals—clients—who may have competing interests. Most often encountered when one agent in a real estate company has a listing on a property and represents the seller, and another agent has a buyer-agency relationship with a buyer interested in the same property. Technically speaking, the managing broker is the agent of both parties and acts as a dual agent.

dual contract   The illegal and unethical practice of providing two different sets of contracts for the same transaction—usually one at an inflated price so that 80 or 90 percent financing will, in actuality, pay 100 percent of the true purchase price. This practice constitutes fraud.

due care   A legal concept meaning just, proper, and sufficient care under the circumstances. It is the care that would be taken by a reasonable person. For example, tenants are required to take due care of leased property and not use a barbecue grill in the living room.

due diligence   The process of investigating all facts, conditions, rules, laws, regulations, financial considerations, or any other such matters as would affect one's decision to purchase property. The various types of investigations as would comprise due diligence will vary from property to property. With the purchase of a home, it might include nothing more than a home inspection, termite report, and a review of any restrictive covenants. When purchasing raw land for development, it could include zoning issues, possible environmental contamination, surveys, soil compaction studies, analysis of cost to develop versus value when completed, and so on as far as the imagination can go.

due-on-sale clause   A clause in almost all mortgage loans providing that the entire balance of the loan will be due and payable if the property is sold, even if all payments are current and there has never been a default; effectively destroyed former widespread ability to assume mortgages. The clause allows lenders to control their interest rate exposure in a rising market, so they are not left with a portfolio full of low-interest-rate loans in an era of high interest rates. It also allows lenders to fully investigate any purchaser and make independent underwriting decisions about that purchaser and whether to extend a loan or not. A due-on-sale clause is not enforceable against someone who inherits property from a relative and intends to live in that property as a principal residence. See also *assumable loan*.

dummy   A straw man, as when a developer desires to purchase a number of properties in order to assemble them and build a shopping center but is afraid that owners will increase their asking prices if they know the true name of the buyer. Owners sell to the dummy, who then transfers to the developer.

duplex   A building separated into two homes.

durable lease   A lease with an annual rent and a term "for as long as the grass grows or the water runs." In most states, leases over 20 years in length must be recorded or they are void for their period beyond 20 years, and leases longer than 99 years are void for any longer periods, even if properly recorded.

durable power of attorney   A power of attorney instrument gives one person—the attorney in fact—the power to act for another in a general manner for all things, or for specifically listed things or areas described in the power. The power ceases as soon as the person granting it—the principal—dies or becomes legally incompetent. A durable power of attorney is different, in that it continues even though the principal becomes incompetent, but still terminates upon death. Used by many elderly people to allow children to manage their affairs in the event of mental disability, but without the stigma, expense, and court oversight of a formal declaration of incompetence and appointment of a guardian.

duress   Unlawful pressure, force, or threats by one person against another. If one is the victim of duress, then any contract or agreement entered into as a result of the duress is void. The operative word in the definition is "unlawful." Many people claim economic duress when a lender, for example, threatens foreclosure unless a borrower signs a new loan agreement with onerous terms, a high interest rate, and large fees for attorneys and other expenses. Usually, if the lender had the right to foreclose, then the threats cannot be unlawful and duress does not exist.

Dutch auction   An auction in which the asking price is lowered gradually until someone is willing to pay at that level, and the property is then sold to that person. Contrast with the typical auction practice in which the auctioneer asks a high price, lowers it until someone places a bid, and then the auctioneer attempts to obtain higher bids to increase the price from there.

duty to disclose   The legal responsibility of a seller, broker, or agent to tell a potential buyer about a defect in the premises. Some states have laws requiring disclosure of certain named and described conditions in addition to anything else that might constitute a defect.

dwelling   A place of habitation.

dwelling defense   In most states, people are allowed to use some degree of force to protect their dwelling and the inhabitants. They may not set traps for intruders, and they are usually entitled to use only the force reasonably necessary under the circumstances to deter the intruder. Some states allow deadly force, however, without any requirement that the home occupant first attempt to escape, or "otherwise avoid using force with complete safety." The defense is based on 500 year-old English court decisions that one's home is one's castle and entitled to defense. See *castle—man's home as*.

DWV (drain-waste-vent)   The section of a plumbing system that carries water and sewer gases out of a home.

E

early occupancy   If agreed among the parties, the ability of a purchaser to take possession of property before closing. Under some circumstances, a buyer who takes early occupancy may be considered as assuming the risk of loss if there is a fire or other destruction of the property. In other words, the buyer may be obligated to proceed to closing at the full purchase price, even if the seller has no insurance coverage.

earnest money   A deposit of money made by the purchaser of real estate. It can serve the following purposes:

- It shows evidence of economic resources and the probable ability to proceed to closing.
- It provides hostage value because of the usual contract provision that seller may retain the earnest money in the event of default.
- It may allow enforcement of a contract that might be defective on purely technical grounds. For example, some states allow enforcement of an oral real estate contract when there has been partial performance by the payment of earnest money. This occurs often, as when a buyer submits a written offer for property and an earnest money check. The seller makes a verbal counteroffer, and the buyer verbally accepts. The seller deposits the check. No one ever thinks to prepare a new written contract for signatures. Standing alone, this is an oral contract that is unenforceable under the Statute of Frauds.

earnest money contract   A real estate purchase contract with a provision for earnest money.

earnings before interest, taxes, depreciation, and amortization (EBITDA)   (pronounced "ee-bit-dah") Net earnings of a business before deductions for interest, taxes, or depreciation. It often provides the standard for purchase of income-producing properties or going-concern businesses, with buyers and sellers conducting negotiations in terms of multiples of EBITDA, such as an offer to buy at "seven times EBITDA."

earthquake strap   A metal strap used to secure gas water heaters to the framing or foundation of a house; intended to reduce the chances of having the water heater fall over in an earthquake and cause a gas leak.

easement   A nonpossessory right to use another's property. Easements may be created by express words of grant in a written document, by prescription (unrestricted usage over time resulting in property rights), or by necessity, as when the law will force the grant of ingress and egress rights for landlocked property.

- Easements are said to be appurtenant or in gross. If appurtenant, then the easement benefits one property and burdens another one. The property being benefited is called the dominant estate, dominant tenement, or dominant hereditament—they all mean much the same thing. The one with the burden is called the servient estate, tenement, or hereditament.
- Easements appurtenant stay with the land, no matter who owns it or how many times the land changes hands. An example is a right-of-way easement.
- If the easement is in gross, then it is personal to someone and does not benefit a particular property. A common example is a power line easement. The easement stays in effect no matter who owns the land burdened by the easement, but typically expires with the death of the owner of the easement.
- An easement may not unduly burden the property.

Example: *A right-of-way easement may have been originally granted so one farmer could cross the property of another to reach another field. Later, one farm is sold to someone who plans to build a 250-home subdivision and use the right-of-way as the construction entrance. Courts will not allow this.*

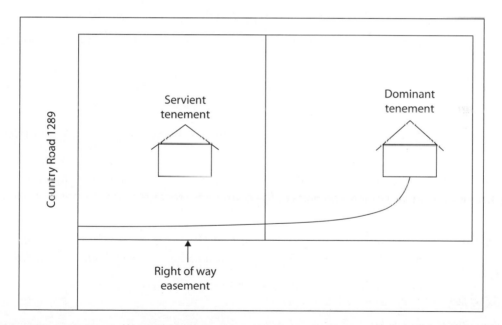

easement by necessity   The legal ability of a property owner to use a right-of-way over the lands of another because the owner's property is landlocked and has no direct access to any public roads. Generally, the right-of-way must be a route that places the least burden on the other property, even if it is inconvenient for the landlocked property owner. See *easement*.

EBITDA   (pronounced ee-bit-dah) See *earnings before interest, taxes, depreciation, and amortization*.

echo boomers   Children of baby boomers; a distinct demographic with identifiable buying habits.

economic feasibility   See *feasibility study.*

economic life   The period of time during which an improvement has value in excess of its salvage value; the useful life span of an improvement.

economic obsolescence   A factor that reduces the value of an improvement because of something external to the property itself. A well-built and well-maintained house may suffer economic obsolescence because it is located on one acre of land in the middle of a fast-food area on a major suburban road. The improvement—the house—no longer has any value at all. In this example, though, that hardly matters because the land is worth vastly more than the original homeowners ever dreamed.

economic rent   The rent reasonably to be anticipated in the marketplace as opposed to the actual rent. For an investor familiar with economic rents in an area, there are usually many opportunities to buy properties at values based on contract rents, and then raise the rents and realize immediate growth in equity and the ability to refinance for amounts in excess of the original purchase price. Also called market rent.

effective age   The apparent age of an improvement rather than its actual age.

effective gross income   The anticipated gross income from a rental property after deducting an estimated amount for vacancies and bad debt.

effective interest rate   The actual interest rate of a loan, regardless of the face interest rate or the rate quoted. See *annual percentage rate.*

effective procuring cause   The broker who first obtains the serious attention of a buyer and brings the parties together.

effective rental rate   True rent, after taking into account rent concessions; usually expressed as a dollar amount per square foot. Some parts of the country quote rents as dollars per foot per month; others use dollars per foot per year.

> **Example:**   *If 5,000 square feet of office space normally rents for $20 per foot per year, but the landlord gives 6 months' free rent on a 5-year lease, then the effective rental rate is calculated as follows:*
>
> *5,000 feet × $20 per foot = $100,000 per year*
>
> *6 months free rent = $0*
>
> *4.5 years paid rent @ $100,000 per year = $450,000*
>
> *$450,000 paid rent spread over a 5-year term = $90,000 per year effective rent*
>
> *$90,000 effective rent ÷ 5,000 feet = $18 per foot effective rental rate*

effective yield   A calculation of the return on an investment that considers the price paid, the time held, and the interest received.

efficiency apartment   A small apartment with living, sleeping, and cooking areas all contained in one room.

efficiency ratio   The ratio of leasable space to gross space in a building. When planning a building, it is important to balance the need to maximize the efficiency ratio in order to lease the maximum amount of space possible, against the aesthetic need to have wide corridors and open spaces.

efflux   The expiration of a prescribed period of time, such as the end of a lease.

egress   An exit.

EIFS   See *exterior insulation and finish system*.

ejectment   A legal action to restore possession of property to the party entitled to it.

ekistics   The science of how people settle land areas, including urban development.

elasticity   The ability of the real estate market to respond to price increases over a fairly short period of time.

elderly housing   Housing occupied by persons 62 or older, or housing designed and marketed for persons 55 and older. Under the Fair Housing Act, elderly housing does not have to be made available to families.

election of remedies   The necessity that injured parties make a selection of only one method of being compensated for their loss, rather than collecting multiple times in different ways. For example, if a certain lender behavior is a violation of the Equal Credit Opportunity Act and of local laws, the borrower may recover damages under one law, but not under both. In addition, some courts hold that when a seller breaches a contact to sell real estate, the buyer must choose between suing for damages or suing to force the seller to proceed with the sale. This does not prevent parties from suing for as many different theories as their lawyer can imagine, but they can have only one remedy at the end of the trial. (The concept of election of remedies is similar to the concept of double jeopardy—one can't be punished twice for the same wrong.)

elective share   The ability of a surviving spouse to elect to take a specified percentage of the decedent's estate rather than the amount left by the will. Most states make some sort of provision so that a surviving spouse cannot be completely disinherited. The vehicle may be the common law rights of curtesy (the widower's share) or dower (the widow's share). Because of archaic concepts about the relative needs of surviving spouses, dower and curtesy did not provide the same benefits to husbands as to wives. As a result, many states passed statutes modifying the rules or even completely abolishing them in favor of a statutory scheme. The statutory system usually allows a surviving spouse to elect between taking what was provided in the will or taking a certain preset percentage of the decedent's estate.

electric lateral   The trench or area in the yard where the electric service line (from a transformer or pedestal) is located, or the work of installing the electric service to a home.

electrical rough   Work performed by the electrical contractor after the plumber and heating con-tractor are finished; normally the installation of all electric wires. The electrical contractor usually receives a substantial payment on its contract price at the completion of the electrical rough. Contrast with *electrical trim*.

electrical trim   Work performed by the electrical contractor when the house is nearing comple-tion. The electrician installs all plugs, switches, light fixtures, smoke detectors, appliance "pig tails," and bath ventilation fans and wires the furnace and "makes up" the electric house panel. The electri-cian does all work necessary to get the home ready to pass the municipal electrical final inspection.

electronic signature   A method of sending identity verification over the Internet, usually through the use of a personal identification number (PIN).

eleemosynary corporation   A nonprofit corporation. Also called a 501(c)(3) corporation.

elevation   An orthographic (flattened; nonperspective) drawing of the various faces of a building, component, or improvement, showing examples of relevant details and something to indicate scale. One may have elevations of each side of a building, usually with a person standing nearby to illustrate scale; elevations of cabinets in kitchens or offices; or elevations of a storm sewer system showing a representation of the incline.

eluviation   The movement of soil caused by excessive water within the soil.

emancipated minor   (1) A child who is under the age of majority—18 or 21, depending on the jurisdiction—but who has taken advantage of state laws and obtained a court order to remove the disabilities of nonage and be declared a legal adult. As a result, such a child may enter into enforce-able contracts and may, if not disallowed in the emancipation order, be allowed to sell real property. There is a difference of opinion among states about whether an emancipation order in one state will be given effect in another state. In other words, a child who has been emancipated in New York may or may not be allowed to enter into contracts or sell real property in another state. (2) A minor child may become emancipated from his or her parents when the child marries or enters the military serv-ice. The parents no longer have any rights or responsibilities concerning the child, but the child still may not enter enforceable contracts or sell real property until he or she has reached the legal age of majority or has obtained a court order removing the disabilities of nonage, as described earlier.

emblement   A growing crop. Emblements are personal property and do not automatically pass with the land when a deed is executed. See also *fructus industriales*.

emerging markets   A loosely defined term generally referring to countries with relatively stable governments, developing economies, and an increasing ability to spend money on consumer goods.

eminent domain   The power of government to take land for the public good with the payment of just compensation. See *condemnation*.

empty nesters   People whose children have matured, left the home, and established homes of their own. This demographic segment generally has disposable income, homes with large amounts of equity, and a desire to change living arrangements either by going smaller, by moving to a completely different locale, or by the addition of a second home.

encapsulate   To remediate hazardous waste by surrounding it, such as spraying a special coating on asbestos.

encroachment   The trespass of an improvement upon the land of another.

encumber   To place a burden or a charge upon property. Commonly used to mean placing a mortgage, but may include other liens, easements, covenants, and restrictions. The burden is called an encumbrance.

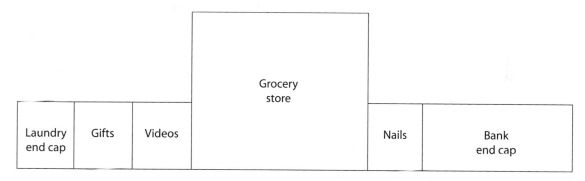

Endangered Species Act   A federal law originally intended to protect endangered species on federal land, but expanded to include protections wherever found, including private property. The existence of a protected species on one's land may prevent development or dramatically increase the expenses. This is not considered a condemnation, so there is no government compensation.

end cap   In a strip shopping center (long and rectangular with large amounts of road frontage), the retail space at either end is called the end cap. Chain restaurants usually desire freestanding space, but will accept end cap. Any establishment requiring a drive-through window, such as a fast-food restaurant, dry cleaning store, or bank, will need end-cap space.

end loan   (1) A permanent mortgage financing placed after construction financing. (2) A loan to buy stock in a cooperative apartment so one may rent a particular unit under a proprietary lease.

end money   An amount of money held in reserve in case project costs exceed estimates in a development. Called over-and-above money in FHA rental housing projects.

endorsement   (also spelled indorsement) Placing one's signature on the back of a check or other negotiable instrument in order to transfer ownership to another. Endorsers warrant payment of the instrument unless they sign with the additional words "without recourse."

energy efficient home tax credit   IRS income tax credits granted when a taxpayer installs energy-saving components in a residence. The amount of credit varies with the type and cost of the particular equipment or features. Contractors who build new homes are eligible for some of the credits. For more information, see IRS Publication 553, "Highlights of 2005 Tax Changes," at www.irs.gov.

enhancement   An increase; a betterment.

enjoin   To issue an order from a court commanding one to take some action or cease some action. See *injunction*.

enterprise zone   An area with the availability of tax incentives, grant money, or low-cost loans offered by local government in order to assist in revitalization.

entertainment complex   A shopping center that features theaters, restaurants, amusements, and related retail stores.

entire tenancy   A sole possession by one person. See *tenancy in severalty*.

entitlement   (1) To be owed something under the law, such as federal entitlement programs. (2) That portion of a VA-guaranteed loan that protects the lender in case the veteran defaults.

entity   A legally created person as opposed to a natural person. May include corporations, partnerships, limited liability companies, associations, joint ventures, real estate investment trusts (REITs), and traditional trusts.

entrants   Newcomers; people who enter a market.

entrepreneur   One who assumes risk in order to combine knowledge, capital, and resources to create a venture that will hopefully return a profit.

entry for marriage in speech   An ancient court order (writ) to recover land given to a man in consideration of his promise to marry a woman, but if he did not marry the woman within a reasonable time, married another woman, or entered the priesthood, he was obligated to return the land.

environmental assessment   A study of land to determine if there are any factors such as would possibly give rise to concerns about hazardous materials, protected species, historic remains, or other such factors.

environmental impact statement   A written report containing an analysis of the ecology and general environment of an area, together with projections regarding how that will change during construction of the project and after completion and public usage. These statements were originally required by the National Environmental Policy Act of 1969, but only for federal projects. Today, most state and local governments require these statements for all large projects and selected smaller ones. The vast collection of federal environmental impact statements, for projects ranging from Alaska to Antarctica, may be accessed online at the Web site for the Transportation Library of Northwestern University, nucat.library.northwestern.edu.

environmental obsolescence   Same as *economic obsolescence*.

Environmental Protection Agency (EPA)   A U.S. government agency established in 1970 to coordinate all federal activities relative to safeguarding the nation's air, water, and land from dangerous substances. Its oversight includes research, monitoring, standard setting, and enforcement matters.

The EPA Web site at www.epa.gov offers information regarding all programs, educational tools, enforcement actions, and current and pending legislation.

The most significant programs from a real estate perspective are the

- Clean Water Act
- Comprehensive Environmental Response, Compensation and Liability Act (CERCLA)
- Resource Conservation and Recovery Act

environmental site assessment (ESA)   A report by an environmental engineer or other qualified professional regarding the existence of any environmental hazards or concerns.

EOY   Abbreviation for "end of year."

EPA   See *Environmental Protection Agency*.

epitome   An abstract of title in book form.

Equal Credit Opportunity Act   A federal law that ensures all consumers and businesses are given an equal chance to obtain credit, assuming they meet legitimate and legal underwriting guidelines. Enforcement is by a number of different agencies depending on the identity of the credit grantor. The FTC may bring an enforcement action against retail stores, utilities, and small loan companies, to name a few. The Office of the Comptroller of the Currency would be responsible for bank violations. No agency will intervene in private disputes, but it will monitor the patterns of violation and could make a decision to take action. Private individuals who believe they have been victims of a violation may bring private or class-action lawsuits against offenders. Among other things, it is illegal to

- Discourage an applicant because of sex, marital status, age, race, or national origin, or because they receive public assistance
- Ask an applicant to reveal his or her sex, race, national origin, or religion, except that it may ask that this information be voluntarily revealed in connection with a mortgage loan in order to compile statistics to assist the government in making sure discrimination does not take place
- Inquire about an applicant's plans to have or raise children
- Ask if an applicant receives alimony or child support, unless the applicant intends to rely on that income in order to qualify for the extension of credit
- Consider sex, marital status, race, national origin, or religion in making a decision to grant credit
- Consider whether you have a phone listing in your own name, although a creditor may consider whether you have a phone or not
- Consider the race of people in the neighborhood where the applicant wants to buy, refinance, or improve a house with borrowed funds
- Refuse to consider public assistance income the same as any other income
- Refuse to consider alimony or child support the same as any other income

It is not illegal to consider military status, citizenship, or sexual orientation, although specific state laws may extend protections to such groups. For more information, visit the FTC Web site at www.ftc.gov.

equal dignities rule   A rule of law that if a contract must be in writing in order to satisfy the Statute of Frauds, then the authority of an agent to enter into such a contract must also be in writing.

equalization board   A state or county agency responsible for ensuring consistency and fairness in real property tax assessments.

Equifax   One of the three major credit reporting bureaus. It maintains a Web site at www.equifax.com. The other two bureaus are Experian and TransUnion. See also *Fair Credit Reporting Act*.

equitable conversion   A doctrine commonly applied when death intervenes between the signing of a contract regarding real property and the actual closing. The purchase money and the real property are converted, or changed, into each other for purposes of determining the rights of heirs and surviving spouses. If a will left all personal property to one child and all real property to another, and the seller of real estate died before closing, then that particular parcel of property would be treated as if closing had taken place before death and the cash received, so that the child inheriting personal property would take the sale proceeds.

equitable lien   A lien or charge on property arising because of some technical defect in a legal instrument such as a mortgage or because a court determines that the lien is only fair and just under the circumstances after considering all the facts.

equitable mortgage   The declaration by a court that an instrument by which one is to pay money to another and, as a result, receive title to real property when all payments have been completed is in reality a mortgage, and the parties will be treated as if they had all the rights and responsibilities of a mortgage relationship. The exception is if an innocent third party buys the property; then the equitable mortgagor—the person making the payments—cannot recover the property but may only sue the seller for damages. See also *equitable lien*.

equitable ownership   Describes the rights of a trust beneficiary in property, as opposed to the legal ownership resting in the name of the trustee.

equitable servitude   A restriction on the use of land that runs with the land. It is often asserted when there is no writing and no legal document imposing any restrictions. Proponents will argue that the restriction is fair and just under the circumstances. If a court agrees with them, then an order will be issued describing the servitude and binding the land to it.

equitable theory of mortgages   An operative theory in states that treat mortgages as instruments granting security rights to a lender, but legal title remains with the borrower at all times. These are called lien theory states. In lien theory states, lenders must usually resort to judicial foreclosure and obtain a court order authorizing sale of the property to satisfy a debt. The alternative is the title theory of mortgages and title theory states, in which the borrowers transfer legal title to the lender, who holds it in trust for the borrower under a deed of trust. Foreclosure in such states is non-judicial because the lender already has the legal title. Some states are called hybrid theory states and transfer title to the lender in an instrument called a mortgage rather than a deed of trust but allow nonjudicial foreclosures.

equitable title   (1) The interest held by one who has agreed to purchase property but has not yet closed. (2) The title held by a trust beneficiary, because the trustee has legal title but the law recognizes the beneficiary as having rights. See also *equitable conversion*.

equity   (1) The difference between the value of a property and the mortgage debt on it is said to be the equity. Under federal law, when one's equity in property reaches 22 percent of the value of the property—when the mortgage has been reduced to 78 percent of the value of the property—then private mortgage insurance is supposed to be automatically cancelled if it is in place. (2) The ability of a court to do what's fair under the circumstances, without regard to many of the technical require-ments of the law. Because real estate has always enjoyed a protected status in the courts, it is usually easier to obtain equitable relief when real property is involved. As an example, in a boundary line dis-pute there might be no legal theory to find in favor of a property owner who accidentally builds part of his house on his neighbor's land. Nevertheless, almost no court will require the property owner to tear down the encroaching part of the house. Instead, the court will usually "do equity" and require the landowner to sell, and the house owner to buy, the small amount of land necessary to fix the problem.

equity buildup   The gradual increase in a person's equity in property because of the monthly payments of principal that reduce a loan amount.

equity dividend   The annual cash flow that an equity investor receives.

equity loan   A line of credit secured by the equity in the borrower's home. It is open ended, mean-ing the borrower may take advances, pay down the line to reestablish it, and then take advances against it as needed; usually renewed on an annual basis, with adjustable interest rates tied to the lender's prime rate. (Often called a HELOC—home equity line of credit.)

equity of redemption   The rights a mortgage borrower has to reclaim property after default and before foreclosure. It is a right in real estate and may be transferred by deed, but a bill of sale of the right to another will be unenforceable. Contrast with *right of redemption*.

equity REIT   A real estate investment trust (REIT) with underlying investments in income-producing properties. Contrast with a mortgage REIT that invests in mortgages, but not physical properties.

equity participation   See *participating mortgage*.

equity sharing loan   See *participating mortgage*.

equity stripping   A term applied to a variety of sleight-of-hand practices, most often:

- Offering to assist homeowners facing foreclosure through buying their home and then selling it back to them, usually at rates and on terms guaranteed to result in default and loss of all equity

- Protecting assets from creditors by encumbering the equity with loans from friendly creditors, such as relatives, who won't foreclose if you miss a few payments

equity yield rate   The rate of return on the equity portion of an investment, taking into account the periodic cash flow after debt service and before taxes, plus proceeds from a sale.

erosion   The slow wearing away by natural forces such as water and wind.

errors and omissions (E&O) insurance   Insurance that protects against malpractice. Especially when working with a buyer's broker, who has a high degree of responsibility to anticipate problems and warn the client, one should ask for proof of E&O insurance before hiring a real estate professional.

escalation clause   A clause in any of a wide variety of contractual or real property arrangements that allows one party to increase the price upon the happening of certain specified events. Long-term leases often have rent increases at 3- to 5-year intervals, with the adjustment being a certain stated amount, a percentage of then-current market rents, or an increase based on some index with the first year of the lease representing the benchmark and against which the index is measured.

> **Example:**   *The parties agree that rent will increase in 5 years in the same proportion as the consumer price index (CPI) in 5 years bears to the current consumer price index. If the rent today is $4,000 per month and the CPI is 179, and in 5 years the CPI is 192, then the new rent is calculated at follows:*
>
> *192 ÷ 179 = 1.0726%*
>
> *$4,000 × 1.0726% = $4,290.40 per month*

Other escalation clauses are used to increase the interest rate in a loan when there has been a default and to increase rent when a tenant remains in possession after expiration of its term.

escalator clause   See *escalation clause.*

escalator mortgage   See *adjustable-rate mortgage.*

escape clause   A clause that allows one party or the other to cancel a contract without penalty upon the happening of certain described events or conditions. The most common ones in real estate are the ability to cancel a purchase contract if the buyer cannot secure acceptable financing or if the buyer cannot sell his or her own home.

escarpment   A long, steep face of rock or dirt.

escheat   The reversion of property to the state because of the lack of anyone to inherit it.

escrow   The process in which money and/or documents are held in trust by a disinterested third party who will consummate the instructions of the parties as expressed in their contracts. The third party is called the escrow agent. The escrow agreement usually contains a clause providing that if the parties disagree about something and are unable to resolve their differences, the escrow company will pay all money on hand into court in an action called an interpleader, name the disputing parties as defendants, disclaim any interest of its own in the property except for reimbursement for costs and expenses of bringing the interpleader action, and then let the parties battle it out in court. This effectively takes the escrow company out of the middle of any disputes and avoids liability on its part.

escrow account   (1) A separate bank account for keeping money that is the property of others. Attorneys and real estate agents are required to keep escrow accounts for client money and not commingle client money with their own funds. (2) An accounting entry by a mortgage lender showing the amount on hand from the borrower's monthly budget loan payments to pay real estate taxes and insurance when those bills become due.

escrow agent   A person or firm who agrees to hold funds for others and disburse them according to lawful instructions.

escrow analysis   With a budget loan, the mortgage lender's annual analysis of funds collected each month from the borrower for insurance and real estate taxes, the amount actually expended for those bills at year end, and the amount the monthly payments must increase or possibly decrease in the next year to provide the appropriate level of funds to pay the next year's bills.

escrow closing   See *closing.*

escrow payment   That portion of the monthly payments in a budget loan that will be accumulated by the lender and then used to pay insurance and real estate taxes.

estate   (1) All the property of a person who has died. (2) The degree, quantity, nature, and extent of legal interest that a person has in real and personal property. The most common estates are

1. In fee simple absolute. This is the greatest degree of ownership possible, in which a person owns all rights to a property and may freely dispose of them to purchasers or heirs.
2. At sufferance. In this type of estate a tenant continues to retain possession past the expiration of the lease.
3. At will. A tenant is put into possession by the owner of land, but the possession may be terminated at the will of the owner.
4. By the entirety. This is a joint estate held by two persons who are married to each other at the time of creation and which cannot be destroyed by either one of them or by the creditors of the other. In some states, a divorce court may not even divide the property, but the parties must agree on its disposition.
5. For life. In this estate, someone has an interest in property that lasts only as long as some life named or described in the granting instrument.
6. For years. This is typically a lease.
7. In remainder. In this type of estate a person takes property after the death of a person with a defining life in a life estate.
8. In reversion. That portion of an estate that remains in a grantor who transfers less than full ownership of a property. For example, if the owner of property transfers a life estate

to another, the owner retains an estate in reversion and will regain full ownership when the life tenancy ends. If that future interest were also transferred to another, it would be called a remainder, but since it is retained by the grantor it is called a reversion.

9. In severalty. This term can be confusing, because it means the opposite of our common understanding of the word "several." An estate in severalty is an estate owned by one person, alone.

estate tax   A tax imposed on the value of the estate of a decedent. The conceptual justification is premised on a peculiarly American notion that it is undesirable for generations to accumulate wealth by passing it to each other in a manner similar to that of English aristocracy and that each generation should make its own mark and earn its own way. As a result, it is considered advantageous to remove wealth from each generation by way of estate taxes and use the money for the common good. For details, see Publication 554, "Survivors, Executors and Administrators" available at the IRS Web site, www.irs.gov.

estoppel   A doctrine that stops one from denying facts or taking a course of action because it would be unfair under the circumstances. It may be because someone else relied on former statements regarding the facts or because someone else relied upon a situation allowed to exist by a party, so that the party cannot now be allowed to change that situation. The concept commonly arises in three situations:

1. Before the sale of an income-producing property, the tenants sign estoppel certificates acknowledging they have no claims against the landlord, no defenses to any of the terms or conditions of their lease, and no outside or "side" agreements varying the terms of the lease. After the sale, the tenant cannot claim otherwise, even if all parties agree that there has been
a wrong done to the tenant by the prior landlord and the tenant would otherwise be able to cancel the lease if it were not for the estoppel certificate.

2. A subdivision with restrictive covenants grows lax in the enforcement of them and permits many violations over the years regarding, for example, parking boats and motor homes in
driveways. If one buys a home in the subdivision and keeps a motor home in the driveway,
the principle of estoppel will prevent the homeowners association from suddenly deciding
to enforce that particular covenant.

3. A government employee tells someone one thing, and it later turns out to be wrong. The citizen has already taken action on the incorrect information. In most circumstances, courts will not allow estoppel against a government or government agency.

estoppel by deed   A legal concept that comes into play when someone deeds real property to another, even though not having title at the time—usually due to a technical defect. When the sellers later gain legal title through clearing up the technical defect or otherwise, they cannot claim the property as their own because of estoppel by deed.

estoppel certificate   See *estoppel*.

estovers   The right or privilege of a tenant to take so much from the land as is necessary for support, such as the right to cut timber for heating.

et con   From the Latin et conjunx, meaning "and husband." Used in deeds and deed records. Also called et vir.

et ux   From the Latin et uxor, meaning "and wife." Used in deeds and deed records. Usage arose in the 1300s in England, when wives had no legal identity and therefore were not named in legal instruments. Despite the dramatic change in circumstances today, one still sees deed references to "John Jones et ux…"

et vir   Latin for "and man," it is often used interchangeably with "et con" to mean "and husband."

evaluation   A study of potential property uses, but not value.

eviction   The process of denying possession to a tenant. It may be one of the following:

- Actual, as when the landlord obtains a court order that the tenant vacate the premises or have his or her goods and person removed by law enforcement officials.
- Constructive, as when the landlord allows a condition to continue that renders the premises, or a part of the premises, incapable of possession and enjoyment.

evidence of title   Proof that one has title to property; may be deeds, court orders, probate estate proceedings, or Torrens certificates.

examination of title   The process of investigating title to real estate, usually confined to recent records.

exception   (1) Estates or described lands specifically spelled out in a deed as not passing to the grantee. (2) Liens and claims specifically excluded from the coverage of a title insurance policy. (3) Liens and claims specifically excluded from a contract of sale.

excess land   Land taken by eminent domain in a condemnation proceeding, but which is greater than the amount actually needed for the project in mind. A government may condemn excess land because the portion remaining after the amount actually needed may be rendered completely useless. In such a circumstance, the authority would have to pay for the condemned land and pay damages for the loss in value of the remaining land. It may be cheaper to simply take all the land and then attempt to sell the excess, especially if there are several excess parcels that are contiguous to each other.

excess rent   A contract rent that is in excess of current market rents. In a bankruptcy proceeding, a bankrupt tenant may renegotiate a lease in order to remove the excess rent.

exchange   Parties may exchange like-kind properties and not pay any income taxes at the time of the exchange but, instead, defer them until the later sale of the exchanged property. See *1031 exchange*.

exclusionary zoning   Zoning that has the effect of excluding persons protected by law from discrimination.

exclusive agency   Same as exclusive agency listing.

exclusive agency listing   A relationship with a seller of real estate in which a broker has the exclusive right to list the property and receive a commission except that if the owner sells the property to one not obtained by the listing agent or its advertising and marketing efforts, then the owner need not pay a commission. Contrast with *exclusive right to sell listing*.

exclusive right to sell listing   A relationship with a seller of real estate in which a broker has the exclusive right to list and to sell the property, so that even if the owner sells to his or her child, with no involvement whatsoever from the broker, the broker is still entitled to a commission. This is done to avoid disputes over who procured a particular buyer. Sellers who wish to exclude certain persons from the effect of the agreement should describe them, such as "except for the following named potential buyers …" or "except for sales to family members related in the third degree… ." Contrast with *exclusive agency listing*.

exculpatory clause   (1) A clause in a mortgage that allows the borrower to surrender the property to a lender without any further personal liability for a deficiency. (2) A clause in a trust instrument or in a will excusing the trustee or executor from liability when powers are exercised in error but in good faith.

execute   To complete, as by signing a contract or signing and delivering a deed.

executed contract   A contract that has been fully performed by all sides; contrast with *executory contract*.

executive suite   An older term for a business center, a business arrangement granting no leasehold interests but allowing persons to enjoy the use of office space with a sharing of amenities such as conference rooms, lobby, phone system, copiers, and network facilities, as well as a sharing of clerical, support help, and facilities and personnel management.

executor   One named in a will to fulfill the wishes of a decedent regarding the disposition of assets. Today, the word refers to both males and females serving in that capacity. At one time, executor referred only to males, and the female was called an executrix.

executory contract   A contract under which one or more parties has not yet completed their performance.

executory interest   A general term used to describe all future interests other than reversions or remainders; an interest that will shift from one owner to another or spring into being upon the happening of some event in the future.

executrix   An older term meaning a female executor.

exemplary damages   The same thing as punitive damages. See *damages*.

expansion option   A right granted by the landlord to the tenant where the tenant has the option to add more space to the premises according to the terms of the option, which may contain restrictions as to the time, proximity, and rental rate, or the restriction that the option is available only if another named or described tenant fails to exercise its expansion option first.

expense ratio   A comparison of the operating expenses to potential gross income of a property in order to obtain a ratio that can be compared to other similar properties. In this manner, the owner may receive advance warning that rents are below market or expenses are too high. In addition, a potential buyer familiar with the ratios for similar properties may be forewarned if there is an unusually small ratio in a property under consideration. This could be the result of a seller not spending the proper sums to maintain and manage property, a seller performing its own maintenance without booking any expenses that might be incurred after the buyer takes over the property, or the seller omitting expenses. Purchasers interested in buying self-managed and maintained property will generally estimate a reasonable maintenance and management expense, and then reevaluate the estimated net income and the asking price in light of that information.

expenses   The cost of maintaining property or generating income.

expense stop   In a commercial lease, a provision that annual rent escalations due to increasing building operating expenses will be stopped, or capped, at a certain amount of increase per year or over the lifetime of the lease.

Experian   One of the three major credit reporting agencies. The other two are TransUnion and Equifax. The Web site for Experian is at www.experian.com. See also *Fair Credit Reporting Act*.

expire   To end; to die.

exposure   (1) In finance, the amount that one may lose in an investment; the potential loss, which could be the capital invested plus any personal liability on loans in excess of the value of the property securing the loans. (2) In the market, the process of making a property known to the marketplace as available for sale or lease. (3) Physically, the direction of an improvement; for example, "The southern exposure of the house had all the best views."

express condition   See *condition*.

express notice   The actual delivery of information to a party. Contrast with *constructive notice* and *implied notice*.

express warranty   Specific promises made by a party regarding the quality of something sold and the remedial actions that will be taken if the property sold does not conform with the promises.

expropriation   The seizure of private property for public use by condemnation.

ex-situ   Off-site; most commonly used in the context of ex-situ remediation of contaminated soil, which means removing the soil and replacing it with clean soil.

extended coverage   Insurance that covers specific risks not covered in a normal policy.

extender clause   A clause in a listing agreement that says the broker may be entitled to a commission after the expiration of the listing period if a buyer originally procured during the period later buys the property within a certain time span afterward, usually 6 months. When hiring a new broker after no success with an earlier one, an owner should always disclose a copy of the former contract and advise both brokers, in writing, that if there are any disputes as to claims for commission, the brokers must share rather than the owner being liable for double commission payments.

extension   An agreement to defer the time for doing an act or for termination of a lease.

extension option   An agreed-upon continuation of occupancy under the same conditions, as opposed to a renewal, which implies new terms or conditions. In a lease, it is a right granted by the landlord to the tenant whereby the tenant has the option to extend the lease for an additional period.

exterior insulation and finish system   A cement-based synthetic material that resembles stucco and is used in the same way. It is usually abbreviated as EIFS. One widely known manufacturer is Dryvit.

external obsolescence   Same as *economic obsolescence*.

eye appeal   See *curb appeal*.

F

facade The front of a building; what one sees from the street. Sometimes a building is constructed of metal, but the facade is brick or some other attractive treatment. Zoning regulations, subdivision restrictions, and historic district requirements may specify particular building facades.

facade easement Typically, rights granted to historic groups so they can maintain control over the appearance of the exterior of a building.

face interest rate The interest rate shown on the face of a promissory note and used to calculate the monthly payments on a loan. In order to help borrowers compare apples to apples when shopping for a lender, the federal Truth in Lending Act requires lenders to reveal an annual percentage rate which includes the "face interest rate" plus the value of some closing costs and prepaid expenses.

face value The value of an instrument (promissory note, bond, stock, etc.) as stated on the face of the instrument. The face value does not always equal the market value.

> **Example:** *A 5-year-old mortgage note with a face value of $100,000 and an amortization term of 20 years at 2.8 percent interest is worth far less than $100,000 for two reasons: (1) The principal balance is now a little under $80,000. (2) Why would anyone invest even $80,000 to earn 2.8 percent interest when he or she can get better returns in the marketplace? For both reasons, an investor would pay much less than the $100,000 face value to buy the mortgage.*

facilitator Someone who helps out in a real estate transaction but owes no responsibilities to the buyer, the seller, the lender, or the borrower. A facilitator in a real estate transaction might contact a home inspector, arrange for a survey, assist with removing underwriting problems on a mortgage loan, and explain the computations for the buyers' and sellers' costs at closing. When working with people in a real estate or mortgage loan transaction, it is extremely important to ask them to disclose, in writing, their exact role and their responsibilities to you. Someone you might assume to be your agent, with the responsibility to work for your best interests, might actually be only a facilitator, with little or no responsibilities.

facilities management Taking care of what's called the physical plant of a property—repairs, maintenance, security, janitorial, groundskeeping, etc. Formerly this was considered a janitorial-type career choice. Today, with rapidly changing technology, environmental concerns, government regulations, terror-related security issues, and other such matters, a career in facilities management is seen as a white collar, high-dollar choice. For more information go to the FMLink Group Web site at www.fmlink.com.

factory-built home   Generally, a home that is largely built someplace else and then shipped to a site for completion and/or simple installation. Mobile homes (also called manufactured housing) generally come to mind first, although the term also includes modular homes, panelized homes, and log-cabin kit homes.

Fair Credit Reporting Act   A federal law intended to remedy abuses by credit reporting agencies. The law is enforced by the Federal Trade Commission, which maintains information on its Web site, www.ftc.gov. Generally, the law prohibits reporting erroneous or outdated credit information. The following adverse information cannot be reported:

- Civil suits, civil judgments, or arrest records older than 10 years or the statute of limitations, whichever is longer;
- Paid tax liens older than 7 years. (Note: Credit reporting bureaus and the Federal Trade Commission take the position that unpaid tax liens can be reported forever. This seems to be against the plain language of the statute.)
- Accounts placed for collection more than 7 years ago. When in doubt, the FTC assumes that an account will be placed for collection 180 days after it first becomes delinquent.
- Anything else, other than crimes, older than 7 years.

An important exception allows reporting of older information if the consumer is applying for a loan of $150,000 or more, life insurance with a face value of $150,000 or more, or a job with an annual salary of $75,000 or more.

Consumers may obtain one free credit report per year from each of the three major credit reporting agencies—Equifax, TransUnion, and Experian—by going to their centralized site of www.annualcreditreport.com.

(Beware of firms promising to "clean up your credit" for a fee. Many times, they employ illegal tactics that involve you committing fraud or perjury. The Federal Trade Commission has been very aggressive in suing such services.)

Fair Debt Collection Practices Act   A federal law designed to curb abuses in the debt collection industry. The law applies to debt collectors, who are defined as persons or companies who collect debts for another. If you owe money to Smith's Marina and Mr. Smith himself or one of his employees contacts you to collect the money owed, that person is not a debt collector under the Act because they are trying to collect money due to themselves, not money due to a third party.

Generally speaking, collectors cannot call you before 8 a.m. or after 9 p.m. They can't threaten you with arrest, bodily harm, or public exposure as a "deadbeat." They can't imply they are connected with law enforcement. Collectors cannot harass you with repeated phone calls on the same day. They can't call you at work if you tell them you are not allowed to receive such calls at work.

Consumers may sue and collect damages and attorneys' fees for violations of the Fair Debt Collection Practices Act. (It may be found at 15 USC §1601 and subsequent sections.) You must file suit within one year of the violation.

Fair Housing Act   A federal law originally passed in 1968. The law prohibits discrimination by landlords, real estate agents, municipalities, lenders, and homeowners' insurance companies, if the discriminatory practices make housing unavailable to people because of race or color, religion, sex, national origin, family status, or disability. Discrimination includes such things as steering, redlining, and imposing greater requirements on some groups than on others. Limited accessibility that makes housing practically unavailable for persons with disabilities is a form of discrimination. Housing providers may not unreasonably limit the number of people living in a unit or restrict families to only certain areas of a complex. It is, however, legal to limit a project to people over 55, as allowed by the Housing for Older Persons Act of 1995. The many faces of discrimination are varied and sometimes subtle. It is recommended that all persons involved in real estate become thoroughly familiar with the law.

The Department of Justice may file civil or criminal actions for violations. Individuals who have been discriminated against may file a complaint with the Department of Housing and Urban Development or file suit in state or federal court. There is currently a thriving litigation industry in consumer protection groups using individuals to attempt obtaining housing, lending, or insurance and then suing under the Act when they encounter discrimination. (More information may be found at the Web site for the Department of Housing and Urban Development, www.hud.gov/offices/fheo/index.cfm, and at 42 USC §3601 and subsequent sections.)

Fair Isaac Company (FICO) score   A credit score, based on the name of the company that wrote the software that calculates the scores.

fair market value   The amount that a willing buyer would pay a willing seller for property after reasonable exposure to the marketplace.

false advertising   Advertising that contains blatantly false or misleading statements, whether intentional or not. False advertising may be grounds for rescission, or cancellation, of a contract, and it may also provide the basis for an award of compensatory and punitive damages.

FAMC   See *Federal Agricultural Mortgage Corporation*.

familial status   Under the Fair Housing Act, a protected class of people who live in a household with one or more persons under the age of 18 years and are the parent, legal guardian, or custodial adult for the minor. The concept includes pregnant women and people attempting to gain custody of a minor. Except for elderly housing, one may not discriminate against someone on the basis of familial status.

family   Traditionally, people who are related by blood or marriage. The term can mean many different things depending on the circumstances. Most statutes have a section devoted to "definitions" that will tell you the intended definition of words used in the law. For example, the concept of what constitutes a family may be important in zoning cases for single-family housing or apartment restrictions against non-family members living in the apartment with the tenant.

family limited partnership (FLP)   A special type of limited partnership recognized by some states as an estate planning tool. A donor establishes a family limited partnership and then transfers into it property expected to appreciate in value over the years. The donor then makes gifts of small percentages of the partnership to children or other family members. The gifts are small enough to escape gift taxes and may be doubled if the donor makes the first gift to the spouse, and then each of them makes gifts each year. As the property grows in value, the appreciation belongs to the person receiving the gifted shares and so is not in the donor's estate at death.

Fannie Mae   A popular name for Federal National Mortgage Association.

Farm and Land Institute   Now known as the REALTORS® Land Institute.

farm area   A specific geographic area or condominium complex receiving intense marketing efforts from a real estate agent in order to obtain listings. The agent specializes in the area, learning everything there is to know. Over time, communities will always have agents identified with particular parts of town, such as "Myra the lake lady" or "Lyman the land man."

farm assets   All the assets of a ranch or farm, including the residence, outbuildings, barns, irrigation systems, trees, and fencing. Farm assets receive special treatment under the Internal Revenue Code if there is sale, exchange, or lease. Farmers are also exempt from the requirements to pay quarterly estimated taxes. (See Publication 225, "Farmer's Tax Guide" at the IRS Web site, www.irs.gov.)

Farm Credit Administration (FCA)   An independent agency (www.fca.gov) responsible for regulating and examining banks in the Farm Credit System, including Farmer Mac. It is funded through assessments made against the FCS institutions.

Farm Credit Council   A federated trade association representing the Farm Credit System.

Farm Credit System   The oldest government-sponsored enterprise (GSE) (www.farmcredit-ffcb.com) in the country, created in 1916. It is a nationwide network of borrower-owned lending institutions and affiliated service entities that makes loans to agricultural and rural borrowers. The members do not take deposits. The funds for loans are obtained through the issuance of Farm Credit debt securities on a worldwide basis in the domestic and global capital markets.

Farmer Mac   A nickname for the Federal Agricultural Mortgage Corporation (FAMC).

Farmers Home Administration (FmHA)   A federal agency that formerly operated under the United States Department of Agriculture (USDA). The Federal Crop Insurance Reform and Department of Agriculture Reorganization Act of 1994 replaced FmHA with USDA Rural Development.

fashion/specialty centers   Shopping centers devoted to retail and dining establishments attractive to a higher-end, fashion-oriented concept. They usually contain 80,000 to 250,000 square feet of space on 5 to 25 acres, with a primary trade area of 5 to 15 miles.

fastrack construction   Construction that begins before all plans and specifications have been completed. For example, the builder may have full architectural and structural engineering drawings sufficient to pour footings and a concrete pad, before the electrical plans have been completed.

FCA   See *Farm Credit Administration*.

FDIC   See *Federal Deposit Insurance Corporation*.

feasibility study   An analysis of the marketplace to determine if it is economically practical and desirable to develop a particular project. Contrast with a market analysis, which merely identifies whether a defined market or trade area desires what you propose to build. A market study determines demand for the real estate development; a feasibility study determines whether that demand is willing to pay what the project will cost, plus a profit.

> **Example:** *The demand for first-class office space in downtown Elm City exceeds the available space. There are no vacancies, and potential tenants must take space in the suburbs or settle for less desirable space downtown. The market analysis determines that a market exists for a new midrise office building. The feasibility study then analyzes all acquisition and construction costs, the length of time until a new building would be at break-even occupancy, the cost of funds for construction financing, and the expenses of operating such a building. According to the feasibility study, the building would have to command rents in the range of $28 to $30 per square foot per year in order to be a viable project. Current market rents downtown for similar space range between $19 and $23 per square foot per year.*

This constitutes the feasibility study—what will it cost, what must I charge, what will the market pay? The portion of the study that asks "What will the market pay" is the portion with the most risk, the most in need of salesmanship when one is talking to lenders and investors, and the truest test of a seasoned developer with good instincts. In the preceding example, the market may very well respond positively to a new building with rental rates significantly higher than anything else downtown. On the other hand, it might not. One has to choose, in the end, after all the analysis has been completed.

Federal Agricultural Mortgage Corporation (FAMC)   Commonly called Farmer Mac (www.farmermac.com), it is one of the system entities in the Farm Credit System. Its purpose is to attract new capital for the financing of agricultural real estate and to provide liquidity to agricultural lenders.

Federal Crop Insurance Reform and Department of Agriculture Reorganization Act of 1994   Federal legislation passed in order to streamline and modernize the Department of Agriculture.

Federal Deposit Insurance Corporation (FDIC)   An independent agency (www.fdic.gov) created by Congress in 1933. It supervises banks, insures deposits up to $100,000 per depositor per institution, and acts as a receiver and liquidator for failed banks.

Federal Emergency Management Agency (FEMA)   Formerly an independent federal agency that became part of the Department of Homeland Security on March 1, 2003. FEMA's mission statement is to "lead the effort to prepare the nation for all hazards and effectively manage federal response and recovery efforts following any national incident." FEMA (www.fema.gov) also initiates proactive mitigation activities, trains first responders, and manages the National Flood Insurance Program.

Federal Financial Institutions Examination Council   A federal interagency body (www.ffiec.gov) that establishes uniform standards and reporting requirements for the examination and auditing of financial institutions supervised by the Board of Governors of the Federal Reserve System, the Federal Deposit Insurance Corporation, the National Credit Union Administration, the Office of the Comptroller of the Currency, and the Office of Thrift Supervision.

Federal Home Loan Banks (FHLBanks)   The largest source of residential mortgage and community development credit in the United States. This group consists of a regional cooperative of 12 FHLBanks, each with its own president and board of directors. Its primary business consists of FHLBank Advances, which are low-cost loans made to member institutions. This gives those members the liquidity to make mortgage loans. The FHLBanks (www.fhlbanks.com) regenerate their own liquidity by selling debt consisting of consolidated bonds with maturities of one year or more, and consolidated discount notes which mature within 360 days.

Federal Home Loan Mortgage Corporation   A stockholder-owned corporation chartered by Congress in 1970 to assist home mortgage lenders with a steady flow of money. Called Freddie Mac (www.freddiemac.com) for short, it buys home mortgages from loan originators such as local financial institutions and then sells mortgage backed securities and debt securities. In order to realize one of its goals, to stabilize the mortgage industry, Freddie Mac has transformed the industry by standardizing mortgage documents, introducing automated underwriting, creating the market for conventional mortgage backed securities, and leading the fight against unfair and predatory lending practices. Its primary competitor is Fannie Mae; both are regulated by the Office of Federal Housing Enterprise Oversight in HUD.

Federal Housing Administration (FHA)   Created by Congress in 1934 and later added to the Department of Housing and Urban Development's (HUD) Office of Housing in 1965. The FHA (www.fha.gov) says it is the only government agency that is entirely self-supporting and receives no taxpayer funds at all. It provides mortgage insurance on loans made by FHA-approved lenders, making those loans risk-free for the originators.

Federal Housing Finance Board (FHFB)   Regulates the 12 Federal Home Loan Banks.

Federal Insurance Administration (FIA)   A federal agency that administers several insurance programs, including flood insurance.

Federal Land Bank   The former name for institutions established by Congress in 1917 in order to provide long-term mortgage credit to farmers and ranchers, and later to rural home buyers. The Federal Land Banks merged with the Federal Intermediate Credit Banks after the Agricultural Credit Act of 1987. It is now known as a Farm Credit Bank.

federally chartered banks   Financial institutions authorized and regulated by the federal government rather than the state government. They have the word "national" in their name, or the initials

"N.A." at the end. Supervision is by the Office of the Comptroller of the Currency (OCC) at www.occ.treas.gov.

federally related transaction (FRT)   FDIC regulations define the term as "any real estate-related financial transaction entered into on or after August 9, 1990, that the Board or any regulated institution engages in, contracts for, or regulates." FDIC regulations require an appraiser for any FRT except those under $250,000 and other narrowly defined exceptions.

Federal National Mortgage Association (FNMA)   Popularly known as Fannie Mae. A former government agency that was privatized in 1968, Fannie Mae's mandate is to increase the availability and affordability of homeownership for low-, moderate- and middle-income Americans. It does this by purchasing mortgages in the secondary market and then selling and insuring securities comprised of packages of mortgages. These are usually single-class mortgage backed securities known as Fannie Mae MBS. Contrast with multiclass mortgage backed securities described under *real estate mortgage investment conduit* (REMIC). The association's Web site is www.fanniemae.com; shares in the company are traded on the New York Stock Exchange as FNM.

Federal Reserve System   Often called "the Fed," it is the central bank of the United States, created in 1913. It regulates credit through the interest rates it charges for short-term loans to financial institutions, supervises and regulates banking institutions, and provides advisory services to the government. Funding comes from interest on investments, fees for services to depository institutions, and interest on loans. The public usually comes into contact with the Fed in two ways: When the Federal Reserve chairman announces interest rate changes for loans to member financial institutions, almost all financial institutions change their interest rates within days afterward. In this way, the Fed controls the cost of credit to consumers. Additionally, it provides a central clearinghouse for checks drawn on different banks across the nation, making it possible for your bank in your home town to give you credit for a check drawn on another bank on the other side of the country.

federal rule for condemnations   A method of appraising property taken by the federal government via condemnation under its rights of eminent domain. It is employed when less than an entire parcel is taken. The entire parcel is given a value as it would be before condemnation. Then the parcel to be taken is subtracted, and the remaining parcel appraised. The difference is the condemnation award. This differs from the method used by most states, which value the property condemned and then award damages for the decrease in value suffered by any leftover property. See *before-and-after rule*.

Federal Savings and Loan Insurance Corporation (FSLIC)   A former quasi-governmental agency that provided insurance for deposits at savings and loan institutions. FSLIC (pronounced fizz-lick) went bankrupt in the 1980s banking crisis, and was replaced by the Savings Association Insurance Fund, administered by the FDIC.

federal tax lien   A lien or encumbrance upon all of a taxpayer's real property located in the county where the lien is filed. Tax liens may be for unpaid income taxes, or for the 100 percent penalty assessed against controlling shareholders when their small corporations do not pay withholding taxes for employees. Lenders who foreclose on real estate must send notices to the IRS regarding impending foreclosures, or the property will still be subject to the tax lien after the foreclosure, even if the lien was filed after the mortgage and would ordinarily be destroyed by the foreclosure. (For more information, go to the IRS Web site, www.irs.gov, and search on "IRC 7425 notice.")

Federal Trade Commission (FTC)   Created in 1914, the FTC (www.ftc.gov) was the successor to the old Bureau of Corporations. It was formed in response to widespread concerns about monopolies and their impact on consumers.

Today, it is comprised of three bureaus:

1. Bureau of Consumer Protection. Created to protect consumers from unfair, deceptive, or fraudulent practices. It enforces a variety of consumer protection laws enacted by Congress. It also maintains the consolidated consumer Web site (www.consumer.gov) with information and links to over 170 government agencies.
2. Bureau of Competition. The antitrust arm.
3. Bureau of Economics. Helps the FTC evaluate the economic impact of its various policies.

fee appraiser   One who furnishes appraisals of real property for a fee. Contrast with review appraiser, who is typically an employee of a financial institution or institutional investor and who reviews the work of fee appraisers.

feeder road   See *arterial street.*

fee simple   The maximum possible interest (estate) one can possess in real property is the fee simple absolute. It is unlimited as to duration, transferability, and descendability to heirs. Lesser types of fee simple estates include the fee simple defeasible and the fee simple determinable, both of which may result in loss of the property upon the happening of some event in the future.

fee simple defeasible   An interest in real property that may be defeated upon the happening of a certain described event. In other words, someone must take an action in order for the estate to come to an end.

> **Example:**   *"I grant Blackacre to First Methodist Church 'so long as' (or 'while' or 'during the period') the property is used for religious services." If the property ceases to be used for religious purposes, then the grantor or the grantor's heirs have a reasonable amount of time to declare their rights and retake possession of the property. If they do nothing, they eventually lose their rights and the property stays with First Methodist Church, to do as it chooses with it. Contrast with* fee simple determinable, *which is an automatic termination.*

fee simple determinable   An interest in real property that will automatically terminate upon the happening of a certain described event.

> **Example:**   *"I grant Blackacre to First Methodist Church 'for so long as it is used as' (or 'but only if the property is used for') a church." When the property ceases being used for the purpose granted, then title automatically reverts back to the grantor or the grantor's heirs. It is said that the grantor retains a possibility of reverter. Contrast with* fee simple defeasible.

fee tail   An ancient form of ownership and restriction on land, in which property could pass only to members of the direct male line of a family, and when a time came when there were no direct male members to inherit, the property reverted to the state.

felony   A crime that carries the possibility of a sentence in excess of one year. Violation of some real estate laws is classified as a felony.

FEMA   See *Federal Emergency Management Agency*.

feng shui   The art and science of placing buildings and specifying the use of components, finishes, and furniture in such a manner as to create harmony and balance.

feudal system   An ancient system of land ownership. Under old English common law, the king owned all lands. All other people were mere tenants, who enjoyed possession solely by virtue of the goodwill of the overlord above them. By the seventeenth century the system was replaced by the allodial system we know today.

FF&E   See *furniture, fixtures, and equipment*.

FHA   See *Federal Housing Authority*.

FHA approved   An activity, development, lender, or construction method which meets all requirements of the FHA and will qualify for FHA-insured mortgage loans.

FHA insured   A single-family or multifamily mortgage loan that is insured by the Federal Housing Authority. If the borrower defaults, the FHA will either pay the lender the insurance proceeds, up to the balance remaining on the loan after foreclosure, or it will pay the loan in full and take an assignment of the collateral.

FHFB   See *Federal Housing Finance Board*.

FIA   See *Federal Insurance Administration*.

fiber to the curb   An important amenity in a development; the existence of fiber-optic cable from the phone company's central office to the edge of the development, so that all properties within may make use of advanced telecommunications services.

fictitious company name   A trade name or assumed name for a company, rather than the actual legal name of the person or entity that owns the business. Many states require fictitious party filings so that consumers and others may determine the true ownership of a business simply by knowing the trade name.

fidelity bond   A special insurance policy that covers losses caused by dishonest employees. Property management companies and others with employees who handle money belonging to clients should generally obtain fidelity bonds. Also called a surety bond.

fiduciary   A person who enjoys a relationship of trust or confidence with respect to another such that the law will impose greater than normal responsibilities on the fiduciary for honesty, integrity, candor, and scrupulous good faith even if it means sacrificing the interests of the fiduciary. Typical fiduciaries include attorneys, real estate agents representing principals, trustees, and guardians. Because of the fiduciary relationship between an agent and principal, it is difficult to understand the concept of dual agency, in which the broker may represent both the buyer and seller. A seller's fiduciary must keep all the client's information confidential, not volunteer anything unless absolutely required by law, and attempt to gain the highest possible price for the property. A buyer's fiduciary must ferret out all secrets, volunteer all information regarding anything at all that might affect property values, recommend the most thorough home inspectors, and attempt to obtain the lowest possible price for a property. These positions are extremely difficult to reconcile in one person.

fiduciary obligations   Very high responsibilities of care, concern, representation, and confidentiality owed by one in a special relationship to another. An agent owes fiduciary obligations to the principal, who is also called the client.

field fit   The practice of taking measurements for building components as an improvement is undergoing construction, rather than relying on precise written plans and specifications. Sometimes small amounts of field fitting are necessary, as when tolerances can vary by fractions of an inch. Other times, although the practice is widespread and commonplace, it is not recommended.

file   To place a document in the public records. All such documents are time and date stamped when received; this is important because the priority of deeds and of liens is usually on a race-to-the-courthouse, first-to-file basis. In many states, if a judgment is recorded against a seller only minutes before a deed to the buyer is recorded, then the buyer's new property is subject to the lien, which must be paid or the judgment creditor may execute and take the property and sell it for satisfaction of the debt.

filled land   An area where the grade—the level of the land—has been raised, preferably by depositing clay, soil, rock, and gravel and then compacting the fill at regular intervals as the grade is raised. Less ideal, but more common in areas with little regulatory oversight, is the practice of dumping tree stumps and other vegetation, covering them with 6 feet or so of clay, and then compacting only the top 6 feet. The property will pass most compaction studies, which bore down only 6 feet. In time, however, the vegetation will rot, the land will settle, and the owner will see potholes and foundation cracks.

final injunction   A court order entered after trial on all issues, directing that the losing party take some action or stop doing something. If the losing party disputes the decision, it may appeal. Contrast with a temporary restraining order, which is a court order intended to be effective for a very short time until there can be a hearing. Contrast also with a preliminary injunction, which is a court order intended to be effective only until there can be a full trial, usually several years later.

finance charge   The total of all direct and indirect costs associated with obtaining credit.

finance fee   A charge by a mortgage broker to cover costs and expenses associated with placing a loan. With VA and FHA loans, the fee is limited to 1 percent of the amount financed. Other loans vary between one-half of 1 percent and 3 percent depending on the competition to obtain loans, credit risk, and other such business factors. The fee is generally negotiable. See *origination fees*.

financial institution   An organization that obtains money from deposits and earns money from loans.

Financial Institutions Reform, Recovery and Enforcement Act (FIRREA)   (pronounced "fie-ree-ah") Federal legislation passed in 1989 in response to the banking and savings and loan crisis, the FDIC bailout, and the bankruptcy of the Federal Savings and Loan Insurance Corporation (FSLIC). It reorganized much of the oversight and regulatory framework for financial institutions and created the Resolution Trust Corporation (now defunct) to receive and liquidate assets from failed financial institutions.

financial management rate of return (FMRR)   A method of evaluating the performance of a real estate investment, FMRR is a modified version of the internal rate of return tool. FMRR uses two different rates for its calculations: (1) the cost of capital rate to discount future negative cash flows back to the present (in other words, what would it cost you to borrow the money to cover losses in future years?) and (2) a specified reinvestment rate for compounding future positive cash flows to the end of the projection period (in other words, what if you took your profits and reinvested them at a certain rate, how would they grow?)

financial privacy rules   See *Gramm-Leach-Bliley Act*.

financial purchase   A buying decision that involves insurance or other financial products, such as a home mortgage.

financial statement   A semi-itemized list of the assets and liabilities of a person or entity as of a point in time, and the revenues and expenses over a representative month or over a period of time such as one year. Do not confuse with *financing statement*.

financing   Borrowing money to buy property. See *leverage*.

financing statement   A document filed in the public records; gives notice that a secured party claims a security interest in certain described goods and other personal property owned by a named debtor. It is also called a UCC-1 after the form provided by the Uniform Commercial Code. The purpose of the statement is to put other creditors, or purchasers, on notice that the security interest exists and will remain on the property even if sold and even if another creditor loans money against the same property. The financing statement does not give the security interest; it merely provides notice of the existence of a security agreement. If a creditor fails to obtain a signed security agreement, the financing statement will be useless. (Do not confuse with *financial statement*.)

finder's fee   A fee for finding someone to buy, sell, or rent real estate. It is illegal in most states unless the finder is a licensed real estate broker or agent. There is some question about whether existing tenants may receive small gifts or rent credits for referring new tenants. The states that allow this limit the compensation or gift to something minimal.

finish-out allowance　See *tenant improvement allowance*.

fire insurance　A type of property insurance covering losses caused by fire and by damage caused in putting out the fire. Premiums will often depend on proximity to a fire station (within 5 miles is best), the rating of the fire department (all volunteer personnel with minimum equipment up to full-time personnel with all equipment), proximity to a fire hydrant, and method of construction of the property.

fireproof　Having all surfaces covered with a noncombustible material such as concrete or brick. Contrast with *fire resistant*.

fire resistant　Able to withstand exposure to a fire of a specified intensity for a specified period of time, usually 1, 2, or 4 hours. Contrast with *fireproof*.

fire sprinkler system　A system for the delivery of water to locations registering a certain heat and to surrounding areas. Local building codes sometimes change the requirements for fire sprinkler systems, requiring larger sprinkler heads than before. Even if a property has a sprinkler system in place, you will need to check the pressure, the size of the heads, and any other matters required by local law in order to ensure that the system will be in compliance.

fire-stop　Obstructions placed in open areas above a ceiling in order to stop a fire that could otherwise easily spread to all parts of a building.

fire wall　A fire-resistant wall required by local health and safety codes. Depending on the particular code adopted, a property owner may need to erect fire walls between every 3,000 square feet of space, between spaces rented by separate tenants or owned by separate condo owners, and along exterior walls within a certain distance of a property line. The code will detail the hours of fire retardant required under different circumstances. Doors allowing passage through fire walls must be fire doors.

firm commitment　A lender's unqualified and irrevocable promise to grant a loan for a specified amount, which may be a firm amount or a certain percentage of the appraised value. The commitment will also specify the interest rate, term, and collateral. For commercial mortgages, the borrower should ask that the firm commitment include a statement of anticipated legal fees and other fees and expenses and, if possible, negotiate an upper limit to attorneys' fees.

FIRREA　See *Financial Institutions Reform, Recovery and Enforcement Act*.

first-generation space　Office space in a new building. First-generation space lacks walls, floor covering, ceiling tiles, and lighting; it has never been built-out. When comparing tenant improvement allowances among buildings under consideration for leasing office space, it is important to note if the space is first generation or second generation, because the build-out will typically be much more expensive in first-generation space. Even if second-generation space has to be completely reconfigured, there will still be some savings by the ability to reuse doors and light fixtures.

first mortgage   A real estate loan made to the borrower and recorded in the public records by the lender, before any other mortgages.

first refusal, right of   The right to buy or rent real property if and when the owner decides to sell or lease. The owner is under no obligation to ever sell or lease, though. Contrast this with an option, in which the the person who wants to buy or lease (optionee) has a legal right to require the owner (optionor) to sell or lease, but the optionee does not have any obligation to buy or lease. With a right of first refusal, control is in the owner. With an option, control is in the other person.

Care should be taken when drafting a right of first refusal. The parties should specify an expiration date, a price or method of calculating the price, and what happens if the purchaser-lessee declines to buy or lease at a particular point: Does the right of first refusal end, or does it continue to the next time?

The parties should give particular thought and attention to describing the triggering event. What gives rise to the ability to exercise the right of first refusal? Is it the owner merely soliciting offers, or must there be a bona fide offer from a third party before the party will be notified and given the first opportunity to buy or lease? What if the owner dies? Does the party have a right to buy the property before it passes to the heirs?

first-year depreciation   See *additional first-year depreciation.*

fiscal year   Accounting year. Many companies use accounting years ending on June 30 or September 30, rather than the calendar year ending on December 31.

fixed assets   Items on a company's balance sheet—the tangible property used in the business and not for resale; would include buildings, furniture, fixtures, equipment, and land.

fixed bid   A firm price for completing a job.

fixed expenses   Expenses that continue at relatively stable levels, month after month or year after year, regardless of occupancy levels, retail sales, or other areas of revenue, including property rent or depreciation, some minimal level of personnel expenses, and some minimal level of utilities. Contrast with variable expenses, which are more or less directly tied to revenue; as revenues increase, so will the expenses.

fixed lease   See *gross lease.*

fixed-rate loan   A certain percentage rate of interest that will not change over the life of the loan. Contrast with adjustable-rate loan or mortgage.

fixed-rate mortgage   See *fixed-rate loan.*

fixed-term mortgage   A real estate loan for a definite period of time, such as 15 or 30 years.

fixer-upper   Usually a polite way of describing a property in need of extensive repairs, renovations, or cosmetic improvement.

fixture   An item of personal property that becomes part of the real property.

fixturing period   A time period before a lease begins, when the tenant is allowed access to make improvements, deliver furniture, install phone systems, and other such matters.

flag lot   A parcel of land shaped like a flag, with a narrow strip providing access to a public street or waterway and the bulk of the property containing no frontage. When planned, it is a way to maximize property density without having to install additional streets. Some jurisdictions require subdivision platting and approval for any project that includes building additional streets. Flag lots are a way around the platting laws.

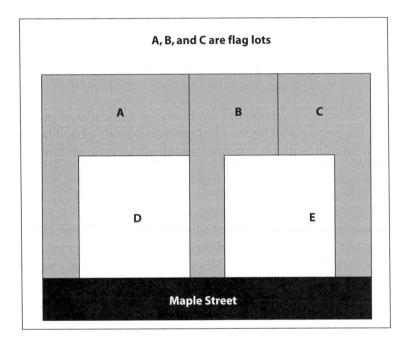

flat   An apartment.

flat-fee broker   One who charges a set fee rather than a percentage of the sale price of a property. Flat-fee brokers typically offer unbundled services, or no-frills services, and almost always exclude any services connected with showing property, handling negotiations, responding to consumer inquiries, or assisting with closing.

For a flat fee, one may usually obtain some combination of the following:

- Listing on the local multiple listing service
- Yard signs and subdivision entrance signs

- An assigned phone number with voice mail for callers
- Placement on a Web site
- Packages of forms, instructions, videos, or DVDs
- A personal consultation for a specified time period
- An initial walk-through inspection with recommendations

flat lease   See *gross lease.*

flat-rate tax   A tax calculated as a certain percentage of income, with all persons paying the same percentage.

flexible payment mortgage   A mortgage with payments that are allowed to vary, but which will always be sufficient to pay the loan over a certain amortizing period. An adjustable-rate mortgage is one example, and a graduated payment mortgage is another.

flex space   Originally, industrial space that could be configured as needed for offices, manufacturing, assemblage, or warehousing. Today, the term usually refers to flexible office arrangements such as movable walls, offices shared by different people during different time slots, or any number of other flexible arrangements.

flip   To buy low and sell high in a fairly short period of time; sometimes associated with predatory practices such as securing an option on property about to be foreclosed and then exercising that option only if able to find a purchaser who will pay enough to generate a profit. In the meantime, the consumer cannot sell to anyone else.

- Condo flipping is accomplished through buying reservation rights in condos to be built in the future, and then selling those rights, not the actual condo, shortly before project completion. There are many Web sites devoted to nationwide markets for condo flipping.
- House flipping usually refers to the practice of buying a home at a price substantially below market because of the need for repairs and then making the renovations and selling in a short period of time, at a substantial profit. Acquisition and renovation is typically financed with a mortgage note due in six months. The practice is risky for those unfamiliar with construction, because delays can be catastrophic.

float   (1) The amount of movement in a variable-rate mortgage, as in "the loan can float 1 percent per year or a maximum of 5 percent in a lifetime." (2) The period of time after a check is deposited but before the funds have been collected or credited. If a depositor receives credit immediately, even though it may take several days for the maker's bank to transfer funds to the depositor's bank, then the depositor takes advantage of the float because it has use of the money. If a depositor does not receive credit for several days, but the bank has already received its money from the maker's bank, then the bank takes advantage of the float.

floating lien   Sometimes refers to the lien of an anaconda mortgage that attaches to additional property acquired after a mortgage loan is originated. More properly refers to a lien on goods or inventory that change constantly, as in financing for a retail establishment. The lien floats among items as they come into the store and are available for sale, detaching itself as the goods are sold to consumers.

floating rate   A loan interest rate that is not fixed and does not have specified times for increase or decrease, but which floats and changes as the index changes.

floating zone   A land area described in the text of zoning regulations but not placed on the zoning map until a developer applies for rezoning.

flood insurance   The popular name for the National Flood Insurance Program (www.floodsmart.gov) administered by the Mitigation Division of the Federal Emergency Management Agency. Flood insurance is intended as an alternative to disaster assistance, by providing better assistance at cheaper net costs to the government. Policies are available in three forms: dwelling (most homes), general property (apartments and businesses), and residential condominium association. They cover structural damage; furnaces, water heaters, and air conditioners; flood debris cleanup; and floor surfaces such as carpeting and tile.

flood insurance rate maps   Maps maintained by the Mitigation Division of the Federal Emergency Management Agency. They locate and describe areas having a 1 percent risk of flooding in any given year. They can be viewed online at the FEMA's Map Service Center Web site, http://msc.fema.gov.

flood plain   Any normally dry land that is susceptible of being covered by water from any natural source.

flood-prone area   An area that has a 1 percent probability of flooding in any given year. Although popularly known as an area that will flood sometime in a 100-year period, this characterization is technically inaccurate.

floor   Other than the obvious, refers to the bottom of something. Variable-rate mortgages may provide a minimum interest rate, called a floor, even if the rate would otherwise be less if the index dropped. Percentage leases with rent partially based on gross revenues might have a minimal amount, or floor payment.

floor area ratio   The ratio of floor space in a building to lot size; used in zoning regulations to restrict the size of buildings.

floor duty   The practice of assigning responsibilities to real estate agents for spending time in the office in order to be available for walk-in customers or general phone inquiries not directed to a particular agent.

floor joists   Horizontal boards laid on edge and resting on the beams that provide the main support for the floor. The subflooring is nailed to the joists, and then the flooring is installed. It is increasing common to use engineered floor joists—wood and binding material rather than traditional lumber—in order to gain strength and stability.

floor load   (1) The weight per square foot that the floors in a building can support, if the weight is evenly distributed. (2) The weight per square foot of a particular piece of equipment or machinery that will be installed in a building, frequently regulated in leases so as not to exceed a stated amount.

floor loan   The minimum amount a lender will fund on an approved loan, with the balance payable if and when the borrower meets certain conditions, such as minimum occupancy levels or preleasing. If the borrower fails to meet the requirements, the borrower will have to secure gap financing or mezzanine financing in the interim, which can be extremely expensive.

floor plan   Architectural drawings showing the layout of the floor(s) in a building, locations of load-bearing walls and/or required fire walls, dimensions for all walls, locations and swings (inward, outward, which side the hinges are on) for all doors, and locations of windows.

flyspecking   A slang expression for reviewing every word, every comma that might make a difference between dependent and independent clauses, every pronoun and its antecedents (does "he" refer to the grantor or the grantee in a sentence, for example), and sketching every property description in every deed in a chain of title to make sure the same land is always described and the description makes an enclosed parcel. Comes from the expression "picking the flyspecks out of the pepper," which is an exceptionally tedious job.

FMHA   See *Farmers' Home Administration*.

FNMA   See *Federal National Mortgage Association*.

folio   In some states, refers to the page number of the book in which real estate documents are recorded.

foot-candle   A measure of light intensity. One foot-candle is the illumination measured on a surface one foot from the source of one candle. Many worker-safety regulations specify the minimum foot-candles of light required in work areas. Zoning variances for commercial properties near residential areas might place a restriction on the maximum foot-candles of lighting after a certain hour at night.

footing   A concrete support for a wall, chimney, or pillar, usually wider than the structure being supported and intended to distribute the weight evenly over a larger surface area. Local building codes will specify minimum footing size for various buildings, although the better practice is to employ a structural engineer to determine the proper size, which may be in excess of the minimums.

footprint   The area of land physically occupied by a building, including its square footage and shape.

forbearance   The act of restraining from exercising a right.

1. Typically encountered in leases and other contracts specifying that a forbearance by one party who fails to declare a default when entitled shall not entitle the other party to rely on future forbearances and will not constitute a waiver of any rights.

2. After a loan default, lenders will sometimes enter into formal forbearance agreements with borrowers, agreeing not to foreclose if the borrowers will agree to a new payment plan, pay all attorneys' fees associated with drafting the agreement, usually agree to a higher interest rate and more collateral, and almost always agree to waive any and all claims against the lender.

forced sale   An involuntary sale resulting from foreclosure, execution on a judgment, partition action by a cotenant wanting to sell the property and divide the money, or a divorce proceeding. See *distressed sale*.

force majeure   Something outside the control of parties to a contract and which could not have been foreseen or planned for. Usually found in construction contracts, suspending the time limits in the event of a force majeure. It can include Acts of God, such as tornadoes and hurricanes, or acts of humans, such as a strike, terrorist attack, or other such disruptive event.

foreclosure   The destruction of a borrower's rights in mortgaged property, except as may be allowed under statutes giving a post-foreclosure right of redemption. The foreclosure process varies among states, but generally segregates into judicial foreclosures and nonjudicial foreclosures.

- Judicial foreclosures involve filing a petition with a court, asking that court to enter an order as to the amount due under a mortgage loan, and then granting the lender permission to sell the property and apply the proceeds to the debt.
- Nonjudicial foreclosures are accomplished by providing some sort of public notice of the default and scheduled auction of the mortgaged property, and then carrying out the auction process.
- Some states allow a statutory right of redemption after foreclosure. This gives the borrower, and sometimes other creditors of the borrower, a certain amount of time to redeem the property by paying the foreclosure purchaser the full amount of the purchase price plus interest at a rate defined in the statute. This is different from the equity of redemption.
- The term equity of redemption means all rights of the borrower before foreclosure, but which are extinguished at foreclosure. If the borrower has any rights after foreclosure, they are granted by specific statutes giving a right of redemption.
- Some states have consumer protection statutes to guard against predatory purchasers taking advantage of foreclosure panic on the part of homeowners.
- If a borrower deeds the mortgaged property to the lender in order to avoid a foreclosure, that is called a deed in lieu of foreclosure. It is a risky route for the lender because all liens remain on the property, even those that might have been cleared off by a foreclosure.
- In most states, if a foreclosure sale does not bring enough money to satisfy the debt, the lender may sue the borrower for something called a deficiency judgment. Exceptions occur in states that limit that right when the debt is a first mortgage on the borrower's primary residence. Another exception would be if the borrower has negotiated a nonrecourse mortgage that insulates it from any personal liability.
- A foreclosure obliterates the rights of the owner (except as noted previously) and virtually all creditors who might have filed claims after the mortgage was foreclosed. This includes second mortgages, if the first mortgage is being foreclosed.

The five major categories of parties who may still have claims on property after a foreclosure are

1. Those who hold mortgages or have other claims which were filed before the mortgage that was foreclosed.
2. The IRS, if the foreclosing lender did not give it the proper notice required by federal law.
3. Those holding mechanics' and materialmen's liens, which might be for work started on the property before the mortgage was taken, but perfected by filing documents after the mortgage was recorded.
4. Local or state governments to which real estate taxes are due.
5. A bankruptcy trustee, who may set aside a foreclosure under the proper circumstances.

foreign corporation   Any corporation organized under the laws of another state or country. Foreign corporations may sue and be sued in the courts of a state only if they are registered and licensed in that state. Normally, if a foreign corporation does business in a state without registration, it may not use the courts of the state to sue the defaulting party.

foreign investment in real estate   The U.S. government closely tracks foreign investment in many critical sectors of the U.S. economy, including banking, technology, and real estate. Foreign investors seeking real estate opportunities may gain information at the Web site of the Association for Foreign Investors in Real Estate, www.afire.org. The U.S. Department of Commerce, Bureau of Economic Analysis (www.bea.gov), requires annual reports from all foreign direct investors in U.S. business enterprises, including real estate.

Foreign Investment in Real Property Tax Act (FIRPTA)   A federal law designed to assist in the collection of income taxes when foreign owners and investors sell real property or shares in entities that own real property.

Purchasers are required to withhold 10 percent of the sales price unless either of the following occurs:

1. The IRS is asked to calculate the exact taxes that would be due, in which case that amount will be withheld.
2. The purchaser will use the property as a residence and the selling price is less than $300,000.

Purchasers must report the withholding on IRS Form 8288 or 8288-A and must report and pay over the money within 20 days after purchase. If purchasers do not withhold, they may be liable for the taxes themselves. Almost all real estate closings today require the seller's signature on what's called the FIRPTA affidavit, stating that the seller is not a foreign person. (For more information, see Publication 515, "Withholding of Tax on Nonresident Aliens and Foreign Entities," available at the IRS Web site, www.irs.gov.)

forfeiture   The loss of rights to something as a result of a failure to perform an obligation. Courts often view forfeitures as penalties, which are illegal. As a result, one who is buying property under a bond for title and will receive a deed only when all payments have been made may be protected from a forfeiture if there is a default after a substantial amount of money has already been paid.

forgery   A counterfeit signature or instrument. A forged deed is void and gives no rights, even to innocent purchasers for value. If title insurance was purchased by an owner, however, that owner may make a claim for compensation, or the title insurance company may take steps to buy out any competing claims.

formaldehyde   A colorless liquid with a distinctive odor, classified as a volatile organic compound because it can be emitted as a gas from certain solids and liquids, even at room temperature. Almost every building component contains formaldehyde in some amount. It is used as a component in glues and adhesives, and in paints and other coatings. Some claim it is a cause of sick building syndrome.

form contract   There is no such thing. Consumers often request a form contract for a real estate sale, lease, or other transaction, thinking to obtain some universally recognized, perhaps government-approved document with a few blanks for variables such as parties' names. Office supply stores, local associations of realtors, books in law libraries, and computers in real estate offices may all have forms that are in widespread use, but each is capable of negotiation and customization. One should never rely on a form to protect one's rights—every document should be read in its entirety, even the boring parts that seem like boilerplate, and changed as necessary.

formosan termite   See *termite bond.*

fortress mall   A shopping mall of superior quality, with at least one fashion department store, at least four anchors having minimum sales of $500 per square foot, and surrounded by a "moat" consisting of acres of parking. The goal is to capture consumers inside the fortress, where they will remain to conduct all their shopping and dining. Still a strong market segment, but seeing erosion by the newer lifestyle malls.

forum shopping clause   A clause in an agreement specifying the state and county where any disputes will be heard. All states have rules regarding jurisdiction, meaning the ability of particular courts of the state (circuit, district, probate, justice of the peace) to hear particular disputes and to issue orders that are binding on the parties. All states have rules regarding venue, meaning the county in which a dispute must be heard. Forum shopping clauses alter the normal rules. They are frequently included by financially strong parties who are afraid of the whims of local lawyers, judges, and juries and would prefer that disputes are handled in their own backyard. Such clauses will be upheld where reasonable under the circumstances.

The contractual agreement to a particular forum does not necessarily mean that forum's law will apply. Choice of law is another totally different concept. Many contracts with forum shopping clauses also have choice of law clauses stating that the law of a certain state will control any disputes.

foundation inspection   An examination of the support for a building to make sure it is sufficient for the size and weight of the building and the character of the soil under it. Also, the examination of an existing building to discover evidence of any defects in the foundation, such as cracks in exterior walls or sinkholes.

fourplex   A small apartment building containing four residences. Many FHA loan programs are available for fourplexes.

four quadrants of the real estate capital markets   An expression describing the following:

1. Private equity. Direct, private, real estate investments
2. Public equity. REITS and other publicly traded vehicles
3. Private debt. Whole loan mortgages
4. Public debt. Collateralized mortgage backed securities and other similar vehicles

four-three-two-one rule   One appraisal method that says commercial property of uniform depth and with road frontage has 40 percent of its value in the front quarter of the parcel, 30 percent in the next quarter, 20 percent in the next quarter, and 10 percent in the rear quarter.

fractional interest   Some interest in real estate less than the entire bundle of rights.

franchise   (1) A contractual relationship whereby one party (franchisee) is entitled to use the trade name, image, procedures, and trade secrets of another (franchisor) usually in return for paying an initial purchase price and a percentage of gross revenues over the period of the arrangement. In most instances, there is a separate fee for the franchisee's share of national and regional advertising campaigns. Real estate franchises include Century 21, RE/MAX, and ERA. (2) A government grant of some privilege, such as the ability to operate as a corporation or the ability to sell drinks and sandwiches in the county courthouse.

fraud   A deceitful practice. Fraud consists of a misrepresentation of a material fact that is relied upon by another party to his or her detriment. There is no requirement that the misrepresentation be intentional. The thing misrepresented must be a fact; it is very difficult to prove fraud when one fails to fulfill his or her obligations but had good intentions in the beginning.

There are three types of fraud:

1. Intentional fraud. Punitive damages may be assessed for this type of fraud.
2. Negligent fraud. As when one makes a statement recklessly but without any intention to deceive, and someone relies on that statement and is injured when it turns out to be false. One example would be a real estate agent telling a buyer that all appliances are new when, in reality, the agent didn't know but thought they looked new. Depending on the degree of recklessness involved, this type of fraud may or may not support punitive damages.
3. Innocent fraud. As when one takes steps to confirm facts but is perhaps mistaken or given mistaken information, and then relays that information to someone else who relied on it and was injured.

The Statute of Frauds is a rule that says certain contracts must be in writing, including contracts having to do with real estate. It has nothing to do with fraud, per se, except to protect against possible fraud by requiring a writing.

Freddie Mac   See *Federal Home Loan Mortgage Corporation.*

free and clear title   Title to real property that is absolute without any liens, mortgages, adverse claims, or other encumbrances.

freehold   An estate in land for life or in fee. The duration of the interest is undeterminable. The estate may end at some point in the future, but no one can predict the date of termination. Best understood by reference to its opposite, which is a leasehold.

free market system auction   An auction process used by the Federal National Mortgage Association (Fannie Mae) to accept bids from approved lenders as to the amount, price, and terms of existing mortgages those lenders desire to sell to Fannie Mae. Once Fannie Mae decides how much it can spend to buy mortgages, it notifies the winning bidders, who have a certain amount of time within which to deliver the mortgages. The servicing agent continues to service the loans and receives a fee from Fannie Mae.

friable   Crumbly, brittle. When asbestos is friable, it is hazardous.

frontage   The length of a property line along a road, street, waterway, or important amenity such as a state park.

front-ending   Doing something in advance of the economically prudent time, taking into consideration all risks. Local governments may front-end the streets in a project and require the developer to build all of them, even though the rearmost lots might never sell. Metropolitan development boards might front-end incentives and pay them to a developer in advance, in order to help defray start-up costs, rather than the more normal method of giving tax breaks over time.

front-end ratio   A mortgage qualification calculation prepared by taking the proposed monthly mortgage payments, plus real estates taxes and insurance, and dividing that number by the borrower's gross monthly income without reduction for taxes.

> **Example:**   *Steve makes $4,000 per month. The mortgage for a home he would like to buy would result in payments of $1,100 per month. His front-end ratio is $1,100 ÷ $4,000 = 27.5%. This is an acceptable ratio for lenders, who would prefer to keep it at 29 percent or lower.*

front foot   A method of describing or pricing commercial real estate by the number of feet of road frontage the parcel has. The drawback is that there is no widely recognized standard for depth, so a property selling for $1,500 per front foot might be half the depth of one selling for $2,400 a front foot, but no one can tell just from the price.

front-loading   See *front-ending*.

front money   Cash needed to start a development, as opposed to borrowed funds. See *seed money*.

frost line   The depth of frost penetration into the soil. It varies from area to area, depending on the soil quality in a particular location, but can average 3 to 4 feet below the surface. Building foundations should penetrate below the frost line in order to avoid the shifting caused by frost heaving.

Many local building codes allow an exception with the use of a frost-protected shallow foundation, which uses insulation and drainage techniques to raise the frost line to just below the surface.

frost-protected shallow foundation   A construction method that uses insulation and drainage to artificially raise the frost line of soil to a level that allows relatively short—shallow—foundations. In cold climates, building foundations must extend below the frost line to a depth of soil that does not freeze. Freezing causes soil to heave upward and then sink back again, shifting everything on top of the soil. It does not result in a very stable building base unless one takes steps to prevent soil movement.

FRT   See *federally related transactions*.

fructus industriales   The fruits of industry, meaning crops and other annual plants that must be sown each year in order to produce. At common law, these things were considered the tenant's, who could make claim for them at the end of a tenancy. The terms fructus naturales and fructus industriales are not representative of modern agribusiness or ranching, but come from a time before the industrial revolution.

fructus naturales   The fruits of nature, meaning things produced by nature without the help of humans, such as fruits, wool, offspring of animals, and milk. At common law, these things did not belong to a tenant, who could not make any claim for them at the end of a tenancy. The terms fructus naturales and fructus industriales are not representative of modern agribusiness or ranching, but come from a time before the industrial revolution.

FSLIC   See *Federal Savings and Loan Insurance Corporation*.

FTC   See *Federal Trade Commission*.

full capacity   Able to enter into contracts without any disabilities at all, such as would be attributable to age or mental abilities.

full disclosure   A requirement to reveal all information relevant to a transaction. Some states have full disclosure laws requiring transmittal of property condition information to buyers.

full reconveyance   A mortgage concept used in title theory states, where the borrower transfers title to the real property to another, usually a trustee, and is entitled to full reconveyance, or a return of the legal title, when the debt has been paid in full.

full service   In connection with a lease, this indicates that the landlord provides janitorial, parking lot cleaning, and waste removal services, but the tenant may have to pay for these services through its pro rata portion of the building maintenance expenses. Contrast with *full-service gross lease*.

full-service gross lease   A lease requiring the landlord to provide and pay for all maintenance, upkeep, repairs, janitorial services, waste removal, utilities, insurance, taxes, and other operating expenses for a property in return for a fixed periodic rent from the tenant.

fully amortizing loan   A loan calling for periodic payments that include some amount of interest and some amount of principal reduction, such that, at the end of the loan term, the entire principal amount of the loan plus all accrued interest will have been paid in full.

functional obsolescence   A loss of value from all factors within a property except for physical deterioration. This may include a poor floor plan, the lack of a garage, high ceilings that dramatically increase heating costs, or the lack of central air conditioning in the South. Contrast with economic obsolescence (factors outside the property that depress its value) and physical obsolescence (deterioration).

funding (a loan)   The act of a lender paying money under a loan.

funding fee   (1) A fee charged to the borrower by the Veterans Administration for guaranteeing a loan. (2) A fee charged by lenders as additional profit, and which may be negotiated downward.

funds from operations   A measure of the profitability of any business, but particularly a real estate investment trust. It is net income without downward adjustments for depreciation or amortization and without considering any extraordinary revenues such as from the sale of an asset.

furniture, fixtures, and equipment (FF&E)   All the property at a location, except for the real property itself. Usually referred to by the initials only (FF&E). Lenders will often take security interests in the FF&E of a business borrower, in addition to a mortgage on the real property, so as not to encounter a possible post-default battle over what was covered by their lien.

future-advances mortgage   A real estate loan that contemplates some portion being funded—advanced—at the beginning of the loan, usually for a purchase of property. The amount advanced is not the full allowable amount under the loan so that future monies may be obtained as necessary for construction, renovation, or other uses in or for the property.

future interest   Interest in land in which the possession and enjoyment are deferred until a future date.

FY   Fiscal year, as in FY07.

G

GAAP (pronounced "gap") Generally accepted accounting principles declared by the Financial Accounting Standards Board (FASB).

gain The profit on the sale of an asset. One may *realize* gain, as when property is taken in condemnation, but not *recognize* gain for tax purposes until a later date. When reading tax advice, it is extremely important to differentiate between these two concepts, as authors sometimes assume that all readers understand the difference.

game theory The science of evaluating the relationships among parties and the optimal choices for participants in any given situation. Game theory is an important tool in negotiating. Two frequently encountered game theory models are the prisoner's dilemma and chicken.

- The prisoner's dilemma model involves parties trusting each other to make the best choice for all, without prearranging their plans, rather than making the best choice for an individual. This is seen in the real estate world in quoting commissions, which involves informal, nonverbal negotiations among real estate agents. Although there is no price fixing going on, all brokers understand that if they cooperate and refuse to lower prices, they will all make a good living. If one or a few lower commission rates in order to capture a lot more business, those few will do well until all brokers lower their prices and get into a price war, after which all will do poorly.
- Chicken is the "sport" of two cars racing against each other, head-on, with the first one to swerve being labeled chicken and losing the match. The best way to win a game of chicken is to remove your ability to swerve and to let the other side know that you no longer have any freedom to move—no freedom of negotiation, in other words. For example, the common use of the chicken theory is to tell a seller that you do not have, and cannot borrow, enough money to meet the asking price. The seller will have to reduce the price, or you will have to find another property.

gap A time period when an additional title search is being conducted to determine if any adverse findings have occurred since the original title search and the recording of the deed or mortgage.

gap financing A loan that covers the difference between the construction loan and the permanent financing. See *bridge loan*.

gap in title A break in the chain of title, as when one finds a deed into party A, and then later a deed out of party B, with never any more claims or deeds from party A.

Example: *You see a deed into Ralph and Anna Brown in 1974, but no deed out of their names. On the other hand, the same property suddenly has a deed in 1985 from "Anna B. and Thad Morton" to Mirriam Waites, but you can't find a deed into Anna B. and Thad Morton. This is a gap in title. Most likely, Ralph Brown died and his widow, Anna Brown, married Thad Morton, but you will need additional research to clarify this.*

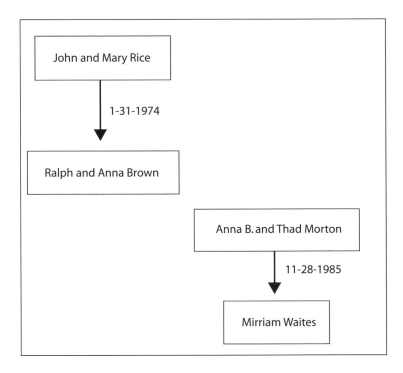

garage mahal   A slang expression for an opulent parking garage.

garnishee   A party who owes money or holds property belonging to the judgment debtor.

garnishment   A process involving three parties:

- Judgment creditor. The party who takes a judgment against a debtor (can also be the IRS or a state's Department of Revenue).
- Judgment debtor. The party who owes the debt.
- Garnishee A party who owes money or holds property belonging to the judgment debtor.

In this legal process, the judgment creditor obtains a court order requiring the garnishee to turn over funds or property to the judgment creditor instead of to the true owner, the judgment debtor. The most common garnishments are against employers, requiring them to withhold a portion of wages and salary and pay it to the creditor rather than to the employee. The second most common garnishment is against a bank, ordering it to turn over bank account funds to the judgment creditor or the IRS.

gated community   A fenced and gated community of homes. Most local governments require public access to all roads maintained by the government. As a result, gated communities must usually assess homeowners in order to maintain their own roads.

gatekeeper   A slang expression to describe the person you must persuade or impress just to get your proposal in front of a decision maker.

gazump   An action by a seller to increase the purchase price of goods or property after the buyer is emotionally invested but immediately before the paperwork is signed. Contrast with *gazunder*.

gazunder   An action by a buyer to lower the offer for goods or property after the seller has already mentally spent the purchase money and is emotionally invested in a sale at that time, but immediately before the paperwork is signed. Contrast with *gazump*.

GC   General contractor. Also can be written as G/C.

general agency   See *agency*.

general agent   See *agency*.

general and administrative expenses   Usually a pro rated portion of general overhead, charged to a particular project although not capable of segregation into goods or services provided for that project. An example could be the cost of paper, toner, office equipment maintenance contracts, phone lines, and office space.

general bill of sale   A document transferring ownership of personal property to another. There are no particular requirements, so long as someone can identify the parties involved and the thing being sold. It is not necessary to spell out the amount paid, but it is usually a good idea to include it.

> **Example:** *"John Jones sells to Lydia Lang, for $200, one 10x15 foot hard plastic portable shed located at 135 Elm Street, Pleasant, New York."*

general contractor   One who is responsible for construction of a building or other improvement for an owner or a developer. Most states have educational, experience, and insurance requirements as a condition of obtaining a general contractor's license. They also prohibit unlicensed persons from constructing improvements for another unless the project is under a certain specified size. The trade association is the Associated General Contractors of America (www.agc.org), established in 1918. You may check licensing requirements and the status of local contractors at www.contractors-license.org, maintained by the Craftsman Book Company.

general lien   A lien that attaches to all property of a debtor located within the area where the lien was recorded. Judgments and IRS liens are general liens, which may be satisfied from the sale of any property found. Contrast with specific lien, which is upon specifically described property only.

generally accepted accounting principles (GAAP)   (pronounced "gap") Established by the Financial Accounting Standards Board (FASB), these are the guidelines for proper accounting practices.

general partner   One who may enter into contracts for a partnership, is liable for all partnership debts, is entitled to vote on all partnership affairs, and is entitled to a pro rata share of all partnership profits. The general partner may be an individual or a corporation. A partnership may be comprised entirely of general partners, or it may have one or a few general partners with the remainder of the investors being limited partners.

general partnership   A partnership in which all partners are general partners. Contrast with *limited partnership*.

General Services Administration (GSA)   A government agency established in 1949 with the passage of the Federal Property and Administrative Services Act, consolidating several earlier agencies. The GSA's areas of responsibility are public buildings, federal supply, and national archives and records. It has been responsible for establishing the Federal Citizen Information Center in Pueblo, Colorado; bringing the government into the credit card age for employee expenses; and creating www.firstgov.gov, the official portal for all government Web sites. The GSA Web site is at www.gsa.gov, which is the starting point for all inquiries regarding surplus property sales and auctions.

general warranty deed   An instrument transferring ownership of real property, and which warrants—promises—that the seller has good title with no adverse claimants and that the seller will defend the title against other parties should that prove necessary. Contrast with *special warranty deed*, which simply promises that the seller has not done anything to cause a problem with the title. Contrast also with *quitclaim deed*, which makes no promises at all, but simply transfers any interest the seller might have, if anything.

gentrification   The informal process of revitalizing an older and deteriorated neighborhood into more upscale homes owned by more affluent occupants. The first step is usually taken by young professionals seeking affordable housing in an urban setting, who immediately begin using disposable income to upgrade their properties. Their efforts attract other like-minded home buyers. Eventually the neighborhood reaches a point where the existing homeowners can afford to sell their properties and buy elsewhere, but they can't afford to pay the increasing property taxes. The process gains momentum at that point, with former apartment buildings being converted to condos, single-family residences undergoing complete renovations, and the entire neighborhood changing to middle class or upper-middle class. It is controversial, with some claiming it destroys the ethnicity and integrity of many older neighborhoods, all in the guise of ethnocentric notions of "improvement."

geodetic survey system   A national coordinate system for mapping the lands, waters, coastlines, and even the ionosphere. Geodetic coordinates are indispensable for routing transportation and delivery of goods, locating underground utility equipment for repairs, excavating, and restoration of the earth's surface. The entire Internet depends on global positioning system (GPS) clocks for the precise timing necessary to avoid instant, perpetual gridlock. Without the spatial coordinates supplied by the geodetic survey system, which are necessary for minute adjustments in the delivery of time information, the Internet, the financial sector, and a host of other necessary sectors of our economy would be in the Dark Ages.

geographic information system (GIS)   A computer mapping program in which land characteristics and/or demographic information may be revealed and printed as color-coded overlays.

gerbil tube   Slang for a glass-enclosed pedestrian overpass connecting two buildings.

ghetto   A term with its origins in eastern Europe, used to designate the part of town occupied by Jewish citizens. Now the term ghetto is used to describe any urban area suffering significant deterioration, often predominated by one or a very few ethnic or racial groups. Disputes often arise regarding whether lenders, insurers, and other service providers are engaged in illegal discrimination when they redline these neighborhoods, or whether they are assessing risks based on the quality of the infrastructure and not on any judgments regarding the inhabitants.

GI Bill   Now called the Montgomery GI Bill, it offers support for veterans seeking postsecondary education.

gift causa mortis   A gift in contemplation of death. This was an important term at one time because the IRS required such gifts, made within 3 years of death, to be included in the gross estate for estate tax purposes. You will still encounter the word, but the legal significance is no longer important because such property is no longer included in the estate.

gift deed   A deed with love and affection as the consideration, but nothing else of generally accepted monetary value.

gift letter   A letter provided to a lender or government agency stating that money to be used as the down payment for a home loan was a gift and not a loan from the donor.

gift tax   A federal tax that must be paid by a donor. The tax is based on the value of lifetime gifts made to others except in the following situations:

- For the base year of 2004, one can make gifts of up to $11,000 of cash or property per year to each recipient without incurring gift taxes; spouses may give up to $22,000 per year to each recipient. After 2004, there is a cost-of-living adjustment. This is an important aspect of estate planning. See *family limited partnership* for details.
- Tuition or medical expenses paid directly to the educational or medical institution are not counted as gifts, regardless of the relationship with the student or patient.
- Gifts to spouses are not taxable; there are no dollar limits.
- Gifts to political organizations or charities are not taxable.

For more information, see Publication 950, "Introduction to Estate and Gift Taxes," available at the IRS Web site, www.irs.gov.

GI loan   GI is a slang term for armed services personnel—"government issue." A GI loan is a loan program for armed services personnel. See *Veterans Administration*.

Ginnie Mae   A corporation formed in 1968 and placed under the control of the Department of Housing and Urban Development (HUD). Ginnie Mae makes no loans, nor does it buy or sell mortgages. Instead, it guarantees pools of federally insured or federally guaranteed loans. It is almost never called by its true name, which is the Government National Mortgage Association (GNMA) (www.ginniemae.gov).

going-concern value   The value of a business in operation, taking into account the goodwill and the value of the income, in addition to hard assets, such as real estate and equipment. When appraising a project to develop income-producing property, the appraiser will usually provide two numbers—one for the project on the day of completion, with no tenants, and one when it reaches stabilized occupancy and is a going concern. Lenders who take mortgages on income-producing property with intensive management aspects—such as hospitality properties—usually obtain a going-concern rider for the title insurance so that coverage will be increased above the value of the real property.

going dark   A slang expression for a retail store closing its doors and discontinuing operations at a particular site. Many shopping center and strip center leases prohibit an anchor store—the one that draws traffic to the center and assists the smaller stores with business—from going dark. Without the clause, the anchor store would be able to move to another location, close operations at the old location but continue paying rent, and effectively destroy the business of all other tenants because of the reduction in traffic.

going-in capitalization rate   A total obtained by dividing a project's first year's net operating income by the purchase price or development cost.

gold plating   Including unnecessarily expensive items in a construction or renovation project to justify a large budget or a substantial rent increase.

good and marketable title   A title to real estate, free of any liens or adverse claims.

good and merchantable title   See *good and marketable title*.

good consideration   Usually signifies something founded on moral obligation or affection for the value necessary to support an enforceable contract. Many deeds will recite they are in consideration of love and affection. This is good consideration, and is sufficient, but it is not valuable consideration.

good faith   Honesty.

good-faith estimate   An initial estimate of expected closing costs, net proceeds to seller, gross cash required of buyer, or loan expenses. By virtue of various state and federal laws, a seller's real estate agent may be required to provide a good-faith estimate of net seller proceeds to accompany every offer; the closing company may be required to provide a good-faith estimate of closing expenses to the buyer, and a lender may be required to provide a good-faith estimate of loan costs to a borrower.

good funds   Collected funds in a bank account and usable immediately by the owner of the account.

good title   See *good and marketable title*.

goodwill   An intangible asset consisting of the public esteem in which a business is held. When a business is sold, the difference between the value of the hard assets and the value of the income stream is often attributed to goodwill. One may not depreciate goodwill, but it can be amortized over 15 years because of its inclusion in the IRS definition of Section 197 intangibles.

Government Accountability Office (GAO)   An investigative arm of Congress, formerly called the General Accounting Office. Members of Congress may request a wide variety of reports, analyses, and raw data, which is supplied in a nonpartisan manner by the GAO. It also recommends actions to be taken by Congress as a result of findings in the reports. Its Web site, www.gao.gov, contains an excellent search engine to find reports on housing, financial services, and natural resources, to name a few topics.

A few interesting reports related to real estate include

- ''Financial Institutions: Issues Regarding the Tax-Exempt Status of Credit Unions'' (important because credit unions usually offer lower interest rates because of their tax-exempt status, but banks are crying "no fair" over the situation.)
- ''Real Estate Brokerage: Various Factors May Affect Price Competition''
- ''Title Insurance: Preliminary Views and Issues for Further Study''
- ''Catastrophe Risk: U.S. and European Approaches to Insure Natural Catastrophe and Terrorism Risks''
- ''Consumer Protection: Federal and State Agencies Face Challenges in Combating Predatory Lending''
- ''Residential Care Facilities Mortgage Insurance Program: Opportunities to Improve Program and Risk Management''
- ''Public Housing: Information on the Roles of HUD, Public Housing Agencies, Capital Markets, and Service Organizations''
- ''Elderly Housing: Federal Housing Programs and Supportive Services''

Government National Mortgage Association (GNMA)   Almost always referred to by its popular name—see *Ginnie Mae*.

government patent   The original deed out of the government and into the first private individual to own a particular parcel of land. A thorough title search will trace the title of real property all the way back to a government patent.

Government Printing Office (GPO)   The federal government's primary, centralized resource for gathering, cataloging, providing, authenticating, and preserving published information in all its forms. It maintains a 1.5 million square foot facility in Washington D.C. for processing, printing, and distribution of materials. Unless one knows the specific government agency responsible for particular materials, GPO's Web site, www.gpo.gov, is the best place to start any search regarding laws, regulations, procedures, forms, advice, or virtually anything else prepared by or collected for the U.S. government.

government rectangular survey system   See *public land survey system*.

government-sponsored enterprise (GSE)   One of a group of financial services organizations created by the government. Some are owned by the federal government, some are owned by private individuals, and some are owned by corporations that use their services. All of them enjoy exceptionally low loan rates and exceptionally high sales prices for their bonds and other debt instruments because of the implicit backing of the U.S. government. They include

- Federal Home Loan Banks. Owned by over 8,000 community financial institutions that use the services of the FHLBs.
- Federal Home Loan Mortgage Corporation (Freddie Mac). A stockholder-owned, publicly traded corporation listed on the New York Stock Exchange as FRE.
- Federal National Mortgage Association (Fannie Mae). A stockholder-owned, publicly traded corporation listed on the New York Stock Exchange as FNM.
- Government National Mortgage Association (Ginnie Mae). A wholly owned (by the government) corporation within the Department of Housing and Urban Development.
- Farm Credit Bank. Federally chartered and borrower-owned financial institutions.
- Federal Agricultural Mortgage Association (Farmer Mac). A stockholder-owned, publicly traded corporation listed on the New York Stock Exchange as AGM.
- Student Loan Marketing Corporation (Sallie Mae). A stockholder-owned, publicly traded corporation listed on the New York Stock Exchange as SLM.

government survey method   See *public land survey system*.

GO-Zone   Certain named states and counties in the southern United States, as designated in the Gulf Opportunity Zone Act of 2005. This legislation was passed by Congress in the wake of the devastating 2005 hurricane season to provide tax benefits in hurricane-ravaged areas. Among other benefits, improved property purchased and put into use after August 25, 2005, and before January 1, 2009, may have 50 percent of the value of the improvements depreciated in the first year. In addition, demolition expenses may be written off as expenses rather than capitalized, and the Section 179 expense limits were increased dramatically. Neither the properties, nor the investors, need to have suffered any hurricane damage. The program is similar to the now-defunct Liberty Zone tax benefits enacted after 9/11. For more information, see Publication 4492, "Information for Taxpayers Affected by Hurricanes Katrina, Rita and Wilma," available at the IRS Web site, www.irs.gov.

grace period   The allotted time during which a payment can be made without penalty and without entry upon credit records as delinquent or in default.

Grade   (1) A designated ground level. (2) To change the contours of land.

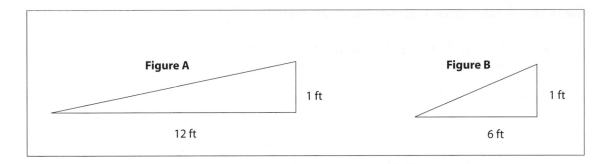

Gradient   The slope, or change in elevation, of land or improvements such as a pipe or a road. It is expressed as the ratio of inches (or feet) of rise or fall over a specified distance. It is similar to the concept of pitch in roofing. Figure A (above) has a gradient of 1:12 because the grade increases by 1 foot over a distance of 12 feet. Figure B has a gradient of 1:6.

Graduate REALTORS® Institute (GRI)   An education program developed by the National Association of REALTORS® (www.realtor.org) and offered through state REALTOR® boards. Members may earn the designation after completion of 90 hours of coursework.

graduated payment mortgage   A home loan structured to provide lower payments in the early years, growing as the homeowners' financial situation hopefully improves. The FHA-insured graduated payment mortgage plan is called a 245 loan. (Do not confuse with the FHA-insured 245(a) program, called a growing equity mortgage.)

graduated rental lease   A commercial lease that offers low rental rates in the early months or years, increasing over time to reach market rates. Sometimes the later rents are greater than market rates, as when the low early rent must be recouped in later years; usually offered as an incentive to secure tenants for a new building or one suffering the recent departure of an exceptionally large tenant. Other times it is offered when a large tenant vacates but continues paying rent for the unexpired term of the lease—the old tenant will make an arrangement with the landlord and effectively subsidize the new tenant's rent for some period of time.

Gramm-Leach-Bliley Act   Contains privacy provisions regarding consumers' financial information. Financial institutions are required to provide information to their customers regarding information-gathering and information-sharing practices. Consumers may opt out if they do not want their information shared with nonaffiliated third parties.

grandfathering   An expression used to describe a statutory or contractual willingness to allow some activities or former rights to continue even though not technically allowed under current conditions. For example, downtown zoning regulations no longer allow gas stations in the area, but Fred's Fuel was doing business before the zoning laws went into effect, so it is grandfathered and can stay in business.

grand list   A name for tax rolls in the New England states.

granny flat   A slang expression for accessory apartments in areas of single-family zoning; also called mother-in-law apartments or maid's quarters, they may or may not be allowed under zoning regulations.

grant   The act of conveying title to real estate via a voluntary transfer. In some states, use of the words "grant, bargain, and sell" in a deed automatically incorporates some or all of the typical deed warranties. (See *warranty deed*.) In order to avoid the consequences of such statutes, if a grantor wishes to convey title without any warranties, it should use a quitclaim deed or the words "bargain, sell, and quitclaim" rather than "grant, bargain, and sell."

grantee   A person who receives the title of real estate via a deed.

grantor   A person who gives title to real estate via a deed.

grantor-grantee index   A method of tracing ownership of real property. Before widespread use of computer databases, all deeds in the abstract system of recording were recorded in deed books, but indexed in grantor-grantee indexes and grantee-grantor indexes. These are large books divided into alphabetical sections such as "Aa through Ad," "Ae through Al," and so on. Each deed was recorded by the grantor's name and then by the grantee's name in the appropriate section of the index. Depending on the volume of transactions over time, an index book might contain entries for a few or for many years.

gratuitous agent   An agent who acts without compensation, but who still owes full fiduciary responsibilities to his or her principal.

grave dancer   See *bottom feeder*.

greater fool theory   An investing theory that supports buying overvalued property in a hot market because a greater fool will come along and buy it from you at a profit. Like the game of musical chairs, the greater fool theory breaks down when one misjudges when the music will stop and there won't be enough fools (chairs) to go around.

greenbelt   An area of natural vegetation around a development, intended to provide a buffer and natural setting. It may be required by zoning or restrictive covenants or may be simply an aesthetic choice.

green space   A natural area in or around a development, intended to provide buffer, noise control, recreational use, and/or wildlife refuge, all in order to enhance the quality of life in and around the development.

GRI   See *Graduate REALTORS® Institute*.

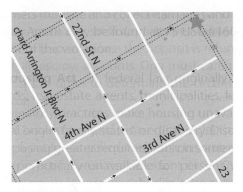
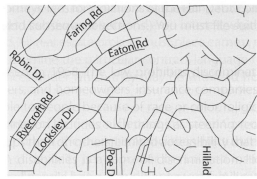

Gridiron system.　　　　　　　　　　Street hierarchy system.

gridiron　Used to describe the numbered rectangular street and avenue system once popular with urban planners. For example, 101 1st Avenue would be on 1st Avenue, between 1st Street and 2nd Street. Contrast with the *street hierarchy system* (above), which is a more disorganized street system consisting of neighborhoods with very limited entrances and exits, and streets with names rather than numbers.

grid system　See *gridiron*.

gross area　A term that must be defined with each use; sometimes it means the total heated and cooled floor area of a building, measuring from the exteriors of all walls and including all floors. Other times it is used to signify space measured from the inside of the exterior walls.

gross income　The total revenue of a business or individual before deduction for expenses, allowances, depreciation, or other adjustments.

gross income multiplier　A rule of thumb for evaluating the reasonableness of an asking price. One compares the monthly or annual gross income to the asking price and evaluates how that compares to typical ratios for similar properties. For example, some investors will not pay more than 100 times the monthly gross income for a property. If a house rents for $900 per month, the investor will pay $90,000 but no more. The method is not a good indication of value and would never be employed by an appraiser, but it has its uses as a preliminary qualifier or disqualifier of properties.

gross lease　A lease for a set amount of rent each month, with the landlord paying all expenses of the property and its management. It is the typical form of lease for residential properties. Contrast with a net lease in which the tenants reimburse the landlord for some or all of the expenses of ownership and management. (Net leases are common in commercial transactions.)

gross leasable area (GLA)　A total amount of floor space available for rental to tenants; typically encountered in the retail development industry, although it also applies to office space.

gross potential income   The total rent possible from a property if it were 100 percent leased at market rates (with no deductions for bad debt,) plus ancillary income such as from laundry machines and late fees. Contrast with *gross potential rental income*.

gross potential rental income   The total rent possible from a property if it were 100 percent leased at market rates (with no deductions for bad debt,) but does not include ancillary income like laundry machines or late fees.

gross rent multiplier   See *gross income multiplier*.

gross square footage   The total number of square feet of a building, measuring from the outside of the exterior walls and including all floors. The term is generally encountered in an institutional setting where the ratio of head count to gross square footage of buildings is important for determining capacity and the need to construct more buildings.

gross up   To artificially increase operating expenses in a project for accounting purposes in order to calculate each tenant's pro rata share of those expenses. Most commercial leases provide that actual operating expenses will be increased—grossed up—to what they would be if the project were 95 percent leased. That figure is then divided among the tenants according to their pro rata share of expenses, as determined by their pro rata share of leased space.

ground area   See *footprint*.

ground lease   A long-term lease of land in which the tenant will erect improvements at its own expense. Not a desirable arrangement from the tenant's point of view, but sometimes the only way to gain access to extremely valuable real estate in an excellent location. The owner may be unwilling to sell, or the owner may have received the property by gift or deed (such as a church or university) and be prohibited from selling for some period of time. At the end of the lease term, the improvements become the property of the landowner.

ground rent   The rent paid under a ground lease.

groundwater   Water below the earth's surface, saturating soil and rock at the level of the water table and below. It supplies approximately 35 percent of the drinking water in the country and, as such, is a source of much concern for the Environmental Protection Agency. If one purchases a property with contaminants, and those contaminants have leached into the groundwater, then remediation will usually be required before development can proceed.

group boycott   An illegal practice in which two or more real estate brokers or agents refuse to cooperate and split commissions with another one, usually a discount broker.

group home   A residence for a group of persons with similar special needs, such as developmentally challenged adults or abused women with small children.

growing equity mortgage (GEM)   A home loan arrangement in which the payments are increased each year by a specific amount, with the additional money credited to additional principal reduction. As a result, the loan is paid in full earlier than the normal amortization period. The FHA-insured GEM program is called a 245(a) loan.

grow your own buyer strategy　When seeking out occupants for a single-tenant building, searching for one that is likely to desire purchasing the building in 3 to 5 years.

GSE　See *government-sponsored enterprise*.

guarantee　The act itself, or also the document, whereby one agrees to pay a debt if the principal obligor does not. Under common law, creditors had to exhaust their remedies against a debtor before pursuing a guarantor. Today, almost all guarantee instruments contain clauses allowing the creditor to seek payment directly from the guarantor if there has been a default by the debtor. Guarantee agreements must be in writing to be enforceable. Usually, there must be some consideration passing to the guarantor unless the instrument creating the obligation (note, lease) is signed at the same time as the guarantee, in which case the law assumes the guarantor has some interest in the transaction.

guardian　A person who operates under court supervision and handles the affairs of a party—the ward—who is incapable of doing so. Wards may be minor children or those adjudged incompetent. Guardians may execute deeds on behalf of their wards. In some states, a guardian may not place a mortgage on property owned by the ward, nor may the guardian buy property subject to a mortgage.

guide meridians　Lines placed every 24 miles in the public land survey system in order to correct for the earth's curvature. Meridian lines are imaginary lines running north and south. They cannot be parallel because the earth curves as it approaches the poles. As a result, they cannot be a uniform 6 miles apart, as they should be. The guide meridians correct for this.

Gulf Opportunity Zone Act of 2005　See *GO-Zone*.

H

habendum clause   The part of a deed that begins with the words "to have and to hold" and that defines the quantity of estate granted, such as "to have and to hold for and during her natural life and thereafter to grantor." This example gives a life estate to the grantee and a remainder to the grantor.

habitable   Living quarters capable of being occupied without danger to health or safety and in a manner generally consistent with minimum living conditions for the community. Many states require landlords to provide habitable dwellings to tenants.

half section   See *public land survey system* for a full explanation.

> **Example:**   *A section of land is 1 square mile, being 5,280 feet on each side and containing 640 acres. A half section can be the north or south half, or it can be the east or west half, but it can't be an arbitrary 320 acres somewhere in the middle. A half section would have one side of 5,280 feet and the other side of 2,640 feet.*

2,640 ft	2,640 ft
1/2 section	1/2 section

5,280 ft

handicap   The Fair Housing Act prohibits discrimination on the basis of a handicap. A handicap has been defined as having the same meaning as disability. Persons with disabilities are persons with mental or physical impairments that substantially limit one or more major life activities. The term mental or physical impairment may include conditions such as blindness, hearing impairment, mobility impairment, HIV infection, mental retardation, alcoholism, drug addiction, chronic fatigue, learning disability, head injury, and mental illness. The term major life activity may include seeing, hearing, walking, breathing, performing manual tasks, caring for one's self, learning, speaking, or working. The Fair Housing Act also protects persons who have a record of such an impairment or are regarded as having such an impairment.

handyman's special   In real estate advertising, generally indicates a building with substantial deterioration and in need of extensive repairs beyond normal paint-up/fix-up aesthetic improvements.

harbor line   Also called the navigable line, it is an arbitrary line set by local authorities for the farthest extent wharves and other structures may intrude into the rivers and other waterways so as not to interfere with navigation.

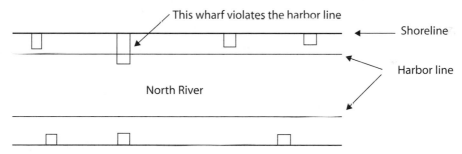

hard costs   See *direct costs*.

hazard insurance   A form of property insurance that protects against physical damage to property, such as by fire or tornado.

hazardous substance   Generally defined as a substance posing imminent and substantial danger to public health and welfare or the environment. The Superfund hazardous substances are specifically defined by inclusion lists within the following legislation:

- Comprehensive Environmental Response, Compensation and Liability Act (CERCLA)
- Clean Water Act
- Resources Conservation and Recovery Act
- Clean Air Act
- Toxic Substances Control Act

hearing   A legal proceeding conducted by an administrative agency in order to take testimony and arguments for or against a proposed action. Parties may have attorneys present but are not required to do so. Unlike the court system, most agencies permit corporations to appear through an officer or majority shareholder, without requiring an attorney.

heavy industry   A concept usually important in zoning regulations, where it will be defined for the particular purposes of those laws. In common parlance, heavy industry is usually understood as that requiring extensive capital investment in land and machinery and thus not easily relocated. This is contrasted with light industry, which is usually more labor intensive and relatively easy to move. Other times, the term "heavy industry" is intended to convey an image of severe environmental impact through normal operations.

hectare   A land measurement under the metric system, equal to 10,000 square meters, or roughly 2.471 acres.

height, building   Generally held to be the height from the street to the surface of a flat roof or the average height of a pitched roof, without taking into account roof structures, air handling equipment, antennas, or satellite dishes. The term is most often significant when attempting to meet zoning restrictions, which usually contain their own definitional sections. If so, then it is irrelevant what the general public considers as the true measurement of building height; the method of measurement specified in the statute will control.

heir   One who inherits property.

heirs and assigns   Because of peculiarities in old English common law, these words when used in a deed, "To Harry Smith, his heirs and assigns," indicate an intention to transfer the maximum possible estate in land.

hereditament   Any real or personal property that may be inherited. It would not include a life estate in oneself—meaning a right to land during one's own life but no longer—because that obviously can't be inherited. The word had more importance under older English law because of the ability to place a greater variety of restrictions on land than is possible today. It is often encountered in wills, leaving "all my lands, tenements and hereditaments to my daughter… ." As a practical matter, only the word "hereditament" is necessary because it includes the other two.

hiatus   A break or gap. In discussions of land, an area of land that lies between two parcels but appears from legal descriptions and public records to not be a part of either.

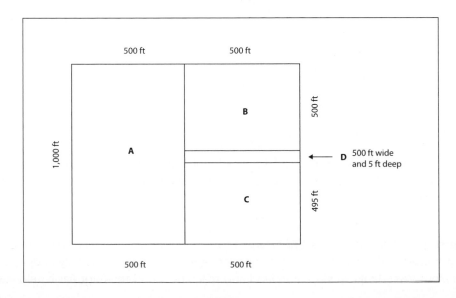

Example: *A parcel 1,000 feet by 1,000 feet has been divided. In writing the deeds, though, parcel C's description started at the southeast corner and proceeded northward only 495 feet rather than the full 500 feet necessary to meet the boundary with parcel B. The missing 5 feet is the hiatus. A court might hold that property C's grantor still owns the 5-foot parcel, or it might reform the deed, or it might find that the owner of parcel B adversely possessed the 5-foot parcel.*

hidden defect   (1) A title defect that is not obvious from examining the public records, such as a forgery. (2) A defect in property that is not observable by the untrained eye and must be disclosed by the seller or seller's agent if known.

hidden risk   See *hidden defect*.

highest and best use   In public appraisal and tax appraisal, that use of land which would be the most economically advantageous over a given period of time, while at the same time being legally, financially, and physically possible. A 5-acre residential estate within minutes of downtown Houston would have a highest and best use if it were developed for offices, and therefore should be appraised with that use in mind. Many property tax laws allow exemptions and appraisal at current use rather than highest and best use.

high-rise   A concept with no fixed definition except as contained within specific fire codes or building codes. In commercial real estate, it is generally understood by reference to what it is not. It is not a low-rise, which is a one- or two-story structure. It is not a midrise, which could be anything between three and six, perhaps eight stories high, depending on the community. A high-rise is anything taller than a midrise. The meaning of high-rise in Asheville, North Carolina, will be different than that in New York City or Chicago.

high-water mark   The line on shore marked by the reach of the medium tide and which usually determines the boundary between private property and public property. Some jurisdictions limit private property to the shoreline, which is the highest reach of the waves inward to the land.

historic cost   The cost of a structure when it was first built. Contrast with original cost, which is the price paid by the current owner.

historic district   A designation given by local government to particular parts of town deemed historically significant or containing a large concentration of older buildings considered worthy of preservation in an historically accurate condition. Properties located in historic districts are usually the subject of dramatically increased scrutiny by planning and zoning authorities. The approval of an historic board may be required before a building permit for repairs or renovations for these properties is issued. Many are also eligible for federal historic preservation credits.

historic preservation credits   A common name given to the IRS concept of rehabilitation tax credits, allowing tax credits equal to 10 percent of the cost of renovation, reconstruction, and restoration of buildings placed in service before 1936. A larger credit, 20 percent, is allowed for certified historic structures. There is a special increase for properties in the Gulf Opportunity Zone (named counties suffering hurricane damage in the 2005 hurricane season) with 13 percent allowed for pre–1936 buildings and 26 percent for certified historic structures. The properties do not need to have suffered any hurricane damage, as long as they are in the specifically named states and counties. See Form 3468, "Investment Credit," and the attached instructions, available at the IRS Web site, www.irs.gov.

holdback   Retainage; amounts withheld from payment until certain goals have been reached.

> **Example:**   *A lender holds back funding the balance of a loan until stabilized occupancy has been reached, or a homeowner holds back the final 10 percent of a construction contract price until after completion of all inspections.*

holder in due course   A party who acquires possession of an instrument (usually a check, promissory note, or installment sale contract) after giving value for it, in good faith, and without notice that there are any defenses; the holder in due course takes free of any claims. It was common at one time for health clubs, home improvement companies, vinyl siding installers, and many others to provide financing for their customers. The company would then sell the promissory notes to a holder in due course. When the consumer complained of high-pressure sales tactics, services inferior to those represented, or shoddy workmanship and refused to continue making payments, the holder in due course would sue and win a judgment because it was not subject to any defenses against the original party. State legislation has now exempted purchasers of consumer contracts from holder in due course status, so that defenses good against the original party are also good against the purchaser of the paper. There is still a very lively industry in buying consumer paper, but purchasers now include clauses making the purchase with recourse, meaning that if the consumer asserts any defenses, the original contracting party must buy the paper back and deal with the consumer directly.

hold-harmless clause   A contract provision that if one party is harmed, injured, subjected to claims, sued, or has a judgment against it, the other party to the contract will reimburse the first party for all such costs, expenses, and claims. It is a common clause in commercial leases, because the law imposes liability on both owners and occupiers of land for a wide variety of injuries caused by defects in or on the property. By the time an innocent landlord, tenant, or other party to a contract is able to obtain a dismissal of charges as to them, the bills for legal fees could amount to many tens of thousands of dollars. To control this situation, landlords usually require hold-harmless clauses from tenants. On the other hand, if the tenant has the superior bargaining position, the tenant will refuse to indemnify the landlord and, in addition, require the landlord to indemnify the tenant! Also called an indemnity clause.

holding company   A company that owns or controls another company.

holding costs   See *carrying charges.*

holding period   (1) A time period important in the law of adverse possession, with its own peculiar rules for calculation. See *adverse possession* for more information. (2) A period of time one owns property, important in tax law for determining tax rates and benefits and for disallowance of some benefits.

Examples:

- Property exchanged in a 1031 exchange by related parties has a 2-year holding period before it can be sold; otherwise there will be adverse tax consequences.
- Banks have a 21-day holding period before sending taxpayer bank deposits to the IRS pursuant to a garnishment.
- Property sold after a holding period of 1 year or less will result in short-term capital gains or losses.
- Property sold after a holding period of more than 1 year will result in long-term capital gains or losses.
- Property sold after a holding period of more than 5 years will result in super-long-term capital gains or losses.
- Property acquired by inheritance will be treated as if it were held for longer than 1 year.

holdout   A property owner who refuses to sell to a developer who is purchasing a number of separate parcels in order to put them together—an assemblage—for development. Sometimes the practice results in an offer vastly in excess of market price, because the holdout controls the success of the entire project. Other times, developers go back to the drawing board and redesign the project, leaving the holdout with no offer at all and what could turn into very unpleasant living conditions due to being surrounded by parking lots and 24-hour high-intensity lighting. Developers often avoid the problem by purchasing options rather than properties, so that if a critical property owner refuses to sell, the developer can abandon the entire project with a minimal expenditure.

holdover tenant   A tenant who remains in possession of leased premises beyond the expiration of a lease term. Most commercial leases, and many residential leases, provide that a holdover tenant will be responsible for rent in an amount 125 to 200 percent greater than current market rents, but accepting the rent does not sacrifice any of the landlord's rights to obtain an eviction. (State laws may place a cap on the amount of increased rent charged to consumers.)

hollday   A day set apart for commemorating an important event. The term is used often in contracts and leases when computing time, as when a certain number of days are allowed for an action, but if the due date falls on a weekend or holiday, it will be the next business day. Leases, in particular, limit delivery of certain services, such as heating and air conditioning, on weekends and holidays. The better practice is for the contract or lease to define the holidays meant by it. In the absence of such a definition, holidays will usually include federal holidays, when federal offices are closed, and may include state holidays when state offices are closed, if different.

holographic will   A will written by the testator's hand but bearing no witness signatures. Regular wills must be witnessed, and the testator and all witnesses must sign in the presence of each other; otherwise the will is void. The holographic will is an exception recognized by some states. Contrast with nuncupative will, which is an *oral* will made shortly before death before witnesses and later reduced to writing by them.

home cooking   A slang expression indicating the fear held by out-of-state or out-of-town defendants in a lawsuit that they will not receive a fair trial because of jury prejudice or because judges will not accord out-of-town lawyers the same credibility and leniency granted to local lawyers. This is the reason for most forum shopping clauses in contracts between local persons and large, usually nationwide, companies. The forum shopping clause requires any lawsuits to be brought in the other party's jurisdiction, thus presumably giving them the advantage of home cooking.

home equity conversion mortgage (HECM)   An FHA-insured reverse mortgage loan allowing persons to borrow money against the equity in their home with no repayment usually necessary until after death. The money may be taken in one lump sum, or in payments over time.

The important elements are

- The borrower and any other current owners of the home must be aged 62 or over and live in the home as their principal residence.
- The home must be a single-family residence in a one- to four-unit building, a condominium, or part of a planned unit development (PUD). Some manufactured housing is eligible, but cooperative apartments are not.
- The home must be at least 1 year old and must meet HUD minimum standards, except that the HECM can be used to make necessary repairs.
- Applicants must discuss the program with a HUD-approved counselor before making any decision.
- Repayment in full is due (1) when the last surviving borrower dies, (2) when the home is sold, (3) when the borrowers permanently move elsewhere or fail to live in the home for 12 months, or (4) if there is a default in mortgage terms, such as failing to pay property taxes or keep the property insured or allowing it to deteriorate below HUD minimum standards.

home equity line of credit (HELOC)   A revolving credit line secured by a mortgage on the borrower's residence. The borrower may draw down the loan—obtain funds—and then repay the principal later and restore the full borrowing ability for the maximum amount of the loan. The loan is often for amounts represented by the surplus above the first mortgage up to 125 percent of the appraised value of the home. These are high-risk loans because a foreclosure after default will not provide a sale price high enough to pay off the HELOC. As a result, the loans carry fairly high interest rates and, despite widespread advertising for 125 percent loans, only the most credit-worthy borrowers are able to secure the maximum loans. IRS rules allow the deduction of the interest on up to $100,000 of home equity line of credit debt.

home improvement loan   A loan to make improvements on one's principal or secondary residence; may be a home equity line of credit or a traditional loan in a fixed amount. Both are secured by a second mortgage on the property.

home inspection   Usually a professional, third-party inspection of a home prior to purchase in order to discover defects and report them to the purchaser.

home loan   See *mortgage*.

Home Mortgage Disclosure Act   A federal law requiring lenders with federally related loans to report the number of mortgage loan applications and the number of actual mortgage loans in different parts of their service areas. The Act is designed to shed light on discriminatory practices and thereby eliminate them. Reports are available on the Web site of the Federal Financial Institutions Examination Council, www.ffiec.gov/hmda.

home office   An area of one's residence used for office purposes. Home offices may be eligible for tax benefits—see *home office tax deduction*. Some states allow real estate brokers to maintain their principal office in their homes under certain circumstances.

home office tax deduction   The ability to deduct a portion of the cost and upkeep of a home because of the use of some space for business purposes. Generally,

- You must use some portion of the home regularly and exclusively as your principal place of business, or a place where you meet with clients, or
  - If using some structure separate from your home, you must merely use it in connection with your business.
  - If you are an employee, the use of a portion of your home for business must be for the convenience of your employer, not for your own convenience.
- The space must be used exclusively for business, but it does not have to be separated by walls or other partitions from other space.
- The deduction will be calculated using a percentage determined by comparing the space used for business purposes with the total space in the home. For example, a 150-square-foot room in a 3,000-square-foot house, or 150/3,000, will equate to 5 percent.
- Direct expenses used for work, materials, or repairs only in the business portion of the home are fully deductible; indirect expenses used for the entire home, such as utilities, cleaning, insurance, and real estate taxes can be deducted in a pro rata amount as determined from the percentage of space; unrelated expenses for nonbusiness parts of the home, such as painting other rooms, landscaping maintenance, or pool care are not deductible.
- Your use of home office business deductions cannot result in a business loss that will shelter other income.

For more information, see Publication 587, "Business Use of Your Home," available at the IRS Web site, www.irs.gov.

homeowners association   An organization of the homeowners in a subdivision or a group of related subdivisions. In order to have the ability to collect dues and enforce rules, the association must be created by a legal document that was drawn up and filed before the first lot or home is sold, or by a legal document signed by 100 percent of the property owners and then filed in the public records.

- The associations sometimes own common areas. They also enforce restrictive covenants for the subdivision, such as setback lines, prohibitions against parking motor homes in driveways, restrictions on home-based businesses, and even architectural and landscaping restrictions. Often, one cannot cut trees, paint a house, add a porch, or make any other changes without first submitting detailed plans to an architectural review committee.

- The associations generally collect monthly dues in an amount barely sufficient to pay for common area maintenance and an annual party. Maintenance could be as minor as buying new flowers for the entrance or as pervasive as maintaining private roads in a gated community; siltation control and dredging for a private lake; costs of a security system and/or guard; and the care and upkeep of swimming pools, tennis courts, and other recreational facilities. In the absence of a fund for attorneys' fees, or the ability to assess additional dues for attorneys' fees in order to take rule breakers to court, the result is that rules generally go unenforced except as may be possible through peer pressure.

- Most homeowners associations have the right to impose fines and to place liens on property and force a sale if the fines are not paid, but this route is rarely successful without long and expensive litigation. Usually, the liens remain in place until the property is eventually sold, and then they are collected, but this has little deterrent value when trying to stop current rule violations.

homeownership rate   The ratio of owner-occupied units to total residential units in a specified area.

> **Example:** *For an area with 20,000 units, 17,000 of them are owner-occupied and 3,000 are occupied with renters. This means that the ratio of owner-occupied units is 85 percent and the ratio of rentals is 15 percent.*

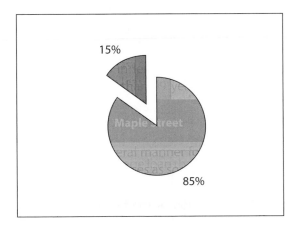

homeowner's insurance policy   An insurance policy tailored for most homeowners with a package of coverages and endorsements designed to address most risks. Usually includes coverage for the main structure, a certain percentage of that in additional coverage for outbuildings, a certain percentage of additional coverage for contents, reimbursement for rental expenses and cleanup costs in the event of significant loss, and liability coverage in case anyone else is injured on the property as a result of a condition or defect of the property.

Homeowners Protection Act of 1998 (HOPA)   Legislation passed in response to abuses in the private mortgage insurance (PMI) industry. Home purchasers who wish to borrow more than 80 percent of the purchase price of their property must usually purchase private mortgage insurance, which pays the lender in the event of default and a foreclosure. The purchaser pays the premiums through additional fees added to the monthly mortgage payment. Once the loan is paid to an amount less than 80 percent of the purchase price or the fair market value, there should be no need for the insurance. Despite this, PMI companies would continue to collect insurance premiums. The Act requires PMI companies to notify borrowers of their right to cancel the insurance when the loan is no more than 80 percent of the value of the home, and it requires them to automatically cancel the insurance when the loan is no more than 78 percent of the value of the home. The value is based on the purchase price or can be based on a recent appraisal if the borrower is willing to order and pay for an appraisal. There are exceptions to the cancellation rules, primarily when there has been a history of loan delinquencies. Also called PMI Cancellation Act.

homeowners' warranty program   An insurance program offered by a subsidiary of the National Association of Home Builders. If purchased, the policy provides the buyer of a new home with a 10-year warranty against named physical defects.

home rule   The power granted to local governments to pass ordinances regulating matters particularly local in nature. Some states have limited home rule, so matters that would seem to be local in nature must still be submitted to statewide referenda for approval and passage.

homestead   The dwelling house and adjoining land forming the permanent residence of the head of household. Under modern law, a person's homestead is given a very specific definition within each state's statutes and is then granted protections from creditors and against excessive real estate taxes. The term homestead may also apply to the rights granted to a widow or widower to use real property for their remaining lives if they elect to take advantage of homestead laws rather than provisions made in a will. The protections may be unlimited, only up to a certain dollar value of equity, or limited in area. Each state's laws are different, and homestead may be defined differently in the various statutes within a state.

homogenous   The same. The value of property in a homogenous neighborhood is relatively easy to determine because of ample evidence regarding recent sales of comparable sites.

HOPA   See *Homeowners Protection Act of 1998*.

Horizontal Property Acts   Name given by some jurisdictions to their statutes regulating the creation of condominiums.

hostile possession   See *adverse possession*.

hotel   A concept that seems relatively straightforward, as a place where people rent rooms for the night. Local business codes, tax laws, and zoning ordinances will all have their own definitions, however, contained within particular statutes. If in doubt regarding whether a particular use will be considered a hotel, one should refer to the appropriate laws.

house   In real estate jargon, generally indicates a detached dwelling on a parcel of its own land.

house fluffer   A decorator who recommends improvements and renovations designed to maximize a home's sale price.

house poor   Also called land poor; a situation in which all of one's wealth is in the home (or land) and there is very little cash or income to pay for anything other than necessities.

house rules   Everyday-conduct rules adopted by a condominium association to cover things such as hours of pool usage, number of allowable guest parking places, prohibitions against drying towels on balcony railings, and other such matters.

housing affordability index   Developed by the National Association of REALTORS® to track the financial ability of consumers to buy homes. Many state organizations publish similar indices for their local markets. The benchmark is 100, sometimes expressed as 1.0. It means that a family earning the median income has exactly enough money to qualify for a mortgage to buy a median-priced home in that market. It assumes a 20 percent down payment, and that mortgage payments will not exceed 25 percent of income. A figure less than 100, or less than 1.0, means that the median income family cannot afford the median house. A greater figure means the median income family can afford a home more expensive than the median home. When a trend line is declining, it indicates that housing is becoming less affordable. Upwardly trending numbers mean housing is becoming more affordable. National figures may be obtained by going to the National Association of REALTORS® Web site, www.realtor.org, and clicking on Research, then Housing Statistics, and then Housing Affordability Index.

housing code   A local ordinance that establishes minimum health and safety levels for existing housing. Contrast with building codes, which address new construction.

housing completions   A statistic tracked by the U.S. Census Bureau (www.census.gov) and by many local real estate and builder organizations. It indicates the number of new homes made ready for occupancy within a certain time period, usually one month and one year.

housing counseling agency   A nonprofit organization that provides advice and credit counseling to individuals wishing to purchase housing. Many low-income loan programs require completion of a housing counseling course as a condition of obtaining the loan.

housing finance agency   A state or local organization that provides housing assistance through low-interest mortgage loans to qualifying buyers, including loans to fund down payment and closing costs due after the application of traditional mortgage money.

housing for the elderly   Any project specifically designed for persons 55 years or older and marketed to that demographic group. Housing for the elderly is exempt from Fair Housing laws prohibiting discrimination against families.

housing permit   See *building permit*.

housing starts   A statistic tracked by the U.S. Census Bureau (www.census.gov) and by many local real estate and builder organizations; indicates the number of new homes on which construction has started within a certain time period, usually one month and one year.

housing stock   The total number of dwelling units in a defined area.

Howey rule   A rule of securities law articulated by the Supreme Court in the case of Howey v. Securities and Exchange Commission. The Howey company sold real estate interests in orange groves that it managed. As a practical matter, one could not buy the real estate and make any profit from it unless Howey handled all the details of cultivation, harvesting, and marketing. The SEC claimed Howey was selling "investment contracts" and therefore had to register with the SEC. The Supreme Court agreed.

The Howey rule, as it has come to be called, says that an investment contract is

1. A contract, transaction, or scheme whereby one person invests his or her money
2. in a common enterprise
3. led to expect profits solely from the efforts of a third party.

HUD   The United States Department of Housing and Urban Development. This federal cabinet-level department has a wide variety of responsibilities, including

- Enforcing fair housing laws
- Assisting community development through block grants, loan guarantees, and disaster recovery assistance
- Regulating Fannie Mae and Freddie Mac
- Supporting health care through providing mortgage insurance for hospitals, nursing homes, and assisted living facilities
- Aiding Native Americans with specialized housing programs
- Educating citizens about hazards such as lead paint
- Overseeing the Federal Manufactured Housing Program
- Providing public housing assistance
- Making available housing counseling
- Administering a number of mortgage insurance programs for multifamily housing
- Providing mortgage insurance for single-family houses
- Handling witness relocation for people who have testified about crimes in their public or assisted housing buildings

HUD-Code home   A manufactured home. The word "code" refers to the HUD regulation requiring all manufactured homes built after 1976 to meet the minimum requirements of the HUD Code, as contrasted with local building codes, which usually don't apply to manufactured housing.

HUD–1 form   *See closing statement.*

hundred percent commission   A real estate office arrangement in which the qualifying or managing broker keeps none of the real estate commission earned by the office, but instead pays 100 percent to the agent who secured the listing, the buyer, or the tenant. The broker makes his or her own money by competing against the agents, contrary to the typical practice in most other real estate offices. The broker also charges each agent a monthly fee to cover office space, advertising, and operating expenses and to provide a profit to the broker. This is in contrast to the more widespread practice in which commissions are paid to the broker, who is the only person legally authorized to enter into an agency agreement with another. The broker then splits the commission, paying some portion to the agent actually responsible for the work performed to earn the money.

hundred percent location   Refers to the best location with the highest land value.

HVAC   Heating, ventilation, and air conditioning.

hybrid mortgage   A mortgage that combines the benefits of an adjustable-rate mortgage and a fixed-rate mortgage, such as adjustable rates in the early years and then an automatic conversion to fixed rates after a stated period of time. For example, the 5/25 (adjustable for 5 years and fixed for 25) and the 7/23.

hypothecate   To give a security interest in specific real or personal property while retaining possession of the property. Contrast with a pawnshop, in which one surrenders possession of the security, or a loan against negotiable securities such as stocks and bonds, which could be sold by the borrower if the lender did not require possession in itself.

hypothetical condition   A condition that does not currently exist in fact but has some probability of existing in the future. An appraisal may determine the value of property in its current condition, and then also determine a value based on a hypothetical condition, such as a state's plans to build a new highway exit at the property.

I

idem sonans   Sounding the same, or alike. The rule of idem sonans is that absolute accuracy in spelling names is not required in a deed or other legal document, so long as the spellings sound the same and there is no intent to deceive. Without the rule, typographical errors in a deed would result in title not passing, creating a nightmare in writing title insurance and in litigation over competing claims.

>   **Example:**   *Jayne Smith is idem sonans with Jane Smith.*

illiquidity   (1) The condition of having insufficient cash to meet anticipated requirements, such as a business loan that is turned down because of the borrower's illiquidity, not because of problems with the borrower's credit rating or the value of the collateral. (2) The relative ease with which an asset can be converted to cash. The more difficult, the more illiquid the asset is.

impact fees   Fees imposed by local government on new construction projects in order to compensate the government for the increased costs of delivering services. Impact fees can sometimes be extremely high, having the result of chilling development.

implied agency   An agency relationship that arises out of the conduct of the parties and the impressions they give to the world, rather than because of a written or oral agreement. It is extremely rare to have an implied agency in real estate because of the rule that real estate contracts must be in writing, so agency relationships regarding real estate must also be in writing.

implied authority   A principal grants the agent implied authority when there is an implied agency. See *implied agency.*

implied condition   A provision not specifically spelled out in a contract, but considered an important underlying assumption of the parties. In most states, there is an implied condition in a new home sales contract that the home will be habitable and can be safely occupied in relative comfort with working hot and cold water with no leaks, a working sanitary sewer system, operational heating, and relative security from intruders.

implied contract   A contract that arises out of the actions of the parties rather than any express words or writings by them. For example, when one names a price for a service and another accepts that service without any comment about the price, there is an implied contract to pay the quoted price. Almost all real estate transactions must have a written contract, by law, to be enforceable. Only the major terms need be in writing, however—the parties, a description of the property, a description of the estate granted (forever, for life, lease for years, etc.), and the consideration. Minor terms may be determined by reference to the actions of the parties, and so can be the subject of an implied contract.

implied easement   An easement recognized by the law, although not expressly agreed upon by the parties or their predecessors in title. This situation usually arises when the owner of a parcel of land sells a portion to someone else. At the time of the sale, there might have been common roads, irrigation, or other uses. After the sale, courts will sometimes recognize an implied easement allowing all owners of the sold parcel to continue to enjoy those uses that technically belong to the other parcel, such as a right-of-way easement or an easement to use water from a lake or stream. This should not be confused with an easement of necessity, which generally requires that there be no other method of ingress or egress, for example. The better practice is to identify such matters ahead of time and include them in the purchase agreement and deed. Unfortunately, these issues usually arise long after the amicable relationship between the original seller and purchaser has deteriorated or the land has changed ownership and conflict results.

implied listing   A listing agreement for the sale of property that arises out of the conduct of the parties, rather than any express written or oral contract between them. If there were an implied listing, then the listing broker would be entitled to the normal and customary commission available in the marketplace. As a practical matter, most states require listing agreements to be in writing to be enforceable and many states subject brokers to disciplinary action for entering into unwritten listing agreements.

implied notice   A situation in which the law considers someone as having notice of a particular fact because they knew of sufficient other facts such as would cause a reasonable person to make inquiries and then gain additional knowledge.

> **Example:** *Zack finds a house he wants to buy. The owners live out of town, but every time Zack visits the house to review and inspect it, he sees evidence that someone is living in the house. Despite that, he signs a contract to buy the house, goes through with the closing, and is surprised when the current tenants tell him they have a 5-year lease on the property. Zack had implied notice of this fact. When he saw evidence of occupancy, he should have asked more questions and is not entitled to simply sit in ignorance and hope everything works out for the best.*

implied warranty of habitability   (1) A legal doctrine that imposes on a landlord the obligation to make leased premises ready for occupancy in a safe, healthy, and nonhazardous condition and with the minimal amenities necessary for the provision of heat and water, although not including the utilities themselves. Many states have passed uniform landlord tenant laws, changing the implied warranty into an expressly articulated and defined legal obligation of the landlord. (2) State law may also imply similar warranties for new home builders.

impound account   See *escrow account*.

improved land   Land that has some improvement from its natural state, such as grading, added structures, planted timber, or crops.

improvements   Valuable additions to land intended to increase its value.

imputed interest   A common term for the IRS expression "unstated interest" or sometimes "original issue discount." It applies to the situation in which a promissory note calls for no interest or insufficient interest under the circumstances. In an audit, the IRS will calculate an interest rate, impute that to the transaction, and declare each year's imputed interest as additional income to the lender, on which the lender must pay income taxes, penalties, and interest. (The rules are found at 26 U.S.C. §1273, 1274 and 483.)

imputed notice   The concept that notice to one person will be considered notice to another in a special relationship to the first person. For example, notice to an attorney is the same as notice to the attorney's client. In circumstances allowing oral contracts (usually not the case with real estate), if a seller makes an offer and a buyer accepts that offer via a communication to the seller's agent, then the acceptance makes a binding contract as of that moment. The seller cannot withdraw the offer before actually learning of the acceptance, because the contract has already been formed when the agent received the notice.

inactive license   A mechanism under some state real estate licensing laws for a real estate agent to withdraw his or her name from licensing under any broker and hold the license in an inactive status until the agent is ready to return to active practice with the same, or another, broker. While on inactive status, the agent may not engage in activities requiring a real estate license and may not accept compensation for buying, selling, or referring buyers or sellers. Normally the inactive licensee is able to pay a smaller licensing fee and is relieved of some or all continuing education requirements during the inactive status.

inchoate   Incomplete, impartial, not completed. Inchoate property rights include mechanics' and materialmen's liens, which come into possibility when work is commenced on a property but might never ripen into actual existence if all bills are paid for the work.

inclusionary zoning   Zoning that requires inclusion of low- or moderate-income housing in new residential developments.

income   (1) For IRS purposes, income is never precisely defined, but it apparently includes all moneys received from any sources unless specifically excluded by some IRS Code provision. (2) In business, all the revenues derived from the business, less all expenses. Many people use the word income interchangeably with revenues, but revenue implies a gross figure without deductions, and income implies an amount after expenses.

income and expense report   See *financial statement*.

income approach   A method of valuing real property by determining the net operating income over the useful life of the property and then translating that number to the present value via a discount rate. The present-value concept depends on the assumption that $1 today is worth more than 10 cents a year for the next 10 years, because of the purchasing power of the $1 to buy other investments that will yield a return over the next 10 years, and because of the effects of inflation, which decreases the amount of goods or services $1 will buy over the years. In order to compensate for these considerations, one would say that the value of 10 cents a year for the next 10 years is worth less than $1 today. How much less is the art and science of discounting.

income averaging   A tax tool formerly given to all taxpayers and now available for just a few classes, such as farmers and fishermen. It allows taxpayers to average their income over 3 years and pay taxes on the average income, rather than no taxes one year and then high taxes at a high bracket in the next year, for example. (Calculated on Schedule J of IRS Form 1040.)

income capitalization approach   See *income approach*.

income limits   The maximum amount a family can earn and still be eligible for certain government housing assistance programs.

income-producing property   Whether or not it actually produces a profit, a property that is intended to generate rental or other revenues for the owner.

income property   Property purchased for the income it generates, such as rents.

income statement   See *financial statement*.

income stream   A steady flow of money from a property. When evaluating the property, one has to evaluate the strength and durability of the income stream.

> **Example:** *Is the tenant a national tenant with good financial strength, excellent prospects for continued health, and a 20-year lease on the property with rent adjustments annually to reflect cost-of-living increases, or is the tenant a start-up business with a 1-year lease in an area already saturated with similar businesses? Those two income streams are markedly different from each other.*

income tax   A tax on income. A simple concept, but one that requires thousands of pages of IRS statutes, regulations, revenue rulings, and court interpretations to explain. See the IRS Web site at www.irs.gov.

incompetent   Legally not able to make decisions, enter into contracts, or execute wills. This may be a result of a permanent mental impairment, as when one is declared non compos mentis or incompetent, or it may be for temporary reasons, such as a minor child's inability to make binding contracts.

incorporate   To form a corporation by filing documents in the appropriate state authority, which may be one's own state or a corporation-friendly state such as Delaware. Once having formed the corporation, one must pay annual franchise taxes to the state for the privilege of existing as an artificial entity, and one must observe all the forms and conventions of corporate existence. In other words, the sole shareholder cannot form a corporation and then never have meetings, never sign documents in the corporate name, take all corporate money for personal use without accounting for it on the books and records of the corporation, and generally behave as if the corporation did not exist. If the shareholder(s) behave as if the corporation does not exist, then creditors may be able to *pierce the corporate veil* and seize assets of the individual shareholders.

incorporation by reference   A method of including all the terms of one document into another document without having to spell everything out. Deeds will frequently make reference to restrictive covenants on file in the real estate records at a certain book and page number and incorporate them by reference into the deed itself. In that manner, any purchaser of the land is bound by the restrictive covenants, without getting into arguments about whether or not they had constructive notice because of the public filing. A renewal lease may be a one- or two-page instrument incorporating the original lease by reference, with the exception of changes to the rental rate and the term.

incorporeal rights   Property rights that are inheritable but not tangible or visible, such as easements, licenses, mining claims, and franchises.

increment   A portion, as of property or time. Developers build subdivisions in phases or increments, completing one section in order to gauge market demand before starting another section. Lawyers bill in minimum increments of 6, 10, 15, or 30 minutes depending on the particular lawyer and local custom, so a 3-minute phone call might be billed as any of these time increments.

incubator space   Office, industrial, or high-tech space usually owned or managed by a local government development board and intended to provide an economical and supportive environment for new business start-ups. The rental rates are usually below market, there is some sharing of services and amenities, and mentoring services are provided. The new business is usually kicked out of the nest after it reaches a certain volume of business or after it achieves a previously approved and agreed upon business plan.

incumbrance   Same as encumbrance. See *encumber*.

incurable obsolescence   See *functional obsolescence*.

Indemnification   The process of shifting a loss from one party to another either because of an express agreement by the parties or because the law requires it under the circumstances.

> **Example:**   *A purchaser of real estate discovers the property is subject to a lien that was placed against it prior to sale and pays the lien in order to avoid foreclosure; then the purchaser is entitled to indemnification, or reimbursement, from the prior owner who breached the warranties in the deed.*

indemnity clause   See *hold-harmless clause*.

indenture deed   A deed in which the buyer and seller bind themselves to certain obligations, such as an agreement that any liability for environmental cleanup expenses will be paid by the buyer and not the seller. Under ordinary circumstances, only the seller need sign a deed, because only the seller has any obligations regarding transferring good title. Leases are often called indentures, because they are a conveyance of an interest in real estate with both parties having continuing obligations.

The name indenture deed comes from ancient times, when such deeds were torn in half in an indented or jagged manner and could be proved by matching the two pieces.

independent appraisal   An appraisal conducted by a disinterested person.

independent contractor   One who is hired to reach a certain goal or perform a certain task, but who has the ability and the right to determine the methods and times for reaching that goal or task, so long as it is not illegal and is within the limits of the contract. This is an important concept because

1. Employers must take withholding taxes and pay matching taxes for employees but not independent contractors. The IRS has significantly tightened the definition of independent contractor so that most work relationships do not qualify. Under certain circumstances, real estate agents have been held to be employees for tax purposes.
2. If an independent contractor is negligent or commits an intentional tort, then the person who hired the contractor is not generally liable for the resulting damage. If an employee did the same thing, the employer would be liable so long as the employee was acting within the line and scope of his or her employment, which is usually a fairly easy hurdle for plaintiffs' lawyers to overcome.
3. An exception exists for the general rule of nonliability for the actions of an independent contractor, and that is in the area of real estate brokerage. Most real estate agents are independent contractors working for the broker. Real estate licensing laws, however, usually hold the broker responsible for the actions of agents.

index   (1) A statistical indicator that measures changes in the economy in general or in particular areas. An example is the cost-of-living index. (2) A reference point against which measurements are taken for purposes of making future adjustments. An adjustable-rate mortgage might begin with an interest rate of 6 percent and provide that it will increase or decrease in a like percentage as the increase or decrease between today's quoted price for 10-year U.S. Treasury bonds and the price on the loan's annual anniversary date. We would say that 10-year T-bonds are the index.

Some leading loan indices include

- Wall Street Journal prime
- Federal discount rate
- Fed funds rate
- 11th District Cost of Funds
- 10-year Treasuries
- One-year LIBOR

index lease   A lease that makes some or all of the rent dependent upon calculations with reference to some index, such as the cost-of-living index or the whole price index.

index loan   See *adjustable-rate mortgage.*

index rate   See *index.*

indicated value   The bottom line in an appraisal; the appraiser's opinion of the current value of real property after reconciliation of all methods and approaches to appraising the property.

indirect costs   Costs of construction not directly related to the sticks and bricks. Examples include

- Real estate taxes
- Administrative costs
- Professional fees
- Insurance
- Lease-up expenses

individual retirement account (IRA)   A retirement savings program entitling the individual to deduct contributions from gross income for purposes of calculating income taxes. The contributions are said to be from before-tax dollars.

Generally speaking, first-time home buyers can withdraw up to $10,000 from their IRA or Roth-IRA accounts, penalty free, in order to pay qualified home purchase expenses such as a down payment. Spouses can withdraw up to $20,000. There's a lifetime limit, though. Once you use up your distribution "free passes," you can't put the money back in your account and then use it again in the future. (For more information, see Tax Topic 428, "Roth IRA Distributions," and Publication 590, "Individual Retirement Accounts," available at the IRS Web site, www.irs.gov.)

indorsement   See *endorsement.*

industrial broker   One who specializes in industrial properties, also commonly called distribution properties.

industrial park   An area zoned for industrial use. Often developed by local industrial development boards in order to provide low-cost real estate with shared rail lines or other amenities to attract employers to an area.

industrial property   (1) Property designed for or used by companies or persons for manufacturing, warehousing, or assemblage of components. (2) In zoning, environmental, and building codes, the term "industrial property" will be defined within the statutes or codes for the specific purposes of those laws. The phrase may include uses not typically considered industrial and may exclude uses normally considered industrial.

in-fill development   Property development within the boundaries of an area rather than moving outward and contributing to sprawl. The concept carries with it connotations of demolition of older buildings in order to make way for new construction, usually with a greater height and/or increased densities, rather than simply finally getting around to developing vacant land. In-fill development generally takes place in older neighborhoods outside the central business district but inside the ring of modern suburbs.

inflation   A loss in the purchasing power of money. Inflation is generally measured by the consumer price index.

inflation guard   An insurance policy endorsement that automatically increases coverage over time in order to keep up with the effects of inflation.

information reporting   Reports provided to the IRS but which do not carry with them any liability for income taxes from the reporting entity. Partnerships and subchapter S-corporations must file information returns, closing agents must report real property purchase price information regarding the seller (Form 1098), and real estate brokers must report earnings of their agents (Form 1099).

☐ CORRECTED (if checked)

RECIPIENT'S/LENDER'S name, address, and telephone number	* **Caution:** The amount shown may not be fully deductible by you. Limits based on the loan amount and the cost and value of the secured property may apply. Also, you may only deduct interest to the extent it was incurred by you, actually paid by you, and not reimbursed by another person.	OMB No. 1545-0901 **2006** Form **1098**	**Mortgage Interest Statement**
RECIPIENT'S federal identification no.	PAYER'S social security number	1 Mortgage interest received from payer(s)/borrower(s)* $	**Copy B For Payer** The information in boxes 1, 2, and 3 is important tax information and is being furnished to the Internal Revenue Service. If you are required to file a return, a negligence penalty or other sanction may be imposed on you if the IRS determines that an underpayment of tax results because you overstated a deduction for this mortgage interest or for these points or because you did not report this refund of interest on your return.
PAYER'S/BORROWER'S name		2 Points paid on purchase of principal residence $	
Street address (including apt. no.)		3 Refund of overpaid interest $	
City, state, and ZIP code		4	
Account number (see instructions)			

Form **1098**   (keep for your records)   Department of the Treasury - Internal Revenue Service

informed consent   Consent given after being provided with fair and full disclosure of all the facts necessary to make an intelligent decision after weighing the relative pros and cons of the situation and the possibility of realistic alternatives. Real estate agents may sometimes represent both buyers and sellers in the same transaction if all parties agree after informed consent.

infrastructure   The basic amenities and services that must be in place for a particular activity or pursuit. The infrastructure in a subdivision would consist of roads; storm sewers; and mechanisms for the transmission of water, waste products, electricity, telecommunications, and possibly natural gas. References to the infrastructure of a community might also include basic services, such as fire and police protection, schools, and libraries.

ingress   A way of entry.

in gross   See *appurtenance.*

inheritance tax   See *estate tax.*

in-house sale   One in which the listing broker also brought the buyer to the closing table. There is no other broker involved, and no one is entitled to a share of the commission except as the broker and the agent working for the broker may have agreed to between themselves.

initial interest rate   In an adjustable-rate mortgage, the first interest rate charged.

injunction   A court order requiring a party to do something, or to stop doing something, until further notice. If the party fails to perform according to the injunction, then the party will be required to appear in court, defend his or her actions, and show cause why he or she should not be held in contempt of court. If held in contempt, the party may be ordered to pay a fine, may be jailed until the contempt is cured, or could suffer both consequences.

Injunctions come in three varieties:

1. Temporary restraining order (TRO). Usually obtainable with little or no notice to the defendant, sometimes as quickly as within an hour or so if the complaining party can convince a judge that there is immediate risk of irreparable harm if the restraining order is not issued.
2. Preliminary injunction. Usually issued after a TRO, if the judge decides that an injunction should remain in effect until such time as there can be a full trial on the merits of the case. Failure to obtain a TRO does not mean a judge will not issue a preliminary injunction; it simply means the judge did not agree with the plaintiff's evaluation of the necessity for urgent action.
3. Final injunction. The final order issued by a court after it has heard all the evidence and legal arguments for and against the injunction. The order is a final order, from which the parties may appeal.

inner city   Technically refers to the densely populated area just outside the central business district, but usually connotes a blighted area near the city center.

innocent misrepresentation   See *fraud*.

innocent purchaser for value   See *bona fide purchaser*. The words "for value" are sometimes added to bona fide purchaser, also, in order to emphasize the requirement for valuable consideration as opposed to mere "good consideration," which might consist of love and affection.

in perpetuity   Forever.

inquiry notice   That legal notice presumed to exist when a person is in command of sufficient facts as would cause a reasonable person to make further inquiries.

> **Example:**   *If one buys real property and knows that it is occupied by someone other than the seller, then the buyer has an obligation to make inquiries to find out the character of the rights of the occupant, whether the occupant has a long-term lease, no lease at all, or is claiming title to the property as his or her own. But, having failed to make any inquiry, the purchaser cannot make a claim against the seller if the occupant claims rights in the property.*

in rem   Meaning "against the thing." Lawsuits regarding title to real estate, or claims against real estate, are said to be in rem, so they must be filed in the state and county where the property is located.

inside lot   Any subdivision lot except the corner lots.

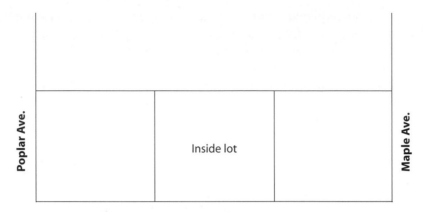

Elm Street

in situ   In place, on-site, such as EPA provisions for remediation in situ of contaminants rather than a requirement the contaminated soil be excavated and disposed of in an approved facility. To illustrate, the following is a diagram showing the process of chemical oxidation as an in situ solution to contamination.

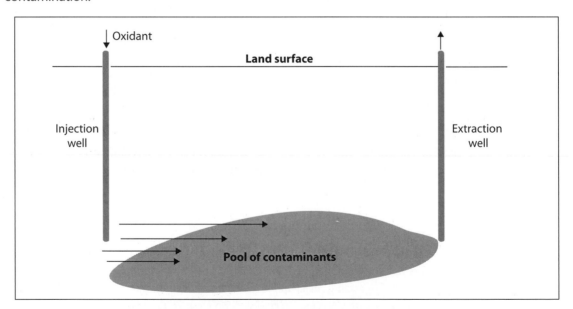

Source: EPA.

insolvent   The condition that exists when (1) one's liabilities are greater than assets, so that a complete liquidation even at fair market value would not pay all debts, or (2) one's current income is not sufficient to pay current bills, resulting in the need to contribute more cash to the organization or default on some payments.

installment contract   A contract providing for payment of the purchase price to the seller over time. Installment contracts are given favorable treatment by the IRS (www.irs.gov), which allows the seller to declare gain only as the seller receives principal payments each year, rather than requiring the seller to immediately take into income the entire gross amount of the purchase price. Interest is counted as income in the year paid.

installment note   A promissory note requiring payments over some period of time. Contrast with a single-pay loan, in which all principal and interest are due at maturity.

installment sale   See *installment contract*.

Institute of Real Estate Management (IREM)   An affiliate of the National Association of REALTORS®, this association (www.irem.org) is devoted to the needs of multifamily and commercial property managers.

institutional investor   A large corporate investor in real estate and real estate securities, such as a pension fund, university, or insurance company.

institutional lender   A federal- or state-regulated entity that loans money.

institutional lender financing   Loan funds provided by a federal- or state-regulated entity that loans money as one of its core business activities. Contrast with seller financing, and with private investors who loan money for particular projects.

institutional property   A zoning category authorizing schools, hospitals, and nursing homes.

instrument   A written legal document.

insulation disclosure   Also called the R-value rule, a Federal Trade Commission (FTC) requirement that persons selling new houses must disclose in their sales contracts the type, thickness, and R-value of the insulation installed in the house. Failure to make the required disclosure constitutes a deceptive trade practice and subjects the party to fines by the FTC.

insurable interest   A right or interest in property or in the life of another that would cause the person to suffer a monetary loss if injury came to the property or to the other person. One must have an insurable interest in order to buy insurance, because the insurance is intended to compensate one for a loss.

insurable title   A real estate title that can be insured by a title insurance company.

insurance   A commercial contract agreeing to compensate one for loss in the event of specifically named or described risks.

insurance binder   Evidence of property insurance coverage. Some insurance agents will bind coverage before receipt of payment for the premium. Lenders usually require proof that the premium has been paid for one year.

intangible property   Something that is nonphysical, noncurrent, and exists only in connection with something else. Business goodwill is intangible property—it does not exist by itself; it cannot be seen, touched, smelled, or heard; and it cannot be sold separately from something else, because even the goodwill built up in a particular business name cannot be sold separately from the name. Intangible property is usually exempt from property taxes.

intelligent building   A building equipped with the telecommunications infrastructure to easily and economically adapt to changing conditions through the use of automated control systems for heating, air conditioning, ventilation, lighting, power, and a variety of health, safety, and security conditions. Contrast with *smart home*, which usually refers to home automation systems that can be controlled by a centralized panel or device, or by dialing in to the control panel from outside the home.

intentional fraud   A misrepresentation of a material fact which is intended to deceive another, does actually deceive another, and which causes harm to the one deceived. The law allows punitive damages. See also *fraud*.

interest   Sums paid or earned for the use of money.

interest deductions   The IRS allows various interest payments on loans secured by real property to be deducted: Some of these deductions are as follows:

- For business loans, 100 percent of the interest paid each year is a deductible expense.
- For homeowners, the interest on up to $1,000,000 of combined primary and secondary residence home mortgage debt can be deducted.
- Home equity line of credit interest is deductible up to the interest attributable to $100,000 of debt.
- Interest on loans to buy stock in a cooperative building are deductible within the same limits as home interest.
- Co-op apartment owners may deduct their pro rata share of mortgage interest on underlying debt on the building.

For more information see Publication 936, "Home Mortgage Interest Deduction," at the IRS Web site, www.irs.gov.

interest in property   The extent of ownership in property.

interest-only loan   A loan on which one pays periodic interest payments without any reduction in principal, and the entire principal balance is due and payable upon maturity of the note.

interest-only securities (IOs)   Instruments created from collateralized mortgage obligations from which the monthly interest payments have been stripped out and converted into securities.

interest rate   The cost of borrowing money, expressed as a percentage per year of the money borrowed.

interest rate cap   In an adjustable-rate mortgage, a ceiling on the amount the interest rate may increase during any described period, such as one year, or over the lifetime of the loan.

interim financing   A short-term loan arranged in order to buy time until something changes. At the end of the original construction loan period, a developer may wish to seek interim financing rather than permanent financing because of an expectation that interest rates will fall in the future, or because the developer's plans have changed and the property will be sold rather than retained. The problem with permanent financing and many development projects is the existence of very large prepayment penalties—one cannot simply refinance when interest rates go down or simply pay off the loan when there is a sale. A borrower may also seek interim financing because the borrower's financial strength, or that of income-producing property serving as collateral, is not currently sufficient to justify attractive financing terms.

interim use   A use for property until it can be put to its highest and best use. Land that is not quite ready for development because of insufficient population densities may be used as a sales lot for manufactured housing, for example. An empty freestanding department or discount store might be used as a flea market.

interlocutory decree   A court order that is provisional, temporary, or not final. Interlocutory decrees are usually not appealable unless one obtains permission from the court.

intermediate theory state   See *hybrid theory state.*

intermediation   The normal flow of money into financial institutions in the form of deposits, which are then loaned out to earn income. Contrast with disintermediation, which occurs when depositors take their money out of financial institutions because they can earn more money, relatively risk free, in other investments.

internal rate of return   The annual rate of earnings on an investment equates the value of cash returns with the cash invested, taking into consideration the power of compounding interest. The following formula requires a trial-and-error method for solution. The fallacy with the method is its assumption that all cash flows are reinvested at the internal rate of return.

$$0 = C F_0 + \frac{C F_1}{(1+r)^1} + \frac{C F_2}{(1+r)^2} + \frac{C F_3}{(1+r)^3} + \frac{C F_n}{(1+r)^n}$$

Using this formula, CF is the cash flow in each period, with one subpart of the formula for each investment year until you reach *n*, the final year of the investment. You have to solve for R, the annual rate, by trial and error.

Internal Revenue Service (IRS)   A bureau within the United States Department of the Treasury, the IRS is charged with the responsibility of collecting the taxes imposed by Congress. In furtherance of that responsibility, it provides a wealth of resources to assist law-abiding persons in understanding and complying with the complicated tax laws of the country. An excellent search engine at the IRS

Web site, www.irs.gov, gives access to thousands of online publications, forms, instructions, and even internal IRS manuals.

International Code Council   A membership association (www.iccsafe.org) that develops the codes used in the construction of residential and commercial buildings.

International Council of Shopping Centers   A global trade association (www.icsc.org) of the shopping center industry.

International Facility Management Association   A global association (www.ifma.org) for facilities management. The organization defines facilities management as "a profession that encompasses multiple disciplines to ensure functionality of the built environment by integrating people, place, process and technology."

interpleader   A legal proceeding in which one holding money and making no claim to it, but unsure as to which of several claimants should receive the money, pays the money into court. This is the normal route taken by an escrow agent or someone else holding earnest money when the buyer and seller both demand the earnest money. The escrow company will name both the buyer and seller as defendants; ask that it be reimbursed out of the money for its costs, usually a small attorney's fee and a court filing fee; and that it be allowed to exit from the fight. The buyer and seller then battle over the funds.

interrogatories   A set of written questions by one party in a lawsuit to another party in the lawsuit, which must be answered under oath.

interstate   A concept with many different interpretations depending on which federal law is being considered. Usually relevant in determining if an activity has a sufficient connection to interstate commerce, and thus the Commerce Clause of the Constitution, to warrant federal intrusion or oversight of the activity. Article I, Section 8, Clause 3 of the United States Constitution is known as the Commerce Clause and empowers the United States Congress "To regulate Commerce with foreign Nations, and among the several States, and with the Indian Tribes." Representative areas of federal power may include

- Matters *in* interstate commerce
- Matters *affecting* interstate commerce
- Agencies and instrumentalities of interstate commerce
- Local laws that discriminate against interstate commerce
- Crimes that interfere with or obstruct interstate commerce

Interstate Land Sales Full Disclosure Act   A federal law passed in response to abuses in the sale and development of large subdivision projects. Developers often took large deposits or even sold lots and then did not begin development for many years. The law requires registration of the subdivision with the federal government and mandates certain disclosures and rescission (contract cancellation) periods to consumers. Subdivisions of less than various size limits or those that will be completed within specified time limits are exempt, as are subdivisions in states certified as having substantially similar laws.

interval ownership   Also called time-share ownership, in which a person shares ownership of property but is entitled to exclusive possession only for a particular time period each year.

inter vivos branch   A theory that is applied to transactions entered into during one's lifetime. Some legal principles have differing rules depending on whether property was disposed of during the owner's lifetime or by provisions in the owner's will. The rule that applies for lifetime transactions is called the inter vivos branch of the rule.

inter vivos trust   A trust established during the granting party's lifetime, rather than by virtue of the party's will.

intestate   Without a will. All states have laws specifying the rules of intestate succession, or who will receive property, and in what shares, when someone dies without a will. If there is no one to inherit, then the property escheats to the state.

intestate succession   The order of distribution of property when one dies without a will.

intrinsic value   An appraisal term meaning an intangible value based on a property's proximity to certain features and amenities, such as good schools, health care, and shopping.

inventory   (1) The total listings controlled by a real estate broker. (2) The total property for sale or lease in a defined area. (3) Property held for sale in the ordinary course of business or to be used in the manufacture of goods held for sale. (4) An itemized listing of personal property.

inverse condemnation   A lawsuit brought against a government agency because of some action claimed to have damaged property to such a degree as to amount to a condemnation, even though there was no official exercise of the right of eminent domain and no compensation offered or paid to the property owner. This situation often comes up when governments increase the level or degree of regulation of property in such a manner as to make it economically incapable of development and thus worthless to the owner.

investment analysis   A study of the potential return on a real estate investment to the owner, without reference to a potential sales price but strictly limited to the earnings and investment returns on the property. There are several different methods of analysis, some of which might be appropriate for particular properties and others not, or some of which are easier to use and favored by investors. The most common methods include

- Cash-on-cash return
- Payback period
- Internal rate of return

investment contract   "Any contract, transaction or scheme whereby a person invests money in a common enterprise and is led to expect profits solely from the efforts of the promoter or third party," is the definition used by the Securities and Exchange Commission (SEC). Investment contracts related to real estate come within the definition. Nationwide litigation is currently under way to say that purchases of units in hotel condominiums—condotels—are also investment contracts. If something qualifies, it is possibly subject to registration, reporting, and disclosure requirements imposed by the SEC.

investment-grade property   A term used to describe property felt to be of sufficient size and quality to be an attractive purchase target by one of the large institutional portfolios, such as retirement funds or insurance companies.

investment interest   An IRS phrase meaning the interest incurred on debt for an income-producing property. Investment interest is deductible only to the extent of investment income; you can't use investment interest to shelter other income. Unused investment interest may be carried over to subsequent years.

investment life cycle   The time period from acquisition of an investment to its final disposition.

investment property   Property held for the production of income or for an increase in value, as opposed to property held as a personal residence, use in a business, used for pleasure, or held in inventory.

investment value   The value of property to a particular investor, aside from the property's general market value. Often encountered when a person sells appreciated real estate and must identify another property to purchase within 45 days in order to take advantage of the 1031 tax exchange vehicle for deferring taxes. Because of the short time limits, that investor is willing to pay a higher price than someone else, because the investor must buy something in order to avoid paying income taxes on the earlier sale.

investor   One who uses his or her money to purchase property in the expectation of earning periodic cash flows from the property, making a profit on the eventual resale of the property, or both.

involuntary alienation   Loss of property for nonpayment of debts, such as foreclosure, tax sale, or execution on a judgment.

involuntary conversion   An IRS term meaning the involuntary loss of property through destruction or condemnation. The event can be a tax loss or a tax gain, depending on any proceeds received as a result of the involuntary conversion. If there is a gain, the taxes can be deferred. See *condemnation*.

involuntary lien   A lien on real estate that results without the property owners' voluntary cooperation in the placement of the lien. Examples include tax liens and judgment liens. Contrast with a mortgage, which is voluntary.

ironclad agreement   A mythical contract that can't be broken—like the Loch Ness Monster, often reported but never confirmed. As a practical matter, there is no agreement that can't be broken if the parties have sufficient resources, well-qualified legal talent, and plenty of time.

irrevocable Not capable of being revoked. An offer to sell at a certain price can be revoked at any time before acceptance. An irrevocable offer to sell cannot be revoked, but it should always have an expiration date.

ISO 14000 Refers to a series of voluntary standards for implementation and auditing of environmental controls previously agreed upon by a community or required by statute. The term is internationally recognized. In the United States, the Environmental Protection Agency (EPA) refers to the standards as Voluntary Environmental Management Systems/ISO 14001.

J

jeopardy (1) Danger, hazard, peril. Mortgaged property is said to be in jeopardy because it might be taken by foreclosure. (2) Subjected to the possibility of criminal punishment, including fines. The constitutional protection against double jeopardy has been held to apply to fines, such as might be levied against a company for violation of housing discrimination laws.

joint and several liability Having full liability for the whole of a debt or injury. Comakers on promissory notes have joint and several liability, so that the lender may collect the entire amount due from only one borrower and is not limited to collecting one-half from each borrower. The following usually have joint and several liability unless required otherwise by a specific state law or contractual agreement:

- Partners in a general partnership
- Taxes owed by husbands and wives who file joint returns
- Multiple persons who commit one wrong and injure another
- Tenants under one lease, such as roommates
- Cosigners on promissory notes
- Cosigners on guarantee agreements

joint ownership Ownership of property by two or more people or entities. It includes tenants in common, joint tenants with right of survivorship, tenants by the entireties, and community property interests.

joint tenancy A short version of the term "joint tenants with right of survivorship." A method of taking title to real property; commonly used by husbands and wives, or by others, as an estate planning tool. The parties each own a fractional share and, at the same time, own the whole of the property. If a joint tenant dies, the others do not inherit that tenant's share, but simply see the removal of an obstacle in the way of taking everything. This is a subtle point, but it is the heart of the estate planning tool—no one inherits anything as a result of the death of the other joint tenant(s). As a result, the property does not pass through probate and cannot be used to satisfy claims against the estate of the decedent. However,

- The property may be includable in one owner's estate for purposes of calculating estate taxes. The rules are different depending on whether the parties were married or not.

- A joint tenancy may be destroyed if one owner transfers his or her interest to a third party. If that happens, the new owner becomes a tenant in common, not a joint tenant. If there were originally more than two joint tenants, the remaining ones may still be joint tenants as to each other's interest.

joint venture   A legal entity somewhat similar to a partnership, except that its purpose is the pursuit of a single transaction for the mutual benefit of both joint venturers. Each joint venturer has equal rights of direction and control. For tax purposes, the joint venture is treated as a partnership and must file a partnership tax return.

judge-made law   Legal decisions by appellate courts that are binding on all future generations unless overruled by a later appellate court, but which are directly contradictory to specific statutes or earlier case authority. This happens rather often in real estate law, much of which arose out of peculiarities of life in the Middle Ages and before. When faced with a situation that would result in a seemingly unfair conclusion under applicable principles of law, the judges sometimes simply change the law.

judgment   An order of a court.

judgment creditor   One who has obtained a judgment against another. The original claim did not have to arise out of a debt—it could have been an automobile accident, a promissory note, an award in a divorce case, or anything at all.

judgment debtor   One who has had a judgment rendered against him or her. The original claim did not have to arise out of a debt—it could have been an automobile accident, a promissory note, an award in a divorce case, or something similar.

judgment, foreign   A judgment taken in another state. Once the judgment has been entered and becomes final in the other state, it may be domesticated—filed of record—in any other state where the debtor may have property. The judgment debtor may not relitigate the original issues at that time, unless there are very extraordinary circumstances.

judgment in rem   A judgment against property, rather than against a person. One example would be a judgment establishing a right-of-way easement in favor of one property and over another property. The judgment binds all people to the extent of their interaction with the property.

judgment lien   A lien on all property of a judgment debtor as a result of the entry of a judgment, the failure to appeal, and the filing of some document in the public records as evidence of the judgment.

judgment-proof   Having no assets out of which a judgment may be satisfied. In some states, a judgment debtor may have substantial assets, but they are legally beyond the reach of creditors. In other states, judgments can remain liens against property for as long as 20 years. Today's judgment-proof debtor may be wealthy in 5 or 10 years and have assets that can be seized at that time.

judicial foreclosure   A foreclosure mechanism used in some states. An action must be filed with a court to begin the foreclosure process. The court will then fix the amount of the debt and order foreclosure of the property.

judicial landmark   A tool available in some states for marking court-established boundary line corners after a lawsuit between contiguous property owners. The applicable statute will usually specify a certain size monument, such as a concrete block at least 12 inches per side; a depth at which it should be buried; and a requirement for an engraved notation that indicates that it is a judicial landmark, the date set, and the name of the surveyor setting the landmark.

jumbo mortgage   A loan in an amount greater than the size limits for Fannie Mae or Freddie Mac purchase. The loans must remain in the lender's portfolio or be sold to other investors. Because the loans cannot be sold easily, some banks charge a higher interest rate for them.

junior lien or mortgage   Refers to the priority of payment if a property must be liquidated to satisfy the debts against it. The first recorded lien or mortgage will be paid first out of sale proceeds, up to the entire amount of the debt, including principal, interests, legal fees, and expenses. If there is any money remaining, junior lienholders (which include junior mortgages) will be paid in full in the order of their priority until the money runs out.

junk fees   A popular term for lender fees and expenses that are disguised additional profit. They are usually relatively small, but can add up to significant income if enough borrowers pay them. Sample junk fees are loan processing, document handling, fund maintenance, review appraisal, underwriting review, and other such items.

jurisdiction   Power. The concept that a court or government authority may exercise control over a person or property because of the location of the property, the activities of a person within a geographic area, or a person's request for assistance from that authority, thereby voluntarily subjecting themselves to jurisdiction.

jury trial, right to   In many states, there is no right to a jury trial on disputes relating to real property. This is because of rules with their roots in English courts dating back to the time of the Norman invasion in 1066. Before making any litigation decisions based on what you think a jury of your peers would decide, be sure to see if you are entitled to a jury.

just compensation   A requirement of the United States Constitution that no owner be deprived of private property without payment of a value which is fair to the owner, and fair to the taxpayers who must pay the compensation. This concept forms the basis of eminent domain law and condemnations.

just title   A title that seemed to be proper and legal, although defective in some regard. In some states, persons with a defective title may gain full title to the property if they use the property for a certain period of time, claim it as their own, and have such title such as would give rise to a good-faith belief that the property was theirs.

K

Kelo   One of the most important real estate cases of modern history, *Kelo v. City of New London* tested the limits of the government's right to condemn private property for public use, and concluded with the United States Supreme Court granting wide latitude to local government.

The issue involved a desire by the city of New London, Connecticut, to condemn 90 acres of private property and offer it to a developer as part of a larger urban revitalization plan. Historically, eminent domain has been used to build roads, schools, and public buildings. In the Kelo case, the overall development plans called for a resort hotel and conference center, retail space, residences, and a new state park.

The case finally ended up in the United States Supreme Court. On June 23, 2005, Justice Stephens wrote the majority opinion, finding in favor of the city of New London. Justice Stephens said that local governments should be given wide latitude in local condemnation cases. "The city has carefully formulated a development plan that it believes will provide appreciable benefits to the community, including, but not limited to, new jobs and increased tax revenue." Under the particular facts of the Kelo case, the condemnation was for a permissible public purpose and not a private purpose.

There have been two types of backlash to the *Kelo* decision.

Many local governments immediately passed laws prohibiting the use of eminent domain for private development. The Supreme Court decision left open the likelihood that such laws would be constitutional and, in fact, practically invited states to pass new laws.

Small towns across America began plans to condemn undeveloped property owned by Wal-Mart within their borders. City leaders and citizens claimed it would be for the public good, because a Wal-Mart store where planned would be a blight on the community, much the same as the 90 acres in New London was considered a blight. (At this writing, it is too early in the judicial process to see where this will go.)

key tenant   See *anchor tenant*.

kickback   An illegal fee or rebate paid to someone in order to gain that person's decision or recommendation for the award of business. Under the Real Estate Settlement and Procedure Act (RESPA), federal law prohibits kickbacks to real estate agents from mortgage companies.

kiosk   A small, freestanding retail location within the confines of another business or in the common areas of a shopping center. Kiosks represent a method of significantly expanding real estate income without raising rents or building more space. The term is sometimes used to denote only self-service locations, with the attended sites called carts. (For more information see the Web site of the Self Service and Kiosk Association, www.selfservice.org.)

kit homes   Structures that arrive as prefabricated components to be erected on-site. Includes the familiar log cabin kits, geodesic dome houses, and post and beam houses.

L

laches   A doctrine of equity, or fairness, holding that people cannot sleep on their rights and then, after the passage of time and possibly the intervening claims of other people, suddenly demand that the law fix everything. The concept is similar to a statute of limitations, except that it has no fixed time period and is totally dependent on the particular circumstances of a case.

> **Example:** *Ruby plants 10 pecan trees on the wrong side of her property line with Jake. Jake knew this when the first shovel of dirt was turned, but he remained silent. Seven years later Ruby begins harvesting pecans to supplement her income, but Jake sues her and claims the pecans belong to him. Most likely the court will rule that Jake's claims are barred by laches and Ruby may harvest pecans until the trees stop bearing.*

land   In the law, the surface of the earth, descending down in a cone shape to the center of the world and upward to the heavens, along with all natural things thereon, such as minerals, water, vegetation, and rights to the air. This is less than the concept of real property, which includes land but also all rights in and to land or its use, and all artificial things attached to the land.

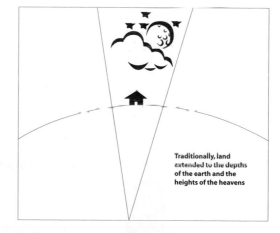

Traditionally, land extended to the depths of the earth and the heights of the heavens

land bank   Land purchased and held for future development.

land contract   Also called a bond for title, land sale contract or contract for deed. It is a financing arrangement for real property, in which the seller holds the financing and the legal title and does not give the buyer a deed until all payments have been made in full. For many people with the inability to secure financing, it is the only practical way for them to own a home. The practice is perilous, though, and could result in the loss of the property, and substantial money spent over the years, simply because of one late payment.

land court   A specialized court to hear real estate matters. The details vary from state to state.

land description   Any instrument granting or relinquishing rights in real estate must contain a description of the real estate. The description must be precise enough so that a stranger, relying only on the writing in the instrument and perhaps some training as a surveyor, could go out in the world and locate the exact piece of property covered by the instrument. That being said, it is not at all uncommon for old deeds to recite, "Starting at the midpoint of the old logging road, thence proceed 500 feet, more or less, to a stream... ." Allowances are made for such descriptions if one can determine the boundaries with other evidence. It is not acceptable, however, to describe real property by a street address, by a tax assessor's parcel identification number, or as something similar to "one acre of land near the north end of Joe Jones's property." Acceptable land descriptions appear in one of three ways:

1. Subdivision lot and block number, as recorded on a master plat in the local real estate records.
2. Metes and bounds, which includes a recognized starting point and then gives the angle and direction of turns, and the length of lines, for the various sides of the property until returning to the beginning.
3. Aliquot part, which starts with a particularly described 640-acre section, and then describes particular fractions of that section to arrive at the description of the parcel.

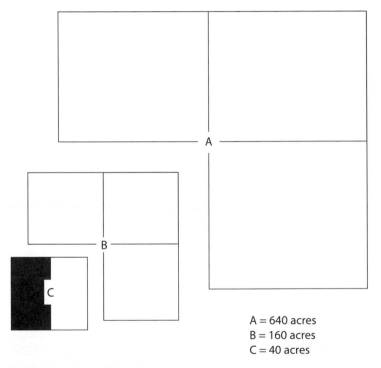

A = 640 acres
B = 160 acres
C = 40 acres

Example of an aliquot part.

The diagram "explodes" out the relevant quarters of each square, to make it easier to follow the description. We start with the largest parcel, which is a section—labeled "A" on the drawing. It contains 640 acres. The part in which we are interested is the southwest (SW) quarter ($^1/_4$) of the section—labeled "B" on the drawing. Within B, we are interested in that SW $^1/_4$—labeled "C". Within C, we are interested in the west half (shaded black in the drawing). Putting all the pieces together, we would name the particular section according to the government numbering system, and then start with the smallest piece and work our way backward to the whole. In this case, the description is, "The W ¹/₂ of the SW ¹/₄ (C) of the SW ¹/₄ (B) of Section 8 (A)." If a section is 640 acres, then B must be one-fourth of that, or 160 acres. C is one-fourth of that, or 40 acres, and the black part is 20 acres.

land economics   (1) The study of land use, natural resources, public utilities, housing, and urban land issues. (2) A prestigious journal, Land Economics has been published since 1925 by the University of Wisconsin Press (www.jstor.org/journals/00237639.html).

land grant   A grant of public lands by the government, usually for roads, railroads, or agricultural colleges.

land hook   A method of indicating on a survey map the existence of contiguous parcels with the same ownership. In the diagram, the symbol connecting parcel A to parcel B is called the "land hook." It may also show the connection of properties across public roads or waterways.

land lease   See *ground lease.*

landlocked   Without access to public streets or roads. The owner of property that is landlocked may file suit to obtain an easement by necessity across another's land, but it must be a route that places the least burden on the other property.

landlord   The owner of property rented to another. The landlord's interest is called a reversionary interest, while the tenant's interest is possessory.

landlord tax stop   See *tax stop.*

landlord-tenant code   See *Uniform Residential Landlord and Tenant Act.*

landlord-tenant law   A general name given to the area of law that concerns itself with the creation of leasehold estates, the rights and responsibilities of the parties afterward, and the termination of the estates.

landmark   In surveying, a permanent feature on the land, used as a reference point. If it is necessary to remove a landmark for development or other purposes, the best practice would be to contact the local government engineer or mapping office and ask that a witness monument be set in the place of the former landmark. (Some states require this by law.)

land measurement conversion   (1) Most often necessary when translating acreage measurements into square feet, because as land becomes more valuable people begin quoting prices in terms of dollars per square foot rather than dollars per acre. There are 43,560 square feet to an acre. (2) Older deeds often contain descriptions with property lines expressed as "chains" or "rods," which must be converted to feet and inches to be meaningful today. Tables and calculators are available online at www.onlineconversion.com to perform virtually any type of measurement conversion. This Web site is privately maintained through voluntary contributions.

land poor   Having substantial real estate assets but little cash. It historically referred to agricultural land, but it no longer has that restricted definition.

land sale contract   See *land contract*.

land, tenements, and hereditaments   In keeping with attorneys' practice of using three words when one will usually suffice, you often see the expression "land, tenements, and hereditaments" in real estate instruments. It is meant to describe all the rights capable of being owned and enjoyed. Land is the dirt and everything natural under it, attached to it, and the air above. Tenements are any structures attached to the land, and hereditaments are any interests in real estate capable of being inherited.

land trust   A trust in which land is the only asset. See *trust*.

land-use intensity system (LUIS)   A concept that certain uses of land share common characteristics as far as population densities and traffic generation, and that the best method of zoning or imposing development restrictions is with regard to those characteristics. Densities are controlled by reference to floor area ratio, open space ratio, livability space ratio, and/or recreational space ratio.

> **Example:** *Rather than zone separate areas for office use, multifamily residential use, and retail use, one LUIS zoning area might permit all three, since all three involve large numbers of people in small spaces needing multilane roads with separate turn lanes and synchronized traffic control devices.*

land-use plan   A plan submitted by a developer to local planning or zoning authorities as a condition of obtaining a demolition or a construction permit.

land-use regulation   A system of government-enforced restrictions on the development and uses of properties. Well-planned regulations should complement each other, although in the real world there is often overlapping of jurisdictions and conflicting laws. The primary vehicles of land-use regulation are

1. Federal and state government environmental protections for species, types of habitats, erosion control, siltation, etc.
2. Preemption by federal agencies for specific purposes, such as Federal Aviation Administration (FAA) restrictions on building heights near airports
3. Federal and state highway restrictions regarding signage and curb cuts
4. Federal and state tax incentives or tax burdens for particular uses of property
5. State health department regulations regarding sanitary waste disposal
6. State and local historic preservation laws
7. Local zoning ordinances
8. Local building codes
9. Local fire department regulations regarding safety issues
10. Subdivision restrictions

larger parcel   A concept relevant in condemnation cases in order to determine if the taking of land by eminent domain has caused damage to the larger parcel. Usually the concept is limited to one piece of property out of which a portion is taken by eminent domain, but courts have described the larger parcel as including noncontiguous properties.

Example: *A resort community has a golf course one-half mile away. If the golf course were taken by eminent domain, its loss would certainly affect the value of the resort community as a whole. Damages attributable to the loss in value of the larger parcel are called severance damages.*

late charge   A fee to compensate a lender for the additional administrative expenses and general inconvenience suffered when payments are not received on time. If the late charge is excessive, the courts will construe it as a penalty, and penalties are illegal. Many industries have had to reduce their customary late charges because of class-action litigation resulting in millions of dollars of refunds and reimbursement for attorneys' fees.

latent defects   Real property defects not discoverable by reasonable and customary inspection. If known to the seller, or to the real estate broker representing the seller, then each of them has an obligation to reveal such defects to a prospective purchaser.

lateral and subjacent support   All property is entitled to support from the sides (lateral support) and from underneath (subjacent support). In the diagram, A owns the surface of the land and all the mineral rights underneath. C owns the surface rights only, because the mineral rights were sold to B, many years ago. A may not dig a strip mine and slice down the property line many feet, because B's and C's land would crumble at the edges and fall into the strip mine. A has a duty of lateral support to B and to C. By the same token, B cannot carelessly dig deep mines and cause the surface to cave in, because B owes the duty of subjacent support to C.

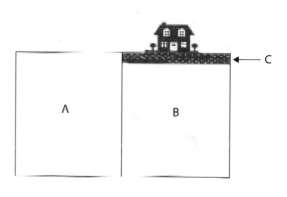

law day   (1) An old term meaning the date an obligation was due. (2) May 1 of each year, a special day first recognized by President Eisenhower in 1958 in order to provide a date to reflect upon and celebrate the rule of law in our country.

lawful condition   See *condition*.

lawful interest   The maximum interest rate allowed by law. Any amount higher is called usury and is illegal. Contrast with *legal rate of interest*, which is the amount set by state law when the parties fail to establish a contractual rate.

law of capture   Under this theory, a landowner does not own migratory substances (such as oil and gas) under the land but does have the exclusive right to drill for, produce, or in some other manner gain possession of the substances. Contrast with *unitization*.

lead   A heavy metal shown to cause learning disabilities, behavioral problems, seizures, and even death in children. The Environmental Protection Agency (EPA) estimates that 3 to 4 million children had elevated lead levels in their blood in 1978. The number has now been reduced to several hundred thousand, but elevated lead levels in blood is still the leading environmentally induced illness in children.

Federal law that went into effect in 1996 requires sellers and landlords of properties built before 1978 (when lead-based paint became illegal) to do the following before any contract or lease becomes final:

1. Provide a copy of the EPA booklet, "Protect Your Family from Lead in Your Home."
2. Disclose any known information concerning lead-based paint or lead-based paint hazards.
3. Provide any records and reports on lead-based paint and/or lead-based paint hazards.
4. Include an attachment to the contract or lease (or language inserted in the lease itself) that includes a lead warning statement and confirms that the seller or landlord has complied with all notification requirements.
5. Provide home buyers a 10-day period to conduct a paint inspection or risk assessment for lead-based paint or lead-based paint hazards.

lead lender   Most often, a lender who originates a loan and then sells part of the loan to another financial institution—called the participant—but remains in control of the relationship with the borrower. Sometimes, the originating lender will also sell the "lead position" and will simply retain a passive, participation interest in the loan.

leakage   A measure of retail sales lost by a community to a competitive market, indicating the need for more retail development in an area.

leaking underground storage tank (LUST)   An underground tank that is leaking or spilling hazardous fluids into the soil or groundwater. In 1986 Congress established the Leaking Underground Storage Tank (LUST) Trust Fund to

- Oversee cleanups by responsible parties
- Enforce cleanups by recalcitrant parties
- Pay for cleanups at sites where the owner or operator is unknown, unwilling, or unable to respond or which require emergency action.

lease   An oral or written agreement transferring the right to exclusive use and possession of property for some period of time. Some important lease concepts are

- The normal requirement that all contracts having to do with real estate must be in writing does not apply to contracts that are capable of performance in one year or less. In most states, an oral lease for less than one year is enforceable; an oral lease for a longer period is not.
- A tenant is not relieved of responsibility to pay rent if the premises are damaged, destroyed, or partially or totally unusable unless the lease allows it, or unless consumer protection laws applicable to residential leases allow it.
- If a tenant transfers the entire remaining term of a lease to someone else, that is an assignment. If a tenant transfers less than the remaining term, that is a sublease. Either way, the

original tenant is still fully responsible for complying with all lease terms, even if the new one does not. In most states, a landlord may require its approval before assignment or subletting, but may not unreasonably withhold its approval.

- A tenant's interest under a lease may be insured, in addition to coverage for the contents. The interest may also be mortgaged, although that would be extremely unusual except in the case of valuable improvements built on leased land under a long-term lease.

leased fee   The name given to the landlord's rights in real estate after the landlord signs a lease with a tenant. It consists of the right to receive rental payments and the right to retake possession of the premises at the end of the lease term—the reversionary right.

leasehold   A name given to the tenant's rights in real estate after signing a lease. The leasehold estate is classified as a less-than-freehold estate.

leasehold estate   The interest a tenant has to possess and use property by virtue of a lease.

leasehold improvements   Improvements made by tenants to leased premises. The cost must be depreciated over a 39-year term, even if the lease will last only 5 years. At the end of the lease term, the tenants then write off on their taxes all the remaining undepreciated balance. For a short period of time between November 2004 and January 1, 2006, leasehold improvements could be depreciated over 15 years rather than 39. (Beware of tax advice indicating this is still the law.)

leasehold interest   The interest a tenant has to possess and use property by virtue of a lease.

lease option   A contractual arrangement in which the tenant is given the right to buy the leased property under certain circumstances. An option is a right to buy, even if the seller later changes his or her mind and does not wish to sell to anyone at all. Contrast with a right of first refusal, which is the right to buy if and when the owner ever decides to sell.

Persons negotiating the terms of a lease option should consider the following:

1. Do you mean to grant an option or a right of first refusal? Be specific; call it by the right name and then describe what happens if the landlord wishes to sell to someone else.
2. What are the earliest and the latest dates on which the option can be exercised?
3. If the option can be exercised any time during the lease term, does it continue if there is a renewal or an extension of the lease? Renewals are new leases. Extensions are continuations of old leases.
4. Can the tenant sell the option to someone else without also assigning the lease to someone else? If not, may the tenant at least sell the option to another entity in which the tenant (or specifically named person) is a controlling or 100 percent shareholder?
5. Will the price be set in the agreement, will the parties agree to a fair market value (usually a bad idea because of the almost certainty of arguments), or will the parties agree to a formula that employs some index that is independent and easily verifiable?
6. What events will allow the option to be terminated by the landlord, even if the lease continues? This could be late payment of rent, the tenant's failure to cure a nonmonetary default after notice by the landlord, or any other factors the parties may negotiate.

lease-purchase agreement   An installment sale. The tenant sometimes pays a higher-than-market rent for the property, with a portion of the monthly payment earmarked as rent, another portion as principal payments, and another portion as interest.

Landlords should not rely on a lease-purchase agreement as a mechanism to keep all payments and bypass foreclosure if there is a default by the tenant. Courts are very antagonistic to such forfeitures. By planning ahead and classifying the different aspects of the monthly payments, you can avoid the possibility of a court deciding things for you or the IRS deciding how to treat the income.

lease-up   The time period for a newly available property to attract tenants and reach stabilized occupancy.

leasing commission   See *commission*.

legal age   The age at which a minor may enter into binding contracts.

legal description   See *land description* and *boundary line disputes*.

legal name   One's first name given at birth and one's last name, or family name. It is good practice, but not required, to include a full middle name and, for married women taking their husband's name, their former surname or "maiden name," usually preceded by the word "nee," meaning "born."

legal notice   Bringing something to another's attention in a legally recognized method. What is required under the circumstances may depend on specific provisions in a contract or lease between the parties. It may depend on what is the standard custom or practice in a geographic, professional, or other community. It may depend on laws that say, for example, all persons are deemed to have notice of anything appearing in the real estate records and/or all things appearing in the legal sections of the newspaper classified ads. If in doubt about the proper way to give notice, give it in all ways you can imagine. (If in doubt about whether you have received legal notice, assume you have if you know about the fact, however you came to know about it.)

legal rate of interest   The rate of interest set by state law in the absence of an agreement by the parties. It is usually the same rate established for interest on judgments. Contrast with *lawful interest*.

lender   One who advances money to another in the expectation of receiving repayment of the money plus a fee for the use of the money, called interest.

lender liability   An area of the law devoted to various theories of wrongdoing by financial institutions in their relationships with third parties, not just borrowers.

lessee   A tenant; the person or entity entitled to possession under a lease.

less-than-freehold estate   The technical definition includes many real estate interests rarely seen any more. Today, the term largely refers to leasehold interests. For sake of historical reference, a less-than-freehold estate is any estate in land or improvements which is capable of determination as to its length or duration. Contrast with a *freehold* estate, which is inheritable or is measured by a lifespan.

let   To rent out.

letter of attornment   A notice from a landlord to a tenant that the property has been sold and which directs the tenant to pay rent to the new owner.

letter of credit (LOC)   (Pronounce each letter of the abbreviation; it is not pronounced as a word.) An instrument issued by a bank or other financial institution (issuer) agreeing that it will pay money to another (beneficiary), on behalf of the bank's customer (account party), upon the happening of certain named events. There is usually an issuance fee of 1 to 2 percent of the face amount of the LOC. Modern banking regulations require the same underwriting as for a commercial loan. The LOC will set out the exact prerequisites to be met before the bank will issue payment. These usually include a particular time and place to present the original letter of credit and the exact documents that must accompany the letter. Some states still follow the old "strict compliance" rule holding that any deviation from the instructions, no matter how minor, will justify the bank in refusing to pay. Others follow a "substantial compliance" rule, so that minor typographical or syntax errors in the presenting documents will not justify nonpayment. See also the two types of letters of credit: *documentary letter of credit* and *standby letter of credit*.

letter of intent (LOI)   A signed document between parties setting out the deal points on which they agree and leaving for later negotiation the minutia over which the lawyers will argue. In the absence of any limiting language in the LOI, it can be construed as a binding contract between the parties. Usually, however, the LOI will recite that it is only an expression of interest regarding the parties' mutual intent, that the parties have not reached an agreement regarding any terms or provisions of a contract, and the LOI is neither a contract, nor an offer capable of acceptance, nor evidence of a contract, but merely the current status of negotiations that might possibly lead to a contract.

letter of patent   A legal document transferring ownership out of the government—federal or state—to a private individual. The following sample is an excerpt from a patent out of the United States to Robert Sage, on May 6, 1812, for 160 acres of land, signed by President James Monroe.

President of the United States of America,

TO ALL TO WHOM THESE PRESENTS SHALL COME, *GREETING:*

Know ye, That, in pursuance of the Acts of Congress appropriating and granting Land to the late Army of the United States, passed on and since the sixth day of May, 1812, *Robert Sage*

having deposited in the General Land-Office a Warrant in *his* favor, numbered *11167* there is granted unto *the said Robert Sage* late a *private in Turpins Company of Light Dragoons* —— a certain Tract of Land, containing *one hundred & sixty acres* being the *North East or*

letter report   (1) A short appraisal report with only the property description and characteristics, valuation, and recommendation, but without all the area information and without details regarding the method of reaching the valuation. (2) A report by a title company regarding the condition of the title on a particular date, but without issuing any insurance.

letter ruling   A written statement from the IRS to a particular taxpayer, containing an interpretation of tax law as it applies to that taxpayer's situation. Letter rulings are issued in response to a request from a taxpayer and are not binding on the IRS as it relates to other cases.

level-payment mortgage   A mortgage note with periodic payments in equal amounts. Usually, a fully amortizing mortgage, with each payment including some portion for principal reduction and some portion for currently accrued interest, so that at the end of the agreed-upon term the note will be paid in full. The concept is not restricted to fully amortizing mortgages, though, and may include payments made according to an amortization schedule but with the entire balance due at an earlier date, or simply payments in a fixed amount with the entire balance due in 3, 5, or 10 years, or whatever the parties agree to.

leverage   The effect borrowed money has on an investment; the concept of borrowing money to buy an asset that will appreciate in value, so that the ultimate sale will return profits on the equity invested and on the borrowed funds.

> **Example:**   *Mark and Amy each have $100,000 to invest. They can buy rental houses for $100,000 per house and collect rent of $1,100 per month for each house. At the end of 5 years, they will be able to liquidate and sell their houses for $150,000 each. Amy uses leverage and Mark does not.*

Mark	Amy
Buys one house for $100,000 cash	Buys five houses with $20,000 down for each one
Mortgage debt: $0	Mortgage debt: $400,000 at 6%
Monthly rental income: $1,100	Monthly rental income: $5,500
	Subtract monthly interest: $2,000
	Net monthly income: $3,500
Total rent income over 5 years: $66,000	Total net rental income over 5 years: $210,000
Total sales profit: $50,000	Total sales profit after paying off mortgages: $250,000
Total money from investment: $66,000 + $50,000 = $116,000	Total money from investment: $210,000 + $250,000 = $460,000

leverage, negative or positive   Negative leverage occurs when the cost of borrowing money is greater than the return a party makes on an equity investment. This could occur with an adjustable-rate mortgage on a commercial investment during a time of rapidly rising interest rates. Construction loans, and development loans, are usually at adjustable rates of interest and do not have any ceilings or limits on the interest rate. Positive leverage occurs when the cost of money is less than the return on an investment.

levy   (1) To assess. One may levy a tax or fine, which means to impose it. (2) To seize or collect, as when a creditor levies on assets by execution.

liability   (1) A debt or obligation. (2) A potential loss, such as a poorly trained, poorly supervised real estate agent who may be a liability.

LIBOR   (pronounced "lie-bore") London Interbank Offered Rate. The rate that European banks use to charge interest to each other on large loans. LIBOR is used as an index for many commercial loans in the United States, rather than a reference to the prime rate. Often quoted as something similar to "135 basis points over 1-year LIBOR," so that if LIBOR on 1-year loans is currently at 5.66 percent, then the quoted loan rate for the customer will be 5.66 percent plus 1.35 percent, or 7.01 percent.

license   An authorization for a particular person or entity to do some act on the land or property of another. Licenses are revocable at will, grant no exclusivity, and are not assignable. The one who receives the license is the licensee; the one who grants it is the licensor.

license laws   Particular state laws having to do with qualifications, licensing, and oversight of real estate or other professionals within the state in order to (1) ensure minimal levels of expertise, (2) promulgate enforceable standards to protect consumers from fraud, abuse, or negligence, and (3) provide mechanisms for self-policing of the industry. One can check the license status of any purported real estate broker or agent by going to the Web site of the Association of Real Estate License Law Officials, www.arello.org, and clicking on License Registration Verification.

lien   A legally enforceable claim on the property of another as a result of a debt or obligation. It may be voluntary, such as a mortgage, or involuntary, such as a tax lien. It may be general, such as a judgment lien on all property within a county, or specific, such as a mortgage lien on the described property. One of the most important concepts in lien law is the priority among competing liens if property is insufficient to pay all claims or if the owner files for bankruptcy. The general rules are as follows (however, there may be local variations among the various states):

1. The first lien to be recorded is paid first, and so on in the order of recordation.
2. A statutory lien, such as a mechanics' and materialmen's lien, may be given artificial priority even though recorded after another lien.
3. Lien priority may be reshuffled if a debtor files for bankruptcy. The rules are too complex to examine here.
4. Lien-stripping takes place in bankruptcy when an asset is not worth as much as the accumulated liens placed upon it. Junior lienholders are stripped out and turned into unsecured creditors. Even mortgage liens may be reduced in amount, if the real estate is not worth as much as the loan balance.
5. A landlord's *statutory* lien for unpaid rent can be avoided, or set aside, by a bankruptcy trustee, but a landlord's *contractual* lien cannot be avoided unless lien-stripping comes into play.

lien-stripping   See *lien*.

lien-theory states   States that treat a mortgage solely as a security interest in real property, with title to the property retained by the borrower. Contrast with title theory states, in which the actual title to the property passes to the creditor, who then has an obligation to reconvey it to the debtor when the loan has been paid in full. Contrast also with hybrid theory, a mixture of the two.

life and safety systems   See *life-support systems.*

life-care facility   A residential development offering varying levels of housekeeping support, medical care, and community dining for senior citizens. Also called a continuing care retirement community, the concept allows residents to remain on campus but in differing residency styles, as they age and their needs change. Residents may begin in a garden home indistinguishable from other homes in the community at large, progress to something similar to a hotel suite with community dining, and then perhaps to bedridden full-time nursing care. Frequently a person will purchase a housing unit and then also pay monthly dues to cover communal services for the rest of their life. The American Association of Homes and Services for the Aging, www.aahsa.org, has additional information and directories.

life cycle   The various phases of a project—predevelopment, development, leasing, operating, and rehabilitation.

life estate   The right to use and enjoy real estate for a limited time measured by someone's life—either the owner of the life estate or someone else. Often used as an estate planning tool so that elderly people can sell their property or give it to relatives, but still retain the right to continue living in it.

> **Example:**   *Mary Smith, who is 85 years old, has a life estate in Blackacre, but it's for the life of 10–year-old Ashley Brown. As a result, Mary and her heirs will be able to use the property until Ashley dies, hopefully some time in the distant future.*

life-of-loan cap   The maximum amount an adjustable-rate mortgage can increase. If the initial interest rate is 6.5 percent with adjustments allowed every 3 months, but there is a life-of-loan cap of 5 percent, then the highest interest rate that can be charged will be 6.5 percent plus 5 percent, or 11.5 percent. Also called "lifetime cap."

life safety systems   See *life-support systems.*

lifestyle mall   A shopping mall concept that first became popular in the late 1990s. The term was copyrighted in May 1997 by Memphis, Tennessee, developers Poag & McEwen Co. The lifestyle mall features an open-air architecture, typically high-end retailers, may or may not include anchor stores, and has a large concentration of dining and entertainment facilities. The properties are usually well landscaped and offer outdoor artwork, music, and trams or trolleys for on-site transportation. It is intended to support a "shopping as entertainment" mindset and has become highly popular in affluent communities.

life-support systems   The fire alarms, smoke detectors, sprinklers, exit lights, hoods, portable fire extinguishers, and other such warning and protection systems in commercial buildings. Most recently, halon (nonwater) fire-extinguishing systems became an important component, because of the need to protect sophisticated computer and telecommunications equipment in the event of a fire. Industry leaders are now calling for inclusion of protections, or at least warnings, for chemical and biological contaminants associated with possible terrorist attacks. Sometimes called life safety systems.

life tenant   One who has a life estate in a property, being the right to enjoy the property for a period of time measured by that person's life or some other designated person's life. The rest of the bundle of rights is called a reversion or remainder interest. Life tenants may sell, gift, or will their property to another, but when the defining life comes to an end, so do the rights of those other people. At that point, the remainderman may take possession of the property and enjoy it fully.

> **Example:**   *Aunt Esther, who is 80 years old, sells her farm to Acme Agribusiness. She retains a life estate, measured by the life of her 40-year-old nephew, Mark. Esther dies two days later, with a will that leaves everything she owned to Texas A&M University. Mark has no rights in the property; he's just a measuring life. Texas A&M may use the farm until Mark's death, at which time it will pass to Acme Agribusiness.*

lifetime cap   See *life-of-loan cap.*

lifting clause   A provision in a second, third, or other junior mortgage that allows the liens ahead of it to be paid off and refinanced for the same or a lesser amount, without sacrificing their priority in lien positions. Without this clause, investors with second mortgages could never refinance the first ones because, the instant the first mortgage was paid off, the second lienholder would immediately advance to first position.

lift the automatic stay   In bankruptcy, all collection activities by creditors must cease as soon as the creditor receives notice of the bankruptcy proceeding. This is called the automatic stay. Creditors may proceed with foreclosure or repossession of collateral only if they obtain permission from the bankruptcy judge to do so. That request is called a request to lift automatic stay, the process is called lifting the stay.

lifting the stay   See *lift the automatic stay.*

light and air   At English common law, property owners were entitled to light and air if they had "ancient windows" through which they had historically enjoyed such things. If an adjoining property owner erected a tall fence, or built a pigsty and fouled the air, this was a violation of what came to be called the ancient lights doctrine. American courts initially followed the doctrine and then rejected it when it seemed to stand in the way of development and "progress."

The landmark case in this country involved two resort hotels in Florida, one of which planned an expansion that would cast the other's pool, cabana, and sunbathing area into the shadows. The court refused to find any rights in light and air and allowed the expansion to continue. Today, especially as regards rights to sunlight for solar energy collection, American courts are reexamining the principles of rights to air and light, and finding ways to enforce them.

light industry   A term usually encountered in the context of zoning regulation, with local statutes or ordinances providing their own definitions. Generally, however, light industry is understood to mean that which is more labor intensive and less machinery intensive than heavy industry. Light industry usually consists of nonpolluting users with moderate energy demands engaged in assembling products, sewing, baking, or cleaning.

like-kind exchange   Under IRS regulations, property held for productive use in a trade or business or for investment that is exchanged solely for similar property. Any real estate (except your personal residence) is considered like-kind to any other real estate. Encountered in the context of a 1031 exchange, if you sell a piece of real estate, and then buy another piece within certain strict time limits and following very specific rules, then you will not have to pay income taxes on the first sale. Taxes will be paid when you sell the second property, unless you do another 1031 exchange. In that case, tax payment will be delayed again. See also *1031 exchange*.

> **Example:**   *In real estate, all real estate except one's personal residence(s) is considered "like kind" to all other real estate. City property is "like kind" to farm property; unimproved real estate is "like kind" to improved real estate. On the other hand, shares in a REIT are not considered real estate for the purposes of a like-kind exchange. In addition, a long-term lease of less than 30 years is not considered real estate, and a life estate expected to last less than 30 years is not considered real estate, for purposes of these rules. (For more information, see Publication 544, "Sales and Other Dispositions of Assets," available at the IRS Web site, www.irs.gov.)*

limitations of actions   Rules for the time limits after which one may not file a lawsuit on particular theories of recovery. Also called statutes of limitations, all states have legislation specifying the time limits. As an example, one state may say that claims for negligence must be brought within 1 year of accrual of the cause of action, claims for fraud within 1 year of discovery of the fraud, claims for breach of contract within 6 years of the breach, and claims for the recovery of land within 10 years of the trespass or other wrong to land. A cause of action accrues when the wrongful conduct has occurred and you have suffered a harm.

> **Example:**   *A carpenter does a poor job building some stairs, but you have no way of knowing until the stairs collapse 5 years later. Then the cause of action for negligence accrued when the stairs fell, causing injury to you or to your property. In this situation, you would have one year from that date to file a suit. If you discover the problem earlier, your cause of action is for breach of contract, for breach of the warranty to perform in a good and workmanlike manner.*

limited appraisal   An outdated expression due to the July 1, 2006, amendments to the Uniform Standards of Professional Appraisal Practice (USPAP). Real estate appraisals typically use three separate approaches to arrive at various values, and then the appraiser reconciles the approaches to reach one opinion of value. The approaches are income approach, comparable sales approach, and the cost-to-rebuild approach. In a limited appraisal, one or more of the approaches might have been omitted. (There is nothing shoddy about this.) Raw land cannot have a cost-to-rebuild analysis, for example. Under older standards, an appraiser would be required to specify that the appraisal was limited and then designate the appropriate departure rule. Today, appraisers are allowed more latitude, as long as they and the client have a clear understanding of the scope of the work requested. The term limited appraisal is no longer necessary.

limited capacity   See *capacity*.

limited common elements   In a condominium project, individual owners own the airspace within their exterior walls, the ceiling, and the floor of their unit. Everything else is owned in common with all other owners in the project. The theory requires some modification because things like balconies, front doors, and windows really provide benefit for only specific unit owners. There may also be assigned parking places, boat slips, or storage lockers. Such things are called limited common elements and must be defined in the condominium documents.

limited equity condominium   Government-subsidized homeownership of condominiums. Low-income consumers are allowed to buy such condos at below-market prices with little or no down payment and very low interest rate financing. When ready to sell, they must sell to other qualified low-income consumers, at a predetermined price that takes into account general inflation, but not rapidly increasing real estate prices in the area.

limited liability company   A cross between a corporation and a partnership, the limited liability company must be created by documents filed in the same place as corporations. This type of organization enjoys much of the informality of a partnership, the tax benefits of a partnership with all income taxed at the shareholder level but not at the company level (see *double taxation*), and the limited liability granted to corporate shareholders, who cannot be held personally liable for a corporate debt or transgressions. Be aware, however, that members of a limited liability company may well be safe from contractual claims against the company, but most claims for negligence or wrongdoing will include some theory of personal liability against the members also.

> **Example:** *A claim against a limited liability company may be for its negligence in allowing mud and water to remain on the floor, leading to a customer slipping and falling and sustaining back injuries. The plaintiff in such a case may claim the individual members were also personally liable for their failure to develop policies and procedures to keep the floors clean or because they were also the employees and had personal responsibility to mop the floors.*

limited partners   Persons who invest in a limited partnership upon the condition that their maximum exposure to liability, if the venture is unsuccessful, is the loss of their investment. Contrast with *general partner*.

limited partnership   A partnership agreement in which one person acts as the general partner, with unlimited liability for all partnership debts, and all other investors have a status similar to stockholders. Such people, called limited partners, may lose their investment if there is a loss to the project, but no creditor may reach their personal assets. The vehicle was much more popular before tax law changes took away most of the tax advantages of real property syndications.

limited power of appointment   A power granted by will, authorizing the recipient to choose who among a group of named or described persons may receive property.

limited power of attorney   The authority granted to another under a written power of attorney, specifying or describing the particular acts the attorney in fact may do, and no others. Contrast with a general power of attorney, which allows all things the person could do himself or herself. Limited powers are usually given to do things like transfer stock, obtain information from the IRS or Social Security Administration, sign all documents necessary for a real estate closing, or other such tasks.

limited referral agent   A real estate agent who refers leads to others in the office in return for a referral fee, but does not actually work the listings or assist a buyer with finding properties.

limited service broker   A real estate broker who offers less than all the traditional brokerage services. Typically, the limited service broker provides sellers with listings on the local multiple listing service, and perhaps some advice and yard signs, in exchange for a flat fee that is fully earned whether the property sells or not.

lineal heirs   Descendants in a direct line, such as children and grandchildren.

line of credit   A revolving loan issued by a financial institution; it may be secured by a mortgage or other collateral, or unsecured. The borrower may draw down the line, up to the maximum limits, at any time and pay interest each month. If the principal is repaid during the time period of the line, then the maximum amount or any lesser amount may be drawn down again. Lines of credit are typically for one year, and then extended from year to year afterward. If a borrower draws down the maximum amount and then does not repay any of the principal, the lender will eventually refuse to renew the note and may require payment in full or conversion to an amortizing loan with regular monthly payments that will eventually pay it in full. Lines of credit are best used by persons with reliable income arriving at sporadic times or by persons awaiting the sale of an asset but needing cash in the meantime.

line-of-sight easement   An easement to preserve a view. The owners of the servient estate may not do anything on their property that would obstruct the line of sight of the dominant estate.

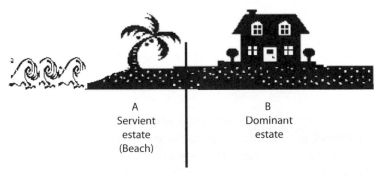

A
Servient
estate
(Beach)

B
Dominant
estate

link   A surveying measurement still seen in older deeds or in deeds using descriptions from earlier times. A link is 7.92 inches. See *land measurement conversion*.

liquid asset   An asset that is cash or can be converted to cash on very short notice.

liquidated damages   Damages agreed upon in advance by contracting parties. The parties will recite that if one or the other breaches the contract, it will be difficult to determine damages at that time. This is often true in situations where construction is delayed and a business cannot open on time or homeowners cannot take possession of their home when anticipated. Liquidated damages are used in a wide variety of cases, though, not just construction contracts. The parties will agree to an amount of damages, or a method of calculating damages, such as a certain amount per day. Most real estate sale contracts stipulate the earnest money deposit as the amount of liquidated damages. The catch with this system is that courts will not enforce penalties, which are illegal. If the liquidated damages do not bear some relationship to reality and the probable damages suffered by the innocent party, then courts will recharacterize them as penalties (completely unenforceable) or will reduce them to an amount deemed reasonable under the circumstances.

liquidity   The ability of a person or company to readily and easily obtain cash from its assets in order to meet obligations or make purchases.

lis pendens   A document recorded in the real estate records, putting all people on notice that a lawsuit has been filed that will affect title to the described property. If someone buys the property after the filing of the lis pendens notice, then that person takes it subject to any claims that might prove successful in the lawsuit.

listing   A written agency agreement between a property owner and a licensed real estate broker, authorizing the broker to market the property, solicit offers for its purchase or lease, and engage in negotiations pursuant to the owner's instructions. It imposes fiduciary responsibilities on the broker, who owes duties of care, loyalty, and confidence to the property owner.

Important concepts include

- Most state licensing laws require listing agreements to be in writing.
- The most common type of listing agreement is an exclusive right to sell, under which the broker receives a commission even if the owner sells the property to a relative.
- Some brokers offer exclusive right to list contracts, giving the owner the right to sell to anyone without paying a commission, but no other real estate broker may earn a commission directly from the owner, only as a cooperating broker paid by the listing broker.
- Most states require a definite termination date in the listing agreement, which may be renewed by mutual agreement of the parties.
- Most states prohibit net listings, in which the owner agrees to pay the broker all sums received over a certain minimum amount wanted by the owner.
- Some listing agreements have a clause entitling the broker to the agreed-upon compensation if the property sells within a certain time period—usually 6 months—after listing expiration, but to someone introduced to the property by the broker during the listing period.

listing agent   The real estate agent who obtained a listing contract from a property owner, authorizing the broker for whom the agent works to market and solicit offers to buy the owner's property on specified terms and conditions. See also *listor*.

listing agreement   See *listing*.

listing broker   The real estate broker who enters into an agreement with a property owner to market and solicit offers to buy the owner's property.

listing contract   See *listing*.

listor   The real estate agent who obtained a listing agreement for his or her broker. Technically, only the qualifying broker, managing broker, or similar statutorily designated person for a real estate company, may enter into listing agreements. The broker will then split any commission with the listor in an agreed-upon amount ranging from 25 percent to as much as 100 percent.

littoral land   Land bordering an ocean, sea, or lake. Contrast *riparian land*, which is land bordering a river or stream.

littoral rights   The rights of landowners who own land bordering an ocean, sea, or lake. Generally speaking, the rights consist of the ability to take fish from the water, to build structures such as piers for a limited distance into the water, and the right to use so much of the water, for irrigation and other purposes, as is allowed under state law and local regulations.

livability space ratio   See *land-use intensity system*.

live load   The amount of additional weight that can be safely added to a building without structural failure or stress. It includes furniture, equipment, and people. Contrast with *dead load*.

livery of seisin   A term that hasn't been used in centuries but is still encountered in real estate literature. It was an ancient ceremony for transferring ownership of land to another by means of the delivery of possession—called "livery of seisin."

lives in being   Persons who will be alive at the time a transfer of real estate takes place. Under highly technical and infrequently encountered rules of real estate having to do with something called the *Rule Against Perpetuities*, certain time limits start to run by reference to lives in being. If a gift of real estate is made in a will, then the time limit is measured by the persons alive at the time the will is effective—when the testator dies—not when the will is first signed.

living trust   A trust that goes into effect during the lifetime of the person who created it, called the settlor. Contrast with a will that goes into effect after the settlor's death, called a "testamentary trust." See *inter vivos trust*.

load-bearing wall   See *bearing wall*.

loan application process   The creation and transmittal of all information a lender might find necessary to assist it in reaching a decision to loan money to a borrower or not. At a minimum, the process usually consists of

- A list of assets and liabilities
- Current cash flows showing a present ability to repay the loan, or pro forma projections showing future income sufficient to repay the loan, such as if the loan proceeds will be used to buy income-producing property
- A Social Security number and present address so that the lender can obtain a credit score

Depending on the complexity of the purpose for the loan, or the handicaps a borrower must overcome because of a poor credit score, the process can become much more complex. All lenders have their own specialized requirements and procedures; even individual loan officers within an organization may have differing requirements for the process.

loan broker   See *mortgage broker*.

loan commitment   In real estate, a formal promise by a lender to loan up to a specified amount of money, depending on the appraised value of the collateral, with additional details regarding the interest rate, term of the loan, property on which mortgage will be taken, and a date on which the commitment will expire.

loan constant   See *constant*.

loan correspondent   (1) One who originates a loan. (2) One who services the loan by collecting payments from the borrower, disbursing funds to investors or the mortgage owner, monitoring insurance status and real estate tax payments, and handling phone calls and inquiries from the borrower.

loan officer   An employee of a financial institution, charged with the responsibility of generating loan business for his or her employer and assisting in all details necessary to complete the loan application process. Sometimes the loan officer also monitors the relationship with the borrower after the loan closes; other times this is taken over by someone else.

loan pool   See *collateralized mortgage backed securities*.

loan servicing   See *servicing*.

loan-to-value (LTV) ratio   The relationship between the principal amount of a loan and the appraised value of the property serving as security. A loan of $80,000 on a property appraised at $100,000 is an 80 percent LTV. Residential mortgages with an LTV of 80 percent or less qualify for FHA insurance; if the ratio is higher, then borrowers may be required to obtain private mortgage insurance. Generally speaking, the higher the LTV, the higher the interest rate will be because the lender has assumed more risk. Those risks are as follows: (1) When there is little equity in the property, it has a low hostage value; the borrower is more likely to default and walk away from the property because the borrower has little to lose. (2) At foreclosure, the property may not bring a price sufficient to pay off the principal balance of the loan, much less the accrued interest and costs of foreclosure.

lobby   To work for or against the passage of legislation. Currently, the two strongest lobbies in the real estate industry are the National Association of REALTORS® and the American Bankers Association. They are squared off on opposite sites of legislation that would give financial institutions the right to offer real estate brokerage services.

local improvement district   A mechanism for property owners with common concerns to band together and assess themselves for purely local improvements such as sidewalk repair, neighborhood park rehabilitation, irrigation, and flood control. The local improvement districts must be authorized by state law and follow specific state procedures for formation, governance, and the issuance of bonds to finance the projects.

locally unwanted land uses   Halfway homes for prisoners, waste disposal sites, electric power plants, and other things generally considered good but in someone else's part of town.

locational obsolescence   See *external obsolescence*.

location intelligence   Generally refers to the use of computer-aided mapping and demographic tools, including market characteristics, locations of competitors, traffic counts, zoning, growth characteristics, and other such data important to site selection.

lockbox   (1) A special box placed on the door of homes listed for sale, with a key to the property inside the box. The box is accessed via a code or a key, available only to licensed real estate agents. (2) An arrangement whereby customers of a business send their payments to a PO box which is actually controlled by the business's lender rather than the business. The lender takes all receipts, pays itself any loan payments and fees, and then remits the balance to the business.

locked-in interest rate   An agreement by a lender to grant a particular interest rate on a loan that is funded by the expiration date. For consumers, the lock-in is sometimes free, sometimes there is a charge, and sometimes the initial lock-in is free but any extensions will require payment of a fee. On commercial loans, there is almost always a commitment fee for an interest rate lock.

lock-in clause   A clause in a promissory note that prohibits prepayment.

lock-in period   (1) The period of time during which a loan may not be prepaid. (2) The period of time during which a lender will guarantee a certain interest rate on a loan to be extended by it in the future.

London Interbank Offered Rate   See *LIBOR*.

long-term capital gain   A gain on the sale of an asset held for more than one year. Currently long-term capital gains enjoy reduced tax rates over those imposed on short-term capital gains.

long-term debt   Technically, that portion of any debt that will come due after 1 year from the current date. A newly made 30-year mortgage would have 1 year of payments posted to short-term debt on the accounting books of the borrower, and 29 years posted to long-term debt. In common parlance, though, it is simply any debt with a maturity greater than 1 year from the time of making.

long-term loss   Losses on real property sold more than one year after purchase. Compare with long-term capital gains, which are profits earned on real property sold more than one year after purchase. Long-term losses must be deducted against long-term gains.

loss factor   The ratio between the total square footage not available for lease in a building and the total square footage in a building. When comparing rents among buildings, be aware that owners may account for the loss factor differently. Some may quote a per-square-foot rate for usable space—the space you can count as "yours." This may be higher than another's quote for a rate per square foot of rentable space—the space you can count as "yours" plus your share of the loss factor. For example, a building has 50,000 square feet, but only 40,000 square feet may be rented to tenants. The remaining 10,000 square feet is devoted to the lobby, elevators, corridors, and utility rooms. Then the loss factor is 10,000/50,000 or 20 percent.

loss payee   A person entitled to payment from an insurance policy, even if the person is not the insured. For property insurance, the mortgage lender is usually the first loss payee and will be paid to the extent of the principal balance of its loan, with the remainder of the money to the homeowner. Lenders may waive payment if there is an insured loss and allow payment to the borrower to make repairs. In the alternative, it may accept payment and then disburse funds as repairs are made, as a method of making sure the insurance money goes back into the property.

lost-grant doctrine   One theory underpinning adverse possession and prescription, that one who occupies and uses property for the required period of time really had good title, or grant, at one time in the past, but the documents have been lost. (1) This is important in determining exactly when someone gains title by adverse possession. Was it from the date of first possession, at the date the statute of limitations expired, or the date of a court's order recognizing the successful adverse possession? Using the lost grant doctrine, title is effective on the date of first possession. (2) This doctrine is used to get around statutes prohibiting adverse possession against the government. Courts will say there was no adverse possession; someone must have just lost the original deed.

> **Example:**   *In the case of normal adverse possession, Tootsie and Ben are adjoining property owners who are arguing over a strip of land that each claims. Ben cuts down the trees on the strip of land. Tootsie claims they were her trees and sues for damages. She claims her survey is the correct one and, even if it were not, she has adversely possessed the land for 20 years and it is now her land. Ben claims his survey is the correct one. If the court rules that Ben's survey is the correct one, but Tootsie has adversely possessed the land, when did Tootsie gain title? If it was at the time of the court ruling, then Ben could not be liable for cutting the trees because they didn't belong to Tootsie at the time he cut them. But, because of the lost-grant doctrine, courts will treat the trees as if they had always belonged to Tootsie, so Ben is liable.*

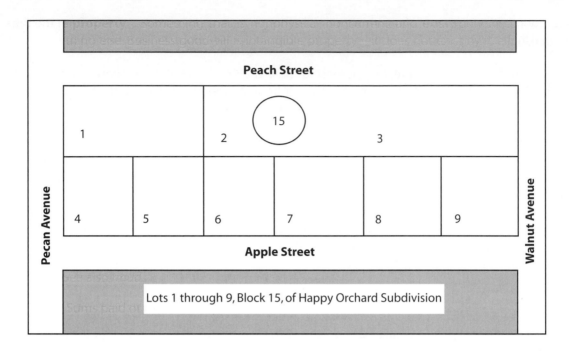

Peach Street

15

1　　2　　3

4　　5　　6　　7　　8　　9

Pecan Avenue

Walnut Avenue

Apple Street

Lots 1 through 9, Block 15, of Happy Orchard Subdivision

lot, block, and subdivision　　A method of identifying property within a platted subdivision. The developer files a map, or plat (see above), with local authorities. It shows the exact legal description of the entire parcel of land, and then shows how the developer will install streets, number the blocks within the subdivision, and number the lots within each block.

love and affection　　The usual recited consideration when there has been a gift of real estate to a family member or other loved one. Love and affection is good consideration under applicable statutes, but it is not valuable consideration. Important concepts include the following:

- A transfer of land to a child for love and affection during the parent's lifetime will often be deemed an advancement under the parent's will and can reduce the amount the child will inherit under the will.
- Love and affection will support a deed and make it valid, but it is not sufficient consideration so as to make a contract enforceable. In other words, a contract to transfer real estate upon love and affection is not enforceable; a deed with recited consideration of love and affection cannot be set aside.
- One who takes property for a consideration of love and affection cannot be a bona fide purchaser for value, because the consideration is only *good*, it is not *valuable*.

low-income housing　　(1) Generically, any housing that is limited to occupancy by persons whose family income does not exceed certain preset maximum levels. (2) For purposes of special tax incentives provided to persons who build or rehabilitate "qualified low income housing projects," the IRS defines the term as (a) any project in which 20 percent or more of the units are both rent restricted and occupied by persons whose income is 50 percent or less of the area median gross income or (b) one in which 40 percent or more of the units are both rent restricted and occupied by persons whose income is 60 percent or less of the area median gross income.

low-income housing limited partnerships   Partnerships formed to take advantage of the tax credits offered for investing in low-income housing.

low-income housing tax credits   A package of allowed tax credits issued by the IRS to state housing agencies. The IRS has formulas for determining the size of credits issued to each state. The state housing agency then reviews applications from developers who wish to build or rehabilitate low-income housing and receive the benefit of the tax credits. If approved, the state agency will then award a certain amount of tax credits to the developer, who may use them on its federal income taxes.

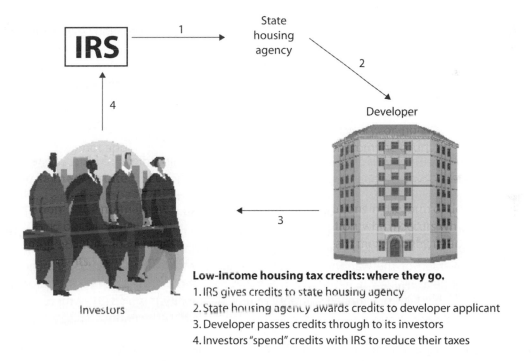

Low-income housing tax credits: where they go.
1. IRS gives credits to state housing agency
2. State housing agency awards credits to developer applicant
3. Developer passes credits through to its investors
4. Investors "spend" credits with IRS to reduce their taxes

low-rise   Usually a one- to four-story commercial building. The meaning changes depending on custom and usage in a particular market.

LTV   See *loan-to-value ratio*.

LULUs   See *locally unwanted land uses*.

lump-sum payment   A payment of all principal and interest at the maturity of a promissory note.

LUST   See *leaking underground storage tank*.

L/V   See *loan-to-value ratio*.

M

Maes, the   Used generically to refer to Maggie Mae, Fannie Mae, Sallie Mae, Ginnie Mae, and Munie Mae.

Maggie Mae   Common name for Mortgage Guaranty Insurance Corporation (www.mgic.com). It is the leading provider of private mortgage insurance for loans in excess of an 80 percent loan to value. It also purchases, pools, and then sells interests in sub- and no-performing mortgage debt, and it purchases and services charged-off consumer debt such as unpaid credit cards and Chapter 13 bankruptcies.

magnet store   See *anchor tenant*.

Magnusson-Moss Act   A federal law passed in 1975, governing disclosures in connection with written warranties on consumer goods, including goods attached to or installed on real property. It does not require warranties, but if one is given, (1) the title of the document must clearly state whether it is a full warranty (imposing no conditions on the buyer, such as routine maintenance every 3 months) or a limited warranty (requiring the borrower to meet certain requirements, that can be spelled out in the body of the warranty itself); (2) the warranty must disclose certain information about the coverage of the warranty, explained in an easy-to-read and concise manner; (3) the warranty must be available where the goods are sold so that consumers can read it before buying. It is unlawful to disclaim the implied warranty of merchantability. It is also unlawful to say that use of unauthorized parts or repair services will automatically void the warranty.

MAI   Member, Appraisal Institute; a designation awarded to appraisers who meet stringent educational, testing, and experience requirements imposed by the Appraisal Institute.

maid's quarters   See *granny flat*.

mailbox rule   A rule of contract law that says if an offer is made in such a manner that it would be reasonable to assume that another person would accept the offer by placing a letter or other writing in the mail, then acceptance is deemed to have occurred when the writing was placed in the mail, not when it was received by the person making the offer. For example, this is important when a property owner offers, in writing, to sell a particular property for a specified sum. The potential purchaser decides to accept the offer and mail the acceptance to the owner. Before the owner receives the letter, but after it is mailed, the owner decides to withdraw the offer and takes the property off the market or increases the price. In this example, the owner cannot do so because the purchaser has already accepted the offer; it cannot be withdrawn. There is now a contract; there is no longer an offer capable of revocation.

maintenance   The care and upkeep of a building to keep it in roughly the same condition as when it was first built, except for natural changes in the patina of finishes.

maintenance fee   Another name for a condo association fee and homeowners association fee, and sometimes used to describe the rent charged to a co-operative apartment owner.

majority   The age at which a person is able to enter into legally binding contracts in a particular state.

maker   The person who executes a promissory note.

malfeasance   Doing an act that is wrongful. Contracts will often have default clauses for a party's malfeasance, misfeasance, or nonfeasance. Malfeasance is a wrongful act, misfeasance is a proper act done in a wrongful manner, and nonfeasance is the failure to act when one had a duty to act.

management agreement   A contract between the owner of income-producing property and another, who will manage the property. Management companies offer a wide variety of services and fee schedules, some charging a percentage of collected rents in return for a package of services and others charging a different fee for minimal services and then a menu of extras for varying charges. There is often a minimal monthly fee. (Always determine if there are additional charges for any of the services.)

Services can include some or all of the following:

- Collection of rents
- Leasing space to new tenants
- Collection activities including evictions
- Management of on-site personnel such as resident managers (who may be the employee of the property owner or the employee of the management company)
- Management of outside repair and maintenance service providers
- In-house repair and maintenance services
- Preparation and filing of all tax reports, such as rent taxes
- Payment of all or some bills
- Physical property inspections
- Periodic reporting of the property condition, revenues, and expenses
- Periodic recommendations regarding changes to the property or rental rates
- Brokerage services for the acquisition of additional properties or the sale of existing properties.

mandamus   In the nature of an appeal, mandamus is a command from a court ordering a government authority, or a lower court official, to do some act that is within their power to do and they are supposed to do without exercising any discretion. One would appeal a decision to deny a building permit for construction with minor or inconsequential variances from code requirements. However, one would seek mandamus if the permitting office acknowledged that all requirements had been met, but still refused to issue the permit. The decision of proper remedy—mandamus or appeal—is highly technical, and the wrong choice could result in the loss of all rights to reverse a decision.

manufactured housing   Housing that is manufactured off-site and then installed on real property with minimal assemblage except as pertains to the various sections of a double-wide or a triple-wide home. All such housing manufactured since 1976 must meet a sort of national building code established by HUD for the industry. The industry trade association is the Manufactured Housing Institute (www.manufacturedhousing.org).

marginal land   Land with little immediate usefulness because of problems with access, water control, topography, environmental restrictions, or other such factors.

marginal release   A method of noting the satisfaction of a mortgage or other lien by making a notation in the margin of the recorded instrument.

marginal tax rate   The percentage of income that must be paid to the IRS for a particular range of incomes, called tax brackets. As one's income increases, the marginal tax rate increases but only for that portion of one's income within the higher bracket. Portions of income within the lower brackets are taxed at the lower marginal tax rates.

marital deduction   For estate tax and gift tax purposes, the 100 percent deduction granted for assets passing to spouses.

market   A defined area from which one's customers may be drawn. The market size and boundaries will depend on the product offered (student housing, self-storage, estate lots for custom homes, professional offices for attorneys, etc.). A market can be defined in various ways. For example, it can be defined

1. By a radius from a certain point, such as the market within a 1-, 3-, or 5-mile radius of a development
2. By reference to natural boundaries consumers will not typically cross for goods and services, such as a highway, a particular city street, or even a bridge.
3. As an entire city
4. As all persons of a particular type within a city

An accurate description of one's market is essential to any development planning in order to assess the competition already existing in the market and the need for additional entrants. Market identification and description is also important for advertising and marketing services. (For example, there is no point in spending a large budget on citywide print advertising in newspapers and local magazines if your market lives and works within 3 miles of your location.)

marketable title   Clear title to real estate without any liens, encumbrances, or adverse claims such as would be considered defects. A power line easement is technically an encumbrance, but most would not consider it such an impediment as to prevent marketable title unless the property was zoned for residential use and the power line easement covered so much of the lot that property became unbuildable.

market comparison approach   A method of appraising property by analyzing the prices of similar properties sold in the recent past and then making adjustments based on differences among the properties and the relative age of the other sale. More properly called the direct sales approach. See also *comparables*. The other two methods are the cost approach and the income approach.

market cycle   A period of time during which real estate prices increase steadily and then level off or decrease.

market data   Information about a defined geographic area or demographic (college graduates, young families, retirees, etc.) and the timing, characteristics, total volume, and individual size of buying activity within that area or group.

market data approach   A former term for the direct sales comparison method of appraisal.

marketing period   A measure of time between listing property for sale and closing. The average marketing period in an area is a good indication of the strength or weakness of the seller's market.

market rent   See *economic rent*.

market rental rates   Rents that are relatively consistent with other rents in the same area for comparable properties. For example, in downtown Metro City, the market rental rate for class A office space is $42 per square foot per year, with a tenant improvement allowance of $25 per square foot on a 5-year lease.

market value   There are many different definitions of market value, depending on the organization finding it necessary to write a definition. Most definitions include the following: the price that would be paid by a motivated buyer to a motivated seller after a property's exposure to a marketplace of equally capable buyers, each with full information about the property and the market place and neither operating under any sort of outside influences.

Mark-to-Market program   As used by the Department of Housing and Urban Development, a HUD program to eliminate higher than market rental rates for low-income housing owned by private developers. There was nothing wrong with this, originally. HUD wanted to encourage developers to build such housing, so it offered to subsidize the rents and pay developers the difference between the income-based rents paid by the tenants and a developer-set unit rent that could be higher than local market conditions. If developers could receive above-market rents and income guaranteed by HUD, anyone would naturally start building lots of low-income housing. Now, however, the properties have been enjoying above-market rents for many years, and HUD wants it to end. The Mark-to-Market program is a staged termination of those incentives, requiring low-income housing facilities to charge market rents, and no higher.

marriage benefit   The concept that married persons enjoy a de facto tax benefit not given to other couples because the married filing jointly tax rates are lower than the ones for single persons.

married, filing jointly   The ability of husbands and wives to file a joint tax return that allows them to aggregate their incomes into one total and pay taxes at a somewhat lower rate than if a single person earned the same amount of income. It is not necessary that both spouses earn income.

master   (1) Employer-employee law is sometimes called master-servant law. (2) A person appointed by a court to perform a specific function, such as to sell real estate that is in dispute or to assist with evidentiary issues or other duties. (The practice is rare in federal court, but very common in some state courts.)

master deed   A document used by condominium developers to record the project; its division into condominium ownership; and the grant of common areas to the condominium owners. Also called the declarations, the condominium declaration, or the declaration of condominium. (Do not confuse with *master's deed*.)

master lease   A lease between the owner of property and its direct tenant, with all other leases subject to the first one. A tenant may sublease or assign part or all of its space on its own terms and conditions, but the parties will always be bound by the master lease because they are subordinate to it.

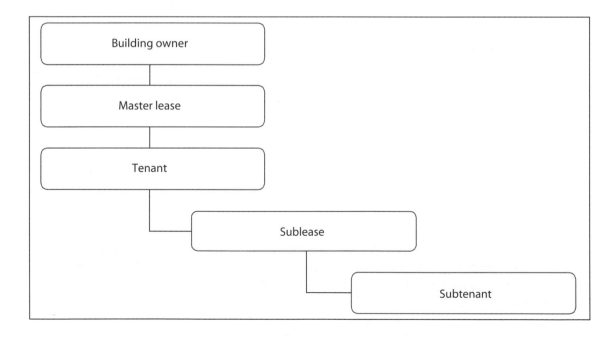

master's deed   A deed from a judicial officer given as a result of a foreclosure, a tax sale, or sometimes a divorce, depending on the state and its customs. Do not confuse with *master deed*.

material fact   Any fact that is relevant to a reasonable person making a decision. For example,

- Real estate agents must disclose material facts known to them about the condition of property.
- Some facts, although they may be material, cannot be disclosed unless the seller gives his or her permission, such as the fact that the seller or a prior owner or occupant of the property was HIV-positive or had AIDS.
- Legally actionable fraud is a misrepresentation of a material fact. If there was a misrepresentation, but the fact was not material, there is no liability for fraud.

materialman   See *mechanics' and materialmen's liens*.

maturity   The date on which the remaining balance of a promissory note is due.

McMansion   A derogatory term for a large house on a small lot; the term is intended to give a sense of uniformity and pretension. Also called starter castle.

mean   The average of a set of numbers. Contrast with median, which is the middle figure in a set of numbers, and mode, which is the value that appears most often in a set of numbers.

> **Example:**   *A survey of home values in a neighborhood of nine houses obtained the following values:*

House	Value
1	$139,000
2	139,000
3	139,500
4	139,750
5	139,850
6	140,000
7	140,500
8	140,800
9	169,000

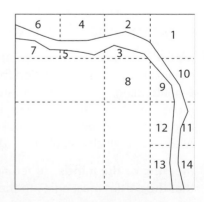

The mean, or average, is the total of all values divided by 9, or $143,044. The median is the middle number when the numbers are all arranged from highest to lowest, which would be house 5, or $139,850. The mode is $139,000, because it is the number that appears most often.

meander line   An artificial line placed on a survey to describe the meandering course of a river or stream that forms a boundary of property. The use of a meander line indicates that the boundary is the waterway and changes if the waterway changes. If the surveyor does not use a meander line, then the boundary line is fixed and constant.

measurements   See *land measurement conversion.*

measuring life   The person whose life span determines the duration of a life tenant's entitlement to possess and use real property. Typically, property is given or left by will to someone to use "for and during their natural lifetime" and then the document specifies who gets the property afterward. In the typical case, the life tenant is also the measuring life; when the life tenant dies, the right to use the property also dies at the same time.

> **Example:**   *A different variety of life tenancy might give property "to Alice and her heirs, for and during the lifetime of Nate," with Nate being a baby born two days earlier. Nate is the measuring life. When Nate dies, Alice or her heirs will cease to have any interest in the property. It does not matter if Nate dies one week later or 100 years later, the life estate ends when he dies. At the end of the measuring life, the property passes to a previously specified remainderman.*

mechanics' and materialmen's liens   Statutory liens granted in some states to specifically describe persons who provide goods or services contributing to the improvement of real property under a contract with the owner or the owner's representative, such as a general contractor. Such a lien will attach in favor of subcontractors even if the owner paid the general contractor, but the general contractor did not pay the subcontractors. It can take priority over a mortgage if the work was started before the mortgage was recorded, even if the lien document was not filed until after the mortgage was filed. Most statutes grant a very short time after nonpayment for the lien documents to be filed, or the lien will be lost. After that, one claiming under the lien must promptly take steps to foreclose the lien, or it will be lost. Property owners may protect themselves in some states by posting notices of nonresponsibility on the property, advising all subcontractors and vendors that they must look only to the general contractor for payment. A commercial service (Wallace W. Lien, P.C.) provides access to the lien laws for all 50 states at its Web site, www.lienlaw.com.

median   The middle number of a series. See also *mean*, which includes examples.

median cut   A break in the concrete or landscaped dividing area separating opposite lanes of traffic, enabling persons to turn at that location. The placement of median cuts is extremely important when looking for locations for retail establishments. If it is not easy for the public to turn into a place of business and to leave from that place of business, they will not shop there.

mediation   An alternative dispute resolution (ADR) process in which a trained person assists disputants in coming to a solution that will be the best one under the circumstances for all involved. It is not binding, but many courts are now imposing mandatory diversion to mediation and a requirement that the parties negotiate in good faith to reach a settlement. Failure to settle may subtly impact a judge's decision regarding the party most at fault in a dispute. The American Arbitration Association, which also offers mediation services, maintains a Web site at www.adr.org.

meeting of the minds   A requirement for the formation of a valid and enforceable contract is that the parties must agree to the same thing. If there is a mutual mistake of fact regarding one of the critical elements of a contract, there has been no meeting of the minds and the contract may be set aside.

megalopolis   A densely populated urban area that sprawls across two or more large, independent cities. The photo is a night-time satellite image showing population concentrations in megalopolis areas in the United States.

Examples include the Bos-Wash megalopo-lis from Boston to Washington, D.C., with an estimated population in excess of 41 million people; Chi-Pitts from Chicago to Pittsburgh; and San-San from San Francisco to San Diego. The largest megalopolis in the world is the 1,200-mile Taiheiyo Belt in Japan.

menace   (1) A threat of violence used to secure a contract. Such a contract can be set aside, just as a contract secured by duress. (2) A threat of violence to another, such as a trespasser. Some state statutes allow the use of force to protect one's home, but do not include the ability to menace another in order to protect one's home.

merchantable title   See *marketable title*.

merger   (1) With regard to corporations, a legal joining together of two or more corporations into one entity or an entity with common ownership. A horizontal merger occurs between or among competitors, and a vertical merger occurs when suppliers, shippers, retailers, and such in a common industry join together. (2) With regard to real estate: (a) The joining of two or more interests in real estate into one owner, so that the separate interests, or estates, disappear. If a property owner with a right-of-way easement over her neighbor's land then purchases the neighbor's land, the easement is extinguished. If she then sells her first property to another, the new owner cannot now claim the benefit of the old right-of-way easement, because it was merged into land ownership. (b) The concept that a real estate contract becomes merged into the deed, so that provisions in the contract, but not in the deed, are not enforceable. This is almost always a question of intent, which means a jury gets to decide. The better course is to specify in the contract that all representations and warranties and all promises and agreements survive the deed. (c) The concept that negotiations are merged into a final contract and cannot be used to vary the terms of the contract.

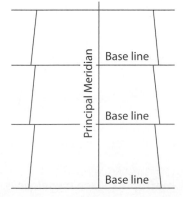

meridian   One of the imaginary lines running north and south and used by surveyors for reference in locating and describing land. Each area has a principal meridian as the reference for all other lines. Because of the curvature of the earth, though, meridian lines cannot remain an equal distance apart, because they converge as they approach the North Pole. As a result, correcting lines, called guide lines, are run at 24-mile inter-vals. The correcting lines break and then re-form at each base line. See also *public land survey system*.

mesne profits   Damages due from one who is in wrongful possession of property, usually meas-ured by the fair market rental of the property during the time period of the wrongful possession. This is damage for the possession itself; not damage for injuries to the property such as cutting down trees, destroying carpet, or flooding the basement. If the trespasser made improvements to the prop-erty, in good faith and believing himself or herself entitled to possession, then the value of the improvements may be used to set off any judgment for mesne profits.

messuage   A house and the surrounding land and buildings used by it; the term is encountered in older laws granting a widow the right of quarantine after her husband's death, being the ability to use the mansion and messuage for a certain period of time until her other rights are settled.

metes and bounds   A method of describing real property by starting with some universally recognized point, usually a specified corner of a 640-acre section but sometimes a monument. The description then specifies turning in a certain direction—northwest or southeast, for exam-ple—and at a certain angle, such as 35 degrees. The description will then specify the distance one should proceed at that direction and angle for one of the property lines, before making a turn. The process continues until the entire parcel is described and one has returned to the beginning point.

> **Example:**   *Beginning at the Northwest corner of Section 16, Township 19 South, Range 10 West, being the Point of Beginning (POB) thence proceed southerly along said section line for a distance of 100 feet to a point; thence turn 90 degrees 0 minutes west and proceed for a distance of 130 feet to a point; thence turn 90 degrees 0 minutes north and proceed for a distance of 100 feet to a point; thence turn 90 degrees and 9 minutes east and proceed for a distance of 130 feet to the POB, containing 0.229 acres, more or less.*

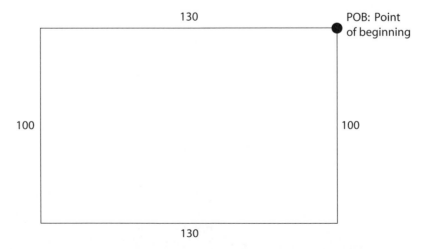

metroplex   See *megalopolis*.

metropolitan area   (1) Generally, any area in or around a city. (2) A concept developed by the federal Office of Management and Budget (OMB) in order to standardize the descriptions of geographical areas so that comparisons of data among various federal agencies could be on an apples-to-apples basis; all data regarding a particular metropolitan area would apply to the same geographical area and the same population density and profile. Today, the concept is called core-based statistical areas, which include metropolitan statistical areas and micropolitan statistical areas. One may find statistical information about each at the Web site of the U.S. Census, www.census.gov/population/www/estimates/aboutmetro.html.

- Metropolitan statistical areas contain at least one urbanized area of 50,000 people or more.
- Micropolitan statistical areas contain at least one urbanized area and a population of 10,000 to 50,000 people.

metropolitan division   See *metropolitan area.*

metropolitan statistical area   See *metropolitan area.*

mezzanine financing   A hybrid of debt and equity funding. Usually shortened to "mezz financing." The provider loans money on a second or even third mortgage basis and may either take an ownership interest in addition or may reserve the right to take over an ownership interest if the loan is not paid on time and in full. The loans are generally extended in emergency situations, such as to buy property quickly before bank lending can be arranged, or to engage in expansion activities and "grow" a company out of a cash crunch that is preventing it from securing a conventional loan. Because of the subordinate nature of the debt, the risky nature of the activities being funded by the money, and the lack of time to perform due diligence, mezz lenders usually want a high return on their money, in the 20 to 30 percent range.

mezzanine investors   Persons or companies who advance money to a business and receive, in return, a combination of promissory notes and preferential ownership shares in the business. Just as the mezzanine is the balcony-type partial floor of a building, between the ground floor and the second floor, so too a mezzanine investor occupies the middle ground with more risk than the first and second mortgage lenders, but not as much risk as the owners and other investors. See also *capital stack.*

MGIC   See *Maggie Mae.*

micropolitan statistical area   See *metropolitan area.*

midrise   Usually a four- to seven-story building, although definitions vary among markets. Contrast with *low-rise* and *high-rise.*

military protections and benefits   There are a number of protections and benefits for current and former members of the armed services, the reserves, and the national guards. They include

- The Homeowners Assistance Program for military personnel stationed at or near a military installation scheduled for closure or realignment. It is administered by the U.S. Corps of Engineers, which may purchase homes, reimburse persons for losses on the sale of their homes, or pay off mortgages if such markets are depressed. See the Web site for the Savannah District of the U.S. Corps of Engineers, www.sas.usace.army.mil/hapinv/index.html, for details.
- The Soldiers and Sailors Civil Relief Act, passed by Congress at the start of World War II, requires automatic reduction of home mortgage interest rates to 6 percent under certain circumstances and a variety of other protections from eviction, lapse of life insurance, garnishments, and lawsuits. See the entry for *Soldiers and Sailors Civil Relief Act* for details.
- Mortgage guarantees by the Veterans Administration.
- The GI Bill (www.gibill.com), now called the Montgomery GI Bill, which offers support for veterans seeking postsecondary education.

mill   One-tenth of one cent, or $0.001. Ad valorem (property) taxes are usually expressed in terms of a certain number of mills. A rate of 12.4 mills means that a property assessed for $100,000 would have ad valorem taxes of 12.4 (rate) $\times$ 0.001 (mill) $\times$ $100,000 (assessed value) for a tax of $1,240.

mineral rights   The right to take things beneath the soil. One may sell land and mineral rights separately from each other, which works a severance of the interests. In some states, sand, gravel, and clay are not considered minerals, even if they exist below the surface. One frequently contentious issue is whether a grant of mineral rights includes the ability to take them by strip mining or other open-air operations, such as quarrying. (The answer differs from state to state and also depends on the precise language of the deed.)

minimum lot area   A zoning ordinance specifying the smallest size lot on which something can be built. Sometimes, the restriction may be because of health department requirements for septic tanks, requiring a minimum of one acre.

minimum property requirements   An FHA requirement that a mortgage loan be secured by a property that is livable, soundly built, and suitably located as to the site and neighborhood. If the property does not meet the standards, the FHA may require repairs before providing funding.

minimum rent   The smallest amount of rent due from a tenant with a variable rental rate, such as a rent calculated as a certain percentage of gross sales, with a minimum rent of a certain amount per month.

mini-warehouse   A term sometimes used interchangeably with self-storage by consumers, but with differing meanings in zoning statutes. Typically, a mini-warehouse is defined as small storage space of 200 to perhaps 1,000 square feet, designed for commercial customers, while self-storage would be something of 25 to 200 square feet and designed for storage of household goods by consumers. Each zoning regulation will provide its own definition.

minor   A person who has not yet reached the age of majority required to enter into binding contracts.

misfeasance   An action that was legal and proper, but which was performed in an improper manner. A real estate agent who innocently deposits an earnest money check in the real estate company's business account instead of the escrow account, but who does not spend the money or use it in any manner, is probably guilty of a misfeasance. If the agent spent the money, that would be malfeasance, or doing something improper and illegal. If the agent put the check in a desk drawer and did not deposit it in any account, that would be nonfeasance, or the failure to take an action when the law required that some act be done.

misrepresentation   See *fraud*.

mitigation of damages   A legal principle that those who are injured by a breach of contract have a duty to take all steps necessary to decrease their damages, rather than simply sitting idly by and suing the defaulting party for all sums due under the contract. A landlord has a duty to mitigate its damages and find another tenant for property, with the defaulting tenant to be given credit for the value of the replacement lease.

mixed use   The use of real property for more than one type of use, such as residential property and small offices in close proximity. The modern trend of land use is toward mixed use.

MLS   Short for multiple listing service. A service whereby real estate brokers agree to make information about their listed properties available to each other and to split a commission with any other broker who provides the buyer. Most local boards require an exclusive listing agreement with a broker as a prerequisite for placement in the multiple listing service.

- At one time, this exclusive access to information about properties currently on the market, and historical information regarding selling prices of former properties, gave real estate brokers tremendous advantages over nonmembers and over consumers trying to sell property without the assistance of a broker. Today, with easy access to information on the Internet, including limited MLS information at the Web site of the National Association of REALTORS® (www.realtor.com), consumers are able to negotiate more competitively.
- The Antitrust Division of the Department of Justice has been scrutinizing MLS agreements that exclude brokers who are not members of the local board of REALTORS® (associated with the National Association of REALTORS®) or brokers who accept limited-services agreements.

mobile home   See *manufactured housing*.

modular housing   A type of housing in which the components are manufactured elsewhere and then assembled at the building site. It allows the construction of semicustom or even custom homes at very economical prices. The industry's trade association is the Modular Building Systems Association (www.modularhousing.com). The above photo is of a custom, modular home.

month-to-month tenancy   A leasehold interest that is terminable at the expiration of any given month, although state consumer protection statutes may require the landlord, the tenant, or both to give one month's notice before termination. Oral leases are assumed to be month-to-month, because the tenant pays rent one month at a time. If a tenant remains in possession of property at the expiration of a typical 6-month or 1-, 3- or 5-year lease, courts in the various states are divided in their opinions regarding whether the new arrangement is a month-to-month tenancy or a renewal for a like term as the original lease, not exceeding 1 year.

monument   A physical object, either natural or artificial, used by surveyors as a reference point. It may be a concrete block, iron pin, rod, stone marker, or other such thing set in place in order to bear witness to the reference point, or it may be a tree, bridge, river, or fence.

moral turpitude   Under all real estate licensing laws, as with other professions, a real estate license can be denied or it can be revoked if a person is guilty of a crime of moral turpitude. There are many definitions, including baseness, vileness, depravity; contrary to accepted and customary rules, depraved or vicious motives, or acts done contrary to justice, honesty, modesty, or good morals. An examination of the various licensing statutes shows that the term is rather free-floating and is intended to convey a sense that if the commission of a particular crime bears a reasonable and substantial relationship to the qualifications, functions, or duties of a real estate broker, then it is a crime of moral turpitude.

moratorium   A temporary cessation. Usually encountered in real estate when a local government suspends issuance of building permits in a particular area because, for example, the existing water line or sewer line capacity will not accommodate new growth.

more or less   Words used in a deed description to indicate that the given size or dimensions of the property may not be precisely as stated. Without such words, a parcel that differs in size from the representations could result in the rescission—setting aside—of a deed because of a mutual mistake of fact.

mortgage   A written document that provides a lender with rights in real property as collateral for a loan. The loan itself is evidenced by a promissory note, which is a written promise to repay money on certain terms and conditions. In common language, people refer to the whole relationship with the real estate lender as a mortgage, and you will see references in writing to "mortgage interest rates." Technically, though, the reference should be to "mortgage loan interest rates."

- In some states, the security instrument is called a deed of trust. The property owner actually deeds the property to a third party, who holds the naked legal title in trust for the owner and will reconvey (retransfer) it when the debt has been paid in full. If there is a default and foreclosure, the trustee will convey the property to the successful bidder. Such states usually allow nonjudicial foreclosures.
- In other states, the instrument called a mortgage creates only a lien on real property. The borrower is called the mortgagor, and the lender is called the mortgagee. In order to foreclose, the lender usually has to obtain court permission to conduct a sale. These are called judicial foreclosures.
- In a very few states, called hybrid states, the instrument called a mortgage transfers legal title to the lender itself. The title is extinguished when the debt has been paid in full. The lender may take advantage of nonjudicial foreclosure.
- If foreclosure nets less money than is owed on the note with all interest and costs of collection, then the lender can usually sue the borrower in state court for the balance, called a deficiency. Exceptions occur if the note provided that it was nonrecourse, meaning without any personal liability by the borrower, or if state laws prohibit deficiency judgments for first mortgages on a consumer's principal residence.
- In some states, a debtor has a grace period after foreclosure within which to buy the property back for the amount of the winning bid price plus interest at the legal rate for that state. These rights of redemption may also be extended to junior lienholders and even unsecured creditors, who may wish to invest the money necessary for redemption because they believe they can sell at a profit and recoup their losses.

mortgage backed security (MBS)   See *collateralized mortgage backed securities.*

mortgage banker   One who is not an institutional lender (bank, credit union, etc.) but who loans their own funds for mortgage financing. The mortgage banker might borrow the money on a line of credit, in order to fund the loans, but it is still responsible for providing the cash. Contrast with a mortgage broker, who acts only as an intermediary.

mortgage broker   One who acts as an intermediary between borrowers and lenders, but who is not personally involved in underwriting, funding, or servicing the loans.

Mortgage Guaranty Insurance Corporation (MGIC)   See *Maggie Mae.*

mortgage lender   A person or company that loans money and takes a security interest in real property. The lender can provide more than just real estate loans, but it is referred to as the mortgage lender when someone is talking about a real estate loan.

mortgage REIT   A real estate investment trust (REIT) that purchases mortgage debts as investments, rather than income-producing property. Contrast with equity REITs, which invest in office buildings, hospitals, apartments, and other real properties, but not mortgages.

mortmain   Literally means "dead hand." Originally referred to statutes passed in England in 1279 and 1290 to prevent transfers of property to the Church, which would keep the land in its "dead hand" forever and prevent the king from ever realizing any tax income from it. In modern times, mortmain statutes invalidated deathbed gifts to charities, upon the theory that the recipient may have been guilty of undue influence by promises of a rosy hereafter, making the gift suspicious. Today, most such statutes have been repealed. (Unhappy heirs wishing to contest last-minute charitable gifts may use the general theory of undue influence to make their case.)

most-favored-tenant clause   A clause in a lease promising an existing tenant the same concessions as may be granted to future tenants, for a specified period of time. Frequently encountered when a new building wishes to secure a large tenant, but that tenant wants to wait and see if the concession package gets any better with the passage of time. As a compromise, the landlord will agree that future tenants will never receive a better deal than the existing one. As a practical matter, the first large tenant in a building will almost always receive the best deal, so the clause is in the nature of a "feel-good clause."

Mother Hubbard clause   See *anaconda mortgage*.

mother-in-law apartment   See *granny flat*.

multifamily residential property   Properties consisting of five or more connected dwelling units.

multiple listing service   See *MLS*.

municipal mortgage enhancement (Munie Mae)   A Fannie Mae program in which its mortgage backed securities are exchanged for the underlying mortgage on a tax-exempt multifamily project, thereby enabling the developer to obtain loan money at the lowest possible rate.

Munie Mae   See *municipal mortgage enhancement*.

muniment of title   (1) A legal document evidencing title to real property. (2) Under the muniment of title doctrine, when parties have litigated the title to real property, the loser cannot take a second bite of the apple, sue the next owners, and thereby attempt to regain title.

N

NAEBA See *National Association of Exclusive Buyer Agents*.

naked title Bare legal title to property, carrying with it none of the benefits of ownership. Usually the title held by a trustee, with the beneficiary holding equitable title.

nanoacre Related to real estate only because space on a computer board is referred to as real estate. A nanoacre is about 2 square millimeters, or 0.003 square inches.

NAR See *National Association of REALTORS®*.

narrative report A self-contained appraisal report.

NAREB See *National Association of Real Estate Brokers*.

National Association of Exclusive Buyer Agents (NAEBA) Established in 1995 as an organization for brokers and real estate agents who represent buyers. In the normal situation, the listing agent represents the seller, and most other agents "working with buyers" act as subagents for the seller. The situation is not well understood by the public. The NAEBA Web site is at www.naeba.org.

National Association of Real Estate Brokers (NAREB) A national trade association with a Mission Statement "to bring together the nation's minority professionals in the real estate industry to promote the meaningful exchange of ideas about our business and how best to serve our clientele." The NAREB Web site is at www.nareb.com.

National Association of REALTORS® (NAR) The largest real estate organization in the world, with over 850,000 members in all 50 states plus Washington, D.C.; Guam; Puerto Rico; and the Virgin Islands. The association promotes ethical standards, educational growth, professionalism, and the effective use of modern tools and technology. It has positioned itself as "The Voice for Real Estate," a theme it adopted in 1989 and has followed since that time. It maintains a Web site primarily for members at www.realtor.org and another devoted to consumers at www.realtor.com.

National Conference of Commissioners on Uniform State Laws Founded in 1892 to study the laws of the various states, recommend areas that should have uniform laws around the nation, and then write laws that may serve as models for legislation by the individual states. The current real estate–related laws written and proposed by the National Conference of Commissioners on Uniform State Laws (www.nccusl.org) include topics on landlord-tenant law, condominiums, conservation easements, residential time-shares, and nonjudicial foreclosure.

National Flood Insurance Program   A federal program allowing people to purchase flood insurance. It is administered by the Federal Insurance Administration (FIA), which is a branch of the Federal Emergency Management Agency (FEMA). See *flood insurance.*

National Trust for Historic Preservation   A private, nonprofit organization (www.nationaltrust.org) dedicated to saving historic places and revitalizing America's communities. Each year it publishes a list of the country's most endangered places. For 2006, one of the top 11 most endangered places was a descriptive locale rather than a specific place. It was the corner of Main and Main, being the heart of downtown urban life and the hottest, most desirable redevelopment site for demolition of older buildings and construction of chain stores.

natural disaster   Any destructive activity not caused by human forces or interventions, including hurricanes, tornadoes, flooding, and volcanic eruptions, to name a few.

natural person   An individual, as opposed to an artificial person like a corporation, partnership, or association.

natural vacancy rate   The normal, average, or traditional percentage of rental properties in a community that are not leased or occupied.

navigable line   That portion of a river that can accommodate boat traffic in safety.

navigable waters   According to the Code of Federal Regulations section dealing with the U.S. Army Corps of Engineers (www.usace.army.mil/), which is given jurisdiction over them, navigable waters are "those waters that are subject to the ebb and flow of the tide and/or are presently used, or have been used in the past, or may be susceptible for use to transport interstate or foreign commerce. A determination of navigability, once made, applies laterally over the entire surface of the water body, and is not extinguished by later actions or events which impede or destroy navigable capacity." Property owners wishing to build boat piers or other structures extending into navigable waters must obtain a permit from the Department of the Army.

NECTAs   See *New England city and town areas.*

negative amortization   The situation that exists when one's monthly loan payments are insufficient to completely pay currently accrued interest. The unpaid interest is added to the principal balance. Rather than the normal situation of a principal balance becoming smaller with a fully amortizing loan, this situation results in a larger balance, hence the name negative amortization. It occurs most often when a borrower has a variable-rate loan but with fixed monthly payments for a short period of time.

negative cash flow   Having insufficient cash to pay all operating expenses of a business or an investment. The situation is common with new developments and is solved by the developer using its own money to help pay bills or, more often, by borrowing enough money in the development loan to cover cash shortfalls until the project reaches stabilized occupancy and the break-even point.

negative easement   (1) A prohibition of some activity on a property, so as to enhance the value or enjoyment of another property. For example, a beach-front property might have a building-height restriction so that inland property owners can enjoy an unobstructed view of the ocean. (2) Subdivision covenants and restrictions on the use of land are sometimes called reciprocal negative easements. For example, the restriction that no property may have fences around the front yard enhances the value of all properties because of the open nature of the community.

negative equity loans   Government-insured mortgage loans for up to 125 percent of the value of the property. The money may be used only for improvements to the property.

negative leverage   See *leverage.*

negligence   A breach in the performance of a legal duty, proximately resulting in harm to another. Central to the concept of negligence is the problem of determining the exact duty owed. For example, does one owe any duties of care regarding the condition of property so as not to injure trespassers? If there is no duty, there can be no negligence, no matter how sloppy and careless the act.

negligent fraud   A false statement of a material fact, made without any intention to deceive, but upon which someone else relies to their detriment and is injured. An example would be a real estate agent telling a buyer that all the appliances are new when, in reality, the agent didn't know, but thought they looked new.

negligent waste   See *waste.*

negotiable instrument   A document signed by the maker or drawer, containing an unconditional promise to pay a certain sum of money on demand or at a definite time to the bearer or to order but without any other promise, order, obligation, or power. (See the Uniform Commercial Code, Article 3.)

negotiation   (1) Under the Uniform Commercial Code, it is a voluntary or involuntary transfer of possession of a negotiable instrument by someone other than the issuer, to another, who thereby becomes a holder. (2) More commonly, it is the art and science of bringing two or more parties to an agreement that each views as delivering at least some of his or her goals.

When negotiating in real estate, keep some of these thoughts in mind:

- Price and terms (amount of earnest money, contingencies, time to close, what personal property stays behind, seller financing, etc.) are like two ends of a street. The closer you get to one, such as the price you want to pay, the further you are away from the other, such as the ability to also obtain seller financing. (Common wisdom says you can negotiate price or terms, but not both. That is not true, but they do tend to have an impact on each other.)
- The better armed you are with facts, the more likely you will succeed in your negotiations. If you think a price is too high, be prepared to give examples of similar properties that sold recently for lower prices. You may learn about features making the subject property more valuable. The seller may drop the price. You may find that, while you think the price is high, it is actually below market compared to similar properties.

- In commercial lease negotiations, there is always a certain amount of money the landlord is willing to spend—the deal money. It might be spent in the way of rent concessions, renovation of the leased property, or real estate commissions. Rent concessions consist of free rent for some time or reduced rent for the entire time. Free or reduced rent that is paid back later in the lease is not a true rent concession and shouldn't reduce the amount of available deal money. Learning about other rent concessions in the marketplace, and the amount of leasing commissions typically paid by a particular landlord, will give you a good idea of how to calculate the deal money. (The easiest negotiation in leasing is to tell the landlord how you want the deal money spent. After that, the measure of a good negotiator is how much more you can get.)

- Learn everything you can about the person or company on the other side. Negotiation is not always about reaching an agreement on price. Many times it is discovering and meeting unspoken goals or needs of the other party.

- Don't bid against yourself. If your offer is rejected, wait for a counteroffer.

- Never be embarrassed by a low offer if you think that's what the property is worth. It is far more common than you would think for properties to have asking prices well above what the owners are willing to accept. See *bottom-fishing*.

- In negotiations over specific wording of a written contract or lease, draw a red "X" on the first page of each version as it is rejected, but keep all rejected versions in a safe place. It may become important later—even years later if there is a lawsuit—to reconstruct what terms were discussed and rejected by the parties.

- Be aware that written negotiations, even by e-mail, can be interpreted as an enforceable contract under some circumstances. All writings, even e-mail messages, should contain a line saying, "For negotiation purposes only." See *Uniform Electronic Transactions Act* and *Statute of Frauds*.

- Letters of intent can be construed as binding contracts. If you want to avoid this, say so in the LOI. If you want the LOI to be a binding contract as to its deal terms, with details to be worked out later, say that. But, the devil is in the details, as they say, so be prepared to find contract or lease language particulars that become deal breakers. If your LOI is a binding contract, then you may find a court deciding the other contract terms for you.

- Be aware that popular word processing programs may keep track of all changes to a document. If you send that document file to someone else, that person may be able to click a menu item and view all your changes, thereby being able to track your thoughts. If in doubt regarding this feature, click on the Help button for your program and enter "track changes," "compare documents," or similar words.

neighborhood shopping center   Generally a straight-line strip center with a grocery store anchor, sometimes a drugstore, and other small retailers. It caters to shoppers in the immediate neighborhood for convenience items, such as laundry, hair and nail care, video rental, tanning salons, mail and package stores, and gift items.

net annual income   Income after payment of taxes.

net income Operating income after deduction of all expenses. See *net operating income*.

net income figures Loosely defined as a listing of after-tax income from various sources.

net lease A lease in which the tenant pays rent plus some portion of the maintenance and operating expenses of a property. The term triple net lease means the tenant pays all expenses associated with the property—maintenance, repairs, insurance, and real estate taxes. Beyond that, though, the expression net lease has no particular definition regarding the tenant's exact responsibilities. Every lease will be different and should be scrutinized for exact tenant expenses. One should always obtain a detailed list of expenses that are within the landlord's control, such as office overhead and salaries. Otherwise, expenses may increase dramatically merely because the owner's son-in-law, for example, has been given a high-paying job for mowing the lawn each week.

net listing An arrangement in which a property owner pays the listing real estate agent all purchase price proceeds over and above a minimum figure required by the owner. Because the real estate agent is usually the one to recommend an asking price to the owner, the practice is very susceptible to abuse. As a result, it is illegal in some states.

net-net-net lease See *triple net lease*.

net operating income (NOI) The foundation of almost all analyses of income producing property such as apartments, office buildings, and retail space. The number is the result of taking all rental and other revenues from the property and then subtracting all reasonably necessary operating expenses. Loan payments do not count as expenses for purposes of the NOI. If you, as the owner, pay yourself a salary of $100,000 a year but your job could be filled by someone at $35,000 a year, it is legitimate to make that downward adjustment in the expenses when presenting figures to a potential purchaser or lender. On the other hand, if you take no salary, do all the office work, make all repairs, and mow the lawn, then you will have to estimate what those expenses would be if a third party owned the project and enter that number as an imputed expense.

Example:

Difference between Cash Flow and Net Operating Income				
	Real Numbers: Annual		**Used to Calculate NOI: Annual**	
Revenues		+$250,000		+$250,000
Utilities		−2,000		−2,000
Maintenance crew	Self:	0	Reasonable third-party expense	−32,000
Office personnel	Spouse:	−100,000	Reasonable third-party expense	−40,000
Taxes and insurance		−20,000		−20,000
Loan payments		−24,000	Not relevant	0
	Cash flow =$104,000		NOI =$156,000	

net present value   An analytical tool for evaluating whether or not to purchase an investment. The tool does not tell you if an investment is good or bad; it tells you if the investment will meet your predetermined objectives or not.

Example of Net-Present-Value Calculations

A, B, and C each have $100,000 to spend on a rental house. By the end of year 1, whoever buys the house will have earned $9,000 in rent after paying all expenses, and the owner will then sell the house and earn $103,000 after paying all closing expenses. Each of them has different requirements for their investments. A would like to earn a 4.5% return, B would like to earn 12%, and C would like to earn 13%. Whose investment needs will be met by buying the rental house?

	A	B	C
	4.5%	**12%**	**13%**
Initial investment	$100,000	$100,000	$100,000
Cash income from rent by end of year 1	9,000	9,000	9,000
Cash income from asset sale at end of year 1	103,000	103,000	103,000
Total year 1 income	112,000	112,000	112,000
Present value of year 1 income at the selected discount rate	107,177	100,000	99,114
Net present value, or the difference between present value and necessary investment of $100,000	7,177	0	(886)*
	Buy	Buy	Don't buy

A's net present value is positive, which means the investment will exceed A's requirements. B's net present value is 0, which means the investment will exactly meet B's requirements. C's net present value is negative, which means the investment will not meet C's requirements.

---

*The parentheses indicate a negative number, in this case −$886.

- Critical to defining your objectives is setting the equivalent of an interest rate you would like to earn on your initial cash investment. This is called the discount rate. The discount rate may change from investment to investment, depending on your assessment of the risk. The safest investment is an FDIC-insured savings account, but it returns the lowest interest rate. You, the investor, decide what rate you would like to earn. You use the net-present-value tool to calculate whether a particular investment will earn the rate you want.

- Having said all that, the official definition of net present value is as follows: using a preselected discount rate, net present value is the present value of all cash incomes, less the present value of all cash outflows (including initial investment). If this is not clear, it will become so with the example below.
- If the net present value is 0 or a positive number, the investor should go forward. If the answer is negative for the discount rate selected, then the investment should not be made because it will not meet the investor's objectives, not because it is a "bad investment" in the ordinary sense of that phrase.
- The Excel formula for present value is
    =pv(rate, cashflow, cashflow, cashflow)
  "Rate" is the cell with the interest rate the investor would like to earn. Each of the "cashflow" entries is a cell address for cash flows by the end of each year, such as year 1, year 2, year 3, and so on. If an asset is sold in a particular year, the net sales price (after expenses of the sale) is entered as part of the cash flow for that year. One flaw of the system is that it assumes all cash flows are received at year-end, when they are really received over time, but that is usually a relatively minor problem.

net return rate   All the profits from a property, including the profit on a resale, as compared to the initial investment.

net usable acre/net usable feet   The portion of a property that is usable for ordinary purposes. If 5 acres of land slopes downward dramatically into a ravine, the listing agent might say the price is $12 per square foot, but $20 per net usable foot.

net worth   The financial value of a person or company after adding all assets and subtracting all liabilities.

New England city and town areas (NECTAs)   Areas defined by the U.S. Census Bureau with reference to traditional city and town designations in the six New England states.

new town   In keeping with the expression "all things old are new again," modern residential development is focusing on a small-town atmosphere called the new town concept. It includes sidewalks and community parks plus offices, retail, places of worship, and schools within the project itself and usually within walking distance of residential areas. It may even include some home-above-retail or home-above-office concepts and satellite offices for government services such as license renewal.

NIMBY   A derogatory term; an acronym for "not in my backyard." It is intended to convey the sense that people are generally in favor of socially desirable programs such as half-way houses for felons, or unsavory but largely necessary uses such as waste disposal sites, as long as they are located in or near someone else's neighborhood.

no bid   When a property with a Veterans Administration (VA) guarantee goes into foreclosure, the VA must perform an analysis regarding whether it would be cheaper to pay the guarantee amount or to buy the house from the servicer and then sell the house itself. When it chooses to pay the guarantee amount, it is called a no bid.

no buy, no pay clause   A clause in a real estate listing contract that excuses the seller from paying a real estate commission if the broker produces a buyer who is ready, willing, and able to purchase the listed property for the asking price, but the seller changes his or her mind and refuses to sell at all, or refuses to sell to that particular buyer. Without such an unusual clause, the broker has earned the commission when he or she produced such a buyer, and the owner will have to pay even though the owner declines to sell the property.

no deal, no commission clause   See *no buy, no pay clause.*

no further action letter   Written confirmation from an environmental oversight board that a property requires no remediation for possible contaminants.

NOI   See *net operating income.*

nominal consideration   A token payment or promise given in exchange for something else of greater value. Courts will usually not "look behind the value of consideration," and even a nominal consideration (such as $1) will support a contract and make it enforceable. It will also support a deed, so that it cannot be set aside.

nominal interest rate   The stated interest rate in a note, which may differ from the true (effective) interest rate because of discounting or fees.

nominal partner   One who lends his or her name to a venture or business and appears to be a partner, but in truth is not. Care should be taken because nominal partners may be held liable for partnership debts and liabilities, especially if someone can prove they would not have done business with the partnership but for their mistaken belief that the nominal partner was a true partner.

nominee   One who is designated to act for another in a limited sense. It could be a trustee, an agent, or a straw man.

nonaccrual   The actions of a lender making a change in how a loan is accounted on its books. Normally, the lender will treat itself as receiving income as interest comes due—accrues—on the loan. Under normal circumstances, the lender can expect to actually receive the cash in a very short period of time afterward. When a borrower defaults and does not pay its interest, and the default continues for several months, the lender will reach the point where it begins to doubt if it will ever receive the cash for the interest that is accruing. At that point, it does not make business sense and, in fact, might be against federal regulations, to keep acting as if the lender were receiving income. As a result, the lender places the loan on nonaccrual, and stops posting income from the loan. This is a bookkeeping and accounting action only. It does not mean the lender will not attempt to collect every nickel of money due to it.

nonassumption clause   See *due-on-sale clause.*

noncapital expenditures   Money spent on repairs, supplies, payroll, and other operating expenses.

noncategorical taking   In an inverse condemnation case, a property owner complains that government regulations have rendered his or her property worthless, thus amounting to condemnation under eminent domain powers and therefore entitling the owner to compensation. There are two approaches to analyzing the taking—a categorical taking or a noncategorical taking. The noncategorical taking standard starts by finding the property has not been rendered economically useless. That being said, the courts must engage in complex analyses and balancing of interests across a wide variety of factors, including the extent to which the regulation interferes with reasonable investment-backed expectations of the property owner. See also *categorical taking*.

noncompetition clause   (1) A contract provision usually required by a buyer when purchasing a business. It prohibits the seller from engaging in a similar business in competition with the buyer. Courts will usually enforce such agreements if they are reasonable in a geographical area and time period. For example, Jack sells his property management business to Irene and agrees he will not open another property management firm anywhere in the same county for the next 3 years. In this way, Irene can be sure she will not lose existing or potential clients to Jack, and she will receive the full benefit of her bargain. (2) Some noncompetition clauses are designed to prevent employees from working for competitors. Courts disfavor such clauses. Most likely, if Irene wanted her employees to agree not to work for any other property management company in town, such a clause would be unenforceable.

nonconforming use   The use of a property in a manner that was permitted at one time but that now violates a zoning or other restriction. The use is allowed to continue—is grandfathered—as a nonconforming use. Depending on the particular laws of the jurisdiction, a nonconforming use may not be allowed to continue after a sale, long-term lease, substantial destruction of the property, or abandonment for a period of time.

nondisclosure   The failure to reveal a fact, whether or not there is an intention to conceal that fact. A person may be liable for nondisclosure if they had a duty to disclose, such as the duty to reveal latent (hidden) property defects.

nondisturbance clause   (1) A mortgage term that guarantees leases will be allowed to continue uninterrupted if there is a foreclosure. (2) A clause in a mineral lease or sale of mineral interests that the buyer will not disturb the surface in its operations.

no-doc loan   Short for "no document" loan, it typically covers three situations in which borrowers cannot or will not provide the documentation typically necessary to evaluate their ability to pay back a loan: (1) a borrower who has regular self-employment income but no tax forms from an employer, (2) wealthy individuals with complex financial lives showing large tax losses every year but an amazing ability to live lavish lifestyles (also called no-ratio loans), and (3) wealthy people with substantial assets but who want maximum privacy and refuse to supply any documentation. All three groups are going to pay high interest rates as a result of their lack of documentation.

nonfeasance   A failure to act when the law required an action. Real estate brokers are supposed to deposit earnest money checks as soon as possible. If the broker neglects to deposit the check, he or she is guilty of a nonfeasance, even if there was no improper motive and no misuse of the funds. Likewise, if local fire codes require fire extinguishers in the hallways of an office building, and the owner fails to install them, it is guilty of nonfeasance and may be liable for injuries and damages if there is a fire. Contrast with misfeasance, which is doing a legal and proper thing but in an improper manner, and malfeasance which is doing something improper or unlawful.

nonfreehold estates   Any interest in land without seisin. Historically, the nonfreehold estates were everything except the fee simple, fee tail, and life estate. Today, it usually refers to a lease.

nonhomogeneic   A term used to describe real property; no two are alike.

nonjudicial foreclosure   A foreclosure under a power of sale in a mortgage. It enables the lender to give the appropriate notices required under state law and then sell the mortgaged property to the highest bidder, which could be the lender itself.

nonperforming loan   Under banking regulations, a loan that is more than 90 days past due, that has been placed on nonaccrual, or that is current on its payments but being handled as a workout.

nonprofit corporation   A corporation formed for a nonprofit purpose, such as charitable, educational, political, social, or trade organizations. Usually called a 501(c)(3) corporation after Section 501(c)(3) of the Internal Revenue Code. All such corporations with tax-exempt status are required to file annual reports with the IRS on Form 990. You may view the tax deductibility of contributions and past 990 forms for particular organizations free of charge at the Web site for Philanthropic Research, Inc., www.guidestar.org. See also *eleemosynary corporation*.

nonpublicly traded REIT   See *private REIT*.

nonrecourse loan   A loan that includes no personal liability for the borrower. The lender has agreed that the collateral is sufficient and, if there is a foreclosure and the property brings less than the amount due under the loan, then the lender will suffer the loss and not sue the borrower. Even nonrecourse loans typically have carve-outs imposing personal liability on the borrower if there are environmental problems or the borrower is guilty of some sort of fraud.

nontraded REIT   See *private REIT*.

no-ratio loans   See *no-doc loans*.

normal wear and tear   That amount of physical deterioration that occurs with normal use of a property as contemplated by the parties. It could be dramatically different between a day-care facility and an upscale clothing store. Most commercial leases require the tenant to return the premises in like condition as when rented, normal wear and tear excepted. Consumer protection laws in many states prohibit withholding a tenant's deposit if there is only normal wear and tear to the premises. The best practice is to define the term in the lease. For example, "Normal wear and tear shall mean the necessity to shampoo carpets and paint walls, but not the necessity to replace carpet or repair walls for anything larger than a small picture hanger."

notary public   A person authorized by law to take oaths and witness signatures on documents. In some states, the notary must post a fidelity bond. In some states, notaries must keep complete logs of all documents notarized and the type of identification provided by the party signing the instrument.

note   See *promissory note*.

notice   See *legal notice*.

notice of assessment   A notice sent to property owners advising them of the current assessed valuation of their property for real estate tax purposes. The assessed value is usually based on a formula that starts with the fair market value and then decreases it to reach an assessed value. Property owners normally have a specific period of time within which to contest their assessments and should not be complacent just because the assessed value is less than the fair market value.

notice of completion   A notice typically given by contractors performing construction or improvement work for state or local governments; advising of the completion of the work and the necessity to file any liens within the required time period afterward. Many times the notice will run in the legal section of the local newspaper, although there may be a central location for filing them.

notice of default   A written notice sometimes required by state law or sometimes required within particular leases, promissory notes, or other contracts, advising the defaulting party of the existence of the default and a time period within which to cure it. Most documents require no notice of monetary default, although the better practice is to require it just in case checks are lost or misplaced. Notices of nonmonetary default would include matters such as failure to maintain insurance, subleasing space without the landlord's approval, or any number of other things prohibited under the parties' agreements.

notice of nonresponsibility   An official notice by property owners that they are not responsible for debts incurred to improve property, and that vendors and subcontractors must look solely to the general contractor for payment. Proper posting of the notice prevents the imposition of mechanics' and materialmen's liens in the event the general contractor does not pay the subcontractors or the suppliers.

notice-race statute   A law in some states that establishes the relative priority of claims when deeds or mortgages are not recorded in the public records in the chronological order in which they were executed. It provides that if a second mortgage lender provides money to a property owner without notice that there is already a first mortgage on the property, and the second mortgage lender records its mortgage before the first mortgage is recorded (usually because of some accident or oversight), then the second mortgage lender will have the first lien on the property.

> **Example**   *Ralph borrows $140,000 from Big Lender to buy a home. He signs a mortgage. Big Lender makes a mistake and files the mortgage in the wrong county in Ralph's state. This has the same effect as not filing at all. A year later, Ralph borrows $25,000 from Easy Internet Loans. It takes a mortgage and files it in the right place. Two days later Ralph takes the cash*

and disappears. In a notice-race state, Easy Internet Money may foreclose on the property and take the first $25,000 in proceeds from the sale. The balance will go to Big Lender, who will usually not see enough money to pay the loan in full. Contrast with pure-race statutes *and* pure-notice statutes.

notice to quit A legal notice to a tenant to vacate the premises; one of the steps in an eviction process.

novation The substitution of a new contract, debt, or obligation for an existing one. Usually encountered when a tenant assigns the lease to another, or when a new building owner requires all existing tenants to execute novation agreements. The effect is to extinguish all obligations under the old agreements and replace them with the new obligations.

nuisance An activity that arises from the unreasonable, unwarranted, or unlawful use of one's own property resulting in an obstruction or injury to another property owner or to the public and producing such material annoyance, inconvenience, and discomfort that the law will presume resulting damage. It may consist of noise, smoke, odors, pollution, vibration, interference with rights of passage, maintaining an offensive business, discharge of water, or maintaining a building in a manner that makes it unsafe for others because of falling debris or because of rats or vermin. (Do not confuse with *attractive nuisance*, a theory of negligence liability for maintaining features attractive to children but likely to harm them.)

null and void Having no legal effect.

nuncupative will An oral will stated by the testator before witnesses shortly before the testator's death and reduced to writing by the witnesses shortly after death. Such wills are unenforceable in many states. Contrast with *holographic will*, which is one prepared entirely in the testator's handwriting but without any witnesses.

O

OAR See *overall capitalization rate.*

obligee A party to whom an obligation is owed. A lender is an obligee.

obligor A party who owes an obligation. A borrower is an obligor.

obsolescence A loss in value of an improvement because something makes it undesirable or no longer useful, even though it might be structurally sound.

- Functional obsolescence occurs because of factors within a property, such as a poor floor plan or lack of modern amenities. A three-bedroom, one-bathroom house with a one-car garage would generally be considered as suffering from functional obsolescence.
- Economic obsolescence, also called environmental obsolescence and external obsolescence, occurs because of factors outside a property. Examples include construction of an airport near a residential area or a change in highway access leaving a retail area stranded.

OC3 The next level of telecommunications requirements for offices and distribution centers. Previously, users wanted local T1 access for broadband needs, with speeds greater than the more familiar digital subscriber line (DSL) service. Even T3, equivalent to 28 T1s, is now sometimes inadequate for intensive voice and data needs. Today, fiber-optic OC3 (optical carrier 3) is the minimum requirement for sophisticated shoppers, with speeds of up to 155 megabytes per second, or the equivalent of 84 T1s or three T3s.

OC12 High-speed data provisioning at speeds up to 622 megabytes per second, equivalent to 414 T1s. See *OC3.*

OC48 High-speed provisioning at speeds up to 2.5 gigabytes per second. It is most often used by large enterprises or as an Internet service provider (ISP) backbone. See *OC3.*

occupancy agreement An agreement that allows a buyer to take possession of property prior to closing on the purchase. Except for the most unusual of circumstances, it is usually a poor idea because of the risks involved if the sale falls through.

occupancy certificate See *certificate of occupancy.*

occupancy level See *occupancy rate.*

occupancy permit See *certificate of occupancy.*

occupancy rate   The ratio of rented property to the total available for rent. It is the flip side of the vacancy rate. Occupancy rates may be calculated by number of units, number of square feet, or by dollar value of rentals, also called the economic occupancy rate.

Example: *A 10-unit apartment complex has the following units and occupancies:*

Style	Number of Units	Size each (ft^2)	Rent each	Number Rented	Number Vacant
One bedroom	4	1,000	$800	3	1
Two bedroom	4	1,200	$1,000	4	0
Studio	2	600	$700	1	1
Totals	10	10,000 sq feet of space available for rent	$8,600 total possible monthly rental income	8	2

Occupancy rate by number of units: 8 units are rented out of a total of 10 possible = 80% occupancy.

Occupancy rate by square footage: 8,400 square feet are rented (3 @ 1,000 feet; 4 @ 1,200 feet; 1 @ 600 feet) out of a possible 10,000 square feet = 84% occupancy.

Economic occupancy: a monthly income of $7,100 (3 @ $800; 4 @ $1,000; 1 @ $700) out of a possible $8,600 = 82.5% occupancy.

occupancy report   See *rent roll.*

Occupational Safety and Health Administration (OSHA)   (pronounced as a word) A federal agency within the Department of Labor, OSHA (www.osha.gov) performs workplace inspections, engages in education and partnership to improve workplace safety, and enforces compliance with workplace safety standards. It is a common misperception that OSHA has the right to conduct surprise inspections of the workplace, including construction sites. In reality, OSHA may inspect only what it is given permission to inspect, or the particular portion of the premises described with particularity in a search warrant.

OEA   See *operating and easement agreement.*

off-balance sheet lease   See *operating lease.*

offer   A commitment to do some act, usually to buy or sell something, upon specified terms which, if accepted, would create an enforceable contract. The person making the offer is the offeror; the person receiving it is the offeree. Some important concepts include

- An offer may be withdrawn at any time before it is accepted, unless the offer by its terms stated it would be irrevocable for a specified period of time or other conditions.

- The mailbox rule states that if an offer is made via the mail, or if an offer does not limit acceptance to some vehicle other than the mail, then it may be accepted by mail. If so, then acceptance is effective when it is placed in the mail, not when received by the offeror. As a result, the offer may not be withdrawn once acceptance has been placed in the mail.
- The Uniform Computer Information Transactions Act provides that e-mail offers are accepted when the return e-mail has been received by the offeror, not when it is sent.
- Some states have held that fax transmissions of acceptance are effective when faxed.
- An offer that is "accepted," but with changes in some of the terms or conditions, is a counteroffer and is not an acceptance. A counteroffer is a new offer that must be accepted or rejected. The old offer may not be resurrected at that point.
- A property auctioned without reserve is an offer that may not be withdrawn. Unless specified otherwise, all auctions are presumed to be with reserve and the property may be withdrawn at any time before acceptance.
- Upon receiving an offer from a potential purchaser, an agent is obligated to transmit it to the client as soon as possible, even if the agent thinks it is a poor offer that will not be accepted. Further, an agent may not retain an offer until receipt of another, in order to present them together, unless the client has given specific instructions to act in that manner.

off-grid Property that has no commercially available electricity. It is "off the power grid." There are three power grids in the United States: the Eastern Interconnect, Western Interconnect, and Texas Interconnect.

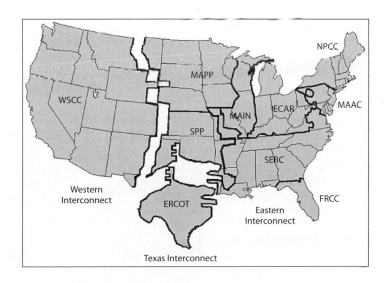

Courtesy U.S. Diesel Engines.

office building   A building used primarily for office space.

Office Business Center Association   A trade association (www.obcai.org) for owners and managers of business centers, also called executive suites and shared tenant services. See also *business center*.

Office of Federal Housing Enterprise Oversight (OFHEO)   An independent entity (www.ofheo.gov) established in 1992 within HUD. It provides oversight for Fannie Mae and Freddie Mac and is funded through assessments against those two corporations.

Office of Interstate Land Sales Registration   Oversees implementation of the 1968 Interstate Land Sales Full Disclosure Act, with provisions similar to securities laws. The Act requires registration of subdivisions with 100 or more nonexempt lots and the provision of a Property Report Disclosure Document to each purchaser. The most common exemption is for improved lots, either with habitable structures completed when offered for sale or to be completed within two years. For more information go the HUD Web site, www.hud.gov.

Office of Management and Budget   A White House office (www.whitehouse.gov/omb) charged with assisting the president in preparation of the federal budget and supervising its administration. It also evaluates the effectiveness of agency programs, policies, and procedures.

Office of Property Disposal   A part of the Public Building Service of the General Services Administration. The Office of Property Disposal (www.propertydisposal.gsa.gov) handles the disposal of all surplus federal property, including real estate.

Office of Real Property Management   Provides asset management, analysis, and reporting of government real property holdings, and regulatory oversight and recommendations. Part of the General Services Administration (www.gsa.gov).

Office of Thrift Supervision (OTS)   A primary regulator of federal- and state-chartered savings associations. OTS (www.ots.treas.gov) was established as a bureau of the Department of the Treasury in 1989.

office park   A development designed specifically to attract office users, usually with scenic views, walking trails and restaurants, multiple entrances to ease traffic flow, and preferably at least one median cut and a traffic light to facilitate left turns out of the property in the evenings.

Many office parks are built around water features

off-site costs   Construction expenses that are incurred away from the construction site. Examples include the cost of bringing in utilities, storm and sanitary sewer lines, and roads.

off-site improvements   Development improvements that are not located on the lots being sold. Examples include roads and street lighting.

off-street parking   The necessity to provide parking places on one's own property, rather than using city streets. Many zoning ordinances establish a minimum number of off-street parking places depending on the zoning and on the particular use of a structure on the property.

OFHEO   See *Office of Federal Housing Enterprise Oversight*.

oil and gas lease   An arrangement granting the right to explore for and extract oil and gas and possibly related minerals. Some important concepts are

- Oil and gas are considered minerals, but the law pertaining to them is different from solid minerals because oil and gas are said to be "fugitive" and capable of traveling from place to place to the lands of different owners.
- Because of the fugitive nature of gas and oil, it is possible for one person to drill many wells on his or her property and effectively drain the gas and oil from all surrounding lands. As a result, many states have laws enforcing pooling of interests or unitization if the property owners cannot agree on a fair way to cooperate in production. Such laws have been held constitutional.
- Because oil and gas are considered such important natural resources, most states with significant deposits heavily regulate exploration, drilling, production, and the rights of various parties to contractual arrangements. (Such legislation must be read into contracts between the parties.)
- Leases fall into two broad categories: "or" leases and "unless" leases. "Or" leases obligate the lessee to drill or to pay "delay rentals," but if the lessee does neither, there is not an automatic termination of the lease. By contrast, the "unless" lease says that if the lessee does not drill by a certain time, the lease will terminate unless the lessee pays delay rentals. Nonpayment and nonproduction will result in forfeiture.
- Rent under the lease is generally paid in the form of royalty payments; lessors generally reserve a one-eighth royalty interest.
- A lease on a pooled tract of land may provide for offset royalties, meaning that if no well is drilled on the subject land, but one is drilled within a certain distance of the land, then the lessor will still be entitled to royalty payments based on the production of the other well.

OILSR   See *Office of Interstate Land Sales Registration*.

once a mortgage, always a mortgage   A maxim signifying the rule that an instrument originally intended as a security instrument cannot be converted to a deed. It has reference to the practice of amending a mortgage to give up a right of redemption or an equity of redemption and thereby give permanent legal title to the lender. Parties may accomplish the same result, but they must do so in a separate legal instrument with its own consideration and the passage of title as of that date and time. Otherwise, the lender must foreclose to obtain full legal title.

one-hundred percent location   The best spot in an urban area, where the land values and the rents are the highest.

on-site   On the property itself, such as an on-site manager for an apartment complex or on-site waste management for a large subdivision.

open and notorious   In the theory of adverse possession, parties who do not have legal title to property may gain it if they use the property in a certain manner for specified periods of time and the true owner does nothing to stop them. See *adverse possession*, generally. One of the requirements is that the possession be open and notorious. This means such acts upon land as are consistent with the ordinary and customary uses of the land and which would alert the true owner that someone is claiming rights to the property. Adverse possessors may not furtively sneak upon land and leave behind subtle indications of their presence—they must act as if the land were theirs and behave accordingly.

open-end fund   An investment fund that does not have a finite life, continually accepts new investor capital, and makes new property investments.

open-end mortgage   A mortgage loan that may allow future advances as the value of the property increases, up to a certain percentage of loan-to-value. The legal problem with this arrangement occurs when loan 1 is an open-end mortgage, lender 2 loans money to the borrower and takes a second mortgage, and then lender 1 advances additional money under its open-end mortgage. If there is a foreclosure or bankruptcy, and not enough money to pay everyone, in what order are the loans paid? The answer depends on the borrower's state, the precise language of the open-end mortgage, and/or whether lender 2 gave notice to lender 1 of the new loan. See *future advances mortgage*. Do not confuse with an *open mortgage*.

open house   In residential real estate sales, an opportunity for prospective home buyers to tour a home offered for sale, or a model home, during a time period when it will be open for all visitors. Shoppers trying to refine their ideas regarding housing needs should not hesitate to attend open houses—they are not wasting the agent's time. Real estate agents and brokers welcome opportunities to tell prospective buyers about other properties if the present one is not appropriate and are also eager to assist prospective sellers who are just checking out the market and possible prices to ask for their own homes.

open housing   The opportunity for housing units to be purchased or leased without discrimination on the basis of race, gender, family status, or any of the other prohibited classifications. The 1866 Civil Rights Act and the 1968 Civil Rights Act did not take the place of local open-housing legislation, which may provide for even greater protections. On the other hand, the constitutional rights of property owners must be recognized under local open-housing laws. The typical battleground for state open-housing laws relates to statutes prohibiting discrimination based on marital status, and the conflict caused with landlords who refuse to rent to unmarried couples for religious reasons.

open listing   An offer by a property owner to pay a commission to any real estate broker who brings a buyer to the closing table. Rather than pay a 7 percent commission to a listing broker, with the listing broker then splitting that commission with the broker who provides the buyer, an open listing will agree to pay the entire 7 percent to any broker who brings the buyer.

open mortgage   A mortgage that may be prepaid at any time without penalty. Do not confuse with an *open-end mortgage*. Further, an *open mortgage clause* does not have anything to do with an open mortgage.

open mortgage clause   An insurance clause providing that the mortgagee (lender) will be paid in the event of a loss "as its interest may appear." This is far less protection to the lender than a union mortgage clause, which stipulates that the policy will be payable to the mortgagee unless it, or its agents, were the cause of the loss. In other words, if the homeowner burns the house to the ground and no insurance is payable to the homeowner as a result, then the lender with only an open mortgage clause will also receive nothing, but a lender with a union mortgage clause will still be paid.

open space   Land that is intentionally left undeveloped as an amenity for a project.

open the kimono   A slang expression used to describe revealing all one's financial and other confidential information to a suitor who has expressed an interest in purchasing a company or some of its assets. The danger, of course, is gauging whether the suitor is serious or merely engaging in a spectator sport.

operating and easement agreement (OEA)   An agreement between a shopping center developer or owner and usually major tenants regarding matters outside the formal lease.

operating budget   A good-faith estimate regarding the size and sources of future income, and the amounts and types of future expenses necessary for the day-to-day operation of a business or project. Contrast with a capital budget, which is an estimate of the capital needs of a project, such as new equipment, unusual repairs, additional property, or other such matters.

operating capital   See *working capital*.

operating expense escalation   An increase in rent because a clause in the tenant's lease provides that as the building operating expenses increase above what they were in a base year, the tenant will pay its pro rata share of those increased expenses. Wise tenants negotiate an expense stop in order to place a ceiling on the escalations. Landlords are reluctant to agree because they generally have no control over real estate taxes or insurance premiums. As a result, tenants will typically put a cap on controllable expenses. Were it not for such restrictions, unscrupulous landlords could employ a large staff of overpaid relatives to perform work on the property and pass that expense on to all the tenants. Whether or not such practices would be attackable on the grounds of a lack of good faith would depend on the landlord's facially reasonable explanation for the practice and on the relative skill of each party's lawyers.

operating expense ratio   The ratio between operating expenses and potential gross income. Such ratios will generally be similar among properties or businesses in the same geographical area with the same or similar characteristics. Knowledge of such ratios allows a developer or entrepreneur to create a pro forma estimate of future income and expenses for a new business. It also allows a property owner to conduct a reality check of its own operations, to see if its own operating expense ratios are consistent with those of other properties in the local marketplace. (An operating expense ratio that is higher than expected may be an indication of inefficiency, embezzlement, or pricing one's goods and services too cheaply.)

operating expenses   Necessary expenses for the normal day-to-day running of a business or income-producing property. It does not include financing expenses, depreciation, or capital expenditures.

operating income   See *net operating income*.

operating lease   An important accounting and income tax concept having to do with the determination of whether a lease (usually of personal property, but sometimes of real property) is a true lease, or whether it is a disguised lending arrangement. The operating lease is the true lease, and 100 percent of the payments are treated as expenses for accounting purposes and tax deductibility purposes. Sometimes called an off-balance sheet lease, meaning not that the lease is hidden or disguised, but it appears on the profit and loss statement rather than the balance sheet. Contrast with *capital lease*. In order to qualify as an operating lease, the transaction must meet the following requirements:

- The lease term is less than 75 percent of the estimated economic life of the equipment.
- The present value of lease payments is less than 90 percent of the equipment's fair market value.
- The lease cannot contain a bargain purchase option (i.e., purchase option for less than the fair market value).
- Ownership is retained by the lessor during and after the lease term.

operating leverage   The phenomenon of inflation leading to increased income and expenses each year, at the same time that financing (leverage) expenses remain the same if the borrower has fixed-rate financing. The result is that cash flows increase over time.

operating statements   Financial statements regarding the cash flow of a business.

operation of law   The application of rights and responsibilities because of a person or property's status, relationships, location, or other such factors independent of one's express agreement to assume responsibilities or another's express agreement to grant rights. Here are some examples of things that happen by operation of law:

- When a premises owner takes possession of mislaid personal property, he or she becomes a gratuitous bailee with a duty to use ordinary care to return the property to the true owner.
- The death of the principal terminates an agency relationship.
- Bankruptcy of the principal terminates an agency relationship.
- Joint tenancies with rights of survivorship are severed when one joint tenant transfers his or her interest or a creditor seizes his or her interest.
- In some states, when property has been dedicated to public usage, such as a park, and that usage is abandoned or relinquished, the property reverts back to the original grantor or his or her heirs.
- Title to real property is said to be acquired by operation of law when it is acquired by adverse possession, by intestate succession (descent), or by virtue of another's will (devise).
- A domicile by operation of law is an assigned domicile for persons who are incapable of making legal choices, such as minor children and persons declared mentally incompetent.
- Title to condemned property taken under a power of eminent domain passes on the day the condemnation declaration is filed, whether or not the parties have agreed upon a price or the former owner has signed any documents.
- A gift made in contemplation of death is automatically revoked if the donor recovers or if the donee dies before the donor.
- A will leaving property to one's spouse is considered revoked in some states if the parties obtain a divorce.

opinion of title   A letter, certificate, or other writing containing a report regarding title to real property and all encumbrances upon it, as of a certain date and time. The opinion of title is not the same thing as title insurance. If the preparer, usually an attorney, makes a mistake, then one's only recourse is to sue for malpractice.

opportunistic investment strategy   A strategy characterized by targeting underperforming and/or undermanaged properties, or properties that are temporarily depressed, and then using high degrees of leverage (borrowed funds) to acquire the property, hold it for a short period of time, and then sell it at an expected profit of at least 20 percent.

opportunity cost   The value of the opportunity given up in order to take advantage of the one you decide to take. The classic opportunity cost evaluation is the "rent or buy decision." If a person buys a home, the person gives up the opportunity to invest the down payment money in something else. Because mortgage payments and maintenance costs are usually higher than rent, the new homeowner must also spend more money each month rather than investing it. On the other hand, the analysis must take into account tax savings because of the deductibility of home mortgage interest payments. Conducting an analysis of opportunity costs in the "rent versus buy" situation might cause one to buy immediately, buy later, or decide not to buy at all for the foreseeable future. Ginnie Mae has an excellent rent versus buy calculator at www.ginniemae.gov.

option   The right to purchase or lease property for an agreed-upon price. The person who owns the property is called the optionor and is the one who grants the option. The recipient is called the optionee. The optionee has the right to take advantage of the opportunity, but does not have the obligation to do so.

option contract   A contract granting an option.

option risk   All American consumer mortgage loans give the borrower the option to pay the loan off early, usually because of a sale of the property or because the borrower decided to refinance. This is bad news for the investors who purchased that mortgage as part of a pool, because now the income stream they intended to purchase has ended. The investor's risk, that the prepayment option may be exercised and the income stopped, is called the option risk and sometimes the prepayment risk.

option to purchase   See *option*.

oral contract   A verbal agreement that is enforceable unless it falls within the Statute of Frauds. The problem with most oral contracts is not one of technical enforceability; it is one of proof. Unless both parties to a dispute have a clear recollection of the exact terms of the contract, and they are both truthful, a jury will have to decide whether a contract exists and the terms of that contract.

oral lease   See *month-to-month tenancy*.

ordinances   Municipal laws.

ordinary and necessary business expenses   An IRS term limiting the deductibility of expenses to those that are ordinary and necessary. Excessive compensation to insiders may be re-classed as only partially ordinary and necessary, with the balance treated as dividends, which are not deductible.

ordinary annuity   A series of equal payments, made at the end of each payment period. Contrast with *annuity due*, which is a series of equal payments made at the beginning of each period. A mortgage payment is an ordinary annuity, because the payment is made after a month's worth of interest has accrued. Rent payments are annuities due, because payment is made in advance at the beginning of each month. The difference is important for proper formula entries in financial calculators, or for Excel, as the formula is slightly different if the payments are ordinary annuities or annuities due.

ordinary income   Income subject to full or ordinary taxation rates. Contrast with *capital gains*.

ordinary loss   A loss that is deductible against ordinary income on one's taxes.

ORE, OREO   Other real estate, other real estate owned; a lender's portfolio of properties on which it has foreclosed.

orientation   Positioning of a structure on a site. Decisions regarding orientation should take into account prevailing winds, solar energy and passive solar heating through windows, the impact of the setting sun on afternoon workers, views, and any other relevant factors.

original cost   The cost to the current owner. Contrast with historic cost, which is the original construction cost.

original equity   An amount of cash originally invested by a property owner.

original face value   The principal amount due on a mortgage at its inception.

original issue discount   See *imputed interest*.

originate   To make; all the steps necessary to attract a potential borrower, process a loan request, prepare all necessary paperwork, and place the loan on the books of the lender.

origination fees   Charges to a borrower to cover the costs of originating a loan.

orphan lot   A subdivision lot that is unbuildable at the current market value of homes (for some reason or another). The lot may be too steep and site work too expensive for current development. Or the lot could have a power line easement crossing the middle, with overhead lines, so that no structure can ever be built under the lines. As land and home values increase, investors search for orphan lots that may become economically viable under new market conditions.

orthographic   A three-dimensional image represented in two dimensions with no perspective, as if the original were truly flat. Architectural drawings of elevations—the different sides of a building—have no perspective detail but are orthographic. Many local tax assessor's offices and online property information services include orthographic aerial or satellite photographs of properties, corrected for the earth's curvature.

orthos   See *orthographic*.

OSHA   See *Occupational Safety and Health Administration*.

ostensible authority   The illusion of having the authority to act as an agent on behalf of a principal. It can be created because the agent gives that impression and the principal does nothing to correct the misperception, or because the principal itself creates that impression in others. Either way, the principal will be bound by the actions of the agent if a court finds that ostensible authority existed.

other people's money (OPM)   A common expression used when talking about the multiplying effect of using borrowed funds to purchase property rather than paying all cash. Investors will say, "I'm using OPM for the deal."

outlet center   A shopping center devoted to discount outlets for brand name manufacturers. They are most often located in rural areas or tourist locations. If rural, the market can be drawn from a radius as large as 200 miles, although a 25- to 75-mile market area is more common.

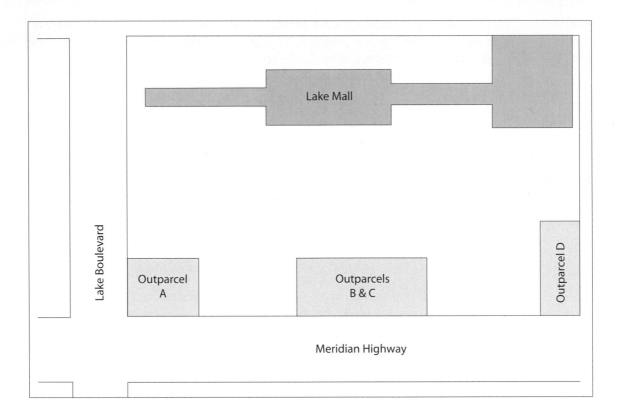

outparcel   (1) A small lot at the outer edge of a shopping center, usually reserved for later sale to a fast-food outlet or chain restaurant; also called a pad site. Many important mall tenants will reserve some control over outparcel development by virtue of agreements in their operating and easement agreement with the mall owner. (2) A small lot the original developer could not obtain when purchasing a large site for a shopping center. The problem with outparcels is the impact future development will have on existing mall tenants, who may find visibility obstructed with new construction, common area maintenance expenses increased because of dramatically increased lighting requirements, and parking problems if the outparcel customers use mall parking places. (See example above.)

outstanding balance   The amount owed on a debt, as of a particular date. Title companies will obtain an outstanding balance for liens on property being sold, as of the anticipated date of closing, with a daily accrual for additional interest due each day the closing is delayed.

overage   Additional rent for retail stores, based on a percentage of gross sales.

overall capitalization rate   (1) Sometimes referred to as the "going-in capitalization rate." It is the first year's net operating income divided by the acquisition cost of the property. (2) In appraisal, it is the proper discount rate to account for the timing and amounts of all future cash flows from an income-producing property.

overall rate of return (OAR)   See *overall capitalization rate.*

over-and above money   Money that is held in reserve in case a project goes over budget. Also called end money.

overbuilding   A situation that occurs when the rate of construction is faster than the market can absorb new construction. Developers often cannot anticipate the amount of competition until it is too late. The lead time between placing land under contract with a lengthy due diligence period to the first signs of excavation or construction that would alert people of new development can be as long as a year on small projects. The typical market cycle is a period of perceived need for "product"—offices, houses, malls, whatever—and then a seeming explosion of new projects "coming out of the ground" almost simultaneously. By the time developers see the signs of large numbers of competing projects, it is too late to back out of their own plans. As a result, all projects go full steam ahead and hope that something other than price will differentiate them from competitors, allowing the current project to fill up quickly while competitors go begging. This hope is usually misguided, and a price war results.

overimprovement   Erecting improvements at prices that are out of proportion to the land value or to the area. Each market will have its own rules of thumb regarding ideal ratios of land cost to improvement construction costs.

override   (1) A carve-out from oil and gas lease royalty payments, usually a gross dollar amount per barrel of oil or per cubic foot of gas without diminution for costs of extraction. The override may be payable to the broker on the deal, to the attorney, or to some person other than the lessor with the mineral rights. (2) A name given to a clause, in a real estate listing contract, that requires payment of a commission to the listing broker if a buyer introduced to the property by the broker purchases the property within a certain time period after the listing agreement expires. The clause is to protect the broker for sales activities at the very end of the listing period that do not come into fruition until later. It also serves to protect the broker from buyers who learn about the property from the broker, take the broker's time in securing additional information and property inspections, and then attempt to time their offers until after the listing expiration in the hopes the seller will accept a lower price because then the seller does not have to pay a commission from the sale proceeds.

Overseas Private Investment Corporation   A federal agency (www.opic.gov) established in 1971 to assist American businesses desiring to invest overseas. It provides medium- to long-term funding for projects in developing countries and emerging markets, including housing, hotels, airports, and natural resource extraction. It also provides political risk insurance for currency inconvertibility, expropriation, and political violence. The corporation is self-funding through fees for services and uses no taxpayer money.

owner financing   A seller of real property holding a first or second mortgage for some or all of the purchase price.

owner-occupant   An owner of real property who also uses that property for his or her own business purposes. The truism is that owner-occupants will pay a higher price for real property than investors, because owner-occupants have limited choices for an ideal location, while investors may place their money anywhere. Contrast with an investor, who owns property in order to derive rental income from it.

owner of record   The person recorded on public real estate records as the owner of real property. The term is sometimes defined to mean the person reflected on the tax assessor's rolls. The exact definition is important when dealing with statutes that require notice to the owner of record of real property. An example is a tax sale statute with such a notice provision. If notice is given to the wrong person, the tax sale may be set aside even if the statutory time period for objection has passed.

owners and occupiers (owners and occupants)   Parties who own real property or occupy it in some legally permitted status, such as a tenant. There are a wide variety of responsibilities imposed on owners and occupants, such as compliance with the Americans with Disabilities Act. Other than such statutory requirements, the area of law concerned with duties of owners and occupiers is called premises liability. The most frequent application of the duties is in slip and fall cases. The duty of care owed to people coming on the property will usually depend on the status of those people as invitees, licensees, or trespassers. Some states merge invitees and licensees into something called entrants, who are lawfully on property, versus trespassers who should not be on the property. A few states impose the same standard of care as to all persons on real property, being a duty of reasonable care under the circumstances.

- An invitee is a person who enters upon property at the express or implied invitation of the owner in order to conduct some business with the owner or engage in some activity the owner conducts or permits to be conducted on the property. The owner and the occupier of property owe a duty to protect invitees against all known dangers and any dangers that should have been discoverable with reasonable care.
- A licensee is a person who has permission to enter on property, but for the person's own purposes rather than that of the owner. Typically, social guests are classed as licensees. In most states, owners and occupiers owe a licensee the duty of reasonable or due care; in some states the only duty is to refrain from wanton, willful, or reckless conduct.
- A trespasser is a person who does not have permission to enter on property. Owners and occupiers owe the duty to not set traps for trespassers and not to willfully or wantonly injure them.

ownership form   See *title*.

ownership in severalty   See *tenancy in severalty*.

ownership rights to realty   One who owns real property in fee simple has the right to possession, enjoyment, control, and disposition of the property.

owner's title policy   Title insurance that protects the owner against loss if there is an adverse claim against the owner's property and that provides legal counsel to defend against adverse claimants.

Typically, the mortgage lender will require a mortgagee's policy that will protect it, but the owner fails to specify that he or she also wants an owner's policy. The increased premium is usually negligible. If there is a mortgagee's policy but no owner's policy, and if there is an adverse claim to the property that is found to be good and not defeatable, the title insurance will pay off the mortgage lender to the full amount of its loan, but the owner will receive nothing and suffer the loss of its equity.

P

package mortgage   A mortgage that includes financing for real estate and for personal property. The plan is usually promoted as beneficial to consumers because it allows them to buy appliances, for example, at low mortgage interest rates and pay just a small amount each month, as compared to typical finance or credit card companies that charge higher interest rates and provide shorter terms for payoff, leading to higher monthly payments. Promoters also tell consumers that with a package mortgage, interest payments for appliances are deductible from taxes, while finance company or credit card interest is not deductible.

> **Example:**   *The following table compares $3,000 worth of appliances financed by a package mortgage, a typical credit card, and a finance company.*

Appliances Financed in Package Mortgage versus Other Choices

	Package Mortgage	Finance Company	Credit Card
Amount financed	$3,000	$3,000	$3,000
Interest rate	7%	20%	15%
Term	30 years	3 years	3 years
Payments	$19.96	$111.49	$104.00
Total interest paid by end of 3 years	$620.50	$1,103.64	$744.00
Unpaid balance at end of 3 years	$2,901.94	$0	$0
Total interest at end of 5 years	$1,021.68		
Total interest at end of 10 years	$1,969.69		
Total payments by end of term	$7,185.60	$4,103.64	$3,744.00

Remember: The package mortgage and finance company will both require additional filing fees for the security interest in the appliances; you will not have that expense with a credit card. Calculate your own tax deductions using the highest rate you'll have to pay. Do the deductions compensate for the higher total interest paid?

pad site   (1) A freestanding parcel at a shopping center; generally leased or sold to financial institutions, fast-food outlets, or chain restaurants. Also called an outparcel. (2) A space rented for placement of a manufactured home.

paid-but-unaccrued   Money paid in advance, before it has been earned or accrued. The person paying the money may be entitled to a refund.

paint-to-paint   Expression used to describe ownership in a condominium building. The condo owner does not own the exterior walls of the unit, only from the interior paint and inward.

paired sales   An appraisal technique used to find the value of a particular feature within a property, such as a two-car garage. If the appraiser can find two recently sold houses that are virtually identical except that one has a two-car garage and one does not, these are called paired sales. If the two-car garage is the only significant difference in the two, then the difference in the sale price must be attributable to the garage. In that manner, one may assign a value to a two-car garage. As a result, when employing the comparable sales method of appraising a house, the appraiser may confidently assign values to the various features that differ in the house under consideration from the houses that sold recently.

panelized home   A home built of preformed panels. A series of rectangular panels arrive at the job site and are put together to form the exterior of the home. Sometimes the panels have exterior siding and interior wiring in place already; other times they do not.

panic peddling   The illegal practice of inducing people in a neighborhood to sell their homes because of fears that minorities are, or will be, buying homes there.

P&I   Abbreviation for principal and interest, being the two components of all payments under an amortizing mortgage loan.

P&L   An abbreviation for a profit and loss statement.

paper   Slang for promissory notes. If a seller is willing to provide some or all of the financing for a property, the seller would say, "I'm willing to hold some paper." Lenders who specialize in loans to borrowers with less-than-ideal credit histories are said to specialize in B paper.

paper profit   (1) An increase in the value of real property, so one has a profit on paper even though the property has not been sold. (2) The profit from an income-producing property that has an accounting profit on which the owner has to pay income taxes, but that has a negative cash flow requiring cash infusion from the owner in order to pay bills. This can occur if debt service payments are high, because only the interest portion is a deductible expense, even though the owner must write checks for interest and principal. It can also happen if customers or tenants are not paying their bills on time, so that the receivables are large, or if the property owner must expend large sums of money making upgrades or repairs that must be capitalized rather than written off as expenses.

paper the file   (1) To document one's own file regarding all events, meetings, who said what, who did what, and anything else, because of a fear that there will be a problem in the future and it will be important to reconstruct exactly what happened. Warning: Papering the file preparatory to firing a real estate agent who might claim discrimination is also discrimination if the broker does not routinely paper everyone's file. (2) Providing every possible projection and all research, analysis, maps, drawings, and photographs to a lender for a commercial loan application. One cynical school of thought says this comforts lenders and makes a loan more likely. Others say that the complicated financial analyses required of lending personnel will be easier with a wide array of data from which to choose, thus speeding up the approval process.

parcel   A piece of real property with its own distinct legal description.

parcel register   The abstract index for a property registered in the Torrens system of land registration.

pari passu   In equal portions. Used to describe distributions to creditors if they will each take a pro rata share of a debtor's assets.

parking ratio   The number of parking places per some other variable. Landlords will sometimes offer a certain number of reserved parking places per thousand square feet of leased space. Zoning regulations may require a certain number of off-street parking places per apartment, per thousand square feet of office space, or per employee.

parol evidence   A rule that parol (oral) evidence will not be admissible to vary the terms of a written contract. On the other hand, if some term of the written contract is ambiguous on its face, then parol evidence is admissible to explain that term. Under the Uniform Commercial Code, if the contract has to do with the sale of goods, more latitude is granted to explain or supplement the contract by parol evidence of typical business practices. Much less latitude is given with real estate contracts.

partial interest   Ownership of some portion of the ownership rights to real estate, such as mineral rights.

partially amortizing loan   A loan with periodic payments of interest and principal, but for a shorter term than necessary to pay the principal balance in full at that rate. Partially amortizing loans have a balloon payment at some point, requiring repayment in full or through refinancing.

partial release   A mortgage lender's release of its lien from only some portion of the land mortgaged. Usually encountered in subdivision development. The lender and the developer will have a prearranged ratio for division of proceeds from the sale of each parcel.

partial taking   A condemnation of only part of a parcel of land. Often, if there is a partial taking, then the condemning authority will also have to pay damages for the decrease in value to the remaining portion. For example, if the partial taking resulted in the city gaining most of a store's parking lot, then the store itself will probably suffer a loss of revenues because customers can't find parking. The property not taken will have decreased in value because of the partial taking.

partial write-down   See *write-down*.

participating mortgage   An older term that is still sometimes encountered; it is a mortgage in which the lender takes a share of the profits during operations and on the sale of the property. Today, this would most frequently be called mezzanine financing.

participation   The practice of a lead lender selling portions of a loan to other lenders, called participants. It may be done because the loan is larger than the regulatory limits for the lead lender, or because the loan is very attractive but rather risky, so several lenders will pool their efforts and spread the risk. FDIC regulations that went into effect on January 1, 2002, dramatically changed the structure and accounting for many participations. Formerly, lead banks could agree to repurchase a bad loan from a participant. As a result, it was easier to sell shares to other banks because the participants had no risk. Today, such a repurchase agreement will cause the transaction to be treated as a loan from the participant to the lead, rather than a sale, with the result that the lead may be in violation of banking regulations regarding loan size.

parties   In litigation, the various people or companies with grievances or defenses that wish to be heard by the court. Types of parties include

- Plaintiff. Files the lawsuit.
- Defendant. The person the suit is against.
- Counterplaintiff. A defendant who has claims against the plaintiff.
- Counterdefendant. The plaintiff who is also sued by the defendant.
- Cross-claimants. Defendants who sue each other.
- Third-party defendants. When a defendant decides someone else should be added to the lawsuit because the defendant has claims against that person and it is all related to the same dispute. (Typically occurs when the defendant seeks indemnity from another.)

partition   The division of real property into separate parcels for joint owners who no longer wish to own the property together. If possible, a court must physically divide the property into shares of equal value and quality. If not possible, the court will order a sale of the property with the proceeds to be split among the owners. Partition actions are encountered most often when an owner of real property dies without a will but with several heirs. If they cannot agree on a disposition of the property, it will be partitioned. In the alternative, investors will often buy an undivided interest from a minority heir for very little money and then petition a court for partition. Usually the investor will be able to buy the property at the partition auction, because none of the other owners can afford to purchase the whole. The strategy is not intended to obtain a bargain price for property, because the court will usually order an appraisal and prohibit any owner from buying at a price less than the appraised value. Rather, the practice is intended to force property onto the market even though some or most of the other owners have no desire to sell.

partition auction   An auction held when co-owners want to divide property they own in common but cannot agree on a physical division into parcels. As a result, the property is auctioned and the sales proceeds are split among them according to their percentage of ownership. Any co-owner is free to bid at the auction, but usually must bid an amount at least equal to the appraised value of the property.

partnership   A legal relationship between two or more persons, each of whom may act as an agent for the partnership and legally bind it and the other partners.

party wall   A wall built on the line between two properties and necessary for the support of structures built on either side of the property line. Each owner owns the one-half of the party wall on his or her own property and has a support easement in the one-half on the other person's property. Neither person can demolish the one-half of the wall on his or her own property because that would damage the neighbor's building. Townhomes usually share party walls.

passive activity   An IRS phrase meaning two different things: (1) A trade or business activity in which the taxpayer does not materially participate during the year. (2) A rental activity, even if the taxpayer does materially participate in it, unless the taxpayer is a real estate professional. One wants to avoid something being characterized as a passive activity, because that limits the deductions that can be taken on tax returns.

> There are many ways to satisfy the material participation test and avoid characterization as a passive activity. The most common one is by working in the business for more than 500 hours a year. To be a real estate professional, you must work more than 750 hours a year in the real estate trades or businesses, and that must be more than one-half of the personal services you provide for the year for all trades or businesses.

passive activity expenses   Generally consists of mortgage interest on a loan used to acquire an investment classified as a passive activity under IRS regulations.

passive activity income   Income earned from a passive activity. The IRS segregates certain types of income and expenses so that passive activity expenses are deductible only from passive activity income. If expenses are greater than income, the taxpayer may not use additional deductions to shelter other income (such as regular payroll income), but must carry the losses forward and use them in a future year. As a general rule, there are two types of passive activities:

1. Trade or business activities in which the taxpayer does not materially participate (less than 500 hours, generally) during the year.
2. Rental activities, even if the taxpayer does participate in them, except for the following:
   a. The taxpayer is a real estate professional.
   b. The rental is a dwelling the taxpayer uses for more than 14 days per year or 10 percent of the days the dwelling was available for rental, whichever is greater.
   c. Taxpayers may deduct up to $12,500 in losses ($25,000 if married) from passive activities if they or their spouse actively participated in it. There is a phaseout for various income levels.
   d. Low-income housing credits are available up to a maximum of $25,000.

(The rules are extremely complicated, and there are many exceptions. For further information see Publication 925: "Passive Activity and At-Risk Rules" and Tax Topics 425: "Passive Activities—Losses and Credits" at the IRS Web site www.irs.gov.)

passive activity loss   The situation when expenses are greater than income from a passive activity.

passive income   See *passive activity income*.

passive income generator (PIG)   The name given to an investment offered to taxpayers who have excess passive activity losses and need some passive activity income to offset the losses. (Be careful of any investment touted as a PIG—if the only reason for an investment is the tax benefits it might produce, then the investment should be made with great caution.)

passive investor   One who does not actively participate in a trade or business. Generally, a passive investor may not take advantage of certain tax deductions, such as the Section 179 deduction allowing the full deductibility of some capital expenditures—up to certain dollar limits—in the current year rather than the normal method of capitalizing and then depreciating them.

passive solar heating   Design features in a structure allowing it to maximize the use of sunlight to heat interior spaces, but without any mechanical devices to distribute that heat throughout the building. Contrast with *active solar heating*.

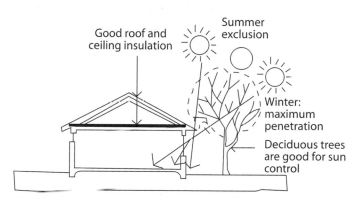

pass-through certificates (or securities)   Interests in a pool of mortgages sold to investors.

pass-throughs   Landlord operating expenses that can be billed to tenants, either as part of their obligation to pay a pro rata share of operating expenses, their obligation to pay a pro rata share of common area maintenance, or a particular tenant's obligation to pay for goods and services benefiting only that tenant.

patent   The first transfer of title out of the government to a private individual or company.

payback period   An estimate of the time that will be necessary for an investor to recoup the initial investment. It is used to compare investments that might have different initial capital requirements.

payment   Funds given to another in exchange for goods or services or as reimbursement for money loaned. A mortgage payment may consist of interest only; it could be a combination of principal and interest; or it could also include sums for real estate taxes, property insurance, and/or private mortgage insurance. In order to use Microsoft Excel to calculate your monthly principal and interest payment for a mortgage, do the following:

1. In cell A1, place the annual interest rate.
2. In cell A2, place the number of months of the loan to fully amortize it.
3. In cell A3, place the principal amount of the loan.
4. In cell A4, write the following formula exactly:
   =pmt(A1/12,A2,A3)
5. Cell A4 will calculate your monthly payment.

payment cap   A limit on the allowable increase of mortgage payments under an adjustable-rate mortgage. The typical horror story used to illustrate this principle envisions interest rates increasing dramatically so that a capped payment is no longer sufficient to pay accrued interest, much less any principal reductions. In such a situation, the accrued but unpaid interest is added to the principal, making the loan grow larger over time rather than smaller. In most of the real world, loans with payment caps also have interest rate caps, so it is contractually impossible for interest rates to climb to an amount causing negative amortization.

payoff   The amount necessary to pay a loan in full, with all accrued interest and fees and the prepayment penalty, if applicable. Payoff figures are usually provided to a closing company as correct on a given day. If closing is delayed, the lender has also provided a per diem charge to increase the payoff for every day of delay.

PCBs   (1) Polychlorinated biphenyls. (2) Pollution control bond.

penalty   A payment required as a result of breaking the law or sometimes for breaching the terms of a contract. Most contract drafters assiduously avoid the term because private penalties are not enforceable. Instead, contract drafters use the terms liquidated damages, delay payments, or late fees. Even the prepayment penalty is really not a penalty but compensation to a lender for the loss of income suffered when a loan is paid off earlier than the terms allow.

pencil out   A slang expression for a rough analysis of the viability of an investment.

penthouse   Originally, a home built on the roof of a high-rise building, giving the occupant complete privacy. By definition, each building could have only one penthouse. Today, the word is used for any number of apartments or condos on the topmost floors of a building, usually finished out in a very luxurious manner.

per annum   Each year.

per capita   Per head; per person. The term is most often encountered in estate planning, where assets may be left to heirs, per capita. In a per capita distribution, a predeceased heir's portion is shared equally among other heirs at the same level.

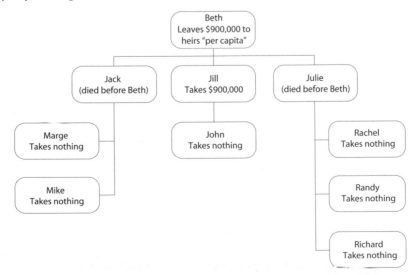

Example: *Beth leaves $900,000 to her heirs, per capita. She has three children, but two of them die before her. Each child would have received $300,000 if alive. Because the gift was per capita, the money is divided among only the children who survived Beth. In the following diagram, one child will receive the entire $900,000. The grandchildren—children of the predeceased children—receive nothing. Contrast with per stirpes, in which the share belonging to predeceased heirs would go to their own heirs. Using per stirpes distribution in the example, Jill takes only $300,000, Jack's children share $300,000, and Julie's children share $300,000.*

percentage lease   A lease that requires rent payments based on a percentage of the gross sales of the tenant. It is common with retail leases and food and beverage leases. Most contain a minimum payment clause so that if gross sales drop below a certain level the rent will be the minimum payment rather than a percentage of sales.

percentage of debt   The ratio of debt secured by property as compared to the value of the property. Most home loans start out with debt equal to 80 percent of the value of the home.

percentage of equity   The ratio of equity in a property (the difference between the value of property and the debt secured by that property) as compared to the total value of the property. Most home loans start out with equity equal to 20 percent of the value of the home.

percolation test   A test to determine the drainage characteristics of soil. Drainage is essential to the proper functioning of a septic tank waste disposal system. Usually called a "perc test."

per diem charge   In mortgage loans, the amount of interest earned by the lender for each day the loan remains unpaid. For purposes of such calculations, some promissory notes define a year as containing 360 days; others define a year as containing 365 days.

> **Example:** *For a 365-day year, if one borrows $100,000 at 7 percent interest for one year, $7,000 in interest will be due at the end of the year. The per diem is $7,000 ÷ 365 = $19.18. Disregarding late charges, for each day the borrower is late in paying the loan, the borrower will owe an additional $19.18. For a 360-day year, for the same loan, the per diem is $7,000 ÷ 360 = $19.44.*

per door   A common method of referring to the number of units in an apartment complex. One might say, "The annual maintenance expenses for my apartment projects generally run in the range of $150 per door."

perfect   (pronounced with the emphasis on the second syllable, not the first) To complete all steps necessary to establish a security interest in property that will take priority over later lenders. As between a lender and a borrower, a mortgage is effective and enforceable even if it is never recorded in the real estate records. If a third party, such as another lender, loans money to the debtor and records its own mortgage, then the second lender will have first rights in the property. The recordation of the mortgage, or of a UCC–1 for personal property, is called perfecting a security interest. Note: The UCC–1 is named for the Uniform Commercial Code form used to record notice of a security interest in personal property.

perfecting title   Curing title defects in real property.

performance   In contracts, the substantial completion of all duties and responsibilities. Note: The exact meaning of the word "substantial" is the cause of much litigation in contract law.

performance bond   An insurance policy often required on government construction projects. If the contractor does not perform the work it contracted to do, the insurance company will either hire someone else to complete the job or will pay off the resulting damages, up to policy limits. Sometimes it is inaccurately called a performance and completion bond. Technically, liability under a performance bond is contingent on the contracting party paying according to the terms of its construction contract. Contrast with completion bond, where the contracting party does not have to pay anything to the insurance company, even though it might have been obligated to pay the contractor. As a result, most bonds are performance bonds and it is very difficult to obtain a completion bond.

performing loan   As defined by the Federal Financial Institutions Examination Council, a loan that is less than 90 days past due, has not been placed on nonaccrual, or is not in workout status.

performing nonperforming loan   A loan on which all payments are made on time but the collateral has decreased in value so that it is no longer sufficient to support the loan. FDIC regulations require the lender to classify the loan as nonperforming. In such a situation, the lender will require additional collateral or will demand payment in full.

periodic cash flow   See *cash flow*.

periodic estate   A lease with a definite period of duration.

periodic tenancy   A tenant's right to possess and use property for periods defined by the amount of rent paid. If rent is paid on a monthly basis, then the tenancy continues month to month as the tenant chooses to stay and the landlord chooses to continue accepting rent. If the tenant pays rent on an annual basis, for an entire year at a time, then the tenancy continues on a year-to-year basis. Consumer protection laws define the amount of notice necessary to terminate a periodic tenancy for residential properties. Usually, the landlord must give 10 days notice for a week-to-week tenancy and 60 days notice for a month-to-month tenancy.

period of redemption   See *right of redemption*.

perks   (1) Slang for perchloroethylene or tetrachloroethylene. These chemicals, used in dry cleaning, are highly toxic and will contaminate soil and groundwater. When buying property on or near the site of a present or former dry-cleaning plant, the investor should be concerned about the presence of perks and should order the appropriate tests to determine the existence and extent of contamination. (2) Slang for perquisites, meaning nonmonetary benefits. In commercial leasing, building perks might include a fitness club open only to employees of building tenants.

perk test   Proper pronunciation, but technically spelled "perc test"; a percolation test.

permanent lender   One who makes permanent loans on real property. Contrast with construction lender or bridge lender. In the field of commercial properties, many permanent lenders include large prepayment penalties in their loan documents. (Unlike consumer lending, which includes no prepayment penalties, the choice of a permanent lender for a commercial loan can have long-lasting adverse consequences.)

permanent mortgage   A mortgage for an extended period of time, usually 10 to 25 years.

permeability   The measure of a material's ability to transmit liquids. The passage of soil contaminants into groundwater increases as soil permeability increases. On the other hand, in situ remediation—removal or decomposition—of groundwater contamination is easier as permeability increases. For a color map of the United States showing the relative permeability of soils across the country, see the Web site page of the Environmental Protection Agency at www.epa.gov/iwi/1999sept/iv20_usmap.html.

permit   A document issued by a government authority giving permission to proceed with some action. In real estate, one may need some or all of the following permits, to name a few:

- A demolition permit before destroying a structure
- An excavation permit before doing site work
- An environmental permit for erosion and siltation control on land about to be disturbed
- A utility disturbance permit to move utility lines
- A construction permit for construction
- A health permit for an on-site waste management system
- A health permit for removal of asbestos-containing building components
- A highway department permit for on-site signage visible from state or federal highways
- An occupancy permit before a structure can be used

perpetuity   Never ending; forever. A legal principle called the rule against perpetuities says that transfers of interests in land must vest, if at all, within lives in being plus a gestational period and 21 years, or they are void.

perquisites   Special nonmonetary benefits, often offered by landlords in order to attract new tenants. Examples include reserved parking places for company executives, an exercise club for tenants or employees, or free high-speed Internet service.

person   Legally, any natural or artificial person, which would include corporations, partnerships, associations, and limited liability companies. If it is important to distinguish among the "persons" who may do something or who are prohibited from doing something, relevant contracts, leases, or statutes will usually define the term.

personal assistant   An unlicensed assistant in a real estate office who may work under the supervision of a licensed broker or agent, but who is prohibited from doing anything that specifically requires a license under applicable state law.

personal liability   The responsibility of a person to pay a debt or other obligation. If an individual signs a promissory note, that individual usually has full personal liability for the debt. An exception is the unusual situation of a nonrecourse individual loan, in which the lender agrees to look only to the collateral for recovery in the event of default. Some states protect consumers from liability for a first mortgage loan on a personal residence, and require that the lender must be satisfied with taking the home by foreclosure, but may not sue for a deficiency. If a corporation signs a promissory note, the individual shareholders will not have personal liability unless they signed a guarantee agreement or unless the lender is successful with an alternate legal theory such as "piercing the corporate veil."

personal property   Any property except for real property. Personal property may consist of physical objects, or it may be intangibles such as copyrights, patents, or securities. Personal property is also called personalty.

personal residence   One's customary and normal place of habitation, as claimed for voting and income tax purposes.

personalty   See *personal property*.

per stirpes   A method of distributing an estate when one of the beneficiaries dies before the testator. The predeceased beneficiary's share is divided equally among that person's own heirs.

> **Example:**   *Beth leaves $900,000 to her heirs, per stirpes. She has three children, but two of them die before her. Each child would have received $300,000 if alive. For the children who died*

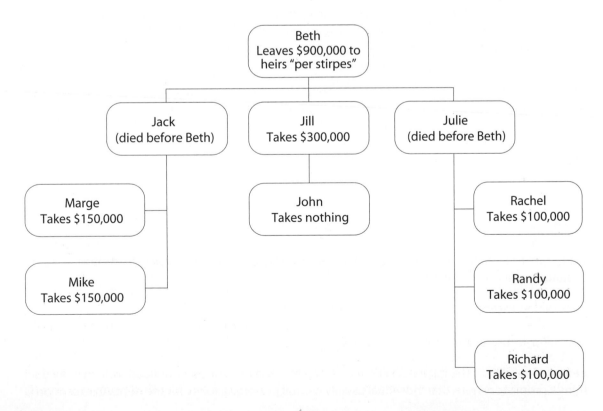

first, each one's $300,000 share will be split equally among their own children. Grandchild John receives nothing, because his mother was still alive to receive her gift. Contrast with per capita, in which all members of a generational class take equal shares.

petitioner   A person who files a complaint in an equity court, such as a divorce court, or who requests relief from an administrative body. In many states, all persons who initiate lawsuits are now called plaintiffs.

phantom income   Reportable or taxable income that does not generate cash flows to pay the taxes on the income. A disclosure that "taxable income may exceed economic income" is the clue that an investor may receive phantom income.

Phase I Environmental Site Assessment   Investigation of real property to determine the possibility of contamination, based on visual observation and property history, but no physical testing. Under new Environmental Protection Agency regulations that went into effect on November 1, 2006, a Phase I, as it is called for short, will be mandatory for all investors who wish to take advantage of CERCLA defenses that will shield them from liability for future cleanup, should that prove necessary. The new Phase I rules, called "All Appropriate Inquiry" or AAI, also require more investigation than previously mandated. Investors can expect to see dramatic price increases over prior experiences.

Phase II Environmental Site Assessment   Investigation of real property through physical samplings and analyses to determine the nature and extent of contamination and, if indicated, a description of the recommended remediation method.

Phase III Environmental Site Assessment   Design and implementation of a plan of remediation for a contaminated site, together with all necessary reports demonstrating successful remediation.

phase out   To bring to an end in stages. Typically encountered with tax benefits that are phased out—decreased or diminished—over the course of several years.

physical depreciation or deterioration   A loss of value in an appraised property because of all causes of age and the action of the elements.

physical life   The time period during which a real property improvement can be expected to remain in existence. Contrast with *useful life*.

physical obsolescence   The deterioration of a property due to wear and tear or abuse.

piggyback loan   A combination of a construction loan and a permanent loan commitment.

piercing the corporate veil   A theory used to reach the assets of individual shareholders when there is a judgment against a corporation but the corporation has no assets to satisfy the judgment. In general, if the shareholders operated a business in complete disregard of the corporate form, meaning they never had shareholder meetings, never voted on anything, never used the corporate name on stationary or paperwork, commingled personal funds and corporate funds, and generally behaved as if the corporation did not exist, then a court will impose personal liability for corporate debts.

pipeline   (1) A system for carrying fluids or gases. (2) A popular expression for things that are in process. For example, "There are over 10,000 condo units in the pipeline, in various stages of construction or conversion." Or "I'm not worried about apartment move-outs this summer because I have a number of prospects in the pipeline."

pipeline risk   A slang expression for the risk a lender takes when it makes a loan commitment at a certain interest rate, but knowing that before the loan closes interest rates might increase.

pipestem lot   See *flag lot.*

pitch   The slope of a roof, sidewalk, or other surface. The Americans with Disabilities Act has specific requirements for the pitch of access ramps leading to building entrances.

> **Example:** *Figure A has a 1:12 pitch because the slope rises 1 foot for every 12 feet of distance. Figure B has a 1:6 pitch.*

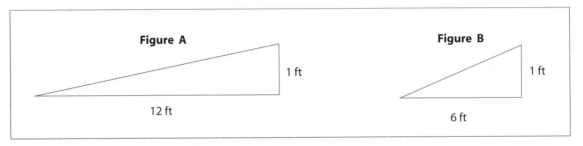

PITI   A mortgage loan term for principal, interest, taxes, and insurance.

placed in service   The date when property was first made available for its intended purpose. This concept is extremely important for tax purposes. Most tax benefits depend on proper determination of when an improvement was first placed in service.

plaintiff   The person who files a lawsuit. See also *petitioner.*

planned unit development (PUD)   A project or subdivision that has individually owned parcels and homes, together with recreational or landscaping elements owned by a homeowners association and managed for the mutual benefit of all homeowners.

planning commission   A government agency or an appointed group of citizens with varying degrees of responsibility regarding the use of land within a jurisdictional limit. Some commissions have the authority to make decisions regarding permitted uses and variances from permitted uses. Some commissions are merely advisory in order to provide citizen input into the process. The authorizations and the delegations of authority for a particular commission will determine the extent of its powers.

plat   A plan or survey map of a parcel of land. Developers file subdivision plats showing block and lot numbers, the dimensions and locations of individual lots, and the dimensions and locations of dedicated streets. Legal descriptions for properties within the subdivision are then made by reference to the recorded plat, such as "Lot 2, Block 3 of Harper Downs II as recorded in Plat Book 213, Page 82, of the Judge of Probate of Jefferson County, Alabama."

pledged account mortgage   A mortgage loan program in which money is placed in a savings account and the interest earned on the account is used to subsidize interest payments in the early years. It allows a borrower to buy property with much less equity while still enjoying a relatively low interest rate. The downside is for the person who put up the pledged account, because the money is at risk in the event of default, and it is not earning any interest for the investor.

pledged asset mortgage   A mortgage loan program allowing a purchaser to grant a security interest in other assets rather than having to liquidate them to pay a down payment. It allows the borrower to continue receiving income and other benefits from those assets, and also avoids the possibility of the borrower having to pay income taxes on sale proceeds if the assets had to be sold to make a down payment.

> **Example:**   *Fannie Mae has three pledged asset mortgage programs: (1) 30 percent of the purchase price in pledged assets from a family member results in 100 percent financing and no PMI insurance; (2) a 10 percent pledge by a family member, with certain borrower income and other requirements, results in the borrower needing to pay at least 3 percent of the combined purchase price and closing costs, and PMI is required; and (3) a 10 percent self-pledge by the borrower will gain 100 percent financing with PMI required.*

plot plan   A diagram showing the anticipated placement of improvements on real property, employed as part of the approval process.

plottage value   The increased value of land due to assembling small parcels into something larger capable of development. Also called assemblage value.

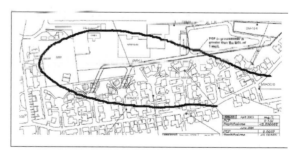

A plume of groundwater contamination. (Source: EPA.)

plume   Contaminated groundwater that flows and spreads from a single source.

PMI   See *private mortgage insurance*.

PMI Cancellation Act   See *Homeowners Protection Act of 1998*.

pocket card   A card issued by a state real estate licensing authority for each licensed salesperson. Many states require licensed professionals to have the card in their possession at all times.

pocket listing   A private agreement between a property owner and a broker, in which the owner agrees to pay a commission if the broker produces a buyer, but there is no listing agreement, no obligation to market the property, and no signage or advertising.

point of beginning   In a metes and bounds description, the starting corner of the property.

point of entry   The place where water service enters private property. If there is a leak on the homeowner side of the point of entry, the homeowner must pay a plumber to fix it and is responsible for payment of all water usage attributable to the leak. If the leak is on the water company side of the point of entry, the water company must make the repair and the homeowner cannot be charged for the cost of leaking water.

points   Charges in connection with a mortgage, calculated with reference to the amount of the loan. One point is equal to one percent of the loan. A fee of three points on a $100,000 loan is $3,000.

- See *discount points* for an explanation of the use of this device to reduce the interest rate on a loan.
- Origination points are the same as *origination fees,* and are charges to cover lender or mortgage broker expenses and profit.

pollution control bond   A tax-exempt security issued by a state, certain agencies or authorities, a local government, or a development corporation in order to finance the construction of air or water pollution control facilities or sewage or solid waste disposal facilities in accordance with federal law. These bonds are backed by the credit of the pollution control entity, not the issuer.

polychlorinated biphenyls (PCBs)   Highly toxic synthetic chemicals.

pool   A group of mortgage loans used as security for a bond issue. See *collateralized mortgage backed securities.*

portable mortgage   A new product first offered in 2003 and still relatively rare; it allows a borrower to move a mortgage from property to property as he or she sells and then buys new homes. This saves significant loan and closing fees. Interest rates are somewhat higher than conventional loans, the borrower must have nearly perfect credit, and the savings decrease the longer the time period is between sales.

portfolio   A group of investment assets.

portfolio loan   A mortgage loan the financial institution keeps in its own portfolio rather than selling on the secondary market.

positive cash flow   See *cash flow.*

positive leverage   See *leverage.*

possession   Exercising dominion or control over property. There are two varieties of real property possession. Actual possession occurs when property is in the immediate physical control and

310

occupancy of a party. Constructive possession exists as to the whole of a property when someone is in actual possession of a part.

possessory interest   The right to immediate use and occupancy of property.

possibility of reverter   See *reverter, possibility of.*

postforeclosure redemption rights   In some states, the right to repurchase one's own property after it has been foreclosed, by paying the full bid price plus interest within a defined time period. Sometimes, creditors of the former owner also have the same rights.

potential gross income   The maximum rental income possible from a property without vacancy or credit losses.

potentially responsible parties (PRPs)   Under federal law, persons who may be responsible for the cleanup of a contaminated site, either because they were an owner, operator, transporter, or disposer of waste products for that site. The Environmental Protection Agency looks for evidence of the identity of potentially responsible parties by reviewing documents, performing a site investigation, conducting interviews, using "information request letters" to gather information, and by performing title searches. (PRPs are not limited to the persons who caused the contamination, but may include all subsequent owners or occupiers of the property.)

power center   A shopping center that dominates its market; it usually has several anchor tenants.

power of attorney   A document executed by one person (the principal) authorizing another to act as his or her agent and on his or her behalf for any legal purposes or for specifically defined tasks. The agent is called an attorney in fact.

power of sale   A mortgage or deed of trust clause granting the lender the right to sell mortgaged property in the event of a default.

power of termination   See *reentry (deeds).*

preapproval   The practice of obtaining lender approval for a mortgage loan up to a certain specified amount and then shopping for an appropriate property.

predatory lending   Strictly speaking, it consists of loaning money to consumers in the hope and expectation they will default and the lender will be able to take the collateral. Modern usage has expanded the term to include any lending practices that rely on a consumer's lack of sophistication, or gullibility, for the imposition of unnecessarily high interest rates, large lending fees, or both. HUD maintains a Web site for researching reports of predatory lending, and resources for persons who believe they have been victims of predatory lending: www.hud.gov/offices/hsg/sfh/pred/predlend.cfm.

predecessors in title   All those who owned a parcel of real property before the current owner.

preexisting use   See *nonconforming use.*

prefabricated components   Ready-to-attach sections of buildings, such as structural insulated panels, tilt-up concrete walls, or roof trusses.

preferred equity   Corporate shares of stock that have greater rights than normal shares. Owners of preferred equity may be entitled to dividends—income—when there is not enough money to pay all shareholders. If the company is liquidated and all assets sold, preferred equity holders will receive their predetermined share before other equity holders.

prelease   To secure tenants for a property before it is completed and ready for occupancy.

preliminary injunction   A court order that orders a party to do something, or to refrain from doing something, until such time as the court decides otherwise after a full trial on all issues. Contrast with *temporary restraining order* and with *final injunction*.

preliminary title report   The initial title report showing the current owners of real property and all liens and encumbrances on the property. It is not title insurance.

premises   Land and improvements, generally, but the definition depends on context, case authority, and statutory description. Premises may be narrowed to one room if a search warrant gives the right to search certain described premises. It could be the entire house and surrounding 160 acres under other circumstances.

premises liability   Responsibilities placed upon owners and occupiers of property to keep the premises in a reasonably safe condition so as not to injure persons coming on the property. The term is descriptive of a field of law; lawyers might specialize in construction litigation, lender liability cases, or premises liability lawsuits, for example. Some states have different standards of care depending on whether one must guard against injury to licensees, invitees, or trespassers. See *owners and occupiers*.

premium   (1) An amount paid for an insurance policy. (2) An advance payment of several months or even years of rent to a landlord. (3) The value of a mortgage in excess of its face value. For example, if a $100,000 mortgage cannot be prepaid and is bearing interest at 10 percent when prevailing interest rates are only 6 percent, an investor might pay more than $100,000 to buy the mortgage because of the high return.

prepaid expenses   Expenses that represent goods or services delivered over a period of time, but which are paid in a lump sum at the beginning of that time period. If one paid $12,000 for an insurance premium on property for one year, that $12,000 would be entered on the accounting records as a $12,000 asset called prepaid insurance expense. Each month the property owner would reduce the asset account by $1,000 and show a corresponding $1,000 expense for that month for insurance. At the end of the year, the prepaid expense account would be $0 and the books and records would show $12,000 worth of total insurance expenses. When conducting the due diligence to purchase an income-producing property, the potential buyer should inquire about the handling of expenses for which the seller receives bills only a few times a year. Sometimes, such expenses never show up on the monthly profit and loss statements, but are artificially placed in something called the thirteenth month accounting period.

prepaid interest   An interest paid in advance of the time it is earned, as with discount points. Prepaid interest is not tax deductible unless all the following specific requirements are met:

1. The loan is secured by the taxpayer's primary residence.
2. Paying discount points is an established business practice in the area.
3. The points paid were not more than customarily charged in the area.
4. The taxpayer uses the cash method of accounting.
5. The points were not a substitute for normally itemized expenses such as the appraisal fee, survey fee, property taxes, and attorneys' fees.
6. The funds provided at closing by the buyer and by the seller, if applicable, were at least equal to the points (in other words, you didn't roll the points into the loan).
7. The loan is used to buy or build the primary residence.
8. The points were computed as a percentage of the loan.
9. The settlement statement (HUD–1) clearly shows the item as points.

prepaids   A word used to describe items that must be prepaid at closing, such as one year's property insurance premium.

prepayment clause   A loan provision allowing the borrower to pay the loan in full before the maturity date without penalty, or to make principal reductions faster than originally envisioned by the parties. Consumer mortgages all have prepayment clauses. Large, commercial loans typically prohibit prepayment.

prepayment option   See *prepayment clause.*

prepayment penalty   A fee paid to the lender for the privilege of paying off a loan earlier than originally agreed upon by the parties. In commercial lending, this is called the defeasance fee and is the amount necessary for the loan manager to take the proceeds of the borrower's payoff, plus the prepayment penalty, and go out in the marketplace to buy an investment with the same return and the same maturity. (Usually that investment will be a government bond.)

prepayment privilege   See *prepayment clause.*

prepayment risk   See *option risk.*

prepayments   See *prepaids.*

preplanning   An early stage of real estate development. The term has different meanings to different people, so one should not make any assumptions when hearing that a development is in preplanning. It may mean that stage when the project is under consideration, but before any money has been expended on research or due diligence. It may mean that stage before generation of any site plans or architectural plans, but after expenditure of significant sums for due diligence and research.

prequalify   To estimate the most expensive home a borrower can afford to buy with the assets, income, and expected loan amount and terms for which the borrower might be eligible.

presale   A sale of improved properties before they are built; common with condos and subdivisions. Presales are binding contracts. If the construction is completed, the buyer must purchase the property. Defaulting purchasers could risk more than the loss of their earnest money or their reservation fee. Under certain circumstances they could be liable for additional damages if the market takes a downturn and the property cannot be sold for a sum equal to or greater than the presale price.

prescription   The loss of rights because of a failure to assert them over a lengthy period of time. This is similar to a statute of limitations, but the time period is not established by statute, but by court interpretation and the particular circumstances of the case.

present value   Today's value for income to be received in the future. Two factors affect the analysis: (1) the perceived risk that one might receive nothing at all in the future, or a smaller amount than expected, and (2) the potential income from alternative investments that could be purchased if one were paid the present value for a future income stream. (Discounting is the mathematical calculation used to arrive at present value.)

present value of annuity   See *ordinary annuity*.

present value of one   The value today of an amount to be received in the future, based on a compound interest rate.

preservation district   A zoning district designed to protect areas that are sensitive to change, either because of environmental concerns, historic preservation, or scenic areas. There is usually a heightened degree of government oversight for development or renovation of these areas.

pretax income   Income from an investment before income taxes. If there are significant tax advantages to an investment, such as low-income housing credits or bonus depreciation, the after-tax income will sometimes be larger than the pretax income.

price   An amount of money exchanged for something of value.

price fixing   An agreement among competitors to charge roughly the same price as each other, denying consumers a meaningful choice in the marketplace. The practice is illegal under the Sherman Antitrust Act. In the real estate area, the most famous application of this principle has to do with real estate commissions and the complaint that local REALTOR® association members agreed to all charge the same rate. It is the reason for the disclaimer that appears on most real estate company form listing contracts and purchase contracts, "The commission is negotiated among the parties and is not set by…."

primary distribution   See *public offering*.

primary lease   The lease between a landlord and a direct tenant. Contrast with a *sublease*, which is between the tenant and a subtenant.

primary market   Any market in which the original issuer receives money, such as an investment house that purchases all securities for an original issue and then resells them on the stock market. Also called the *loan origination market*. Contrast with *secondary market*, where mortgages are pooled and then sold to others.

primary metropolitan statistical area (PMSA)   Now obsolete but still encountered in trade literature. The term was adopted by the U.S. Census Bureau in 1990, as part of a hierarchy that started with something called a metropolitan area (MA). The MA included metropolitan statistical areas (MSA), consolidated metropolitan statistical areas, and primary metropolitan statistical areas (PMSAs). The entire hierarchy was changed in 2000, with the new concept being a core-based statistical area, which includes metropolitan statistical areas and micropolitan statistical areas. For historical reference, a PMSA consisted of two or more communities that would qualify by themselves to be an MSA (1 million or more inhabitants) but that were so closely tied together economically that they should be treated as one unit.

primary mortgage market   The portion of the mortgage market that originates loans and then either keeps them or sells them on the secondary market.

prime   To come before another creditor in terms of priority of payment should there be insufficient assets to pay all creditors. A first mortgage holder primes a second mortgage holder, who primes a later judgment creditor, who primes a general unsecured creditor. Filing for bankruptcy reshuffles the deck, as the bankruptcy trustee primes large categories of creditors.

prime contractor   See *general contractor*.

prime rate   Traditionally defined as the rate of interest charged by a financial institution to its best customers. In reality, many commercial loans are quoted in terms of "prime minus one quarter," for example, which indicates there are better rates than prime. In addition, many lenders offer rates based on the London Interbank Offered Rate (LIBOR), resulting in interest rates less than prime. Today, prime rate is often just a published rate by a financial institution, called its prime rate whether it is the lowest offered rate or not.

prime tenant   Usually the largest, most important tenant in a shopping center or office building.

principal   (1) One who has permitted or instructed another—called an agent—to act on his or her behalf and according to his or her instructions. (2) One who is primarily liable for an obligation, as opposed to a surety, who is secondarily liable. (3) With a promissory note, the principal is the unpaid balance of the funds borrowed, not including any interest or other fees. (4) In a trust, the property of the trust that generates income. Principal can be real property or personal property.

principal and interest payment   The typical mortgage loan payment includes all accrued interest on the principal balance and some reduction of the principal; the borrower pays principal and interest. Only the interest portion of the payment is deductible on the borrower's taxes.

principal balance   That portion of the original loan amount which remains unpaid. It does not include accrued interest or fees.

principal broker   A name given in some states to the responsible party in a real estate office; sometimes called the managing broker or the qualifying broker. It is the person legally authorized to enter into agency contracts with consumers, and the person legally responsible for supervising the agents who work under that supervision.

principal, interest, taxes, and insurance payment   Usually a consumer mortgage loan arrangement that allows the borrower to pay small amounts each month toward anticipated annual expenses for taxes and insurance. The lender keeps the tax and insurance portions of the payment in an escrow account, ready to pay the bills when they come due. If the borrower sells his or her home before the taxes or insurance are due, the borrower may be entitled to a refund of monies in the escrow account.

principal limit   The maximum lifetime amount an elderly borrower can take out on a reverse mortgage. Calculation of the principal limit is a formula that uses the age of the youngest borrower, the maximum claim amount (the lesser of the house's appraised value or the FHA's maximum loan amount for houses in the area), and the expected average mortgage interest rate.

principal meridian   One of the imaginary lines running north and south, used as references for the public land survey system. There are 37 principal meridians in the United States. Each one has a name, and the names are used to distinguish the various surveys that eventually made up the public land survey system.

principal-only securities (POS)   Collateralized mortgage obligations issued by the Government National Mortgage Association (Ginnie Mae) that have been stripped out into bonds based only on interest payments (interest-only securities) and those based solely on principal payments (principal-only securities).

principal residence   The place one declares as his or her primary domicile; the address used on a driver's license, for voting, and for income taxes. The choice of a principal residence can make a difference regarding liability for income taxes, estate taxes, creditors' rights, homestead exemptions, and other such legal and economic consequences.

principle of balance   See *balance, principle of*.

prior appropriation theory   A theory of water use that holds that the first user of water has the unrestricted right to take it, even if it works to the detriment of the neighbors. Contrast with *reasonable use theory.*

priority   An order of payment of creditors if there are insufficient assets to pay all creditors.

privacy law   There is no single statute called the privacy law; however, a variety of statutes attempt to protect the privacy of citizens. They include as follows:

- The Buckley-Pell Amendment to the Family Educational Rights and Privacy Act denies federal funds to educational institutions that do not maintain the confidentiality of student records.
- The government may not obtain bank records without first informing the account holder and giving the account holder an opportunity to protest, by virtue of the Privacy Act of 1974, found at 5 U.S.C. §552a.
- Privacy of medical records and health information is guaranteed under the Health Insurance Portability and Accountability Act of 1996, typically called HIPAA (pronounced "hip-uh" for short). See 42 U.S.C. §3201.

private covenant   See *covenant.*

private letter ruling   An official IRS decision regarding how it will treat a transaction contemplated by the particular taxpayer who requested the private letter ruling. Private letter rulings are binding on the IRS for that one taxpayer, but other taxpayers are not entitled to rely on the position articulated in the ruling. Another taxpayer with an identical fact situation could find the IRS taking a completely different position.

private mortgage insurance (PMI)   Insurance to cover a lender's risk if it extends a loan for more than 80 percent of the fair market value (or purchase price, whichever is less) of property. Usually, the borrower pays the premiums for the PMI insurance. See also *Homeowners Protection Act of 1998,* which is popularly called the PMI Cancellation Act.

private offering   An investment offered to a small group of investors. Section 4(2) of the federal Securities Act exempts from registration "transactions by an issuer not involving any public offering." What qualifies as "not involving any public offering" is complicated and differs depending on a wide variety of circumstances. Generally, Regulation D (Rules 501 through 508) provides a safe harbor. If the issuer follows the rules for the circumstances described in Regulation D, then the issuer won't get in trouble.

private REIT   A real estate investment trust that is not traded on the national stock exchanges. Investments typically last for a set time period, usually 10 to 12 years. At the end, investors cash out through an initial public offering, a merger, or a liquidation. The investment usually lacks the liquidity of a publicly traded REIT—it is often difficult to redeem the shares or sell to a third party. Also called unlisted REIT, nontraded REIT, and nonpublicly traded REIT.

private sector   A portion of the economy composed of businesses and households, but excluding government.

privity of possession   (1) In successive possession of property, one possessor after another without a break. It is an important concept in adverse possession, which requires possession of property for a certain period of time before gaining title. Possessors who cannot meet the time period requirements are allowed to tack (combine) their time with earlier possessors who were in privity. (2) Having a direct contractual relationship between parties.

> **Example:**   *If Joe surveys land for Bill, then Bill and Joe have privity. If neighboring property owner Sydney is unhappy with the results of the survey, he cannot sue Joe for breach of contract or failure to perform the survey properly, because there is no privity between Joe and Sydney. Other legal theories may get around that problem, but not a breach-of-contract action.*

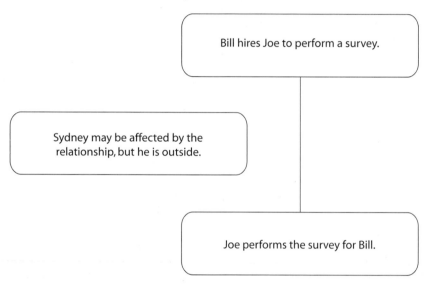

probate   To prove the validity of a will. Probate courts generally oversee decedents' estates, the payment of bills, and the distribution of assets. Some states have exemptions for small estates, which may avoid probate. Other states have no exemptions. Probate will need to be opened in every state in which a decedent owns assets, including real estate, unless there is a specific state exemption.

proceeds from resale   See *resale proceeds*.

procuring cause   A broker is considered the procuring cause of a sale and is entitled to a commission if the broker's efforts are the foundation on which negotiations resulting in a sale are begun.

producing cause   See *procuring cause*.

profit and loss statement   A semi-itemized list of all revenues and expenses of a person or company over a stated period of time, such as one month, one quarter, or one year. The items on the list are generally broad categories, but the selection of categories is a matter of personal preference for most small businesses. As a general rule, one should design a profit and loss statement so that it gives a snapshot of important revenue categories and the expenses associated with those particular revenues.

profit a prendre   A right to take substances from the soil of another.

profit margin   The difference between the cost of a unit (house, subdivision parcel, condominium) including a pro rata share of all overhead and other such expenses, as compared to the sales price for that unit.

pro forma   See *pro forma statement*.

pro forma statement   Anticipated revenues and expenses of a business. Development projects will include a pro forma statement (pro forma for short) for each month or quarter until the project reaches stabilized occupancy, and then a separate pro forma for a representative 12 months at stabilized occupancy. Many developers prepare three pro formas for every project: best case, worst case, and most likely case.

progressive tax   A tax that imposes a greater burden on the wealthy than on those with low incomes because the tax rate percentage increases as one's income or assets increase. Income taxes and estate taxes are progressive taxes. Contrast with a regressive tax, such as sales tax, that charges the same percentage to all taxpayers but results in a heavier burden to low-income citizens.

progress payments   Payments to a contractor or developer based on the stage of completion of the project.

projection   A forecast of future trends in a business, based on past experiences or on other currently available data. A projection that senior housing needs will increase at 12 percent per year for the next 5 years may form the basis for a pro forma profit and loss statement for development of a retirement community.

projection period   The time period of a projection. It might be the next 5 years, it could be the life span of a real estate development from breaking ground to selling out all properties, or it could be one year from today. The projection period is always defined when making projections.

promissory note   A binding contract—promise—to pay a definite sum of money to someone upon specified terms and conditions.

property   Any tangible or intangible thing that is or may be owned by someone.

property condition addendum or clause   A clause in a real estate purchase contract permitting the buyer to cancel the contract without penalty or loss of the earnest money if an inspection reveals defects. Wise sellers will insert a basket clause, specifying that minimal defects, such as those that would cost no more than $500 to repair, may not be grounds for cancellation and that anything estimated to cost between $501 and $2,000 (or wherever the seller's comfort level is) may be repaired by the seller within a reasonable time and the contract may not be cancelled.

property depreciation   See *depreciation*.

property description   See *land description*.

property line   The boundary line between two properties.

property management   See *management agreement*.

property report   A summary of facts about undeveloped land that must be given to purchasers of nonexempt properties under the Interstate Land Sales Full Disclosure Act.

property tax   See *ad valorem tax*.

proportional tax   A tax that charges the same percentage of income, regardless of the amount of income; also called a flat-rate tax.

proprietary lease   In a cooperative apartment, residents buy shares of stock in a corporation that owns the apartment building. They then rent a particular unit from the corporation, under a document called a proprietary lease.

proprietorship   Ownership. Those who own their own business in their own personal name, without a corporation or partnership or other such business structure, is said to have a sole proprietorship.

pro rata   Proportionate to one's interests or claims. In bankruptcy, unsecured creditors will receive their pro rata portion of any money left after paying secured creditors, attorneys' fees, and costs of administration. If the unsecured claims total $1,000,000, and the money left for distribution is $10,000, then each creditor will receive 1 cent for each dollar of their claim.

prorate   The process of determining the pro rata portions. In real estate, the term comes up frequently at a closing, when allocating certain property expenses. Usually real estate taxes are paid in arrears and homeowners association dues are paid in advance. The new owner will pay 100 percent of the real estate tax bill when it is presented after the closing, but a portion of that bill represents time periods when the seller owned the property. Likewise, the seller will have already paid the association dues for the month, but will own the property for only a portion of the month. At closing, these expenses are prorated between the buyer and seller. The buyer will receive a credit for the accrued-but-unpaid property taxes. The seller will receive a credit for the paid-but-unaccrued association dues.

prospect   A person who has indicated some interest in buying and who appears to have the desire and the ability to purchase. Contrast with suspect, who is someone identified as possibly having an interest in buying, but who has not yet been contacted or has not yet given any evidence of interest.

prospective appraisal   A licensed professional appraiser's estimate of the value a property will have after certain conditions come to pass. Before lending development money for a project, lenders will require a prospective appraisal of the completed project.

prospectus   A legal document describing something that is being offered for sale, with all disclosures required by applicable state and federal laws.

proximate cause   The primary or moving cause of an injury.

proxy   A person who stands in the place of another. (1) Normally used in the context of a share-holder granting permission for another shareholder or board member to vote his or her shares of stock. (2) In bankruptcy, creditors may give their proxies to other creditors, to the trustee, or to the debtor's attorney to vote for or against a plan of reorganization. (3) Marriage by proxy is still allowed in a very few states, in which someone stands in for the bride or the groom in the wedding ceremony, usually because one party is in the military service and deployed to a combat area.

PRPs   See *potentially responsible parties.*

public auction   See *public sale.*

public domain   (1) Land belonging to the government and not reserved for a specific use. (2) Things belonging to all persons to share, use, and enjoy, such as music and literature for which the copyrights have expired or ideas that are freely exchanged in the public domain.

public housing   Housing owned and operated by the government, usually for rental to low-income families. Contrast with low-income housing, which is privately owned but government supported through a variety of incentives.

public lands   Land owned by central or local government in trust for its citizens. Most federal lands are managed by the following agencies, depending on a grant of jurisdiction to each:

- Bureau of Land Management (www.blm.gov)
- U.S. Fish and Wildlife Service (www.fws.gov)
- U.S. Forestry Service (www.fs.fed.us)
- National Park Service (www.nps.gov)
- National Oceanic and Atmospheric Administration (www.noaa.gov)
- Bureau of Reclamation (www.usbr.gov)
- U.S. Army Corps of Engineers (www.usace.army.mil)

public land survey system (PLSS)   A way of subdividing and describing land in most of the United States. Texas, Hawaii, and most of the original 13 states are not described by the PLSS. The system starts with a principal meridian, which is a north-south line. There are 37 principal meridians in the United States. Each principal meridian has a base line that runs east and west through it.

Land is described as being east or west of the principal meridian, and north or south of the range line associated with that meridian. Land is typically divided into 6-mile-square townships. Townships are described with reference to their principal meridian and base line.

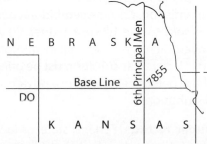

> **Example:**   *A township "2 North, Range 3 East, Mount Diablo Meridian" would mean the township is in the*

second tier north of the base line, and the third column east of the Mount Diablo Principal Meridian.

Each township is then divided into 36 sections. Each section is 1 mile square and contains approximately 640 acres, making allowance for unsophisticated measuring tools employed at the time of creation.

6	5	4	3	2	1
7	8	9	10	11	12
18	17	16	15	**14**	13
19	20	21	22	23	24
30	29	28	27	26	25
31	32	33	34	35	36

Sections may be further subdivided into quarter-sections (160 acres), quarter-quarter sections (40 acres), or any other mathematical subdivision. The gray square in the figure on the bottom right might be described as "the northeast quarter of the northwest quarter of the southeast quarter of Section 14, Township 2 North, Range 3 East of the 6th Meridian.

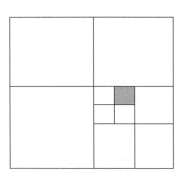

public offering　(1) Offering of new securities to the investing public after registration with the Securities and Exchange Commission. (2) A sealed-bid auction where oil sands rights are sold to the highest bidder. (3) A requirement by some governments, educational institutions, and others that property declared as surplus must be offered to the public for purchase before being sold in a private sale. Also called a primary distribution.

public record　Federal, state, or local records that are available for inspection by the public. In real estate, it refers to the practice of filing copies of all real estate documents in a central depository, where they are indexed and preserved for viewing by members of the public.

public sale   An auction of property after notice to the public. Notice requirements will vary depending on the reason for the sale.

public sector   That portion of the economy consisting of the government and corporations owned by the government. Contrast with *private sector*.

public street   Any street, road, or way dedicated to public use. Most cities have strict requirements for roads built by developers and then dedicated to public use.

PUD   See *planned unit development*.

puffing   An expression of opinion regarding positive traits and superior qualities of a property, but not intended as a statement of fact.

punch list   The list of completion, correction, and repair items necessary after construction has been completed on a project and before acceptance by the owner, tenant, or purchaser. The item can be as minor as, "Switch plate in master bathroom is not straight," to things as important as, "All the carpet is the wrong color."

pur autre vie   Literally, "for another life." An ownership interest in land, but only for a period of time measured by the lifetime of a named person.

purchase agreement   See *contract for purchase or sale*.

purchase contract   See *contract for purchase or sale*.

purchase money mortgage   (1) A mortgage loan used to purchase real estate. It may be seller-financing, institutional lender financing, or any other type, as long as the loan proceeds were used to purchase the property. Some states prohibit lenders from suing borrowers on purchase money mortgages if a foreclosure sale does not result in enough money to pay the debt in full. (2) Sometimes used to refer to a purchase money security interest in personal property. Personal property security interests are sometimes called chattel mortgages, hence the expression purchase money mortgage. (3) In bankruptcy, the debtor may not keep normally exempt assets without paying the creditor if the creditor has a purchase money security interest.

purchase option   See *option*.

purchase price   The contractually agreed upon price for a property, before credits, adjustments, or concessions.

pure debt   An obligation to repay money, but without any sharing of profits or increases in value. Most mortgages are pure debt; the lender does not own any part of the property nor does the lender receive any profits from the property.

pure notice statute   Refers to recordation statutes that say, as between competing claimants to real property or to liens on real property, priority is given to a subsequent claimant who takes its interest without notice of the prior interest. Contrast *pure race statute* and *notice-race statute*.

pure race statute   Refers to recordation statutes that provide that the first lender, lienholder, or purchaser to record their instrument take precedence over all others, even if when they were recording they had knowledge of prior claims that were simply unrecorded. It is a race to the courthouse to record. Contrast *pure notice statute* and *notice-race statute*.

Q

QLIP   See *qualified leasehold improvement property*.

quadraplex   An apartment building with four units. Also called fourplex.

qualified buyer   One who is actively seeking property to purchase and has the financial ability to complete a purchase. If a seller refuses to sell property to a qualified buyer procured by a real estate broker during the listing period, then the seller will be liable for payment of the full commission unless there is a no-buy, no-pay clause.

qualified intermediary   A person or entity permitted to hold funds in a 1031 exchange, which is a vehicle for selling a property and buying a replacement property, thereby deferring payment of taxes until sale of the second property. Anyone may be a qualified intermediary as long as that person does not fit the description of a disqualified person. Disqualified persons are those who are the agent of the taxpayer at the time of the exchange or who acted as an agent for the seller at any time in the 2 years prior to the exchange. See *1031 exchange* for the mechanics of the transaction.

qualified leasehold improvement property (QLIP)   An IRS term meaning any improvement made or to be made by a tenant taxpayer to the interior part of nonresidential real property more than 3 years old, in space occupied exclusively by the tenant. For QLIPs placed in service after August 27, 2005, and before January 1, 2009, in the GO-Zone (hurricane damaged states and counties), 50 percent of the cost of the QLIP may be taken as a depreciation deduction in the first year, rather than the $^1/_{39}$ deduction allowed under normal tax law.

qualified real estate professional   An outdated IRS term related to the passive activity rules. See *real estate professional*, which is the modern term.

qualifying broker   In some states, the person legally responsible for a real estate office, the training and supervision of all licensed real estate persons in the office, and the one who must sign all agreements with clients. Also called broker in charge or managing broker. See *broker*.

qualifying ratio   The maximum ratio of debt to income that will still allow a borrower to qualify for a loan. Lenders use two different ratios. The front-end ratio compares housing costs to income. The back-end ratio compares all consumer debt to income. Each lender has its own preferred ratios, which are usually dictated by demands placed by the secondary market or by loan guarantors such as the Veterans Administration. The numbers are not secret, but they change too often to include in a book. Be sure to ask a lender about its qualifying ratios and what exactly is included in the numbers.

quantity survey   An appraisal method used to calculate the reproduction cost of a structure by quantifying all materials, labor and overhead necessary to reproduce it.

quantum meruit   (pronounced like "merit") Means "as much as he deserves." It is the principle that if someone has benefited from the work and goods of another, but without a formal contract, then the one supplying the labor or materials is entitled to a reasonable compensation as long as they did not lead the other to believe it would be free. The theory arises often in construction projects, which seem to have a high percentage of people working on a handshake and an implied understanding of the normal fees in the area.

quarantine   An ancient right of widows to enjoy their deceased husband's home and property for a period of time after death and before allocation of the widow's other common law rights. Today, the concept has been codified in many state probate codes, which grant an allowance to the widow during the pendency of the estate probation.

quarter   One-fourth of a year. For 2007, January, February, and March would be written as 1Q07; April, May, and June would be 2Q07, and so on.

quarter-quarter section   A parcel of land described by starting with a 640-acre section, dividing it into quarters, and then dividing one of the quarters into fourths again. It has a size of 40 acres. In the figure, 1, 2, 3, and 4 are each quarter-quarter sections. A, B, and C are quarters, of 160 acres each. See *public land survey system*.

quarter section   A parcel of land described by starting with a 640-acre section and then dividing it into four equal quarters, each with 60 acres. In the figure, A, B, and C are all quarter sections, and 1, 2, 3, and 4 together make a quarter section. See *public land survey system*.

```
+----------------+----------------+
|                |                |
|       A        |       B        |
|                |                |
+----------------+--------+-------+
|                |   1    |   2   |
|       C        +--------+-------+
|                |   3    |   4   |
+----------------+--------+-------+
```

quash   To annul, vacate, void, abate, dispel, or overthrow. One quashes an indictment, a rebellion, or fears that a zoning variance will ruin the neighborhood. Use of the word "squash" instead of "quash" is inappropriate.

quiet enjoyment   The right to enjoy leased or owned property without disturbance. The covenant of quiet enjoyment is one of the typical warranties made in deeds and leases. Some states will not find a breach unless there has been an actual or constructive eviction of the owner or tenant. Other states are more lenient. Most controversy arises in the context of landlord-tenant disputes, in which the landlord has done something the tenant views as damaging to the tenant's business. Examples include extremely noisy construction on the floor above for an extended period of time; barricades erected in front of a tenant café's entrance, or the landlord failing to furnish heat.

quiet title action   A court action to determine the true owner of real property when there is a dispute among parties or when there might be an adverse claim by parties who cannot be found.

It is common in the case when a prior owner might have been the cause of a technical title defect, but the prior owner has died and no one can find the prior owner's heirs. In such a case, the purported owner will file a quiet title action and publish notices requiring anyone with claims to come forward or be forever barred.

quitclaim deed   A deed with no warranties at all. The grantor conveys anything it might own at the moment, but makes no representations or warranties it owns anything. It is the normal vehicle for clearing up title defects.

quit title suit   See *quiet title action*.

quotient verdict   One in which jurors cannot agree on an award, such as for a contested condemnation. They agree to each write down the amount they think should be awarded, and then someone takes the average of all those numbers. By agreement among themselves, the jury awards the average amount to the plaintiff. (Quotient verdicts are illegal and may be set aside if the jurors were foolhardy enough to leave their slips of paper and calculations in the jury room when they depart.)

R

race to the courthouse In a pure race state, the first party to file a deed, mortgage, or other instrument will take priority—will be given effect—before instruments filed afterward. As a result, a situation sometimes arises when there is a possibility of competing claims, such as a spouse or creditor who wants to file a claim against property before it is sold to another. In such situations, there is a race to the courthouse to file first—before anyone else.

racial steering See *steering*.

rack rate Slang for rent at full asking price with only the minimal build-out or other allowances usually quoted to prospects. No concessions.

radius clause A shopping center lease clause that prevents a tenant from opening another store within a certain radius of the current shopping center. The purpose is to prevent a competitor from duplicating the landlord's tenant mix in a nearby mall. In the drawing, a 5-mile radius clause would not prohibit the second store, even though they probably have overlapping market areas. Most courts require the restriction to be reasonable in duration and geographical area in order to be enforceable. Contrast with *reverse radius clause*.

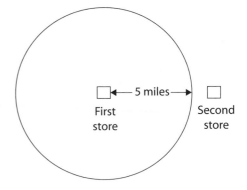

radon Colorless, odorless gas that occurs naturally due to the breakdown of minerals in the earth. It tends to become trapped in our modern, nearly air-tight homes. Since there has been some correlation between radon and lung cancer, the EPA recommends levels no higher than 4 picocuries per liter (pCi/L), although generally acceptable levels are in the range of 4 to 8 pCi/L. The EPA Web site at www.epa.gov has information on testing for radon and reducing it.

RAM Short for reverse annuity mortgage. See *reverse mortgage*.

range A division of land in the public land survey system. Each range line is approximately 6 miles apart and is identified according to its distance east or west from the principal meridian for the area. Range 1 West is in the column immediately west of the principal meridian for the area. See *public land survey system*.

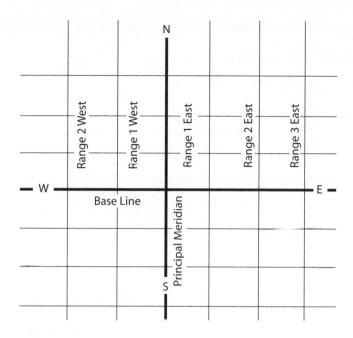

RAP   See *remedial action plan*.

rate guarantee   See *locked-in interest rate*.

rate improvement mortgage   A fixed-rate mortgage with one opportunity, at a time of the borrower's choosing but in the early years of a loan, to reduce the rate to market interest at that time. The loan will then continue at the new interest rate, which cannot be changed again.

rate of return   The ratio between the earnings and the cost of an investment.

rate of return of investment   See *recapture rule*.

rating agency   A company that evaluates the creditworthiness and strength of other companies and assigns a score to them, such as A, AA, and so on.

raw land   Land with no improvements, no infrastructure, and no grading or site development.

RBC   See *risk-based capital requirements*.

ready, willing, and able   One who has the desire and the ability to act. If an owner has an exclusive right to sell listing contract with a broker, and the broker produces a buyer who is ready, willing, and able to buy, but the seller refuses to sell, the broker has earned the commission.

real estate   Land and everything above and below the soil.

real estate agent   See *agent*.

real estate board   See *board of REALTORS®*.

real estate broker   See *broker*.

Real Estate Brokerage Managers Council   See *Council of Real Estate Brokerage Managers.*

real estate commission   See *commission.*

real estate contract   See *agreement of sale.*

Real Estate Educators Association (REEA)   A professional organization (www.reea.org) dedicated to its mission statement of providing "resources and opportunities for professional development to individuals and organizations involved in Real Estate education to better serve their customer base."

Real Estate Information Professionals Association (REIPA)   A national trade association (www.reipa.org) for professionals and corporations involved in providing real estate and public record information in the United States. It has spearheaded the drive to deal with standards in automated valuation model (AVM) technology, which is being used more and more by home lenders for property evaluation, rather than traditional appraisals.

real estate information system (REIS)   A computerized system for tracking property location, description, ownership, and any other information considered important by the entity creating the system. Today, almost any major and midsize city in the United States has online REIS access for property taxes, past and current property ownership, and recent sales prices.

real estate investment trust (REIT)   Congress passed the Real Estate Investment Trust Act of 1960 to allow small investors to pool their money into real estate investments and receive the same benefits as wealthier Americans who were able to purchase real property directly. REITs are special corporations that must invest only in real estate and must distribute at least 90 percent of their net income in the form of dividends, 95 percent before 1999. In exchange, they are allowed to escape any income tax liability at the corporate level.

Many people describe REITs as real estate mutual funds, which is conceptually true except for one big difference: REITS are closed-ended funds, meaning investors cannot demand redemption of their shares, but can only trade them on the open market. With a real estate mutual fund (REMF) investors may demand redemption from the fund, even if the public market isn't buying. There is a wide variety of REITs:

- Overall, they are either equity REITs that invest in property or mortgage REITs that invest in mortgages.
- They are not allowed to operate high-management properties like hospitals or hotels, but they can hire outside companies for the management.
- REITs generally specialize in one of the following sectors: retail, health care, lodging, industrial, office, residential, or specialty (self-storage centers, restaurant properties, etc.). Some diversify across several sectors.
- Some are publicly traded on the stock exchanges, some are private, and some are unlisted. Unlisted REITS are also called non-exchange traded REITS; they file reports with the SEC but do not trade on the national stock exchanges. Private REITS do not file any reports with the SEC and are not traded on any national stock exchange.

real estate mortgage investment conduit (REMIC)   An entity that holds a fixed pool of mortgages and issues multiple classes of mortgage backed securities. All interests must be classified as regular or residual. Regular interests are entitled to principal and interest income, through bonds, stock, or some other vehicle. Residual interests provide income that is less certain. There are almost 50 different classes of certificates, all with varying rights and risks. The Freddie Mac Web site has an excellent discussion of all available certificate types at www.freddiemac.com/mbs/docs/remic_glossary.pdf.

real estate mutual fund (REMF)   Similar to a REIT but with technical differences that make the REMF like any other mutual fund. The REMF invests in real estate assets, including REITs and REOCs and pays dividends to investors. A REMF is open ended, meaning investors may demand that their shares be redeemed and can then cash out and pursue other investments.

real estate operating company (REOC)   A publicly traded company that specializes in real estate investments but does not meet the strict requirements to be a REIT, particularly the requirement to pay at least 90 percent of net income out to investors. As a result of the ability to retain funds, REOCs can invest in expansion opportunities.

real estate owned (REO)   Foreclosure property held by a lender.

real estate professional   Usually refers generically to a trained and licensed person who makes his or her living in some aspect of buying, selling, or managing real estate. The IRS has a specific definition applicable to whether one is exempt from the passive activity rules. For IRS purposes, a real estate professional is any person who meets the following requirements:

1. More than half of the personal services the taxpayer performed in all trades or businesses during the tax year were performed in real property trades or businesses in which he or she materially participated.
2. The taxpayer performed more than 750 hours of services during the tax year in real property trades or businesses in which he or she materially participated.

real estate salesperson   See *sales associate*.

real estate securities   Various methods for people to invest in real estate without having to buy land and/or buildings. Some of the various methods are the following:

- Bonds for a particular project. One of the earliest issuers was the American Real Estate Company, organized in 1888 with $100,000 worth of capital, it issued almost $15 million in bonds and certificates with installment payments to purchasers. It went bankrupt soon after the 1914 market downturn.
- Stock in a corporation that owns a particular building or project. Early development pioneers sold stock in buildings to be constructed, thus largely eliminating the need to borrow construction money.
- In the 1950s, real estate syndication emerged, with limited partnership interests being offered to the public. They were popular for a few years and then interest waned.

- By 1960, Congress authorized creation of real estate investment trusts (REITs) which would produce favorable tax advantages for investors. Most early REITs were mortgage REITs (ownership of mortgages) rather than equity (ownership of property) investments.
- In the 1980s limited partnerships and syndications became popular again as large, nation-wide firms entered the picture as underwriters and promoters. Passage of dramatic tax law changes in 1986 took away many of the tax incentives for this vehicle, leading to its near demise.
- In the 1990s, investment in equity-REITs took off, with that becoming the predominant real estate security for investors.
- Today, tenancy in common investments (TICs) are the favored medium.

Real Estate Settlement Procedures Act (RESPA)   A federal consumer protection statute supervised and enforced by the Department of Housing and Urban Development (HUD). First passed in 1974, it requires various disclosures in order to help consumers make more informed decisions when shopping for settlement (real estate closing) services. It also seeks to eliminate kickbacks and referral fees, which unnecessarily increase the costs of certain settlement services. It applies to mortgage loans on single-family housing, duplexes, triplexes, and four-plexes (generally described as "one- to four-family residential property"), whether the loan is for a purchase, refinance, property improvement, or home equity line of credit.

- When borrowers apply for a purchase loan, they must be given a special information booklet regarding various real estate settlement services, a good-faith estimate of settlement costs, and a mortgage servicing disclosure statement regarding whether the lender will service the loan or transfer it to another.
- There must be an affiliated business arrangement disclosure whenever a closing company recommends a particular attorney, appraiser, surveyor or others if that third party is not independent from the closing company. The closing company cannot require use of a particular third party, but the *lender* can do so in order to protect its interests.
- The settlement agent must provide the consumer with the HUD–1 Settlement Statement, which clearly shows all receipts, all disbursements, all credits and charges, and all fees in connection with the transaction. The borrower may request to see the HUD–1 one day before closing.
- Loan servicing companies must supply an annual escrow statement to borrowers at least once a year. It summarizes all escrow account activity for taxes, insurance, and other escrow items.
- If the loan servicing is transferred, the borrower must be given a servicing transfer statement at least 15 days before the effective date, including a toll-free number and address for the new servicer. If the borrower makes timely payments to the old servicer during the first 60 days after transfer, the borrower cannot be penalized.
- Kickbacks and referral fees for settlement service business involving federally insured loans are prohibited, with civil and criminal penalties for violation.

- Sellers may not specify the buyer use a particular title insurance company, either directly or indirectly, as a condition of sale. Buyers may sue a seller who violates this provision and receive an amount equal to three times all charges made for title insurance.
- Escrow deposit payments cannot be excessive. Lenders may require borrowers to pay no more than one-twelfth of the total annual disbursements each month, plus a cushion that cannot exceed one-sixth of the total disbursements for the year.

real estate tax   See *ad valorem tax*.

realized gain   A tax concept meaning the taxpayer has received a profit—a gain—on the sale of real property, but, for various policy reasons codified into the Internal Revenue Code, the IRS chooses not to *recognize* the gain and, as a result, requires no payment of taxes at that time. The reason could be because the taxpayer took advantage of a 1031 exchange, because the gain was from the sale of a home and was less than the current exclusions, or because the property was taken by eminent domain and the proceeds reinvested within the required time period.

real property   See *property*.

real property trades or business   Under the Internal Revenue Code, losses from passive activities have limited deductibility unless one is a real estate professional. The test for a real estate professional is whether the person spends the required amount of time in real property trades or businesses. With that background in mind, the expression includes development, redevelopment, construction, reconstruction, acquisition, conversion, rental, operations, or management and brokerage of real estate.

realtist   A member of the National Association of Real Estate Brokers (www.nareb.com), comprised primarily of minority brokers and salespersons.

REALTOR®   A member of the National Association of REALTORS® (www.realtor.org).

REALTORS® Land Institute (RLI)   An affiliate of the National Association of REALTORS®; it focuses on brokerage of farms and ranches, undeveloped tracts of land, transitional and development land, subdivision and wholesaling of lots, and site selection and assemblage of parcels. (Originally named the Farm and Land Institute.) The RLI Web site is at www.rliland.com.

realty   See *real estate*.

reappraisal lease   A lease in which the rent is adjusted based on an independent appraisal of the value of the property; frequently seen with long-term ground leases.

reasonable consent   In most leases, a landlord's reasonable consent is required before the tenant may make an assignment of the lease or sublet to another tenant. The concept is naturally vague, as it must cover a wide variety of circumstances. It is intended to be understood by its negative—the landlord must have a stated reason for withholding consent, and, considering all the circumstances, that reason cannot be arbitrary, foolish, unfair, illegal, or unethical.

reasonable time   A fair and just amount of time to complete an act or fulfill a contract, taking into consideration all the circumstances. Unless a contract provides that time is of the essence, then the parties will be given a reasonable time after a due date within which to comply.

reasonable use theory   Riparian owners (owners of land located beside a river or stream) may make reasonable use of the water flowing past their land for either natural or artificial wants, but may not use it in such a manner as to affect the quality or quantity of water available to downstream owners. Contrast with *prior appropriation theory*.

reassessment   Reviewing or updating the value estimates of real property for the purpose of calculating ad valorem taxes.

rebate   (1) A refund. (2) A kickback. Kickbacks from settlement providers are illegal under the Real Estate Settlement and Procedures Act.

rebuttable presumption   A law of evidence that something will be considered true (the presumption) until it is proven untrue (rebutted). When a rebuttable presumption has been created, it normally shifts the burden of proof to a different party than would normally have it. For example,

- In some jurisdictions, if a bankrupt debtor company owns only one asset, and that asset was transferred to the company shortly before it filed for bankruptcy, then there is a rebuttable presumption that the transfer was fraudulent and intended to isolate that one asset and its creditors from other assets belonging to the original owner. The debtor must prove the transfer was not fraudulent, rather than the creditor being required to prove it was fraudulent.
- In some states, when spouses take property as joint tenants with rights of survivorship, but one spouse provided all the money for the purchase, there is a rebuttable presumption that a gift was intended to the other spouse. As a result, if the one providing the money wishes the whole of the property upon divorce, and the state is not a community property state, then the paying spouse has the burden of proving it did not intend a gift to the nonpaying spouse.
- If there is a boundary line dispute and one party destroys evidence, such as tearing down a fence or removing markers or pins, there is a rebuttable presumption that the evidence would have been adverse to the party who destroyed the evidence.

recapture (tax)   Same as *depreciation recapture*.

recapture clause   (1) A clause in a lease setting out conditions under which the landlord may recapture the premises even without a default by the tenant. A common usage occurs when the tenant wishes to sublease or assign its space for a profit—the new occupant will pay a higher rental rate than the tenant is paying to the landlord. In such a circumstance, the landlord will want to recapture the space and rent it directly to the new tenant or it will want to share in the lease profits. (2) A clause in a statute that provides exceptions to an exception. For example, one clause in the Clean Water Act grants an exception to the requirement to obtain a permit. But, the recapture clause "recaptures" the permit requirement under certain limited circumstances.

recapture of depreciation   Same as *depreciation recapture*.

recapture rate   In appraisal, used to describe the rate of recovery of an investment in a wasting asset—one that becomes less valuable because it is used up, like an oil lease.

recasting   Renegotiating a loan in the face of an impending or actual default. See *workout*.

receivables   Money due from tenants or clients. Receivables are listed as an asset on the balance sheet. One can have a profit on paper, because all the rent charged to tenants counts as income, whether collected or not. One can also have a large amount of assets and be worth a lot of money, on paper, because unpaid rents—receivables—are listed as an asset. At the same time everything looks rosy on paper, you can be going broke because tenants are not paying their rent, you don't have any hope of ever collecting the past-due receivables, and there is no money to pay the bills.

(Remember this when reviewing financial information for a rental property: you must see the balance sheet and the financial statements at the same time to figure out what is really happening.)

Sample Balance Sheet Showing Assets	
Assets:	
Current Assets	
Cash on hand	500
Cash in banks	4,500
Receivables	28,000
Fixed Assets	
Furniture and equipment	16,000
Land and buildings	200,000
Total Assets	249,000

recession   Technically, two successive quarters of falling gross domestic product as judged by the National Bureau of Economic Research, a private nonprofit, nonpartisan research organization founded in 1920. Commonly, a time of general economic slowdown.

reciprocal negative easements   Another name for *restrictive covenants*.

reciprocity   A mutual agreement to accept another's judgment on a matter. Some states offer reciprocity of real estate licensing, so that an agent or broker licensed in one state may become licensed in another without meeting the minimum education, testing, or apprenticeship requirements.

recital   Statements of fact, usually appearing at the beginning of contracts and leases. Usually the recitals start with the word, "Whereas ..." Most attorneys and almost all parties give very little thought to the recitals, but they can be critically important. The recitals are the facts considered important in the formation of the agreement. They may be as innocuous as a statement that the tenant is a corporation duly organized and existing under the laws of the state of California, for example. They can also include such things as specific representations made by each party to the other. If there is a later dispute about the parties' intentions, or whether a misrepresentation was material or not, reference to the recitals can often make the difference in the dispute.

reclamation   (1) The process of converting unusable lands to beneficial use, such as reclamation of strip mine sites, swamps, and gullies. (2) A bankruptcy remedy allowing a vendor who sold goods on credit to one who filed bankruptcy shortly afterward to reclaim those goods and obtain their return from the bankrupt buyer, but only if the buyer was insolvent at the time of receipt and the seller makes demand for reclamation within 10 days of the buyer's receipt.

recognized gain   That portion of a sale profit that is taxable. When a person has a gain on the sale of property, it is said the person realizes gain. Under certain beneficial tax provisions, the seller may not have to pay taxes because the gain is not recognized at that time—the IRS chooses to ignore it for one reason or another. Normally, all gain is recognized unless it falls within one of the exceptions allowing deferral until a later date, such as a 1031 exchange, or excluded completely, such as sale of a principal residence for less than the ceiling amount of gain.

reconciliation   In appraisal, the process of considering values calculated from the various apprais- al methods and weighting the strength to be given to each approach in order to arrive at a final value for the property.

reconfiguration   Changing the physical layout of something, such as a work space, a golf course, or the sizes and layouts of rooms in a hotel.

reconveyance   When a mortgage debt is retired, the lender conveys (transfers) the prop- erty back to the borrower in a title state.

recording   Entering something into the real estate or probate records so that it serves as constructive notice of its contents to all the world. Many jurisdictions have specialized requirements before they will admit docu- ments to recording, such as the name and address of the person who prepared the docu- ment, the book and page numbers of the source of title for the property, and prohibitions against strike-through marks or other editorial revisions apparent on the face of the docu- ment. See the sample recording information that appears to the right.

2006 16959	
Recorded in the above	
DEED Book & Page	
08-02-2006 03:33:57 PM	
Source of Title: 1998 / 13964	
W. Hardy McCollum - Probate Judge	
Tuscaloosa County, Alabana	
Book/Pg: 2006/16958	
Term/Cashier: SCAN2 / hazeln	
Tran: 6B30.458511.552066	
Recorded: 08-02-2006 15:34:09	
DFE Deed Tax	13.50
PJF Probate Judge Fee	2.00
REC Recording Fee	6.00
SOT Source of Title	1.00
Total Fees: $ 22.50 Page	

recording acts   State statutes that govern the official recording of deeds and other real estate documents and the effects of such recording as to creditors, subsequent purchasers, and other interested parties. There are three varieties of recording statutes:

1. Notice acts provide that a person with notice of an unrecorded instrument is barred from claiming priority over it, as of the date the person received notice.
2. Race acts ("race to the courthouse") provide that the first person to record takes priority, even if that person had notice of a prior unrecorded instrument.
3. Race-notice acts provide that the first to record without notice of a prior unrecorded instrument has the better rights.

recording fee   A fee charged by the office that accepts real estate–related documents for recordation. The term is used generically and is meant to include the actual recording fee, the transfer taxes, the indexing fees, and other such related costs.

record owner   See *owner of record*.

recourse   (1) The ability of a lender to demand payment from a borrower if the collateral is insufficient to pay the debt in full, or even if the lender chooses not to attempt foreclosure of the collateral. (2) The requirement that the seller of a promissory note repurchase it if the borrower defaults.

> **Example:**   *Vic's Vinyl Siding agrees to install siding on Nellie's house in exchange for her agreement to pay $300 a month over the next 5 years, for a total of $18,000. Nellie signs a promissory note with those payments, and a mortgage. Vic does the work and then sells the note and mortgage to Quick Cash Company, with recourse, for $10,000. Three days later the siding falls off the house and Nellie refuses to make any more payments. Under federal law, she can refuse to pay Quick Cash Company even though her dispute is with Vic's Vinyl Siding. Because the sale was with recourse, Quick Cash can force Vic to repay the $10,000 to them and take back Nellie's promissory note and mortgage. Nellie and Vic may then battle over the quality of the work.*

recovery fund   A fund maintained by many state real estate commissions to assist in compensating victims who have suffered as a result of a breach of a real estate agent's or broker's responsibilities but were unable to recover because there was no insurance and no discoverable assets. The fund is typically maintained by dues from agents and brokers.

recreational lease   (1) Separate ownership of recreational facilities at a condominium project or planned unit development, with the owner leasing their use to the residents. (2) Leasing of land for recreational purposes such as hunting, fishing, snow sports, and motor sports. It is a method of keeping land largely natural and still enjoying some sort of income.

rectangular survey   See *public land survey system*.

reddendum clause   A deed clause that reserves something for the grantor, such as a life estate. Contrast with *habendum clause*, which describes the quality and quantity of the estate conveyed.

redeem   (1) In mortgages, to cure a default by paying all past-due sums and penalties after receiving notice of default, but before acceleration. (2) To exercise the post-foreclosure right of redemption, if allowed. (3) Under federal law, the IRS has 120 days after foreclosure to purchase property on which it had a lien—to redeem the property. (It rarely does this, and would only do so if it believed it could sell the property at a profit large enough to justify the time and trouble.)

redeemable rent   Under lease with a purchase option and the ability to use a predetermined amount of the rent as payment on the purchase price, the payment portion is called redeemable rent.

redeemable ground rents   Homeowners sometimes own their house, but must rent the land on which the house sits—called a ground lease. This is fairly common in Maryland and some other states. The homeowner may deduct redeemable rent paid for the ground lease, the same as mortgage interest, but only if

1. The ground lease, including renewal periods, is for more than 15 years.
2. The lease can be freely assigned.
3. The homeowner has a present or future right to end the lease and buy the land at a specified price.
4. The lessor's interest in the land is primarily a security interest to protect the rental payments to which he or she is entitled.

redemption, equity of   See *equity of redemption*.

redemption rights   See *right of redemption*.

redevelop   To rebuild after substantial demolition of the old structure.

redevelopment agency   A government subdivision created to improve blighted, depressed, deteriorated, or otherwise economically depressed areas; to assist property owners displaced by redevelopment; and to issue bonds or other instruments necessary to fund the programs. Goals are normally accomplished in partnership with private developers.

red herring   A proposed prospectus that has been filed with the Securities and Exchange Commission (SEC) but not approved by it. Its purpose is to determine the extent of public interest in an issue while it is being reviewed by the SEC. Called a red herring because of the red ink around the border of the front page.

rediscount rate   An interest rate charged by the Federal Reserve to member banks who borrow money. See *discount rate* (also called bank rate).

redline prints   Blueprints with changes marked in red ink. At the completion of construction, the redline prints should be combined into as-built drawings.

redlining   Commonly used to communicate an illegal practice of refusing to make loans or sell insurance in certain areas. In reality, the practice is common and is legal, but only if the disqualifying criteria do not include race, religion, gender, family status, disability, or ethnic origin, or some disguised criteria intended to discriminate on those grounds. Many insurance companies will not sell insurance in entire states viewed as being plaintiff-friendly with outrageous jury awards. This is a form of permissible redlining.

reentry (deeds)   Sometimes called the power of termination, or the right of entry, it is the retained right of a grantor who conveys property subject to a condition to subsequently enter and retake the property when the condition has been broken. An example would be a deed to the city of particular land "on condition that it be used for a school and for no other purposes." If the city uses the property for something else, the land does not automatically go back to the grantor, but the grantor has the right to retake the property—the right of reentry—should the grantor choose to do so.

- Even if the grantee or subsequent purchasers mortgage the property, the grantor still has the right to reenter and regain the property free and clear of any liens or claims, including the mortgage.
- The right of reentry can be exercised only by the grantor and his or her heirs, but not by third parties such as creditors of the grantor.
- Some states hold that the right cannot be transferred to others by the grantor during his or her lifetime.
- Some states require the holder of a right of reentry to file a statement in the real estate records regarding that specific right, rather than simply rely on deed language as sufficient notice to the world.

reentry (leases)   The right of a landlord to enter premises upon a breach and retake possession. Contrast with *reversion*, which is the right the landlord has in premises at the expiration of a lease.

referral   Recommending a particular broker to someone. Brokers may legally pay referral fees, but only to other brokers.

refi   Shorthand for *refinance*.

refinance   Obtain a new loan to pay off an older one.

reformation   A legal action to correct an instrument to comply with the intentions of the parties. If the grantor in a deed will not agree to sign a corrective deed, it may be necessary for the buyer or a subsequent owner to file a reformation action.

regional shopping center   In common language, a large shopping center that draws customers from outside the part of town where it is located. According to the International Council of Shopping Centers, it is one with general merchandise including a high percentage of fashion stores, with 400,000 to 800,000 square feet of space sitting on 40 to 100 acres and two or more anchor tenants taking up 50 to 70 percent of the available space. The typical market area is a radius of 5 to 15 miles, or approximately 80 to 700 square miles.

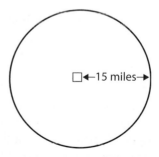

registered agent for service   See *resident agent*.

registrar   A person charged with maintaining official records, such as deeds and mortgages.

regression   (1) A statistical technique for creating a mathematical equation to explain the relationship between known variables so that the model can be used to predict other variables when one has insufficient data. Multiple regression analysis is the basis of computerized automatic valuation models (AVM) employed instead of appraisals by many mortgage lenders. (2) An appraisal principle that if properties of relatively unequal value are located near each other, the one with the lower value will depress the value of the other. (3) A withdrawal of the sea from the land due to an uplift of the land or a drop in sea level.

regressive taxation   A tax burden that falls more heavily on those with low income. Contrast with *progressive tax* and *proportional tax*. Sales taxes are regressive taxes if imposed on all sales, because the straight percentage imposed on all sales takes away a higher percentage of a low-income household's available income. Some states attempt to lessen the regressive effect of sales taxes by exempting purchases of food and medicine. In the following table, the low-income household spends almost 5 percent of its disposable income on sales taxes, because all income after paying for housing must go to buy things that are taxable.

Comparison of Effects of Sales Taxes

	Low-Income Family	High-Income Family
Income	$15,000	$150,000
Housing costs	7,200	48,000
Taxable purchases	7,800	36,000
Sales taxes @ 9%	702	3,240
Percentage of income spent on sales taxes	4.68%	2.16%

Regulation D (Reg D)   A Securities and Exchange Commission regulation that can apply to real estate investments that constitute a security. Reg D provides two types of limited offering exemptions from the registration requirements of federal securities laws, neither of which are dependent on the nature or sophistication of the purchaser. The first exemption is for offerings of up to $1 million and an unlimited number of purchasers; the other is for offerings of up to $5 million to a limited number of investors. It also allows exemptions for private offerings to accredited investors or to a small number of sophisticated investors. Even if an offering is exempt under Reg D, the company must still file a Form D with the SEC, providing the names and addresses of the company's owners and stock promoters. If investors are offered a Reg D investment, they should check with the SEC (publicinfo@sec.gov) to see if a form is on file; the lack of a Reg D form may be a warning of possible illegality in the investment. (These are important safe harbors to the real estate investor and developer because sales of interests in real estate–related businesses can constitute securities. The full text may be found at 17 CFR 230.504 through 506, retrievable at the U.S. Government Printing Office Web site at www.gpoaccess.gov/cfr/retrieve.html.)

Regulation CC ("Reg Double C")   A federal banking regulation regarding the availability of funds and collection of checks, Reg CC sets limits for the length of time a financial institution may place a hold on the use of funds after a check has been deposited to an account. People commonly think funds must be available immediately if checks are drawn on local financial institutions, but that is not true. Large checks, such as are often received for real estate transactions, may have a hold time as long as 7 days for local checks, except that the first $5,000 must be made available on the first business day.

Other than the deposits described in the following list, checks drawn on local institutions must be credited on the second business day after deposit, and checks drawn on nonlocal institutions must be credited on the fifth day after deposit. A local institution is one in the same check processing region. The financial institution may increase the hold times for large deposits or for any number of factors causing it reasonable concern. The deposits described in the following list must be made available for withdrawal on the first business day after deposit except that items 3 through 7 can be made available on the second day after being deposited if the deposit is to one of the financial institution's own ATM machines, or on the fifth day after deposit if made to any other ATM machine:

1. Electronic payments
2. U.S. Treasury Department checks
3. Cash
4. U.S. Postal Service money orders
5. Federal Reserve and Federal Home Loan Bank checks
6. State or local government checks
7. Cashier's, teller's, or certified checks
8. Checks drawn on an account at the same financial institution

Regulation Q   A federal law having to do with interest on bank deposits. Today, it provides that banks cannot pay interest on demand deposit accounts—checking accounts.

Regulation Z   A regulation issued by the Board of Governors of the Federal Reserve System in order to assist in implementation of the Truth in Lending Act. It requires certain disclosures regarding the cost of credit and rights of rescission (discussed at length under *rescind*). Additional disclosures must be made for *reverse mortgages*, discussed within that topic. The disclosure box appearing on all consumer promissory notes is called the Reg Z Box (see the diagram).

Annual Percentage Rate	**Finance Charge**	**Amount Financed**	**Total of Payments**
The cost of your credit at a yearly rate	The dollar amount the credit will cost you	The amount of credit provided to you or on your behalf	The amount you will have paid after you have made all payments as scheduled
A%	$**B**	$**C**	$**D**

Regulatory Information Service Center   A centralized Web site (www.reginfo.gov) for research on all federal government regulations and deregulatory actions.

regulatory taking   A legal theory that a particular government regulation has so adversely affected the value of real property as to amount to a condemnation of the property, for which the owner is entitled to compensation. There are two varieties: categorical and noncategorical takings. In order to establish a case of categorical taking, the Supreme Court has held that the property owner must show (1) that the land-use regulation does not substantially advance legitimate state interests, and (2) that it denies an owner all economically viable uses of his or her land. These are both heavy burdens to overcome. A noncategorical taking does not require elimination of all economically viable uses of property, but does require a case-by-case analysis of the regulation regarding its character and nature, the severity of its economic impact, and the degree of interference with the property owner's reasonable investment-backed expectations.

rehab   Short for *rehabilitate*.

rehabilitate   To restore a structure to good condition after deterioration.

rehabilitation tax credit   Credits against income taxes for expenses associated with the renovation, restoration, or reconstruction of certain buildings. The credit is 10 percent of the expenses for buildings placed in service before 1936, and 20 percent for certified historic structures. For properties located in the GO-Zone (certain named states and counties suffering 2005 hurricane damage) the credit was increased to 13 and 26 percent, respectively, for expenses incurred after August 27, 2005, and before January 1, 2009.

Reilly's law of retail gravitation   Proposed by William J. Reilly in 1931, it says that people in a larger city will travel farther to shop than people in a smaller city. Reilly created a formula for calculating the precise point of geographical equilibrium between two nearby trade areas—the point at which one-half of the population shops in either trade area. Its weakness is that it assumes no natural or human-made boundaries. Modern retail theory recognizes that populations will usually not cross boundaries—such as major highways, bridges, or even some streets—in order to shop on the other side, even if more convenient than perceived "local" choices.

reinvestment rate   When analyzing the value of an income-producing property, it is the rate an investor is assumed to be able to earn on intermediate cash flows. The number is necessary for inclusion in the formula for the financial management rate of return.

> **Example:**   *Ryan owns two rental houses. After payment of all expenses and debt service, Ryan has cash flows of $300 per month, which is a 15 percent return on his money. The internal rate-of-return analysis for these properties assumes that Ryan will take his entire $300 per month and reinvest that money in something else at the same 15 percent rate he is earning on the apartments. The formula assumes a reinvestment rate of 15 percent, which is highly unlikely. The financial management rate-of-return formula still assumes Ryan will reinvest the entire $300 per month, but allows the person doing the analysis to pick a reinvestment rate. If Ryan puts the $300 per month in a savings account earning 2.5 percent, then his reinvestment rate is 2.5 percent.*

REIS   See *real estate information system*.

reissue rate   A discount given by a title insurance company when the prior policy on the same property was from the same title company. In some markets, even competitor companies will offer a reissue rate if the property purchaser can provide a copy of the prior title policy, thus saving some work for the current company.

REIT   See *real estate investment trust*.

related party transactions   A business deal, transaction, or conveyance among parties that have a special relationship with each other, either through family ties, related corporations, or other possibilities. Related party transactions require certain regulatory disclosures in order to avoid the appearance (or the actuality) of wrongful insider conduct. In addition, the IRS disallows or limits tax benefits if the underlying transaction is between related parties, because of the possibility of manipulation.

relation back doctrine   (1) The principle that something done today will be treated as if it were done earlier. A document held in escrow and then delivered later will be treated as if delivered when it was put into escrow. This is not because the escrowee is the agent of the person receiving delivery, but because of the doctrine of relation back. This is an important distinction when someone dies after escrow, but before delivery, because agencies are automatically terminated upon death. (2) Some jurisdictions follow a relation back doctrine regarding lawsuits, so that if the plaintiff sues the defendant on a breach of contract claim for some transaction between the parties (normally a 4- to 6-year statute of limitations) and the defendant has negligence claims against the plaintiff arising out of the same transaction (normally a 1- to 2-year statute of limitations), then the defendant may assert his or her claims even though the time limit may have otherwise expired.

release   See *release of lien*.

release clause   A mortgage clause that allows a partial release of some of the collateral when the borrower pays off a portion of the loan. Typically found in subdivision development mortgages, because the development lender must release its lien in order for the purchaser-homeowner to secure his or her own first mortgage financing.

release of lien   A recordable document showing that a lender, judgment creditor, the IRS, or other secured creditor no longer claims a lien upon real property.

reliction   A gradual withdrawal of waters, leaving dry land. Riparian owners (owners of land located beside a river or stream), and sometimes littoral owners (owners of land at the edges of lakes and ponds), have the right to any new land caused by reliction. Some states hold that a sudden reliction creating large quantities of land results in the land being owned by the state. See also *dereliction*.

Religious Land Use and Institutionalized Persons Act of 2000   Federal legislation that prohibits any government from imposing or implementing a land-use regulation in a manner that imposes a substantial burden on the religious exercise of a person, including a religious assembly or institution, unless the government demonstrates that imposition of the burden on that person, assembly, or institution (1) is in furtherance of a compelling governmental interest and (2) is the least restrictive means of furthering that compelling governmental interest.

relinquished property   The first property transferred in a 1031 exchange. The property received is called the replacement property.

relocation clause   A lease clause that allows the landlord to move a tenant to another location within the building, usually to accommodate the entry of a new tenant requiring a large quantity of space or for the expansion of an existing tenant. Tenants requiring site-specific locations, such as retail tenants next to a particular anchor, or office tenants with ground-floor space needs, usually negotiate the deletion of a building's standard relocation clause. If the clause is present, landlords typically pay for all expenses of the move but may not pay for new stationery, change-of-address notifications, or business interruption unless these items are negotiated and included in the lease.

relocation exception   An exception to the Housing and Urban Development (HUD) regulation denying FHA insurance to properties flipped in less than 90 days, and requiring additional documentation for properties purchased and then sold within 91 to 180 days after initial purchase. The exception is for properties purchased by an employer or relocation agency in connection with the transfer of an employee who needs to sell his or her home in order to relocate.

relocation network   A group of independent real estate brokers that agree to cooperate and exchange information regarding potential customers moving into their various geographical areas.

relocation service: A company that assists with advice and possibly handling of the details of a move, usually to another city. Most commercial relocation services contract with employers in order to assist transferred employees. Services may include packing, moving, and unpacking services; purchase of the employee's old home; and assistance with finding a new home. Free services are provided by many specialty support groups.

remainder   An estate in property that takes effect at the termination of a life estate. One may transfer property to another for their lifetime or for the lifetime of a third party. The named person who defines the duration of the life estate is called the measuring life. The person who has the life estate is called the life tenant. When the measuring life ends, even if the life tenant is still alive, the person who owns the remainder is entitled to the full possession and enjoyment of the property. The interests may be contingent remainders, vested remainders, or vested remainders subject to divestiture. The rules of construction are complicated.

> **Example:**   *A clause in a will leaving property to an only child for life, and then the remainder to grandchildren alive at the time of the child's death, creates a contingent remainder in the grandchildren until they are born, and then vested remainders as they are born, but subject to divestiture if they die before their parent, the testator's child. One should seek legal counsel well versed in specialty real estate law if setting up or interpreting life estates and remainders.*

remaining balance   See *outstanding balance*.

remaining economic life   The number of years between the date of an appraisal and the date a property improvement will cease to have any economic value, even if it will still be structurally sound. A solidly built parking deck with short ceiling heights, narrow lanes, and tight turning radii might have a limited remaining economic life because most modern cars, particularly trucks and SUVs, cannot use the deck.

remaining term   An amount of time left before a loan matures or before a lease expires.

remedial action plan (RAP)   A plan required by the Environmental Protection Agency for cleanup of hazardous waste sites.

remediation   The process of cleaning up environmentally contaminated sites. It may be active, which requires some human intervention, or it may be passive and accomplished through the normal processes of nature. It may be ex situ, in which contaminated material is removed, or in situ, which relies on cleaning mechanisms in place on the property. Processes can include mechanical, chemical, thermal, magnetic separation, manual separation, use of biologic agents, or flushing, to name a few.

REMF   See *real estate mutual fund*.

REMIC   See *real estate mortgage investment conduit*.

remodel   To change the appearance or utility of a building.

rendering   A drawing or painting showing a perspective view of a building, also called a rendition. Contrast with *elevation*, which shows only a two-dimensional view of one or more faces of a building.

> **Example:** *At their simplest levels, Figure A is a rendering and Figure B is the east elevation, both of the same house.*

rendition   (1) A report generally required of businesses, listing their personal property subject to property taxes. The system relies on honest and accurate reporting, because personal property is not as easily discovered and valued as real property. Cheats may be discovered through the services of tax ferrets. (2) Another name for a rendering.

Figure A   Figure B

renegotiate   An agreement to revise the terms of a contract. Promissory notes, mortgages, leases, and other contracts can typically be renegotiated if failure to do so will result in default and that default would be economically disadvantageous to the other party. This power to renegotiate is exemplified by the old saying referring to loans from small banks, "If you owe the bank $10,000, they own you. If you owe the bank $1,000,000, you own them." A debtor in bankruptcy can force renegotiation of onerous contract terms, such as a long-term lease at above-market rental rates.

renegotiated-rate mortgage (RRM)   Sometimes called a rollover mortgage, it is a type of balloon mortgage. The interest remains fixed for some period of time, usually 3 to 5 years. At the end, the parties may renegotiate the interest rate and, if they come to an agreement, the lender will change the rate with a minimum of fees and expenses. If they do not agree, the borrower is free to move the loan, but may not choose to simply keep the existing loan and its terms in place.

renewal lease   The lease term after tenants exercise their renewal option. See *renewal option* for more in-depth treatment.

renewal option   A right that may be given to a tenant to continue in the leased space at the expiration of the current lease, on specified terms and conditions. A renewal is a new lease agreement. Contrast to an *extension*. The difference is important because

1. Oral agreements to extend a lease may be enforceable under the Statute of Frauds, but oral agreements to renew may be unenforceable unless there is some writing evidencing the agreement.
2. A previously agreed upon rental rate for a renewal would indicate adjustment of the base period for the tenant's share of operating expenses to the renewal year, while the same rental rate for an extension would indicate use of the original base year. If the tenant must pay a pro rata share of building operating expenses in excess of what they were in year 1 (first lease year) versus what they were in year 6 (first renewal year), it could amount to a significant amount of money each month.

renewal probability   The average percentage of tenants in a building that are expected to renew at market rental rates at the expiration of their current leases. The figure is used to estimate leasing-related costs and downtime.

renovate   To repair and upgrade, with a sense of changing something. Contrast with rehabilitate or restore, which imply keeping the same general character and appearance. Differences among the words are important when making modifications to historic structures, because renovation may not be allowed. A property owner's imprecise use of terminology regarding his or her plans could result in unintentional animosity by neighbors and historic preservation commissions.

rent   Payment for the privilege of possessing space one does not own.

rental growth rate   The expected trend in market rental rates over the period of projection, expressed as an annual percentage increase. In the chart, rents are expected to be at $43 a foot for 2007, climb rapidly to $50 a foot for 2008 because of a lack of new buildings coming online, remain at $50 a foot during 2009 because of the opening of new buildings, and then climb moderately afterward.

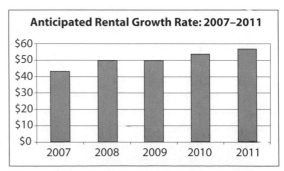

Anticipated Rental Growth Rate: 2007–2011

rental income   Money collected from tenants for the use of space. On financial statements, money collected as late fees, from the use of laundry machines, or as forfeited deposits (unless credited to rent) should not be included in rental income but should be listed separately or under "miscellaneous income."

rental pool   An arrangement in which condo owners or other such ownerships in a large community agree to make their units available for rental by a common leasing agent or property manager according to the good business judgment of that agent and then to all share in the overall revenues and expenses according to a predetermined formula. The arrangement may constitute a security under federal securities laws and require registration and appropriate disclosures.

rental rate   The periodic charge per unit for the use of property. The rental rate may be a certain amount per square foot per year (even though paid monthly), per square foot per month, per room, per apartment, or any number of other variations.

rent concession   See *concession*.

rent control   Laws that regulate the rent that can be charged for space. Rent-control laws were originally enacted as emergency measures after World Wars I and II, because many returning service personnel emigrated to urban centers. This caused housing shortages and dramatic rent increases, with a resulting increase in evictions. Today, rent control is seen as a legitimate exercise of a government's police power and usually does not require an emergency situation. The state of New York differentiates between rent-controlled apartments and rent-stabilized apartments because of the dates of differing legislation. Rent-controlled apartments are still operating under laws enacted in 1947. They require that the tenant have continuously occupied the apartment since before July 1, 1971. As those apartments vacate, they become rent-stabilized under other legislation, or they become decontrolled under some circumstances.

rent escalation   See *escalation clause*.

rent-free period   A sometimes misleading term indicating a landlord concession regarding a period of time during which the tenant will not have to pay any rent. It is truly rent-free if the uncollected rent is not rolled into the back end of the lease or otherwise recaptured over the term of the tenancy. If the tenant must pay the rent, but simply at another time and in smaller increments, then it is more properly called deferred rent. Even landlords often misuse the two words, so persons shopping for space should specifically inquire about the free-rent versus deferred-rent issue when receiving quotes.

rent multiplier   See *gross rent multiplier*.

rent roll   A list of tenants, usually including the lease expiration date and rental rate for each one.

December Rent Roll: Fernwood Apartments

Tenant	Apartment	Lease Start	Lease End	Rent
Anderson, John	F	1/1/2005	12/31	$900
Chabannes, Norbert	A	6/1/2000	5/30	$1,000
Freeman, Larry	B	11/1/2005	10/31	$1,100
Lucas, Patricia	E	4/1/2003	3/31	$990
Malone, Paulette	C	6/1/2004	5/31	$1,050
Woodruff, Joseph	D	9/1/2006	8/31	$1,100

rent stabilization   See *rent control*.

rent strike   A group of tenants banding together and refusing to pay rent until necessary repairs have been made to a building. Typically, the rent is paid into an escrow account or into a court clerk's office in conjunction with a lawsuit against the landlord.

rent-up period   The time it takes new properties to reach stabilized occupancy.

REO   See *real estate owned*.

REOC   See *real estate operating company*.

reorientation   A change in direction or focus of a business in response to changing market conditions or in order to attract a different market.

repair and retreatment bond   If available, an agreement by a pest control company that if a property has been treated and continuously protected by it against termites or other wood-destroying insects, but an infestation occurs and results in damage, the company will repair all damage and eradicate all such insects, at no charge to the property owner, with the possible exception of a deductible.

repairs   Work to return a property to its former condition without extending its life. Repairs are fully deductible on the current year's tax returns.

replacement cost   (1) In appraisal, the cost to erect a new building substantially similar to the current one. (2) In insurance, the cost to purchase a new item substantially similar to the one damaged, destroyed, or stolen. Contrast with *fair market value*.

replacement property   A property received in a 1031 exchange. The first property given up is the relinquished property.

replacement reserve   An amount of money set aside because building components or equipment will wear out in a relatively short time and need to be replaced. Replacement reserves can be a mere accounting entry as a phantom expense item reducing net operating income each month, or it can be money actually deposited into an account and earmarked for replacements. If the money is set aside into a separate account, any contract for the purchase of that property or business should include a clause addressing who gets the money—the purchaser or seller. When purchasing a condo or co-op, or a home in a planned unit development, the buyer should make sure there are adequate cash replacement reserves for the future. If not, then repairs will not be made or they will be made only after assessments against all owners.

replacement value protection   Insurance that will provide payments to replace insured goods, whatever that cost might be, rather than insurance in the amount of the current fair market value of the used goods. This could be important for personal property protection, but also for building insurance. Especially with historic homes built of high-quality durable materials with a great deal of hand-crafted and decorative detail, the replacement value could be far in excess of the fair market value.

replevin   A type of lawsuit to recover personal property, such as when a landlord takes possession of leased property due to a default and refuses to return personal property located on the premises.

repo   Slang for repossess.

reporting requirements   IRS requirements that certain transactions or financial information be reported to it, even if there are no tax consequences. Settlement agents are required to report sales or exchanges of all real property, or a statement of exemption. If there is no settlement agent, the order of responsibility is attorney, title company, mortgage lenders, and real estate brokers. The IRS also requires reporting returns for partnerships, S corporations, and limited liability companies, even though none of those entities has to pay taxes; instead, individual members report their share of income and losses.

repose, statute of   See *statute of limitations*.

repossession   The actions of a lender to take possession of personal property in which it has a security interest, or the actions of a landlord to take possession of leased premises after default. Repossession may be by court order, or it may be self-help, as when the automobile repo person takes a car in the dead of night. Self-help repossession is generally allowed unless prohibited by specific consumer protection statutes, but it must be accomplished without a breach of the peace. Some courts define "breach of the peace" as shouting, threats of violence, or any sort of public disturbance. Others hold that repossession in the face of the debtor's oral statements to cease and desist is a breach of the peace, but that does not preclude the creditor from returning later to attempt repossession when the debtor is not present.

reproduction cost   The cost of exactly duplicating an improvement as of a certain date. Contrast with replacement cost. An example is an historic building with high coffered ceilings and deep solid-maple crown molding that has been converted to office space with a drop-in grid ceiling that hides the older details. The reproduction cost would include the cost to build a structure with the same high ceilings and the same crown molding. The replacement cost might be the cost to build a structure with normal 8-foot ceilings constructed of ceiling tiles.

repurchase agreement   An agreement to buy something back from the purchaser. This is encountered most often in two situations: (1) The thing purchased turns out to be less valuable than originally thought, such as when someone buys a promissory note, or a partial interest in a promissory note, and the obligor then defaults. (2) Especially with condominium units in facilities specializing in elder care, the seller of the units will agree to buy them back at a preestablished price if the owner dies or becomes so disabled as to require nursing home or similar care.

request for proposal (RFP)   Ideally, a tightly written list of requirements and specifications upon which contractors, vendors, or service providers are invited to place bids. The goal is to write the specifications in such a manner that bids can be compared equally, without making adjustments among them. For example, an RFP for floor covering might specify the exact maker and pattern name for a carpet, or it might specify a generic carpet of a certain weight, with or without a pattern, and with or without a pad of a specified thickness. It would include scale drawings of the space to be carpeted so that waste could be calculated, and it would include special instructions such as the need for installation to take place between certain dates or over a weekend.

request for qualifications   In a public sector–private sector partnership for development or redevelopment of property, a call by the government entity in charge for submission of the qualifications of those interested in being involved in the partnership.

resale price   In a projection regarding the performance of a real estate investment, it is the anticipated price the property will bring upon eventual sale at a point in time.

resale proceeds   Upon the sale of real property, the money remaining after payment of expenses of the sale, any mortgage debt on the property, and sometimes after payment of income taxes. The term is imprecise and is usually defined in context. Under some programs administered by the Department of Housing and Urban Development, property owners who received assistance for their home purchase must reimburse HUD for some of the resale proceeds.

rescind   To withdraw or undo. The act itself is called rescission. If a party has a right of rescission, the party may rescind a transaction. Important rescission rights include the following:

- Under the Truth-in-Lending Act, consumers may rescind a loan transaction if the lender failed to provide all required disclosures.
- Certain state laws give homeowners the right to rescind sales contracts for properties in danger of foreclosure.
- Most states still allow insurance companies to rescind policies if there was a fraud in the representations made to secure the policy.
- A contract may be rescinded if there was fraud in the inducement, meaning a fraud with the underlying transaction and not with the nature of the contract or document signed.
- Under the Truth-in-Lending Act, consumers refinancing their principal residence or taking out a home equity line of credit may, with certain exceptions, rescind the loan within 3 business days and not owe any interest or fees.

rescission   See *rescind*.

Research Institute for Housing America   A nonprofit organization (www.housingamerica.org) that is a division of the Mortgage Bankers Association. It provides research grants for projects regarding expanding rental opportunities and homeownership for the underserved.

reservation   The retention of some right by the grantor in a deed. Grantors may reserve a life estate, the mineral interests, or a right-of-way across the property, for example. Reservations appear in the reddendum clause of a deed.

reserved water rights doctrine   Holds that when the United States withdraws land from the public domain and reserves it for a private purpose, it also withdraws all water rights necessary to support the purpose, including the rights to groundwater if other waters are inadequate. This includes Indian lands and lands owned in the Territories before statehood. The U.S. may sell or assign those rights to others. The reservation allows the government (or persons to whom it sells those rights) to prevent upstream owners from taking water, even if otherwise allowed under state law. Assignees of federal reserved water rights enjoy greater protections and privileges than other citizens of the state. Whether or not there was a reservation is a question of federal law and must be determined in federal court.

reserve for bad debt   An expense item on a profit and loss statement for the current period's pro rata share of anticipated annual credit losses due to unpaid bills or defaulting tenants.

reserve for credit and collections   See *reserve for bad debt*.

reserve for losses   An accounting entry made to set aside a fund for payment of possible future liabilities as a result of litigation or similar claims. If a tenant is injured after falling from a defective balcony at an apartment, that tenant might sue for damages. The apartment complex might have liability insurance, but there could be a very large deductible. If there is no doubt about the fall, no doubt about the landlord's liability, and the only issue is regarding the size of the check to the tenant, the landlord knows he or she will eventually have to pay up to the deductible limits for the injury. As a result, the landlord will probably set aside a reserve for losses in that amount.

reserve fund   A physical fund with money for anticipated future needs. A reserve fund should appear on a company's or property's balance sheet as an actual bank account, earmarked for a particular use.

reserve price   The price below which auctioned property will not be sold. If a property is advertised with reserve, then the owner may withdraw it from auction at any time before sale. If it is advertised without reserve, then the seller must go through with the auction.

reserves   See *reserve fund*.

residence   The place where one lives.

resident agent   A name given in some states to the person authorized by law to accept service of process (lawsuits, for example) for a corporation or other artificial person. There are many commercial services that will provide this service for companies. Also called "registered agent for service."

residential   Pertaining to housing. Many tax laws and consumer protection statutes turn on whether a property is residential or not.

residential broker   A real estate broker who specializes in single-family homes. A broker who specializes in multifamily residential, such as apartments, is usually called a commercial broker.

Residential Communities Initiative   A Department of Defense program to upgrade housing for military personnel by partnering with private industry for renovation, construction, and management.

residential development   The preparation of land and infrastructure for dwelling places and may also include construction of the dwellings.

residential mortgage   A loan secured by real property used for a personal residence or dwelling.

residential property   (1) In real estate brokerage, commonly used to signify an owner-occupied residence, even though a rental house is technically a residential property. (2) For tax purposes, any rental property in which at least 80 percent of the income is from dwelling units. Residential property enjoys a 27.5-year depreciation period, while normal commercial property must be depreciated over 39 years.

Residential Sales Council   See *Council of Residential Specialists*.

residential service contract   An insurance policy that will cover repair or replacement of major home systems, such as plumbing, heating, air conditioning, or electrical. Either the buyer or seller can purchase the contract, although sellers usually do so as an incentive for a buyer to purchase that property rather than another.

resident manager   A person who supervises an apartment complex or self-storage facility while living on the premises. The practice usually provides excellent management and early detection of problems, but can have some drawbacks, including the possible need to go through an eviction proceeding if the manager is fired or quits and refuses to leave the dwelling. In addition, there may be overtime pay issues if the manager is "on call" for emergencies outside normal business hours. From a psychological standpoint, some resident managers report burnout because, even during their off-hours, they are never truly free of the tenants and the need to interact with them.

residual   (1) An amount remaining from an investment after payment of all operating expenses, debt service, reserve funds, and income taxes. The residual remains for payment to the investor. (2) The value of leased personal property at the end of the lease term. Under an operating lease, a lessee may be given the right to purchase the property for the previously agreed upon residual value. Car leases, copier leases, and heavy equipment leases all work on this principle.

residuary   Everything not specifically mentioned in a will. After all named and described gifts have been made, whatever is left is in the residuary. If the will makes no provision for the residuary, that portion of the estate will pass by intestate succession.

Resolution Trust Corporation (RTC)   A corporation that no longer exists, but had a major impact on U.S. real estate markets. The RTC was formed in the wake of the banking and thrift crisis and bailouts of the mid to late 1980s. As lending institutions were declared insolvent and closed by their various regulatory agencies, the Federal Deposit Insurance Corporation (FDIC) or the Federal Savings and Loan Insurance Corporation (FSLIC, pronounced "fizz-lick") arranged for payments to depositors and then took over the assets of the failed institutions. The assets could include performing and non-performing loans, real estate, vehicles, equipment, furniture, and often rare and expensive artwork and accessories. The task of managing and liquidating the assets proved too much, so the government created the RTC to take over those functions. The mandate of the RTC was to liquidate assets, including real estate, as quickly as possible, even if a higher price might be obtained by holding the assets and managing sales over a longer period of time. Billions of dollars of real estate came into the hands of the RTC. The real estate was then sold, often for pennies on the dollar, and as a result many real estate markets were seriously depressed and took years to recover.

Resource Conservation and Recovery Act (RCRA)   (pronounced "rick-rah") A federal law that establishes a system for managing hazardous wastes in an environmentally sound manner from the point of origin to the point of final disposal, called cradle-to–the-grave management. It also promotes resource recovery and waste minimization. The Act gives citizens the right to file suit against violators to enforce its provisions, and the right to file suit against the Environmental Protection Agency administrator to require enforcement of the rules. More information is available at the EPA Web site at www.epa.gov.

RESPA   See *Real Estate Settlement Procedures Act.*

respondeat superior   One of the many methods of finding someone vicariously liable for the wrongful actions of another. It is the legal theory that an employer is responsible for the negligent or wrongful acts of its employees performed within the line and scope of their employment, and a principal is responsible for the negligent or wrongful acts of its agent performed within the line and scope of its agency. It is not a theory of contract law—meaning who has authority to bind whom—but rather a theory of tort law and injuries to persons or property. It is extremely rare to find a case in which a property owner has been held liable for the wrongful conduct of its broker. More often, brokers have been accountable for actions of their salespersons.

restatement of laws   Works prepared by the American Law Institute (www.ali.org) in order to set out the law on various subjects with commentary regarding changes and anticipated growth. The Restatement of the Law of Agency, for example, is not itself law, but may become so when a court refers to a rule in the restatement and adopts that rule of conduct or interpretation within the state. Other restatements related to real estate include

- Restatement of the Law of Contracts
- Restatement of the Law of Property
- Restatement of the Law of Trusts

restore   To return a structure to its original appearance, although the use of modern and updated materials may be employed.

restraining order   See *temporary restraining order*.

restraint on alienation   A restriction on the ability to transfer real property, such as a gift of land to a church or university with the requirement that it not be sold for 99 years. Restraints on alienation are generally disfavored by the law and will only be enforced if they are reasonable in scope and duration.

restricted appraisal report   A report in which the information that forms the basis of the appraisal is not included within the document itself, but is available for reference should that prove necessary.

restriction   A limitation on the use of property, usually contained in the deed, in restrictive covenants appearing in the real estate records, or by virtue of local ordinances.

restrictive covenant   A deed restriction. See *covenant*.

resulting trust   A trust that is implied by law as necessary to carry out the true intentions of the parties involved. It typically arises when one transfers legal title to another for various reasons, but both parties intended the grantor to retain all benefits from the property. If an elderly person transferred her home to a child as an estate planning tool, but continued to live in the residence, the law would not allow the child to sell the home and keep the proceeds. It would, instead, impose a resulting trust. Contrast with a *constructive trust*.

retail anthropology   The study of consumers' shopping habits in order to choose the best locations for new retail sites and the best designs for the development itself and for the space within each store.

retail gravitation   The ability of a shopping center to draw business away from other shopping areas. See also *Reilly's law of retail gravitation*.

retail installment contract   A contract that provides compensation for consumer goods or services by making payments over time, usually at a high interest rate.

retail investor   An individual investor who buys securities through a stockbroker on online service. Contrast with *institutional investor*.

retail property   A zoning classification that allows stores or shopping centers.

retainage   Money withheld and not paid until completion of a project and inspection of the goods or services provided. Typically, 10 percent of a construction contract price will be withheld until final inspection.

retaining wall   A support to prevent collapse of earth embankments. Many local governments have landscaping requirements to disguise retaining walls over a certain height and restrictions on the materials that can be used for retaining walls.

354

retaliatory eviction   A landlord's refusal to allow a tenant to remain after the tenant has made a good-faith complaint about the landlord, the property, or the landlord's manner of management. (This is illegal in many states.)

retention pond   A human-made pond where storm water is directed and retained until it can be absorbed into the water table or slowly released without flooding downstream property owners. The modern trend is to prefer absorption into the natural water table, so many local governments impose retention pond requirements as a condition of development, even if storm sewer facilities are available. Many modern office park water features, such as small lakes with fountains, are government-required retention ponds.

retire (a debt)   To pay off a loan.

retreatment bond   An agreement by a pest control company that it will not charge to eradicate an infestation, usually by termites, if insects appear between regularly scheduled treatments.

retrospective appraisal   The estimated value of property at some point in the past; may be necessary to value a gift.

return on equity   See *equity dividend*.

return on investment (ROI)   A generic term to define a number of analytical tools for measuring the financial benefits of an investment, including cash on-cash, internal rate of return, equity dividend, and financial management rate of return.

revaluation or reevaluation   See *reassessment*.

revaluation clause   See *reappraisal lease*.

revaluation lease   See *reappraisal lease*.

revenue   The total rent, sales, or earnings of a company. When negotiating for the purchase of income-producing property, be sure to inquire about the seller's definition of revenue rather than make the assumption that the seller is using the correct terminology to describe figures supplied to you. Contrast with *income*.

revenue ruling   Advice from the IRS national office regarding application of the law to a particular fact situation on which a taxpayer has requested guidance. Any taxpayer may rely on a revenue ruling as guidance for similar conduct, but courts are not bound by them if a court thinks the IRS was wrong. Contrast with *private letter rulings* (also called letter rulings) which issue from a local IRS office and which can be relied upon only by the taxpayer to whom the letter was addressed. Contrast also with a *technical advice memorandum* issued under different rules but still binding on the IRS only as regards one particular taxpayer.

revenue stamps   Stamps affixed to deeds and some other real estate documents as evidence of payment of the appropriate recording or transfer taxes.

355

reverse annuity mortgage   See *reverse mortgage.*

reverse exchange   A tax-deferred exchange in which the taxpayer acquires the replacement property before selling the relinquished property. See *1031 exchange.* (It is far more common to sell a property and then begin looking for a replacement property to take advantage of Section 1031 of the Internal Revenue Code.)

reverse leverage   A situation in which the interest rate on a mortgage is so high that one cannot obtain any financial benefits from a property because of the debt service.

reverse mortgage   A financial tool that allows senior homeowners to withdraw money from the equity in their home in a lump sum, or in payments over time, in the form of a loan that is not payable until after the last spouse dies or the homeowners cease using the home full time. Because this is a loan transaction, federal truth-in-lending laws require certain disclosures to the homeowners before they enter into such a transaction. They include, among other things, the following:

- An itemization of the loan charges, appraised value of the home, and age of the youngest borrower.
- All advances to and for the benefit of the consumer, including annuity payments that the consumer will receive from an annuity that the consumer purchases as part of the reverse mortgage transaction.
- Any additional compensation to the lender, such as the right to share in the increase in value of the home.
- The assumed annual appreciation of the home at 0, 4, and 8 percent per year.
- The assumed loan period of 2 years, one based on the actuarial life expectancy of the home owner, and one based on the actuarial life expectancy times 1.4 (in case the homeowner beats the odds and lives longer than expected).
- All other normal disclosures required in any consumer lending transaction (see *Regulation Z*).

reverse radius clause   In a shopping center lease, a clause that prevents the center owner from buying or building another one nearby and thus providing competition for the tenant's customers.

reverse redlining   Another name for predatory lending. The lender does not refuse to do business inside the redlined area, but instead targets the residents for predatory lending practices.

reversion   The interest retained by a grantor after transferring some of its interests but not all. A landlord transfers some of its interests when it executes a lease; the right retained is the reversion. Also called a reversionary interest. Contrast with *right of reentry.*

reversionary factor   The mathematical factor that indicates the present worth of one dollar to be received in the future. It is the same as the *present value of one.*

reversionary interest   See *reversion.*

reversionary value   The value of property at the expiration of a certain time period.

reverter, possibility of   The interest retained by a grantor after transferring a determinable fee (one that will automatically end on a specified event, such as "to Mary until her thirtieth birthday or marriage, whichever comes first) or an estate in fee simple conditional (available in only some states, it says that a gift to A "and the heirs of his body" retains a possibility of reverter in the grantor because A might never have any heirs of his body).

review appraiser   Usually an employee of a lender or institutional purchaser, the review appraiser is responsible for checking the reports of fee appraisers to make sure they have been properly prepared and documented and do not seem out of line with the review appraiser's own estimate of property value.

revocation   A cancellation of a power or authority, such as a power of attorney or an agency.

RevPAR (revenue per available room)   A value used to compare investments in comparable hospitality facilities. It is the total room revenue for the period divided by the average number of available rooms.

rezoning   To change the permitted uses of property within an area. If only one property is rezoned, it is called spot zoning. When property is rezoned, then all future owners can use it for any purpose allowed by the zoning classification. Contrast with *variance*, which allows one particular use not otherwise allowed by the zoning regulations.

RFP   See *request for proposal*.

RFQ   See *request for qualifications*.

Rho Epsilon   At one time a national organization of real estate clubs for students at colleges and universities. Today, there is no longer a central headquarters or a coordinating entity, but there are many local Rho Epsilon real estate clubs at schools of higher education. See also *Alpha Sigma Gamma*, which is the national real estate honor society open to college seniors.

rider   (1) An amendment or attachment to a contract. (2) Commonly used to indicate additional terms or coverages for standard insurance contracts.

right of contribution   See *contribution*.

right of entry   See *reentry (deeds)*.

right of first offer; right of first opportunity   If specifically granted in the lease, the tenant's right to obtain additional space in the building or in the office park, or to buy the building if the landlord agrees. Unlike a right of first refusal, an offer from a third party is not required in order to trigger the right. The landlord may simply advise the tenant that space is available, or that the building is for sale, and solicit an offer. If the tenant does not make an offer, or if the offer is unacceptable, the right terminates as to that space.

right of first refusal   The right to match a third-party's offer and purchase property if it is offered for sale. The owner has no obligation to sell to anyone, however. The term "right of first refusal" is often used interchangeably with option, but an owner who grants an option is obligated to sell if the recipient of the option chooses to exercise it. Contrast *right of first offer*.

right of prospect   See *views, right to*.

right of redemption   The statutory right to redeem property either after it has been set for foreclosure or sometimes after the foreclosure itself. Postforeclosure redemption rights typically belong to the borrower, to any other persons with interests in the property, and to creditors of the borrower. It gives such persons the right to buy the property from the foreclosure purchaser, even if the purchaser was the lender, for the foreclosure price plus accrued interest at a statutorily set rate. The right of redemption may extend as long as one year in some states.

right of survivorship   The right to enjoy full and undivided ownership of property after the death of another. It may apply to real property, or to personal property, including bank accounts. In real estate, the right is incidental to an estate called joint tenancy or sometimes joint tenancy with right of survivorship. The estate can be destroyed in most states if one of the joint owners, without the knowledge or consent of the others, conveys (transfers) his or her interest to someone else. The purchaser does not enjoy a right of survivorship with the other remaining joint tenants, but has only an undivided interest that will pass to his or her heirs upon death.

right-of-way   (1) The right to use another's land for ingress or egress, which is a type of easement. (2) Either deeded rights or easement rights in the government for public roads, streets, and highways. Government rights-of-way may extend for many feet outside the paved boundary or even beyond the shoulder of the road. Typical rights-of-way are measured from 30 to 50 feet from the centerline of the road and may be larger if the government secured enough land for future road widening. (Before building, excavating, or even planting trees along the side of a road, one should check with the local road department for right-of-way measurements.)

Right to Financial Privacy Act   Guarantees that a bank customer will be given notice and an opportunity to object before bank records will be revealed to the government. There are some exceptions for things such as drug trafficking. (Do not confuse with the Financial Privacy Rules of the Financial Modernization Act of 1999, which protects disclosure of information to nongovernment entities, such as other companies wishing to sell goods and services to the bank customer.)

riparian owner   One who owns land along a river, stream, or other watercourse. Contrast with *littoral owner*. Often, riparian is used to signify all things having to do with water, rather than in its technically accurate sense. As a result, care should be taken to read in context when the word is encountered.

riparian rights   Rights pertaining to the use of water in, on, near, or flowing over land. The most common rights are the right to a reasonable use of the water, the right to use the shoreline and have access to the water, the right to any land formed by accretion or relication, the right to have the water flow to the land without obstruction, the limited right to build piers in the water, and the right to catch fish, although the land owner does not own the fish. Although the word "riparian" typically applies to rivers and streams but not lakes, the expression "riparian rights" generally means to imply any rights having to do with water, including surface runoff.

risk   Uncertainty regarding the possibility of loss.

risk of loss   Responsibility for damage to improvements, typically after signing a contract for sale and before closing takes place. States that have adopted the Uniform Vendor and Purchaser Risk Act place the risk of loss on the seller. As a result, if the property is damaged before closing, the buyer may cancel the contract, recover all sums paid, and not have any liability, provided the buyer has not taken possession. Contracts may, of course, vary the terms of the uniform law, and not all states have adopted it.

risk-free rate   An interest rate on the safest investments, which would generally be short-term federal government obligations or savings accounts in amounts less than the FDIC insurance limits.

risk management   A systematic approach to identifying insurable and noninsurable risks, evaluating the risk of loss versus the cost of insurance, and minimizing the possibility of loss through well-planned and regularly followed systems and procedures. Especially in construction, which typically has the very highest premiums for workers' compensation insurance, well-planned and well-executed risk management programs can result in significant savings on premiums.

risk-based capital requirement   Evaluation of the capital adequacy of a financial institution according to the amount of risk attached to each type. One dollar in cash is much less risky than an unsecured promissory note for $1 from a con artist. Everything in between is a matter of degree. That is the premise that forms the basis of risk-based capital requirements. The Board of Governors of the Federal Reserve System sets the requirements for American financial institutions. This impacts the sizes and types of real estate loans financial institutions are willing to make. Internationally, the Basel II Accord provides guidelines for measuring risk when evaluating capital.

risk versus reward   A financial analysis comparing the potential gains from a project or property against the potential losses. The greater the risk, the greater the reward should be.

Robert's Rules of Order   Rules for the conduct of meetings in an orderly manner. First used in 1876 by American army officer Henry Martyn Robert, who was asked to preside over a church meeting and discovered that neither he, nor anyone else, knew a proper or consistent way to conduct meetings. Today, almost all organizations, including those for condominiums, co-op apartments, homeowners groups, and others, adopt Robert's Rules of Order in their bylaws. (The official Web site at www.robertsrules.com warns that the earliest editions of the Rules are no longer copyright protected, and so may be found in reprint, masquerading as current editions.)

rod   A linear unit of measurement equal to $16^{1}/_{2}$ feet.

rollback   A retroactive claim for a higher ad valorem (property tax) rate when property is sold or put to a higher use than the one for which it was assessed. The rollback period can be as great as 10 prior years of recalculated taxes.

Example: *Farmer Brown owns 100 acres of land at the corner of a busy road used by almost all commuters in the area. The land is worth at least $200,000 an acre, but because of state law favorable to agricultural uses, it is appraised for tax purposes at only $10,000 an acre. Farmer Brown sells the land to Doris Developer, who is surprised when the real estate tax bill comes due a few months later and there is a rollback for 5 years. Doris will owe 5 years of prior real estate taxes calculated on an appraised value of $200,000 per acre. In all likelihood, Farmer Brown had an innocent-sounding clause in his sales contract that said, "The parties will prorate real estate taxes as of the date of closing, except that seller shall not be responsible for any increase in taxes as a result of the sale." Without the clause, if they had simply agreed to pro-rate taxes (as most form contracts provide), then Farmer Brown might have to reimburse Doris Developer for over four years, worth of the taxes.*

rollover home sale   An older income tax concept referring to the ability of homeowners to defer payment of taxes on the sale of their principal residence if the money were rolled over into a new residence. Today, taxpayers may exclude from income up to $250,000 of gain ($500,000 for married persons) on the sale of a principal residence, with no necessity that they buy another one.

rollover loan   (1) A construction loan that automatically converts to permanent financing upon completion of construction. (2) A loan from a person's own retirement plan that continues into a new retirement plan if one changes jobs. (3) Short-term loans (as short as 14 days) that automatically renew if not paid, but incur substantial fees in connection with the renewal. The most common type is the payday advance loan.

rollover risk   The risk that a tenant will not renew the lease.

roof rights; roof rental   A lease of space on building rooftops for satellite dishes or other telecommunications equipment. It can be a significant source of additional income, which is why building tenants are now finding it difficult to include roof rights within their space lease at no additional charge.

root deed   The first undisputably error-free, claim-free conveyance in a chain of title. In many jurisdictions, it is the first deed (the patent) out of the government into a private owner. Other states have statutes that cure any title defects that are older than a certain number of years. In such states, the root deed is the first deed older than the cutoff period.

row house   See *town house*.

royalty   Compensation for the use of property, usually copyrighted material or minerals, including oil and gas. Payment is generally calculated as a percentage of receipts and may be paid in cash or in kind.

RRM   See *renegotiated-rate mortgage*.

rule against perpetuities   See *perpetuity*.

rule in Shelley's case   An ancient rule of law designed to plug a loophole used in the fourteenth century to avoid paying the historic equivalent of estate taxes. The rule involved a transfer of land to A for life and then to A's heirs. Worded in that way, A's heirs did not take by inheritance; they took by virtue of the original deed. As a result, no inheritance tax was due. This is common estate planning stuff today, but it was fairly revolutionary in the 1300s in England. The word "heirs" could not be defined until A died, so no one had any real rights in the property until A died. As a result, A could do whatever he or she wanted with the property and no one could complain. The rule in Shelley's case said that, in such an instance, the transfer to A for life was really completely to A, not just for his or her life. A had all rights to the property, and there were no remainder interests. When A died, the heirs had to pay the inheritance tax. Virtually all states have abolished the rule in Shelley's case. Some have abolished its application in all instruments, some only in wills, and some only in deeds. An understanding of the rule in Shelley's case is the hallmark of one knowledgeable about obscure points of real estate law.

rule of 5   A rule of thumb used by subdividers to estimate development costs. Generally, one-fifth goes to land acquisition; one-fifth to site improvement, engineering, and legal; one-fifth to miscellaneous charges such as loan interest; and two-fifths to advertising, administration, commissions, and profit.

rule of 72s   A quick calculation of the approximate time it would take money to double when earning compound interest. Divide 72 by the interest rate to obtain the approximate answer.

Example:

Time Needed for an Investment to Double at Various Interest Rates

Interest rate	4.5%	6%	7.5%	9%
Math	72/4.5	72/6	72/7.5	72/9
Approximate years to double	16	12	9.6	8
Actual years to double	15.5	11.5	9.25	7.75

rule of 78s   A method for computing the refund due when a borrower wants to pay off an add-on interest loan at an earlier time than the maturity date. The reason there would be any refund at all is because all the interest is calculated up front, for the entire loan, and then paid in equal monthly installments. If the loan is repaid early, some portion of the interest has not been earned, but it has already been paid. Use of the rule of 78s results in the lender "earning" more of the interest than one might otherwise think. To calculate, you need to use a fraction that changes every month. For the first month, the numerator (top number) is the number of months remaining in the loan. The denominator (bottom number) is the sum of the digits for the number of months of the original loan. If the loan is for 1 year, then you add $1 + 2 + 3 + 4 + \ldots + 11 + 12 = 78$. For the first month, with 12 months remaining in the loan, the fraction is $12/78$. According to the method, $12/78$ of the interest has been earned in the first month, or 15.38 percent. You might think that only $1/12$ of the interest—8.33 percent—has been earned, since only one month has passed, but that's the way the rule of 78s works—to the lender's advantage. The next month, you change the numerator by adding the number of remaining months (11) to last month's numerator of 12. The numerator is then $11 + 12 = 23$, so $23/78$ of the interest has been earned, or 29.48 percent. For month 3, the numerator is $10 + 23$, and so on.

Example: *Danielle buys a used car for $6,000 and finances it with the dealer for one year at 18 percent interest. The dealer adds $6,000, plus the $1,080 for one year's interest, to arrive at $7,080. Then the dealer divides that number by 12 to arrive at Danielle's monthly payment of $590. Of that number, $90 is the add-on interest. The following table shows what Danielle's interest refund would be if she paid off the loan in full in each of the following months after buying the car. (The rule of 78s is a common term used with car loans; it is rarely used with real estate loans.)*

Month	Months Remaining	Interest Paid	% of Interest Earned	$ of Interest Earned	Refund
1	12	$90	12/78	$13.85	$76.15
2	11	90	23/78	26.53	63.47
3	10	90	33/78	38.08	51.92
4	9	90	42/78	48.47	41.53
5	8	90	50/78	57.60	32.40
6	7	90	57/78	65.77	24.23
7	6	90	63/78	72.70	17.30
8	5	90	68/78	78.46	11.54
9	4	90	72/78	83.07	6.93
10	3	90	75/78	86.54	3.46
11	2	90	77/78	88.85	1.15
12	1	90	78/78	90.00	0

run with the land   Passes with the transfer of the land. Covenants and easements run with the land. They are binding on the land—and through the land, binding on the owners. This is true even if subsequent owners do not agree or have no knowledge of the easement or covenant.

rural   Concerning the country. Contrast with *urban* or *suburban*.

rurban areas   A term coined in the early 1970s by French philosopher Henri Lefebvre; meant to describe areas that combined intensive agricultural uses with suburban living sites and some industrialization. In much of the world except the United States, it is used generally to describe areas that derive economic benefit from the nearby city, but which maintain the ability for people to grow foodstuffs on their own land for personal consumption and minor amounts of sales in the city. In the United States, it is meant to be synonymous with exurban—another component of suburban sprawl, being estate-sized lots usually with ancillary country clubs, located past the suburbs and before the country.

R-value   A measure of the heat conductivity of material. The higher the R-value, the better the insulating qualities. The Federal Trade Commission, in something called the R-Value Rule, requires certain disclosures regarding insulation. Among other things, new home sellers must put the following in every sales contract: the type, thickness, and R-value of the insulation that will be installed in each part of the house. Failure to make the required disclosures amounts to a deceptive trade practice and is punishable by fines. For full text of the rule, see 16 CFR 460 available at the Government Printing Office Web site at www.gpo.gov.

R-Value Rule   Also called "insulation disclosure." See *R-value*.

R/W   See *right-of-way*.

Rylands v. Fletcher   A very famous case that should be known and understood by all real estate developers. It was the precursor of the doctrine that a property owner is strictly liable for all damages caused by abnormally dangerous things and activities on his or her land, without any need to show negligence, contractual responsibility, or any neglect or omission at all. In this 1865 English case, Rylands was building a pond to supply water for his mill. During excavation, his engineers discovered five abandoned and filled mine shafts in the bed of the pond site. They seemed unimportant. Upon completion of the pond, the shafts started filling in with water. Shortly afterward the water burst through the abandoned shafts and traveled underground until it flooded Fletcher's mines. Fletcher sued, but Rylands defended by saying he had done nothing wrong, that it was a freak accident, and, anyway, it was all the engineers' fault for not investigating further. The court held Rylands liable, stating that if one brings upon his land something that will cause injury if it escapes, then he is strictly liable for the consequences if it does escape.

S

safe harbor   A system of rules that, if followed exactly, will provide protection from the effects of other laws. For example, in a 1031 like-kind exchange, the use of a qualified intermediary and compliance with strict IRS deadlines will result in the ability to avoid paying taxes at the time of a sale. This is the safe harbor from normal tax liability rules. There are other ways to complete a like-kind exchange without paying taxes, but the seller embarks upon those uncharted waters at its own peril. A very slight miscalculation could result in the imposition of large taxes, penalties, and interest at a later date.

safe rate   The interest rate obtainable from relatively risk-free investments, such as U.S. Government Treasury Bonds.

sale leaseback   The simultaneous purchase of a piece of property and the lease of the same property back to the former owner. This practice is common with professional associations, such as doctors and lawyers, who wish for a core group of senior partners to own the real estate despite the entrance and exit of other partners in the business. Other times, banks or other owners with long-term plans will sell their property to investor groups and sign long-term leases.

sale pending   A term used by real estate brokers to indicate that a contract has been signed but not yet proceeded to closing.

sales associate   A licensed real estate agent who works under the supervision of a qualifying or managing broker.

sales commission amounts   Typically a percentage of the gross sales price of the property, although some brokers are now offering flat-fee commission structures for minimal services, with add-on fees for additional services selected from a menu of items. It is illegal for any organization or group to establish a standard commission rate, because that would amount to price-fixing. Individual brokers may decline to accept any listing for less than a certain minimum commission level or percentage, though. The average commission for a home sale is in the range of 4 to 7 percent, except that a more difficult property might require a commission as high as 10 percent in order to interest a broker. Commercial, industrial, and farm and land properties typically have higher commissions, but there may be complex formulas for calculating them, rather than a simple percentage of the sale price.

sales comparison approach   See *market comparison approach*.

sales contract   See *agreement of sale.*

sales kit   A package of materials about a listed property and the area in which it is situated.

salesperson   See *sales associate.*

sales price   The contractually agreed upon price for real estate.

Sallie Mae   Popular name for Student Loan Marketing Association. This organization has nothing to do with real estate, but it is defined here because there is sometimes confusion with all the other "Maes" that are related to real estate finance—Fannie Mae, Ginnie Mae, Maggie Mae, and Munie Mae.

S&L   See *savings and loan association.*

salvage value   The estimated value a property will have at the end of its useful life. (1) It is an important consideration when demolishing a structure in order to build a new one. Especially with older buildings, architectural components such as molding, trim, doors and hardware, windows, and even antique brick can command a very high price. (2) It was important at one time for income tax depreciation, but there is now a different system in place, the modified cost recovery system, which does not rely upon establishing a salvage value.

sandwich lease   The lease that exists between a tenant and subtenant when one subleases space.

SARA   See *Superfund Amendments and Reauthorization Act.*

Sarbanes-Oxley Act of 2002 (SOX)   Also known as the Public Company Accounting Reform and Investor Protection Act of 2002. This Act is a federal law that was passed in response to the major accounting scandals and resulting corporate crashes in the beginning years of the twenty-first century. The law imposes enhanced accounting and disclosure standards on public companies, including REITs. In particular, the balance-sheet treatment of real estate values to reflect economic obsolescence, potential contamination, and short-term lease expirations with key tenants are critical issues. It has an indirect impact on private companies because many insurers and lenders are imposing the same requirements on all customers. Further, an exit strategy that depends on selling real estate assets to public companies will need to implement SOX-compliant controls early to facilitate due diligence and obtain the highest price.

satellite city   A self-supporting city planned within the natural growth pattern of another major city. It is intended to stop urban sprawl, supply an alternate mini central business district, and provide high-speed (preferably mass-transit) access between the major city and its satellites.

satellite tenant   Any tenant except the anchor tenants in a shopping center; usually a national or local tenant occupying smaller space.

satisfaction of mortgage   The process of making a notation in the public records that a mortgage debt has been paid in full and is no longer a lien upon the described real estate. When paying off a loan, one should make sure the lender records the satisfaction information. Failure to do so could result in later title problems for the owner as he or she attempts to hurriedly obtain the satisfaction in time for a closing. It can also subject the lender to a cause of action for slander of title.

satisfaction piece   The instrument that provides notice of the satisfaction of a mortgage.

save-harmless clause   See *hold-harmless clause* or *indemnity clause*.

savings and loan association   A financial institution that specializes in consumer deposits and residential mortgages.

savings bank   Originally organized under individual state supervision as a vehicle for cash workers to deposit their earnings. The industry remained small until the mid–1980s, when savings banks became a federally chartered alternative to the savings and loan associations, whose insurance fund was bankrupt. Savings banks could be protected under the Bank Insurance Fund of the FDIC.

SBA   See *Small Business Administration*.

scale   The relationship between measurements on a plan or map and the dimensions of the physical object represented. One inch might represent 10 feet or 10 miles. Topographic maps contain two scales, one for distance and one for change in elevation.

scenic easement   A voluntary, but permanent and legally enforceable restriction on the use of land that maintains it in a more-or-less natural state. See *easement*.

schematics   (1) Preliminary drawings prepared in order to obtain regulatory approval of plans for construction or development. They lack the details necessary to actually build the project because the project may not go forward at all, or because the details may change dramatically after regulatory approval is conditioned on certain changes. (2) Final electrical plans showing locations and types of all fixtures, switches, outlets, junction boxes, and load centers, together with labeling of circuits and identification of elements on each circuit.

scienter   Knowledge regarding the wrongful nature of an act. Some criminal or civil penalty statutes require scienter, and some do not. For example, the shareholders of a small corporation are liable for the 100 percent IRS penalty if the treasurer fails to pay over employee withholding taxes, whether or not the shareholders knew of the practice. One may be liable for discriminatory housing advertising, without a showing of scienter, if ads show all-white human models and target advertising media not likely to be viewed by nonwhites.

scire facias sur mortgage   Foreclosure. In some states, foreclosure proceedings are started by a judicial writ (scire facias) requiring the debtor to appear in court and show cause why there should not be proceedings upon the mortgage (sur mortgage). See *judicial foreclosure*.

scope of appraisal   An explanation of the work done to complete an appraisal, including physical inspection of the site and comparable properties, industry research for standard ratios, operating incomes and expenses, and other such matters.

scope of authority   The boundaries of an agent's ability to take actions in furtherance of the objectives of the agent's principal, or client. Those same boundaries will also impose liability on the principal if the agent does something wrongful, without knowledge or approval by the principal, but within the scope of the agent's authority. (1) In most states, a purchaser of real estate must take steps to determine the scope of the agent's authority to bind its client-seller; otherwise the purchaser deals with the agent at its own peril. (2) The owner of real estate may be liable if its sales or leasing agent engages in discriminatory or other wrongful conduct that is within the scope of the agent's authority. (3) The owner of real estate may be liable if the agent fails to disclose unsafe conditions known to the seller and the agent, but concealed by the agent from the buyer.

scope of employment   The actions taken by an employee in furtherance of the employer's business objectives or the employee's job description. Wrongful conduct within the scope of employment will subject the employer to liability, even if it had no knowledge of the wrong and had specific rules prohibiting such behavior.

>   **Example:**   *A receptionist who places minority callers on "hold" for long periods of time before transferring them to an apartment leasing agent, but who transfers white callers immediately, is engaging in discriminatory behavior that is within the scope of his or her employment as a receptionist. Answering calls and making decisions to transfer those calls is within the scope of employment. How people make decisions within the scope of their employment can result in liability to the employer. If, in this example, the receptionist shot and killed a minority applicant entering the reception area, that would not be within the scope of employment for a receptionist, although it might be for a security guard.*

scope of work   Under the July 1, 2006, changes to the Uniform Standards of Professional Appraisal Practice (USPAP), the phrase means the type and extent of research work an appraiser performs to develop the results for an assignment. Under prior requirements, all clients had to be provided with a complete appraisal unless the client signed off and approved a limited appraisal noting specific departure rules. Today, the new Scope of Work Rule allows the appraiser to choose the analytical methods necessary to meet the client's objectives, but the client does not have to approve the methodology.

Scope of Work Rule   A July 2006 amendment to the Uniform Standards of Professional Appraisal Practice (USPAP) which changed the emphasis of rules already in place and removed some technical requirements formerly necessary for appraisals. The Rule provides that for each appraisal, appraisal review, and appraisal consulting assignment, an appraiser must

- Identify the problem to be solved
- Determine and perform the scope of work necessary to develop credible assignment results
- Disclose the scope of work in the report

S-corporation   See *subchapter S-corporation*.

scrape   A slang expression for a property with improvements that should be bulldozed because they detract from the value of the land. Example: "That old shopping center is a scrape."

scrivener   One who drafts a document. Under the "doctrine of scrivener's error," parties may correct a deed, mortgage, or other instrument by the use of oral evidence that the draftsperson made a mistake and did not express the intention of the parties. By virtue of the parol evidence rule, such testimony would ordinarily not be allowed.

seal   (1) An embossed impression created by a metal die pressed upon paper. A notary public seal, a corporate seal, or a government agency seal are all proof that the signature of that person is genuine and authorized, because they would not otherwise have access to the embosser to create the seal. (2) Originally, an impression made in wax upon a contract. It took the place of reciting consideration, having a signature, or having witnesses for the contract. Today, some statutes allow certain symbols, such as the initials "l.s." to take the place of a seal, transforming a standard contract into one "under seal." Where still recognized, contracts under seal may have a longer statute of limitations than others.

seasoned loan   A loan that has been paid on time for a sufficient amount of time to give a lender the reasonable belief that it will continue in a like manner.

SEA street   A road that uses <u>s</u>treet <u>e</u>dge <u>a</u>lternatives.

SEC   See *Securities and Exchange Commission*.

secondary easement   A voluntary but legally enforceable restriction on land that is necessary in order to assist in the rights granted under another easement. This is typically encountered in the context of one's ability to enter on the land of another to maintain a right-of-way easement. It is sometimes difficult to repave a road while remaining only on the road—the easement—so a secondary easement is necessary.

secondary financing   See *junior lien* or mortgage.

secondary market   A general description for the sale and purchase of financial instruments. The New York Stock Exchange is a secondary market for shares of stock. Although there is not a similar central exchange vehicle, trading in existing mortgages is also called the secondary market.

secondary mortgage market   The market for the purchase and sale of existing mortgage loans as long-term investments. Fannie Mae purchases many mortgages, as do other private investment groups. See *collateralized mortgage backed securities, REMIC, Fannie Mae*, and *collateralized mortgage obligation*.

second bite of the apple   A second chance at an argument or negotiation previously lost. The law typically frowns upon second bites of the apple and does not allow them. For example, in a dispute over the breach of a real estate sales contract, the unhappy purchaser may not sue for damages, lose, and then file another lawsuit for specific performance to enforce the terms of the contract.

second-generation space   A term typically applied to office space that has had a prior tenant and so has some improvements that are reusable by a subsequent tenant, such as some walls, doors, ceiling treatments, and light fixtures. Contrast with first-generation space, which has never been customized for a tenant and consists of wide-open space with support columns, concrete flooring, and the concrete bottom of the floor above.

second home   A residence that is not one's principal residence. The IRS allows mortgage interest deductions for up to two residences.

second mortgage   A mortgage (or deed of trust) that is placed on property after another mortgage. Typically, the first mortgage provides security for the loan used to finance the bulk of the purchase price. The second mortgage could be seller financing for some portion of the purchase price, a home equity line of credit, construction cost overruns, or any other reason. In a foreclosure, no money can be paid to the second mortgage holder until all principal, interest, and expenses of the first mortgage have been paid in full. This results in a greater risk that the second mortgage lender might not receive payment of its debt, so it usually charges a higher interest rate than the first.

secret profit   The practice of real estate agents making money on the sale of their client's real estate above the amount paid as a commission. This typically occurs when an agent recommends a sale to a friend, relative, or a corporation in which the agent owns an interest, and then the agent profits on a resale or development of the property. Secret profits violate the fiduciary responsibilities owed to the client, making the agent liable for punitive damages, payment of the profit to the client, and possible loss of the agent's real estate license.

section (federal code)   A particularly numbered subpart of some federal law. The text of any federal law may be found by going to the Office of the Law Revision Counsel at uscode.house.gov and clicking on "Search the U.S. Code." Laws written as, for example, "26 U.S.C. Section 121," "26 U.S.C. §121," or sometimes "U.S.C.A." or "U.S.C.S." consist of a "title" (26 in the example) and a "section" (121 in the example). Entering the appropriate title and section will bring up the text of the law. See also *U.S.C.*

section (of land)   A section is a specific area of land measuring 1 square mile. See *public land survey system*.

Section 8 housing   Low- and moderate-income housing subsidized by the federal Department of Housing and Urban Development. There are two primary methods of subsidy: (1) Tenant-based subsidies consist of rental vouchers and rental certificates that are portable—the tenant can use them for any approved rental housing offered by landlords willing to participate in the programs. The program certificates may also be used to assist with mortgage payments under current rules. (2) Project-based subsidies consist of housing complexes that offer reduced rental rates to qualifying applicants, usually as a condition of the developer receiving tax credits, low-interest-rate loans, and high loan-to-value ratios for mortgage lending.

Section 121 (26 U.S.C. §121)   The Internal Revenue Code section that addresses taxable income upon the sale of a principal residence. An unmarried individual may exclude up to $250,000 of gain from income; married persons filing joint returns may exclude up to $500,000 of gain. The taxpayer must have owned and occupied the property for at least 2 of the prior 5 years and this exclusion can be used as frequently as every 2 years. For many Americans, this ability to buy a home, fix it up, sell it in 2 years for a large profit, and then do it all over again is their primary investment vehicle and "savings account." As a result, statistics regarding the low level of savings in the United States are somewhat misleading. To find the law's text, see the instructions at *Section (federal code)*.

Section 167 (26 U.S.C. §167)   The Internal Revenue Code section that addresses depreciation deductions. To find the law's text, see the instructions at *Section (federal code)*.

Section 1031 (26 U.S.C. §1031)   The Internal Revenue Code section that addresses tax-deferred exchanges, also called like-kind exchanges. See *1031 exchange*. To find the law's text, see the instructions at *Section (federal code)*.

Section 1221 (26 U.S.C. §1221)   The Internal Revenue Code section that defines a capital asset by explanation of things that are not capital assets. To find the law's text, see the instructions at *Section (federal code)*.

Section 1223 (26 U.S.C. §1223)   The Internal Revenue Code section that defines the various holding periods for property, important in determining tax benefits. To find the law's text, see the instructions at *Section (federal code)*.

Section 1245 (26 U.S.C. §1245)   The Internal Revenue Code section that establishes rules regarding gains and losses on certain depreciable property, including real property. It is important because it contains definitions for something called "Section 1245 property." This, in turn, is important in other tax laws defining benefits available for Section 1245 property. To find the law's text, see the instructions at *Section (federal code)*.

Section 1245 property   Under IRS statutes and regulations, depreciable real and personal property.

sector theory   A land-use theory that says development tends to grow along transportation corridors outward from the city, forming wedge-shaped areas that follow the path of least resistance and most economy.

Securities and Exchange Commission (SEC)   A federal agency charged with the supervision of publicly traded securities and the protection of the public from fraud, manipulation, and other abuses. Real estate may constitute the primary or most important assets of many publicly traded companies such as REITs. In addition, the direct sale of interests in real estate may qualify as a sale of a security and subject one to SEC registration and oversight. As a general matter, certain persons must register with the SEC and certain investment vehicles must be registered with the SEC. On any given transaction, one or the other may be exempt but not both. The SEC has four divisions:

1. Division of Corporation Finance, which oversees disclosure of important information to the public
2. Division of Market Regulations, which regulates the participants in the securities markets, such as broker-dealers and stock exchanges

3. Division of Investment Management, which regulates the $15 trillion investment management industry, including mutual funds.
4. Division of Enforcement, which investigates possible violations of securities laws, conducts civil enforcement actions, and works closely with law enforcement when it appears there has been criminal activity

securitization   The process of taking many individual assets and combining them into a group, or pool, so that investors may buy interests in the pool rather than in the individual assets. The creation of collateralized mortgage backed securities is one example. The process increases the number of possible investors due to the ability to sell shares in the pool at relatively modest prices. In addition, because of the high degree of predictability inherent in large groups of things, the process of securitization increases predictability, lowers risk, and therefore increases value.

> **Example:**   *On a single flip of a coin, how much would you bet that the coin would land heads up? On 20,000 flips of a coin, how much would you bet that it would land heads up fifty percent of the time, give or take two percent? This is a fundamental concept of securitization.*

security   (1) Property that serves as collateral for a debt, such that defaulting on the debt will result in the creditor seizing and selling the property. (2) Under what has come to be known as "the modified Howey rule," an investment contract or other instrument commonly known as a security is defined as "an investment in a common venture premised on a reasonable expectation of profit to be derived from the entrepreneurial or managerial efforts of others." This definition includes many real estate investments that, if not specifically exempted under some provision of federal law, are susceptible to SEC regulation and oversight for the investment itself, the persons marketing the investment, or both. The Howey rule arose out of a Supreme Court case interpreting sales of interests in an orange grove in Florida—a real estate sale arrangement held to be a security.

security agreement   A contract that grants a creditor a lien in personal property belonging to the debtor. Every state has passed some version of the Uniform Commercial Code, Article Nine, which addresses security agreements and their consequences. A mortgage lender will often require a separate security agreement and UCC–1, which is the document filed in the public records to provide evidence of a security agreement. Lenders do this so that if there is later a default and argument regarding whether specific additions to the real estate constitute real or personal property, the lender is covered both ways. Formerly known as a chattel mortgage.

security deposit   Money required to be paid to a landlord or to service providers in order to protect them against possible default. The law varies from state to state regarding the following questions: Must the deposit be kept in a separate account from the operating account? Must it earn interest? May it be used to pay for damage to the property, or just default in the payment of rent? How much money can a landlord require? How soon does it have to be refunded? Most states maintain excellent Web sites with information about consumer protection laws, including landlord-tenant law and the requirements related to security deposits.

security instrument   A generic name for something that gives a creditor rights in property for the protection of a debt from the borrower. It may include a security agreement for personal property, or a mortgage or a deed of trust on real property.

security interest   Rights in property, voluntarily granted by a borrower to a lender, so that the property may serve as collateral for a loan and be subject to seizure and sale in the event of default.

seed money   The amount of money necessary to begin a real estate development prior to the acquisition of any financing. It will cover the costs of market studies, feasibility studies, loan application expenses, and accounting and legal fees. Also called front money.

see-through building   A new office building with a high vacancy rate. As a result, many floors have never been built-out, so they contain no interior walls. At night, with the lights on, one can literally see through the building to the other side.

seisin   The possession of real property by one who claims to own a freehold interest, which is generally everything except a leasehold interest.

seized   To have seisin, as in "He was seized of certain real property described as…."

self-amortizing mortgage   See *fully amortizing loan*.

self-contained appraisal report   According to the Appraisal Standards Board requirements for Uniform Standards of Professional Appraisal Practice (USPAP) it is an appraisal report that should contain all information significant to the solution of the appraisal problem. The emphasis is upon the word "significant"; the appraiser need not include *all* information.

self-employment tax   A federal tax similar to the Social Security and Medicare taxes deducted and matched by employers. It is equal to 15.3 percent of net earnings from self-employment and must be calculated on Schedule SE and reported on Form 1040. Real estate agents, brokers, mortgage brokers, and all other self-employed individuals are required to pay self-employment taxes. (See Tax Topic 554, "Self-Employment Tax" and Publication 334, "Tax Guide for Small Business," at the IRS Web site, www.irs.gov.)

self-help   Refers to the ability of a creditor to take steps to gain control of property currently in the possession and control of a debtor. Self-help repossession of personal property is generally allowed if it can be done without breaching the peace. Self-help eviction is generally frowned upon and may expose the landlord to liability in damages to the tenant. The time-honored but illegal practice of removing a tenant's front door in order to "paint" it is a form of self-help eviction.

seller financing   The practice of a seller of real property holding some or all of the debt necessary to purchase the property. It is widely believed that seller financing is the last resort of borrowers who cannot obtain financing elsewhere, and the last resort of owners who cannot sell their property without offering it to buyers who cannot obtain financing. In reality, many property owners prefer to finance the sale of their properties, thereby earning a better rate of return on their money than if they obtained cash and then attempted to invest that cash in the marketplace. By the same token, many purchasers are able to secure somewhat cheaper mortgage loan interest rates than generally available in the marketplace if a seller will hold the financing.

seller's market   A market in which there is very little desirable property for sale and a multitude of buyers attempting to purchase. Sellers can afford to demand low commission rates from agents who are hungry for listings, refuse to negotiate the price, and refuse to allow contract contingencies. Contrast with *buyer's market*.

selling broker or agent   The one who provides the buyer for a piece of property. The other side of the transaction is the listing agent, who provided the seller.

sell the paper   A slang expression meaning to sell mortgage notes on the secondary market or to another investor.

semiannual   Occurring twice each year. Same as *biannual*.

senior mortgage   See *first mortgage*.

Senior Residential Appraiser (SRA)   A designation granted by the Appraisal Institute. An SRA may refer to himself or herself as a member of the Appraisal Institute, but may not use the designation MAI, which, confusingly, stands for Member, Appraisal Institute. An MAI must meet more rigorous education, testing, and experience requirements than an SRA.

sensitivity analysis   Use of spreadsheets to analyze an income-producing property or a development project, and then changing key assumptions in order to view the changes this causes. The creation of a best-case, worst-case, and most-likely-case pro forma is one type of sensitivity analysis.

separate property   Property owned by either spouse before marriage, or inherited by one or the other after marriage. Contrast with *community property*. In other states, a divorce court will take into consideration the separate nature of property when making decisions to divide property or award alimony. One tricky aspect of the separate property issue is the interest in minerals, oil and gas, crops, timber, or postmarital improvements on or under separate land. Such interests do not always carry with them the separate property characterization.

septic system   An on-site system for the disposal of wastewater.

sequestration order   A court order authorizing the seizure of personal property, or the rents or other income from real property, to be kept in safety under court supervision pending the outcome of litigation between the parties. The order is usually issued only when the creditor can prove that the debtor intends to fraudulently remove or spitefully damage the property to the detriment of the creditor. Normally the creditor requesting the order must post a bond in order to reimburse the debtor for his or her damages if it later turns out that the order was wrongfully entered.

service of process   Completion of all legal requirements to give official notice to a person regarding a lawsuit filed against that person. After service of process, the defendant will have a certain number of days to file an answer. It is critical to determine the correct service date and to keep track of the deadline to file an answer, which could be as short as 14 days in most states. Failing to file an answer will result in a default judgment in which the court will give the person filing the suit—the plaintiff—everything that person asked for, no questions asked. When the judgment becomes final and not appealable, after the passage of another period of time, the plaintiff may begin efforts to seize any real or personal property he or she can find to satisfy the judgment.

service release premium   The commission a lender pays a loan broker in return for placing a loan with that lender rather than another. Also called yield spread premium.

servicing   Providing management, oversight, payment receipt, property insurance monitoring, and all other functions related to ongoing loan activities after origination. Most loan originators sell the servicing to third-party companies.

servient estate   See *servient tenement*.

servient tenement   Property upon which an easement exists in order to benefit another property, called the dominant tenement. Also called servient estate.

set-aside letter   A letter from a lender stating that funds have been "set aside" to pay for specific improvements. It is sometimes given to the contractor of a financially troubled project advising that the lender will set aside money to fund completion, even though there may be problems with the owner. It is also sometimes given to a local government authority as a condition of issuing subdivision development approval. The set-aside letter from the lender guarantees availability of funds to complete common areas of the development. The developer may obtain a commercial bond to achieve the same results, but the set-aside letter may be cheaper.

setback   The distance between the edges of property and improvements located on the property. Local governments and subdivisions usually have minimum setback requirements for aesthetic and for safety reasons.

set off   To deduct debts from each other. Oftentimes defaulting debtors will claim that they have not paid their obligations because of a right of setoff against injuries suffered as a result of wrongdoing by the creditor. Lenders with bank deposits in the name of their borrower may set off the bank account against the mortgage debt if there is a default.

settlement   See *closing*. See also *Real Estate Settlement Procedures Act*.

settlement date   Closing date.

settlement statement   See *closing statement*.

settling   Movement of an improvement because of movement in the soil supporting the improvement. It could be caused by compaction of the soil, erosion of pockets due to underground streams or springs, or the aftereffects of frost heave pushing frozen ground upward and then settling back.

settlor   The person who establishes a trust.

sever   To separate, as when the mineral interests are severed from the surface rights in real property.

severally   This is one of those words that means the exact opposite of what you might guess. It means individually, although you might think it has something to do with several people. It is most often encountered in two situations. Property may be owned severally, or "in severalty" meaning that there is one owner with no co-owners. In addition, one might see legal liability expressed as "jointly and severally," such as roommates who sign a lease together. They are both liable for the entire rent (jointly), and they are each individually liable for the entire rent (severally). If there is a default, the landlord may sue both of them and collect from whoever has money, or the landlord may choose to sue only one tenant and collect the entire amount from that one tenant, not simply one-half of the debt.

severalty   Sole ownership of real property.

severance damages   The compensation to a property owner after the government takes some portion of real property by condemnation under its eminent domain rights and, as a result, causes a decrease in value to the remaining property.

> **Example:** *Annie's Corner Grocery received a $135,000 condemnation award when the city took one-half of the grocery's parking lot in order to expand the library, and an additional $200,000 in severance damages because the grocery store itself was now much less valuable with the smaller parking lot.*

sewer   A system for the transmission of storm water to a controlled discharge point or for the transmission of sanitary wastewater to a treatment facility.

shadow anchor   Understood with reference to an anchor store, which is a retail store that generates a great deal of traffic and attracts business to the shopping center in which it is located. A nearby shopping center would say it is shadow anchored by the same store— the anchor is nearby, but not part of the same center.

shall   When used in a contract, lease, mortgage, or statute, it means that the thing is required; it must be done. Shall implies a complete lack of discretion. Contrast with *should*.

shared appreciation mortgage (SAM)   A mortgage arrangement that virtually disappeared for many years and is now making a reappearance. The borrower receives a lower interest rate on the mortgage loan in exchange for agreeing to pay the lender some of the profits when the property is sold. Every agreement will be different, but one example would be a reduction of one-half of 1 percent in the interest rate in return for 20 percent of the profit from a sale. Under IRS Revenue Ruling 83–51, the shared appreciation paid to the lender when the property is sold will be deductible interest in the year in which it is paid, but only if the lender is paid in cash, not via a refinance of the mortgage.

shared equity mortgage   A mortgage loan in which the lender pays a portion of the equity for the borrower and in return receives a portion of the increase in value of the property when it is sold. It is most commonly seen today in use with public programs that assist first-time home buyers; the practice is intended to discourage flipping in a rapidly rising real estate market. The longer the homeowner keeps the property, the lower the percentage of equity that must be shared with the lender.

shared tenant service provider   A short-term, small office space on flexible terms with bundled services such as telecommunications, secretarial support, meeting rooms, and other business necessities. Also called business center or executive suite.

shareholders   See *stockholders*.

sharing the market uplift   An expression used to describe a recapture clause in a lease, allowing the tenant to sublease space at a profit in an escalating rental market, but with the necessity to share some or all of the profit with the landlord.

Shelley's case, rule in   See *rule in Shelley's case*.

shell lease   A lease for unfinished space, typically for retail or distribution purposes, with the tenant to make all improvements to the property. Sometimes called a dark shell lease.

sheriff's deed   A deed from a court after an execution on real property to satisfy the judgment obtained by a creditor.

Sherman Antitrust Act   One of the antitrust laws designed to encourage competition and discourage monopolies.

shopping center   According to the International Council of Shopping Centers (www.icsc.org), "a group of retail or other commercial establishments that is planned, developed, owned and managed as single property. On-site parking is provided. The center's size and orientation are generally determined by the market characteristics of the trade area served by the center."

shoreline   The mean high-water mark dividing water from land.

short form   A one- or two-page instrument with important deal points sufficient for recording, so that a lengthier document need not be placed in the public records.

short rate   The relatively higher insurance premium rate charged for coverage when one cancels a policy earlier than originally agreed upon. Rather than receiving a pro rata refund of the unearned premium, the property owner receives a smaller amount.

short sale   In real estate, the lender's agreement to release its lien upon property so that the property can be sold, even though the sale price will not generate enough money to pay off the loan. Investors who specialize in purchasing preforeclosure properties will often negotiate a short sale price with the lender as part of their strategy. Oftentimes, the lender will agree to forgive the balance of the mortgage debt.

short-term capital gain or loss   A gain or loss on the sale of real estate or other capital assets that were held for one year or less. Disregard advice that short-term capital gains are for holding periods of less than one year; a holding period of exactly one year is still short term. To calculate the holding period, start counting on the day following the date of acquisition; the day of sale is considered part of the holding period. Short-term capital gains are netted against short-term capital losses. If the net result is a gain, it is taxed at ordinary income rates, not the more favorable long-term capital gain rates.

short-term debt   That portion of debt that is payable within one year. Consumers typically include only debts maturing in one year in their schedule of short-term debts. Businesses usually segregate debt into the current year's portion of all debt, with the balance, if any, categorized as long-term debt. When completing a form financial statement for a lender, it is important to find out that lender's definition of short-term debt. Placing debts in the wrong category could result in a failure to meet certain critical ratios, and denial of the loan.

should   In a lease, mortgage, contract, or statute, it is language of recommendation rather than something that is required. Contrast with *shall*.

show-cause order   A judicial or government agency order to appear before it and present evidence regarding why a specific order should not issue from that authority. When one is charged with violation of an injunction prohibiting certain actions on real property, for example, the order is to appear and show cause why the defendant should not be held in contempt of court.

shut-in royalty   In oil and gas leases, a royalty paid to keep a lease in effect, even though there is no oil or gas production.

sick building syndrome   A combination of symptoms—rashes, respiratory problems, fatigue, headaches—that appear when one is in a building or a portion of a building and diminish when one is away from the building. The symptoms cannot be traced to any single cause, but they typically manifest in office buildings and very rarely in residential properties. Contrast with a *building-related illness*, which can be traced to a particular source, such as Legionnaires' disease.

side letters (leases)   Written agreements that vary the terms of a lease. All contracts for the purchase of income-producing property should provide for full review of leases and any side letters before closing.

siding   Materials used to clad the outside of building walls. Siding is not structural and does not support the roof or upper floors. It may include wood, brick, shingles, vinyl, and other materials. Many zoning regulations stipulate the types of siding that must be used, or cannot be used, for buildings in particular zone classifications. For example, metal siding may be prohibited in certain residential areas.

sight line   An imaginary line extending from an observation point to a view beyond that. Many neighborhood restrictions prohibit obstruction of sight lines to scenic views.

signature elevator link   A fancy elevator, such as the glass ones that ascend and descend on the exterior of buildings.

silent partner   A partnership investor without any voting power or authority. See *limited partnership*.

silent second   (1) A second mortgage placed on a home, usually in favor of the seller, so that a purchaser can buy the home even without a sufficient down payment. They are called silent because the first lender does not know about the second mortgage and might not have approved the first mortgage if it had known the borrower did not have enough money for a down payment. (2) Shared equity second mortgage programs offered by some state housing assistance authorities. The housing authority loans money to a qualifying moderate-income home purchaser, with repayment due only when the home is sold or refinanced. This is called the silent second, meaning an invisible second mortgage. The housing authority then shares in the profits due to the increase in value. Sometimes there are restrictions requiring sale only to another qualifying moderate-income home buyer.

simple interest   Interest on the principal balance of a loan or debt, but without compounding due to also charging interest on past-due and unpaid interest.

simple loss payable clause   See *open mortgage clause*.

simple majority   Fifty-one percent of the voting members or shares. Contrast with *supermajority*.

simulate   To create an artificial environment or circumstance that closely resembles reality so that people may test their predictions about behavior or practice their skills. One may purchase simulation software to help new real estate agents learn how to interact with buyers and sellers or house-flipping simulation software to learn the tricks and perils of that process.

Simultaneous Death Act   A law enacted in most states providing that when persons die at the same time or perhaps within a described number of hours of each other, and one or both would inherit from the other if only they had survived, then each will be treated as if he or she had died before the other. As a result, property does not pass through one estate briefly and then into another estate.

simultaneous death clause   Usually in wills made by husbands and wives, the clause says that if one does not survive the other by a certain time limit, usually 6 months, their properties will be disposed of in an alternative manner specified in the will.

single agency   The practice of representing only one side in a real estate purchase rather than engaging in dual agency.

single-asset entity (SAE)   See *single-purpose entity*.

single-family housing   Relatively freestanding dwelling units, but may include townhomes that share a common wall. The exact definition will be important for zoning purposes and for some loan programs that are restricted to single family housing. In each instance, the law or program itself will have a definition of the word for their particular purposes.

single load corridor   A hallway that has apartments, condo units or offices on only one side.

single pay loan   Usually a short-term loan with all principal and interest due at maturity. There are no monthly interest payments. It is the typical loan for a house flip, with a quick purchase, rehab, and resale anticipated within 6 months. May also be used for a bridge loan made when an old home has not yet sold but a new home must be purchased, with the bridge loan being payable in full when the old home sells.

single-purpose entity (SPE)   A limited liability company or corporation that holds title to real estate and owes money to a lender as the result of a mortgage on the property, but which has no other assets or liabilities. The SPE will usually lease the property to another company, comprised of the same owners. That second company then executes leases to tenants, hires a management company or provides for necessary services, and generally incurs all liabilities associated with managing the property. This structure is usually required by a lender as a condition of extending a mortgage loan. It insulates the collateral from claims of other creditors. If the second company must file for bankruptcy because it is not able to pay creditors, that does not stop the lender from foreclosing unless the SPE also files for bankruptcy. If the SPE files for bankruptcy, it is much easier for the lender to lift the automatic stay and proceed with foreclosure because it has the only vote for issues such as approving a plan of reorganization under Chapter 11 (see *bankruptcy*). If there were many creditors, consisting of the janitorial service, utilities, tenants, and others, then those other creditors could force the mortgage lender to acquiesce in a plan of reorganization that is not in the lender's best interests. That process is called a cram-down. With only one creditor, the mortgage lender, there is no chance of a cram-down. (Do not confuse with a *special-purpose entity*, also abbreviated as SPE, which is much broader than a single-purpose entity.) Also called a single-asset entity (SAE).

single-room occupancy (SRO)   A type of housing in which residents have a private bedroom, but share other communal features such as a kitchen, bathrooms, or entertainment areas. It may be very-low-income housing, student housing, or elder housing. Some very expensive condo and co-op projects include SRO space set aside for domestic help employed within the buildings, because the employees could not otherwise afford to live near where they work.

sinking fund   Money set aside in a special account to which regular contributions are made by way of additional money and/or interest on the money, with the plans that by a specified date the fund will be sufficient for a particular purpose. Prospective homeowners may set up a sinking fund for a house down payment, and companies usually establish sinking funds to pay off bonds.

SIOR   See *Society of Industrial and Office REALTORS®*.

site   A property location. Typically refers to one planned for development, but does not necessarily have such a restrictive meaning.

site assessment   See *environmental site assessment*.

site-built home   A home built primarily at the location where it will be inhabited. The extreme opposite is a manufactured home, which is built elsewhere and simply moved to the location. Modular homes are more of a gray area because components are built elsewhere and then assembled at the house site.

site improvements   Any alterations or additions to land that enhance its utility or value.

site plan   A drawing that shows the boundaries of a parcel of land, the topography, important landscape elements that impact design (such as a large oak tree), and the placement of all anticipated major improvements, including buildings, roads and driveways, storm and sanitary sewer lines, and utility connections.

site selection   The process of choosing the best location for an anticipated use. Large national chain retailers and restaurants typically have very specific criteria regarding demographic profiles and densities, traffic counts, access and proximity to competitors, and amount of land required. Smaller companies usually piggyback on those requirements or simplify them dramatically. One rule of thumb for site selection says that a prospective retail site from which one can see a McDonald's and a branch bank is a good site. Persons skilled in the complex statistical and mathematical calculations and projections necessary for some industries are able to command high salaries. Also called location intelligence.

siting   Establishing placement of future improvements upon land so as to make the best use of whatever features are important. These might include using existing contours, vegetation, and routes of access. Items that might need to be contemplated are prevailing winds, solar energy or satellite access needs, and desirable and/or objectionable views and zoning regulations.

situs   Location.

skin in the game   An expression reputed to have been coined by investor Warren Buffett, referring to a situation in which high-ranking insiders use their own money to buy stock in the company they are running. Most often, it refers to a lender aversion to 100 percent financing, even if the property is worth well more than the loan, because the lender wants the owner or developer to "have some skin in the game" and some equity to lose if the deal goes bad.

sky lease   Lease of air rights above land.

skyscraper   A multistory building with a steel skeleton that supports the weight of the building.

slab   A building foundation of poured concrete, lacking a basement or crawl space.

slander of title   See *defamation of title*.

slant drilling   A method of drilling for oil and gas from an adjacent property.

sleeper note   See *single pay loan*.

slip and fall cases   A generic type of litigation referring to injuries sustained when someone fails to maintain his or her property in a safe and clean condition. Many states differentiate among types of persons when evaluating the duty of care owed by an owner or occupier of property. For such states, legal responsibility for the injury may depend on whether the injured party was an invitee, a licensee, or a trespasser. See *owners and occupiers* for a description of the various parties and responsibilities to them.

slum   A heavily populated urban area with widespread and massive deterioration of buildings and infrastructure, a lack of meaningful social or police services, and an exceptionally high degree of poverty, unemployment, and crime.

small-bay retail   Businesses with a size of 1,000 to 2,500 square feet, such as nail salons, video stores, sandwich shops, and other similar tenants.

Small Business Administration (SBA)   A federal government agency created in 1953 to "aid, counsel, assist and protect… the interests of small business concerns," including real estate related industries. It provides training and counseling and financial assistance through loans and guarantees. The SBA (www.sba.gov) also negotiates small business set-asides with federal agencies requiring outside goods and services, meaning that a certain predetermined percentage of those contracts will be awarded to small businesses.

small claims court   A court of limited jurisdiction, meaning it will not hear disputes larger than a certain dollar amount. It is usually intended to be fast, informal, and not dependent on technical rules of procedure or evidence that would give an advantage to persons with lawyers. Matters pertaining to title to real estate, rights of occupancy under leases, or requests for injunctions normally cannot be heard in small claims courts, but suits for real estate commissions, collection of unpaid rent, or minor property damage would be appropriate. Normally the losing party may appeal to a somewhat higher court and automatically obtain a completely new trial. Most states allow corporate officers or employees to represent the corporation in small claims court, even though this technically constitutes practicing law.

smart building   A building that includes the most modern telecommunications amenities generally available in the marketplace, allowing occupants easy access to bandwidth and switching services. Do not confuse with *intelligent building*, which is one able to sense its environment and make heating, cooling, lighting, health, and safety decisions without human input.

smart home   Usually refers to home automation systems that can be controlled by a centralized panel or device or by dialing in to the control panel from outside the home.

SMSA   See *standard metropolitan statistical area*.

societal marketing concept   The idea that a real estate project has an impact on more than just the people who will use the project and must be marketed to the collective satisfaction of the entire community of neighbors and regulators.

Society of Industrial and Office REALTORS® (SIOR)   An association (www.sior.com) of industrial and commercial real estate professionals, including brokers, corporate executives, lenders, and educators. It is affiliated with the National Association of REALTORS®.

soft costs   Construction costs that cannot be visibly seen, such as professional fees for architects, surveyors, engineers, lawyers, and accountants; government fees and permits; utility hookup fees; and construction period interest and loan fees.

soft market   A real estate market characterized by more sellers or lessors than buyers or tenants.

soft money   (1) A slang expression for creative financing techniques that involve no cash changing hands, such as seller financing. (2) Money invested in a real estate acquisition or development that is written off as an expense rather than added to the basis to increase equity.

soil bank   A former federal government program that paid landowners to keep their agricultural lands fallow—unfarmed—for 5 to 10 years in order to prevent overproduction in specified commodities. Today, many of the same functions are administered by the Conservation Reserve Program of the Farm Service Agency (www.fsa.usda.gov).

soil boring tests   Tests performed by a geotechnical engineer by drilling holes into the soil in order to determine some or all of the following: (1) ability of the soil to support structures on the surface with or without additional assistance from footings, piers, and other aids; (2) permeability of the soil to determine whether it will percolate sufficiently for an on-site septic system; (3) discover and monitor leakage from underground storage tanks or the presence of other contaminants.

soils engineer   A licensed professional who is responsible for determining the soil's load-bearing capacity, sizes and depths of footings, groundwater levels, presence of any contaminants, and advice regarding fill and compaction preparatory to construction. Also called a geotechnical engineer.

solar easement   The right to prevent an adjoining landowner from building a structure that will block the sunlight and diminish the effectiveness of solar energy features on one's own property. Such easements are normally voluntary and agreed upon between the property owners, but they may be imposed by a court of law under the proper circumstances.

solar heating   A system using the energy of the sun to heat a structure. Active solar heating uses some type of motor to move heat; passive solar heating relies on the design of the structure itself to move the heat. Use of solar heating can result in tax credits. For more information, see "Notice 2006–27" at the IRS Web site, www.irs.gov.

Soldiers and Sailors Civil Relief Act (SSCRA)   A federal law providing protections for persons who may be handicapped by active military service. Protection is extended to active-duty military personnel (and sometimes their dependents), and to reservists and members of the National Guard who are called up to active federal services. Benefits of the Act include the ability to request interest rate reductions on all debt incurred before entering military service, including mortgage debt but excluding student loans; stop eviction proceedings if the monthly rent is under a preset amount; terminate a residential lease without penalty if the lease was entered into before active military duty; and delay civil lawsuits such as collection cases, bankruptcy, foreclosure, child custody, paternity, and divorce proceedings until after the service member is able to attend proceedings.

sole proprietorship   Ownership of a business by an individual rather than a partnership, corporation, or limited liability company.

solid waste   All types of waste material, not necessarily contaminants.

SOX   See *Sarbanes-Oxley Act of 2002.*

space planning   Configuring the interior of a building for the optimum use of interior spaces in order to meet the needs of the owner or occupant. It is usually a good idea to meet with a space planner before designing a building or leasing space because a good planner can minimize the square footage necessary for one's needs, thus saving expenses.

space pocket   A portion of leased premises set aside to accommodate future growth on the part of the tenant. Typically, no rent is due on the pocketed area until the earlier of actual use or a specified future date.

SPE   Either a *Single-Purpose Entity* or a *Special-Purpose Entity.* These two are not the same thing.

spec   Speculative; built without a purchaser or a tenant, but in anticipation of securing one when the project is completed.

spec house   A residence built without a particular buyer in mind or under contract, but designed to appeal to the maximum market possible. Spec houses are typically built in an inexpensive manner, but with decorative finishes commensurate with the tastes of the target market. For example, an upper-bracket spec home might have a marble entryway, but wire shelves in the closets, inexpensive lighting and plumbing fixtures, and other contractor-grade materials.

special agent   Someone employed to represent another person the principal—In a clearly defined and limited activity. A real estate broker hired to sell a property is a special agent.

special assessment   A charge to property owners in order to pay for some improvement benefiting all assessed owners in common. Local government sometimes makes special assessments to pay for road or sewer work. More commonly, condo associations and neighborhood associations will levy special assessments for the repair or expansion of recreational or other community amenities, or for structural repairs such as a new roof or road repaving.

special assessment district   A specifically defined geographical area of property owners who have requested some public improvement and agreed to pay for that improvement through pro rata charges levied against owners within the district.

special benefits   The improvement in value certain properties experience after condemnation proceedings under the government's eminent domain authority. They are different from the general community benefits enjoyed because of the improvements planned after condemnation.

>   **Example:**   *The city condemns a 100-foot-wide strip of land for road building. As a result, for-merly landlocked property now has valuable road frontage. It has received a special benefit.*

special conditions   See *contingency clause.*

special-purpose entity (SPE)   Usually a limited liability company formed in order to separate profits, losses, and risks from the corporation that created it. The most spectacular example of the use of special-purpose entities was Enron, which used SPEs to siphon off losses and "cook the books." The use of SPEs is legitimate and necessary in many circumstances, though. (Do not confuse with *single-purpose entity*, also abbreviated as SPE, which is more specialized and is typically a lender requirement before it will extend mortgage financing on large projects.) Also called special-purpose vehicle.

special-purpose property   Real property improvements that are designed in such a customized way that they are usable only by a limited number of owners or occupants. An automobile dealership is a special-purpose property. It would be extremely expensive to convert the dealership to some other use.

special-purpose vehicle   See *special-purpose entity*.

specialty investments   Property types that are not considered conventional institutional-grade real estate investments. Examples include congregate care facilities, self-storage facilities, mobile homes, timber, agriculture, and parking lots.

specialty shopping center   A shopping center devoted to a particular market segment. The most common type has upscale fashion and home accessory stores. It may or may not have an anchor, but usually does have a number of restaurants for the "shopping as entertainment" market segment. Another type caters to certain demographic groups, such as a shopping center with largely Hispanic-themed merchandise and restaurants, and a high percentage of Hispanic shop owners.

special-use permit   Local government permission to use property in a certain manner allowed under applicable zoning regulations, but only after a case-by-case analysis of the intended use and the issuance of the special-use permit. For example, a group home intended for two, three, or four adults who are developmentally challenged might be a permitted use in an R–1 residentially zoned area, but the regulations might require a special-use permit. This allows authorities to assure themselves regarding the existence of safeguards and assistance for the residents and to limit densities of such facilities so that one area or another does not tend to a high concentration of group homes.

special-use valuation   For purposes of ad valorem (real estate) taxes, and for estate taxes, property may sometimes be valued at its current use rather than the highest and best use. This is called special-use valuation, as opposed to fair market value. Most often, this special consideration is granted for agricultural land, so that farmers and their families are not forced to sell their land because they are unable to pay the taxes that might be imposed if the property were valued as a potential subdivision development, industrial park, or shopping center, as examples.

special warranty deed   A deed that provides warranties against the consequences of any actions by the grantor, but makes no representations, warranties, or promises regarding what title defects might exist because of the actions of prior owners. Contrast with *general warranty deed*.

specifications   The detailed requirements for some or all aspects of a construction or development project. For example, cabinet specifications might detail the type and quality of wood for the doors, drawer bottoms, and cabinet fronts and sides; full-extension or limited-extension drawer glides capable of supporting certain weights; the type and thickness of paint or other finishes; and the quality and type of hinge and pull hardware.

specific performance   A court order requiring one to comply with the terms of his or her contract rather than the typical legal remedy of paying monetary damages for breach of contract. Real estate is considered unique, and the theory is that a buyer can never take money damages, go out into the marketplace, and replace the property when a seller defaults. As a result, the law gives to the buyer of real estate the remedy of specific performance. Under very exceptional circumstances a court has been known to grant specific performance to a seller and force a buyer to go forward with purchasing real estate.

speculation   Investment decisions based on the hope and expectation there will be a profit, but no firm evidence that this will be the case. As a general rule, the more speculative the venture, the greater the reward should be, commensurate with the risk taken.

spendable income   Gross salary minus taxes, housing costs, and savings.

spite fence   A high fence erected between neighbors, for no other reason than to obstruct one's light, air, and view. The law will sometimes force a party to remove a spite fence, even though property owners normally have no rights to light, views, or air from across an adjoining property.

split-rate capitalization   Estimating the value of income-producing property using more than one discount rate because of differences in lease expirations or tenant quality

spoliation of evidence   The destruction of evidence necessary for pending or contemplated litigation. The practice is illegal under common law and under Sarbanes-Oxley (SOX) regardless of the motives or intention of the party responsible for maintaining the evidence.

> **Example:**   *Landlord Larry has a problem tenant who constantly complains about various unsafe conditions at a 6-year-old apartment complex, attributing them to poor design and construction. The tenant threatens to file suit if Larry does not fix all the defects and give the tenant 6 months free rent. Two days later, as she does on the same date every year, Larry's assistant destroys all noncurrent files more than 5 years old. This includes many of the original development and construction records for the complex. SOX probably does not apply because the apartment complex is not owned by a publicly traded company, but Larry is more than likely guilty of common law spoliation of evidence.*

sponsor equity   The cash investment by the owners of a project.

spot zoning   Changing the zoning for a particular parcel of property in order to allow uses not ordinarily permitted under the regular zoning for that area. This is a very unusual step; the more common method of reaching the same goal would be to grant a variance for a particular owner for a specific use. In an area zoned for residential use, local government might grant a variance so that a parcel can be used for a doctor's office. With spot zoning, that parcel's zoning would be changed to General Business or something similar, and any business permitted under such zoning could operate on the parcel.

spread   (1) The difference between the asking price and an offer. For example, if the seller was asking $1.5 million but the offer was only $1.2 million, the spread would be $300,000. (2) The difference between the cost of money and the earning rates.

> **Example:** *A mortgage banker is able to borrow money at 7 percent interest because of its excellent credit and high net worth. It then loans that money out on moderately risky ventures at 15 percent interest. The spread is 8 percent.*

spreading agreement   A separate agreement spreading the reach of a mortgage to other properties and sometimes even to other borrowers or lenders. It was once common in New York, in particular, to use spreading agreements rather than executing new mortgages because of the ability to thereby avoid paying large mortgage recordation fees. Such loopholes have largely been closed, however.

sprinkler system   A system of overhead pipes, valves, heads, and sensors that will cause the release of water if a fire develops. Under most building codes, certain types of structures are required to have sprinkler systems. If present, but not required, the owner may usually have fewer fire walls, greater occupancy levels, and/or fewer exits and greater distances between exits.

spur track   A segment of railroad line connected to the main line at only one end. Contrast with *drill track*.

square footage   The area of a space measured in feet. A rectangular parcel of land 100 feet wide by 150 feet deep is 100 $\times$ 150 = 1,500 square feet. For buildings, the measurements are usually taken at the outside walls. Leased space is measured in usable or in rentable square feet, which differ from each other. Usable square feet consist of the space capable of being occupied by the tenant. Rentable square feet may include a percentage add-on, such as ten percent increase over usable square feet, so that the tenant is paying rent on its proportionate share of the common areas in addition to its own space. Space is generally quoted as a certain number of square feet, "more or less." This is because there have been successful lawsuits for fraud against real estate agents who represented that, for example, a house contained 2,050 square feet when it really measured out to only 2,000 square feet—a difference of one large closet.

square footage of living area   The heated and cooled space in a dwelling, except that a heated garage is generally not included.

square foot method   The practice of estimating the cost of construction work by reference to the number of square feet in a structure. For example, houses of a certain quality might cost $100 per square foot to build. One might obtain a wide variety of bids for subcontracting work, such as plumbing and painting, because of the ability of some subcontractors to review plans and calculate the labor, materials, overhead, and profit necessary for them to accept the job, while others use a simple square footage method and hope that it all works out okay.

square yard   A space that measures out to the equivalent of a square 1 yard (3 feet) wide by 1 yard long. There are 9 square feet to a square yard. Most real estate measurements are in acres, square feet, or cubic yards, rather than square yards.

squatter's rights   See *adverse possession*.

SRA   See *Senior Residential Appraiser*.

SRO   See *single-room occupancy*.

stabilized income   The income from a property once it reaches stabilized occupancy.

stabilized occupancy   The occupancy levels reached by a new property after the initial lease-up period, and that are reasonably expected to continue into the future with the proper marketing, management, and maintenance. Conventional wisdom says that stabilized occupancies in excess of 90 or 95 percent are not good, but merely indicate a failure to charge enough rent.

stabilized value   The value of a property after it reaches stabilized occupancy. Most appraisals of property to be developed include one value for the day the project opens its doors and then a separate stabilized value.

Stachybotrys chartarum   See *black mold*.

stacking plan   A two-dimensional representation of a building showing the general shape of the building and the space availability and tenants on each floor, for use as a marketing piece on a Web site. Management may have its own version that includes color coding for lease expiration dates, current rental rates, and target rental rates.

    Example: *Stacking plan for an office building.*

Floor	Tenants				
8	Columbia Spectrum Mgmt 15,035 sf		Great American Title 3,140 sf		Vacant 2,866 sf
7	Friedman & Fuller 4,825 sf	VTEL 2,276 sf	Equifax 5,340 sf	MetLife 6,022 sf	Vacant 2,578 sf
6	Network Equipment Technologies 21,041 sf				
5	Interoffice of Tysons 21,041 sf				
4	Westbourne Investments 1,389 sf		Americredit 1,137 sf	Adobe 7,965 sf	FCEDA 10,550 sf
3	Pharmaceutical Research 4,766 sf		N.E.T. Federal 5,592 sf	Wiltel 8,098 sf	CalNet 2,585 sf
2	Charles Schwab 4,260 sf	Flinn & Beagan 2,241 sf		Transgeneral 3,498 sf	Scitor 4,210 sf
1	Cassidy & Pinkard 6,261 sf	Accustaff 2,000 sf	Dictaphone 4,385 sf	Phillips 13,812 sf	

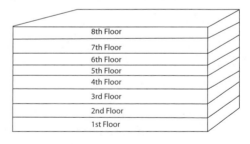

8th Floor
7th Floor
6th Floor
5th Floor
4th Floor
3rd Floor
2nd Floor
1st Floor

stagflation   A slang expression for a period of stagnation and inflation.

staging   Redecorating a home, including the use of rented furniture and accessories, to make it appear more attractive to potential buyers.

stakeholder   Anyone who might be affected by a decision; anyone who has a "stake" in the outcome of a situation. Local government decisions are typically made with reference to the stakeholders in the community, which could include nearby property owners, employers, employees, tenants, lenders, and community service programs.

standard depth   The depth of a lot considered normal for appraisal purposes. For residential appraisal, 100 feet is considered the standard depth.

standard metropolitan statistical area (SMSA)   A former U.S. Census Bureau term outdated since 2000, but still sometimes encountered as referring to a large city and its economically related environs. See *metropolitan area.*

standard mortgage clause   A clause in a fire and casualty insurance policy providing additional coverage for the mortgage lender and also providing that the lender's rights to recover proceeds will not be compromised if the borrower is guilty of wrongdoing relative to the insured loss. Also called a union mortgage clause. Contrast with an *open mortgage clause.*

> **Example:** *Ted cannot make his mortgage payments and fears foreclosure, so he burns down his house to collect the insurance proceeds. Unfortunately, his neighbor saw the whole thing and alerted the police. Ted will not be able to collect any insurance money, but his mortgage lender will because it was not involved in the wrongdoing.*

standard of care   The duties and responsibilities expected of people by virtue of their status, their relationship with another person, or the situation in which they find themselves. Real estate licensing boards establish standards of care for their members regarding duties of honesty, integrity, disclosure, and professionalism. A property owner may have differing standards of care relative to persons on his or her property, depending on whether those persons are licensees, invitees, or trespassers.

standard practices of the trade(s)   The way in which construction work is normally done by the average professional in the field in that general locale. Most construction contracts include a clause holding the contractor and subcontractors to the standard practices of the trades. Unfortunately, most property owners don't know what that means until it is too late. The better practice is to have a detailed set of specifications and to delete the standard practices clause. For example, standard practices may indicate the use of plastic electrical outlet boxes, but a property owner might prefer to pay the additional $1 or $2 each to have metal ones.

standby commitment   A lender's promise to make funds available to a borrower for a specified period of time. Different from a line of credit because the standby does not contemplate a revolving relationship in which the borrower obtains money, repays some or all of it, and then has that same amount of credit available again for new borrowings. The standby is intended to be drawn down and then repaid according to normal promissory note terms. The most typical use is when a developer needs a takeout loan—permanent financing that will "take out" the construction loan—in order to obtain a construction loan. Rather than lock in possibly high interest rates and prepayment penalties for permanent financing, the developer will pay a fee for a standby commitment. When the project is completed, the developer can then elect to fund under the standby and then wait and see if interest rates drop or if it will sell the project rather than retain it, or proceed with permanent financing.

standby fee   A fee charged for a standby commitment.

standby letter of credit   Usually shortened to standby or to LOC. It is the agreement by a lender to disburse funds to a third party if the lender's customer defaults on its obligations to that third party (called the beneficiary).

Rather than pay a large security deposit for a lease, a tenant might offer the landlord a standby letter of credit (LOC) issued by the tenant's bank. For all but the most exceptionally credit-worthy customers, the bank will usually require cash collateral in the form of a certificate of deposit or comparable asset.

The issuance fee is generally in the range of 1/2 to 2 percent per year for the issuance of the standby, which should be less than the money earned by the cash collateral.

The LOC will usually specify the exact manner in which the beneficiary must collect funds, such as presentation of the original LOC at a certain branch location to a particular officer at that location, accompanied by a statement regarding the customer's default. Normally, the statement must be worded exactly in the manner specified within the body of the LOC and any paraphrasing at all will result in denial of payment. The LOC will also have a date and time of expiration.

Landlords (or anyone else) accepting standby letters of credit should be aware that the law in this area is very precise in its requirements. In many states, minor errors in wording the documents presented in order to collect on a letter of credit might result in the bank's legally justifiable refusal to pay. Presenting documents to the wrong person, or at the wrong location, could result in refusal to pay. That refusal might not be curable because of the expiration of the time limits within which to make the claim. The better practice is to pay a lawyer with good malpractice insurance to review the documents and prepare the request for payment.

standing   Having a sufficient stake in the outcome of a dispute so as to justify a court in believing that the party will vigorously defend or pursue the rights at issue in litigation. The concept of standing used to be very narrow, so that if a property owner contracted for selective cutting of timber, but the timber company clear-cut and left a devastated wasteland behind, only the property owner could sue for damages because he or she was the only one with standing. Today, the concept has been expanded and would probably include adjoining landowners and even public interest groups who would be recognized as having standing and the ability to sue the timber company.

standing timber   Timber that has not been cut or sold. Standing timber is considered part of the real estate. In some states, once a landowner signs a contract to sell the timber, it becomes personal property even if it has not yet been cut. As a result, a sale of the real property after the timber contract will not include the timber.

stapled stock   A relationship between a real estate investment trust (REIT) that owns real property, such as a hotel, and a standard corporation that leases or manages that property, ostensibly for a profit. But the arrangement is set up so the stockholders are the same for the REIT and for the operating company—the stocks are "stapled" together. As a result, they hypothetically do not care which company makes what size profit, as long as the aggregate profit is an acceptable number. There is one problem: the REIT profits are not taxable at the corporate level, but the corporation profits are taxed. As a result, the ideal situation would be for the operating company to pay exceptionally high rent, forcing it to just barely break even every year and owe no taxes, while the REIT collects high rents, makes large profits, and pays no taxes. Of course, distributions to shareholders are taxed as income to the shareholders for either entity. The practice was once widespread but now represents a now-closed loophole that is seldom encountered except for older transactions. It is necessary to understand the concept, however, because there are always novel arrangements attempting to accomplish the same goals and that describe themselves as similar to stapled stock.

Starker transaction   Named for T. J. Starker, who successfully claimed the benefit of IRS like-kind exchange and tax-deferral rules even though there was a significant time lapse between selling one property and buying the replacement property. Section 1031 of the Internal Revenue Code establishes a safe harbor for similar transactions, guaranteeing the IRS will not contest a delayed exchange if all parties follow the rules exactly. See *1031 exchange.*

starter castle   A derogatory expression for a large house on a small lot, generally considered pretentious and often containing minimal furniture and accessories because all disposable income must go toward the mortgage payments. Also called a McMansion.

starter home   A home that is smaller than the typical homes in an area, and thus less expensive and easier for first-time home buyers to acquire.

starts   See *housing starts.*

state rule   One method of calculating compensation for condemnation of property under a government's eminent domain powers, it calculates the value of the land taken, the damages caused to any property not taken, and the special benefits enjoyed by the remaining property as a result of the condemnation. The numbers are all combined in the calculations to arrive at an award amount. Contrast with the federal method, which is a straight before-and-after analysis: the difference in the value of the entire parcel before condemnation and the value of the remainder after condemnation is the award.

statute   A law enacted by a state or by the federal government.

Statute of Frauds   A statute setting out certain contracts that are not enforceable within the state. The most significant provisions for real estate purposes are those that require almost all contracts and transfers related to real estate to be in writing and all guarantee agreements to be in writing. This does not mean there must be a formal "contract" or "agreement" signed by all parties. The Statute is usually satisfied if there is some writing signed by the party sought to be held liable.

> **Example:**   *A letter from Sam Seller to Betty Buyer says, "Dear Betty, I'm glad you like the home so much. Your offer of $150,000 was more than I was expecting, so I'll be out shopping for a new home while you get ready for closing. I'm looking forward to seeing you again at the end of the month; do you mind terribly if I don't move out until a day or two afterward? Warmest regards, Sam." This might be sufficient to allow Betty to enforce a sale contract.*

Even a combination of e-mails, read together, could suffice for Statute of Frauds purposes in some states. See also Uniform Electronic Transactions Act.

statute of limitations   State and federal laws that place a time limit on the ability to make certain claims in a lawsuit. The various statutes are usually fairly clear and might provide 6 years for breach of contract, 2 years for negligence, and 10 years for rights to real property. The part that causes all the litigation is the question of "when does the time period start to run?" As a general rule of thumb, the clock starts ticking when there has been a harm that would give rise to the ability to sue. If a stairway is erected improperly in year 1, but there is no way to know this until it collapses in year 5, then the statute of limitations begins to run in year 5.

statute of repose   See *statute of limitations*.

Statute of Uses   A statute passed in England during the reign of King Henry VIII and expressly or by implication adopted by all American states. Formerly, one could not create an estate in land that would begin in the future. After the statute, such estates were granted legal recognition. One often sees frequent references to the Statute of Uses although it is seldom a point of contention between parties. However, as recently as 2003 the issue was raised in a California case in the context of determining rights of various parties in a trust.

statutory dedication   The granting of public rights in roads, parks, or other improvements by virtue of recording a subdivision plat on which the developer indicates those areas dedicated to the public use.

statutory foreclosure   See *judicial foreclosure*.

statutory lien   A charge or claim upon property that arises by virtue of specific statutes that address the relationship between the property owner and the party given the ability to place the lien. A mechanics' and materialmen's lien is a statutory lien; a mortgage is a voluntary lien; and a lease giving the landlord rights in property located in the leased premises is a contractual lien. In bankruptcy, statutory liens are not enforceable but contractual and voluntary liens are. As a result, even if state statutes grant a landlord's lien, for example, the better practice is to also include those rights in the lease itself.

statutory right of redemption   A right given in some states for mortgage debtors to repurchase their property after foreclosure and before expiration of the allowed time period. The same rights are also sometimes given to spouses and other creditors of the debtor. In order to redeem, the former owner must pay the full bid price at the foreclosure, plus interest. Under some statutes, the right can be lost if the property owner does not vacate the foreclosed property within a certain time period after receiving notice from the purchaser. Rights of redemption may be bought and sold.

stay, automatic   In bankruptcy, the requirement that all creditor collection activities must cease immediately upon receiving notice the debtor has filed for bankruptcy protection. There is generally a breathing spell during which nothing may happen. Afterward, the creditor may apply to the court to lift the automatic stay and allow collection proceedings, usually foreclosure, to go forward.

steering   The illegal practice of limiting housing choices, and thereby engaging in discrimination, through a variety of subtle and not-so-subtle techniques. An agent working with minority buyers is guilty of steering when he or she fails to provide information about houses within the buyers' price range that are located in predominantly white neighborhoods.

step-in-the-dark rule   A rule of contributory negligence that says those who enter property in the dark, without first determining if there are any dangers in or upon the property, are not entitled to recover damages from the property owner if they suffer injury or damage.

step loan   A type of adjustable-rate mortgage under which the interest increases in one or some-times two steps only, combining some of the best features of a fixed-rate loan and an adjustable-rate loan.

stepped-up basis   Under current tax law, a tax benefit granted to one who inherits real property, allowing an increase in basis up to the fair market value of the property as of the date of death. Normally, a person receiving a gift has the same basis in the property as the donor.

> **Example:** *If Mary buys a parcel of land for $10,000 and then 20 years later gives it to Jamie, Jamie's basis is $10,000. If Jamie sells the land, the taxable gain is the difference between the sales price, which could be many millions of dollars, and the $10,000 basis. If, however, Jamie received the same property under Mary's will, the property will be valued as of the date of death (or 6 months afterward, depending on which election is selected) and that value will be Jamie's basis. As a result, if the property is worth $1,000,000 on the date of Mary's death and Jamie sells it for $1,000,000, Jamie has no taxable gain. Mary's estate, on the other hand, could have a sizable estate tax it will have to pay. Efforts to repeal estate taxes are usually accompanied by less well-publicized compromises to also repeal the stepped-up basis rules.*

step-up lease   See *graduated rental lease.*

stigma   A negative impression of property because of real or perceived problems. The most com-mon stigma is associated with property that has remained on the market for whatever time period is locally considered "too long." Potential buyers usually think there must be some problem with the property that they might or might not be able to recognize and economically cure, so they avoid such properties. Another common stigma is a commercial property, usually with a restaurant tenant, that has experienced high turnover. The reason might be that the tenants had insufficient financial resources to survive until the break-even point, but the property soon acquires a stigma as a bad location for restaurants. To some extent, the stigma can become a self-fulfilling prophecy if the com-munity fails to patronize any business at that location because of the stigma. Despite that, there are tremendous opportunities for investors who target stigmatized properties and can successfully overcome the bad reputation.

stipulations   The terms of a written contract.

stirpes   See *per stirpes.*

stockholders   Persons who own shares of a corporation. As a matter of convention, persons who own shares in large, publicly traded corporations are called stockholders and persons who own shares of small, subchapter S-corporations are called shareholders. Technically, though, the two names are interchangeable.

stop clause   See *expense stop*.

straight lease   See *gross lease*.

straight-line   To estimate evenly spaced, and regularly increasing, rents or other revenues from a project, although reality may be a little more irregular. In the graph, A (the dark columns) shows a straight-line projection for apartment lease-up over the course of the year. The B columns show a more realistic projection based on an expectation that students will largely fill the apartments in July and August with a small percentage of other rentals coming at various times.

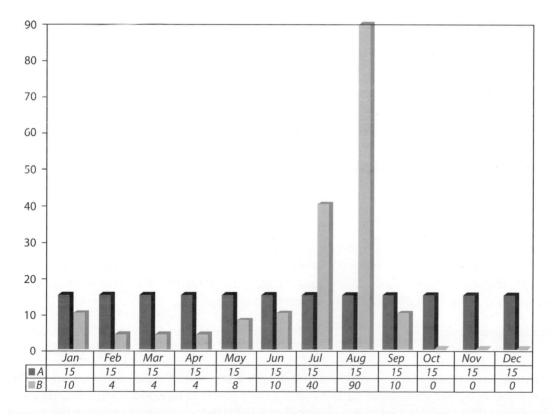

	Jan	Feb	Mar	Apr	May	Jun	Jul	Aug	Sep	Oct	Nov	Dec
A	15	15	15	15	15	15	15	15	15	15	15	15
B	10	4	4	4	8	10	40	90	10	0	0	0

straight-line depreciation   A method of accounting for the gradual loss in value of an asset over time by predicting that the asset's value will decline in equal amounts each year over a specified number of years. The method is also used for tax purposes as an expense allowed each year for the supposed loss in value of an asset, even though it might actually be increasing in value. See *depreciation*.

straw man   One who purchases real property in his or her own name and then holds it for sale to the person who supplied the money for the sale, the intended ultimate purchaser. The technique is often used when a well-known developer, or even a large local property owner such as a hospital or university, wishes to conceal its identity so sellers do not raise their prices.

street edge alternatives   Streets and roads with swales—shallow ditches—lined with rocks and filled with soil and plants to increase absorption and reduce storm-water runoff into nearby streams or ponds. Contrast with the typical curbs and gutters spilling into a storm sewer system.

street hierarchy system   A local government system of classifying streets in order to determine widths, traffic control devices, building setback lines, and other factors. The most common classifications are

- Principal thoroughfare, usually more than 5 miles long and connecting freeways and other major roads, with daily traffic counts in excess of 30,000 vehicles
- Thoroughfare, usually more than 3 miles long and connecting freeways and other major roads, with daily traffic counts in excess of 20,000 vehicles
- Collector, usually 1 to 2 miles long, connecting thoroughfares and local streets, with daily traffic counts in excess of 5,000 vehicles
- Local, usually less than 1 mile long, servicing neighborhoods and accommodating on-street parking and pedestrian traffic, with low traffic counts

strict liability   The liability of a property owner or occupier for injury to others despite the lack of any fault or wrongdoing by the owner or occupier. Typically, when people engage in an inherently dangerous activity on land, such as blasting rock, they are responsible for damage to adjoining property or to persons injured by the blast. This is true even if an independent contractor was responsible for the work and even if everything was done exactly as it should have been done using all possible safeguards and protections and the injury was the result of a freak accident.

strip center   An attached row of stores or service outlets managed as a coherent retail entity, with on-site parking usually located in front of the stores. It may be configured in a straight line or have an L or U shape. There are no enclosed walkways linking the stores. The tenants offer a narrow range of goods and services usually targeted to a local neighborhood.

structural inspection   An evaluation by an engineer of the structural integrity of an improvement or a building foundation.

structural insulated panels   A modular and energy-efficient method of construction that uses large sheets of rigid foam material sandwiched between sheets of plywood. Sometimes the exterior siding material is also attached to the plywood, as is the interior finish wall material. The system is used for economy construction and luxury construction, both, depending on the quality of the interior and exterior finishes, the thickness of the foam layer, and the quality of the plywood. Typically spaces are precut for windows and doors and chases are predrilled for electrical wiring.

structure   Any constructed improvement to a site.

Student Loan Marketing Association   See *Sallie Mae.*

subagency   An agent who operates under the authority of another agent. Typically, the listing broker has the direct agency relationship with the seller of real property. Other real estate brokers may attempt to sell the same property and act as a subagent for the seller rather than acting as the agent for the buyer.

subchapter S-corporation   A corporation just like any other, but that meets certain IRS requirements and is therefore eligible for specifically described tax benefits. IRS Form 2553 must be filed in a timely manner, though. If this type of corporation is elected, there are almost no taxes to the corporation on earned income, although there are some narrow exceptions. Instead, the income is taxed directly to the shareholders according to their percentage of ownership in the corporation. In order to qualify, the corporation must have no more than 100 shareholders, none of which may be another corporation or a non-U.S. citizen.

subcontractor   One who performs services under the supervision of a general contractor. Also called a "sub."

subdivide   To separate property into smaller parcels for sale or borrowing purposes. People normally think of a subdivision as related to development of a residential area, but the definition is not that restrictive.

> **Example:** *A seller wishing to sell only a portion of a parcel of real property may have to apply for subdivision approval before the sale, including assignment of a new tax parcel identification number. Borrowers sometimes subdivide property so that a mortgage will be on only a specific improvement, such as a house, and the land reasonably necessary to support that improvement, rather than have a mortgage encumber more land than is necessary.*

subdivision   Popularly refers to a residential neighborhood developed as an integrated whole and with a specific identity.

subdivision lot and block number   The subdivision plat identification for a particular parcel of land (lot) and the numbered block in which it is located.

subflooring   The plywood or other solid base nailed directly to the floor joists and on which carpeting or other finish flooring is attached.

subjacent   A property that is contiguous to another, but at a lower level.

subject property   The property under discussion.

subject to   Refers to the practice of purchasing real property on which there is an existing mortgage and, rather than paying off or assuming the mortgage, simply allowing it to remain on the property in the original owner's name. Purchasers buying property subject to a mortgage should make sure the loan does not have a due-on-sale clause and that it is not enforceable in the particular circumstances, and they should take whatever steps are necessary to ensure that monthly mortgage payments are made on time.

sublease   The relationship created when a tenant rents some or all of its premises to another for some or all of the remaining term of the original tenant's lease. Technically, if the tenant transfers all of its interest, that is an assignment. If the tenant retains some of the space, or some of the time under the lease, that is a sublease. At all times, the tenant remains liable under its lease with the building owner.

sublet   See *sublease*.

submarket   A small geographical area that is clearly identifiable, at least to local residents, and that contains the logical users of specific goods and services being offered to the public. Submarkets will vary depending on the businesses defining them.

> **Example:** *In Houston, Texas, the Highway 290 submarket may define the customers for billboard advertising. Off 290, the Cypress submarket may define customers for a shopping center, and in Cypress, Enchanted Valley may define the submarket for a convenience store.*

submittal notice   A written notice by a broker to a seller regarding the identity of a person to whom the property has been shown. This is important in order to register prospective buyers in case there is a dispute with another broker in an open listing situation and in case the listing broker is entitled to a commission if a prospect secured during the listing period buys the property within a certain time limit after expiration of the listing.

subordinate   To agree to place one's mortgage or other interests in a junior position relative to another. See *subordinated ground lease* and *subordinated mortgage*.

subordinated classes   Those classes of collateralized mortgage backed securities that have the lowest priority to receive payments from the underlying mortgage loans, and thus the highest risk and the highest rate of return.

subordinated ground lease   An agreement by a property owner in a ground lease situation to allow the tenant's construction lender to have superior rights to the land. The ground lease tenant often builds improvements on the rented land. If those improvements are made with borrowed money, the lender can take a mortgage only on what the tenant owns—the lease rights, not the land itself. If the lender forecloses on the leaseheld interest, it must continue paying rent to the property owner or risk loss of the lease and the improvements. This is generally unacceptable to a lender. It will require the property owner to put the land up as additional collateral for the loan—subordinate the ground lease to the mortgage. In other words, if the lender forecloses, it may take the land and the improvements. Property owners who agree to subordinated ground leases generally obtain higher-than-market rent for their land, to compensate for their increased risk.

subordinated mortgage   A mortgage lien that might have been filed first, but which is agreed among the parties to be treated as a junior lien and inferior to the rights of another mortgage.

subprime loan   A loan at higher interest rates because the borrower does not qualify, for credit or income reasons, for the best rates.

subrogation   The substitution of one party for another. Insurance companies typically have rights of subrogation, so if the insurer pays the property owner for a loss, such as a house fire, and then discovers that loss was the fault of a third party, the insurance company may sue and recover from the third party.

subsidized housing   Residential dwellings that receive some form of government assistance.

subsidy   Benefits granted to persons or groups in order to encourage behavior or outcomes deemed important to society. Rent subsidies encourage construction of adequate affordable housing because the owner can be ensured of an income stream as long as the housing meets government requirements. The same subsidy encourages better consumer choices because of the availability of affordable alternatives. Tax credits to contractors for energy-efficient construction are subsidies to encourage the use of energy-efficient alternatives.

substandard housing   Residential structures that do not meet local health and safety requirements.

substantial completion   The point at which a construction contract has been completed to the point that the owner or tenant may use the property in the manner in which it was intended, even though some work may remain undone. As used in leases for the start date of rent, construction loans for the maturity of the loan, and construction contracts defining the timing of draw schedules, the term may be defined someplace else in the document. That definition, if it exists, will control the rights and responsibilities of the parties, even if the definition is completely different from the normal understanding of the parties.

substitute trustee   The naming of a successor trustee under a deed of trust for real property. Typically, the lender does not name a substitute trustee until immediately before foreclosure. A review of local real estate records for substitute trustee filings may give advance notice of opportunities to invest in foreclosure properties.

substitution   In appraisal, the principle that the value of property may be determined by examining the sales prices of similar properties sold in the past. The theory is that a buyer would be indifferent to the substitution and either property would be acceptable.

subsurface rights   See *mineral rights*.

suburb   An outlying residential area some distance from a city's core.

successor in interest   An owner of property after the one being described.

> **Example:** *Jim executed a mortgage on property that was never paid off, but which never showed up in title searches until recently, despite the fact the property had been sold several times. All of Jim's successors in interest were in danger of losing their property to a foreclosure by the mortgage holder.*

successor trustee   Under a deed of trust, a person or company called a trustee holds the title to the mortgaged property. If that trustee resigns, another one, called the successor trustee, must be appointed.

summary appraisal report   A written appraisal report with a minimum of detail. Contrast with a *self-contained appraisal report.*

summary possession   See *eviction.*

sum-of-the-years digits depreciation   An accounting method of describing the loss in value of an asset over time, sometimes used for personal property that tends to lose more of its value in the early years and then level off.

sunset clause   A provision in a sales contract that sets a date for closing and after which the contract will be unenforceable except for provisions related to damages or earnest money refund or retention.

superadequacy   A component of real estate that is not necessary to the current or anticipated use and so adds no value. In an office building, a private luxury bathroom with a whirlpool tub and steam shower, installed off the office of the president of the company, could be deemed a superadequacy.

superfund   See *CERCLA.*

Superfund Amendments and Reauthorization Act (SARA)   Amendments to the Comprehensive Environmental Response, Compensation and Liability Act (CERCLA) that placed greater emphasis on state and citizenry involvement and coordination, increased focus on human health problems from contamination, and put in place greater enforcement mechanisms.

supermajority   A specified number of votes greater than a 51 percent simple majority. Some condo association bylaws, corporation bylaws, or neighborhood association rules require a supermajority for certain actions, such as making special assessments or amending the bylaws. The rules for the organization will specify the size of the supermajority, which can be anything from 67 to 95 percent.

superpriority   The rights of certain creditors of a bankrupt debtor to receive payment before others that would seem to have superior claims to money or assets; typically granted when a creditor provides much-needed financing after the filing of the bankruptcy petition. Attorneys and bankruptcy trustees have a de facto superpriority because they will always be paid from estate assets before any other creditors.

superstructure   That portion of a building or other structure that is aboveground.

supply and demand   An economic principle that says the price is determined by the point where supply equals demand. As supplies increase and purchasers have more choices of housing or commercial spaces, sellers and landlords will begin to compete on the basis of price and prices will come down. As demand increases and there are insufficient properties in the market to meet the demand, purchasers will begin bidding up the prices or sellers will raise prices until they meet some price resistance.

supported housing   See *congregate housing.*

suprariparian   Upstream; describes the relative position of two properties that border a river or stream. The one that is upstream, in the direction against the current, is the suprariparian property. In some states, suprariparian owners may not take so much of the water from the stream or river as to deny its use to those downstream.

surety   One who guarantees the performance of another. Contrast with a simple guarantee, which is an agreement to pay money if another does not pay money due. A surety, on the other hand, may have to pay money or undertake the responsibility to complete a project.

surety bond   See *fidelity bond*.

surface rights   The right to use and modify the surface of land. Normally, one who has mineral rights may make use of the surface in furtherance of those rights, but may not destroy the value of the surface.

surplus funds   The situation in which a foreclosure sale results in more money than is necessary to pay off the mortgage loan plus all expenses and costs of foreclosure.

surrender   The cancellation of a lease or other contract by mutual agreement of the parties.

surrogate court   In some states, the name given to the probate court that has jurisdiction to supervise the administration of a decedent's estate.

survey   The process by which land is located with reference to commonly agreed upon landmarks or other points of reference, and then measured out for all of its boundaries, including distances and direction-and-degree of turns. Surveys will typically note any indicia of property lines, even if inaccurate, including fence lines and marks left by prior surveyors. A topographic survey will also include land contours. An as-built survey will include all improvements upon the property with their placement and dimensions.

surveyor   A licensed professional who prepares surveys.

surviving spouse's share   The ability of spouses to choose to disregard the will left by their deceased husband or wife and, instead, to take a portion of the estate as specified by the state's laws. The provision for a surviving spouse's share is intended to prevent spouses from being disinherited and left destitute.

survivorship   The right of a joint tenant to attain full ownership rights upon the death of other joint tenants. It is sometimes important to understand that the survivor does not acquire the rights of predeceased joint tenants; rather the deaths of the other tenants remove obstacles to full ownership by the survivor.

suspect   A person identified as possibly having an interest in buying, but who has not yet been contacted or has not yet given any evidence of interest. Contrast with a *prospect*, who has indicated some interest in buying and who appears to have the desire and the ability to purchase.

suspense account   In accounting, a temporary "parking place" for entries one does not know how to classify.

Example: *An apartment project receives a cash rent payment left in its mailbox. There is no indication of the name of the tenant, so the manager cannot post the payment to any particular account. Because of the software accounting system, however, the manager cannot create a deposit slip for the payment unless there is a tenant account. To solve the problem, the manager posts the payment to the suspense account, where it will stay temporarily until someone can find out the tenant's name.*

sustainable site design   Landscaping plans using plants either native to the area or tolerant of local weather conditions and thus requiring a minimum of water and chemical management for diseases and pests.

sweat equity   An increase in the value of property due to the rehabilitation and renovation efforts of the owner, usually acting as his or her own general contractor, subcontractor, and laborer.

sweetener   Something extra included in a transaction to make it more palatable to the other side. For example, Farmer Brown might agree to mow the fields for 5 years if Roberta Rider agrees to buy 10 acres of his land for a horse farm.

sweetheart contract   A contract entered into by related parties who do not negotiate aggressively for the best terms and conditions and which usually has the effect of costing a third party more money than would otherwise be necessary under the circumstances. At one time it was common for developers to retain title to recreational amenities in a subdivision or condo project and charge high rents for their usage. This has largely been regulated out of existence, but such sweetheart contracts always seems to arise in some other guise.

swing loan   A short-term loan that allows homeowners to buy a new home even though their old one has not yet sold.

SYD   See *sum-of-the-years digits depreciation*.

syndicate   A method of selling real property in which a sponsor—the syndicator—sells interests to investors. At one time limited partnerships were the preferred vehicle. Today tenant-in-common properties (TICs) are extremely popular.

synthetic lease   A transaction that appears as a long-term lease from an accounting standpoint but as a loan from a tax standpoint. In the past, such transactions were booked as leases in order to remove loan liabilities from the balance sheets of companies. The company did not have to disclose the duration of the long-term leases, simply the amount of annual lease expenses. Now, the Sarbanes-Oxley Act requires publicly traded companies to disclose the true nature of such off-balance sheet transactions. Unfortunately, many such synthetic leases included both real and personal property. Today, perhaps 10 years after they were originated, the transaction must be reported as a loan liability; the real property posted as an asset at its current value; and the personal property, now practically worthless, posted at its value. The result has been huge losses posted to corporate balance sheets because of the accounting corrections.

T

table funding A lending method employed when a loan originator does not have access to the money necessary to make loans and then hold them until it has enough to sell on the secondary market. As a result, the originator forms a relationship with a lender who provides the funds for closing and immediately takes an assignment of the loan. This is called table funding. Under regulations of the Department of Housing and Urban Development, table-funded loans must disclose service release premiums—profit received by the originator—on the loan closing settlement statement. Loans sold on the secondary market do not have to make those disclosures.

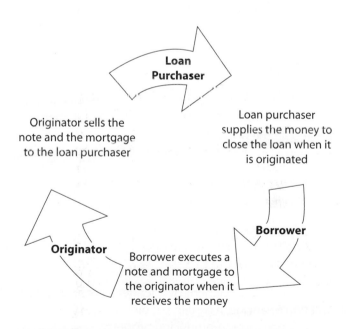

Table funding—everything occurs on the same day.

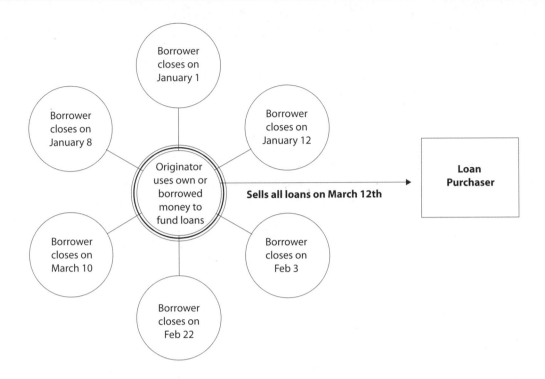

A typical (non-table funded) loan transaction.

tack   To add one time period onto another. When parties are in adverse possession of real property, the possession must be uninterrupted and last for 10 to 20 years before the true owner will be prohibited from trying to regain the property. A current possessor can tack his or her time together with the time of prior possessors in order to accumulate the requisite number of years.

take   (1) A generic term meaning to acquire title by whatever means, such as by deed, by will, by purchase, or by gift, to name a few. (2) A common expression for a condemnation under the power of eminent domain.

take down   To receive money from a loan. A developer or contractor will usually take down its loan in planned stages.

take-out commitment   A binding agreement by a lender to provide permanent financing at the expiration of the construction financing, if certain conditions have been met. These usually include minimum occupancy levels for an income-producing property.

tangible personal property   That which can be seen, touched, and moved, such as equipment, furniture, and vehicles. Contrast with intangible personal property, which includes goodwill, copyrights, and accounts receivable.

tangible property   Real estate plus tangible personal property.

targeted affordable housing   A Freddie Mac (www.freddiemac.com) multifamily lending program.

taxable income   Gross revenues minus almost all operating expenses, depreciation, loan interest, and a few other minor items. Some business expenses, such as entertainment, are not fully deductible.

tax and insurance escrow   A fund maintained by a lender when a borrower makes monthly payments toward the annual property tax and insurance bills. See *PITI*.

tax avoidance   Perfectly legal and ethical strategies for reducing taxes to the lowest possible number. Contrast with *tax evasion*.

tax base   The assessed value of all the property within a taxing jurisdiction. Local governments are always extremely sensitive to the size of the tax base and the need to increase it, and will often offer incentives to developers who will increase the sales taxes in the area, increase the tax base through additional improved properties, or increase the tax base through redevelopment and increased property values.

tax benefit rule   A rule that if one receives a tax benefit from an item in a prior year because of a deduction, such as for an uninsured casualty loss or a bad debt write-off, and then recovers the money in a subsequent year, the money must be counted as income in the subsequent year.

> **Example:** *Acme Inc. suffers a fire a few days after completion of a building that cost $500,000 to build. The building is a total loss. Acme's insurance company refuses to pay the claim, suspecting arson. Acme writes off the $500,000 loss as an expense on its taxes and sues the insurance company. Five years later Acme wins the lawsuit and receives an award of $500,000. The money must be reported as income because it was expensed in the earlier year. If it had never been written off, it would not be income when the judgment was recovered.*

tax bounty hunter   See *tax ferret*.

tax bracket   The highest marginal tax rate to which a person or estate will be subject. Income taxes and estate taxes are calculated as a percentage of adjusted gross income, but the percentage increases as income increases. One's income is divided into brackets with an upper and lower limit to each bracket; the income within the bracket is taxed at its appropriate percentage rate, and then the next bracket is taxed at a higher percentage rate. See *marginal tax rate*.

tax certificate   When a property is sold for delinquent real estate taxes, the purchaser usually receives only a tax certificate. It is not a deed, nor does it transfer title to the property into the purchaser. Rather, it is a right to receive a deed when the statutory time period passes but only if the property owner has not paid all past-due taxes plus interest and costs.

tax court   A specialized federal court established to hear taxpayer claims opposing tax deficiencies assessed by the Internal Revenue Service. There are no juries in the United States Tax Court, but on the plus side, the taxpayer does not have to pay the IRS before filing suit. If a jury is desired, the taxpayer can contest the same issues in the United States District Court for the taxpayer's district, but only to claim a refund. In other words, the party has to pay the taxes first, and then file suit in District Court. If you pay your money, you get a jury. No money, no jury.

tax credit   A direct reduction against income tax liability. Credits reduce taxes dollar-for-dollar. Common tax credits include

1. Earned income credit, used to assist low-income taxpayers.
2. Saver's tax credit, for contributions to qualified retirement plans by low-income individuals.
3. Child-related credits for child- and dependent-care expenses, adoption expenses, and the child tax credit.
4. Education credits, particularly the Hope credit and the lifetime learning credit.
5. Credits for the elderly or disabled.
6. Mortgage credit certificate programs by some state and local governments may be used for tax credits on federal income taxes.
7. Work opportunity credits (for businesses).
8. Rehabilitation credits.

Contrast with a tax deduction, which merely reduces income on which taxes are calculated.

tax deduction   An expense allowed as a reduction of taxable income. The most common individual deductions are for home mortgage interest, ad valorem and sales taxes, moving expenses associated with a job, charitable giving, and health-care costs. Virtually all expenses associated with income-producing property are deductible, including noncash expenses such as depreciation. Virtually all operating expenses for a business are deductible, except that capital expenditures (a new roof, expansion of building, purchase of equipment) must be capitalized and depreciated over time unless falling within the Section 179 limits. Section 179 lets a taxpayer deduct as expenses certain things that would otherwise have to be capitalized.

tax deed   A deed issued to the successful purchaser at an auction for unpaid real estate taxes, but only after passage of a predetermined period of time during which the owner may reclaim the property by paying all past-due taxes, expenses of sale, and interest. See also *tax certificate*.

tax-deferred exchange   See *1031 exchange*.

tax depreciation   See *depreciation*.

tax evasion   The use of fraud or other illegal means to hide income or reduce taxes. Contrast with *tax avoidance*.

tax exemption   A reduction in the assessed rate of real property for purposes of calculating ad valorem taxes. Properties used for religious purposes usually have a 100 percent reduction, resulting in no tax liability. Additional exemptions might be granted for other uses, such as for a personal residence, timberland, or conservation land. One must generally apply for exemptions; they are not granted automatically.

tax ferret   A person who assists property tax collectors, for a fee. Also known as a tax bounty hunter.

tax foreclosure   See *tax certificate, tax deed*, and *tax sale*.

tax-free exchange   A common term for a tax-deferred exchange. It is not tax free; one pays the taxes at a later date. See *1031 exchange*.

tax home   A person's principal place of business or employment. Used for determining if travel expenses are deductible, because they are from the tax home to other business locations, or if they are simply nondeductible commuting expenses from the residence to the tax home.

tax lien   (1) A statutory claim on specific real property for ad valorem or other property taxes; the lien is automatic and nothing regarding a particular property needs to be filed. The tax lien has priority over all other liens—even a mortgage filed before the taxes became due. (2) A claim on all real property of a taxpayer within a certain geographical area, usually a county or parish, because of unpaid federal or state taxes. The lien attaches when the lien documents are filed with the local recording office, and not before. Even though an IRS lien does not take priority over a prior-recorded mortgage, a mortgage lender who fails to give proper foreclosure notice to the IRS may find the property still subject to the lien, even after foreclosure.

tax maps   An official document showing the locations and parcel identification numbers for all property located within an ad valorem (property) tax jurisdiction. Today, many tax maps are maintained online for easy search by citizens, either through a commercial service such as eMapsPlus (www.emapsplus.com) or by the local tax assessor or tax mapping office.

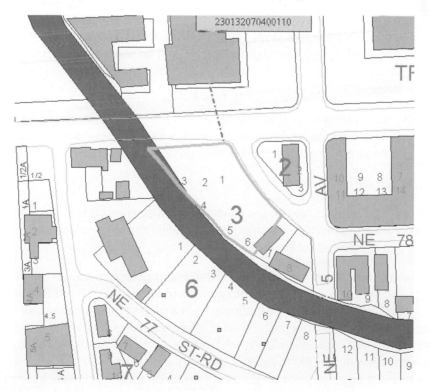

tax on sale of home   See *Section 121*.

tax preference items   Certain types of income or deductions that are used to calculate the alternative minimum tax. The most common item related to real estate is the depreciation deduction.

tax rate   The percentage used to calculate various taxes.

tax redemption   (1) The act of a property owner paying all delinquent real estate taxes, plus expenses and accrued interest after a tax sale but before final issuance of a tax deed to the sale purchaser, and thereby regaining all rights to the property. (2) In some jurisdictions, another name for a tax certificate is a tax redemption certificate. It is the document given to a successful tax sale purchaser, and entitles the purchaser to receive a tax deed after a preset period of time unless the owner pays all taxes before that time expires.

tax roll   A list of all real property parcels located within a taxing jurisdiction, with the names of the owners or those receiving the tax bills, assessed value of properties, and tax amounts due.

tax sale   A public sale because of unpaid property taxes. In most jurisdictions, the successful purchaser receives only a tax certificate, which will entitle the purchaser to ask for a tax deed after the passage of the time period specified in that state.

tax shelter   An investment that generates paper losses or tax credits that may be used to offset other income and thus reduce taxes.

tax stop   A clause in a lease that stops the escalation of tax expenses for either the landlord or the tenant. (1) A tenant tax stop would put an upper limit on the taxes a tenant must reimburse to a landlord under a net lease or triple-net lease. (2) A landlord tax stop would require the tenant to reimburse the landlord if property taxes in any year exceed a certain amount.

tax year   The accounting year selected by a taxpayer for purposes of determining annual taxable income. A new company may select any tax year it desires—July 23 through July 22, for example—and need not use the standard individual tax year of January 1 through December 31.

TDR   See *transferable development rights*.

teaser rate   A below-market rate for the initial period of an adjustable-rate mortgage. It is intended to attract borrowers to this type of loan. Interest usually adjusts to market rates or even somewhat higher on the first allowed adjustment date.

technical advice memorandum (TAM)   A written interpretation of tax law as it relates to a specific problem posed by a specific taxpayer. The question must regard a closed transaction—a dispute over the treatment of something done in the past, not a request for advice on how to proceed in the future. Only an IRS district director or the chief of a local Appeals Office may request a TAM, which is then written by the National Office. TAMs are binding on the IRS for only the transaction at hand. Other taxpayers who use the TAM as guidance for their own actions do so at their own risk, because the IRS may take the opposite position the next time. Contrast with a *private letter ruling*, which has the same effect but the guidance comes from the local office and the advice relates to a future transaction. Contrast also with a *revenue ruling*, which is often issued in response to a particular taxpayer problem but which may be used by all other taxpayers as authority for their actions.

temporary restraining order (TRO)   (Pronounce each of the letters, not as a word.) A court order issued upon application of someone claiming that a state of emergency exists, a defendant must be ordered to desist some action, or a defendant must be ordered to take some action, otherwise irreparable harm will result and the simple recovery of money damages afterward will not be adequate to compensate the plaintiff. Because of the unique nature of real estate and the protections historically granted to it, TROs are usually sought in order to stop developers from cutting trees, clearing land, building or destroying dams, or other such matters.

- The temporary restraining order is a type of injunction.
- Normally the application must be made under oath and must be accompanied by a bond in an amount set by the court. The bond is supposed to provide a fund out of which a defendant may be reimbursed if it later appears that the temporary restraining order was wrongful.
- The TRO may be issued without notice to the other side and without giving the other side an opportunity to argue against it, if certain technical requirements are met. The judge issuing the TRO must set the matter down for hearing on a preliminary injunction within a very short period of time, and notice of the hearing must be given to the other side. At that hearing, the judge will either grant the preliminary injunction or dissolve the TRO. If the judge grants the preliminary injunction, the matter will be set for trial regarding the propriety of a permanent injunction. A judge may determine that there is no emergency, dissolve the TRO, but still set the matter for trial regarding a permanent injunction or money damages.

tenancy   The right of possession to real property; may refer to a leasehold interest or any ownership interest.

tenancy at sufferance   A tenancy established when one who was originally in lawful possession of property refuses to leave once the tenancy expires.

tenancy at will   A landlord-tenant relationship that arises because of some defect in a written lease or because the parties intended to execute a lease but, for some reason, never did. It continues for as long as both parties desire it to continue, usually on a month-to-month basis. Many consumer protection statutes require a minimum of 30 days notice before termination of a tenancy at will. (Do not confuse with a periodic tenancy, which may be from month to month and terminable upon a 30-day notice, but which was never intended to be anything more than a lease for an indefinite time.)

tenancy by the entireties   An estate in land allowed in some states and available only to husbands and wives. Each owns an undivided interest in the whole. When one dies, the survivor takes everything. Unlike a joint tenancy, however, a tenancy by the entireties cannot be destroyed and converted into a tenancy in common when one person attempts to sell his or her interest to an outsider. In addition, creditors of just one spouse may not execute on that interest. Any disposition or mortgage of the property requires both signatures to be valid. (In most states, even most judges may not divide the property or order it to be sold.)

tenancy for life   See *life estate.*

tenancy for years   A leasehold interest for a fixed term, which may be month to month. The more proper term is a periodic tenancy. Do not confuse with a tenancy at will, which is usually a month-to-month tenancy that arose because of some defect in the originally planned lease between the parties.

tenancy in common   Joint ownership of an undivided interest in real property with one or more other people, corporations, or other entities. Tenants in common may each sell their shares to outsiders. If a tenant dies, that tenant's share goes to his or her heirs or as directed in a will. Contrast with *joint tenancy*, sometimes called joint tenancy with right of survivorship, in which one's death causes the cessation of any interest, leaving the survivors to have undivided interests in the property. See also *tenant-in-common properties*, which are a specialized investment vehicle using the tenancy-in-common concepts.

tenancy in severalty   Ownership of one property by one person. That one person may own more than one property, but each property is owned "in severalty."

tenant   (1) One who leases real property. (2) One who has an estate in land, such as a joint tenant with right of survivorship.

tenant improvement (TI) allowance   A negotiated sum a landlord is willing to spend to customize space for the needs of a particular tenant. For second-generation space—that with walls, doors, ceiling tiles, lighting, and electrical already in place because of a prior tenant—the offered TI allowance will typically be enough to replace worn carpets and wallpaper, paint walls, freshen up some cabinetry, and move a minor number of walls and doors. For first-generation space—brand new space—the TI allowance is often insufficient to complete construction with even the most inexpensive quality of components. Construction expenses in excess of the TI allowance must be paid by the tenant.

tenant improvements   Improvements to leased space for the benefit of a nonresidential tenant.

tenant-in-common properties (TICs)   (pronounced as a word) Rarely called by its full name. See *TICs.*

tenant mix   The type and quality of the tenants in a commercial property. Institutional investors typically prefer a mixture of credit tenants from the national, regional, and local levels.

tenant reimbursements   Amounts paid by a tenant to a landlord as reimbursement for operating expenses, taxes, and insurance, if required by the lease.

tenant representative   A real estate broker or agent who represents tenants in locating and nego-tiating space for lease. Typically, the commission is paid by the landlord and is a percentage of the gross value of the lease. If the commission is 4 percent and the rent is $5,000 a month for 5 years, then the gross rent is $5,000 × 12 (months per year) × 5 years = $300,000. The commission would be 4 percent of that, or $12,000.

tenant tax stop   See *tax stop*.

tender   An offer to perform a contract, with the present ability to do so. The term is important when parties dispute the amount due on a debt. Usually, the debtor tenders payment in full, but the payment is refused by the creditor because of an assertion that more is due and the creditor will not accept a partial payment. Because there was a tender, if it is later determined the debtor's calculations were accurate, the debtor will owe no additional interest, costs, fees, or expenses.

tenements   (1) A common expression for apartment buildings in advanced stages of disrepair, located in a generally deteriorated part of town. (2) In its broadest sense, anything permanent that may be the subject of an interest. It is more than just land, but includes all real property that is the subject of a freehold interest and so excludes leases. See *land, tenements, and hereditaments* for differences among the words.

tenure   A time period, as in the tenure of a lease.

tenure in land   The manner in which one enjoys rights or possession, such as a leasehold interest or a fee simple interest.

tenure monthly advance reverse mortgage   A specialized reverse mortgage in which payments continue as long as the owner occupies the property, even if the payments exceed the value of the property.

term   The life of a loan.

term, amortization   The number of years over which a loan will be completely paid by regular monthly payments of principal and interest. Terms of 20, 25, and 30 years are common with residen-tial mortgages. New regulations allow terms as long as 50 years. Especially in commercial real estate, it is very common to have amortization terms longer than loan terms. A lender may offer a "10-year loan on a 30-year am" which means the regular monthly payments will pay the loan in full by the end of 30 years, but the entire loan balance will be due at the end of 10 years.

terminal value   The remaining value of property at the end of a certain designated period.

terminate   To end. (1) For leases, this term implies an ending before the natural expiration time, as by default. When reviewing leases, pay close attention to the rights and responsibilities "upon termination" or "at expiration," because these are two completely different circumstances. (2) For partnerships, it means the end of the partnership business and affairs, although that might tech-nically be before formal dissolution of the partnership. (3) Under the Uniform Commercial Code, it means legally ending a contract, without default by either side.

termination date   Although the verb "to terminate" in a lease usually implies an ending before the natural expiration, termination date is sometimes used to mean the natural ending date of a lease.

termite bond   An insurance policy issued by a pest control company. There are two varieties. The most common is a retreatment bond, which will pay all costs and expenses of eradication and retreatment if termites are discovered. Less common today is the repair and retreatment bond, which will also pay for any repairs necessitated by termite damage. Virtually every bond today excludes Formosan termites from their coverage. The Formosan termite is a particularly voracious termite that exists in large colonies and eats practically anything.

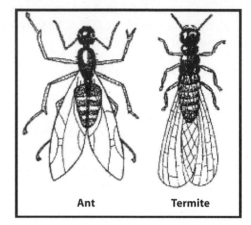

Ant   Termite

termite clause   A provision in a sales contract that allows a buyer to obtain a termite inspection, also called a wood infestation report, and either cancel the contract or require the seller to eradicate and repair as a condition of closing if termites are discovered.

term loan   A loan with a maturity date but no amortization. One pays the interest monthly, quarterly, or annually, as required by the lender, but the principal is not due until maturity. Term loans of short duration, usually less than one year, may be set up as single pay loans. In that case, principal and all accrued interest are paid at maturity.

term monthly advance reverse mortgage   A specialized reverse mortgage plan in which the payments are for a specified term; usually employed by homeowners who do not expect to live very much longer. The advantage over a regular reverse mortgage is the ability to receive larger monthly payments.

terotechnology   A study of costs associated with an asset throughout its life cycle, using analytical tools such as internal rate of return, present value, and discounted cash flow. The results are used to better manage the property.

testament   Originally, an instrument that provided for the disposition of personal property after death. Today, it is simply another word for a will, as in "last will and testament."

testamentary trust   A trust created by one's last will and testament.

testator   The decedent who leaves a will. The feminine form used to be called "testatrix," but today testator includes male and female.

testatrix   See *testator*.

testimonium clause   The clause in a deed that says, "In witness whereof, the parties to these presents have set their hands and seals on this the ___ day of _____, __ __." It is the clause that identifies the grantor(s) and establishes the date of signing.

theme or festival center   A shopping center designed to appeal primarily to tourists, sometimes with unified architectural themes, entertainment, dining, and merchandise. Examples include Pier 39 in San Francisco, Jax Brewery on the riverfront in New Orleans, and Faneuil Hall Marketplace in Boston.

thin corporation   A corporation with large debts to its shareholders and very little equity. In such a situation, the IRS may reclassify the debt as equity investment, meaning payments to shareholders do not include tax-deductible interest but are, instead, dividend payments. Thinly capitalized corporations are used for a variety of sophisticated tax planning vehicles.

thinly capitalized   See *thin corporation*.

thin market   A market in which there are few sales, making it difficult for people to purchase a property or to find comparable sales for an appraisal.

third-party beneficiary contract   A contract formed between two parties, but some or all of the contract is for the benefit of a third party who owes no obligations under the contract. The classic third-party beneficiary contract is a life insurance policy, which is intended to benefit a survivor. In real estate, the concept frequently comes up as aggrieved individuals attempt to claim they are third-party beneficiaries of contracts among property owners, surveyors, appraisers, or developers and therefore are entitled to sue for breach of contract.

> **Example:**   *Linda wants to obtain a home equity loan. The bank hires an appraiser to determine the value of her home. The appraiser finds that Linda has no equity, and the property has actually declined in value since she purchased it 5 years earlier. Linda is turned down for her loan request. She sues the appraiser for negligence and for breach of his contractual obligations to perform his job in a good and professional manner. The court dismisses all claims because the appraiser did not owe any duty to Linda, so there could be no negligence. In addition, she was not a party to the contract between the bank and the appraiser, so there could be no breach of contract. Finally, she was not a third-party beneficiary because the contract was not for her benefit, but for the bank's protection. (Like the insanity defense in criminal law, the third-party beneficiary theory is often employed, but seldom successful.)*

thirteenth-month accounting period   An accounting method that does not seek to make annual corrections or adjustments during any particular month or quarter, because that would skew the financial reporting for that particular period. Instead, an artificial month is created, being the thirteenth month. Bad debts, other write-offs, and income from unusual activities are all booked in the thirteenth month and then flow through for year-end accounting purposes. (Do not confuse with thirteenth-period accounting, which uses 13 periods per year, each with 4 weeks, for a total of 52 weeks or 1 year.)

TICs (tenant in common properties)   Almost always pronounced as a word and very rarely called "tenant in common properties." Investment vehicles that allow persons to buy fractional shares of real estate interests directly, rather than shares of stock, bond certificates, or other intermediate ownership mechanisms. The property may be a high-rise office building on the other side of the country, a retail center, a triple-net lease from a national drugstore chain, oil or gas wells, or any other investment properties. Because of securities and tax law limitations, no more than 35 investors may be involved to jointly own the properties. It allows them to invest in high-quality property that would ordinarily be outside their budgets—most properties that are "tic-ified" cost $30 million or more.

The industry has grown from virtually nothing in 2002—when an IRS ruling clarified the status of such an investment—to many billions of dollars of properties today. An investor has the ability to invest in a TIC as a replacement property in a 1031 exchange.

tie-in contract   A contract in which a vendor conditions the sale of a desirable product on the purchaser's willingness to also buy a less desirable product. The products are said to be tied to each other. The definition includes lenders, who might express a willingness to loan money for a development project at very attractive interest rates and terms, but only if the developer will purchase a piece of foreclosed real estate in the lender's inventory. The slang expression for this practice is called trash for cash. It is illegal under banking regulations and under the Sherman Antitrust Act.

tier   A row of townships extending east and west. See *public land survey system*.

Tier I, II, III, or IV data center   Facilities for the secure maintenance of data computers for government, industry, health care, and finance. Each increase in a tier level represents increased redundancy (duplication of equipment), reliability, power paths, and availability. A Tier IV data center must be able to withstand one unanticipated worst-case scenario with no interruption in service. Because of rigorous site prerequisites for a Tier IV facility, such as distances from certain risk factors, it can be extremely difficult to find an appropriate property for a user.

timber investment management organization (TIMO)   A group that aids institutional investors in locating and managing timberland. The industry grew after legislation in the 1970s that encouraged institutional investors to diversify their portfolios. A 2002 study by Yale's Program on Private Forest Certification showed that approximately $14.4 billion of timberland was managed by TIMOs.

time is of the essence   An expression that often appears in contracts and leases. It is intended to nullify the typical rule that one may have a reasonable amount of time after passage of a deadline in order to do the thing required. If the writing contains a time is of the essence clause, then failure to perform by the deadline will be a noncurable default.

time-price differential   The difference between the purchase price of a property and the higher total price paid if the purchase is financed. The Truth in Lending Act requires disclosure of the time-price differential in an installment sale contract.

time-share ownership   The right to use property for an interval of time each year. See *time-sharing and time-shares*.

time-sharing and time-shares   A temporal division of possessory rights in real property, typically allowing one the use of resort property for a limited time each year. "Owners" may have deeded rights to the real estate with fixed or floating periods of possession, or they may have only a license or other such right-to-use, but no ownership. The rights may be limited in duration, expiring after 5 or 10 years. Many time-share communities offer exchange programs, allowing one to use their time at a different resort than the one of their purchase. Besides the original acquisition price, owners are responsible for their share of the annual dues and unusual expenses. The resale market is limited, so the economic evaluation of a decision to buy should not depend on the ability to recover the purchase price, much less a profit, at some time in the future.

There is currently some regulatory confusion among states and the federal government regarding exactly how time-share interests should be treated. Before developing a time-share project, one should check with local authorities to see if any of the following are required: securities registration with the state Securities Department, subdivision platting, condominium registration, and/or real estate license needed for sales of interests.

title   (1) All the elements that create the highest legal right to own, possess, use, control, enjoy, and dispose of real property or an inheritable right or interest in it. (2) The rights of ownership recognized and protected by the law.

title by estoppel   See *estoppel by deed*.

title insurance   A policy issued by an insurance company to cover defects in legal title to real property, including liens and other adverse claimants. All institutional lenders (everyone except individuals and small private lenders) require title insurance in connection with their loans. One may buy the basic, no-frills policy or add riders for additional protection and higher premiums. (The standard title insurance policy written for closing protects only the lender; owners should request owner coverage in addition.)

Commercial borrowers comparing lending costs among providers should inquire about the standard riders required by each lender: a large number of riders can dramatically increase closing costs and may make the difference in a decision between two lenders. Riders (also called endorsements), can address some of the following:

- Inflation
- Problems with restrictions, encroachments, and minerals
- Zoning problems
- Separate tax parcel problems if the tax parcel includes land in addition to that being mortgaged
- Losses if it turns out the land does not abut a public street
- Last dollar coverage, meaning that if the loan is secured by real property and personal property, borrower payments will be treated as if made to personal property first, so that the lender's real property title insurance is not reduced simply by virtue of loan payments
- Usury, so that if a court rules that the mortgage is invalid because the note's interest rate is too high and violates state usury laws, the title insurance will pay the lender
- Environmental protection, in case a government authority files an environmental protection lien that gains priority over the mortgage
- Going-concern value measure of damages for an operating business, rather than simply the value of the real estate measure of damages

Title I (one) loan   A HUD loan insurance program for light to moderate home improvement loans up to $25,000 for single-family residences, and up to $12,000 per unit, with a total cap of $60,000, for multifamily properties. The loans may be repaid over 20 years at market interest rates. This is not a subsidized-interest program, although some local communities do offer interest subsidies in connection with Title I loans. Eligible borrowers include owners, purchasers under a contract for sale, or tenants with at least 6 months left on their lease. [Do not confuse with HUD's 203(k) loan, also called a HUD rehabilitation and repair loan.]

title I look-alike loan   Same as a Title I loan, except privately funded without government insurance, and the money can be used for other things beside home improvements.

title plant   A collection of information about the ownership and lien history of property, filed according to geographical location rather than by owners' names. The use of a title plant makes it very easy to research the history of ownership of land.

title search   A review of all recorded documents that affect title to a particular piece of real property. Ideally, a title search should proceed all the way backward to the original patent (deed) out of the government into the first private owner, or to the root deed, which is the first deed before a statutorily enacted cutoff date for claims.

title theory of mortgages   See *title-theory states*.

title-theory states   Those states in which mortgages are treated as passing legal title to the lender, with the borrower having equitable title. Typically title-theory states employ a deed of trust instrument rather than something called a mortgage. If the borrower pays the debt in full, then the lender reconveys the property to the borrower. Contrast with *lien theory states* and with *hybrid theory states*.

tolling   A suspension of a statute of limitations time period. In adverse possession, the time period may be tolled while the record owner is a minor child and unable to bring a lawsuit to oust trespassers in possession of his or her property. Parties in disputes often contractually agree to toll all applicable statutes of limitations while they pursue negotiations; otherwise a rapidly approaching expiration date would force them into litigation just to avoid loss of valuable rights.

topo   Short for topographic map.

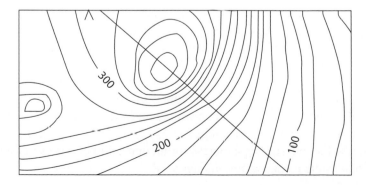

topographic map   A map that shows the contours of the land via a two-dimensional drawing with multitudes of contour lines showing changes in elevations. Each map has its own scale. The contour lines indicate a change in elevation by the scale amount. For example, each line might represent a 1-foot change in elevation. The distance between the lines can be computed by reference to the distance scale. For example, 1 inch might equal 50 feet. Two contour lines that are 1 inch apart would indicate a grade of 1 foot over the course of 50 feet, which is very gentle. The closer the lines on the topographic map, the steeper the incline. (See figure on bottom of page 414.)

topography   The contours of land—such as flat, rolling, or steep.

topping off   A ceremony to celebrate the completion of a building. It is a custom to attach a tree branch to the highest point on the roof at that time. All decision makers and management-level people involved in the project, including lenders, professionals, ownership, important prelease tenants, and construction and development personnel are usually invited to the ceremony, and each are given a complimentary hard hat customized with the name of the building and the date of the ceremony.

tornado bait   A slang expression for a mobile home park.

Torrens certificate   An instrument issued by the registrar of legal titles in a state that employs the optional Torrens system for title registration. The certificate operates much like a car title, listing the name of the owner and any mortgage or deed of trust liens, plus any other liens or encumbrances.

Torrens registration   The process of first entering a property into the optional land registration system known as the Torrens system. For the states and counties that offer this as an alternative to the more traditional abstract method, registration begins as a lawsuit. The property owner sets out all the evidence showing his or her entitlement to the property and any mortgages or other liens against the property. The owner must disclose other persons who might have a claim to the same property. Those persons receive notice of the suit. There is usually also a method of public notice in case other claimants wish to assert their rights. Normally, no other claimant disputes the title and the court orders issuance of a Torrens certificate. If there is a dispute, the lawsuit will proceed just like any other suit, with a trial and a decision.

Torrens system   An optional system for registering title to real property and all claims and encumbrances against the property; available in only a few states. See also *Torrens certificate* and *Torrens registration*.

tort   A legally recognized wrong for which the law provides a remedy. The wrong may be negligent; it might be one of the intentional torts such as defamation, assault, battery, trespass, conversion (broadly, acts that amount to theft), or false imprisonment (preventing someone from leaving a place); or it might be something that can combine elements of negligence, recklessness, or intentional conduct, such as fraud or nuisance. The modern trend of legal theory is to expand concepts of tort liability. As a result, older decisions that find in favor of a property owner, for example, and against someone injured on the property may no longer be reliable when you are trying to determine rules of conduct and the limits of responsibilities. The better practice is to do all things reasonable and fair under the circumstances, regularly consult with insurance advisors regarding risk management practices, keep informed regarding litigation trends in your industry, and always maintain adequate insurance coverage.

total assets   The sum of all cash, investments, furniture, fixtures, equipment, receivables, intangibles, and any other items of value owned by a person or a business entity.

total inventory   A sum of the square footages of particular types of properties within a defined area, regardless of whether vacant or rented.

total return   The sum of periodic income and property appreciation.

town house or townhome   A residential construction type that includes dwelling units with no side yards, but which share a common wall and sometimes common roof structures, sidewalks, and/or driveways with the units on either side. Each property owner has an easement in the shared portion on the other side of the line. A common wall cannot be partially removed, for example, because it would damage the support for the other property, and a common driveway cannot be partially removed because it supplies the access to the others' parking court or garage. See also *party wall*.

township   (1) Primarily in the northeast, a jurisdictional and geographical area within a county. (2) A division within the public land survey system.

toxic mold   See *black mold*.

tract   A parcel of real estate; usually refers to a large area of land.

tract house   A house that is substantially similar to all other houses in a subdivision.

trade fixtures   Personal property attached to a structure and used in a business. Normally, fixtures become part of the real estate and cannot be removed by a tenant. Trade fixtures, however, are recognized as a part of the business itself, not the real estate, and so may be removed at the expiration of the lease term. Despite that, many leases specifically provide that any tenant improvements paid by the landlord must remain on the property, even if they are trade fixtures.

trade-in   The practice of a developer purchasing a buyer's existing home in order to facilitate purchase of one in the developer's new subdivision. Industry groups have asked the Department of Housing and Urban Development (HUD) for exemption of the practice from the FHA antiflipping regulations that deny FHA insurance if a house is purchased and then resold within 90 days, but HUD has been resistant to the idea.

trade libel   The intentional disparagement of a property or a business. The statements must be false and must result in monetary loss in order to give rise to a cause of action.

traditional zoning ordinance   Zoning that specifies the same density for each and every lot within an area.

traditionary evidence   An exception to the hearsay rule. One may use evidence regarding traditions, reputation, and oral histories in order to establish ancient boundaries of land when there are no living witnesses to testify regarding the original parties' intentions.

traffic counts   Statistics regarding the number of vehicles that pass a given point during a 24-hour period. Traffic counts are an important component of site selection for most national companies. There is a science to reading traffic counts, because annual numbers, by themselves, can be deceptive.

trailing twelve   Shorthand for "trailing 12 months of financials," meaning profit and loss information for a property or business for the past 12 months. Also written as the abbreviation "ttm."

tranche   A class of securities. Collateralized mortgage backed securities are usually divided into tranches according to seniority and risk.

transaction broker   A real estate broker or agent who acts as an intermediary for the exchange of information and negotiations regarding the sale or lease of real estate and who may offer marketing and advertising services, but who does not represent either party in the relationship. Transaction brokerage is allowed only when state legislatures specifically provide for its use.

transferable development rights (TDR)   A zoning and land planning tool often used to preserve undeveloped or culturally significant areas. Typically, the local government will identify an area it wants to retain in a natural state, such as farmland, called the sending area. Government will also identify an area in need of development, usually through rehabilitation, called the receiving area. To meet those two goals—preservation one place, development in another—government will buy development rights from the farmers, for example. The farmers will agree to restrict their land so it cannot be developed. In return, they will receive something in the nature of credits that allow zoning variances in the receiving area. The farmer may sell those credits to a developer who wishes to build or renovate something in the receiving area. The farmer gets cash, the developer gets its variance, some land is preserved, and other land is rehabilitated, all with a minimum of bureaucratic involvement along each step of the way.

transfer certificate of title   Used in the Torrens system, it is a duplicate Torrens certificate of title. The owner of property receives a duplicate certificate; the original is retained by the registrar and recorded. When the property is sold, the purchaser receives the transfer certificate of title, which is surrendered to the registrar in order to complete issuance of a new Torrens certificate listing the new owner.

transfer tax   A state or local tax imposed when title is transferred from one owner to another.

transit-oriented development   Development around destinations near public transportation centers, with mixtures of housing, employment, shopping, dining, and entertainment all within walking distance of transit nodes.

TransUnion   One of the three major credit reporting bureaus. The other two are Experian and Equifax. The TransUnion Web site is at www.transunion.com. See also *Fair Credit Reporting Act*.

trash for cash   See *tie-in contract*.

treble damages   A court award of damages in an amount three times greater than some proven value such as actual damages. It is intended as a punishment to a wrongdoer. Most government regulations that grant to the public the right to sue if there is a violation also grant the right to receive treble damages.

trespass   The unlawful interference with someone's personal or property rights. In a lawsuit, the property owner does not need to prove physical damage to the property in order to recover monetary damages, because the damage is to the exclusive ownership and possessory rights of the owner. However, modern courts do require some evidence that the trespass was intentional; older law did not differentiate between intentional and accidental trespass. In many states, the duty of care a property owner has to avoid unsafe conditions that might harm persons coming on the property is much less for a trespasser than for those who are invited.

triple-A tenant   A commercial tenant with excellent credit, extremely low sensitivity to temporary market downturns, and, ideally, national name recognition. Banks are generally included within the examples of triple-A tenants despite the lack of a national platform, because their financial strength and prestige make them very desirable tenants.

triple-net lease   A lease that requires the tenant to pay all costs and expenses associated with ownership of the property, including taxes, insurance, repairs, and maintenance. Contrast with *gross lease*.

TRO   See *temporary restraining order*.

trophy building   A status symbol, landmark building with distinctive design features and the very best construction and finishes. It generally has widespread name recognition and is considered a prestigious address. Since 9/11, the allure of trophy buildings has waned among some tenants, who view the real estate as a mixture of trophy and target.

trunk title   When an owner fails to record a deed, but instead keeps it in a trunk at home, in a dresser drawer, or such, there is nothing in the public records to evidence the owner's right to the property. If necessary for a real estate closing, the owner will have to produce the original of the instrument. In the title insurance industry, such persons are said to have trunk title or sometimes dresser drawer title.

trust   The practice of one party holding legal title to real property or other assets for the benefit of someone else, called the beneficiary. The one with the legal title is called the trustee. The person or entity that set up the trust is called the trustor. Trusts are extremely important in tax and estate planning but should almost never be established without the assistance of a tax attorney who is well skilled in the area. A very slight deviation from the format acceptable to the IRS could prove disastrous.

trust account   A bank account specially designated to hold funds that belong to others. Real estate brokers and attorneys are required to maintain separate trust accounts for client money and for escrowed funds.

trustee's deed   The instrument that transfers legal title to a purchaser after a foreclosure in a state that uses deeds of trust rather than mortgages. See also *deed of trust*.

trustee's sale   A foreclosure in a state that uses deeds of trust as a vehicle for granting rights in real property to be used as collateral for a loan.

Truth in Lending Act   Title I of the Consumer Credit Protection Act. It is a federal law that requires lenders to make certain disclosures to potential borrowers within 3 days after receipt of a written loan application. A final disclosure statement is provided at the time of loan closing. The disclosure is required to be in a specific format and must include the following information:

1. Name and address of creditor
2. Amount financed
3. Itemization of amount financed (optional, if a good-faith estimate is provided)
4. Finance charge
5. Annual percentage rate (APR)
6. Variable-rate information
7. Payment schedule
8. Total of payments
9. Demand feature
10. Total sales price
11. Prepayment policy
12. Late payment policy
13. Security interest
14. Insurance requirements
15. Certain security interest charges
16. Contract reference
17. Assumption policy
18. Required deposit information

truth in lending laws   Various provisions of the Truth in Lending Act and sometimes state laws with similar requirements.

Truth in Negotiations Act (TINA)   A public law enacted for the purpose of providing for full and fair disclosure by contractors in the conduct of negotiations with the government. The most significant provision included in TINA is the requirement that contractors submit certified cost and pricing data for larger contracts.

turnkey project   Construction and furnishing of an improvement to the customized requirements and specifications of a buyer to the degree that the new owner need only turn the key in the lock and start business. The concept may include hiring and training all necessary staff positions, letting contracts for routine maintenance needs, and/or leasing a property up to stabilized occupancy. Contrast with *built to suit*.

turnover rate   The rate at which tenants or clients depart and are replaced.

U

UCC   See *Uniform Commercial Code.*

UETA   See *Uniform Electronic Transactions Act.*

ULI   See *Urban Land Institute.*

underground storage tank   A tank maintained below ground level and holding liquids, usually petrochemicals or waste. The Environmental Protection Agency (EPA) registers and regulates underground storage tanks unless there is an approved state or tribal program in place. The EPA maintains an excellent Web site (www.epa.gov/oust) with information about regulations, cleanup, assistance for development of abandoned gas stations, and links to all individual state programs and resources.

underimprovement   A structure that is less than the highest and best use for a property. A residence sitting on 1 acre of land on a major retail street is an underimprovement; the property would be more valuable with a fast-food restaurant.

underlying mortgage   The first mortgage in a wraparound mortgage arrangement.

undersecured loan   A loan in which the collateral is not worth as much as the debt.

underwater   A popular expression for a property with a debt larger than its value. You will sometimes encounter prime properties for lease, rather than for sale, because the property is underwater. The owners cannot afford to sell, because a sale at market value would require them to bring cash to the closing table to pay off the debt.

underwrite   (1) To evaluate the risk of a situation, as in loan underwriting to determine the borrower's financial strength, ability to repay the debt in the event of an interruption of cash flow, and willingness to repay the debt as evidenced by the borrower's credit score or credit history. (2) To guarantee a sale, such as an investment banker who underwrites the sale of securities and will purchase any that do not sell on the open market. (3) To assume liability, such as an insurance company that underwrites a policy.

undeveloped land   See *raw land.*

undisclosed agency   The failure of an agent to disclose that he or she is working for another, called the principal. Most states require real estate agency disclosure before a person reveals any confidential information.

> **Example:** *Ralph asks his next-door neighbor, real estate agent Beronda, to help him find a house. Beronda agrees, but she must disclose to Ralph that she will work as a subagent for the sellers (the typical situation) and will not be Ralph's agent. She will owe Ralph only the duty of honesty and no other duties.*

undivided interest   Ownership that is shared with other co-owners, but not as to any particularly identifiable portion of the whole.

undue influence   A theory used to set aside contracts, wills, or deeds. It is any improper method of persuasion used to overcome the will of another and induce that person to do something he or she would not otherwise do. Success in using the theory usually depends on proof that someone used his or her position of trust and confidence to overcome the will of a person in a weakened, infirm, or psychologically distressed state.

unearned increment   The amount by which land increases in value because of generally improving conditions in the area, not because of any particular efforts by the property owner. The concept is important to a social theory made popular in the late 1800s by American journalist Henry George, but which still maintains broad appeal. Proponents, often called "Georgists" support the return of the unearned increment to society, in the form of large taxes on that portion of the increase in value of real estate. The concept is diametrically opposed to the current system of long-term capital gains tax breaks, which allow a property owner to retain more of the unearned increment, not less.

unencumbered property   Real estate with no other liens, claims, easements, leases, or anything at all that would diminish free and clear title.

Uniform Commercial Code (UCC)   A system of laws governing commercial transactions such as sales of goods, banking, the taking of security interests in personal property, documents of title regarding personal property, and letters of credit. The word "uniform" is misleading because all states have their own customized versions of the UCC. The UCC is important to real property because many real estate transactions involve a component that includes personal property.

Link to each state's version of the UCC by going to Cornell University's excellent legal resources site at www.law.cornell.edu/uniform/ucc.html. See also *uniform laws*.

Uniform Electronic Transactions Act (UETA)   An attempt to bring commerce into the twenty-first century by recognizing the importance of electronic documents and by providing rules for granting legal effect to them and protecting against abuses. Many states passed local versions of the UETA; some apply to real estate and some do not. The federal version is called the Electronic Signatures in Global and National Commerce Act (E-Sign). It governs in the absence of state laws, or when state laws are inconsistent with E-Sign. The critical issue in real estate is whether an exchange of e-mails or e-mailed documents may satisfy the Statute of Frauds requirement that almost all contracts related to real estate must be in writing. This issue is still unsettled and controversial. See also *uniform laws*.

uniform laws   A misleading term, because it seems to imply a nationwide system of laws, when really it refers to model legislation that may be adopted by individual states with or without local revisions. There is a great variety of uniform laws, which may be found at the Web site of the organization responsible for discussing and drafting them—the National Conference of Commissioners on Uniform State Laws (NCCUSL) (www.nccusl.org).

Uniform Residential Appraisal Report (URAR)   A standard form for reporting the value of a residence, required by most major lenders and secondary market purchasers in order to simplify the underwriting and review process.

Uniform Residential Landlord and Tenant Act   Legislation governing the rights and responsibilities of residential landlords and tenants. Currently, some version of the law has been passed by many states. As a general matter, the laws

- Standardize and simplify the eviction process
- Require the tenant to pay rent into court during the pendency of an eviction if it is contested
- Limit the amount of any security deposits
- Provide for prompt repayment of security deposits
- Require certain minimal conditions of habitability
- Impose penalties for breach of the provisions.

See also *uniform laws*.

Uniform Settlement Statement   The real estate closing form required by the Real Estate Settlement Procedures Act (RESPA) in order to account for all funds received, all disbursements made, and all expenses and all credits at closing. The form is more commonly known as a HUD–1.

Uniform Standards of Professional Appraisal Practice (USPAP)   Requirements of the Appraisal Foundation (www.appraisalfoundation.org) regarding appraisal ethics, record keeping, methodology, research, reporting, and client interaction. The Standards have undergone recent revisions simplifying the appraisal process and conforming its practices to modern realities.

unilateral contract   A contract that is binding on one party but only if the other party chooses to take advantage of it. An option contract is the classic unilateral contract. A property owner (optionor) will give another party (optionee) the right to purchase property, but the optionee is not obligated to purchase if it chooses not to.

unimproved land   See *raw land*.

unincorporated association   A group of two or more persons who band together for a common purpose or goal, but without the formality of creating a corporation or partnership. Many religious groups function as unincorporated associations. The rules differ among states, but a deed to or from an unincorporated association may have specialized requirements to be legal.

union mortgage clause   See *standard mortgage clause*.

unities   A concept having to do with joint ownership of property. The four unities are interest, possession, time, and title. Joint tenancy with right of survivorship requires all four unities—the owners must have obtained their rights from the same deed, must have undivided possession, and the same use over the same period of time.

unitization   A system for controlling proliferation of oil and gas wells. Originally, property owners with oil or gas under their land would each dig one or more wells on their property and try to capture as much as they could of the underlying pool, which drained from many properties. One response was the passage of unitization laws by state governments, establishing spacing restrictions on wells and a sharing of profits and expenses among all the owners of the underground pool.

unlisted REIT   See *private REIT*.

unrealized gain   The current increase in fair market value of a property, which is unrealized because the property has not been sold. Contrast with *unrecognized gain*, which is a tax concept.

unrecognized gain   A gain on the transfer of real property, but for which there is no current tax consequence because of various provisions of the Internal Revenue Code, such as the ability to reinvest proceeds and defer taxes until a sale of the replacement property. See *1031 exchange*.

unrecorded deeds   Deeds that are not recorded with the public official given responsibility for maintenance of real estate records. An unrecorded deed is perfectly legal and passes title from the seller (grantor) to the purchaser (grantee) just like a recorded deed. The problem occurs if there is some event after the transfer, such as the grantor's bankruptcy, grantor's sale or mortgage of the same property to another, or tax or judgment liens against the grantor. If the deed was not recorded, other parties may be able to successfully claim the property, including a bankruptcy trustee who may seize the property and sell it to satisfy the grantor's debts.

unsecured creditors   Persons owed money by a debtor, but who have no collateral as security for the debts owed to them.

unsecured loan   A loan without collateral.

unstated interest   See *imputed interest*.

upper bracket   A slang term describing a home for affluent persons; refers to people with income at the highest bracket of the income tax rates.

upset price   See *reserve price*.

URAR   See *Uniform Residential Appraisal Report*.

urban area   (1) As used by the U.S. Census Bureau, the term refers to all areas that are urban. Since the 2000 census, that includes urban clusters and urbanized areas. An urban cluster is a densely settled territory with more than 2,500 people but less than 50,000. An urbanized area is one "consisting of a central place(s) and adjacent territory with a general population density of at least 1,000 people per square mile of land area that together have a minimum residential population of at least 50,000 people." (2) The Census Bureau's definition of "urban area" has changed several times in the past. If researching a particular subject that uses the term, it may be important to find the definition in effect at the time the book or article was written. (3) In popular speech, any densely populated area of a city or town.

urban cluster   See *urban area*.

urbanized area   See *urban area*.

Urban Land Institute   A nonprofit organization (www.uli.org) that provides research services and publications on land use and development.

urban renewal   Redevelopment of deteriorated and underutilized urban properties, often through the provision of tax incentives, low-interest-rate bond money for loans, and government investment in infrastructure improvements such as roads and public parks in order to spur development.

urban sprawl   A derogatory term for the spread of suburban developments, typically along relatively narrow strips of land following major arteries or highways.

usable area   In commercial leasing, it is the amount of space that can be utilized by tenants within the walls defining their rented space. Contrast with rentable area, which is an artificial measurement of a tenant's usable area plus a tenant's pro rata portion of the common areas. When quoting rent per square foot, landlords usually base the rent on rentable area, not on usable area.

U.S.C.   This is the abbreviation for United States Code. Any reference to, for example, 26 U.S.C. §1273, means Title 26 of the United States Code and section 1273 of that Title. This format is considered the official citation. There are several publishers of the United States Code. An alternate citation might be seen as 26 U.S.C.S. §1273 (United States Code Service, published by Lawyers Cooperative Service and containing cross references to legal aids from the same publisher, including LexisNexis) or 26 U.S.C.A. §1273 (United States Code Annotated, published by West Publishing Company and containing cross references to legal aids from the same publisher, including Westlaw.) To find the complete text of United States Code Sections, visit the Web site of the U.S. Government Printing Office, www.gpoaccess.gov/uscode/index.html. See also *section (federal code)* for an alternate, but still official, Web site for research.

useful life   (1) In accounting and taxation, the time period over which an asset is depreciated. (2) In appraisal, the time period during which one can expect a positive cash flow from a property.

U.S. Government survey system   See *public land survey system*.

USPAP   See *Uniform Standards of Professional Appraisal Practice*.

UST   An abbreviation for "underground storage tank."

usury   An interest rate higher than allowed by state law. The limits usually vary depending on the size of the loan, the term, the use of the money, and/or the status of the borrower as a consumer or other type of borrower. The consequences of usury may range from a reduction of the interest rate, loss of all interest completely, or even civil fines or penalties.

utility easement   A right to use another's property for purposes of laying water and sewer lines, gas lines, or bringing in electric or telecommunications services.

utility notification   See *blue stake*.

utility stop   A cap on the utility expenses used to calculate a tenant's pro rata share of building operating expenses. It may be desired as a lease term by a small-space user who does not wish to assist in paying the power bills for a large user with seemingly excessive utility needs disproportionate to the space it is occupying.

V

VA   See *Veterans Administration*. (It is now called the Department of Veterans Affairs.)

vacancy and collection allowance   When preparing a pro forma estimate of future performance of an investment, the vacancy and collection allowance is an estimate of the amount by which gross scheduled rents should be decreased to account for vacancies and for rents that will be uncollectible. A typical number to use is 5 percent of the gross scheduled rent. Some analysts include rent concessions, or discounts, in the vacancy and collection allowance figure; others prefer to list rent concessions as a separate expense item so management can track how much it is willing to give away in concessions and match that against how much it actually has to spend for concessions.

> **Example:**   *An apartment complex has 10 units renting for $800 per month. It caters to students and sometimes has vacancies during the summer months. The owner is willing to give away $1,500 a year in free rent, reduced rent, or other concessions. The owner anticipates next year will look like this:*

Gross scheduled rent		$96,000
Less V&C allowance		(4,800)
Total anticipated revenue		$91,200
Maintenance expenses	(3,600)	
Concessions	(1,500)	
Other marketing expenses	(1,000)	
Insurance	(8,000)	
Real estate taxes	(11,000)	
Total expenses		($25,100)
Net operating income		$66,100

vacancy factor   See *vacancy rate*.

vacancy rate   The ratio of vacancies to total available rentals, over a particular period of time. There are three primary methods of calculating the vacancy rate: by number of units, square footage, or dollars of rental income. Beyond that, the calculations can be for a moment in time—a particular month—or for experience over the course of a year. Economic vacancy, which is the dollar value of vacancies rather than the number of units or square footage of floor space, is the most accurate indicator of the vacancy rate. When reviewing pro forma projections or past financial records, one must ascertain which method was used to calculate vacancies, however, because each method will result in a different rate unless all units are the same size and rent for exactly the same amount. See Example at *occupancy rates* for an explanation of the various calculations.

vacant land   Land not being used at the present time but that may have utilities and infrastructure in place. Contrast with *raw land*.

vacate   (1) To move out. (2) To release and give up, such as a city agreeing to vacate a public street and return it to private ownership. (3) To set aside, such as a judge vacating a previously entered order.

> **Example:** *At one time residents needed an alley behind their homes so the coal trucks could make deliveries for home heating fuel. Today, there is no longer any need for truck deliveries behind the homes; the residents petition the city for an order vacating the alley and giving the land to adjoining landowners.*

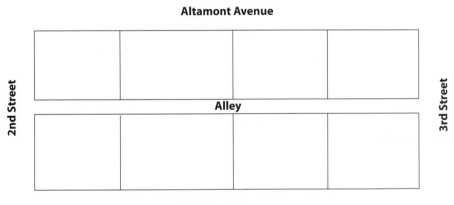

vacation home   A second home used for recreational purposes. Mortgages for vacation homes generally have higher interest rates than those for primary residences because, if there is any economic difficulty, the property owner is more likely to stop making payments on a vacation home than on a primary residence. Vacation home mortgage interest is deductible the same as for a primary residence, but under current tax law there is a $1,000,000 cap on the amount of debt generating deductible interest. The sale of a principal residence will not result in current income taxes if the gain is less than $250,000 for single persons or $500,000 for married people, but this exclusion does not apply to vacation homes. If the vacation home is used for rental income, there are limitations on your personal usage if you want to deduct rental expenses, including depreciation.

valid   Having legal force.

VA loan or mortgage   A home loan guaranteed by the Department of Veterans Affairs (www.homeloans.va.gov/elig2.htm) (known as the Veterans Administration before 1989), which will pay the lender up to certain limits if the borrower defaults. In some instances, the VA will decide to purchase the home from the lender after default and attempt resale, calculating that the profits from a resale will make the transaction cheaper than paying off the loan. By law, it is required to do this analysis on all defaulted loans. Eligibility for a VA guarantee is complicated and depends on the borrower's dates, length, and type of service; whether the borrower is currently active in the military; whether the borrower is in the National Guard or the Reserves; and the number of months the borrower was in peacetime or combat service.

valuable consideration   Any type of promise, benefit, or relinquishment of a right given by a party in order to receive something else in return, and which will result in a contract being legally enforceable. A contract to sell a home in consideration of love and affection is *good* consideration, but not *valuable* consideration. Good consideration is sufficient to prevent a deed from being set aside, but it is insufficient to enforce a contract.

valuation   (1) The process of estimating the worth of something. (2) The estimated worth given to something.

value   The worth of all rights arising from ownership of property.

value before and after taking   A rule used in federal condemnation cases. When the government takes only part of a piece of property, it values the entire parcel before the taking and then it separately appraises the portion remaining after condemnation. The difference in the two numbers is the amount of the award to the property owner. Contrast with the method used by many states, which value the property taken, add any severance damage caused to the remaining property, and subtract any special benefits gained by the remaining property as a result of the condemnation. In an ideal world, both approaches would result in the same number.

value in exchange   The value of property if one were to exchange it for goods and services.

value in use   The worth of a property as it is currently being used. A convenience store allowed to remain in business in a zoning area that no longer allows convenience stores has a high value in use because there can be no nearby competition. A house on the side of a major street in a retail area would have a value in use much lower than its highest and best use as a retail site.

value per square foot   A method of pricing land when it becomes very valuable. Rather than quote $1,176,120 per acre, which is a bit awkward, value will be expressed as $27 per square foot in this example. There are 43,560 square feet per acre: $27 $\times$ 43,560 = $1,176,120.

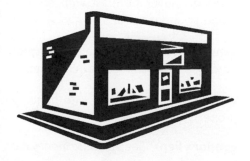

vanilla building   A building suitable for a wide variety of uses and brand names, rather than one with a distinctive architectural style or use such as a Taco Bell or a car dealership.

variable expenses   Property operating expenses that increase and decrease in relatively direct proportion to changes in occupancy. It is important to differentiate between fixed expenses and variable expenses because the fixed expenses must be met every month, no matter what the occupancies. In preparing a pro forma analysis for a new project, one will usually calculate fixed expenses starting with month 1 and continuing unchanged until perhaps another employee must be added to the payroll. Variable expenses, however, are always calculated as dependent on lease-up and tied to each month's occupancy figures if the pro forma is a spreadsheet.

variable interest rate   A loan interest rate that changes as some outside factor, preferably one not within the control of the lender, changes. Commonly seen in adjustable-rate mortgages.

variable maturity mortgage   A mortgage loan with a variable interest rate but a fixed monthly payment. As interest rates increase or decrease, less or more of the payment each month will be used to pay the principal rather than interest. As a result, the maturity of the note will change over time.

variable payment plan   Any loan that contemplates changes in payments, either because of a variable interest rate, graduated payments increasing principal reductions as one's income increases, or some other type of flexibility in the loan.

variable-rate mortgage (VRM)   A precursor to the modern adjustable-rate home mortgage (ARM), and still used in the area of commercial mortgages. With a variable-rate mortgage, the interest rate on the loan changes whenever the index rate changes. The monthly payments usually change every month, also. Most construction loans are variable-rate mortgages. The ARM differs because the interest rate changes at predetermined intervals, such as once a year or once every 6 months.

variance   Permission to use a property in a manner that does not meet current zoning requirements. In order to gain a variance, the property owner usually has to show a hardship on the property—not on the owner—if the requested use is not allowed. It is considered a hardship if the property will otherwise remain vacant or if a structurally sound improvement must be demolished to allow some other use. Buyers with a signed purchase contract can usually petition for a variance; this is commonly one of the steps in a due diligence plan that must be completed in a satisfactory manner before the buyer will purchase property.

vendee   Buyer. Contrast with *donee*, who receives property by gift, and *devisee*, who receives property under a will.

vendee's lien   A lien against real property for the earnest money deposit paid on a contract of purchase. Not enforceable in all states.

vendor   Seller. Contrast with *donor*, who transfers property by gift, and *testator*, who transfers property under a will.

vendor's lien   See *purchase money mortgage*.

venire   The total pool of people summoned for jury duty.

venture capital   A common name given to money raised for investment in high-risk enterprises. Venture capital firms may specialize by industry and/or by stage—seed money for start-ups, mid-stage firms on the brink of success but needing additional capital, or successful firms capable of expansion to a regional or nationwide platform. There is a National Venture Capital Association (www.nvca.org). Sometimes called angel investors.

verbal   Oral. Verbal contracts are enforceable unless they fall within the Statute of Frauds.

- Verbal wills, called *nuncupative wills,* are usually not enforceable.
- Verbal statements made by someone before death, and which would have the effect of increasing or decreasing that person's estate, will usually not be allowed into evidence by virtue of the dead man's statute.
- A verbal agreement regarding the location of the true boundary line between property owners is often enforceable; a verbal agreement to compromise the line between two property owners is usually not enforceable.

verification   A sworn statement before a notary public, or other person authorized to take oaths, that the contents of a document are accurate. Contrast with *acknowledgment*, which is simply confirmation that one's signature was knowingly and willingly placed on an instrument.

vertical development   The philosophy that increasing population density for an area requires construction of taller and taller buildings. Especially since 9/11 and the perceived vulnerability of skyscrapers, vertical development in its traditional form does not enjoy the widespread and enthusiastic support it once did. Today, notions of building down into the earth are gaining acceptance in vertical development planning, as are more sophisticated notions of horizontal development making better use of space.

vertical merger   A merger between companies that supply different goods or services but in a common industry.

vest   To give immediate rights in property, even if possession or enjoyment will be delayed until later. The question of when property rights vest is critical to future interests, taxation, and creditors' rights.

Veterans Administration   A former name for the current Department of Veterans Affairs. The Department was established in March 15, 1989.

vicarious liability   The legal principle that persons who are in a position to control the actions of another will be held liable for any injuries caused by that other person. Liability does not rely on proving there was improper training, instructions, control, or supervision. Rather, it is imposed merely because of the relationship between the parties. Respondeat superior is one type of vicarious liability. In real estate, the concept is most often encountered in claims against an employer (construction contractor, property manager, and sometimes even real estate brokers) for the discriminatory actions of an employee.

views, right to   The theory that one is entitled to a particular view, as of the ocean or something else scenic. Such rights may be granted by particular language in an easement. In the absence of such language, courts are very reluctant to find that any property owner has an inherent right to a view across another's land to something considered of aesthetic value. Also called visual rights or a right of prospect. In the following example, unless local ordinances or zoning provide otherwise, the homeowner cannot prevent construction of the condo project on the grounds it will obstruct the homeowner's view of the ocean. Under some circumstances, though, if the tall building were a government office, school, or some other public structure, the homeowner might be entitled to compensation for the loss of the view, under eminent domain and condemnation theories.

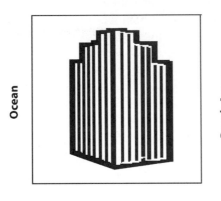

violation   Something prohibited by law.

virtual office   An arrangement with a phone answering and mail receipt company that may or may not also provide meeting rooms, administrative support, and telecommunications services. The practice is popular with small entrepreneurs and with large-corporation employees who live and work in markets that do not need, or will not support, traditional office space with rent, furniture, equipment, and support staff personnel expenses. A step up from the virtual office, but less demanding than conventional office space, is the relatively recent phenomenon of the business center.

visual rights   See *views, right to*.

voice over IP (VoIP)   Technology that allows voice, videophone, cell phone, Internet, and office network traffic to all be usable with the same instrument—a telephone.

The following scenario describes use of VoIP in a real estate office:

A single phone instrument can awaken you in the mornings, read to you your most important voice mail and e-mail messages, respond to voice commands for handling those messages, and tell you your schedule for the day. As you make cellular calls before reaching the office, the phone downloads any new information from the office network, including appointments made by your assistant, who has constant real-time access to your calendar. Incoming calls will carry with them not only caller ID, but full contact information from the office computer, including histories and notes regarding prior calls with the same person. While speaking to the caller, you can e-mail to them photographs or any other information on file at the office. Once you reach the office, the phone will sense your proximity to the network and automatically switch from cellular service to office wireless service, enabling you to take full-size video calls with links to all branch offices or the main office, plus links to special video kiosks set up at shopping malls, new subdivisions, or college campuses.

If you are a real estate sales or leasing agent, people will be able to enter a kiosk, call you and take a virtual tour of all properties meeting their criteria, and then narrow the choices to the few that warrant a personal visit.

The uses of VoIP are limitless and will completely revolutionize how we think about interacting with other people and with information. Because of its growing importance, offices and residential areas unable to accommodate the bandwidth requirements will find themselves at an extreme disadvantage. Today, all real estate decisions must be made with one eye on the IRS and one eye on the telecommunications possibilities and limitations.

void   Without any legal effect from the very beginning. Sometimes written as "void ab initio." A contract by one who has been judged mentally incompetent is void. Contrast with voidable, which is something able to be set aside, should the party so chose.

voidable   Capable of being set aside and rendered not enforceable, but not inherently without legal effect. Contracts made by minor children are voidable when they reach the age of majority, but are not automatically void. Contrast with *void*.

voidable preference   In bankruptcy law, the notion that a transfer of property within a certain time period before filing for bankruptcy may be set aside, because it takes property out of the bankruptcy estate and may diminish the money available for unsecured creditors. There does not have to be any showing of fraudulent or dishonest intent.

voluntary alienation   A transfer of real property through one's intentional actions. Contrast with *involuntary alienation*, such as a foreclosure.

voluntary lien   An agreement to allow the use of specific property as collateral for a debt. Contrast with *involuntary lien*.

voucher system   A method of disbursing money from a construction loan. The developer or the general contractor (general) will give vouchers to subcontractors (subs) or suppliers as they are entitled to payment under their own contracts. The voucher certifies that the work has been performed properly, or the supplies are free from defect and accurate in price and amount delivered. The subs or the suppliers then take their vouchers to the construction lender, who writes checks to them. The drawback is that it is management intensive for the lender, who is usually operating on such tight margins that it can't afford the administrative staff to service a voucher system. The more common system is the draw system, in which the general receives large chunks of money on a prearranged draw schedule and then disburses them to subs and suppliers.

vulture capitalist (1) A person or firm who accumulates cash and commitments for cash in order to take advantage of an anticipated temporary plunge in real estate values. At the proper time, the vulture capitalist will buy virtually every distressed property it can acquire, to resell when the market returns. (2) A derogatory term applied to venture capitalists, some of whom have a reputation of investing in a business in the hopes it will fail, at which point the venture capitalist takes over the assets and liquidates them at a profit.

W

wage earners' bankruptcy   Same as Chapter 13 bankruptcy. See *bankruptcy*.

waiver   The voluntary relinquishment of a known right, remedy, claim, or privilege.

waiver of tax lien   See *certificate of discharge*.

walk-through inspection   An inspection by a buyer or a tenant prior to taking possession, typically to determine that all repairs or improvements have been completed in a proper manner.

ward   See *guardian*.

warehouse   A commercial storage building. Zoning regulations and building codes may place restrictions on the placement and construction styles of warehouses. See *bailment* for the rights and responsibilities of parties.

warehouse fee   A charge to a borrower when a mortgage banker or other small lender must borrow money on a short-term basis in order to loan money on mortgage loans. If the interest rate on the short-term loan is too large to make money on the spread, the mortgage banker will charge a warehouse fee to cover its costs until it can assemble enough loans in its virtual warehouse and sell them to someone else, making enough money to pay off its short-term loans.

warehousing   The practice by a loan originator of packaging large numbers of loans for sale on the secondary market.

warranty   An express or implied promise arising out of a contract or a transfer of interests in real estate. An express warranty would be a manufacturer's warranty that an appliance will be defect free for 12 months. The "warranty of fitness for a particular use and purpose" is an implied warranty, imposed by the law, that a product will be safe if used in the manner in which it is intended. The contents of written warranties on consumer products are covered by the federal Magnusson-Moss Act, passed in 1975. It includes goods attached to or installed on real property. See also *warranty deed*.

warranty deed   A deed containing promises by the seller regarding the quantity and quality of title being transferred to the buyer and some of the responsibilities of the seller if the warranties are breached. A special warranty deed gives assurances that the seller has not done anything to diminish the title but makes no promises about things that happened before the seller took title or things that are outside the seller's control. A general warranty deed gives the most protection to a buyer, and includes both present and future covenants as follows:

- Present covenants:
  - Seisin, meaning the seller (grantor) has legal title
  - Right to convey, meaning there are no restrictions on the right to convey
  - Against encumbrances, meaning there are no other claims such as liens, easements, or other similar matters
- Future covenants:
  - Covenant of warranty, being a promise to indemnify the grantee for any damage suffered as a result of the title being defective. Some courts require an actual dispossession of the grantee before the covenant comes into play, and others do not. Some allow the attorneys' fees paid by the grantee as an element of damage, and others do not.
  - Quiet enjoyment, that grantee will be able to enjoy the estate without adverse claims from other parties.
  - Further assurances, that grantor will take any steps necessary in the future to defend the title or perfect grantee's title if there is a technical defect and a corrective deed required, for example.

warranty of habitability   An implied promise, meaning one imposed by the law and not specifically agreed to by the parties, that the premises will be suitable for habitation in a safe and sanitary manner. It is a change from the old common law rule of caveat emptor, meaning the buyer takes at his or her own risk. The warranty applies to landlords and has been held to apply to sellers of new homes and sometimes to sellers of used homes. (Consumer protection statutes and disclosure statutes in some states expand upon the implied warranty.)

waste   An abusive or destructive use of property by someone who is entitled to possession but who does not have complete ownership rights, such as a tenant, mortgage borrower, or a joint owner. Waste is more than normal wear and tear and implies neglect or misconduct. Contrast with *trespass*, which is damage by one who is not entitled to possession. There are three types of waste:

1. Voluntary waste (also called affirmative waste) is an intentional change to property resulting in damage to the property.
2. Permissive waste (also called negligent waste) is a failure to maintain property, so that it deteriorates in value.
3. Ameliorative waste occurs when the changes increase the value of the property. In some jurisdictions, a court will still award damages because the owner is entitled to have its property remain in the same condition, without being subjected to others' opinions regarding whether it was improved or not. Other jurisdictions refuse to allow damages, finding that the owner has been benefited by the actions.

wasting asset   An asset that is depleted or used up over time, such as oil and gas, minerals under the earth, or timberland. Wasting assets may give rise to income tax depletion deductions, similar to the better-known depreciation deductions.

water line capacity   The volume of water capable of being transmitted by particular sizes of pipes, expressed as gallons per minute. When making zoning decisions, or considering requests for variances, local boards must always consider the water line capacity of the existing infrastructure and whether or not the lines in place will accommodate the anticipated water needs, or if it will be necessary to lay new lines.

water rights   See *riparian rights* (surface waters, rivers, and streams) and *littoral rights* (oceans, lakes, and other large bodies of water).

water table   The upper limit of the saturated area of the earth containing groundwater. The water table will be at varying depths depending on location and time of year.

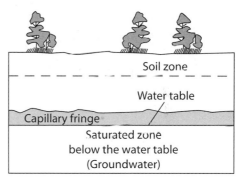

Source: EPA.

waters of the United States   All navigable waters within the United States. The Army Corps of Engineers attempted to expand the definition to include wetlands and waterways that drained into navigable waters, thus allowing it to require permits from property owners under many circumstances. In the landmark decision of *Rapanos v. United States,* the Supreme Court decided, on June 19, 2006, that "The phrase the waters of the United States includes only those relatively permanent, standing or continuously flowing bodies of water 'forming geographic features' that are described in ordinary parlance as 'streams,' 'oceans, rivers, [and] lakes'... and does not include channels through which water flows intermittently or ephemerally, or channels that periodically provide drainage for rainfall."

wear and tear   Physical deterioration of property as a result of normal usage and aging.

Webcam   A camera with an assigned Internet protocol (IP) address, reachable by persons on the Internet and in possession of the IP address or a Web link. Webcams with remotely controlled pan and zoom features are becoming an important tool for the marketing of commercial properties, especially when potential buyers or tenants may come from anywhere in the nation or the world.

wetlands   (1) Land normally saturated with water, such as swamps or marshes. Wetlands are now recognized as an important component of wildlife preservation, water purification, and protection against hurricanes. The federal government currently has no centralized wetlands protection program; the primary vehicle for preservation is the Clean Water Act as administered by the Environmental Protection Agency. Many states do have comprehensive wetlands management programs, however, and care should be taken to review all relevant laws before purchasing property that might be construed as wetlands. (2) An alternative wastewater management system is called constructed wetlands; it makes use of natural cleaning systems found in wetlands. The following diagrammed system, called the subsurface flow system, can handle discharges up to 10,000 gallons a day—enough for a small community.

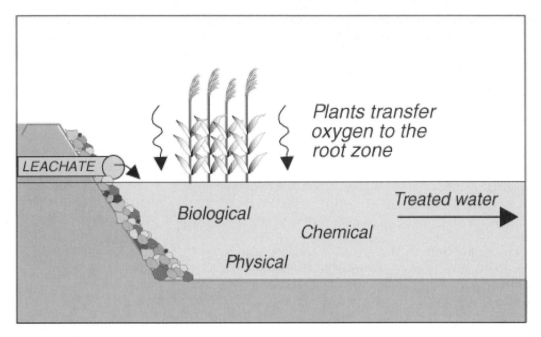

Source: U.S. Geological Survey.

wharfing out   The right to exclusive use of submerged lands by virtue of erecting a wharf over them.

white elephant   Like the legendary white elephants of India, a property that is expensive to maintain, doesn't return any particular value, and can't realistically be sold to anyone else.

wholly destroyed   In leases and insurance policies employing the term, it means an improvement that is no longer usable for its purpose in any part, not a complete obliteration of all pieces and components.

widow's election   In some states a widow may claim a portion of her husband's estate, even if she is intentionally excluded from his will. Normally it is the amount she would take by statute if the husband had died intestate—without a will.

wild deed   Also called a thin air deed, one which appears in the real estate records with a grantor who has never before had recorded title, usually to a grantee who is never heard of again. Unless the state has a statute voiding any claims under such a wild deed after a certain period of time, the effect is to so thoroughly cloud the title that a suit to quiet title will be necessary to bar any future claimants under the wild deed.

will   An instrument by which a person directs the disposition of assets after death. At one time the term will referred to disposition of real property, and a testament was a disposition of personal property, hence the expression "last will and testament." Today, will covers all properties. See also holographic will (handwritten), nuncupative will (oral), intestate succession (dying without a will), and escheat (dying with no will and no heirs).

willing buyer   See *ready, willing, and able.*

without recourse   Words sometimes written on the back of a check when one endorses the check over to another. It has the legal effect of preventing recovery of the money from the endorser in case the check is returned as "not sufficient funds" (NSF) or for any other reason. It would be imprudent for anyone to accept a two-party check with the words without recourse written on the back.

witness monument   A permanent marker used to establish the location of boundary lines or the quarter-quarter section and larger-area corners in the public land survey system.

Women's Council of Realtors (WCR)   Founded in 1938 as an affiliate of the National Association of REALTORS®, the WCR (www.wcr.org) promotes networking, education, and professional development for women with careers in real estate.

wood-destroying insect   Termites, post beetles, carpenter ants, and carpenter bees. Millipedes are technically wood decomposers, but may be included under some circumstances. Home purchase contracts generally require the property to be free from wood-destroying insects. Most termite policies exclude from coverage Formosan termites—a particularly voracious and practically indestructible termite working its way northward from New Orleans and other southern coastal cities. The Pest Control Canada Web site at www.pestcontrolcanada.com is one of the best for identification and further information about wood-destroying insects and other pests, plus there is an opportunity to submit photos of your own unidentified pests in order to ask for assistance.

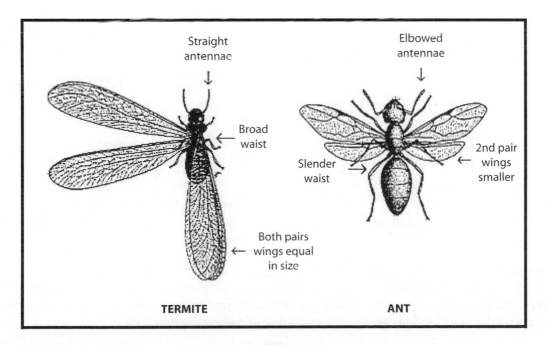

wood infestation report   A report required by almost all lenders of residential mortgages. The report identifies any signs of current or past infestation by wood-destroying insects, and may include reports of mold or water damage. Ideally, the report will state that there is no current wood infestation.

worker's compensation laws   A statutory arrangement granting employers protection from lawsuits by injured employees, in return for granting employees the right to recover specified amounts for injuries, even if due to the employee's own negligence. Most states require employers with a certain minimum number of employees to maintain worker's compensation insurance. Historically, the concept has been thought inapplicable to real estate agents, who were considered independent contractors rather than employees. Recently, though, cases in New Jersey and in Virginia have ruled that real estate agents were employees for purposes of the worker's compensation statutes in those states.

working capital   The difference between cash and other quick assets (current assets) and current liabilities.

Example:

Statement of Working Capital as of January 1, 20____

Assets		Liabilities	
Current		Current	
Cash	$1,000	Payables	$1,200
Receivables	$4,000	90-day note	$1,000
		Bad debt reserve	$200
Total current assets	$5,000	Total current liabilities	$3,200
Fixed		Long term	
Land	$15,000	Mortgage	$22,000
Buildings	$45,000	Equity	$45,800
Equipment	$6,000		
Total assets	$71,000	Total liabilities and equity	$71,000

The working capital consists of the difference between the total current assets and the total current liabilities: $5,000 – $3,200 = $1,800. The bad debt reserve is an artificial number selected by management, based on prior experiences, regarding the amount of accounts receivable that will not be collected during the current period, or perhaps at all.

working drawings   Surveying, topographic, architectural, and engineering plans used in the field to construct improvements, and on which any changes are noted as the work is performed. At the end of the project, the working drawings are then submitted to the persons who originally created them in order to incorporate all changes into a final set of as-built drawings.

working mortgage   A Fannie Mae product employing electronic payment and mortgage terms synchronized with a borrower's schedule of payroll deposits. Whether a borrower is paid weekly, or twice monthly, mortgage payments can be calculated for that time period and automatically deducted from the borrower's bank account on the day after electronic deposit of the paycheck. It assists the borrower with a more levelized budgeting process and will lead to a faster payoff of the loan because of the effective addition of one payment period each year and the decreased amount of time on which interest is paid.

workout   The process of working with a lender to explore alternatives to foreclosure or bankruptcy after a default. This may involve the lender receiving additional collateral, lengthening the term of the loan, writing down part of the principal balance, providing minor additional lending to make the repairs necessary to sell the property at its best price, or any number of negotiated terms and conditions. One of the keys to a mutually beneficial workout solution is for all parties to be well educated regarding the consequences of bankruptcy. One example is the ability of a bankruptcy court to reduce the principal balance of a mortgage loan under certain circumstances. It is also wise for borrowers to understand the limitations of bankruptcy, however, so they don't take an imprudently aggressive stance with their lender.

worthier title doctrine   (1) At common law, if a testator devised (left by will) exactly the same interest in land that an heir would take by descent (laws applicable when there wasn't a will), then the heir would be considered as having taken title by descent rather than devise. Descent was considered the worthier title. The doctrine has its roots in English feudal law and certain rights that passed by land if it were inherited, but not if it were gained "by purchase," which included "by will." Today, most states have overruled this portion of the doctrine or ignored it as irrelevant. It does still sometimes arise in the context of adverse possession and calculation of holding periods. (2) A second portion of the doctrine is called the inter vivos branch; it is still alive and well, although rarely encountered because it is a somewhat exotic theory. This branch holds that a gift by A to a trust for A's lifetime, with the property then given to A's heirs after A's death, is a gift to A's heirs by the worthier title of descent rather than by a lifetime gift. The practical implications are that the heirs have no rights to anything until A dies, so that if an heir has creditors, there is nothing for the creditors to seize until A dies. If it were not for the doctrine, A's heirs would have a remainder interest during A's lifetime, which would be subject to seizure by creditors.

wraparound mortgage   A largely extinct financing tool involving a seller leaving its first mortgage in place while selling the property to another and holding the financing. The new mortgage "wrapped around" the old mortgage, so that the buyer made payments to the seller, who then deducted enough to make payments to the original mortgage lender. The practice has been rendered obsolete by the widespread use of the due-on-sale clauses in mortgage loans, making the entire principal balance of the loan due when the property is sold, whether or not there has been a default. There are a few circumstances when a *due-on-sale clause* is not enforceable (see that entry for details), providing an opportunity for wraparound mortgages.

441

write-down   (1) To reduce the value of an asset on the books and records of a company because of a decrease in value of that asset. Because of the mechanics of double-entry bookkeeping, writing down an asset has the consequence of reducing income for that time period. The timing of write-downs is therefore critical because of the impact on taxable income, earnings reported to shareholders, asset value, earnings reported to lenders, and other instances. Large companies will often write down assets in a quarter that is already disappointing, in an attempt to get all the bad news over with at the same time. (2) A lender's agreement to accept less than the full principal balance of a loan, usually in recognition of the fact that it won't collect the full balance anyway.

write-off   To take an asset entirely off the books because it no longer has any value. If an accrual-basis taxpayer has taken money into income when bills were sent out to customers, but then some of the bills became uncollectible, the taxpayer may write off the uncollectible ones as a deduction against income. Financial institutions are required to write off loans when they become delinquent by a certain amount.

writ of certiorari   A request that a higher court hear arguments that a lower court ruled improperly on some or all issues in a lawsuit. The higher court does not have to honor the request and therefore frequently "denies cert." This is different from an appeal, which must at least be heard by the higher court, even though the court may ultimately rule against the person who filed the appeal.

- In the federal court system, trial occurs at the level of the United States District Court. If one is unhappy with the outcome, one has the right to appeal to the United States Circuit Court with authority over the district court. If again unhappy with the outcome, one petitions the United States Supreme Court for a writ of certiorari.
- The writ orders the Circuit court to certify the record and send it up to the Supreme Court for review. The same system is used in most state courts, to some extent.
- The denial of a writ of certiorari, often called a "denial of cert," does not mean the higher court agrees with the ruling of the lower court. Rather, it usually means the issues presented are not important enough, in the opinion of the higher court, to warrant its consideration. The vast majority of cases are rejected.
- Cert may be granted but limited to one or a few issues. An example appears here.

CERTIORARI GRANTED

04-607   LABORATORY CORP. OF AMERICA V. METABOLITE LABORATORIES, ET AL.

             The petition for a writ of certiorari is granted limited to

Question 3 presented by the petition.

---

writ of ejectment   See *ejectment*.

writ of execution   The vehicle for seizing property in order to satisfy a judgment. The rules are different in every state but can be determined by inquiring at the clerk's office where one ordinarily files lawsuits.

X

xeriscaping Landscaping that uses plants and elements requiring little or no water. The xeriscaping movement is gaining momentum among environmentally conscious corporations making choices for their office landscaping.

Y

yard of concrete   One cubic yard, or a volume 3 feet wide by 3 feet long by 3 feet high. One yard of concrete will cover 80 square feet at the 3^1/$_2$ inch depth required for a sidewalk or a garage floor.

yield   A measurement of the rate of earnings for an investment.

yield capitalization   A method of converting future income from an investment into present value by discounting each year's income using an appropriate discount rate or by using one overall rate that reflects the investment.

yield maintenance premium   A prepayment penalty designed to replace lost income to investors if one of the loans in a collateralized mortgage backed security is paid off early, thereby effectively stopping any future interest income.

yield spread premium   See *service release premium*.

yield to maturity (YTM)   The internal rate of return of an investment, taking into consideration all incomes and expenses and their timing.

YTM   See *yield to maturity*.

Z

zero cost loan   A popular advertising hype for a mortgage loan with no costs to the borrower. The reality is that the borrower pays a higher than normal interest rate on the loan. The normal loan expenses, including the profit to all the intermediaries, are paid out of the higher yield. This could result in dramatically increased overall mortgage costs.

> **Example:**   *The table shows a $150,000 loan at 7.5 percent interest on a 30-year amortization with the borrower paying all closing costs and expenses and a $150,000 loan at 8.5 percent interest with no costs at closing.*

	7.5%	8.5%
Loan amount	$150,000	$150,000
Closing costs	$3,000	0
Monthly payment	$1,048.82	$1,153.37
Interest paid over 5 years	$54,855.12	$62,437.57
Lifetime interest paid	$227,575.20	$265,213.20
Total interest and closing costs	$230,575.20	$265,213.20

The $3,000 in closing costs you "saved" with Option 2 cost you $34,638 in additional interest over 30 years. Even if you sell after year 5, the $3,000 in closing costs you saved cost you $7,582.45 in additional interest.

zero lot line   A type of construction in which the building sits directly on the property lines. It is usually prohibited by setback requirements in local zoning or in deed restrictions.

zone condemnation   The demolition of entire areas for new construction.

zone theory   In the law of trespass as it relates to flights over one's land, the theory is that a property owner has a lower zone of effective possession which should not be invaded by the government or others, but flights in the zone above that are permissible. Traditionally, property owners owned all to the middle of the earth and up to the far reaches of the heavens. Without the zone theory, every aircraft in the skies would be trespassing on someone's property.

zoning   The regulation of the uses of property; the density of populations employing those uses; and the kinds, sizes, and proportions of structures that can be erected on property. Zoning was first put into place in New York City in 1916 as a reaction against the construction of the Equitable Building, because its 41-story height cast shadows over neighboring residences and affected people's quality of life. The concept soon caught on and was enacted by nearly every city and town in America as a function of their police power. Today, Houston, Texas, is the only major American city with no zoning regulations at all.

- A current use of property that is no longer permitted after a zoning change may be allowed to continue for some period of time. Purchasers of such properties should make sure the use will still be allowed, if that is important. Purchasers of nearby properties should not make assumptions about zoning merely because of what already exists nearby.
- Zoning variances—permission for nonconforming uses—are typically granted only if it would be a hardship on the property to do otherwise. An economic hardship on the owner is irrelevant. Hardship is usually found only when the property has no other practical use other than the one planned and there is a need in the community for that use.
- Zoning variances, when granted, usually contain some requirements not otherwise demanded of other property owners, including such things as facade renovation of an older building, the necessity for off-street parking, or any number of other demands.
- Euclidean zoning, also known as building block zoning, is the most common. It is named for the town of Euclid, Ohio, which provided the test case for Supreme Court review and confirmation as constitutional. Land is divided into specific geographical districts with permitted uses within each type of district. Districts are usually designated R1 for single-family residential, R2 for two-family homes, R3 for multifamily, and so on. Its proponents like the long history of interpretation and the ease of implementation. Its critics say it lacks flexibility and fossilizes outdated theories of land-use planning.
- Performance zoning uses goal-oriented criteria to establish guidelines for the intensity of land use and the impact on infrastructure and on surrounding areas. It employs four major concepts: open-space ratio, impervious surface ratio (roads and parking lots), floor area ratio, and density. Zoning districts have descriptions such as wilderness districts, agricultural districts, and development districts. Proponents like the flexibility, but critics say the system is too complicated.
- Incentive zoning is a rewards-based system that seeks to encourage development to meet a city's needs. The system starts with standard restrictions on building size and height and occupancy densities, and then offers bonuses if developers will include needed amenities such as low-income housing, transit access, or beautification features. By agreeing to the bonus items, the developer may increase the densities or gain other variances.
- Design-based zoning is used in newer mixed-use urban planning models. It concentrates on building design and compatibility in an area rather than specific uses. Zoning districts might be called traditional neighborhood, suburban neighborhood, or transit-oriented development.

zoning variance   Permission to conduct a particular activity on real property even though in violation of applicable zoning restrictions for the area. Variances are typically granted only after public notice and a hearing on the subject, and then only if it would be a hardship on the property to disallow the variance. An economic hardship on the owner is irrelevant. Hardship is usually found only when the property has no practical use other than the one planned, and there is a need in the community for that use.

Appendix A

125 Terms All Buyers and Sellers Should Know

(See also List of Consumer Protection Laws and List of Tax Laws that Affect Real Estate)

1. Adjustable rate mortgage
2. Agency
3. All-risks policy
4. Amortization
5. Annual percentage rate
6. Arbitration
7. Back end ratio
8. Balloon mortgage
9. Bargain and sale deed
10. Boundary line dispute
11. Breach of contract
12. Buyer's broker
13. Caveat emptor
14. CC&R
15. Clearance letter
16. Closing costs
17. Commissions
18. Contingency clause
19. Conforming loan
20. Covenants, the usual
21. Credit report
22. Curb appeal
23. Deed of trust
24. Disclosure statement
25. Discount broker
26. Discount points
27. Distressed property
28. Double escrow
29. Dry closing
30. Dual agency
31. Due on sale clause
32. Durable power of attorney
33. Duty to disclose
34. Early occupancy
35. Earnest money
36. Escrow
37. Exclusive agency listing
38. Exclusive right to sell listing
39. Extender clause
40. Facilitator
41. Fair Credit Reporting Act
42. First refusal, right of

(Cont.)

43. Fixed rate loan
44. Flat fee broker
45. Flip
46. Flood insurance
47. Foreign Investment in Real Property Tax Act (FIRPTA)
48. Form contract
49. Formosan termite
50. Fraud
51. Front end ratio
52. Full disclosure
53. General warranty deed
54. Gift letter
55. Good-faith estimate
56. Grantee
57. Grantor
58. Greater fool theory
59. Homeowners' association
60. Homestead
61. HUD–1 form
62. Impound account
63. Individual retirement account (IRA)
64. Installment contract
65. Insulation disclosure
66. Joint ownership
67. Junk fees
68. Latent defects
69. Lead
70. Lease option
71. Lease purchase agreement
72. Limited service broker
73. Loan application process
74. Loan commitments
75. Mailbox rule

76. Mechanics' and materialmen's liens
77. MLS
78. Mortgage
79. Net listing
80. No buy, no pay clause
81. No-doc loan
82. No-ratio loan
83. Occupancy agreement
84. Open house
85. Open listing
86. Option
87. Owners title policy
88. Percolation test
89. Portable mortgage
90. Private mortgage insurance (PMI)
91. Property condition addendum or clause
92. Proprietary lease
93. Pro-rate
94. Quitclaim deed
95. Regulation CC
96. Reissue rate
97. Replacement value insurance
98. RESPA
99. Right of first offer; right of first opportunity
100. Right of first refusal
101. Risk of loss
102. Sale-leaseback
103. Severalty
104. Sheriff's deed
105. Single asset entity (SAE)
106. Special warranty deed
107. Staging

(Cont.)

108. Statute of Frauds
109. Subchapter S corporation
110. Sunset clause
111. Tax certificate
112. Tax deed
113. Teaser rate
114. Tenancy by the entireties
115. Tenancy in common
116. Tenancy in severalty
117. Tenant-in-common properties (TICs)
118. Time is of the essence
119. Time-sharing/timeshares
120. Title insurance
121. Torrens registration
122. Trunk title
123. Walk-through inspection
124. Warranty deed
125. Zero cost loan

Appendix B

105 Words for Landlords, Tenants, and their Agents

1. AAA tenant
2. Absolute net lease
3. Absorption rate
4. Actual eviction
5. ADA
6. Additional rent
7. Anchor tenant
8. Annual bumps
9. Assignment of lease
10. Attorn
11. Back to back lease
12. Base (expense) year
13. Base rent
14. Bay depth
15. Broom clean
16. Building efficiency ratio
17. Building standard
18. Business center
19. CAM
20. Cancellation clause
21. Class A (or B or C) building
22. Concession burnoff
23. Construction allowance
24. Constructive eviction
25. Continuous occupancy clause
26. Continuous operations clause
27. Controllable expenses
28. Core factor
29. Credit tenant
30. Dark store
31. Deferred commission
32. Demising partition or wall
33. Discrimination
34. Disparate impact
35. Dock high building
36. Effective rental rate
37. Efficiency ratio
38. End cap
39. Escalation clause
40. Eviction
41. Expansion option
42. Expense stop
43. Extension option
44. First generation space

(Cont.)

45. Fixturing period	76. Reappraisal lease
46. Flex space	77. Reasonable consent
47. Full service	78. Recapture clause
48. Going dark	79. Redeemable rent
49. Graduated rental lease	80. Relocation clause
50. Gross lease	81. Renewal option
51. Gross up	82. Renewal probability
52. Handicap	83. Rental growth rate
53. Hold harmless clause	84. Rent control
54. Holdover tenant	85. Rent-free period
55. Implied warranty of habitability	86. Rent roll
56. Index lease	87. Rent strike
57. Intelligent building	88. Retaliatory eviction
58. Lease	89. Sandwich lease
59. Leasehold improvements	90. Satellite tenant
60. Letter of credit	91. Section 8 housing
61. Letter of intent	92. Security deposit
62. Life support systems	93. Sharing the market uplift
63. Loss factor	94. Shell lease
64. Master lease	95. Sky lease
65. Mitigation of damages	96. Stabilized occupancy
66. Month-to-month tenancy	97. Surrender
67. Most favored tenant clause	98. Tenancy at sufferance
68. Net lease	99. Tenancy at will
69. Normal wear and tear	100. Tenant improvement (TI) allowance
70. Notice to quit	101. Tenant mix
71. Operating expense escalation	102. Trade fixtures
72. Pass-throughs	103. Triple-A tenant
73. Percentage lease	104. Turnover rate
74. Rack rate	105. Uniform Residential Landlord and Tenant Act
75. Radius clause	

Appendix C

100 Tax Terms Important in Real Estate

1. 501(c)(3)
2. 1031 Exchange
3. 1099
4. Accommodating party
5. Accrued depreciation
6. Active participation
7. Additional first-year depreciation
8. Adjusted basis
9. Ad valorem tax
10. After tax cash flow
11. Alternative minimum tax
12. Arm's length transaction
13. At-risk rules
14. Bargain purchase option
15. Basis
16. Bonus depreciation
17. Boot
18. Burned-out tax shelter
19. Capital gain
20. Capitalized closing costs
21. Capital loss
22. Carryover basis
23. Certificate of discharge
24. Conditional sales contract
25. Conduit tax treatment
26. Constructive receipt
27. Cost allocation depreciation
28. Cost recovery
29. Dealer
30. Dealer status
31. Debt relief
32. Deferred gain
33. Depletion
34. Depreciation methods
35. Depreciation recapture
36. Energy efficient home tax credit
37. Estate tax
38. Family limited partnership
39. Federal tax lien
40. Gift tax
41. GO-Zone
42. Gulf Coast Opportunity Act
43. Historic preservation credits
44. Holding period

(Cont.)

455

45.	Home office tax deduction	73.	Real estate professional
46.	Imputed interest	74.	Realized gain
47.	Income averaging	75.	Real property trades or business
48.	Independent contractor	76.	Recognized gain
49.	Individual retirement account	77.	Redeemable ground rents
50.	Information reporting	78.	Rehabilitation tax credit
51.	Installment contract	79.	Related party transactions
52.	Interest deductions	80.	Revenue ruling
53.	Investment interest	81.	Reverse exchange
54.	Involuntary conversion	82.	S-corporation
55.	Letter ruling	83.	Section 121
56.	Like-kind exchange	84.	Section 167
57.	Long term capital gain	85.	Section 1031
58.	Long term capital loss	86.	Section 1221
59.	Low income housing tax credits	87.	Section 1223
60.	Marital deduction	88.	Section 1245
61.	Modified accelerated cost recovery system	89.	Starker transaction
62.	Operating lease	90.	Stepped-up basis
63.	Ordinary and necessary business expenses	91.	Taxable income
64.	Passive activity	92.	Tax avoidance
65.	Passive activity income	93.	Tax benefit rule
66.	Passive investor	94.	Tax credit
67.	Phantom income	95.	Tax deduction
68.	Placed in service	96.	Tax evasion
69.	Prepaid interest	97.	Tax lien
70.	Private letter ruling	98.	Tax preference items
71.	Qualified leasehold improvement property	99.	Technical Advice Memorandum (TAM)
72.	Qualified intermediary	100.	Thin corporation

Appendix D

80 Slang Expressions Used by Real Estate Insiders

It doesn't matter how much you know about a topic, if you don't use the right "insider's language," you'll be dismissed as a spectator—someone who knows all the rules but has never really played the sport. Learn these 80 bits of "jargon" used in the real estate industry, and you'll be recognized as someone who "talks the talk" and can therefore probably "walk the walk." It's all about credibility. You either have it or you don't. Next to each word is a short-hand definition. Refer to the main Encyclopedia content to find out more.

1. **Administrivia**: seemingly useless language in a document
2. **Alligator property**: a bad deal that's eating up your money
3. **Anaconda mortgage**: one that covers ALL debts with that lender, past and future
4. **Annual bumps**: rent increases
5. **BANANA**: Build Absolutely Nothing Anywhere Near Anyone
6. **Big box**: large square building use by Wal-Mart, Target, Kmart, etc.
7. **Bird dog**: someone who sends you leads
8. **Blackacre**: the example property name always used by lawyers
9. **Boomerangers**: baby boomers' children who come back home to live
10. **Bootstrap financing**: creative financing without a formal lender

11. **Bottom-fishing**: shopping for properties at disgracefully low prices
12. **Bricks and mortar**: having a physical presence, not solely Internet-based
13. **Bricks, clicks, and flips**: having stores, Web sites, and catalogues
14. **Bullet loan**: one that will be due in full in a few years
15. **Burned out tax shelter**: real estate that doesn't have any tax benefits any more
16. **CBD**: Commercial Business District; downtown
17. **Century 21 page**: home web page that pops you over to a new page
18. **Condo cowboys**: condo developers who don't know what they're doing
19. **C-Store**: convenience store *(Cont.)*

20. **Corner of Main and Main**: middle of downtown

21. **Cram down**: bankruptcy court order forcing terms that make creditors unhappy

22. **Crib**: home

23. **Cyberpark**: business park with a lot of high-tech companies

24. **Dark store**: large retail store that's still paying rent but closed the doors at that location

25. **DINK**: Dual Income, No Kids

26. **Dinosaur pen**: a room for high-speed, high-heat computers

27. **Doc-In-A-Box**: retail medical offices for minor emergencies

28. **Dockominium**: cross between a condo and a dock: ownership of a dock

29. **Dog**: crummy property with bad problems, like toxic waste or steep ravines

30. **Dresser drawer title**: deed that stays in a dresser drawer instead of being recorded

31. **Dry mortgage**: mortgage loan with no personal liability for borrower

32. **Dummy**: straw man; someone who fronts for another, secret, buyer

33. **Echo boomers**: children of baby boomers

34. **Empty nesters**: baby boomers whose children have grown up and moved out

35. **Equity Stripping**: (1) buying foreclosures at deep discounts or (2) hiding assets

36. **Fleas**: the things that are bad about "dog" properties

37. **Flyspecking**: checking and re-checking every tiny thing about a document or title

38. **Garage mahal**: pretentious garage architecture

39. **Gatekeeper**: the person who keeps you from getting to the decision maker

40. **Gazump**: increasing the sales price after someone agrees to buy but before contract signing

41. **Gazunder**: decreasing offer after someone agrees to sell but before contract signing

42. **Gerbil tube**: enclosed walkway that connects buildings

43. **Going dark**: large retailer closing its doors but continuing to pay rent

44. **Gold plating**: padding expenses or financials

45. **Granny flat**: apartments within homes, such as over garage, in basement

46. **Greater fool theory**: even if you pay too much, someone else will pay more

47. **Gross up**: artificially increase building expenses to a calculated level

48. **Home cooking**: out of town lawyers and parties getting the shaft from locals

49. **House fluffer**: decorator who makes a house look pretty so it will sell more quickly

50. **House poor**: having a big house, but no cash

51. **Ironclad agreement**: no such thing. Any agreement can be successfully broken

52. **LULUs**: Locally Unwanted Land Uses

53. **McMansion**: pretentious house that looks like all the other pretentious houses

54. **NFL city**: city with an NFL franchise; supposedly has good demographics

55. **NIMBY**: Not In my Back Yard

56. **Open the kimono**: reveal all financial information to a supposed buyer

57. **Paint-to-paint**: what you own in a condo—the insides of the outer walls

58. **Paper**: mortgage notes *(Cont.)*

59. **Paper the file**: generate lots of analyses, spreadsheets, charts and photos for a loan application

60. **Pipeline**: what's coming along right now in the way of prospects, apartments, condos, etc.

61. **Pipeline risk**: lender worry that interest rates will increase after a firm loan commitment

62. **Rack rate**: quoted rent rate, ignoring discounts that might be available

63. **Sandwich lease**: a sublease

64. **Scrape**: a property suitable only for bulldozing and redevelopment

65. **Second bite of the apple**: getting a second chance with a different set of arguments

66. **Seed money**: start up cash before obtaining any loans

67. **See-through building**: new building with no tenants

68. **Skin in the game**: investor/developer with some cash at risk; not 100% financing

69. **Stagflation**: stagnant inflation

70. **Starter castle**: pretentious home built with really cheap components and methods

71. **Sweat equity**: increase in value due to hard work

72. **Tax ferrets**: people who rat out tax cheats

73. **Tornado bait**: mobile home

74. **Trash for cash**: forcing you to buy shoddy stuff in addition to the good stuff you really want

75. **Trunk title**: deed kept in a trunk instead of being recorded

76. **Underwater**: property with more debt than the property is worth

77. **Upper bracket**: making lots of money

78. **Vanilla building**: plain building that could have any brand of tenant

79. **Vulture capitalist**: someone waiting for a crash so they can buy properties very cheaply

80. **White elephant**: property you can't get rid of because it's too nice and can't be afforded

Appendix E

77 Words Important to Developers

1. ADC loan
2. Adequate public facilities ordinances
3. Adverse financial change condition
4. Aesthetic zoning
5. Air rights
6. Annexation
7. As-built drawings
8. Assemblage
9. Bankruptcy
10. Basket loan
11. Bay depth
12. Bid bond
13. Bid shopping
14. Biometrics
15. Builder's risk insurance
16. Capital stack
17. Carrying charges
18. Carve out
19. Cash out refinance
20. Claritas
21. Completion bond
22. Conditional use permit
23. CoStar
24. Defeasance clause
25. Diffused surface waters
26. End cap
27. Feasibility study
28. Field fit
29. Flag lot
30. Floating zone
31. Floor loan
32. Footprint
33. Four quadrants of the real estate capital markets
34. Front ending
35. Front money
36. Future advances mortgage
37. Gap financing
38. Height, building
39. Holdback
40. Holdout
41. Impact fees
42. Inclusionary zoning
43. Indirect costs
44. In-fill development
45. Infrastructure
46. Interim use
47. Inverse condemnation

(Cont.)

48. Joint and several liability
49. Jury, right to trial by
50. Kelo
51. Key lot
52. Land use intensity
53. Land use regulation
54. Location intelligence
55. Mechanics and materialmens lien
56. Median cut
57. Moratorium
58. Operating and easement agreement
59. Outparcel
60. Overbuilding
61. Overseas Private Investment Corporation
62. Performance bond
63. Phase I
64. Phase II
65. Plottage value
66. Potentially responsible party
67. Prime rate
68. Pro forma statement
69. Progress payments
70. Public land survey system
71. Radius clause
72. Reilly's Law of Retail Gravitation
73. Retail anthropology
74. Retention pond
75. Rylands v. Fletcher
76. Schematics
77. Zoning variance

Appendix F

60 Useful Ideas for Analyzing Investments

1. 4-3-2-1 rule
2. Advance payment annuity
3. After-tax cash flow
4. After-tax equity yield
5. After-tax income
6. After-tax proceeds from resale
7. Appreciation return
8. Average downtime
9. Average free rent
10. Average rate of return
11. Balance sheet
12. Before-tax cash flow
13. Break-even point
14. Building efficiency ratio
15. Cap rate
16. Capitalized value of future income
17. Capture rate
18. Cash flow
19. Cash flow before taxes
20. Cash-on-cash
21. Cost benefit analysis
22. Debt coverage ratio
23. Debt/equity ratio
24. Debt service coverage ratio
25. Discounted cash flow
26. EBITDA
27. Economic rent
28. Effective gross income
29. Effective rental rate
30. Elasticity
31. Equity yield rate
32. Expense ratio
33. Financial management rate of return
34. Going in capitalization rate
35. Gross income
36. Gross income multiplier
37. Gross operating income
38. Gross potential income
39. Gross rent multiplier
40. Internal rate of return
41. Loan-to-value ratio
42. Marginal tax rate
43. Negative amortization
44. Negative cash flow

(Cont.)

45. Negative leverage
46. Net operating income
47. Net present value
48. Net usable acre
49. Occupancy rate
50. Operating expense ratio
51. Ordinary annuity
52. Parking ratio

53. Payback period
54. Potential gross income
55. Present value
56. Reinvestment rate
57. Renewal probability
58. Rental growth rate
59. Rental income
60. Stabilized occupancy

Appendix G

50 Words Important to Residential Real Estate Agents

1. Ad valorem tax
2. ALTA
3. Artificial intelligence
4. Assessed value
5. Attractive nuisance
6. Automated mortgage underwriting
7. Automated valuation model
8. Black mold
9. Blockbusting
10. B paper
11. Broker price opinion (BPO)
12. Bubble
13. Comparables
14. Computerized loan origination
15. Conditional offer
16. Distressed property
17. Double escrow
18. Dry closing
19. Easement
20. Fee Simple
21. Fiduciary
22. First refusal, right of
23. Form contract
24. Good-faith estimate
25. Gratuitous agent
26. Group boycott
27. Implied agency
28. Implied listing
29. Independent contractor
30. Limited referral agent
31. Mailbox rule
32. Metes and bounds
33. Open listing
34. Option
35. Package mortgage
36. Panic peddling
37. Parol evidence
38. Pocket listing
39. Price fixing
40. Procuring cause
41. Prospect vs. suspect
42. Qualified buyer
43. Radon
44. Ready, willing, and able
45. Recovery fund
46. Rescind
47. Secret profit
48. Steering
49. Submittal notice
50. Undisclosed agency

Appendix H

50 Federal Laws, and Widespread State Laws that Affect Real Estate

1. AIDS Housing Opportunity Act
2. Adequate public facilities ordinances (APFO)
3. Agricultural Foreign Investment Disclosure Act
4. Americans With Disabilities Act
5. Antitrust laws
6. Arbitration
7. Building Energy Conservation Code
8. Check 21
9. Civil Rights Act of 1866
10. Civil Rights Act of 1964
11. Civil Rights Act of 1968
12. Clean Water Act
13. Color of Title Act
14. Community Reinvestment Act (CRA)
15. Comprehensive Environmental Response Compensation & Liability Act (CERCLA)
16. Consumer Credit Protection Act
17. Davis-Bacon Act
18. Endangered Species Act
19. Equal Credit Opportunity Act
20. Fair Credit Reporting Act
21. Fair Debt Collection Practices Act
22. Fair Housing Act
23. Federal Housing Administration (FHA)
24. Federal Trade Commission
25. Foreign investment in real estate
26. Foreign Investment in Real Property Tax Act (FIRPTA)
27. Gramm-Leach-Bliley Act
28. Home Mortgage Disclosure Act
29. Homeowners' Protection Act of 1998 (HOPA)
30. Howey Rule
31. Interstate Land Sales Full Disclosure Act
32. Occupational Safety and Health Administration (OSHA)
33. Magnusson Moss Act
34. PMI Cancellation Act
35. Privacy laws (see topic for various laws)
36. Private Property Rights Implementation Act of 2006
37. Real Estate Settlement Procedures Act (RESPA)

(Cont.)

38. Regulation CC

39. Regulation Z

40. Religious Land Use and Institutionalized Persons Act of 2000

41. Residential Communities Initiative

42. Right to Financial Privacy Act

43. R-Value Rule

44. Sarbanes Oxley Act of 2002 (SOX)

45. Sherman Antitrust Act

46. Soldiers and Sailors Civil Relief Act (SSCRA)

47. Statute of Frauds

48. Truth in Lending Act (TLA)

49. Truth in Negotiations Act (TINA)

50. Uniform Landlord Tenant Act

Appendix I
20 Ways to Hold Real Estate

1. Community property
2. Condominium
3. Cooperative apartment
4. Corporation
5. General partnership
6. Interval ownership
7. Joint tenants with right of survivorship
8. Joint venture partners
9. Lease
10. Leasehold interest
11. Life estate
12. Limited liability company
13. Limited partnership
14. Ownership in severalty
15. Remainder interest
16. Tenants by the entireties
17. Tenants in common
18. Tenants in common with cross contingent remainders
19. TIC properties
20. Trust

Appendix J
Symbols and Abbreviations

Δ   defendant

Π   plaintiff

§   section

¶   paragraph

©   copyright

®   registered

~   approximately

±   more or less

≤   less than or equal to

≥   more than or equal to

≠   not equal to

<   less than

>   more than

=   (double underline) total of above

A

AAA triple a

ABA American Bankers Association

ABC Associated Builders and Contractors

A/C air conditioning

ACM asbestos containing material

ACRS accelerated cost recovery system

ADA Americans with Disabilities Act

ADC acquisition, development, and construction loan

ADR asset depreciation range

AGCA Associated General Contractors of America

AI artificial intelligence

AIA American Institute of Architects

AIDS acquired immunodeficiency syndrome

ALDA Asset Conservation, Lender Liability and Deposit Insurance Act of 1996

ALTA American Land Title Association

Alt/min alternative minimum tax

AMI alternative mortgage instrument

AML adjustable mortgage loan

AMT alternative minimum tax

ANSI American National Standards Institute, Inc.

APA American Planning Association

APFO adequate public facilities ordinances

APN assessor parcel number

APP appreciation

APR annual percentage rate

ARA Accredited Rural Appraiser

ARELLO Association of Real Estate License Law Officials

ARES American Real Estate Society

AREUEA American Real Estate and Urban Economics Association

ARM adjustable-rate mortgage

ASA American Society of Appraisers

(Cont.)

ASFMRA American Society of Farm Managers and Rural Appraisers

ASHI American Society of Home Inspectors

ASREC American Society of Real Estate Counselors

AVM automatic valuation model

B

BANANA build absolutely nothing anywhere near anybody

BFP bona fide purchaser

BIF Bank Insurance Fund

BLM Bureau of Land Management

BMIR below market interest rate

BNA block numbering area

BOMA Building Owners and Managers Association

BOY beginning of year

BPO broker price opinion

BSPRA builders and sponsors profit and risk allowance

BTU British thermal unit

BTXE benzene, toluene, xylene, and ethylbenzene

C

CAD cash available for distribution

CAD central appraisal district

CAD computer aided design

CAI Community Association Institute

CAM common area maintenance

CBA controlled business arrangement

CBD central business district

CBSA core-based statistical area

CCA chromated copper arsenate

CCIM Certified Commercial Investment Member

CCR conditions, covenants and restrictions

CD certificate of deposit

CERCLA Comprehensive Environmental Response Compensation and Liability Act

CLO computerized loan origination

CMA comparative market analysis

CMBS collateralized mortgage backed securities; sometimes commercial mortgage backed securities

CMO collateralized mortgage obligation

CMSA consolidated metropolitan statistical area

CO or **C/O** certificate of occupancy

COFI cost of funds index

COLA cost of living adjustment

CPI consumer price index

CPM Certified Property Manager

CRA Community Reinvestment Act

CRA credit reporting agency

CRB Certified Residential Broker

CRE Counselors of Real Estate

CREW Commercial Real Estate Women

CRS Certified Residential Specialist

CRV certificate of reasonable value

C-store convenience store

CUP conditional use permit

CWA Clean Water Act

D

D defendant

DBH diameter breast high

(Cont.)

DCR debt coverage ratio

DDA demand deposit account

DINK dual income, no kids

DIP debtor in possession

DOI Department of the Interior

DPP direct participation program

DREI Distinguished Real Estate Instructor

DWV drain-waste-vent

E

EBITDA earnings before interest, taxes, depreciation and amortization

EIFS exterior insulation and finish system

E&O errors and omissions insurance

EOY end of year

EPA Environmental Protection Agency

F

FAMC Federal Agricultural Mortgage Corporation

FCA Farm Credit Association

FDIC Federal Deposit Insurance Corporation

FEMA Federal Emergency Management Agency

FF&E furniture, fixtures and equipment

FFIEC Federal Financial Institutions Examination Council

FHA Federal Housing Administration

FHFB Federal Housing Finance Board

FIA Federal Insurance Administration

FICO Fair Isaac Company score

FIRPTA Foreign Investment in Real Property Tax Act

FIRREA Financial Institutions Reform, Recovery and Enforcement Act

FLP family limited partnership

FmHA Farmers Home Administration

FMRR financial management rate of return

FMV fair market value

FNMA Federal National Mortgage Association

FRT federally related transaction

FSLIC Federal Savings and Loan Insurance Corporation

FTC Federal Trade Commission

FY fiscal year

G

GAAP generally accepted accounting principles

GAO Government Accountability Office

G/C and **GC** general contractor

GEM growing equity mortgage

GIS geographic information system

GLA gross leasable area

GNMA Government National Mortgage Association

GPI gross potential income

GPO Government Printing Office

GPRI gross potential rental income

GRI Graduate REALTORS® Institute

GRM gross rent multiplier

GSA General Services Administration

GSE government-sponsored enterprise

H

HECM home equity conversion mortgage

HELOC home equity line of credit

HOPA Homeowners Protection Act of 1998

HUD United States Department of Housing and Urban Development

HUD-1 settlement statement

HVAC heating, ventilation and air conditioning

(Cont.)

I

ICSC International Council of Shopping Centers

IFMA International Facilities Management Association

ILSFDA Interstate Land Sales Full Disclosure Act

IRA Individual Retirement Account

IREM Institute of Real Estate Management

IRR internal rate of return

IRS Internal Revenue Service

L

LIBOR London Interbank Offered Rate

LLC limited liability company

LLP limited liability partnership

LOC letter of credit

LOI letter of intent

LTV loan-to-value ratio

LUIS land use intensity system

LULU locally unwanted land use

LUST leaking underground storage tank

L/V loan-to-value ratio

M

MAI Member, Appraisal Institute

MBS mortgage backed security

MGIC Mortgage Guaranty Insurance Corporation

MLS multiple listing service

M&M mechanics and materialmen

MSA metropolitan statistical area

N

NAEBA National Association of Exclusive Buyer Agents

NAR National Association of REALTORS®

NAREB National Association of Real Estate Brokers

NECTA New England city and town area

NIMBY not in my back yard

NNN triple net lease

NOI net operating income

NPV net present value

O

OAR overall capitalization rate

OEA operating and easement agreement

OFHEO Office of Federal Housing Enterprise Oversight

OILSR Office of Interstate Land Sales Registration

OMB Office of Management and Budget

OPM other people's money

ORE owned real estate; other real estate

OSHA Occupational Safety and Health Administration

OTS Office of Thrift Supervision

P

P plaintiff

PCB polychlorinated biphenyls

PCB pollution control board

P&I principal and interest

PIG passive activity generator

PITI principal, interest, taxes and insurance

P&L profit and loss

PLSS public land survey system

PMI private mortgage insurance

PMSI primary metropolitan statistical area

POS principal only securities

PRP potentially responsible party

(Cont.)

PUD planned unit development

PV present value

R

RAM reverse annuity mortgage

RAP remedial action plan

RCRA Resource Conservation and Recovery Act

REEA Real Estate Educators Association

REIPA Real Estate Information Professionals Association

REIS real estate information system

REIT real estate investment trust

REMF real estate mutual fund

REMIC real estate mortgage investment conduit

REO real estate owned

REOC real estate operating company

RESPA Real Estate Settlement Procedures Act

RevPAR revenue per available room

RFP request for proposal

RFQ request for qualifications

RLI REALTORS® Land Institute

ROI return on investment

RRM renegotiated rate mortgage

RTC Resolution Trust Corporation

R/W right of way

S

SAE single asset entity

SAM shared appreciation mortgage

SARA Superfund Amendments and Reauthorization Act

SBA Small Business Administration

SEA street edge alternatives

SEC Securities and Exchange Commission

SH shareholders; stockholders

SIOR Society of Industrial and Office REALTORS®

SIP structural insulated panel

S/L statute of limitations

S&L savings and loan association

SMSA standard metropolitan statistical area

SOX Sarbanes-Oxley Act of 2002

SPE single purpose entity

SPE special purpose entity

SRA Senior Residential Appraiser

SRO single room occupancy

SSCRA Soldiers and Sailors Civil Relief Act

SYD sum of the years digits

T

TAM technical advice memorandum

TDR transferable development right

TI taxable income

TI tenant improvements

TIC tenant in common property

TILA Truth in Lending Act

TIMO timber investment management organization

TINA Truth in Negotiations Act

TRO temporary restraining order

U

UCC Uniform Commercial Code

UCC-1 financing statement

UETA Uniform Electronic Transactions Act

ULI Urban Land Institute

URAR Uniform Residential Appraisal Report

(Cont.)

USPAP Uniform Standards of Professional Appraisal Practice

UST underground storage tank

V

VA Department of Veterans' Affairs

VRM variable rate mortgage

W

WCR Women's Council of REALTORS®

WOR without recourse

Y

YTM yield to maturity

Appendix K

Common Land Measurements and Conversions

Author note: Land measurements and conversion tables are available online at www.onelineconversion.com to perform virtually any conversion.

1 mile = 80 chains
    = 320 rods
    = 1760 yards
    = 5280 feet

16 $\frac{1}{2}$ feet = 1 rod, perch, or pole

1 chain = 100 inches
    = 66 feet,
    = 100 links
    = 4 rods

1 link = 7.92 inches

25 links = 1 rod

4 rods = 1 chain

144 square inches = 1 square foot

9 square feet = 1 square yard

30 $\frac{1}{4}$ square yards = 1 square rod

160 square rods = 1 acre

10,000 square links = 1 square chain

10 square chains = 1 acre

1 acre = 208,708 feet by 208,708 feet

1 acre = 43,560 square feet

1 acre = 4,840 square yards

1 acre = 160 square rods

640 acres = 1 square mile or 1 section

36 square miles or sections = 1 township

About the Authors

Denise L. Evans received her law degree from the University of Alabama and is licensed to practice law in the state of Texas, where she specialized in real estate and banking litigation. When she returned to Alabama, she entered commercial real estate, and has been active in various aspects of that field for almost twenty years. Today, she is a commercial real estate broker, adjunct professor in real estate at the Culverhouse College of Commerce and Business Administration at the University of Alabama, and the author of several real estate books. She is married to her coauthor, O. William "Bill" Evans. She founded and is active in her local chapter of CREW, the national organization devoted to women in commercial real estate.

O. William Evans, JD, has over thirty years of experience as a commercial developer, real estate broker, and nationally recognized seminar speaker. He currently serves as Interim Executive Director of the Alabama Real Estate Research and Education Center, and is Vice Chairman of the Board of Trustees of the same institution. He teaches courses in real estate investment and real estate development at the Culverhouse College of Commerce and Business Administration and the Manderson Graduate School of Business, both at the University of Alabama. He currently also serves as Assistant to the Dean of the College of Commerce. He previously served on the Board of Directors of a national real estate franchise company, is a past president of the Commercial Real Estate Club of Birmingham, and a past chairman of the education committee of the Birmingham Association of REALTORS®.

NEED MORE REAL ESTATE INFORMATION ?

www.mhprofessional.com/reencyclopedia

We are excited to offer you a companion Web resource to this book. It can be an indispensable tool for keeping you up to date with the latest concepts, formulas, and resources necessary to keep you one step ahead in the fast-paced world of real estate.

It includes:

- 50 fill-in-the-blank, legally binding real estate forms
- 100 real estate formulas that you can download
- 50 practice problems for most financial calculators
- A downloadable spreadsheet of formulas for common real estate functions
- Links to more than 500 real estate web sites
- Over 125 definitions of words and concepts updated as soon as they come to our attention
- And more!

Hone your skills and stay abreast of the latest developments in the real estate field!

Visit www.mhprofessional.com/reencyclopedia for up-to-date information!